Hazardous Waste in America

Samuel S. Epstein, M.D.
Lester O. Brown
Carl Pope

Sierra Club Books
SAN FRANCISCO

The Sierra Club,
founded in 1892 by John Muir, has devoted
itself to the study and protection of the earth's
scenic and ecological resources—mountains,
wetlands, woodlands, wild shores and rivers,
deserts and plains. The publishing program of
the Sierra Club offers books to the public as a
nonprofit educational service in the hope that
they may enlarge the public's understanding of
the Club's basic concerns. The point of view
expressed in each book, however, does not necessarily represent that of the Club. The Sierra
Club has some fifty chapters coast to coast, in
Canada, Hawaii, and Alaska. For information
about how you may participate in its programs
to preserve wilderness and the quality of life,
please address inquiries to Sierra Club, 530 Bush
Street, San Francisco, California 94108.

Hazardous Waste in America was first published
in hardcover by Sierra Club Books in 1982.
First softcover edition: 1983.

**Library of Congress Cataloging in
Publication Data**
Epstein, Samuel S.
Hazardous waste in America.
Includes index.
1. Hazardous wastes—United States.
2. Hazardous wastes—Law and legislation—
United States. I. Brown, Lester O. II. Pope,
Carl. III. Title.
TD811.5.E67   363.7′28   82-3304
ISBN 0-87156-294-4   AACR2
ISBN 0-87156-807-1 (pbk.)

Book design by Howard Jacobsen
Printed in the United States of America
2 4 6 8 10 9 7 5 3 1

Contents

Foreword
by Albert Gore, Jr.

The problems associated with hazardous waste were virtually unknown a few years ago. In a remarkably short period of time, however, they have climbed to the top of the public opinion polls as a source of concern to the American people. More than 80 billion pounds of toxic waste are dumped in the United States each and every year, and the volume is steadily growing. Moreover, several thousand abandoned sites caused by the indiscriminate actions of past dumpers have already been identified.

Seldom have the American people been so united in their determination to see an environmental problem solved. Their commitment crosses partisan and ideological lines and knows no geographic boundaries. However, in spite of this unprecedented public mandate for action solutions have proven to be elusive and expensive. The economic interest of industries inconvenienced by remedial efforts have often outweighed the public interest when the critical decisions were made.

Yet the problem not only persists, it is growing. For example, since the end of World War II, the production of organic chemicals in the United States has grown from one billion pounds annually to more than 300 billion pounds annually. And of course the volume of chemical waste has grown proportionately. Moreover, with the massive shift of the chemical industry to the use of petroleum as its primary feedstock, and with the increasing sophistication of chemical science and engineering, we witnessed the introduction of powerful new kinds of substances quite different from any mankind had previously encountered.

These new substances, and the new waste streams which accompany them, are capable of ruinous damage to the environment and to living organisms. Nevertheless, 90 per cent of the wastes disposed of each year are dumped in an irresponsible and environmentally unsafe manner.

The exotic new chemical wastes, moreover, make up only a part of the hazardous waste problem. Older and more familiar villains, such as mercury and lead, are also being dumped in larger and larger quantities.

It is as if our civilization has lost a sense of its future. We are so busily engaged in making miracle products for our present enjoyment from substances deposited in the earth over millions of years, we don't stop to consider the environmental burdens we are placing on future generations. We have pillaged the past and pawned the future, telescoping time for the benefit of a fleeting present. Only when the consequences begin to manifest themselves in our own generation do we demand that changes be made.

It is now apparent, however, that industrial society has reached a turning point. The future is no longer an endless, open and empty frontier. Our children and grandchildren will likely face all the problems they can handle even without the environmental ransom we are currently demanding they pay. Our growing numbers and our growing mastery of nature's subtle processes are forcing us to forge a new ethic of "stewardship"—an ethic which insists that we foresee and account for the future consequences of our present actions.

The appearance of this book marks the maturing of the toxic waste issue as the centerpiece of the environmental movement. The authors have gone far beyond the shock treatment so commonly used to make the public aware of a problem and have presented instead a fascinating blend of politics, economics, and history—along with an easy-to-understand, layman's treatment of the legal, chemical, and biological issues involved.

It is not surprising that this book should be as good and as thorough as it is. One of the authors, Lester Brown, was the principal investigator for the first congressional hearings on toxic waste and is in large measure responsible for the national prominence which the issue subsequently and quickly attained.

It is ironic that as this book appears, the political battles it describes are heating up again. The personalities have changed and the stakes are higher, but the fundamental conflict between exploitation and grace is the same. Indeed, the present conflict is illuminated by the authors' decision to describe the contending forces in generic terms.

On one side, the American people are demanding that the toxic waste problem be solved, even if the clean up turns out to be expensive. In growing numbers, they understand that the costs of ignoring the problem will exceed by a thousand fold the cost of facing it.

They know that America's groundwater, upon which 50 per cent of our people rely for drinking water, is one of our most precious resources and must be safeguarded at all cost. It is easy for them to recognize the insanity of actions which systematically poison our groundwater.

On the other side, a small group of industries, including most prominently the petrochemical industry, has resisted the sweeping changes which will inevitably be required. Although responsible figures within the chemical industry had begun to offer welcome leadership, the more reactionary among their colleagues have found new support and encouragement in the Reagan administration which took over EPA and the Justice Department last year.

The new administration seems incapable of perceiving any points of conflict between the public interest and the unrestrained activities of the chemical industry. The painful lessons that most of America learned at Love Canal and similar sites all over the country have evidently been lost on the current stewards of our environmental laws. They seem to believe that the entire problem has been "blown out of proportion," and that industry has matters well in hand.

They have devastated the ability of the Environmental Protection Agency to administer the laws recently passed to deal with hazardous waste. They have suspended requirements that the industry notify the government where waste is being dumped and have virtually halted enforcement of the laws prohibiting irresponsible dumping. While calling on the states to play a larger role in addressing the problem, they have slashed the state assistance and liaison programs.

It is a tragic record that is already beginning to produce a massive political backlash. It is true that narrow special interests often take precedence over the broader, more diffuse public interest when the public is unaware of the battle taking place. In this case, however, the public is keenly aware of the conflict. They have seen its consequences in their own communities in all fifty states. They know the stakes are high and they are going to insist that the problem be solved in a responsible manner.

Those who wish to help them should read this book from cover to cover.

Acknowledgments

Thanks are due to G. Scott Clark, Gary A. Davis, Robert Harris, Zafar Iqbal, Barbara Morrison, Christine Riddiough, and Joel Swartz for helpful comments, and to Catherine Dollive, Mindy Dollive, and Kate Montague Perry for their assistance. We thank Durwood Zaelke, Jeffrey Trauberman, and Barbara Shaw for writing Chapter 10.

It has been a pleasure to work with the staff of Sierra Club Books.

PART I
Introduction

Hazardous waste may be the single most significant health issue of this decade. Many Americans are justly concerned about the problems of disposing of our nuclear wastes. Yet total nuclear wastes produced to date are estimated to be well under 100 million pounds. By contrast, 92 *billion* pounds of non-nuclear waste are generated each and every year; and these wastes are disposed of cavalierly.

CONGRESSMAN ALBERT GORE, JR.
October 30, 1978

CHAPTER 1

The Problem of Hazardous Wastes

On Tuesday, August 25, 1981, construction crews working in downtown San Francisco accidentally drilled into a sixteen-inch natural gas main operated by Pacific Gas and Electric (PG&E). Immediately a huge geyser of natural gas spurted into the air, endangering a major office complex, surrounding streets, shops, and smaller office buildings. Fire officials, deeply concerned that concentrations of the natural gas might fall into the 5–15 percent-range mixture with air, at which natural gas explosions most easily occur, gave immediate orders to evacuate the surrounding area. Thirty thousand office workers and shoppers were evacuated from the immediate vicinity of the gas leak.

Fortunately, although it took a full day to completely seal off the leaking natural gas, PG&E was able to reduce the flow to a reasonably safe level by shutting eight valves in their pipeline system. Police cordoned off the area affected by the slow leak still remaining, while PG&E crews welded a metal cap onto the broken pipeline.

Hours after the initial break, when most workers in the effected area had been sent home for the day, PG&E informed San Francisco Fire Chief Andrew Caspar that natural gas had not been the only substance spurting out of the broken pipeline. The gas, the utility told Caspar, had been mixed with fine droplets of lubricating oil that had accumulated in the bottom of the pipeline. And the oil, the utility reluctantly admitted, was contaminated with polychlorinated biphenyls—PCBs—a chlorinated hydrocarbon used by industry for years in electrical equipment and pumps until it was discovered that it was highly toxic and a potent carcinogen.

Immediately upon being informed that the oil spray was PCB-contaminated, Caspar called in officials from the California Occupational Safety and Health Administration (Cal-OSHA). Initial tests revealed that concentrations of PCB in the spray were approximately 25 parts per million (ppm)—half of the 50 parts per million standard set by the federal Environmental Protection Agency (EPA) as requiring the treatment of PCB-contaminated oil as hazardous. But Cal-OSHA officials and Caspar also knew that the 50 ppm standard had been challenged in court as providing insufficient protection against PCBs, and they immediately issued warnings to those persons who had been exposed to the spray to segregate shoes and clothing they had worn that might have been sprayed, to seal them in large plastic bags, to carefully shower, and to leave sprayed automobiles in the contaminated zone until decontamination procedures had been followed for the cars.

For days, debate raged over how many people needed to have their clothing and shoes shipped to a hazardous waste disposal site and what procedures to follow in cleaning the film of PCB-contaminated oil off of the buildings around the break. Assurances from the utility that all the oil had been safely removed from the streets within twenty-four hours turned out to be false, as three days later Caspar and his inspectors found oil film still remaining in large areas. Pacific Gas and Electric and the contractor whose crew punctured the pipe argued over liability for damages.

It appeared that the PCBs had leaked into the natural gas lines during the years when PG&E, like other utilities, routinely used PCBs to lubricate the huge pumps that push gas through the pipeline. After regulatory agencies required the removal of PCBs from these pumps, the utility complied, but the oil that had leaked was never removed. Within days of the puncture, newspapers reported that the utility had reason to expect that the oil spray was contaminated.

In January, 1981, PCB fluids had clogged residential gas meters on Long Island and were carried into stoves and water heaters fueled by natural gas. In the wake of this incident, the California Public Utilities Commission (PUC) had conducted a survey of gas lines in the state, and this survey had turned up extensive contamination of natural gas pipelines by the substance. Some pipelines in the Bay Area were found to have 150 ppm of PCBs, three times the EPA's hazard level. Utility and PUC engineers insisted that since PG&E's pipelines had drip valves enabling the utility to drain oily condensate that forms in low spots of the pipelines, the fluid was unlikely to build to the level at which it would fill gas meters and enter residential and commercial appliances. But the engineers admitted that no plans had been made to remove the fluids from pipelines and that it would take years to collect all of the oil contaminated by PCBs by draining each drip valve as the condensate collected. Similar problems exist all over the nation.

Thus, a simple, and not uncommon, human error—the puncture of a pipeline—can expose thirty thousand people within a few hours to a substance that is an enormous threat to their health—such a threat that their clothing must be sealed off in plastic bags and shipped to special disposal sites. The potential for repeated incidents is nationwide. Solutions are not in sight and, if adopted, would take years to implement. The toxic material in question was introduced and used in the belief that it was safe, without any serious effort to ascertain whether or not it was, in fact, safe. The threat of contamination results not from present uses of the material, but from the residues of past uses. The problem was discovered at all only because of a particular spectacular manifestation. The menace is hidden, pervasive, and difficult to combat.

Unfortunately, the contamination of natural gas pipelines with residual PCBs is only one of many examples of the hazards and problems posed by toxic materials that are no longer useful —hazardous wastes, they are called, these poisons that nobody wants. They have become a major, seemingly unavoidable side effect of industrial civilization. And finding some way to neutralize the menace they pose has become one of the major challenges in making industrialism safe for human life.

Background

The Environmental Protection Agency (EPA) is the U.S. government agency charged with regulating the disposal of hazardous wastes. The EPA uses a complicated and convoluted definition of this term for legal purposes.* But for practical purposes, the hazardous waste problem is easy to explain.

Every process for producing useful things—food, clothing, equipment, drugs, and housing—also produces materials that are not generally regarded as useful. Either they are by-products of the production process, or they are raw materials that have served their purpose. Most of these wastes are harmless—rice straw, for example, while sometimes difficult for a farmer to remove from his fields, is hardly dangerous. But a small percentage of all these wastes are dangerous. The manufactured product itself may be dangerous—unused pesticides left over after spraying a field, for example, are chemically as harmful as those sprayed on the field, but likely are more concentrated. Or the wastes may be dangerous by-products of manufacturing a nontoxic product, such as cyanide wastes from the refining of gold.

Since hazardous wastes are not useful to the industry producing them,† they have typically been disposed of in the easiest

---

*"A solid waste is any garbage, refuse, sludge or any other waste material which is not excluded under #261.4(a). . . . A solid waste is a hazardous waste if (1) It is not excluded from regulation as a hazardous waste under #261.4(b); and (2) It meets any of the following criteria: (i) It is listed in Subpart D and has not been excluded from the lists in Subpart D under ##260.20 and 260.22 of this Chapter. (ii) It is a mixture of solid waste and one or more hazardous wastes listed in Subpart D and has not been excluded from this paragraph under ##260.20 and 260.22 of this section. (iii) It exhibits any of the characteristics of hazardous waste identified in Subpart C."[1]

†Or, at least, these wastes are seen as not useful. In many cases, these "wastes" actually are useful materials with economic value—but unless the waste generators are aware of this value, they will still view the wastes as useless and try to get rid of them as cheaply as possible, regardless of the problems that may result.

and cheapest way. A major problem now is how to ensure that those who generate such hazardous wastes do not simply dump them, but handle them without creating public health or environmental problems. In some cases, wastes are generated and dumped in large quantities by major industrial producers (producer wastes); in others, it is the consumers of a product who, having used it, get rid of it (consumer wastes). Producer wastes are typically more concentrated than consumer wastes, but their total volume may be smaller. No one really knows, for it is impossible to keep track of the wastes discarded by the ultimate consumers.* At the end of World War II, the United States produced only 1 billion pounds of hazardous (producer) wastes per year. The production of such waste has since increased at a rate of about 10 percent per year.[2] The EPA now estimates that around 80 billion pounds of hazardous waste material are generated annually—about 350 pounds of hazardous waste for every inhabitant of the United States. The EPA further estimates that only 10 percent of this waste is properly disposed of.† A wide variety of industries, led by the organic chemical and metals industries, produce these wastes (Table 1-1), and dispose of them in a variety of ways, mostly unsafe (Table 1-2).

Literally thousands of wastewater lagoons and ponds pose a threat to drinking water. A 1980 EPA survey of industrial im-

---

*The figures that follow, and those found in almost any discussion of this subject, are underestimates, *inter alia* as they relate to producer wastes, not consumer wastes. A March 1983 report of the Office of Technology Assessment estimated the annual generation of industrial waste could be as high as 360 billion pounds, some four times higher than EPA estimates (Office of Technology Assessment, *Technology and Management Strategies for Hazardous Wastes*, U.S. Congress, 1983).

†Tables 1-1–1-5 present a variety of data on current disposal practices, industrial sources, physical form, and chemical composition of hazardous waste streams. Various studies in the last decade have used different definitions of "hazardous waste" and have employed different base years and different data bases. Comparison of the data from different studies is therefore difficult. For example, the data on industrial sources in Table 1-1 are based on the total 1978 estimate of seventy-six billion pounds of hazardous waste. The data on physical form and chemical composition in Table 1-4 are based on an earlier 1973 study, which analyzed only 25 percent of the total waste stream identified in the 1978 study and thus covered only twenty billion pounds of hazardous waste.

poundments (Table 1-3) found that 70 percent of those assessed were unlined; 33 percent of all the industrial sites contained potentially hazardous wastes; only 5 percent of the sites were monitored for groundwater-quality; and 33 percent of the sites were located within one mile of a water-supply well.

Similar dangers exist for the second most common disposal technique—nonsecure landfills. Seventy-five percent of all landfill sites are in areas "particularly susceptible to contamination problems" because they are in wetlands, on floodplains, or over aquifers.[3]

Once disposed of unsafely, hazardous wastes do not remain immobile. Pesticide residues dumped in Hardeman County, Tennessee, ended up in the local drinking water supply (see Chapter 3). Abandoned drums at Chemical Control, Inc. in Elizabeth, New Jersey, exploded in April, 1980, and the toxic fumes drifted off—fortunately away from nearby New York City (see Chapter 7). Toxic chemicals dumped by Hooker Chemical at Love Canal seeped into basements and buildings of residents who lived in houses near the canal (see Chapter 5). Pesticides dumped by Occidental Chemical in Lathrop, California migrated into the water table and contaminated neighboring wells (see Chapter 4). The highly toxic carcinogenic pesticide kepone was washed off the urban lots in Hopewell, Virginia where Life Sciences, Inc. dumped it and was carried into the James River and taken up by oysters and other shellfish. Uranium-mining mill tailings, used as landfill for houses constructed in Grand Junction, Colorado, emitted radon gas which was inhaled by local residents.

Table 1-1. Sources of Hazardous Wastes, 1978

Generating Industry	Pounds (billions)
Organic chemicals	26
Primary metals	29
Electroplating	9
Inorganic chemicals	9
Textiles, petroleum refining, rubber, and plastics	3
TOTAL	76

Source: EPA *Journal* vol. 5, no. 2 (February 1979), p. 12.

Major Sources of Hazardous Wastes

The rate of production of hazardous wastes, both producer and consumer, has increased dramatically in recent years. But the problem is as old as human technology and has been recognized for centuries. For instance, the ancient Greeks knew that the asbestos used in weaving garments was dangerous to the slaves who breathed in the fibers released in making the cloth. Lead leached by wine from lead-lined storage jugs is thought to have poisoned the bibulous Roman aristocracy.

PRODUCER WASTES

Although mining was the first significant source of hazardous wastes, and for centuries the most important, such wastes have been generated by virtually every advance in technology. With the advent of the Industrial Revolution, the mining of fossil fuels became a major source of toxic wastes. In England, coal mining generated a public outcry against the leftover spoils piles, which, after combining with rainwater, formed acids, poisoning streams. In the nineteenth century, as German chemists developed coal-tar dyes—relieving the textile industry of its dependence on expensive, sometimes quirky, and difficult-to-obtain natural dyes—toxic by-products began to make their way into the waterways of industrial Germany. Eighteenth- and nineteenth-century advances in metallurgy required the use of great

Table 1-2. Methods of Hazardous Waste Disposal, 1978

Method	Pounds (billions)
Properly disposed of	7.6
On-site disposal	5
Secure landfill	2.6
Improperly handled	68.4
Unlined lagoons and ponds	34
Nonsecure landfills	20
Ocean dumping, sewers, roads, deep-well injection, ordinary incinerators	14.4
TOTAL	76

Source: Douglas Costle, "EPA Moves to Control Hazardous Wastes" (press release, Dec. 19, 1978).

quantities of acids to strip corrosive materials from the vast new quantities of iron and steel pouring from Henry Bessemer's new furnaces, and these acids had to be disposed of. The invention of photography increased the demand for a variety of new inorganic chemicals, which also had to be disposed of. The new technology of electricity required huge quantities of lead storage batteries. Lead smelters and the battery plants all left toxic lead wastes in the soil, air, and waters. Some of the sulfuric acid used as an electrolyte also ended up as a toxic waste. The development of high explosives resulted in nitrate wastes, while the continuing efforts to find new steels to resist the impact of shells on warships meant that chromium and other metals were employed on a wide scale, and chromic wastes became a significant problem.

After 1850, as the world entered the petroleum age, new chemical techniques were developed to break crude oil down into its component hydrocarbon chains. The new refinery methods, based on the fractional distillation of petroleum, required the use of metal catalysts, themselves toxic. Then it was discovered that the most important of these fractions, gasoline, was more useful as a motor fuel if tetraethyl lead was added to reduce its tendency to explode prematurely (knock) in internal combustion engines—and a vast additional source of lead wastes was created. When William Hall, an American scientist at Oberlin College, discovered how to use electricity to separate

Table 1-3. Wastewater Impoundments Identified by the Environmental Protection Agency, 1979

Category	Sites Located	Impoundments	Sites Assessed
Industrial	10,819	25,749	8,193
Municipal	19,116	36,179	10,675
Agricultural	14,677	19,167	6,597
Mining	7,100	24,451	1,448
Oil/gas brine pits	24,527	64,951	3,304
Other	1,500	5,745	327
TOTALS	77,739	176,242	30,544

Source: EPA, *Groundwater Protection*, WQM CWH-5547, Washington, D.C., 1980.

aluminum from its ores in 1889, he also discovered a technology that released large quantities of fluoride wastes from those ores—and something had to be done with the fluoride.

At the end of the nineteenth century, the pioneering work of the Curies with radioactive materials made it possible to illuminate the dials of wristwatches with radium. However, this new industry left behind the tailing piles from the radium mines, the waste materials of the purification process, and the waste materials from the factories, where workers patiently licked small brushes to pick up the radium paint and apply it to the minute and hour hands.

In the twentieth century, the explosive growth of petroleum-based organic chemistry made possible a host of new and useful materials—synthetic fabrics, pesticides, wood preservatives, plastics, drugs, new paints, and solvents. Each entered commerce and found its place, and each left behind some by-products, waste materials, and intermediate chemicals used in its processing, which had to be disposed of. Tables 1-4 and 1-5 illustrate some of the major components of the waste stream by physical form, chemical composition, and industry producing each.*

Certain regions of the country have high concentrations of industries that produce toxic wastes. According to a 1979 EPA study, the big ten states generating 65 percent of all hazardous wastes are, in order of amount produced: Texas, Ohio, Pennsylvania, Louisiana, Michigan, Indiana, Illinois, Tennessee, West Virginia, and California.[4] These overall figures conceal some major regional variations. Problems from uranium mill tailings, for example, are largely confined to the mountain West—Colorado, Utah, and New Mexico. New Jersey probably has the largest volume of dangerous chemical wastes. Waste problems resulting from oil production and refining are particularly acute in Texas, California, and New Jersey. In 1970, the EPA estimated that the West South Central region of the country produced the largest volume of organic wastes, but only one-third the quantity of aqueous inorganic wastes that was

*For more detailed data on major industrial sources of hazardous wastes, including their major chemical classes, their origin by major geographical area, and their volume of generation, see Appendices I–III.

produced in either the Mid Atlantic states or the East North Central states.* 5

CONSUMER WASTES

It is important to recognize that all the above data focus on producer wastes—that is, materials generated and discarded by industrial and commercial manufacturers. Sources, however, include wastes generated by consumers, which, in most cases, probably comprise much larger volumes, but in much more dilute form. For example, the production of mildew-resistant

Table 1-4. Physical and Chemical Classification of Hazardous Wastes —Based on 20-Billion-Pound Survey, 1973

Classification	Pounds (billions)
Liquid inorganic wastes	7.0
Copper- and lead-bearing refinery wastes	.8
Brine sludges from chlorine production	.1
Steel plant wastes	.5
Organic chemicals	1.0
Gasoline-blending wastes	.4
Solvent-reclaiming residues	.3
Outdated or contaminated tear gas	.3
Aqueous organic chemicals	10.0
Organic pesticide and herbicide wastes	1.0
Dilute drug manufacturing waste	5.0
Solids, slurries and sludges	.7
Sodium dichromate wastes	.3
Arsenic trioxide from smelters	.02
Recovered arsenic from smelters	.04
Battery manufacturing sludges	.05
Refrigeration equipment wastes	.2
TOTAL	20.0

Source: EPA, *Report to Congress on Disposal of Hazardous Wastes* (Washington, D.C., June 20, 1973), pp. 50–53.

Note: Only major categories and subcategories are listed, so totals for both categories and subcategories are less than overall totals. For a detailed characterization of waste streams, see Appendix I. For an overall regional classification of major waste streams, see Appendix II.

*For a listing of the relative quantities of wastes generated in all fifty states, see Appendix III.

paints requires the use of mercury. Paint companies discard some mercury as production waste, which is included in the EPA's estimates for the total paint-industry waste (7 million tons total in 1973). However, most mercury-containing paints are used in painting bathrooms and kitchens. This mercury becomes a waste only when the paint is stripped and discarded or when the house is demolished. Similarly, although petroleum refineries produce massive quantities of lead-contaminated wastes, most of all the tetraethyl lead manufactured becomes a waste, not at the refinery, but as it is emitted in dilute form in automobile exhaust.

No good estimates exist for the total of consumer and producer wastes. In the case of such hazardous wastes as heavy metals, which are nondegradable and thus effectively *immortal,* total waste production over time will be equivalent to total pro-

Table 1-5. Correlation Between Industry and Chemical Composition of Waste

Industry	Chemical Composition of Waste*							
	As	Cd	Cr	Cu	Cn	Pb	Hg	ClHC
Mining and Metallurgy	•	•	•	•	•	•	•	
Paint and Dye		•	•	•	•	•		
Pesticide	•			•		•	•	•
Electrical and Electronic			•	•		•	•	•
Printing and Duplicating	•	•	•			•		
Electroplating	•	•	•			•		
Chemical Manufacturing			•	•			•	•
Explosives	•		•			•		
Rubber and Plastics				•			•	•
Battery		•				•	•	
Pharmaceuticals	•		•	•				
Textiles			•	•				
Petroleum and Coal	•					•		•
Pulp and Paper							•	
Leather			•					

Source: EPA, *Report to Congress on Disposal of Hazardous Wastes* (Washington, D.C., June 20, 1973), p. 5.

*As = arsenic; Cd = cadmium; Cr = chromium; Cu = copper; Cn = cyanide; Pb = lead; Hg = mercury; ClHC = chlorinated hydrocarbons.

duction. *All* the lead, mercury, cadmium, and other heavy metals produced in a given year will eventually end up as hazardous wastes.

Other toxic substances are completely or partly degraded in use. For example, most of the benzene used in gasoline is burned in the engine, and broken down into carbon dioxide and water vapor. Some is, however, released at service stations as benzene vapor and represents an airborne hazardous waste.

Because of the prevalence of such consumer wastes, hazardous wastes are found not only in factories, in mines, in refineries, but also on streets, in the tailpipes of automobiles, and in homes themselves.

Major Chemical Categories

From a practical standpoint, it is conventional to classify hazardous wastes in the following major categories: radioactives; flammables; heavy metals; asbestos; acids and bases; and synthetic organic chemicals.

RADIOACTIVES*

Those elements that are intrinsically unstable and that give off energy or charged particles as they decay into other forms are termed "radioactives" and are collectively known as "radionuclides." Because the energy or small particles that are being emitted by these materials have the potential to damage living tissue, radionuclides are highly hazardous. Among their other effects, they can cause immediate death, burns or injury, and even in small quantities lead to birth defects, cancer, and other chronic disease.

Radionuclides are among the more recent additions to the arsenal of industry. Certain radioactive minerals, principally uranium, thorium, and radium, occur in significant quantities in nature. In the latter part of the nineteenth century, scientists, led

---

*Because the history of public concern over radioactive waste is very different, and much older, than that over nonradioactive hazardous wastes, and because of the extensive literature on radioactive waste disposal, such wastes are not dealt with in this volume. For a good recent discussion on radioactive waste disposal, see R. D. Lipschutz, *Radioactive Waste: Politics, Technology, and Risk*.[6]

by Pierre and Marie Curie, investigated the properties of these materials and learned how to separate them from their natural ores. Initially, radioactive materials were just curiosities. Radium, important though it was in helping physicists to understand the composition of matter, was an industrially insignificant element until well after World War I, and many of its early uses constituted dangerous quackery based on the notion that radiation had "magical" curing properties.

In the 1930s, however, as an outgrowth of experiments in the nature of matter and of efforts to test Einstein's relativity theory, which proposed that matter could be converted to energy, physicists mastered the fission process, in which neutrons emitted from uranium were used to split other atoms, producing new radioactive elements and radioactive isotopes of known elements. Because each of these elements or isotopes has its own special properties, science rapidly developed a variety of uses for many, as radiation sources for x-rays of material welds, as medicinal tracers within the body, in nuclear power plants, as a heat source to power steam-driven turbines. By the 1960s, radioactive materials were being used in a wide diversity of industrial settings, although by far the largest source of man-made radioactive materials remained the nuclear weapons industry and nuclear power plants.

Radioactive materials are unstable. Eventually, they release enough of their matter or energy that they are transformed into stable, nonradioactive elements or isotopes. The length of time this transformation takes varies widely from one radionuclide to another. The amount of time it takes for one-half of the total amount of radiation to be released is called a half-life. The half-life of plutonium 239, the most lethal of the radionuclides, a principal component of nuclear weapons, the fuel of "breeder" nuclear reactors, and a by-product of ordinary nuclear power plants, is 24,000 years. After 24,000 years, that is, one-half of the plutonium 239 will have decayed to a stable form, and one-half will remain. At the end of the next 24,000 years, one-half of the remainder will have reached stability, and one-fourth of the original material will remain in the form of plutonium 239.

Radioactive materials are also classified by the type of radiation they emit. Gamma emitters, for example, emit gamma rays, a form of energy with great penetrating powers. Neutron emitters, principally found in nuclear reactors, also have great penetrating powers. Beta emitters, such as strontium 90 and krypton 85, emit beta particles (electrons or positrons). These are lighter than neutrons, but carry electrical charges that reduce their penetrating power. Alpha emitters release energy in the form of particles consisting of two neutrons and two protons. These particles are heavy and have relatively little penetrating power. Radioactive materials emitting gamma rays or neutrons can affect organisms from a relatively great distance. Beta emitters are most dangerous if they are at very close range, particularly if they come to rest within the body. Alpha emitters are of concern only if they come to rest within the body.

Because of this diversity of characteristics, it is difficult to generalize about the forms in which radioactive waste materials may pose a threat. In general, the faster the rate of decay and the shorter the half-life, the more intense the radiation. Similarly, while alpha emitters do not travel far, because their energy is rapidly absorbed by other atoms they encounter, they do tremendous damage at close range by giving up this energy. Thus, plutonium 239, an alpha emitter with a very long half-life, is of enormous concern because it can become lodged inside the body, in the lungs, if it breaks down into particles. Strontium 90, a beta emitter, poses a threat because it tends to accumulate in the bones in place of chemically similar calcium.

FLAMMABLES

Flammables are a miscellaneous category of chemicals whose danger derives mainly from their tendency to react strongly with other materials—in this case the oxygen in the atmosphere—giving off massive quantities of heat in the process. The most important flammables are petroleum or natural gas by-products. There are also such relatively exotic flammables as pure elemental sodium. But, like acids and bases, their very reactivity makes their hazard short-lived as, once released into the environment, they immediately come into contact with atmospheric oxygen and heat or sparks.

HEAVY METALS

Just as mining was the first significant source of hazardous wastes, heavy metals were for many centuries the major component of hazardous wastes. These metals—among the most important being lead, arsenic, zinc, cadmium, copper, and mercury—were among the first raw materials ever used for technological purposes. They are often found in close conjunction with each other in nature, are relatively easy to separate from their natural ores through smelting, and are relatively easy to shape and mold, either alone or alloyed with other metals.

As science and technology advanced, an ever-greater variety of uses were found for heavy metals, which were mined and processed in greater and greater quantities. For instance, lead, originally prized for its malleability and resistance to corrosion, was later used in a wide range of products and processes: in bullets for its density; in storage batteries, because of the relative ease with which it both yields up and accepts electrons; as a soldering agent to seal tin cans, because of its low melting point and ability to adhere to other metals; as a gasoline additive, to prevent irregular explosion under pressure (knocking); as a base for paints, because of its resistance to weathering; and, finally, in the nuclear industry, because its great mass enables it to absorb neutrons and block radiation.

In older cities, lead can be found in tap water as it leaches from old pipes. It may also be found in old interior and even new exterior paints, or coming out of the tailpipes of automobiles from leaded gasoline, thus contaminating the streets and playgrounds of the neighborhood.

Copper, originally a component of the bronze that early civilizations used to forge weapons and tools, was early prized for its qualities in conducting heat and for its resistance—and that of its alloys, brass and bronze—to the corrosion that made iron unsuitable in ocean-going vessels. With the dawn of the age of electricity, copper wiring became the material of choice because of its excellent qualities as a conductor. Copper salts were also used to kill fungus on crops and fruits.

Mercury, known to the ancients as quicksilver, has been used most widely for its poisonous qualities. Previously used in drugs and medicinals for treatment of various diseases, including syphilis, it is now added to paints to make them resist mildew and to seeds because of its properties as a fungicide; mercury fumes are released from mildew-resistant paints, often sold for use in interior kitchens and bathrooms. Mercury is also widely used in the chemical industry in the manufacture of chlorine; as a common drug ingredient, often contaminating waste waters discharged by hospitals; and in many small batteries sold for electronic appliances and often burned in incinerators or disposed of in ordinary dumps and landfills. Zinc, originally used for alloying into bronze and later for galvanizing iron to protect it against corrosion, is now commonly used in batteries and cosmetics.

Modern industry also makes substantial use of other heavy metals, including selenium, beryllium, and cadmium. Cadmium is often leached from solders and pipes into water supplies, particularly hot water drawn from taps; it is contained in tires and released onto city streets as the treads wear down; and it is used in the electroplating industry, which discharges it into sewers. Sewage sludge from many cities is, as a result, often heavily contaminated with cadmium.

Overall rates of utilization of most heavy metals have increased dramatically over the past century and continue to do so. For instance, worldwide production of mercury has more than doubled since World War II, and worldwide production of lead is doubling every twenty years. Utilization of such metals as cadmium and beryllium for nuclear reactors has increased even faster. This increase in the utilization of heavy metals has happened in spite of the fact that many of their earlier uses have either been superseded by newer technologies or banned as health hazards. Lead, for example, is no longer permitted in interior paints in the United States; methyl mercury fungicides have been banned; and arsenic- and copper-based pesticides have given way to chlorinated hydrocarbons or organophosphates. But, even as old uses are phased out, new uses continue to increase our dependence on heavy metals.

Heavy metals pose a variety of health hazards. Lead, in even very small quantities, is a neurotoxin, causing learning disabilities in children, particularly in major urban ghettos, where exposures to lead are high. Lead also produces other chronic toxic effects involving a wide range of organs. Mercury is an even more powerful neurotoxin and has been implicated in mental illness among nineteenth-century hatters, who used it to treat furs; among families in the American Southwest who accidentally ingested mercury-treated seed; and in Japan, where the population of Minamata Bay and local fishermen were afflicted by a progressive neurological disease due to high levels of mercury that had accumulated in the fish they ate. Cadmium is implicated in high blood pressure and heart disease and is carcinogenic, being implicated in lung and prostate cancer.

As wastes, heavy metals pose particular problems. Their toxicity is a function of the structure of their atoms. As elements, they are toxic. By contrast, many other materials are only toxic in particular molecular or chemical forms. These molecular forms, unlike the atomic structure of lead, are continually changing under the impact of chemical reactions. But lead—and this is the case with all heavy metals—will always remain lead regardless of what other materials it reacts with, or how it is heated or put under pressure. Neither heat nor biological processes can change it into anything else. It may temporarily take a molecular form in which it is not readily available for assimilation into living organisms, and so for a time it may be neutralized. But it will always retain the potential to be converted into a toxic form.

ASBESTOS

Of ancient origin and uses, asbestos is the generic name for a group of minerals composed of calcium or magnesium silicates formed into long, threadlike fibers. These fibers can be woven or spun into cloth and shaped into materials by mixing with cement or other substances. They possess the special qualities of very high resistance to heat and electricity. This combination results in a wide range of uses, including insulation of electrical wiring, hot pipes and furnaces; firemen's suits and theater curtains; and automobile brake linings.

The effects of heavy metals generally depend upon their chemical reactivity; however, it is the fibrous nature of asbestos and its resistance to biological degradation and chemical change that make it so dangerous. Because of its tiny fibers and fibrils, it easily penetrates the exposed surfaces of the lungs; there it provides a continuous irritation and cellular response, which result either in a progressive lung disease known as asbestosis or in a variety of cancers of the lung and other sites, when blood and lymph streams carry the fibers through the body.

ACIDS AND BASES

Acids and bases are not in themselves necessarily hazardous—many common components of the body are slightly acidic or basic, as are foods. Materials that are very acidic or basic are extremely chemically reactive and corrosive. However, their hazards are likely to be relatively short-lived. Once released into the environment, acids begin to encounter bases and vice versa. The acid gives up its hydrogen ions to the base, leaving behind various neutral compounds (salts) and water. In large concentrations, acids and bases can do considerable damage along the way, especially if released into small streams and rivers, where they can kill fish and other aquatic life before becoming neutralized. An additional hazard is that acids, in particular, may dissolve heavy metals out of soils or sediments, and these heavy metals remain in suspension even after the acid itself has been neutralized. While one very powerful base, quicklime, and a number of powerful acids, including sulfuric and nitric acid, have been known and used for hundreds of years, the production of corrosive acids and bases has increased dramatically in the past century.

SYNTHETIC ORGANIC CHEMICALS

While heavy metals, asbestos, acids, and bases have been used for hundreds of years, synthetic organic chemicals are a relatively new category of industrial products. In the nineteenth century, limited quantities of organic chemicals, principally dyes, were developed from coal tar and wood alcohol. The more recent use of petroleum as a basic feedstock has, however, enabled synthesis of organic chemicals in relatively limitless quantities and has thus revolutionized the entire chemical industry.

The basic units of synthetic organic chemicals are hydrocarbons—materials formed through chemical reactions under heat and pressure from the remains of plants and animals and preserved in the form of fossil fuels—coal, natural gas, or petroleum. In coal and petroleum, long chains of carbon and hydrogen are strung together in large, complex molecules. The molecule of natural gas—methane, CH_4—is itself a simple, short chain, but can be easily combined into very large, long molecular chains.

Plants, using chlorophyll and other organic enzymes, do manufacture some fairly complicated organic molecules. Cellulose, for example, consists of very long chains of glucose molecules, often more than a thousand linked in one strand. However, these naturally occurring hydrocarbon chains have been developed through evolutionary processes because they served a necessary function in the organism. Only a small fraction of the possible arrangements of carbon and hydrogen occur in plant and animal species in nature.

For thousands of years mankind has utilized certain processes to produce synthetic organic chemicals from naturally occurring hydrocarbons, principally wood and grain. Alcohol, fermented from fruits and grains, is one of the most important, but the distillation of turpentine from pine resins, charcoal from wood, and pectins from fruit are other examples of very ancient organic chemicals produced from wood and grain bases. Typically, the chemicals produced by these processes were smaller, simpler molecules than those from which they were produced. It is easier to break hydrocarbon bonds than to create them, except with the aid of such biological catalysts as chlorophyll, or through slow and tedious use of heat and pressure, the means by which nature produces oil and coal geologically. Because these synthetic organic chemicals were simpler versions of naturally occurring organic materials, natural systems typically found it easy to break them down and assimilate them. Alcohol can be metabolized directly in the bloodstream, burns easily at low temperatures, and oxidizes into vinegar in the presence of oxygen.

However, beginning with the convoluted, complex hydrocarbon chains of coal and oil, or the easily combinable methane (CH_4) molecules of natural gas, heat and pressure can relatively quickly produce the building blocks of myriads of new com-

pounds that do not occur in nature and that are extremely difficult for natural systems to assimilate, either because of their
complexity, or because of their specific chemical structure.
After World War I, the focus of hydrocarbon production
shifted rapidly from coal to petroleum and natural-gas
materials:

> In 1931, the U.S. National Bureau of Standards and the American
> Petroleum Institute began a systematic study of petroleum hydro-
> carbon synthesis and uses. This culminated after World War II in
> a fundamental shift of organic chemical production to the
> petroleum industry, which, along with increased hydrocarbon
> production from catalytic cracking of petroleum, gave birth to a
> new petroleum industry. Petrochemicals are the quintessence of
> a "process industry," in which a small number of primary
> constituents from crude oil are converted into a large number of
> intermediate chemicals and a still larger number of large scale end
> products.[7]

Petroleum when separated into its various components by
fractional distillation, yields a number of light molecular weight
hydrocarbons that are highly volatile and from which the majority of organic chemicals now in use are manufactured or synthesized. United States production of synthetic organic chemicals
took off sharply after World War II and increased progressively
ever since. The total United States production of synthetic
organic chemicals increased from about 1 billion pounds in
1940, to 30 billion in 1950, to 300 billion pounds in 1976.
Growth rates of 15 percent or more are not uncommon for
organic chemical industries at a time when the rest of the
economy is advancing by only 4 or 5 percent per year.
Synthetic organic chemicals, whether manufactured or synthesized from coal, natural gas, or petroleum, are a diverse
group with a wide range of uses. Products derived from these
chemicals, particularly since the advent of the petrochemical
era, have increasingly supplanted natural materials such as
cotton, wood, leather, and natural rubber. But petrochemical
technology has also made possible the production of a wide
variety of new products that could not otherwise be manufactured in large quantities from naturally available raw

materials. Even when these new products have substituted directly for commercially feasible natural materials—as in the substitution of artificial fibers like rayon and nylon for cotton and wool—they offer substantial commercial advantages to both the producer and the ultimate consumer. However, some of these advantages occur at the expense of natural-product markets, which cannot compete with the economy of scale of petrochemicals and which are thus supplanted, if not destroyed. These advantages have also occurred at the expense of the health of exposed workers and of the general public, and at the expense of the generation and disposal of highly hazardous toxic wastes.

Three major uses of hydrocarbons should be clearly distinguished. First, some are used as *end products* in themselves. These include lightweight hydrocarbon fractions, containing relatively small molecules, such as ethylene, toluene, benzene and styrene, some of which are important industrial solvents. Second, some are used as *intermediates,* such as ethylene and styrene, which can be linked together (polymerized) to form long-chain plastics, such as polyethylene and polystyrene, for use in insulation foam, furniture, and packaging materials. And finally, some are used for the *synthesis of novel molecules* by chemical splicing or molecular engineering, designed to meet specific industrial needs.

Such novel chemicals, with entirely new properties, have never before existed and no natural system has ever been previously exposed to them. Examples of such splicing include a wide range of *halogenated hydrocarbons,* in which atoms of chlorine, bromine, or iodine are added to basic hydrocarbon chains, producing such relatively simple new chemicals as trichloroethylene (TCE) and perchloroethylene (PCE)—used as industrial solvents or degreasing agents, or more complex organic chemicals, such as the pesticides DDT, mirex, and chlordane, which after World War II were widely used against agricultural pests and insect-borne disease, such as malaria, filariasis, yellow fever, and dengue fever. By tacking chlorine onto particular hydrocarbons known as phenols, chemists produced polychlorinated biphenyls (PCBs), chemicals whose greatest value was their ability to resist breakdown from heat and electrical charges when used as insulating fluids in transformers and other electrical machinery.* By adding larger numbers of chlorine atoms, chemists produced pentachlorophenol (PCP), a wood preservative used to resist termites. By using bromine instead of chlorine, an effective fire retardant—polybrominated biphenyls (PBBs)—was produced. By adding halogens, simple precursors of new plastics, such as vinyl chloride (VC), were synthesized; the VC was subsequently polymerized to form polyvinyl chloride (PVC) for use in records, plastic pipe, and a wide range of other products.

By splicing or dividing complex hydrocarbon chains in different places and in different ways, it is possible to reproduce synthetic versions of natural chemicals—as drug companies do in synthesizing hormones or some drugs. But it is also possible to split and divide the hydrocarbon chains in fossil fuels in ways that produce substances that do not naturally occur in living organisms—but which in important ways may mimic them.†

The halogenated hydrocarbons are a particularly important class and exemplify many of the problems of the new petrochemical era. Their most common characteristic is an ability to suppress or alter various chemical reactions involving naturally occurring organic processes. Insecticides like DDT or mirex lethally alter the metabolic processes of insects. PBBs applied as a fire retardant suppress the rapid oxidation of organic materials in the presence of heat.

An additional important characteristic of the more complex halogenated organics is their resistance to degradation by natural biological reactions. Thus, chlorinated hydrocarbon pesticides were favored because they are persistent—they, and their effects, linger in the environment and frequent reapplica-

---

*It is estimated that up to one-third of 35 million oil-containing electrical transformers are contaminated with PCBs.

†Mimicking may be relatively primitive—many organic chemicals are capable of passing through the membrane barriers that separate the lungs and intestines from outside abuses and are dissolved and transported through the body by the bloodstream. A more complex form of such mimicry results in the concentration of strontium 90, a radioisotope, in the bone tissues, because strontium is so chemically similar to calcium. In the most sophisticated forms of mimicry, certain drugs or chemicals seek out and attach themselves to cell receptors originally designed for chemically similar but nonidentical hormones or other constituents of body chemistry.

tion is not necessary. Their toxicity results in part from these same characteristics. Chlorine and bromine—the two halogens most commonly found in industrial hydrocarbons—are very toxic. (Chlorine and iodine, another halogen, are used as disinfectants for this reason.)

In nature, unattached to hydrocarbon chains, the halogens tend to react with other elements in the environment to form biologically less-toxic chemicals, like table salt, sodium chloride. However, attached to a hydrocarbon chain, the halogens can remain toxic and enter into the metabolic system of a wide variety of organisms, whether those be a mosquito or other pest that has been targeted for attack or a nontarget species—a fish or a man.

Once these complex chemicals enter the ecosystem, some other characteristics become critical. Halogenated hydrocarbons, especially the more complex ones, are almost insoluble in water. (This insolubility increases their value for some purposes—it means, in the case of insecticides, that the first rain does not wash them from the farmer's field.) These hydrocarbons, however, tend to be much more soluble in fats. While they are only slowly carried off in stream waters for fish to ingest, once ingested they are stored in the fat cells in the body, to await ingestion by the first predator.

Because of their selective solubility and preference for concentrating in fatty tissues, halogenated hydrocarbon pesticides are thus described as "bioaccumulative," meaning that they tend to accumulate in living organisms in a much higher concentration than in the surrounding ecosystem. Other hazardous wastes that bioaccumulate because they have such favorite target organs in the body include mercury, lead, and certain radioisotopes, such as strontium 90.

However, unlike heavy metals, even the more complex halogenated hydrocarbons are not immortal. Indeed, like the natural hydrocarbons from which they are formed—coal, oil and natural gas—they are fuels. By breaking the bonds between atoms of hydrogen and carbon, energy originally stored as the result of photosynthesis in plants is released. But the presence of the halogen atoms impedes this reaction—again a factor tending to make the material durable, and useful to industrial man. PCBs resist the attacks of electricity and heat on their molecular structure—up to a point. However, they can be incinerated—at temperatures over 900 degrees centigrade—and to ensure complete combustion must remain at such temperatures for a relatively long time. And, while halogenated hydrocarbons resist the attacks of most scavengers that break down other organic molecules—bacteria, yeasts, and fungi—they succumb slowly to some, so that in nature they gradually change their forms. This transformation or degradation can be good—toxic molecules can evolve into less toxic ones—but it can also be troublesome; in some cases, the new materials may be even more toxic than the old, as when PCBs break down into dibenzofurans.

Thus, useful as they are, synthetic organic chemicals are hazardous. For example, benzene induces aplastic anemia and leukemia; VC is a highly potent carcinogen; the entire class of chlorinated hydrocarbon pesticides—DDT, dieldrin, endrin, chlordane—produces adverse reproductive effects in birds and is also carcinogenic, as demonstrated in test animals; PCBs are carcinogenic and impair fertility; and dioxin (TCDD), a contaminant of phenoxy herbicides such as 2,4,5-T, is the most toxic known chemical, inducing cancer and birth defects in experimental animals in parts-per-trillion concentrations.

Indeed, "a disproportionately large number of recognized carcinogens fall into just three families of widely used petrochemicals: aromatic amines, in the form of dyes and synthetic intermediates, particularly epoxy compounds and hydrazines; chlorinated olefins, as monomers and pesticides; and alkyl halides, as solvents and degreasing agents."[8]

The Hazards of Hazardous Wastes

The hazards of hazardous wastes have only recently been recognized. Indeed, the literature on such effects is relatively scanty. However, a recent EPA survey of 350 hazardous waste disposal sites has documented a wide range of damages both to the environment and to the public health (see Table 1-6). These hazards were tabulated under nine major categories, which were not mutually exclusive:

"1. *Groundwater/Water Supply.* These are damages that have resulted in the contamination of water supplies and/or groundwaters. Water supplies are both groundwaters and reservoirs. While most potable water supplies in the Report are groundwaters, not all groundwaters are potable drinking water supplies.

2. *Well Closures.* These are incidents where drinking water wells were actually closed. Instances of contamination but not closure are not included. The citation consists of the number of sites in a particular State followed by the number (in parentheses) of actual wells closed in the State.

3. *Habitat Destruction.* These are incidents where natural habitats such as streams, rivers, lakes, or fields have been rendered unfit for indigenous species or contaminated to the extent that indigenous species, while present, are adversely affected.

4. *Human Health.* These are instances of actual human health damages such as kidney malfunction, respiratory difficulties, or death. Endangerment sites are not included in this category.

5. *Soil Contamination.* While most sites have some degree of soil contamination, only those sites where the major consideration is the hazard presented by the presence of contaminated soils are included. Such sites as those rendered unfit for planned playgrounds or developments are examples of situations in this category.

6. *Fish Kills.* These are cases of documented fish kills caused by the chronic release of hazardous materials from a site.

7. *Livestock.* These are instances of actual loss of livestock due to the ingestion of contaminated vegetation or waters.

8. POTWs *or Sewers.* These are instances of chronic discharge of hazardous materials into sewer systems or to publicly owned treatment works (POTWs) which rendered them unsafe or inoperable.

9. *Other.* These sites include damages to crops or wildlife, air pollution, fire or explosion hazards, and abandoned sites."[9]

The same EPA report summarized available information on the identity of some major classes of chemicals found at the 350

Table 1-6. Incidents: Damages to Environment and Public Health in 350 Hazardous Waste Disposal Sites, 1980

State	Groundwater/ Water Supply Contamination	Well Closures*	Habitat Destruction	Human Health Damage	Soil Contamination	Fish Kills	Livestock Loss	POTWs† or Sewer Damage	Other Damage
Alabama	3		3		3	1			1
Alaska			1		1				
Arizona	3								
Arkansas			3						
California	7	3 (34)							
Colorado	2			2	2				
Connecticut	7	4 (21)		1	2				2
Delaware	2								
Florida	2	2 (6+)	1			1			1
Georgia								1	
Hawaii									
Idaho					1				
Illinois	17	3 (11)	3	1	1	1	3		3
Indiana	4	2 (2+)	1		3	1	1	1	1
Iowa	3				1	1	1		1
Kansas			1						
Kentucky	2		2	1				1	1
Louisiana	3	2 (16+)	1	1	1		1		1
Maine	1		1						
Maryland	4	2 (6)	2	1	1				1
Massachusetts	7	3	2	1	3				
Michigan	7	2 (4)		2	3	1			1
Minnesota									
Mississippi			2	1	1				
Missouri	1								
Montana									

State									
Nebraska	1								
Nevada	9								
New Hampshire		1 (17)				1			1
New Jersey		3 (252)	3	5					
New Mexico				1					
New York	15	3 (41)	9	3	3				4
North Carolina	2	2	1		2	2	1		2
North Dakota							1		
Ohio	3	1	6	1	3	1			1
Oklahoma									
Oregon	1	1	1		1				
Pennsylvania	35	2 (9)	11	11	5			2	
Rhode Island	5	2 (15)	2		3				
South Carolina	2		1						1
South Dakota									
Tennessee	5	3 (22+)	3	2	1	1		1	
Texas	1		4		1				1
Utah	1								
Vermont	1								
Virginia			3						
Washington	6		3	1	1				1
West Virginia									
Wisconsin	4	111 (3)	3						
Wyoming									1
Guam									1
Trust Territories									
TOTAL	168	44 (468+)	74	27	43	12	7	6	29

Source: EPA, *Damages and Threats Caused By Hazardous Material Sites* (Washington, D.C., 1980), p. xv.

*This citation consists of the number of sites in each state, followed by the number (in parentheses) of actual wells closed in the state.

†POTWs = publicly owned treatment works.

hazardous waste sites (see Table 1-7). The EPA listed both sites where the raw material itself (i.e., acetylene) was found and those where derivatives of the raw materials were found. Toluene, benzene, chromium compounds, mercury, and arsenic were among the raw materials most commonly found, while chlorine, ethylene, sodium hydroxide, and sulfuric acid were the most frequent precursors of chemicals found at the sites.

Such information, however, is of limited value because of resource and technical constraints, including incomplete analytic determinations, and cannot necessarily be considered as representative of the broader national scene.

ENVIRONMENTAL FATE

Another way of analyzing the potential toxic effects of hazardous wastes is on the basis of their fate in the environment or living organisms. Some wastes are effectively *immortal*; their toxic qualities are intrinsic to their elemental structure. The heavy metals are in this category, and, in a different sense, so is asbestos, whose toxicity is a function of its physical structure, which, for practical purposes, is indestructible. Some radioactive wastes, particularly uranium and plutonium, retain their radioactive properties for so long that we should also view them as immortal.

A second group of wastes is *semi-mortal*. Destruction or degradation occurs in the environment, but very slowly. Chlorinated hydrocarbons, especially complex ones, are *semi-mortal* in natural environments, but can be destroyed in high-temperature incinerators.

A third group of toxics is very short-lived or *mortal*, including acids and bases and other strongly reactive materials like cyanides, which are rapidly destroyed or neutralized in the environment.

Some *semi-mortal* and *immortal* toxic chemicals, particularly complex chlorinated hydrocarbons and some heavy metals, pose additional problems by virtue of their tendency to be selectively concentrated in living organisms at levels greater than in the surrounding ecosystem and to progressively bioaccumulate in the food chain, ending up with man.

Table 1-7. Major Classes of Chemicals Found at 350 Hazardous Waste Disposal Sites, 1980

Chemical	Sites Containing Raw Material	Sites Containing Derivatives	Total Sites
Petrochemical			
Acetylene	0	56	56
Benzene	19	113	132
Butane	0	8	8
Butylene	0	8	8
Butadiene	0	0	0
Ethylene	0	97	97
Methane	1	44	45
Naphthalene	2	0	2
Propylene	0	14	14
Toluene	23	30	53
Xylene	12	6	18
Waste Oil	35	0	35
Inorganics			
Ammonia	6	22	28
Antimony & compounds	1	0	1
Arsenic & compounds	10	0	10
Barium sulfide	0	0	0
Beryllium & compounds	0	0	0
Bromine	0	2	2
Cadmium	5	0	5
Chlorine & compounds	5	197	202
Chromium & compounds	18	1	19
Cobalt	1	0	1
Copper	6	1	7
Hydrogen fluoride	2	1	3
Lead & compounds	11	0	11
Mercury	16	0	16
Nickel	4	0	4
Nitric acid	1	0	1
Phosphorus & compounds	6	8	14
Potassium hydroxide	1	0	1
Selenium	1	0	1
Sodium hydroxide	0	39	39
Sulfuric acid	3	35	38
Stannic(ous) chlorides	0	0	0
Zinc	9	2	11

Source: EPA, *Damages and Threats Caused by Hazardous Material Sites* (Washington, D.C., 1980), p. xviii.

RISKS TO THE GENERAL PUBLIC[10,11]

The general populace is exposed in daily life to trace quantities of many hazardous wastes. Virtually all Americans carry in their bodies burdens of lead, DDT, PCBs, and other toxic chemicals. Such exposures result from broad environmental dissemination of these hazardous materials in the form of air pollutants, food-chain contaminants, and through direct use of toxic consumer products. But, for the most part, these exposures have not been incriminated in any dramatic and documented incidents of death or disease. High concentrations of hazardous wastes that produce clusters of disease or other adverse effects are relatively easier to detect. These include the adverse health effects in wildlife, cattle, domestic animals, and humans that are discussed in the various case studies in this book.

Some of the general public are also exposed to heavy concentrations of one or more hazardous wastes through random events. In any given neighborhood where utility transformers contain PCBs, some explode, and certain households will be exposed to contamination. Illegal dumpers may pick a particular highway during a rainstorm to get rid of a highly toxic liquid waste. Those who happen to then be driving that highway may receive relatively concentrated exposures.

Most concentrated exposures to hazardous wastes, however, are more predictable. People living in proximity to hazardous waste disposal sites, legal or illegal, publicly known or secret, are at serious risk if the sites are poorly managed or improperly designed or in the event of unexpected accidents or natural catastrophes. Such sites or industrial facilities disposing of wastes on-site may produce localized air pollution; those downwind will be more heavily exposed, and certain seasons will be riskier than others. Transportation of wastes to dump sites and from facilities generating or processing wastes also poses hazards. Normal operations may involve evaporation or spillage of some waste, and accidents are an ever-present possibility, especially on transportation corridors generally known for their high frequency of accidents, such as the notorious Louisville and Nashville railroad line in the southeastern United States.

Other high-risk groups are those exposed to toxic wastes in their drinking water supplies. It has been known for some time that drinking water supplies drawn from rivers and streams were often contaminated with pollutants and waste materials, and it was assumed that groundwaters, normally not the recipients of discharges from urban and industrial sewers, were safer. In some parts of the country, this is still true. But groundwaters in the vicinity of hazardous waste disposal facilities, factories storing substantial quantities of dangerous wastes on their sites or disposing of them in wells or unlined ponds, and mining operations may be heavily contaminated. Meanwhile, surface waters in many areas are being cleaned up. Over time, we may find an increasing number of underground water supplies suffering contamination from waste-disposal operations. Rural well waters in areas with heavy pesticide use or significant concentration of facilities manufacturing agricultural chemicals generally are not monitored carefully, and exposure may be particularly likely to persist unnoted for long periods. From this standpoint, the safest populations at the present time are probably those in large cities that draw their drinking water from aqueducts linked to distant, nonindustrialized mountain watersheds, such as New York and San Francisco.*

An increasingly large group at risk will be those who live or work in areas overlying contaminated soil. As industrial facilities or waste sites are shut down, all too often they leave behind them heavily contaminated soil. If housing tracts, schools, or office buildings are built over these areas, even in the distant future, very heavy exposures are likely to result. Children who play in and around the soil are likely to receive direct exposure. They may also receive such exposure from former dump sites or industrial areas that have not been reused for new construction, as such sites are often particularly attractive to children because of the absence of adult supervision and the presence of such "play" objects as old equipment and barrels and strangely

---

*Even here, though, if the pipes within the city are old, they may either produce wastes themselves, especially heavy metals, or permit contaminants to enter the pipes from the surrounding ground through leaks and cracks.

colored soils. Major lead exposures have resulted from schools being built on the site of old battery factories; children on the playground picked up lead-contaminated soil and ingested it with their candy or lunches. Uranium tailing piles in the Southwest have been particularly attractive "sandpiles" for children.

RISKS TO OCCUPATIONAL GROUPS[12]

Workers in industries generating or disposing of hazardous wastes are probably the group at highest risk. In addition to exposure to airborne wastes, workers are likely to receive direct exposure to skin or clothing from normal operations and, in case of accidents, to suffer large exposures from the accident itself and during subsequent cleanup and decontamination procedures. Workers in the electrical industry, for example, have frequently been exposed to PCBs during routine maintenance processes for removing waste oil from transformers and other equipment for disposal. Utilities also expose many workers in the process of cleaning up waste oil from transformers that have exploded.

Workers in other industries can also suffer heavily from illegal waste-disposal practices. Where toxic materials like PCB-contaminated waste oil are accidentally or knowingly sold as boiler fuel, for example, workers who clean the boilers receive large exposures as may road crews where PCBs are used as road oil. Municipal incinerator and landfill crews, particularly bulldozer drivers, are exposed when hazardous wastes are mixed with ordinary solid wastes for cheaper disposal in municipal dumps or incinerators. When wastes are dumped down drains and sewers, workers in sewage treatment plants may suffer adverse health effects. Firemen and policemen are another occupational group at high risk, since they are often called upon to deal with accidents at hazardous waste disposal facilities.

A group of industries posing particularly high risks from occupational exposures to toxic chemicals has been identified (see Table 1-8). While only part of the risk from these industries is the result of their waste disposal practices, they are the industries, in addition to the waste disposal industry itself, whose work force and neighboring residents are most likely to suffer high exposure to hazardous waste materials. Over 3

Table 1-8. High Health-Risk Industries Using Greatest Number of Hazardous Substances

Industry	Total Employment (thousands)	Production Workers (thousands)	Number of Establishments with 1 to 49 Employees	Estimated Number of Production Workers in Establishments with 1 to 49 Employees (thousands)
Industrial inorganic chemicals	321.9	173.1	866	9.5
Plastics materials and synthetics	229.8	157.2	293	3.4
Drugs	164.7	82.3	804	8.2
Paints and allied products	70.5	38.7	1,172	14.7
Industrial organic chemicals	55.8	34.2	426	5.0
Agricultural chemicals	52.9	32.9	962	10.3
Miscellaneous chemicals products	37.2	22.8	2,053	20.5
Petroleum refining	154.8	94.2	164	2.1
Tires and inner tubes	130.2	94.5	114	1.3
Rubber and plastics hose and belting	92.3	72.9	50	0.7
Fabricated rubber products	92.3	72.9	707	9.4
Miscellaneous plastics products	361.2	290.0	5,897	69.6
Blast furnace and basic steel products	609.0	486.9	481	6.4
Iron and steel foundries	247.3	207.0	591	9.4
Primary nonferrous metals	33.7	37.5	100	1.1
Secondary nonferrous metals	58.3	43.8	272	3.1
Nonferrous foundries	93.5	78.4	1,343	5.9
Miscellaneous primary metal products	79.4	64.0	876	11.3
Miscellaneous electrical equipment and supplies	139.2	108.7	1,043	10.4
TOTALS	3,024.0	2,182.0	18,214	202.3

Source: *A Study of Occupational Safety and Health Training Program Alternatives and Priorities.* U.S. Occupational Safety and Health Administration, October 20, 1977.

million workers are employed in these industries, which run the gamut from such heavy industry as steel foundries to makers of miscellaneous electrical equipment.

PUBLIC HEALTH EFFECTS

There are different types of public health hazards from toxic wastes. Some wastes are *flammable,* prone to ignite or explode with great ease or great force. Others, like acids and bases, are *corrosive,* possessing the ability to eat or wear away materials by chemical action. Some wastes are toxic because they contain disease-bearing organisms. Such *infectious* wastes may result from disposal of hospital waste material and from sewage sludge.

Wastes that are not corrosive, flammable, explosive, or infectious may still be toxic, able to "produce injury upon contact with, or by accumulation in, a susceptible site in or on the body of a living organism."[13] This injury may result immediately from the exposure; materials producing immediate injury are *acutely toxic.* But toxic effects may be delayed. Such effects are *subacute* or *chronic.* The concentrations required to produce acute effects may be so much greater than those producing chronic injury that, for most purposes, the chronic effects are the greatest problem. These subacute or chronic toxic effects can involve any body function or organ system, including the liver, the gastrointestinal tract, and the central nervous system, producing chronic disease, whose cause may not be immediately apparent and whose relation to the past toxic exposure will probably not be detected.

A major category of concern is chemicals that induce specific types of chronic and irreversible effects, such as genetic damage, birth defects, and cancer. *Mutagens* are substances causing a change in the genetic material of a cell, inheritable from cell to cell and sometimes also between generations. *Teratogens* are substances that damage the developing fetus, resulting in birth defects. *Carcinogens* are materials that cause cancer. Additionally, many agents that cause any one of these chronic toxic effects may also cause others. No safe levels or thresholds are recognized for chemicals inducing carcinogenic, teratogenic, or mutagenic effects.

Toxic chemicals may induce a wide variety of effects. Benzene, for example, is very flammable at high concentrations; in lower concentrations it is acutely toxic, causing skin irritation and drowsiness; and even at lower exposure levels it is chronically toxic, leading to a usually fatal blood disease known as aplastic anemia, as well as to acute myelogenous leukemia. Trichloroethylene can induce acute liver and central nervous system damage; its chronic effects include deafness, visual defects, behavioral disturbances, and carcinogenic effects, as evidenced in experimental animals.

The Environmental Problem of the Century

No environmental problem poses more starkly than hazardous wastes the dilemma of industrial civilization. Materials and functions that have come to be taken for granted as fundamental features of modern life are dependent upon an exponentially increasing, proliferating, and dangerous array of heterogeneous chemicals. These chemicals generally serve a useful purpose, but, when the purpose is completed, their dangerous properties often remain in the wastes—sometimes for a brief time, sometimes virtually forever.

As the number of such modern materials and functions increases, the volume and complexity of their hazardous wastes inevitably increase—wastes that no one wants and therefore that no one can be relied upon to safeguard.

Ten years ago, although public consciousness of other environmental concerns was high, hazardous waste was virtually an unknown public health problem. Early air- and water-pollution laws were debated and enacted without awareness or consideration of what to do with waste materials once we stopped dumping them in the air and water.

Awareness of the hazardous waste disposal problem has now dramatically increased, particularly since the late summer of 1978, when Love Canal broke upon the public consciousness. Prior to 1978, disposal of hazardous wastes was seen as so unimportant that most major opinion polls did not even question the level of public concern. In March, 1980, however, when the Roper poll first raised the topic, two-thirds of the responding public expressed a "great deal of concern [about] disposal of industrial chemical wastes that are hazardous,"[14] while only one-third expressed a similar level of concern about air pollution. Not only was the level of concern much higher for hazardous waste disposal than for air pollution—it was also higher than the level of concern measured by the same poll on air and water pollution in previous surveys.

Another measure of public concern tested in the survey was public willingness to accept the location of various industrial facilities in their neighborhoods. Only nuclear power plants generated more anxiety than hazardous waste disposal sites—by but a small margin. Concern for both was much higher than for coal-fired power plants or large factories. Indeed, half the population objected to such a facility being located even within one hundred miles of their homes. These results are particularly striking since interviewees were assured that, at the site in question, "disposal could be done safely and that the site would be inspected regularly for possible problems."[15]

This is a remarkable level of public concern and one that has built up with almost unparalleled speed, in spite of the fact that the overwhelming majority of the public have not personally experienced adverse effects from hazardous waste disposal. It is even more surprising when we consider that only 22 percent of the surveyed public had sufficient information about the problem to know what had happened at Love Canal.

It does not appear that the public has panicked prematurely about hazardous wastes. The dangers and costs of this problem are overwhelming. Legal claims from the one episode at Love Canal exceed $2 billion. Estimates of damages from kepone in the James River are over $500 million. And such figures and episodes largely reflect industrial practices decades ago, when levels of production of materials, such as synthetic organic chemicals, which end up as hazardous wastes, were trivial compared with the present.

Nor can it be assumed that safe disposal techniques will be easy to identify and implement in the near future. After years of debate and research, no clear consensus has yet emerged on whether it is even possible to safely dispose of nuclear wastes

—the one element in the hazardous waste stream that has been subjected to extensive public scrutiny.

Either dramatically different approaches to the hazardous waste problem must be found, or it will turn modern industrial production into a confrontational nightmare between industry and society as a whole. Such approaches, as we shall see, do exist. But public debate and understanding of them has only just begun. Government response, extensive as it is, in many ways has failed to deal with the problem. And with each passing day, more and more people become involuntary and often unknowing victims to past and present habits of dealing with the poisons no one wants.

PART II
Case Studies

CHAPTER 2

Introduction to
Case Studies

In the following five chapters, a series of major episodes of hazardous waste contamination are reviewed.* While each chapter focuses on particular aspects of the problem, analysis of each ultimately leads to a similar conclusion: no area of the entire United States is now safe from the harmful effects of past improper waste disposal practices. Dumping of hazardous wastes from rural towns like Toone, Tennessee to urban cities like Elizabeth, New Jersey has caused major environmental damage and has, so far, cost the public millions of dollars.

These case studies provide some insight into how the various hazardous waste incidents have been perceived and handled by government, industry, the media, and the public.† While some of the case studies (Chapters 3 and 5) are organized

*The case studies were based on information available up to September 1981.

†For other recent case studies, see Michael Brown, 1980;[1] Congressional Research Service Report, 1980;[2] and Ralph Nader and John Richard, 1981.[3]

geographically, others (Chapters 4, 6, and 7) deal with the problem more generically.

Each case study raises a wide range of questions which can only be answered in the context of the facts peculiar to that situation. In many cases, these facts are still emerging. Critical questions that should be used to guide the reader through the details of these case studies are:

1. How was the problem initially discovered?
2. Who first brought it to the public's attention?
3. How quickly and how effectively did local, state, and federal agencies react to this knowledge?
4. What role did the generator(s) and transporter(s) of the waste play in its discovery, analysis, and cleanup or containment?
5. What major types of wastes were involved?
6. Were local or federal environmental laws adequate for protection?
7. Who and what was damaged?
8. Did the victims of these incidents receive adequate assistance?
9. What needs to be done to prevent similar occurrences from taking place in the future?
10. Who should be held accountable for the damage that has resulted?

The last question has no simple answer. Rather, the facts are marshaled in order to highlight the roles of the players and their victims. While society must ultimately decide who will be held responsible for the destruction wrought by unsafe hazardous waste disposal, legislation, notably the Resource Conservation and Recovery Act and the Superfund, provides some guidance. As a result of dozens of recent enforcement actions, the courts have also begun to set some guidelines. Even with these tools, the answers to the questions of who should pay, how much should be paid, and what should be paid for, are still most controversial.

Clearly, the problems of hazardous waste have already seriously affected the lives of thousands of Americans. However, the impact of this problem has only begun to be felt.

At the core of each case study is a fundamental question of politics. How does society allocate responsibility for past and continuing problems of runaway technology? These studies, combined with the more general contents of the book, will provide a framework in which these important questions can be reasonably answered.

I sympathize with each and every
one of you, and truly regret the inconvenience
which this has caused you.

WM. HOWARD BEASLEY III
Vice-Chairman of the Velsicol Board of Directors,
letter to Toone-Teague residents,
November 10, 1978

CHAPTER 3

Dumping in Rural America

Most industries that generate hazardous wastes prefer to dump them on-site. When on-site disposal is not possible, finding sufficient land for off-site disposal may often be difficult. Many companies have selected locations well off the beaten track for their dump sites. These rural areas have become choice dumping grounds for the nation's industrial wastes, resulting in significant, or even devastating, impacts on the community and environment of these sparsely populated areas.

Hardeman County, Tennessee

Woodrow Sterling and his wife Christine had always been healthy, but toward the end of 1977 they began to complain of headaches, nausea, and loss of energy. About the same time, they noticed a strong chemical taste and smell in their drinking water.

At first, they thought that the winter's snow had stirred up dirt and minerals in their well. But the snow stopped and the problem persisted. The Sterlings soon discovered that they were not the only ones with such complaints in the hilly, backroad, rural area where they lived in Hardeman County, Tennessee, a few miles from the town of Toone.

In December, 1977, the Sterlings asked Hardeman County Health Department official George Wallace to examine their drinking water. Wallace, with decades of public health background, only tested for bacteria and shrugged off the problem. "Ah, that's fine," he said after drinking a handful of the Sterlings' water. "Go ahead and drink it."

In the following weeks, the Sterlings' health and that of their close neighbors deteriorated. Their complaints included nausea, abdominal cramping, vomiting, persistent lethargy, weakness in upper and lower limbs, skin and eye irritation, upper respiratory tract infections, and splitting headaches. Christine and several neighbors were hospitalized in Memphis, but no diagnosis could be made. Ona Boyd, Christine's sister-in-law, went into premature labor, and her infant son was found to have an unusual birth defect—exomphalos—in which his intestines protruded into the umbilical cord through a gap in his abdominal wall.

These continuing complaints forced Wallace out to the Sterlings' neighborhood several times. He again took water samples to be analyzed for bacterial contamination, a usual cause of bad taste and odor. These tests were negative, so Wallace confidently insisted that the water was fine. The Sterlings reluctantly continued to use their water, although its taste and smell were getting worse. The shoe-polish-like smell of the water permeated everything, even food and washed clothing. Water from the shower, kitchen faucet, and toilet filled the house with nauseating fumes. "When you run it [the water] through the hot water heater," remarked one of the Sterlings' neighbors, "it almost takes the skin off your nose."

Searching for an answer, Woodrow Sterling decided to replace the well pump, which he thought could be leaking gasoline. One winter Sunday, Woodrow, his father, and several neighbors dismantled the pump, which they found clogged with "a gallon of white jello." They didn't know what the material was; it smelled foul, just like the tap water, but stronger. They then spent hours installing a new pump and cleaning out each section of the pipe. But, "after running it [the new pump] for several twenty-four-hour periods, if anything the taste was worse," Woodrow said.[1]

On March 23, 1978, the Sterlings finally got their answer. Results from the state health department and the Environmental Protection Agency (EPA) revealed that their drinking water was contaminated with very high levels of organic solvents and pesticide wastes.

Velsicol

About a quarter of a mile southeast of the Sterlings, an esti-mated 16.5 million gallons of wastes, in over 250,000 fifty-five-gallon drums, had been dumped between 1964 and 1972. The dump was owned and operated exclusively by Velsicol Chemical Corporation, a Chicago-based subsidiary of Northwest Indus-tries, Inc.* The dump was used as a burial ground for heavily

---

*Besides the Hardeman County dump, Velsicol has been associated with a number of major environmental problems; the EPA has taken strong enforcement action against several products manufactured by the company, and the agricultural use of two carcinogenic Velsicol pesticides, chlordane and heptachlor, is being phased out. Endrin, another Velsicol pesticide, was banned. Velsicol is also responsible for manufacturing an organophosphate pesticide, leptophos (phosvel), a strong neuro-toxin, which allegedly paralyzed workers at Velsicol's Bay Port, Texas plant.

In 1976, Velsicol acquired the Michigan Chemical Company, the largest manu-facturer of polybrominated biphenyls (PBBs). Between five hundred and one thou-sand pounds of this highly toxic flame retardant were accidentally mixed with cattle feed and shipped to dozens of Michigan farms in 1974. Millions of chickens, over thirty thousand cows, and thousands of sheep either died or had to be de-stroyed after consuming PBB-laden feed.[2] The human cost is also high: the health of dozens of farm families was seriously affected, and thousands of Michigan resi-dents now carry significant amounts of PBB in their bodies.

Many who consumed PBB-laden milk, meat, and eggs complained of extreme fatigue, dizziness, headaches, skin problems, including chloracne, stomach ail-ments, unusual nail growth, hair loss, and other ailments, including increased sus-ceptibility to disease.

Michigan Chemical also produced some 54 million pounds of tris (2, 3-dibro-mopropyl) phosphate (TRIS), a flame-retardant chemical used in children's sleep-wear until 1977, when it was banned as a hazardous substance by the United States Consumer Product Safety Commission. TRIS, a potent mutagen and carcinogen,

contaminated residues, by-products, and solid wastes from the manufacture of four carcinogenic chlorinated hydrocarbon pesticides; heptachlor, at concentrations up to 20 percent; dieldrin and endrin, up to 0.6 percent; and heptachlor epoxide, at about 0.006 percent. The wastes included another carcinogen, aldrin, as well as related highly toxic chemicals, such as chlordene, isodrin, hexachlorocyclopentadiene (HEX), and hexachlorobicycloheptadiene (HEX-BCH).

The Hardeman County Dump

The origins of the Hardeman dump date back to 1964, when a major fish kill over the length of the Mississippi River from Memphis to New Orleans was traced to massive contamination by high concentrations of endrin and other organochlorine pesticides originating from a Memphis dump. For years previously, Velsicol had dumped millions of gallons of toxic liquid pesticide waste into the Hollywood dump, a Memphis facility on the shores of the river.* However, the bulk of the contaminants originated from solid residues placed in the dump. During periods of high water, the residues dissolved and flowed into the river.

While Velsicol has never acknowledged that its waste disposal practices were killing fish in the Mississippi, it nevertheless recognized that continued dumping at Hollywood would ensure

was found on unwashed children's sleepwear at concentrations of up to 72,000 parts per million (ppm). Significant quantities of TRIS could be ingested through children's and infants' frequent mouthing of the material or through skin absorption. It is estimated that over 60 million children were exposed to potentially dangerous levels of this toxin.[3]

According to a recent *Wall Street Journal* article, "Velsicol's role in a recent string of incidents involving actual or potential damage to the public—the details of which are still emerging in courtrooms around the country—is unusual for a company of any size." The *Journal* quoted an EPA spokesman as follows: "Velsicol's record of compliance with environment statutes is one of the worst of any company." The *Journal* further quoted an Environmental Defense Fund spokesman: "[Velsicol is] a corporate renegade that seems totally lacking in public responsibility."

*Ironically, the Hollywood dump became a matter of concern only a year and a half after the Sterlings testified before Congress about the Hardeman dump in October, 1979.

continuing bad publicity. The corporation therefore set out to find a new dump in a quiet rural area where its wastes were unlikely to attract attention. The site selected was sparsely populated and located in the wooded hills of Hardeman County, Tennessee, about fifty miles east of Memphis.

On August 24,1964, Velsicol bought a 242-acre farm, just off the Toone-Teague road, about ten miles north of Bolivar, from Wilson and Geraldine Keyes for the traditional Tennessee formula of "$10 and other valuable considerations." Curiously, the deed was notarized in Chicago, not in Hardeman County. The actual purchase price has never been made public. Still more curiously, the Keyes had bought the land only six weeks before from Charles G. Frady, who had owned the farm for many years. The Sterlings believe that the Keyes were hired by Velsicol to buy the farm, and that otherwise Frady would never have sold his land.*

When the Sterlings and their neighbors first learned that a chemical company had purchased the Frady land, they were very pleased, thinking that a plant would be built that would provide jobs for local people. The Sterlings were soon disillusioned. As dozens of trucks rumbled down their narrow road into the farm every day, it became clear that the land was instead being used as a dump. The community became aware that pesticides were being dumped there when they spilled on the road a year after the site was established.

The farm's conversion into a dump required no permits, licenses, or public announcements. Tennessee law, at that time, allowed a landowner to do anything with his own land, as long as he didn't obviously bother anyone else. Velsicol did not have to inform any state or local agency that it had established the dump or what it was dumping. No laws specifically prohibited the dumping of any materials on private land, nor had state and local officials any authority to check on the operation.

Velsicol employed what it termed the "time-honored practice [of] shallow burial of toxic wastes" at its dump. Trucks filled with fifty-five gallon steel drums and fiber cartons of wastes would pull up to the edge of the shallow trenches, ten to

---

*Allegedly, Wilson Keyes was subsequently employed as a contractor by Velsicol.

fifteen feet deep and wide, and dump their loads. A bulldozer would then deliberately crush the drums and cover them and their spilled contents with a few feet of dirt. More drums would then be dumped on top until the trenches were almost filled to the surface. The trenches were not lined with impermeable materials, so nothing prevented the liquid wastes from leaching directly into the underlying soil.[4]

Mounting Concerns

The dumping might have gone unquestioned for years had not certain Memphis and Shelby County health officials been alert. In March, 1965, Everett Hardorf, a Memphis County engineer, first learned about the new Velsicol dump and immediately questioned its safety. Hardorf warned that the site was located in an area where surface contamination could filter down into the artesian aquifer that served as the groundwater source for Memphis' six hundred thousand residents. By June, spot sampling by the Tennessee Stream Pollution Control Board found evidence of contamination of groundwater supplies in three of four shallow wells on the margin of the dump, with endrin, dieldrin, heptachlor, and heptachlor epoxide at scattered areas in the Velsicol farm. The Sterlings' well was also found to be contaminated with low levels of endrin (0.5 ppb) and dieldrin (0.3 ppb).*

Alarmed, the state called on the Water Resources Division of the United States Geological Survey (USGS) for a hydrological survey. The survey, undertaken from 1966 to 1967, found that contamination of surface waters and of the shallowest groundwaters— the perched water zone—had already taken place and that this contamination had almost reached the local water-table aquifer, 90 feet down. The survey also pointed out that the contamination was likely to persist, in view of the permeability of the soil under the disposal trenches. Although the Sterlings

---

*Residents, including the Sterlings, were, however, not informed of these results until the summer of 1978, although county health officials, including George Wallace and D. B. Hale, had been fully informed.[5]

and several other homeowners only about a quarter of a mile west of the dump had wells sunk into the local water table, the USGS concluded that there was "no possibility" that these wells could be contaminated, as the prevailing movement of local groundwaters was easterly. The USGS also concluded that there was no chance that the contamination could reach 200 feet down to the deep water-table artesian aquifer.[6]

Encouraged by the USGS conclusion that there was no apparent danger to local wells, Velsicol expanded its dumping operations from twenty to forty-five acres. Trucks carrying waste to the site began to spill pesticides on the roads almost daily. The dump's oozing trenches allowed chemical fumes to drift over into the surrounding residential areas. "A lot of times you could hardly stay outside at night because when the wind was in the right direction it was a very noticeable odor," one local resident remarked.

While Velsicol's dumping continued to concern state officials, they had no authority to stop it. In December, 1970, E. J. Kennedy, a USGS hydrologist familiar with the dump-site operation, raised new questions about its safety. After reviewing the 1967 survey, Kennedy concluded that "a clear and immediate threat to local water supplies does exist." He noted that the Velsicol operation had expanded well beyond the "safe areas" delineated by the 1967 study, more houses had been constructed closer to the site, more wells had been sunk, which placed greater hydrological pressure on the groundwater, and that the massive dumping had so changed the land surface that the direction of groundwater flow was now in doubt. In March, 1971, Robert Krieger, another Department of the Interior expert, agreed that the 1967 survey was misleading. "[It failed to] consider the change or stress on the system due to the expansion of the dumping area, increased use of water, encroachment on the site by housing [and incorrectly] ruled out [the] bigger problems, possibilities, and other events."

The survey also failed to consider how the "highly acidic nature of the waste may dissolve and open new channels through rock, thereby promoting rapid movement" of the pesticide wastes into the aquifer. Krieger concluded that the contamination of local groundwater could thereby be increased to an extent far beyond that calculated in the 1967 report. Krieger also questioned the basis of the USGS assertion that the ground-water contaminants were moving due east, away from the local residents' wells, a suspicion confirmed by a later USGS study. Stressing the importance of the need for a more thorough evaluation, Krieger concluded that "the pesticide matter, which is very stable, may be worse than radioactive wastes, because the pesticides have no half-life, hence [no] decay rate."

These questions resulted in a high-level, closed-door meeting on March 4, 1971. Representatives of the Tennessee Department of Public Health, the USGS, Congressman Ray Blanton, and Velsicol were in attendance. Neither the press nor general public was informed. The USGS frankly admitted that its 1967 study had failed to recognize the extent of the danger from the Velsicol operation, a danger subsequently exacerbated by Velsicol's expanded dumping. Velsicol officials were unmoved and made it clear that they intended to continue dumping.

During the following year, the Tennessee Department of Public Health tried without success to persuade Velsicol to stop the dumping. Finally, in February, 1972, the state filed a complaint against Velsicol. Velsicol was ordered to halt all dumping, except that of nontoxic wastes, and these only with written approval of the health commissioner. Velsicol was further directed to store all future wastes on site at its Memphis facility until methods for their incineration or other safe disposal could be developed.[7]

While Velsicol began burning some of its wastes out of state, it nevertheless continued dumping at the Hardeman site at a rate of about four truckloads a day. In spite of persistent complaints from local residents, no enforcement action was taken.

By 1975, Velsicol had finally stopped dumping. The Hardeman site was officially closed and given a superficial cleanup, alleged by Velsicol to involve "substantial costs." Velsicol spread fresh dirt over the trenches and seeded the whole site with grass. The local residents, somewhat acclimated to the smell from the dump, gradually relaxed.

The Ban on Drinking Water

In November, 1977, the state health department took samples of tap water for chemical analysis. In December, 1977, the first set of tests proved negative. However, a second batch of tests made in January, 1978 were positive and were confirmed by a third batch three months later; on the basis of the second round of tests, the Sterlings and their immediate neighbors were told in March, 1978 that their well water was highly contaminated with as many as twenty different chlorinated hydrocarbons and must no longer be drunk or used in food preparation.* [8]

Wayne Max of the Tennessee Department of Public Health advised the owners of five wells that their water was contaminated. A total of forty-seven people, including twenty-three children, were left without any drinking water. Under strong protest, the Tennessee Office of Civil Defense and Emergency Preparedness provided the residents with a large tank of drinking water, usually used by the National Guard for field maneuvers. Every day, someone had to haul water from the tank. When the tank ran dry, the residents had to drive twenty miles to an uncontaminated well for water. However, they continued to use their own tap water for cooking, bathing, and washing dishes and clothes.

With the closing of five wells in the neighborhood, several families abandoned their houses and land and moved out of town. When asked why they did not move too, Woodrow Sterling answered, "Move where? My family has always lived here; my grandfather was born here. We've been here for four generations. Where would we go? [Besides], who's going to buy our house? We just can't abandon everything we've worked for."

The Sterlings found that, although everyone seemed to feel sorry for them, no one really wanted to help. There were no

---

*The contaminants, at concentrations ranging from 0.1 to 40 ppb, included chloroform, carbon tetrachloride, naphthalene, methylnaphthalene, chlorobenzene, dicyclopentadiene, trichloroethylene, tetrachloroethylene, hexachloroethane, toluene, hexachlorobutadiene, hexachloronorbornadiene, tetramethylbenzene, dimethyl-ethylbenzene, trimethylbenzene, isodrin, endrin, heptachlor, chlordane, and benzene.

government loans or grant programs for victims of man-made environmental disasters. The Sterlings felt they had suffered as much as many survivors of natural disasters, such as hurricanes and floods, for which there was federal aid available, but they were told that their only recourse was private litigation, which would be very costly and time-consuming. The Sterlings were understandably reluctant to sue anyone, let alone a powerful company like Velsicol.

The Sterlings tried to ascertain the posssible effects of the contaminated water. They were concerned not only about damage to their own health, but also about possible future effects on their children. "We have three daughters. There is a nagging thought in the back of our minds. Are those daughters going to grow up and have cancer because they have been subject to this water for so long, even when we were unaware? Are our daughters going to have deformed children? Is our son going to have deformed children? I am sure that when they grow up, if they knew that their child was going to be somehow affected by these chemicals being taken into their bodies to the great extent that they are, that they would make the decision not to have children—we have got to know this."

Velsicol's Denial of Liability

In spite of the mounting evidence to the contrary, Velsicol continued to staunchly deny any responsibility for the contamination of water in Hardeman County.

In May, Velsicol announced that it was "highly improbable" that the chemicals had come from its dump site. Velsicol plant manager Charles Hanson was quoted as saying, "I can say now I don't believe it's coming from our dump site."[9] Velsicol also insisted that the smell and taste problems were due to small amounts of manganese, iron, and sulfides in the well water, which was perfectly safe to drink.

The Sterlings found inconceivable Velsicol's persistent refusal to admit that the contamination was serious and due to chemicals from Velsicol's dump. Mrs. Sterling was especially angry, since Velsicol's public statements were at complete variance with what she had been told by Velsicol employees who had come to sample her water. "I insisted that they drink the water, with them telling us that it was OK to drink, that it was OK, it was fine. But they refused to drink the water. They would not drink the water because they said, 'I might die before I get back to Memphis.'"[10]

Local Initiatives

The Sterlings and their neighbors finally decided to go it alone. In May, 1978, they hired an attorney and filed a $2.5 billion suit against Velsicol.* They also decided to raise funds to get independent, expert medical and engineering advice. In June, 1978, they organized a dance. Food and drinks were sold, and admission was charged. The event raised $1,045. The amount would not buy much advice, but it was a start.

The Sterlings soon learned that the cost of pure water was high. They were told by local and federal officials that they could qualify for $240,000 in federal funds† to pay for the fresh, clean drinking water, provided the town of Toone would under-write about 15 percent of the costs with a $30,000 loan.

The Sterlings were forced to appeal to their neighbors in Toone for the matching loan. But as soon as they put their hands out, "people got ugly." The Toone town government refused to apply for the loan. Town officials stated publicly that unless they received a "100 percent grant," running a water line to the Toone-Teague Road area was "out of the question." A hurried, secret meeting of the town board was held in July, and the federal government's offer of assistance was rejected out-of-hand.

In the days that followed, private citizens, local media, and even some local officials rallied behind the Sterlings and forced

---

*The suit was filed for property damage, personal injury, and punitive damages on behalf of seventeen families. Subsequent suits were filed and, in February, 1981, were consolidated into a class-action suit on behalf of over one hundred named plaintiffs.

†These funds were composed of a $120,000 grant and a $30,000 grant from the U.S. Department of Housing and Urban Development and a $90,000 interest-free loan from the Farmers Home Administration.

the Toone government to meet publicly to reconsider the issue. Under heavy pressure, the town reversed its former stand, but stipulated that thirty homeowners of the Toone-Teague dump site area would each have to sign up and pay $165 in advance for the water hookup. The residents were given a few days to obtain the signatures and funds.

The Sterlings and their neighbors were faced with having to come up with $4,950, a seemingly impossible task for people who were barely coping on their incomes. As Christine Sterling observed, "There are months that some of these people don't have money for groceries." The Sterlings and their friends appealed to all their neighbors and eventually succeeded. By July, they had obtained the signatures and checks. Some of the money raised for expert medical and environmental advice was used to pay for those who couldn't afford the $165. The Sterlings and their neighbors celebrated their victory. But the celebration was premature.

Shortly after the checks were collected, Toone officials tried to cash them, but six bounced. Since they did not have all thirty payments, city officials said that if the money was not made good by October 24, they would drop the application for the loan, thereby disqualifying Toone for the federal funds. The Sterlings felt betrayed by the Toone officials, who had promised not to cash the checks until the families concerned had time to raise all the money.

Congressional Interest

In September, 1978, the Sterlings received a call from Washington. They were informed that the Oversight and Investigations Subcommittee of the House Committee on Interstate and Foreign Commerce intended to send investigators to Hardeman County in preparation for hearings on hazardous waste disposal to be held on October 30. The subcommittee also informed Velsicol that it wanted full information on the dump.

In early October, a subcommittee investigator discovered unrevealed EPA data, transmitted to the Tennessee Department of Public Health about six weeks earlier, showing carbon tetrachloride (CCl_4) in the Sterlings' drinking water at a level of

4,800 ppb.* A chemist at the EPA's Atlanta laboratory confirmed the test results and told the subcommittee that he was "shocked" by them. He had never before seen such a high level of CCl₄ in drinking water. When a congressional investigator first brought the EPA test data to the attention of David T. Allen, deputy commissioner of medical services of the state of Tennessee, a few days before the hearing, he could not believe it. "They must have misplaced the decimal point," he said. When assured that the tests had been checked and double checked, Allen claimed that the results had never been previously brought to the attention of himself or other responsible state officials. However, the results had, in fact, been attached to an EPA letter dated August 31, 1978, addressed to O.D. Keaton, a member of Allen's own staff.

The state of Tennessee was not alone in its failure to have recognized the critical significance of these findings. Thomas Jorling, then assistant administrator in charge of the EPA's water and waste management programs, was surprised when the subcommittee informed him of the CCl₄ results. Somehow, Jorling explained, the information had not reached the EPA's regional office responsible for the Toone situation until the Saturday before the subcommittee's Monday hearing, two months after the EPA's chemists had completed the test. Jorling candidly admitted that the EPA had taken no action on the matter and added, "I think our behavior in this instance is deserving of criticism."¹¹

Immediately after the hearings, the EPA and the state tested additional samples and found a still-higher level of CCl₄ in the Sterlings' water and a level of 12,000–19,000 ppb in adjacent wells. Of all the hundreds of municipal water supplies tested throughout the country, the EPA had previously found only a handful in which the level of this contaminant exceeded 1 ppb. All the contaminated Toone wells were immediately ordered capped.

---

*CCl₄ is a toxic and carcinogenic organic solvent, widely used in industry, which can induce liver, lung, kidney, and central nervous system damage following ingestion, inhalation, or skin contact. When, following an industrial spill in the winter of 1976, the EPA discovered 100 ppb of CCl₄ in the Cincinnati water supply—a level 48 times lower than that found in the Sterlings' water—the residents were immediately warned not to drink the water.

Carbon tetrachloride was by no means the only chemical contaminating Hardeman County water (see Table 3-1). Unpublicized EPA tests in April, 1978 had shown very high concentrations of other organic contaminants, including tetrachloroethylene, a carcinogenic industrial solvent with toxic effects similar to CCl₄, present in the Sterlings' water at 2,400 ppb—a level some ten thousand times in excess of the maximum level (0.26 ppb) found "acceptable" by the EPA.* Chlorobenzene, another toxic contaminant, was found in a neighbor's well at a concentration of 41 ppb.[13]

In the spring of 1978, Hugh Kaufman, manager of the EPA's Hazardous Waste Assessment Program, had attempted unsuccessfully to get his agency to work on other site problems. "Trying to get the appropriate EPA regional offices to take action against these facilities proved to be an almost insurmountable obstacle," he said. When Kaufman once discussed a serious site problem with regional office personnel, he "was told they have in their files other cases that are even worse . . . and they didn't plan to investigate any of them, let alone take action against them." Kaufman believed that taking strong enforcement action against facilities whose waste practices posed a hazard would "develop a track record in the minds of the public that we [the EPA] intend to take a strong position" in protecting the public. His superiors did not agree, and he was told to put a "hold" on his activities.[14]

When, on July 17, 1978, a member of Kaufman's staff attempted to obtain information on the Toone problem from the EPA's Atlanta office, she was told, "You people up there [in Washington] better stay out of it." Kaufman reported this reaction to Steffan Plehn, deputy assistant administrator for solid waste, and told him that more information was needed to assess the situation. "The local citizens are exasperated," Kaufman said and

---

*As defined by the EPA's water-quality criteria, "acceptable" means the induction of one extra cancer per million population. A recent report by the National Academy of Sciences has estimated that an intake of 1 μg/day of CC1₄ produces a lifetime excess cancer risk of 1/20 million.[12] Assuming a total water consumption of 2 liters/day, Toone residents using well water contaminated with average CC1₄ levels of 5,000 ppb received a daily dose of 10 mg, increasing their cancer risk by at least 10,000 times, assuming linearity down to risks of 1/2,000. This risk estimate ignores incremental contributions of CC1₄ in air and of other carcinogens in air and water.

asserted that immediate enforcement action under the imminent hazard authority of the Resource Conservation and Recovery Act (RCRA) might be necessary. Two weeks later, Kaufman was told by John Lehman, the director of his division, that "a direct link to the Velsicol hazardous waste disposal site apparently has not been established." He was told that the EPA would take no action until Velsicol-funded groundwater studies were completed and that the regional office was already grappling with Velsicol on another pollution problem and didn't want to be "disturbed."

In the course of the October subcommittee hearing, chaired by Congressman Albert Gore, Jr., of Tennessee, it became clear that the EPA's hazardous waste program was understaffed, overworked, poorly funded, and seriously behind schedule in issuing the dump-site regulations mandated by Congress. The program had been given neither the funds nor the personnel to

Table 3-1. Contaminants in Private Wells in Toone-Teague Area of Hardeman County, Tennessee

Compound	NP/NT*	Ppb (μg/liter)	
		Range	Median
Benzene†	7/7	5–15	12
Carbon tetrachloride (CCl_4)†	11/11	1,700–18,700	6,100
Chlordene	5/18	trace–0.81	trace
Chlorobenzene†	18/19	trace–41	9.3
Chloroform†	11/12	16–1,890	500
Hexachlorobutadiene†	20/20	trace–2.53	0.22
Hexachloroethane†	17/23	trace–4.6	0.64
Hexachlorobicyclo-heptadiene (HEX-BCH)	22/23	trace–2.2	0.30
Methylene chloride†	7/9	3.6–160	45
Naphthalene†	13/23	trace–6.7	1.8
Tetrachloroethylene†	20/20	trace–2,405	6.8
Toluene†	14/20	0.1–52	24
Xylenes	2/3	0.07–1.6	0.84

Source: Based on U.S. Environmental Protection Agency, Region IV, *Summary of USEPA and State of Tennessee Chemical Analyses,* March 9, 1979 as modified by C.S. Clark, et al., 1981.

*NP = Number of samples with detectable amounts of the substance tested. NT = Total number of samples tested.

†On National Priority Pollutants Consent Decree List.

search out dangerous dump sites, assess the dangers posed by these sites, or take enforcement action against the owners or operators of the sites. Kaufman, for example, only had one full-time assistant. Additional funding was initially opposed by the Carter administration, which had pledged to reduce the federal budget and shrink the federal work force. Jorling had directed his staff to put all their efforts into drafting the overdue regulations. All current problems, such as the Toone-Teague dump, however serious, would just have to wait.

Velsicol's Acceptance of Liability

Apparently stimulated by congressional interest, Velsicol suddenly reversed its longstanding denial of liability in October, 1978. "Preliminary analyses just received may suggest the former disposal site is the source of contamination via underground migration. . . . A possible seepage was found in what was previously considered by experts a secure landfill," Velsicol announced.

After the October hearing, Velsicol seemed even more contrite. Announcing that they now wanted "to make amends," Velsicol representatives visited the Sterlings in November and asked Christine how much she would settle for. When Christine didn't answer, she was slipped a sealed envelope filled with money and offered a $4,000 check and the appraised value of the house if she and her husband would sign a release indemnifying the company. Christine at first refused. The Velsicol representatives moved on to the next house down the road.[15]

With each passing day, Christine's hostility toward Velsicol lessened. Unlike EPA or the state officials, Velsicol officials seemed most friendly and willing to talk about her problems. They established a local office, and Velsicol personnel visited each family several times a week. Velsicol also replaced the plumbing in most of the homes with contaminated wells, bought new washing machines and dishwashers, connected them to a temporary water supply, and paid the $30,000 water-hookup charge.

Parties to the damage suit against Velsicol began to sign releases. The Sterlings gave in too. They sold their home to

Velsicol and then contracted to rent it. Christine, still unable to obtain information on the likely effects of the chemicals on her family, accepted $1,500 to "sign off healthwise" too.* "There were no doctors who would say anything anyway," Christine said, so it didn't make much sense to continue to hold out. Besides, Velsicol promised to take care of her family and arranged for them to be given a complete medical checkup.

In December, 1978, Velsicol assembled its team of consultant engineers and hydrologists† to attempt further definition of the extent of the contamination and to develop plans to prevent it from getting worse. The consultants issued several reports that were uncritically supportive of Velsicol's past performance.

> In 1978 it was suggested that disposed waste from the landfill site was migrating with the groundwater and was contaminating private water supplies located north and west of the landfill site. Velsicol acted immediately by undertaking a hydrogeologic investigation of the site and surrounding locale. This study showed that groundwater contamination was possible as a result of the land fill site. . . . Velsicol will continue to respond immediately to health concerns regarding contamination.[16]

In July, 1979, Velsicol and its consultants met in Nashville with various state and federal agency representatives to review plans for the "Site Investigation and Monitoring Program" being developed by Velsicol. Velsicol proposed four alternative approaches to preventing further contamination from the Hardeman dump site: removal and incineration of the buried wastes; removal of the buried wastes to another off-site, secure landfill; on-site containment and securing of the wastes by "capping" the dump; and "environmental assimilation." Velsicol strongly favored the latter, which essentially meant leaving the

---

*The EPA's Atlanta office immediately wrote to the Sterlings, congratulating them on their decision. However, the medical release for the Sterling children was subsequently not approved in court.

†Conestoga-Rovers & Associates, Waterloo, Ontario, Canada; Walker Wells, Inc., Champaign, Illinois; Geraghty & Miller, Inc., Annapolis, Maryland; Associated Water and Air Resources, Inc., Nashville, Tennessee; Aware, Inc., Nashville, Tennessee.

wastes where they were, regrading and covering eroded and contaminated areas, and continuing surveillance and monitoring. The rationale for this preference was based on the "limited areal extent of potential contamination" and on the unsubstantiated assumption that the worst of the contamination was over and that the natural environmental assimilation and dilution processes would take care of what was left. The state rejected the "environmental assimilation" approach and also Velsicol's plea for a twelve-month moratorium to collect more data. Instead, the company was given a November 1 deadline to come up with further specific plans.

Meanwhile regional EPA offices were investigating whether the contamination was getting worse. An October, 1979, report made it clear that contamination was increasing. The EPA found that CCl_4 levels in three wells north of the landfill had increased dramatically over the preceding year from an average of 20 ppb to 150 ppb and that fish from the local Pugh Creek and Sandpit Spring had become contaminated with from 170 ppb to 900 ppb of CCl_4 and from 360 ppb to 500 ppb of chloroform. Although no CCl_4 could be detected in the water of nearby Holland Lake, composite levels in fish were in the region of 12 ppb.[17]

By early November, Velsicol submitted its "Closure Plan," concluding that "the hydrogeologic environment . . . is at present attenuating migrating contaminants to a level minimizing environmental impact," but recognizing that nothing could be done at the dump site to eliminate the contaminants that had already been dispersed. The plan recommended that the dump site be capped to reduce further migration of contaminants, that adjacent areas be cleaned up, and that a maintenance and monitoring program be implemented.[18]

The state reacted critically to this proposal, largely because of Velsicol's failure to have detailed the rationale for "capping," as opposed to other alternatives for site closure. The state also emphasized Velsicol's failure to supply it with requested information on a wide range of other critical issues, particularly those having to do with monitoring and hydrogeology, and challenged Velsicol's assertion that the level of contamination in groundwater was decreasing. By March, 1980, Velsicol had failed to answer most of these unresolved questions.

Future Prospects

The EPA estimates that minimal remedial action on the site will cost about $6 million and that complete cleanup will cost about $165 million. The fate of the water supplies is more problematical. According to the 1978 USGS survey, the local water-table aquifer is now contaminated, and contaminants are moving underground at a rate of 80 to 300 feet per year. Moreover, the contamination is spreading toward the north and northwest in the direction of the Toone-Teague wells, rather than to the east and northeast, as predicted by the 1967 survey. Sharp increases in levels of CCl_4 in wells north of the dump have been found; the highest ever-recorded level, 29,500 ppb, was reported in March, 1979. This indicates that contamination of the aquifer is clearly increasing, even with decrease in overall usage of the aquifer as a water supply. Still more seriously, there is now the real possibility that cracks or fissures in the subsurface below the dump site may allow some 16.5 million gallons of highly toxic wastes to filter down into the deep artesian aquifer that supplies Memphis with its drinking water. Furthermore, the dump site sits atop the New Madrid fault line. Since almost all western Tennessee depends on groundwater, continued leaching of pollutants from the dump will continue to endanger this broad geographic area for decades to come.

The long-term health effects are at least as poorly predictable. An EPA-supported, University of Cincinnati Medical School preliminary study initiated in November, 1978, some eight months after five wells were closed because of heavy contamination, found evidence of abnormal liver function in about 25 percent of a group of thirty-six Toone-Teague Road residents.[19] A questionnaire found that these residents had suffered from a variety of acute symptoms and illnesses, including eleven hospitalizations and one birth defect, in the preceding twelve months. While these symptoms could not be easily related to the contamination, their incidence was related to the degree of contaminant-exposure, and their frequency appeared to diminish sharply after their use of contaminated well water for drinking and cooking ceased. In one home tested prior to the survey, levels of CCl_4 in bathroom air when water was running into the tub were over one hundred times higher than before running the water (3,600 μg/m³ compared with 23 μgm³).*

In January 1979, the study was extended to 150 local residents, who were also given a more detailed health questionnaire covering the preceding six months and a physical examination, including routine blood chemistry, blood pressure, liver size, and other physical measurements. No statistically significant differences in acute-illness rates or liver-function tests were found between the 49 residents whose water supply had been contaminated and the 33 others with intermediate exposure or the 57 with no known exposure.[20,21] However, many residents in the contaminated group reported persisting nausea, vomiting, and mucous membrane irritation. A statistically significant increase in the incidence of borderline liver enlargement was found among seven residents who had been drinking the contaminated water. The study concluded:

> It is our opinion that the most likely reason for the presence of abnormalities discovered in the inhabitants of the Toone-Teague Road area was the consumption of water from wells contaminated by the leaching of material from the chemical land dump located in that area. The acute symptomatology and the abnormal liver function tests have in all but a few isolated cases returned to normal and, with no further contamination, should remain normal. However, it is impossible at this time to predict whether there will be any future chronic effects as a result of this exposure. We believe that medical followup of the people studied in this investigation is warranted.[22]

Some Toone-Teague residents are clearly at serious excess risk for various chronic toxic effects, particularly cancer, from prolonged ingestion and inhalation of high concentrations of some carcinogens, such as CCl_4, as well as lower concentrations of other carcinogens, such as tetrachloroethylene and chloroform. Such predictions are, however, further complicated by a wide range of possible interactive effects between the numerous toxic and carcinogenic chemicals in the water and air.

---

*Urine analyses for HEX, HEX-BCH, and three other related pesticide intermediates that had rarely been found in the contaminated wells, at less-than-ppb levels, were negative. Detectable levels of HEX were however found in the air of three of five homes tested, with maximum concentrations of 0.1 μg/m³.

Overview

Rural America has often borne the brunt of the hazardous waste problem. Small towns like Toone are a favored dumping ground because land is cheap and often sparsely populated. Companies apparently believe the chances are slim that anyone would either complain about the dump or even know about its existence. Examples of this extensive and destructive rural dumping are numerous.

In the "Valley of the Drums," between seventeen thousand and one hundred thousand drums of waste were dumped illegally at a farm in a hilly section of Shepardsville, Kentucky, thirty miles south of Louisville. The mountains of drums were abandoned by the owner of the property and left to rot, spilling their dangerous contents into a local creek.

In Byron, Illinois, approximately fifteen hundred containers of industrial wastes were buried on farmland, causing contamination of local surface water, groundwater, and soil with cyanide, chromium, arsenic, and other toxic compounds and heavy metals. Several cows died, and the farmland has been rendered useless.

In Saltville, Virginia, an alkali-processing plant in operation between 1895 and 1972 left huge deposits of mercury-contaminated soils, which have subsequently contaminated the North Fork Holston River.

In Bayou Sorrel, Louisiana, a truck driver employed by a disposal company died of hydrogen-sulfide asphyxiation as he emptied a load of chemicals into a waste pit. Millions of gallons of toxic waste were deposited here in huge open pits, filling the air of the community with toxic pollutants.

In Pichens, South Carolina, an electric company dumped dozens of capacitors and transformers leaking high levels of polychlorinated biphenyls (PCBs) into a local watershed, contaminating local drinking water.

Although it is not known how much waste is shipped to rural areas each year, unsafe pits, ponds, lagoons, and landfills litter the countryside in many areas of the nation. The ultimate destruction of farmland and groundwater will cost billions of dollars. The health costs are incalculable.

The problems faced by the Sterlings are symptomatic of those faced by rural residents throughout the country who live near dangerous dump sites. For years, many states did not require regulation of dumping activities on private lands. From the beginning, the Sterlings were kept ignorant about what was going on at the farm behind their home. They were not provided with sufficient information to be forewarned about possible migration of highly toxic and carcinogenic chemicals into their drinking water. Local county officials were not equipped to properly evaluate the situation. Residents of nearby towns were reluctant to help foot the bill for a new water supply. Federal officials showed little interest in the problem until it had become critical. Finally, the company responsible moved to help only after intense media and political pressure.

The Sterlings learned a hard lesson. They learned that even in the back woods of rural Tennessee, toxic chemicals could devastate their lives. They also learned to be skeptical of the government's ability to protect their health. "You have to trust somebody," Christine said. "We just believed what they were telling us. We trusted them to find out what was wrong. I don't trust government people like that anymore."

> Despite its tremendous importance to our lives,
> our health, and economy, we have almost
> recklessly damaged our groundwater.
>
> CONGRESSMAN TOBY MOFFETT
> July 24, 1980

CHAPTER 4

Dumping and Groundwater

Improper disposal of hazardous wastes is resulting in irreversible destruction of an ever-increasing volume of groundwater. Throughout the country, wastes improperly dumped decades ago are just now beginning to render drinking water supplies unusable. For centuries after the hazardous waste disposal problem has been "solved," its devastating impact on groundwater will persist.

St. Louis Park, Minnesota

Minnesota, like many other major American states, is critically dependent on groundwater. Of its nearly 4 million inhabitants, 67 percent get their drinking water from wells. In the Minneapolis area, for example, most fresh water comes from underground sources (aquifers). Generally, these aquifers have provided an abundant supply of clean water. However, recent events suggest that at least several Minneapolis aquifers are becoming endangered by casual hazardous waste disposal practices dating back some fifty years.

Reilly Tar and Republic Creosote, a coal-tar and creosote manufacturing facility, opened on an eighty-acre site in St. Louis Park in 1916, long before the area became a major bedroom community for Minneapolis. Over five decades of subsequent operations, the company distilled millions of pounds of coal tar to produce liquid wood-preserving oils and creosote, used by Reilly to treat wood. Residue coke and vapors resulting from the distillation process were condensed and separated, yielding other products, including tars, light oil, ammonia liquor, and coke-oven gas.

The first hint of problems from the plant's operations came in 1932, when St. Louis Park contracted for a new well to supply its growing population. A 540-foot well was sunk at the intersection of two main roads. The top 280 feet of the well shaft were encased in iron to ensure against possible contamination from shallow water-bearing strata. Nothing unusual was observed while the well was being drilled. When water was finally pumped up from the well, Fred McCarthy, president of the drilling company, noted that it had a "creosote" taste and smell. A subsequent state health department inspection condemned the water as undrinkable. Other private wells in the area were also found to be contaminated and were closed.

The precise source of the contamination was never firmly established. However, it became clear that wastes from the Reilly operation were somehow responsible. During an investigation into the pollution source, McCarthy discovered "two abandoned wells at the Republic Creosote Company plant about one half mile away [used] to drain creosote down to the ground."[1] It seemed likely that creosote was leaking from the disposal wells into fissures in underlying semipermeable strata, through which the city well was being contaminated.

Assuming that the creosote could eventually be cleaned out of the aquifer, the city continued pumping the well for another two years. Additionally, the lower section of the well was encased in an attempt to seal it off from the polluting creosote. However, the water quality failed to improve, and the well was eventually abandoned. No legal action was taken against Reilly by the city or private well owners, nor was Reilly ordered to improve its waste-disposal practices.

Over the years, Reilly management faced a continuing problem with creosote wastes, which were accumulating much faster than they could be disposed of. In 1956, for example, Reilly employees were directed to unload a 50,000-gallon tank containing process wastes "as quickly as you can," since storage capacity for new wastes was needed immediately. One company official recommended that the materials "could be wasted on the grounds in the yard to treat the soil and kill weeds . . . ."[2]

By 1957, so much creosote waste had been dumped on the plant site that Reilly's own water well became contaminated. Coal tar was found seeping into the well shaft down to 226 feet. Contamination was so severe that the well had to be closed. The company was then forced to buy its yearly millions of gallons of water from the city rather than risk drilling a new well in the creosote-impregnated plant site.

These on-site disposal problems became exacerbated by the rapid growth of the St. Louis Park community. As more houses were constructed around the perimeter of the plant, its operations came under closer scrutiny. Strong odors from the plant swept into nearby houses. Spills and contaminated rain runoff, which often ponded south of the plant, became more and more obvious.

In 1962, the city mayor and engineer sat down with Reilly management and discussed the continuing problems caused by the contaminated runoff from the plant and their fears that local water wells could become contaminated. City officials suggested that the runoff problem could only be solved by filling in the areas "saturated with creosote." Since it seemed unlikely that Reilly would be able to take appropriate action to end its discharges into the ground, air, and surface waters while the plant was in operation, the mayor asked Reilly to plan ceasing operations within ten years.

When Reilly management resisted, the city began to crack down on the plant. A 1969 city investigation discovered that creosote seeping from the plant had extensively corroded buried underground water mains. The study also noted that several city workers had complained of "severe skin reactions" from handling "creosote-bearing soil" while constructing a utility line near the plant and that some local groundwaters were contaminated with creosote. Several samples from city wells contained concentrations of phenol well "above the upper limits" established by the U.S. Public Health Service.[3] A later city study found that there were large pools of contaminated water south of the plant that were "acutely toxic to animal and plant life," and that the plant itself was often waterlogged and "saturated with petroleum products."[4]

In October, 1970, the state of Minnesota Pollution Control Agency and the city of St. Louis Park filed a joint complaint against Reilly Tar, charging the company with polluting local surface waters and fouling the air.* While it denied these charges, Reilly decided that modifications needed to satisfy local government would cost far too much and therefore closed the plant in September, 1971.†

The discharges from the plant ceased immediately. Heartened by this turn of events, the city negotiated with Reilly to purchase the property.‡ On April 14, 1972, an agreement between the two parties solidified the deal. St. Louis Park was about to become the owner of dozens of acres of creosote-saturated land. Reilly management was not, however, interested in giving the property away. Before the deal could go through, they insisted that the state/city suit would have to be dropped. The city readily agreed; the state, however, refused.

Some state officials suggest that the city council of St. Louis Park was so anxious to get the land from Reilly that it acted foolishly. Wayne Popham, then city attorney, disagrees. According to Popham, any fault lies with the state. Popham insists that the city had no idea that the groundwater was severely contaminated. He says the city knew about the phenol problem,

---

*This suit did not contain a provision on groundwater contamination because no substantial evidence of such contamination had then been found.

†While the potential cost of complying with the pollution-control program demanded by the city was a major factor in the management's decision to close the plant, Reilly Tar was also dismayed by city plans to force Republic Creosote to sell the city eleven acres of land as a right-of-way for a newly planned street through the Reilly complex. Construction of the road would have ended Reilly's easy access to the adjacent rail line.

‡The city had actually been negotiating with Reilly before the complaint was filed. Reilly first offered to sell the city the entire property in July, 1970.

but relied on the state's evaluation of the overall problem. Ironically, according to Popham, although the city raised questions about the groundwater, it was the state health department that told the city everything was OK.

Popham says that when the city first sued Reilly for surface-water and air pollution, it strengthened its case by adding the charge of groundwater pollution. The city hired a consultant, who concluded that there was enough evidence of groundwater pollution. The state health department, however, insisted that the consultant was wrong and denied that there was any health threat. Popham and another city attorney were suspicious, but when they attended a meeting with the state health department and asked if the department was "sure," a health department official answered angrily, "Look, I'm telling you, you've got nothing there. We can't make up a case for you lawyers." Given this advice, Popham says, the city moved ahead and eventually paid approximately $2 million for the land.[5] Finalization of the negotiations was far from smooth. First, the land was purchased by the city as part of its development plan under a grant from the Department of Housing and Urban Development (HUD). The HUD grant was delayed and the closing held up for several months. Additionally, before the state would drop its suit against Reilly, it insisted that the city submit a satisfactory plan for cleaning up the surface-water problem. Popham says that a week before the scheduled closing, the state suddenly announced that its review of the cleanup plan would take longer and asked the city to stall the closing for six weeks. When the city presented the dilemma to Reilly's attorney, he was unsympathetic. Reilly wanted an immediate settlement. Its attorney insisted that, since the state would not agree to drop the suit until the plan was approved, the only way the city could get the land was by signing a hold-harmless agreement.

On June 19, 1973, the city signed the hold-harmless agreement and dismissed the court action "insofar as a remedy [was] claimed by the city." The agreement stated that the city would "hold Reilly harmless from *any* and *all* claims which may be asserted against it by the State of Minnesota acting by and through the Minnesota Pollution Control Agency" and that the city would be responsible for "restoring the property, at its expense, to any condition that may be required by the State of Minnesota."

Soon after the deal was closed, the city tried to clean the site up. It soon found that most of the land was so saturated with creosote wastes as to be useless for construction. In September, 1973, St. Louis Park municipal water wells were found to be contaminated with high concentrations of carcinogenic chemicals. Subsequent tests in 1974 found extensive contamination of groundwater with phenols to a depth of over 900 feet and of soil in the southern section of the plant property with wastes to a depth of over 45 feet. At 67 feet below the surface, the soil was so saturated that it exuded a "tarlike odor."[6]

June, 1977 brought more bad news. A study by Barr Engineering reported that 90 percent of the soil samples it had collected from the plant area contained high concentrations of coal-tar derivatives. Samples from the southern end of the site yielded concentrations of benzene at over 1,000 parts per million (ppm) at a depth of fifty feet below the surface. Furthermore the hydrology of the area, Barr concluded, indicated that the groundwater was flowing laterally through the site toward a buried bedrock valley, a recharge area for the St. Peter sandstone aquifer, one of the major area sources of drinking water. Barr found that the "drift" was heavily contaminated with coal-tar derivatives, including polycyclic aromatic hydrocarbons (PAH), such as pyrene at concentrations of 3,400 ppm, besides several carcinogens belonging to this class.[7]

In April, 1978, the state sued Reilly Tar to clean up the plant area and cleanse the groundwater. The state charged that the hold-harmless agreement did not cover groundwater, but only surface-water contamination and air pollution.[8] Reilly claims, however, that the clause relieved it of responsibility for all pollution problems.

According to the state, the aquifers that crisscross the old plant site are in imminent danger of contamination. Approximately two hundred and fifty thousand people obtain their drinking water from those aquifers. "Until the phenols are captured and removed from the soil and groundwater," the state contends, the threat will continue.

By June, 1980, five municipal wells and at least six private wells had been closed because of PAH contamination. Levels of contaminants in the municipal wells continue to fluctuate. Studies conducted by the U.S. Geological Survey (USGS) and state geologists have uncovered numerous abandoned "multi-aquifer" wells that have served over the years as a downward pathway for the creosote. Constant monitoring of area wells has found contamination over two miles from the plant site. All indications are that the contaminants are continuing to move down and toward the southeast. Since the ground is supersaturated with the wastes, every rainfall is likely to force them further into the groundwater.

In September, 1980, the federal government joined the fray by filing a complaint against Reilly and the city's Housing and Redevelopment Authority, as well as several developers.*[9] If successful, the suit would require Reilly to conduct research and monitoring and submit a plan to the Environmental Protection Agency (EPA) for cleanup and containment. Once approved, Reilly would then have to bear the cost of cleanup and reimburse the government for the costs it incurred investigating the problem. Firm estimates are not yet available on the cleanup cost, which could run from a few million to a few hundred million dollars. A massive effort is now underway to plug all the pathways from the surface to the deeper aquifers in the hope that the continuing contamination can be stopped. It is unlikely that the damage already done can be corrected.

Lathrop, California

Lathrop is a small town (population 5,000) in the San Joaquin Valley about seventy-five miles east of San Francisco and ten miles south of Stockton. Several companies have manufacturing plants there, including Libby-Owens Ford, Air Products, Inc., and Occidental Chemical Company. The vast majority of the land in and around Lathrop, however, is utilized

---

*Developers and the city's Housing and Redevelopment Authority were only named in the suit "to ensure that remedial measures sought can be fully implemented."[10]

for agricultural purposes. Water in the Lathrop area is a scarce and valuable resource. Lathrop's residents, farms, and industries rely almost totally on groundwater obtained from wells sunk into the sandy and porous soil.

In 1979, Lathrop was stunned by news that its only water resource was contaminated with dibromochloropropane (DBCP), a soil fumigant known to cause cancer and sterility.* The company suspected to be the source of the contamination was Occidental Chemical, also known as Oxychem, a division of Hooker Chemical Company.

The Lathrop plant began manufacturing fertilizer in 1953. In 1964, it was purchased by Occidental, which greatly expanded its operations. The facility sits less than thirty feet above a major aquifer, which supplies the Lathrop area with its drinking, manufacturing, and irrigation water. The soil in the area is extremely permeable, and liquids dumped on the surface are readily absorbed into the underlying soil. The absence of impermeable strata between the surface and underlying aquifer ensures easy downward migration of pollutants.

Over the years, the plant manufactured thousands of tons of fertilizer and fertilizer constituents, including sulfuric acid, phosphoric acid, ammonium sulfate, and ammonia. The plant also formulated and packaged for sale over fifty pesticides. One of the pesticides formulated at the Lathrop plant between 1963 and 1971, and again between 1974 and 1976, was DBCP.†

*DBCP was initially marketed as Fumazone® by Dow Chemical Company in 1957, following a six-year testing program, and subsequently as Nemagon® by Shell Chemical. The first publication on the toxicology of DBCP in 1961 reported that it induced sterility, testicular atrophy and inhibition of spermatogenesis, in various species and that these effects, together with growth inhibition, were seen in rats inhaling 5-ppm levels, the lowest dose tested.[11] Subsequent studies confirmed its sterilizing effects (1971)[12] and also demonstrated the induction of gastric cancer in mice and rats and breast cancer in rats after only brief periods of exposure (1975)[13] and mutagenicity in bacterial and other systems (1977).[14] Over this twenty-year period, no warning at all was given to the workers at the Lathrop plant or elsewhere concerning the extreme reproductive and other hazards of DBCP.[15]

†In 1977, workers at the Lathrop plant, worried by their infertility, prompted their own medical examination. Of twenty-three workers exposed to DBCP, nine were found to have no sperm at all after working in the plant for fifteen years, while others who had been employed for shorter periods had a marked reduction in sperm count. Following similar findings elsewhere, at Dow and Shell facilities, DBCP production was suspended by the Occupational Safety and Health Admini-

Until 1977, the plant took minimal precautions in disposing of its pesticide wastes. Most were dumped directly on the plant grounds or into an unlined lagoon with a porous base. Both practices were in clear violation of California state law, which requires any company dumping a chemical waste that could percolate into groundwater to promptly report the dumping to the California Regional Water Quality Board. As evidenced by internal memoranda, made public in June, 1979 by Congressman Bob Eckhardt's Oversight and Investigations Subcommittee, company personnel were well aware of this violation but continued to dump and to withhold this information from the state.[16]

The documents demonstrate that, as early as April, 1975, Oxychem personnel were aware that their pesticide operation violated state law.[17] Robert Edson, the facility's environmental engineer, told company officials that allowing waste percolation into the ground was clearly against the law.*

According to Edson, who had been complaining about the problem for years, the situation had already become dangerous. "Our laboratory records indicate," wrote Edson, "that we are slowly contaminating all wells in our area, and two of our own wells are contaminated to the point of being toxic to animals or humans. THIS IS A TIME BOMB THAT WE MUST DEFUSE [emphasis original]."[19]

Impressed by Edson's concerns, Lathrop management informed Oxychem's comptroller at Houston headquarters that it would need immediate funds to stop the pollution before the state caught up with it. M. A. Stanek, the Lathrop plant manager, wrote, "Should the water quality control regulatory agencies become aware of the fact that we percolate our pesticide wastes, they could justifiably close down our entire Ag Chem [Agricultural Chemical] plant operation."[20] Despite these

---

stration (OSHA) in September, 1977. Worker exposure at the Lathrop plant was estimated by the National Institute for Occupational Safety and Health (NIOSH) to be in the region of 0.5 ppm.

*These regulations were spelled out in detail to Oxychem in August, 1968: "The waste discharge shall not cause a pollution of ground or surface waters. . . . The waste discharge shall not cause concentrations of substances in usable ground waters, which are deleterious to human, plant, animal, or aquatic life."[18]

warnings, cleanup money was not made available that year, and the coverup continued.

By June, 1976, Edson was getting very nervous. "I believe we have fooled around long enough and already over-pressed our luck," he wrote. Edson's estimates of the plant's discharges showed that an excessive amount of hazardous wastes had already been dumped. "To date, we have been discharging more than 500 parts per million or about 5 tons of pesticide per year into the ground. The next drop of pesticide that percolates to the ground is a management decision I don't feel we can afford."[21]

Edson was especially concerned about a neighbor's drinking water well, located only five hundred feet from the point of the plant's waste discharge, and warned that he "would not drink from this well."[22] Later that year, the plant sampled this well and found 2,000 parts per billion (ppb) of solvents, a level far exceeding health standards. The neighbors were not informed of the danger.

Further tests taken in 1977 revealed that other plant operations had also heavily contaminated local groundwater. In an April, 1977 memorandum, Edson wrote, "We have destroyed the usability of several wells in our area." This new information, together with the plant's failure to abate the problem, led to Edson's refusal to sign Oxychem's less-than-honest reports to the California Regional Water Quality Control Board. He wrote:

> In the past I have sent a report monthly to the Water Quality Control Board which gives our discharge to the waste water leach pond. This report does not consider the chemicals leached from our gyp [gypsum] ponds and ditches or the chemicals discharged from Ag Chem. I don't believe the Water Quality Control Board is even aware that we process pesticides. Since this report isn't exactly accurate even though the inaccuracy is due to omission rather than outright falsehood, I don't really feel comfortable in signing it. However, I don't think it would be wise to explain the discrepancy to the state at this time.[23]

Faced with this information, Oxychem finally agreed in late 1977 to authorize an abatement program. This program was based largely on the construction of lined concentrator, cooling, and waste-water ponds. No attempt, however, was made to prevent continuing percolation from previously dumped wastes, or to warn the state and owners of contaminated wells.

The state continued in ignorance until February, 1979, when an extensive testing program was mounted. High levels of several pesticides, including DBCP, malathion, methoxychlor, chlordane, ethyl parathion, ethylene dibromide, and DDT, were identified in a waste-water pond and ditch near the Lathrop plant. Local groundwater was also found to be contaminated with DBCP, ethyl parathion, and lindane. In one well, lindane concentrations of 22 ppb, fourfold in excess of the EPA safe drinking water criteria, were found.

Testing for DBCP and other possible contaminants in local wells led to some new discoveries. Norman Hixon, principal of the Lathrop elementary school, was one of the first local residents to find out about the new problem. Hixon received a call from the county health department, informing him that something had been found in the school well water, something the county would tell him about at a meeting shortly. Hixon suspected that the county had found DBCP in the well, but at the meeting he was told the county had found elevated levels of radiation.

The levels of radiation found in the well were nine times higher than the EPA safe drinking water criteria. The water was immediately turned off, and a hookup to the uncontaminated municipal water system was established. While the school district took swift action to correct the problem, Hixon was miffed. "If we had been notified earlier, we would have had the water changed," he said, noting that the findings had been kept "secret."

The state alleges that radioactive water draining from Oxychem's fertilizer-manufacturing operation caused the contamination that closed the school well, a trailer-park well serving over eighty people, and about half a dozen other wells. Small amounts of radium and uranium in the phosphate rock used by the plant are considered the most likely sources of the radiation.[24]

In March, 1979, the California Regional Water Quality Board issued a "cease and desist" order to prevent further discharge of wastes from the Lathrop plant. The order also established a five-month compliance schedule, during which the plant was required to submit a plan to determine the extent of pesticide contamination, to complete a survey of the plant site for pesticide contamination, to remove all contaminated soil to a secure landfill, to seal areas to prevent further groundwater contamination, to submit a report describing areal extent of groundwater pollution, and to recommend remedial action. On December 18, 1979, the federal government, together with the state of California, filed a civil suit against Oxychem, demanding $30 million in penalties and $15 million for cleanup.[25] Additionally, a criminal investigation is now being conducted into the coverup.

On February 6, 1981, the federal government, the state of California, the Regional Water Quality Control Board, and the Occidental Chemical Company signed a settlement agreement that requires Occidental "to clean up contaminated groundwater and soil in the vicinity of the Occidental Chemical Company's facility."[26] Details of Occidental's plan were still being worked out in the fall of 1981.

No firm estimates for the total cost of the cleanup work have been reported. However, the state of California estimated that the cleanup would cost around $16 million. Occidental disputes that figure. All parties agree that completion of the cleanup program will take from twenty to thirty years.

The settlement also required that Occidental pay the federal government $200,000 and the state of California $100,000 for the costs they incurred in investigating the problem. In addition, Occidental agreed to spend $1.5 million on groundwater research and pay the state of California's hazardous waste cleanup program $1 million.[27]

The DBCP contamination and the radiation levels found in local wells have made the many Lathrop residents who depend on their private wells feel "insecure," says the Reverend Mr. Apolinar N. Sangaland. A retired clergyman, and thirteen-year resident of the area, Sangaland had been following the local events with great concern. "Quite a few people are upset about it," Sangaland says about the contamination problem, "especially the people employed by Oxy."

Both Sangaland and Hixon believe Oxychem should have been more careful. They also believe that if the state hadn't been looking for DBCP and other chemicals, people would never have known about the contamination. For Sangaland and Hixon, however, the only long-range solution is self-help. "I don't believe the government is going to take care of us," Hixon said. He pointed out that most area residents used their own well water and didn't have the money to get it tested on a frequent basis. Given the present circumstances, Hixon decided against drinking his well water. "I look at my own water and I'm not too far from the plant, and I can't afford to test it, so we're on bottled water now," he said.

The full extent of the groundwater pollution has not yet been defined. Based on the evidence developed so far, it seems that the pollution plume may move into residential areas north of the plant. Meanwhile, local area residents have the option of continuing to drink contaminated or untested well water or of buying bottled water.

Lathrop citizens remain nervous. "People have been trying to make a joke out of it," Hixon said. "They are selling T-shirts that say 'Lathrop, California—It's the Water.'"

Rancho Cordova, California

Aerojet General Corporation was having difficulty disposing of one of its rocket-fuel wastes in the mid-1970s. The problems occurred at its eight-thousand-acre industrial complex near Rancho Cordova, California. In 1979, tests of the soil in one of the facility's waste lagoons showed extremely high concentrations of a number of dangerous substances, including trichloroethylene (TCE) at 130,000 ppb. Test wells in the vicinity of the disposal ponds and pits yielded 100,000 ppb of chloroform; 42,000 ppb of dichloroethane; 11,000 ppb of dichloromethane; and 2,300 ppb of TCE.

These results prompted testing of other wells in the area. One well serving 120 people at a nearby trailer park contained a TCE level of 480 ppb and was closed as a health hazard. A local fish-hatchery well showed an even higher contamination of

8,500 ppb. Over nineteen rural wells have since been closed as a result of TCE contamination.

While state investigators were reviewing the situation at Rancho Cordova, an Aerojet employee tipped them off to an illegal dumping operation. Investigators allege that a three-thousand five hundred foot pipe had been constructed to bypass an approved disposal well, dumping waste into a bottomless gravel pit. State inspections of the facility also revealed five unlined settling ponds, into which chemical wastes were pumped from the Cordova Chemical Company, a subsidiary of Aerojet. These ponds allowed large amounts of chemical waste to percolate into the ground.

San Gabriel Valley, California

The discovery of pollution in Rancho Cordova groundwater led Aerojet to test the groundwater under their facility in the San Gabriel Valley in southern California. These tests showed 250 ppb of TCE in the well water, and additional tests conducted on wells in the valley showed widespread TCE contamination. Over fifty-eight wells have been closed. TCE contamination ranges from 6 ppb to almost 600 ppb. The state of California estimates that the water supply for some four-hundred thousand persons, including the supply for Azusa, Glendora, Baldwin Park, and Irwindale, has been affected.

Raymond M. Hertel, executive officer of the California Regional Water Quality Control Board for Los Angeles, stated he believes the TCE contamination may have resulted from "practices of 15, 20, or even 30 years ago. We're talking about true contamination from massive pollution," Hertel told the *Los Angeles Times* in January, 1980.

The exact source of this contamination has not been determined. State investigators suspect that Aerojet and a neighboring company, Oil Processing and Solvent Company, Inc., are at least partially responsible for the pollution, but the widespread local use of TCE has so far precluded a conclusion on what is the major source.

The EPA has set a guideline level of 5 ppb for TCE in drinking water. Nevertheless, water shortages in the area have forced some municipalities to use water containing TCE well above the 5 ppb level.

The case studies of groundwater contamination in St. Louis Park, Minnesota and several California sites are by no means exceptional. In fact, they reflect events now commonly seen all over the United States.

Massachusetts

Groundwater contamination in Massachusetts has reached epidemic proportions. A report compiled by the state's Special Legislative Commission on Water Supply concluded that "in total at least one-third of the Commonwealth's communities have been affected to some degree by chemical contamination." The state report documents contamination incidents in twenty-two communities throughout Massachusetts.[28]

In a state where groundwater serves about 1.5 million people and is the only water supply for almost all of its rural population, thousands have been forced to seek new sources of water.

In Bedford, Massachusetts, the closing of four municipal wells in June, 1978 resulted in a loss of 80 percent of the town's water supply. Dioxane, a synthetic organic chemical, was found in one well at a concentration of 2,100 ppb, over one hundred times the recommended "safety level." TCE was also found in the water at up to 500 ppb, fifty times the recommended "safety level." The exact source of the contamination has not been found. Investigations have shown that the recharge area for the town water wells, a swamp located on the property of a local industry, is heavily contaminated with dioxane at concentrations of up to 23,000 ppb.

State and federal health officials examined death certificates for a nine-year period, 1969 through 1978, in an effort to determine whether there was an increased cancer rate in area residents, as suggested by local newspaper reports. A significant increase in cancer deaths was found among women in the town during four years of this time period; the increase was largely due to breast and ovary cancer. Although these data are not conclusive and no causal link between the increase in cancer and the contaminated water has been made, local health officials have urged town women to regularly examine their breasts and watch for any early cancer signs.[29]

Connecticut

Over 1.2 million Connecticut residents, almost 40 percent of the state's population, depend on groundwater.* Almost half get their water from private wells, which are rarely tested for chemical contaminants. A 1981 state hazardous waste inventory indicates that one quarter of the state's towns had already experienced groundwater problems.[30]

Connecticut exemplifies some specific problems faced by older industrial states with high concentrations of small manufacturing facilities. According to a 1979 state survey, many Connecticut manufacturing facilities utilize a "seepage impoundment" process that deliberately allows contaminated waters to seep into the ground "to aid in the dewatering of the metal hydroxide sludges." There are over one hundred fifty active and nineteen abandoned seepage impoundments of this type in Connecticut. The state conservatively estimates that over half the metal-plating and finishing wastes placed in these impoundments could eventually reach groundwaters.

In 1970, students and faculty at Durham High School began complaining about an unusual odor in the school's drinking water. Tests indicated that the water was contaminated with the solvents tetrachloroethylene and chloroform. Subsequent investigations determined that the most likely source of the contamination was an impoundment on the property of Sibbley, Inc., a metal-plating operation located within a few hundred feet of the school water well.[31] Although discharges into the impoundment have been stopped, the school must continue to use an activated-carbon filter system to cleanse the contaminants from the water.

Solvents Recovery Services, of Southington, Connecticut, operated for over twenty years before it was discovered that it

---

*About 18 percent of Connecticut's population is dependent on stratified drift aquifers. These river-basin groundwater sources are highly susceptible to contamination.

had polluted the local groundwater. Leaky drums, direct discharge into the ground, and storage and disposal of millions of gallons of hazardous wastes in unlined lagoons are considered the probable sources of the contamination. For example, Solvents Recovery disposed of its degreasing solvents in an unlined lagoon only 250 feet from a municipal water well.

The solvents in the groundwater have forced the closing of two municipal water wells and threatened a half dozen private wells. Investigators believe more wells will be affected as the plume of pollution from the site expands.

Long Island, New York

Almost 100 percent of Long Island's 2.5 million population depends on the island's abundant groundwater supply. In June, 1979, about twenty-five community wells in Nassau and Suffolk counties were closed as a result of chemical contamination. The island faces an especially acute problem created by the wide use of degreasing agents, particularly TCE, in hundreds of thousands of septic tanks. These chemicals have in recent years found their way in increasing concentrations into the island's highly permeable soil and shallow aquifers. Additional problems are due to heavy use of pesticides and to manufacturing wastes and landfill leachate, as well as salt-water intrusions created by overdrafts of the aquifer. It seems likely that sooner or later the island's population will have to import its drinking water.

New Jersey

Approximately 53 percent of New Jersey's population depends on groundwater. A three-year-long water monitoring program conducted by the New Jersey Department of Environmental Protection found "trace levels" of toxic industrial chemicals in most wells. Organic chemical contamination was especially severe in industrialized areas of the state, and excessive contamination of public water supplies was found in Ocean, Bergen,

Camden, and Middlesex counties. Municipal water wells in these areas were forced to close.[32]

"I have two children. I'd like to see them live. Are they going to live? Somebody has to help us. We need help," James G. McCarthy of Jackson Township testified before a United States Senate subcommittee. Toxic chemicals had been discovered in his drinking water well. McCarthy's nine-year-old daughter had died of a chronic kidney disease, and an unofficial local survey showed eight cases of kidney disease and seven miscarriages in a total of six houses. In 1978, wells serving 165 area families were capped, and the municipality began to supply them with approximately thirty gallons of drinking water a day. McCarthy insists that the community's problems are linked to toxic chemicals dumped nearby.

Overview

All proposed approaches to the protection of groundwater quality rest on its high vulnerability to improper disposal of hazardous wastes and on the critical needs for the development and implementation of strong and coherent national policies. While these policies must ultimately stress the needs to reduce the volume of hazardous wastes generated, they must more immediately focus on the needs for the rigid control, to the extent of complete prohibition, of land use for waste disposal, whether by pits, ponds, lagoons, or even "secure" landfills, especially in areas where vulnerable groundwater aquifers are located.

The development of realistic national groundwater policies requires sensitivity to a variety of regional considerations. These considerations include differences of natural water quality in different aquifers and the possibility of developing differential standards to reflect differences in major intended uses, whether for human consumption, irrigation, or mining. Additionally, national groundwater policies must be integrated with other environmental laws.

In the final analysis, it is unlikely that effective national policies will ever be implemented until there is full realization of the grossly inflationary and delayed impact of the present failure to regulate. Groundwaters in the industrialized areas of the Gulf states, Northeast, and Great Lakes are beginning to show signs of contamination. Hundreds of wells have already been closed. Solvent wastes have begun to appear in groundwater supplies. These wastes may well be only the mobile front of pollution plumes, behind which may come more toxic pesticide and other industrial wastes. It is the responsibility of an enlightened Congress and general public to ensure that effective national regulation is not delayed until it is forced belatedly by catastrophe. A clear national strategy for preventing groundwater contamination is essential, and long overdue.

Our boys are bright and well-to-do
Our girls are smart and pretty
They cannot help it nor could you
If you lived in [Love's] Model City

WILLIAM T. LOVE

CHAPTER 5

Dumping in Niagara Falls

No adequate examination of the hazardous waste problem would be complete without a review of the tragedy at the Love Canal. Much confusion still exists about exactly what happened there. It is unclear whether all the relevant facts will ever surface. Nevertheless, the story of the Love Canal has been etched into modern history as few other events have. It has set the pace. It is the centerpiece of the hazardous waste debate.

In the pages that follow, some of the relevant facts about the Love Canal are displayed, and some personal observations by those who were affected by it are recalled. While it is unlikely that another such occurrence will take place, it cannot be viewed as entirely unique. The mistakes made at the Love Canal have been repeated hundreds of times. Perhaps a better understanding of those mistakes will assist in their future avoidance.

On August 2, 1978, in an unprecedented move, New York state officials ordered the emergency evacuation of 240 families living within two blocks of an old abandoned canal, the Love Canal, in Niagara Falls, New York. Dangerous concentrations of highly toxic and carcinogenic chemicals had been discovered oozing from the canal. Headlines throughout the nation declared the Love Canal the largest manmade environmental disaster in decades.

The Love Canal is a sixteen-acre landfill located just southeast of Niagara Falls. Bounded by Colvin Boulevard on the north, Frontier Avenue on the south, Ninety-Seventh Street on the west, and Ninety-Sixth Street on the east, it spans a large residential community of approximately one thousand small, closely built, low-to-middle-income, single-family homes. The Ninety-Ninth Street Elementary School is located on the canal site, near the intersection of Ninety-Ninth Street and Read Avenue.

On the same day that the emergency was declared, seven-year-old Jon Kenny, who lived a few blocks from the canal, was pronounced in satisfactory condition at Children's Hospital in Buffalo, New York and told that he could go home. Jon was suffering from chronic nephrosis, a kidney disease, whose cause had not been determined. His parents, however, had been assured by one of the hospital doctors that he would recover fully.

Jon returned home to a neighborhood in uproar. Rumors were circulating that people had been poisoned. Some families were preparing to leave, while others had already left. No one knew what, if anything, was going to be done to help them. On August 7, Governor Hugh Carey announced that the state would purchase the homes closest to the canal. The Kennys, however, were not advised to move or offered any help, as they lived just outside the narrow evacuation zone.

Weeks later, after successive brief periods of hospitalization, Jon died quite unexpectedly at Buffalo Children's Hospital. The realization of a possible relationship between her son's nephrosis and the Love Canal disaster did not occur to Mrs. Kenny until well after the August evacuation took place. "At the time of his death we read in the newspaper that the state was planning on investigating his death because of his age and where he lived, but truthfully we really didn't think much about it . . . We were distraught and quite upset and it was hard to even think about that it would be related to chemicals."

The cause of Jon's illness remains unresolved. Nevertheless, the Kennys suspect that chemicals draining from the canal were responsible, since nephrosis can be caused or exacerbated by exposure to toxic chemicals. State investigators tested a creek running through the Kennys' back yard and found high levels of the most toxic synthetic organic chemical known to man, tetrachlorodibenzo-para-dioxin (TCDD), more simply known as dioxin.

The Love Canal

The Love Canal was originally excavated in the 1880s by entrepreneur William T. Love as part of his grandiose scheme to create a sprawling industrial complex between the two branches of the Niagara River. This "model city," he boasted, would take advantage of the massive electric power that could be generated by the water's steep drop from the canal's entrance just above the falls to its terminus at the Niagara River, several miles away and several hundred feet below. At the time Love conceived his model city, use of electricity, then only in direct current (DC) form, was severely restricted, since it could only be transported for short distances. In Love's new city, industries located on the shores of the canal would be able to take full advantage of the abundant hydroelectric power.

Love's plan received enthusiastic support. The state of New York granted him uniquely broad authority to develop his planned city for two hundred thousand people and gave him "authority to condemn properties and to divert as much water from the upper Niagara River as he saw fit, even to the extent of turning off Niagara Falls!"[1]

Unfortunately for Love, just as his plans were reaching fruition, alternating current (AC) was developed, making it feasible to transmit electricity over long distances. The canal's major selling point immediately vanished, and, over the next two decades, Love's model-city plan collapsed. All that remains today is a small segment of the unfinished canal between Frontier Avenue and Colvin Boulevard, some eight miles north of the falls.

During the twenties and thirties, the abandoned canal filled with water and was used as a swimming hole. Art Tracy, a local resident for forty years, remembers, "When we first moved there, the Love Canal was there and it was a beautiful body of water. We used to go and get on cardboard or something else on top of the hill of dirt and slide right down into the water."

The Hooker Chemical Dump

The Hooker Electrochemical Corporation (later Hooker Chemical and Plastics Corporation) began operations in Niagara Falls in 1905. As one of the first industries in the area, it took full advantage of the Niagara's hydroelectric power. Over the years, the Hooker operation expanded to include the manufacture of industrial chemicals, fertilizers, and plastics.*

In 1942, Hooker signed an agreement with the Niagara Power and Development Corporation, the owners of the canal, to dump chemical wastes in the canal. About the same time, the city of Niagara Falls started dumping garbage in the canal. Tracy well remembers those days. There were few people living in the area, and there was little or no opposition to the dumping. But Tracy wasn't happy. He wanted to see the canal area turned into a picnic ground. Instead, the canal became an offensive nuisance. Soon he and his neighbors were "overrun by rats" and constantly overwhelmed by the odors.

In 1946, Hooker purchased the Love Canal from the Niagara Power and Development Corporation and turned it into a chemical dump site. From 1947 to 1952, Hooker dumped over 43 million pounds of industrial chemical wastes into the canal (see Table 5-1). These wastes included over 13 million pounds of lindane (benzene hexachloride), a highly toxic and carcinogenic chlorinated hydrocarbon pesticide; over 4 million pounds of chlorobenzenes, chlorinated derivatives of the highly toxic industrial solvent benzene, which is known to induce aplastic anemia and leukemia; and about half a million pounds of trichlorophenol (TCP), used in the manufacture of herbicides, such as 2, 4, 5-trichlorophenoxyacetic acid, also known as 2, 4, 5-T, and of cosmetic ingredients, such as hexachlorophene (HCP).

*Hooker, now one of the nation's largest chemical manufacturers, was purchased by Occidental Petroleum (Oxychem) in 1969. Hooker has several plants in the United States, of which Niagara Falls is the largest, with about thirty-one hundred employees.

The TCP was heavily contaminated with several hundred pounds of TCDD, formed as an accidental by-product of overheating TCP during the manufacturing process. Less than three ounces of TCDD could kill the entire population of New York City. At parts-per-billion (ppb) levels, exposure to TCDD can result in chloracne, an intractable and disabling chronic skin disease, and a wide range of other diseases and disturbances in metabolic functions. TCDD is also the most potent known carcinogen and teratogen, producing these effects in experimental animals at concentrations as low as 10 to 100 parts per trillion (ppt).*

Table 5-1. Wastes Dumped by Hooker Chemical into the Love Canal

Type of Waste	Estimated Quantity (tons)
Benzene hexachloride	6,900
Benzyl chloride	2,400
Mercaptans	2,400
Sulfides	2,100
Chlorobenzenes	2,000
Miscellaneous chlorinations	1,000
Benzoyl chloride	800
Liquid disulfides	700
Thionyl chloride	500
Metal chlorides	400
Miscellaneous acid chlorides	400
Trichlorophenol	200
Miscellaneous	2,000
TOTAL	21,000

Source: Based on Draft Report Interagency Task Force on Hazardous Wastes in Erie and Niagara Counties, New York, March 1979, pp. III-72–73.

Notes: Levels of benzene hexachloride (BHC) at the site were 1,900 times the EPA-established risk-criteria level for lindane and 20,000 times the EPA risk-criteria level for the alpha isomer. Other toxic chemicals found in the area of the site include: tetrachloroethylene, at 525 times the EPA risk level; trichloroethylene, at 7.6 times the EPA risk-criteria level; and benzene, at 7.3 times the EPA risk-criteria level. For a detailed listing of chemicals identified in the dump, and a summary of toxicological effects, see Appendix IV.

*It has also been alleged that, beginning about 1942, U.S. Army personnel dumped drums of toxic chemicals from various defense contractors, including Hooker and Linde Air Products (now Linde Division of Union Carbide), into the Love Canal. The Army's denial of these allegations has been challenged in a January, 1981 report by the New York State Assembly Task Force on Toxic Substances, on the basis of documentation obtained through the Freedom of Information Act.[2]

The Ninety-Ninth Street Elementary School

While Hooker was turning the canal into a chemical-waste dump, the city of Niagara Falls was expanding rapidly. By the early 1950s, the Board of Education and the city of Niagara Falls became eager for the canal and the land around it. The board wanted to build a school on the banks of the canal, and the city and private developers wanted to use the rest of the land for residential development. In 1952, the school board and the city instituted condemnation proceedings on the property adjacent to the canal and, according to Hooker, threatened to condemn the canal itself.

Hooker knew that it had buried millions of pounds of highly toxic wastes in the dump, that the area should not be used for construction of a school or homes, and that it might be held responsible for any of the canal's problems if the property was condemned. Hooker then decided to take action that it thought would insulate the company from all future responsibility. In April, 1953, Hooker sold the land to the school board for $1 in exchange for the board's signature on a deed with a provision intended to absolve Hooker from all future liability for injury or property damage caused by the dump's contents. Hooker insists that it warned the school board against "any construction activity of any kind going on at that disposal site."[3] However, the deed clause failed to explain that the Love Canal waste dump site contained many chemicals known at the time to be highly toxic.

In January, 1954, while attempting to lay the foundation for the Ninety-Ninth Street Elementary School, the construction company struck "a pit filled with chemicals."[4] Charles Thiele, the school board's architect, expressed grave concern. "It is poor policy to attempt to build over this soil, as it will be a continuous source of odors, and until more information is available regarding the materials dumped in this area, we must assume that it might be a detriment to the concrete foundations," he wrote. The board nevertheless decided to go ahead with its plans. In an attempt to avoid the "chemical pit," the foundation was shifted eighty-five feet north of the originally planned site. Efforts were also made to "clean up and bury as much of the [chemical] debris as possible." Thiele directed his contractors to "fill up the two chemical pits towards the north end of the southerly section of the property." However, he warned that placing fill in these pits would probably cause the chemicals inside to "overflow and cover adjacent areas," and for this reason decided to eliminate the school's planned basement.[5]

The Ninety-Ninth Street School opened in the fall of 1955. About five hundred children enrolled. The canal fascinated and frightened them, and they told each other tales of a monster that lived there, a monster that emerged from the depths of the canal with each full moon.

Barbara Quimby grew up on Ninety-Ninth Street. She attended the Ninety-Ninth Street School and, like her future husband and other local children, spent many years playing in the school yard. In the late fifties, Barbara remembers, she and her friends used to go down to an area behind a house on Ninety-Seventh Street that they called the "quicksand lagoon." There, she and her playmates poked sticks into the surfacing drums of chemicals and skipped rocks over the black sludge that accumulated there. The rocks popped and smoked as they bounced.

The canal, which was mostly a large, swampy field of unkept grasses and gullies, was also a favorite play area for Barbara and the local school children. However, playing there became more and more unpleasant. Barbara explains, "We had special shoes which we kept in our garages to wear over there, because once you wore something, a pair of sneakers or whatever, you couldn't get them clean again." Barbara remembers how children were often burned by liquids oozing from the canal. Neighborhood dogs that spent a lot of time at the canal also seemed affected. Their hair fell out in clumps, some developed severe skin diseases, and others became sickly and died.

Hooker soon found itself involved in these problems, as local parents started calling the company dispensary to inquire about the proper treatment of an increasing number of chemical burns suffered by their children. In June, 1958, Jerome Wilkenfeld, assistant technical superintendent of the Niagara Falls plant, informed the management that several children playing near the dump had been burned by chemicals that had "surfaced" in several areas of subsidence in the northern section of the canal and that "the entire area, [although not] officially designated for that purpose, was being used as a playground."[6]

Although Hooker insists that it warned the school board that children should be kept from playing in areas where chemicals had surfaced, they did not warn local residents about the danger. At congressional hearings many years later, Wilkenfeld claimed that Hooker management could not have given this warning, as "we did not feel we could without incurring substantial liabilities for implying that the current owners were [using] inadequate care on the property."[7]

Hooker's failure to warn the residents, and its explanation of this failure, prompted Congressman Albert Gore to remark:

> Clearly, the concern about exposing the School Board to some legal liability should not have overridden the duty of the corporation to inform the citizens of this area—of this community which has served you [Hooker] so well—of the hazards that they faced, particularly when you had information available to you that children were using the whole area as a playground. Not until 21 years later were they evacuated. . . . I just have to think that the events at Love Canal which we saw last year could have been avoided if the first warnings which were so clear—of children burned playing on top of the ground—had been heeded. This whole incident could have been completely avoided.[8]

The Canal Residential Area

Many prospective residents were attracted to buy houses surrounding the canal by realtors who promised that the canal area would soon be turned into a big park and that owning a home there was an investment in the future. In 1965, the Bulkas were among the couples hooked by this sales pitch. They quickly shed their illusions. The Bulkas' single-story, three-bedroom ranch-style house was on Ninety-Seventh Street. A large, empty lot, an extension of the canal grounds, lay just to the north. This favorite playground of the local children, "the lagoon," was almost always filled with a muddy, black liquid. But the lagoon was a dangerous place to play. Soon after the Bulkas moved in, their son Joey fell into one of the pits. "He was covered with thick, black, sooty stuff," Peter Bulka recalled. A small amount of the sooty material got into Joey's ear. Shortly after, his eardrum was perforated.

The Bulkas complained to the school board and the Niagara city and county health departments about the lagoon. "We called every day. They did absolutely nothing," Peter Bulka said. The children's injuries were not the only reason for the Bulkas' concern. "We called one time because [the fumes from the dump] were taking the bark and everything right off the trees [and] turned the white paint on our house pink." A private developer finally solved the immediate problem. He filled in much of the lagoon and built a house on it, into which Debbie and Norman Cerrillo moved.

"I was one of the suckers," Norman says. The Cerrillos were told the developer was going to "build a beautiful park" on the old canal site. The realtor promised "swings and a ball diamond and things like that. That's what sold us."

The Cerrillos, like their neighbors, soon found that living by the canal was a continuing nightmare. Their problems began when Debbie tried to cultivate the barren expanse of their backyard. "In the last sixty feet of the yard we planted grass; then we planted grass; then we planted grass. We even went so far as putting sod there. Nothing would grow. We tried one year to grow a garden. We planted tomato plants, and they stayed their original size all summer. I also tried my hand at growing summer squash—they never got any bigger than a large tomato. Usually you'd get them sometimes a foot long. The summer squash was as hard as a gourd right from the beginning. You couldn't cut them with a knife." Debbie, known for her green thumb, refused to give in and tried growing other vegetables. "I planted three packages of beets. I should have had hundreds of beets. I ended up with one. It was the size of a pumpkin and hard as wood." Their neighbors, the Bulkas, had worse luck. All they could grow were dandelions.

The Cerrillos paid little attention to the huge holes in the field behind the house. There was one thirty-five by twenty-foot hole that was filled with a pool of brown-black liquid, which, Debbie said, "smelled like Hooker Chemical," and which never dried out. When it rained, the same type of dark liquid would flood the Cerrillos' backyard. After a hard rain, the family would be forced to wade through ankle-deep sludge to get to the backyard swimming pool.

A new problem developed in the early seventies. After each heavy rainfall, homes with basements closest to the canal, on Ninety-Ninth and Ninety-Seventh Streets, began to flood with black sludge. Since the Niagara Falls area gets an average of thirty-six inches of rain a year, flooding became a constant problem. The Bulkas tried to cope by installing a sump pump in their basement. The liquid sludge rapidly corroded it. The Bulkas would ultimately replace their new sump pump many times. "We had sump pumps lined up against the basement wall," Peter remembers. "The stuff would eat out the bottom of the pump. One time I had a stainless-steel pump, and it ruined that one too." The worst problems occurred in the spring, when the ground thawed and the rain was heavy. Peter recalls the smell being so strong "you couldn't stand on the basement stairs —your eyes would water."

Residents on the other side of the canal had similar troubles. In October, 1974, Karen and Tim Schroeder, who lived on Ninety-Ninth Street, watched with alarm while their in-ground swimming pool heaved and cracked. Its fiberglass base sunk, and the pool itself was extruded from the ground. It seemed as if something underneath was trying to fight its way to the surface. As the pool rose higher and higher, it split and filled with the same dark liquid that had appeared in the yards and basements throughout the area. The city of Niagara Falls, reacting to an emergency call from the Schroeders, pumped thousands of gallons of the liquid sludge out of the pool and into the sewer.

The Calspan Report

A barrage of complaints from neighbors about the flooding of their basements, destruction of their sump pumps, and the appearance of offensive black liquid in holes throughout the area finally prompted the city of Niagara Falls to seek help from Calspan, a prestigious Buffalo-based engineering consulting firm. At this stage, Hooker Chemical also offered to help.

The Calspan investigation went into full swing in June, 1977. As soon as the engineers arrived on the scene, they noted that very strong "fume odors from the site are evident at all times," particularly on warm summer days. They also found that water from several monitoring wells sunk around the canal had "an organic-type odor," suggesting that the groundwater had become heavily contaminated.[9]

Calspan, in its final report of August, 1977, concluded that, over the years, the drums nearest the surface of the canal had become increasingly corroded and exposed, and that there had been massive leakage of contaminated liquid from the canal into the sumps and storm sewers of adjacent homes, particularly on the Ninety-Seventh Street side of the landfill. Several samples of groundwater and surface water were found to be heavily contaminated with highly toxic chemicals, including hexachlorocyclopentadiene (C-56), (HEX), a precursor of the pesticide mirex; hexachlorobenzene, a fungicide; and a wide range of other carcinogenic chlorinated hydrocarbons.[10]

Lois Gibbs

At first the Calspan report seemed to interest the local media more than the area residents, with one major exception—Lois Gibbs, who lived several blocks from the canal. Lois was typical of Love Canal mothers. She had no interest in politics and spent most of her time washing, cooking, and cleaning. Her son Mike had had a long history of illness since enrolling at the Ninety-Ninth Street School, including asthma, nephritis, and hepatitis. The press accounts of the Calspan findings convinced Lois that her son's problems were caused by the toxic chemicals in the dump, and she decided it was high time to get him out of the Ninety-Ninth Street School.

In May, 1978, armed with a note from her doctor, Lois petitioned to get Mike transferred to another school. The Board of Education refused. "If they had allowed Mike to transfer, they would have had to let the other kids go too," Lois observed. "They didn't want to set a precedent."

When Lois was turned down, she decided her only remaining course of action was to close the school. As she began an effort to do just that, she soon found that many other parents were equally concerned about their children sitting in classrooms on top of the oozing, toxic wastes. They were also concerned about the children playing in the adjacent fields, where barrels of chemicals were now surfacing more frequently, particularly since the heavy rains and snowfall of 1977 and 1978.

As Lois went from door to door with her petition, neighbor after neighbor expressed concerns about the canal. And much to her surprise, almost everyone had a health problem they couldn't explain. They all wondered if the canal had been poisoning their families over these years. "I finished my half of Ninety-Ninth Street, where I first started, and I decided it was more than the school. It was the immediate area too," Lois recalls. The "parents' movement" now became a residents' movement.

Debbie Cerrillo worked with Lois on the petition drive. Debbie had not previously realized that there were so many sick people in her neighborhood. What she soon learned frightened her. Karen Schroeder had given birth to a daughter with multiple birth defects, including a double row of teeth in her lower jaw and a cleft palate. In one family, three children had all been born with incomplete skull closures, each requiring multiple surgery. In the next house, a young child had to be kept on oxygen most of the time because of severe asthma. Two children in another family had been born with congenital heart defects. Directly across the street, a neighbor recently had a stillborn baby. Between Debbie's house and one corner of Ninety-Ninth Street, she found several hyperactive children. In the first nine houses on her block, five women had had miscarriages. There had also been two crib deaths on the same block.

As the petitioning continued, families several blocks from the canal also began to speak up about health problems. Seventeen-year-old Laurie Nowak, who lived on 101st Street, reported that, when she was thirteen, her hair had begun to fall out, and she had to wear a wig for six months. Laurie married and had three miscarriages while living at Love Canal and a fourth while temporarily relocated in the autumn of 1979. Her only child has a birth defect.

Annie Hillis, who had lived on 102nd Street for over thirteen years, had had a miscarriage. Her ten-year-old son, who attended the Ninety-Ninth Street School, had been hospitalized several times for acute gastroenteritis and suffered from skin rashes and frequent attacks of bronchitis.

Patricia Grenzy had moved to 100th Street in July 1976. Planning a large family, the Grenzys built a major addition on their home. During the construction, they had been overwhelmed with the stench of chemicals. Their two daughters soon developed itchy, red, swollen, runny eyes and bronchitis and have been sickly ever since.

The State Surveys

While Lois Gibbs and other residents were collecting signatures to close the school, the state Department of Health started a survey of local residents, and the state Department of Environmental Conservation initiated tests to determine the extent of the groundwater, soil, and air contamination.

The results of these surveys alarmed state experts. In the southern section of the canal, women between the ages of thirty and thirty-four had a miscarriage rate nearly four times higher than normal. The air, water, and soil of the entire canal area were found to be heavily contaminated with a wide range of toxic and carcinogenic chemicals coming from the former Hooker dump; particularly high levels were found in the air of basements in houses near the canal. Sediment samples from Black Creek, which ran behind the Kennys' house, were found to be contaminated with 31 ppb of TCDD, a level about 700 million times greater than that calculated by the EPA to produce one cancer death per million population. Chloroform was found in the air of one Love Canal home at a level more than one hundred times that considered by the EPA to cause a significant excess of cancer risk.

The state then tried to get the county to close the school and to declare a general emergency in the area. The county medical officer, Francis Clifford, known as "Cancer Clifford" to Love Canal residents, refused to act. Worried by the increasing evidence of danger and angered by Clifford's refusal, state health commissioner Robert Whalen stepped in. In August, 1978, on the day that Lois Gibbs and Debbie Cerrillo arrived in Albany to present their petition, Whalen announced that the Ninety-Ninth

Street School would be closed, dozens of families would be evacuated, and their homes would be purchased by the state. The state believed that this decisive action would satisfy all concerned. Instead, the announcement caused general panic. As eligible families packed to leave, neighbors watched in silence. The Cerrillos, Bulkas, and Schroeders were moved out, while the Kennys, Quimbys, Nowaks, Hillises, Grenzys, Gibbses, and hundreds of others remained behind, frightened and angry. It just didn't seem to make sense. If it was unsafe for someone living just a dozen yards from their home, why was it safe for them to stay? Moreover, health surveys in areas outside the evacuation zone had strongly suggested that there was an excess of miscarriages, birth defects, and chronic disease among the remaining residents.

Lois was convinced that hundreds more families should be evacuated and demanded that the state's first health survey be expanded to cover a wider area. She managed to secure a commitment from the state health department to send a medical team to take blood samples from these families.

On October 17, 1978, the blood testing began. Almost immediately after the doors of a makeshift clinic opened, the four state technicians were overwhelmed. Hundreds of area residents arrived and stood huddled together with their children in frightened groups. Anxieties and tempers ran high. Children were screaming, the heat of an Indian-summer day adding immeasurably to already unbearable conditions.

The technicians gave up and told people to go home and fill out their health questionnaires. The crowd, already near panic, left more disillusioned and frustrated than before. It was an exercise in futility. No one answered questions. No one examined them. No one seemed to care.

Tensions ran high. Some remaining families even sent their children away, at least temporarily. Some abandoned their homes, never to return. But most stayed.

Local Initiatives

Under New York state law, residents were forced to file claims or risk being barred from taking any future action to recover damages. Since the canal was owned by the city, claimants had to file claims against the city. Once the claims were filed, it became difficult for the city government to work with the residents. Any admission of guilt, fault, or concern could now be used against the city in court. Tension between the two groups grew greater each day. Hundreds of residents filed class-action suits and other claims against the city for personal injury and property damages. Altogether the claims against the city amounted to $3 billion. "If these claims for personal injury resulting from exposure to the chemicals in the Love Canal are successful, every man, woman, and child in the City of Niagara Falls will essentially have to pay $30,000 [in taxes]," complained former city manager Harvey Albond.[11]

Home Owners' "Wet"–Area Health Survey

Frustrated by the state's failure to conduct a proper health survey, the Home Owners' Association decided to conduct its own. With the assistance of Beverly Paigen, a cancer researcher at Roswell Park Memorial Institute in Buffalo, the association did a preliminary survey on the health of over eleven hundred residents by telephone.[12] The study was not intended to be formally scientific. The test population was not compared with a control group, the participants were not screened, nor were medical records collected.

At the same time the health survey was being conducted, residents began to compare notes about the old streambeds and marshy areas that had crisscrossed the area over the life of the canal. These areas were dubbed "wet" areas. When Paigen's disease data were correlated with the information on local topography, a distinctive pattern seemed to emerge. People who lived in "wet" areas appeared to have higher rates of miscarriages, birth defects, asthma, and urinary-tract disease than people who lived in "dry" areas.

The most frightening results of Paigen's survey related to birth defects. Nine of sixteen children born to "wet" area parents between 1973 and 1978 had birth defects. One child was born deaf, five children were born mentally retarded, six suffered from severe kidney problems, and three were born with serious heart defects. Paigen concluded that women who lived in "wet" areas had a 56 percent chance of giving birth to malformed children. She advised women living in these areas not to get pregnant.

The survey also suggested that women who had healthy children before they moved to the canal area experienced new problems after the move. One woman, for example, had two normal pregnancies and healthy children before moving to the canal. She then had six miscarriages in a row and mothered a child with a birth defect. Another woman, who had previously given birth to a healthy child before moving to the canal, later gave birth to one child with three ears and another with deformed ears.

The survey also found that many "wet" area residents suffered from severe nervous disorders, resulting, in some cases, in institutionalization and suicide. People in the "wet" areas suffered seven times more nervous breakdowns than those living in "dry" areas.

The home owners' study was presented to the state Department of Health in the fall of 1978. On February 8, 1979, after carefully reviewing the home owners' study and conducting its own limited study, the state Department of Health recommended that all pregnant women and children under two be "temporarily" removed from the canal area. The state acknowledged that its own studies showed higher-than-normal birthdefect and miscarriage rates among the residents of "wet" areas and agreed with several of the basic conclusions of the Paigen study. However, the state still refused to authorize relocation of the over two hundred remaining "wet" area families.

The "wet" area residents were furious. Not only was the state sanctioning the splitting-up of families, but it had failed to consider the danger to which a fetus could be exposed during its most vulnerable period, the few weeks before a pregnancy might be discovered.

The Home Owners' Association demanded to see the state's data, but the state refused, explaining that the data under review by its scientific advisory group were protected under a confidentiality statute. The commissioner of New York state's

Department of Health, David Axelrod, asserted that confidentiality was necessary to protect the panel members. Early advisory group members known to the public had even been threatened with injury and kidnapping, Axelrod added. The situation had become so bad that the Federal Bureau of Investigation (FBI) had been called in. The homeowners were unimpressed.

Congressman John LaFalce, representative from the Love Canal area, and one of the few public figures still trusted by the residents, attempted to mediate. He arranged to have an independent panel of scientists, chaired by David Rall, director of the National Institute of Environmental Health Sciences (NIEHS), review both the Paigen and state findings.

The Rall panel concluded that the data from both studies suggested the existence of some health problems, "the most severe occurring in residents of houses immediately adjacent to the canal and in 'wet' areas." The state's figures for miscarriages "may have been underestimated," the panel added, concluding that further exposure to the toxic wastes should "be minimized to the extent feasible." Evacuating the remaining residents was an option which the panel said should be considered by the state.[13]

Rall publicly rejected assertions that state public-health commissioner Axelrod was playing politics and trying to save the state money and suggested that the uncertainty and disagreements about what the data show stem at least partly from ignorance. "We don't have the appropriate tools or even the appropriate background with scientific knowledge to evaluate these problems," Rall observed. "Scientists probably don't even know what the short-term effect of half to a third of each of the chemicals found in the canal have on laboratory animals. Without this basic knowledge, assessing the immediate effect on people is almost impossible. We have even less understanding of what each of the chemicals may do over a long period of time. The problem is one can have an exposure for five to ten years without effect, but then have a serious outcome twenty or thirty years later. That's only a small part of the problem. We next need to know the effect of combinations of chemicals." This is the "real world," Rall added. "Scientists are only beginning to think about this issue."[14]

The State's Response

Faced with the results of the Rall panel and a mounting barrage of national publicity, the state accelerated its attempts at on-site cleanup. The remedial activities seemed primarily designed to reduce further leakage of toxic wastes from the canal into surrounding homes, rather than to remove the contaminant source itself. Moreover, the construction work involved in the attempted cleanup seemed to be creating still further problems. Holes spewing black ooze were cropping up in new locations. Dirt and odor carried by the wind were spreading through the area. Trucks working at the site carried contaminated materials into the neighborhood on their tires.

The state tried to alleviate these fresh concerns by developing an emergency evacuation plan in case an accident took place during the cleanup. Some thirty buses stood, with their motors running, in locations throughout the surrounding areas, waiting to whisk residents away at the first sign of trouble. Residents were suspicious. When a state official was asked whether he'd wait for the buses in the event of an emergency, he answered, "No, I'd run like hell."

As the summer approached, a new concern developed. How was the cleanup going to affect the children home on summer vacation as they played in the streets? The United Way headed off this crisis by providing a day camp. When the summer ended, new problems developed.

After considerable pressure, the state agreed in late August, 1979 to temporarily relocate those families who, as a result of the construction work, were at special risk. The state only provided other accommodations if the applicant obtained a doctor's letter stating that remaining in the canal area during the remedial work was unhealthful.

Releases for over one hundred families were obtained. More than two hundred people requiring temporary relocation obliged the state to rent dozens of hotel rooms throughout the Niagara Falls area. Temporary relocation cost the state over $7,000 a day.

Hotel life for most families was a nightmare. Conditions were cramped. Families were separated. Parents and children spent hours in line waiting for meals. There was no place for children to play. People were moved from one room to the next, or even to different hotels, as often as several times a week.

Art Tracy, a temporarily relocated resident, was angry and frustrated by the experience. "We're American refugees. We're not boat refugees, but we're American refugees. We have no home. We've been pushed, frustrated, pulled, hauled. I've moved four times in the last month; room to room, floor to floor. We're so frustrated we don't know what we're at."

In early November, the state told Tracy and the other "refugees" to go back home. Tracy felt confused and abandoned. On the one hand, the state told him it was safe to live at home. On the other hand, he was warned by his doctor and outside experts of the substantial health risks of remaining in the Love Canal area. The "refugees" had no choice; they all returned home.

Barbara Quimby, another "refugee," who had lived on Ninety-Ninth Street for twenty years, playing in the canal when she was a child, and then had moved to 103rd Street in 1971, was also frightened about returning home. Barbara's first pregnancy had been difficult. Her oldest child, Randy, was born retarded and with multiple birth defects. Barbara was sure her health and her family's health had been damaged by the chemicals in the canal.

The Quimbys' house sat atop a major "wet" area. They were particularly concerned because both their children spent much of their earlier years playing in the basement, in spite of its offensive odor. However, only recently was Barbara warned not to let her children down there even for a few minutes.

Barbara was also angry because she felt she was never given a choice. "Decisions are being made for my family by people who have probably never been here, who don't even know us," she said. "If I can't decide someone else's life, I don't want someone deciding mine."

The Real Estate Freeze of 1979

The remaining Love Canal residents faced many other setbacks. But the most cruel blow was delivered by the federal government in 1979, when it halted approval of all Federal

Housing Administration (FHA)–insured loans for the purchase of homes in the community. This action essentially froze the sale of all homes in the area. Now even the residents concerned about their health were virtually forced to stay. The Quimbys, after deciding to leave the neighborhood where they had spent all their lives and offering their home for sale at thousands of dollars less than the assessed value, were forced to remain because their otherwise-qualified buyer was refused an FHA-insured loan.

FHA officials in New York were directed to send all applications for Love Canal area homes to Washington, D.C. for special processing. Generally, loan applications are reviewed at the regional level and approved or disapproved within a few weeks. The Department of Housing and Urban Development (HUD), of which FHA is a part, did not know what to do with the applications. Since over 100 of the 239 homes evacuated by the state in August, 1978 were financed by FHA loans, HUD was well aware of the Love Canal problem. The decision was made to review each loan application on an individual basis, to be sure that FHA would not be held liable if a home was determined to be unsafe in the future. HUD was afraid that approving a loan would signal federal endorsement that the home was safe. It did not believe it could afford to make such a determination, except on a case-by-case basis.

"The problem is, nobody knows what the chemicals do and what the sources are," remarked Mary Ann Taranowsky, a HUD staffer. "It seems to us not very sensible to provide a method of getting out which at the same time would be a method of putting someone else in a potentially hazardous situation." A community testing program was not good enough. "It may be safe at 105, 101st Street, but not at 107, 101st Street," explained Bonnie Kasper, an aide to Congressman John LaFalce. Tests would have to be performed on each house before a loan could be approved.

HUD turned to the EPA for help in establishing safety standards. The EPA transmitted evaluation guidelines to HUD that called for a program of testing, costing the seller over $500 and taking approximately two months. The tests were not all-inclusive and, even if positive, could not signal that any house was safe, but rather only provide a measure of the relative risk of living there. This crude evaluation, which could take months to complete, was to be the basis on which HUD evaluated loan applications for Love Canal homes.

To the Love Canal residents, HUD's actions finally sealed their fate. Now there was no escape. How, they wondered, could the government expect them, after offering their homes at a loss, to spend $500 on tests whose results might scare away prospective buyers? For the strife-weary residents, the testing program was an injustice that clearly demonstrated the government's insensitivity toward their plight.

"My rights are gone. The government is keeping me from selling my house," Barbara Quimby remarked bitterly. "This woman [the buyer] knew everything. Morally I'm not sure if I would have backed out at the last minute . . . but she knew the readings. She knew what was here. It was all public in the newspapers . . . , but I was selling the house for $10,000 less than it was worth, and she wanted the house. It was a routine sale, and the papers went to Washington."

HUD's position, though seen as punitive by the Home Owners' Association, was not without precedent. HUD had taken similar action in Montana, when presented with evidence that homes being sold might present a low-level radiation hazard. However, the tests prescribed for the Montana homes were easier to perform, took less time, and only cost about $50.

The safety and sale of homes in the Love Canal neighborhood also concerned city officials. City manager Harvey Albond believes that the houses were safe and blames the homeowners for having frightened would-be buyers away. "They will use every factor at their disposal" to force the state to buy their homes, Albond said in a 1979 interview. Albond also believed that the stories on migration of chemicals from the canal into areas far beyond those already evacuated were responsible for unnecessary questions about safety.[15]

Albond insisted that the remaining "wet" area residents faced no "real" hazard. He also believed that most of the houses that were originally purchased by the state, and which were due to be demolished, were perfectly safe. "Wouldn't it be wonderful," he mused, "if we could move those ninety-nine homes, at a cost probably not to exceed $8,000, to the Griffin Manor area [a public low-cost housing project a few hundred feet from the canal] to make those houses available for ownership to people who could not hope to acquire such a house?"[16]

According to Albond, "All responsible parties believe that nearly all the houses in the neighborhood are safe, but no one will take on the responsibility of certifying them as such." Without certification, Albond's plan and the residents' attempts to sell their homes were doomed. Albond suggested that the only solution would be to have Uncle Sam pick up the tab.[17]

Albond believed that the remaining residents faced no problem and that the Paigen study was biased, at best. When asked about independent confirmation by the Rall panel of some of the Paigen-study results, Albond smiled. "They have accepted a disproven hypothesis," he said. He questioned the panel's motivation and believed the experts involved were wrong. His experts almost completely disagreed with the panel's criticisms.

Serious questions have been raised about the adequacy of the remedial work as well. Albond claimed that all the problems would be solved once the work was complete. The state calls the project a temporary solution, at best. Finally, the federal government remains unconvinced that the work will eradicate the problem. Love Canal residents call it a "rip-off" and add, "It's making the situation worse."

Although Albond refused to discuss the city's actions prior to the evacuation, he admitted the city has a large stake in minimizing the canal problem. The city has been primarily responsible for cleaning up the canal. From 1978 to 1979, out of a total city budget of $45 million, $7 million was spent on the canal problem, mostly for remedial work. Albond believed that failure to accept the remedial work as the solution to the problem will have an increasingly negative impact on the city. House values in the area will continue to decline, tax revenues will decrease, and legal fees will increase.

The Federal Suit

On December 20, 1979, the United States Department of Justice filed a complaint against Hooker Chemical, the city of Niagara Falls, the Niagara County Health Department, and the

Board of Education of the city of Niagara Falls.[18] The federal suit called for immediate action to end the continuing discharge of toxic chemicals into the area surrounding the canal and called upon the defendants to clean up the canal site, provide funds for medical research, relocate remaining residents if necessary, and compensate the federal government for the more than $7 million it had already expended on the canal.* Although the suit is primarily directed at Hooker, it also seeks to force the city of Niagara Falls, the county health department, and the school board to take remedial action under federal direction.

The suit further calls for the establishment of a $45-million annuity account or the posting of a bond to ensure that cleanup funds will be available should Hooker be forced into bankruptcy.

This is one of the largest amounts ever called for in a federal environmental-pollution suit. It will be years before this landmark suit is settled. Never before has the federal government attempted to force action and recover costs from a company that dumped materials over twenty-five years previously, and which then sold the contaminated land to a public entity. The outcome of this case may have an immense impact on future attempts to force industry to pay for the cleanup of their old dump sites.

The suit also revealed, for the first time, that chemical contamination of the drinking water had occurred. The complaint charges that the toxic chemicals in the dump have entered the pipes supplying fresh water to several households.

1980: Year of Confusion and Relief

The fall and winter of 1979–80 brought no new hope for the Love Canal residents. Although public sympathy continued to grow, no one had offered the funds necessary to vacate the area. In the late spring of 1980, all this changed.

The first public sign of a change in the government's attitude about the remaining residents came in May, 1980, at a rare Saturday press conference held by Barbara Blum, deputy EPA ad-

*This $7 million is over and above some $28 million in expenditures by state and federal governments. It is estimated that the original costs of proper disposal of toxic chemicals dumped in the Love Canal would have been about $4 million in 1979 dollars.

ministrator. Blum called the conference to release the results of a pilot study of chromosome changes among Love Canal residents.[19] The study showed that eleven out of the thirty-six residents studied had suffered chromosome damage. Blum noted that this study was merely preliminary and thus could not be used to predict the potential health effects chemicals in the canal had on the population in general. Nevertheless, she said an announcement regarding whether the remaining residents should be moved would be forthcoming by the middle of the next week.

Announcement of the test results set off a new wave of panic in Niagara Falls. The story of the chromosome study was dramatized by the media, and confusion as to what the results actually showed was rampant. Lois Gibbs and the other members of the Home Owners' Association clamored for immediate permanent relocation, stating that the test results proved Love Canal residents were being harmed by the chemicals in the area.

Although appearing cool and collected, personnel at the EPA, the White House, and the NIEHS were working overtime to determine whether the study was valid and what to do next. Unbeknown to the outside world, the pot had been preparing to boil over as early as Thursday, May 15, when the study results were leaked to the New York Times. The Times planned to print the story on Saturday, May 17. Blum was forced, inside observers say, to make the Saturday announcement in order to diffuse any misinterpretation the EPA expected the Times story Saturday morning would generate. Unfortunately, her action had the opposite result. In the press stampede that took place in the days that followed the Saturday conference, many of the facts about the survey and its limits were lost.

The survey, properly labeled a pilot study by its author and project director, Dante Picciano,* was begun in January, 1980. It was undertaken under contract to the EPA in an effort to provide Justice Department lawyers prosecuting the Hooker Chemical case with a preliminary indication as to whether chromosomal abnormalities could be detected in Love Canal–area residents. The Justice Department, before being able to prove that the

---

*A geneticist then with Biogenics Corporation of Houston, Texas.

chemicals in the canal had injured public health, needed a study that would tell them whether injury, in the form of chromosome damage, could be detected at all. The next step would be to show whether there was a causal link, or at least a strong possibility of a link, between the injuries and the chemicals leaking from the canal. Finally, to be sure, the Justice Department would most probably have conducted additional studies to determine whether other residents were likewise affected. In essence, this study was only the first step in a long series and was clearly not designed to show that the chemicals in the canal had induced chromosome damage in the Love Canal residents as a whole.

Since this pilot study was merely designed to discover whether chromosome changes in the subject population could even be detected, the study design was based on residents who would be the most likely to have suffered such damage. The high-risk group included residents who had suffered some "disease situation"; those who had had adverse reproductive effects (spontaneous abortions or children with birth defects); those who lived in houses where toxic fumes had been measured and recorded; and those who lived in "wet" areas. High-risk individuals were selected by Picciano and members of the Love Canal Home Owners' Association.

Limited EPA funding made it impossible for Picciano to obtain a control group with which to compare the test group, although he made every attempt to do so. Instead, he was forced to use control data from other published studies on the background rate of chromosomal abnormalities in normal, healthy populations. Comparison of the Love Canal cytogenetic results with control data from other studies led to the conclusion that eleven of the thirty-six Love Canal residents surveyed had major chromosomal abnormalities, and that this rate was well above normal expected rates.[20]

As a result of these findings, Picciano cautiously concluded:

It appears that the chemical exposures at Love Canal may be responsible for much of the apparent increase in the observed cytogenetic aberrations and that the residents are at an increased risk of neoplastic disease, of having spontaneous abortions and of having children with birth defects. However, in absence of a contemporary control population, prudence must be exerted in the interpretation of such results.[21]

News of the preliminary results reached the EPA before May 5, 1980. The report did not, however, become a subject of controversy until May 15, when it was discovered that the study had been leaked to the press. Knowing that this news would create pressure to evacuate the canal area, Blum, EPA attorneys, and government scientists began round-the-clock discussions with the White House. By Saturday, May 17, it was decided that Blum should make the announcement and that further action should await review of the Picciano data by a team headed by Rall of the NIEHS. While Picciano readily agreed to the review, he raised questions of conflict of interest among members of the team.

Rall's team immediately flew to Houston to review the slides and data, but, when they arrived, Picciano reiterated his concerns, and concerns of local residents, about the conflict-of-interest problem and offered to negotiate the matter with Charles Carter, the team's chairman. However, Carter declined an invitation to visit Picciano's laboratory for discussions, and the review team left in a huff, with little more than the report itself, claiming that the study "provided inadequate basis for any scientific or medical inferences from the data, even of a tentative or preliminary nature, concerning exposure to mutagenic substances because of residence in the Love Canal area."[22] Since then, Picciano appears to have rebutted criticisms of his study,[23] whose results have been reviewed in detail and independently confirmed by several recognized authorities on cytogenetics.* Furthermore, as Picciano has pointed out, "the cytogenetic study of the Love Canal population is totally overshadowed by the outcome of the last eighteen pregnancies among residents: two births were normal; nine children had birth defects; there were four spontaneous abortions and three stillbirths."[24]

While the scientific community battled over the Picciano data, the Love Canal residents became more militant with each passing hour. On the afternoon of May 19, two federal experts,

---

*These authorities include Marvin Legator, Margery Shaw, Sidney Green, Cecil Jacobson, Robert McKinnell, and Jack Killian.

after discussing the situation with area leaders at the Love Canal Home Owners' Association headquarters, were temporarily trapped inside as a large, angry group of residents blocked the exits from the building. The local police surrounded the area, and the FBI was called in. After several tense hours, the "hostages" were allowed to leave. No one was arrested, and no charges were filed.

The EPA kept its word and on Wednesday, May 21, announced that all remaining residents would be temporarily evacuated pending further tests. For Lois Gibbs, Barbara Quimby, and Art Tracy, the fight seemed over. They had won. And although they knew the announcement only discussed "temporary" relocation, behind the scenes, the White House had already committed itself to a more permanent arrangement, including funds for "temporary permanent" relocation.

Puzzled by the events, two congressional committees—the Environment, Energy, and Natural Resources Subcommittee of the House Committee on Government Operations, chaired by Toby Moffett (Democrat-Connecticut), and the Oversight and Investigations Subcommittee of the House Committee on Interstate and Foreign Commerce, chaired by Bob Eckhardt (Democrat-Texas)—held a hearing on the situation. As Moffett, Eckhardt, and Gore noted in their opening statements, the events of the past week clearly indicated that the federal government had no program for systematic review and study of the potential health impact of hazardous wastes. Congressman Moffett warned that the continued *ad hoc* nature of the government's response to the problems would only lead to further hysteria. Gore noted that at the very time more research was needed into the potential health effects of toxic chemicals, the president's Office of Management and Budget had circulated orders to the EPA to cut to zero the funds used for hazardous waste health research.[25]

The record of the hearing indicated that the final evacuation of the Love Canal residents was not based on science, but on politics. Congressman John LaFalce reminded the subcommittees that all the scientific health data referred to by the EPA as looming large in the decision to move the residents, with the exception of the Picciano study, had been performed either by

the state of New York or the Home Owners' Association over a
year and a half before. If it was the EPA's belief that the area was
unsafe, why didn't it act earlier? LaFalce asked.

As a result of this hearing, the Superfund legislation included authorization of up to $10 million a year for scientific
health surveys of the potential impact of hazardous wastes on
surrounding population groups. The amendment put the
National Institute of Health (NIH) at the head of this effort, rele-
gating the EPA to a secondary role.[26]

The Love Canal residents have now been "temporarily permanently" removed. Many have new homes, with the help of
federal and state tax credits and low-interest loans. In the fall of
1980, a $15-million fund was established to purchase 550 homes
within a thirty-square block area surrounding the dump at "fair
market value," usually in the range of $30,000 to $35,000,
which is claimed by some residents to be an underestimate.

Several additional reviews of the Picciano data have since
been made.* Most independent reviewers agree with Picciano
that some abnormalities had been found, but differ on their
precise significance. The canal residents, exhausted after years
of fighting, have resisted any further government attempts to
study their health. No one really knows what impact the chemicals in the canal have had or, more importantly, will have on the
residents.

A report by a special scientific panel organized by Governor
Hugh Carey of New York to review all the scientific information
available on the canal situation concluded that both public and
private efforts to determine the health impact of the chemicals in
the canal on the local population had been botched.[27] First, the
panel found that the data relied upon by the state of New York to
relocate the first 230-plus families from the canal area were,
because of the absence of a suitable control group, no "more
than suggestive."[28] Second, the panel criticized the state for issuing a report calling the Love Canal tragedy an "environmental
nightmare" that threatened "profound and devastating effects."
The panel felt this language was uncalled for and resulted in fur-

---

*These include an EPA outside-panel review, chaired by Roy Albert, of June 12,
1980, which attempted to dismiss the Picciano study on technical grounds.

ther frightening of area residents.[29] Third, the panel criticized Paigen for carrying out a study that was "literally impossible to interpret," and which "cannot be taken seriously as a piece of sound epidemiological research."[30] The panel reserved its most severe criticism for the manner in which the Picciano chromosome study was handled. The report states that "such a poorly designed investigation as this one should not have been launched in the first place. With so much at stake for the residents involved, to have set up experiments that lead to public conclusions of such magnitude, without prior review of the protocol by qualified uninvolved peer scientists, and without any after-the-fact, independent review by competent scientists before release of the results, was a disservice to the citizens most intimately concerned."[31] The panel's final conclusion was that all of these actions "fueled rather than resolved public anxiety," while adding little to the understanding of the threat to public health posed by the chemicals found oozing out of the canal.[32]

The scientific objectivity of the panel report has, however, come under serious question, as has their judgment. Irwin Bross, a leading biostatistician, on the basis of a documented critique of the panel, concluded:

> By current "state of the art" standards in epidemiological field studies, the methodology [of the Paigen study] is acceptable and the quality control on the data exceeds usual standards. The 100 percent increase in reproductive wastage can be compared with corresponding increases in studies of this type. Very briefly, such studies are recognized as one of our best early-warning signals of environmental hazards, particularly of genetic damage. . . . Thus, there is strong evidence here of a very serious health hazard at Love Canal.[33]

The most recent epidemiological study in the Love Canal area by the New York State Department of Health claimed that there was "no evidence for higher cancer rates associated with residence near the Love Canal. . . in comparison with the entire state outside of New York City."[34] However, the total number of cancer cases studied was too small to justify such categorical negative inferences. Even so, the study revealed excess lung cancer rates in the Love Canal area, which were discounted because of the lack of a precise geographic relation of these cancers to the canal. Finally, the study failed to consider a wide range of other adverse effects besides cancer, such as miscarriages and birth defects.

It is of particular interest that the various reports attempting to rebut the Paigen health survey and the Picciano cytogenetic study have ignored or failed to consider the substantial evidence of high levels of atmospheric carcinogens, such as benzene, chloroform, and tetrachloroethylene, found in the air of Love Canal houses by the New York State Department of Health; these results were confirmed by the EPA in 1979. Also ignored were data on high levels of a wide range of organic contaminants and carcinogens in drinking water. On the basis of such exposure data, EPA estimates showed that Love Canal residents are at substantial excess risks of cancer.[35]

Hooker's Defense: A Critique

Hooker maintains that it is fully protected from any liability, not only by the hold-harmless clause in the deed of sale to the school board, but also by its proper care in burying chemicals at the canal and in properly closing the site. Bruce Davis, executive vice-president of the company, told a congressional committee in 1979 that Hooker had used standard industry methods to bury the wastes. Davis went on to describe the site as a "mini-vault," which was especially safe for dumping toxic wastes, as he claimed that the walls and floor of the canal were lined with an impenetrable barrier of thick clay. Hooker also alleges that before the property was sold to the school board, the company sealed the dump by constructing a clay cap over the surface of the entire canal.[36] The truth of this defense is currently in dispute.

Hooker's clay "mini-vault" defense has been challenged by evidence that streams in the immediate area have been fed by fissures in the canal, through which chemical residues could drain away. Eyewitness reports have established that numerous "swales"—old stream beds and marshy ground—crisscrossed the area many years ago. A study conducted by Cornell University's Remote Sensing Program found that, as a result of these swales, contamination outside the walls of the canal may be "rather extensive." Cornell's report noted that, in 1938, several drainage paths passed through the canal proper, emptying into adjacent areas. A 1952 photograph showed that many of the same drainage paths still remained open. Soils along these drainage paths are likely to have become saturated with chemical wastes. Even if the chemical drainage into these swales stopped after the dump was allegedly sealed, a major problem still exists. Toxic chemicals will be leached by heavy rains out of soils lining the swales and will further contaminate groundwater.[37]

Hooker's policies regarding its legal responsibilities for the toxic wastes were not always consistent. In 1968, drums filled with chemicals were unearthed while the state Department of Transportation was building a road through the area. Hooker then not only investigated the matter but, according to R.T. Olotka, Hooker's disposal supervisor at the time, removed approximately "forty truckloads" of waste and contaminated earth.[38] The materials were taken to another Hooker dump site at company expense. No explanation was given as to why Hooker took this action.

In the spring of 1980, Hooker launched a major public relations offensive to combat what it termed the "sensationalized media treatment" of the Love Canal situation. In correspondence with members of Congress, immediately before the House of Representatives was to consider Superfund legislation, Hooker insisted that any legislation based on "false" public perceptions of the Love Canal situation would "likely" result in inappropriate action. Hooker asserted that most of the "facts" appearing in the media concerning the Love Canal were "fictions."[39]

First, Hooker emphasized that the Love Canal "containment would have met current disposal standards" and blamed the problem on the school board's failure "to properly maintain the site" after Hooker sold it.[40] Second, Hooker insisted that the Board of Education "apparently" directed the removal of dirt from the site, or at least did not stop developers from removing it.[41] Third, Hooker blamed the city, the school board, and the New York state Department of Transportation for "putting streets and a highway through the site, digging away the protective cover for use as fill at other locations and installation of sanitary and storm sewers through the chemicals. . . ."[42] Finally, it accused government agencies of "acting on inconclusive and sometimes erroneous technical and medical information."[43]

Superficially, some of Hooker's points appear well taken. Certainly, the school board had some responsibility for making sure the "park" over the site was properly maintained. Whether they allowed the top layer of soil to be taken away, did it themselves, or simply allowed it to wash away over the years, the school board can be blamed for improper maintenance of the land. Nevertheless, the fact that Hooker knew the school board had no "facilities" to maintain a park indicates that Hooker knew its unwritten agreement (that the land not used for the school be used as a park) probably would not result in the proper maintenance of that land.*

Hooker's argument that its protest against the sale of the land to developers in 1957 proves that it warned against the use of the land for any activity that might disrupt the clay cap is not persuasive for the following reasons: 1) Hooker reiterated in 1957 its understanding that the land would only be used for the construction of a school. Obviously, such construction had the potential of disrupting the surface of the canal. Such a disruption was noted by Charles Thiele, the school board's architect, during the 1954 school construction. 2) No prohibition as to the use of the land was contained in the deed. Hooker notes that it was only a "mutual understanding" between the Board of Education and Hooker that the land should only be used for a

* At the Niagara City school board's November 21, 1957 meeting, A. W. Chambers, Hooker's plant manager, appeared again with a letter from Hooker's vice-president and general counsel, Ansley Wilcox II, which also argued against the sale of the land. In his letter, Wilcox said Hooker had provided the school board with the "gift" of the canal property because it "was so important to the school board." Wilcox further wrote that the land was to be used only for "a school and a park. . . . We were thoroughly convinced that, should the property ultimately be used for any other purpose, the residues that had been buried thereon might well have a serious deleterious effect on foundations, water lines, and sewer lines, and, in addition, we felt it quite possible that personal injuries could result from contact therewith. . . ." Wilcox urged the school board to use the remaining land for a park, noting this was not put in the original deed as the school board did not have "facilities for maintaining a park."[44] However, Hooker failed to warn the local community of the dangers of construction on the land.

school and a park. 3) The land in question, on the canal itself, was never sold by the school board and, indeed, was never used for home development. 4) A reasonable person, knowing that the land was to be used for a school, should have realized that if there was no road crossing the canal within a quarter of a mile of the school, one would most likely have to be constructed. 5) Hooker did not warn homeowners living on the periphery of the canal. 6) Hooker has never produced full documentation of its claims of full warnings to the city and its people. 7) When, in 1957, three children were burned by exposed residues on the surface of the canal, the company made no public comment and offered no redress. 8) Hooker's actions at the Love Canal appear consistent with those at other dump sites in Niagara Falls—the "S" area, Hyde Park, and 102nd Street—where local school boards could not be blamed and where there appears no evidence that Hooker warned the local communities. 9) The construction of a road on the edge of the land by the state Department of Transportation took place in an area where few chemicals were supposedly buried. If Hooker was concerned that the construction of the road would change the drainage pattern of the dump, at the time it hauled the forty truckloads of contaminated dirt from the area, it could have made such fears known to the state. There is no record that such a warning was given to the state in 1968. Finally, there is no documented evidence that Hooker actually constructed a clay cap over the Love Canal or indeed at any other of its hazardous waste dumps elsewhere in the USA.

Exactly what Hooker did and didn't do and what the school board did or didn't do have been left for the courts to decide.

Nonfinancial Costs

The names of the people whose lives have been damaged, some irreversibly so, now lie buried under a mass of statistics, reports, and legal briefs. The children have been hit the hardest. "One night last winter," said Ann Hillis, a Love Canal resident, in testimony before a congressional subcommittee in 1979, "I looked in on my son. His bed was empty. I looked all over. It was 2:00 A.M. I heard a cry from under the couch. My son was under there with his knees drawn up to his chin, crying. I asked him to come out, and what was wrong. His reply was 'I want to die. I don't want to live here anymore. I know you will be sick again and I'll be sick again.'" The Hillis family spent the night crying together.

In a recent interview, Mrs. Bulka, the tragedy of the Love Canal behind her, said, "They told us they were going to build a park. But what we got was a killer."

Other Dump Sites

Love Canal wasn't the only place in Niagara Falls where Hooker's dumping operations had been creating problems. At three other locations—"S" Area, Hyde Park, and 102nd Street—Hooker had dumped approximately 350 million pounds of toxic industrial wastes. All of these dump sites are now closed. The federal government's December, 1979 complaint against Hooker claimed that, quite apart from the Love Canal, these three sites posed imminent and substantial hazards to the public health and environment. The federal government further demanded that Hooker clean up these sites, at an estimated cost of $67 million.[45]

"S" Area

The "S" Area dump* is located on highly porous land within two hundred yards of the city's largest drinking water facility, which has been in operation since the early 1900s. From the time this dump first opened in 1947 until its closing in 1975, Hooker used it to dispose of about 148 million pounds of chemical wastes. An eyewitness account by Elliot Lynch, supervisor of the water-treatment facility for nearly thirty years, described the dumping operation: "A series of parallel trenches were dug,

---

*The "S" Area site as used here includes two areas designated by Hooker Chemical around its Buffalo Avenue Niagara Falls plant where chemical wastes were dumped. Data for the "S" Area dump include materials dumped in the "N" area as well.

fifty-five-gallon drums were lined up on the crest of the trenches, punctured in some instances, and rolled into the trenches and covered. Tank wagons would be discharged directly into the pits and the effluent then covered."[46]

Workers at the nearby drinking water facility periodically complained about the fumes drifting over from the "S" Area dump. The fumes were described by Lynch as "nauseous, choking, and lacrimatory to humans, and toxic to plant life." The city, trying to reduce the fumes, planted and replanted bushes and trees on the border of the water facility adjacent to the "S" Area. Within days the plants would turn black and die. Repeated complaints, which grew more constant and vocal, were ignored by Hooker.

Subsequent developments further increased the risks of massive contamination of Niagara Falls' water supply. With the growth of the city's population in the early 1950s, the drinking water plant was enlarged to increase its treatment capacity. Some ten years later, the state's riverfront construction of the Robert Moses Parkway caused the buried liquid wastes to back up and move underground toward the water plant. After Hooker stopped most of the dumping in 1967, not only did the company fail to take any action to determine what steps should be taken to protect the city's water supply, but, in the early 1970s, it further intensified the problem by constructing two large, heavy treatment lagoons directly over the dump site. Federal experts have since concluded that these lagoons exerted increased downward hydraulic pressure on the underlying wastes, "exacerbating their migration" toward the water-treatment plant.[47]

In 1978, the pumphouse operators of the municipal water-treatment plant barraged the city with complaints of offensive odors in the incoming water supply. Howard K. Allen, president of Allen Marine Salvage, the firm hired to investigate the problem, said that when he and his divers were lowered into the forebay area of the water-intake tunnel, they discovered a huge pool of thick, black liquid lying stagnant at the bottom of the shaft. In the course of a thirty-year career, Allen had often been employed to dive into polluted waters, but had never before encountered any material like this. It burned the rubber gloves off

his fingers and ate through his wet suit. Allen and the other
divers were forced to wear coveralls over their suits, change
gloves frequently, and remain in the polluted area for only brief
periods.[48]

Since the pool of sludge stagnated in the same chamber as
the raw water used to supply the drinking water for the city's
fifty thousand citizens, samples of the sludge, sediment, and raw
and finished water were analyzed. The sludge was found to
contain massive amounts of the highly toxic and carcinogenic
chemicals that Hooker had dumped on the other side of the
fence (see Table 5-2). Lower concentrations of these chemicals
were also identified in the raw water entering the plant, and even
smaller concentrations were found in the finished water piped to
homes, schools, hospitals, and restaurants throughout the city.

There is no way of knowing just how much toxic sludge has
gone through the treatment plant over the years and ended up in
drinking water. However, as made clear by a recent federal
report, significant contamination has already taken place.

> Although none of Hooker's hazardous wastes have yet been
> detected in the drinking water supply at the level that would
> require immediately ceasing the use of the Drinking Water
> Treatment Plant, the presence of these wastes in close proximity
> to the plant . . . threatens that, at any moment, a slug of toxic
> waste could migrate from the "S" Area into the drinking water
> supply itself. The detection of some of Hooker's hazardous
> wastes already in the drinking water supply system at high levels
> indicates the very real susceptibility of the Drinking Water
> Treatment Plant to hazardous chemical infiltration. A slug of haz-
> ardous chemicals . . . infiltrating the Drinking Water Treatment
> Plant in high enough concentration could result in a human
> health disaster.[49]

City officials have been accused of undue laxity in their
handling of these problems. As late as 1979, Robert Mathews,
director of water utilities for the city, was still seriously
suggesting that the contaminants found in the plant's intake
tunnels had originated from polluted air.[50] The $225,000 cost of
two cleanup operations in the tunnels, entailing removal of over
one hundred thousand pounds of contaminated materials, was

placed on the shoulders of local ratepayers. Some reasons for the failure of the city to force Hooker to clean up the "S" Area are characterized by the gratitude expressed to the company by Mathews. "Hooker executives have given me good and learned advice. When you are in a situation such as I am in, you need advice."[51]

It was left to the federal government to finally take action on the "S" Area site. In its December, 1979 suit, the government joined Hooker with the city, county, and state. The complaint stated that these codefendants had failed "to protect the public health of Niagara Falls' residents."[52] In addition to the pending

Table 5-2. Wastes Dumped by Hooker Chemical at "S" and "N" Areas

Type of Waste	Estimated Quantity (tons)
Chlorobenzenes	18,900
Hexachlorocyclopentadiene (C-56)	17,400
Mercaptans	8,100
Thionyl chloride	4,200
Sulfides	4,200
Benzoyl chloride	3,300
Liquid disulfides	2,200
Benzyl chlorides	1,600
Metal chlorides	900
Phenol tars	800
Thiodan	700
Anhydride and hetrons	500
Miscellaneous chlorinations	400
Miscellaneous acid chlorides	400
Organic phosphates	200
Trichlorophenol	200
Miscellaneous	6,400
TOTAL	70,400

Source: Based on Draft Report Interagency Task Force on Hazardous Wastes in Erie and Niagara Counties, New York, March 1979, p. II-71.

Notes: Test borings of the ground surrounding the water treatment plant revealed that some areas were saturated with toxic wastes. Among the compounds found in the soil samples on the grounds and sediment samples in the tunnel were: tetrachloroethylene, at 140,000 times the EPA-established risk-criteria level; hexachlorobenzene, at 96,000 times the EPA risk-criteria level; trichloroethylene, at 4,190 times the EPA risk-criteria level; and benzene, at 2,220 times the EPA risk-criteria level.

suit involving the "S" Area, the federal government has instituted a further suit against the city of Niagara Falls for improper management of its water-treatment plant.

The Hyde Park Dump

The Hyde Park site was used by Hooker as a dump for approximately 160 million pounds of toxic wastes from about 1953 to 1979 (see Table 5-3). The major problems caused by this

Table 5-3. Wastes Dumped by Hooker Chemical at Hyde Park

Type of Waste	Estimated Quantity (tons)
Chlorobenzenes	16,500
Sulfides	6,600
Benzoyl chloride	6,200
Benzotrifluorides	5,600
Mercaptans	4,500
C-56 derivatives (includes dechlorane and other dechlorane derivatives)	4,500
Organic phosphates	4,400
Benzyl chloride	3,400
Trichlorophenol	3,300
BTF derivatives	2,900
Anhydride and hetrons	2,100
Benzene hexachloride	2,000
Benzotrichlorides	1,700
Chlorotoluenes	1,700
Miscellaneous chlorinations	1,600
Miscellaneous acid chlorides	1,200
Hexachlorocyclopentadiene (C-56)	1,100
Thiodan	1,000
Hypo mud	1,000
Liquid disulfides	900
Calcium fluoride	400
Dechlorane	200
Metal chlorides	100
Inorganic phosphates	<100
Mercury brine sludge	<100
Miscellaneous (10% of the above)	7,300
TOTAL	80,400

Source: Based on Draft Report Interagency Task Force on Hazardous Wastes in Erie and Niagara Counties, New York, March 1979, p. II-66.

dump are due to its close proximity to an adjacent residential area and to three manufacturing plants bordering the site—the Greif Brothers, barrel manufacturing plant, NL Industries, and Niagara Steel Finishing. Significant amounts of toxic chemicals have been spread into the surrounding area by Bloody Run Creek, a natural runoff area that extends from the dump, under the Greif Brothers' plant, through a local residential area, and then under Niagara University into the Niagara River.

Local residents have been complaining for years to Hooker and the county health department about ill effects of fumes from the dump and about toxic wastes in Bloody Run Creek.

Fred Armagost, who has lived with his family on the banks of the creek for over twenty years, is typical. Fred is convinced that his health and that of his family have been seriously damaged by chemical fumes from the creek and dump site. The Armagosts' family doctor and pediatrician, James Dunlap, agrees.

The most seriously ill member of the Armagost family is Wayne, Fred's twenty-four-year-old son. As Wayne grew up he developed "very serious pulmonary problems," which are progressive and which have made it almost impossible for him to work.

Dunlap has also looked after several of Fred's grandchildren, who have spent many years living with Fred, and two unrelated children who live across the street. "All these children have profound respiratory problems," Dunlap explained. "The children have been exhaustively tested, not only by myself, but by immunologists and pulmonary-function specialists at Buffalo Children's Hospital. . . . We can find no intrinsic causes for the problems the children are having." Dunlap is most concerned because they require "constant" medical attention. Wayne, the grandchildren, and Fred Armagost all suffer from continuous, hacking coughs. Susan Jasper, one of Fred's granddaughters, was only a few months old when she was first affected. Susan had already been hospitalized three times by the age of eighteen months for serious respiratory problems. The neighbors' children have also had many bouts with flu, bronchitis, and pneumonia.

While Dunlap concedes that children in the Niagara Falls area suffer from higher-than-normal rates of respiratory problems, presumably because of the high concentration of local industrial facilities, he insists that the Armagost children and their neighbors are different, as they have failed to improve substantially over time. "I have been having extraordinary difficulties even putting a dent in the incidence of morbidity with these kids," he says.

In October, 1978, Dunlap wrote to the county health commissioner to express concern that the dump might be the cause of the Armagosts' health problems. He received no reply.

Other problems and complaints from Hyde Park residents included leakage from the dump, periodic flooding of local property, and offensive odors. However, the most serious and persistent complaints have come from workers in the three local industries. Carl Sabey, who worked at the NL plant for over thirty years, remembers several times when work had to be stopped because of the fumes. "My eyes would water and my skin would burn. If you could not run away from those fumes, then your throat would burn, also," he said.

The most frightening experience, recalled Sabey, was when fumes from the dump damaged the building in August, 1972. Men arriving at the morning shift on that day were shocked when they observed what had happened to the outside of the plant's newly painted office. It "looked as though somebody took a blow-torch" to the building, Sabey said. The fumes from the dump were so powerful that they sent workers rushing for the exit. The plant manager finally wrote to Hooker, demanding immediate action to prevent the continual disruption of NL's operations.

> We want to acquaint you with what we consider to be an extremely dangerous condition affecting our plant and employees. . . . Again today, the problem was critical. We received a call at 7:15 A.M. that our midnight shift workers had complained of coughing and sore throats from the obnoxious and corrosive fumes permeating from the disposal site and that our day workers were leaving the plant. Upon arriving at the plant, the fumes were obvious, the men were disturbed and there were many indications of physical damage to our buildings.[53]

Workers at the Greif Brothers factory also had their problems. For years, parts of the factory were permeated by the caustic stench of chemical wastes rising from an open manhole overlying the section of Bloody Run Creek that passed under the plant. After it became obvious that Hooker had no intention of cleaning up the creek, Greif management attached a plastic cover over the manhole. Within a few weeks, the fumes had completely eaten the cover away.

Employees at Greif Brothers, NL Industries, and Niagara Steel Finishing are convinced that they are suffering from an excessive incidence of persistent skin rashes, respiratory disease, and cancer because of pollutants from the Hyde Park dump. The National Institute for Occupational Safety and Health (NIOSH) conducted a brief health survey on workers in these plants.[54] Preliminary results show TCDD levels up to 10 ppb in dust samples taken from the rafters of the NL plant and Niagara Steel Finishing. Samples from the manhole of the Greif plant show TCDD levels of 30 ppb; its immediate source is likely to be the Bloody Run Creek, whose sediment has been found to be contaminated with levels of about 200 ppb.

As early as 1969, Hooker was aware that quantities of toxic materials were pooling in areas on the site. Studies by Hooker then indicated that the leachate flowing off-site at certain times contained very high concentrations of toxic chemicals, including 131,000 ppb of phenol and total organics at over 67,000 ppb.[55]

In September, 1971, a Hooker employee, B. J. Carreno, sent to study the problem concluded, "The 1.5 million gallons of contaminated water which are impounded at the Hyde Park dump have created a potentially serious water pollution problem."

Over the years, officials inspecting the dump had noted numerous violations of Niagara County and New York State sanitary codes. In a letter to Hooker dated July, 1971, the Niagara County Health Department concluded:

> Leaching conditions exist from beneath the surface as well as from numerous drain tiles installed at this site. . . . Properties surrounding this area that do not belong to Hooker have been and

continue to be contaminated. . . . This office has received numerous complaints of odors which originate from your disposal site.[56]

A November 29, 1972 letter to Hooker from the state of New York noted that "waste water is in fact being discharged into the drainage ditches tributary to the Niagara River"—and into Bloody Run Creek. By 1976, the state of New York found that polychlorinated biphenyls (PCBs) and mirex from the site had contaminated land outside the site and Bloody Run Creek. Nevertheless, local residents reported that dumping continued until the spring of 1979, two years after the state of New York had ordered the site closed. In January, 1981, Hooker attempted to settle its suit with the U.S. Department of Justice by promising to spend over $16 million to clean up the site. Facing opposition to the proposed settlement, Hooker promised the court to purchase nine homes located nearest to the Hyde Park dump, including the Armagost home, at fair market value. Final court approval of the Hooker plan was still pending in the fall of 1981.

The 102nd Street Dump

Hooker opened the 102nd Street site in the early 1940s and has since, along with the Olin Corporation, dumped about 47 million pounds of toxic wastes there. The site is located on the Niagara River above the intake of the city's drinking water treatment plant, just a few hundred feet away from the Love Canal.

Complaints about this dump date back to July, 1967, when two young boys were seriously burned as they ran across the unfenced site. The burns were caused by chlorates and phosphorus, which lay exposed on the surface of the dump. A full year before the accident, Hooker's insurance agent had advised that the site be fenced to keep local children out. Because of this site's proximity to the densely populated Love Canal area, thick clouds of "coal gas" odors, formed during the dumping operation, occasionally drifted into the Love Canal area, discoloring house paint and prompting complaints from local residents.

In 1970, Hooker was informed by the Army Corps of Engineers that it was operating an "illegal dumpsite." Shortly after, Hooker executives discussed the feasibility of getting rid of the problem by selling the heavily contaminated site, zoned "multifamily/residential," to a local developer. Had this happened, the 102nd Street dump could well have become a second Love Canal.

Internal discussion of disposing of the site mostly focused around its sale to the city for use as a park. In October, 1972, Hooker's works manager, John Judy, noted that the state was about to vote on a $1.15-billion bond issue that included money for parks and recreational facilities. Judy directed his staff to see if it couldn't interest the city in buying the land as an extension of Griffon Park, which bordered the site.

Hooker's 1972 ideas about what to do with the land directly conflicted with its own staff's 1963 assessment of the usability of the land. At that time, M. L. Parker, production manager of Hooker's Eastern Chemical Division, in arguing against the sale of this land to the city as a park, remarked, "Hooker is still being plagued with problems associated with fill at the Love Canal area in spite of their best efforts to shed themselves of any."[57] Parker noted further that, in early conversations with the city, which at that time wanted to acquire the land, Hooker representatives had stated that it "was very questionable whether lands which have been developed through the years by burying chemical fill are suitable for recreational purposes." Parker and his colleagues convinced the city that buying the land would be a mistake. No explanation was given for Hooker's policy reversal nine years later.

Overview

The record seems clear that Hooker was well aware of many of the risks of its dumping operations at its four Niagara Falls sites. Although the question of responsibility for the Love Canal may be controversial, there is certainly no question about the responsibility for the other sites, which are all owned and operated by Hooker.

There also seems little question that the city and county governments have been lax in protecting the health of their citizens and their environment. Their position appears to reflect at least ignorance and, at worst, a desire to protect local revenues.

Is Hooker the worst offender in the nation?* It is difficult to make comparative judgments, as few other large industries have been as closely scrutinized as Hooker. It must also be recognized that Hooker was one of the first companies to make major investments in on-site, high-temperature incineration technology. Today, an increasing amount of Hooker's toxic wastes are being incinerated under controlled conditions, and Hooker is now even accepting wastes from other companies. However, what appears to distinguish Hooker from most other industries is the sheer size of its dumping operation and its constant maneuvering to evade the burden of responsibility for its actions by shifting it to the local citizens.†

---

*Hooker has other problems, such as in Lathrop, California, where it has been accused of defrauding the state and poisoning water supplies (see Chapter 4), and in Montague, Michigan, where self-admitted waste dumping has resulted in a cleanup bill totalling more than $14 million.

†Dr. Armand Hammer, chairman of the board of Hooker's parent company Occidental Petroleum, who told a national audience on *Meet the Press* on October 14, 1979 that the danger of Love Canal was minimal and "has been blown out of context," was appointed chairman of the National Cancer Advisory Panel of the National Cancer Institute by President Reagan on October 2, 1981. A coalition of public interest groups, "Citizens Concerned About Corporate Cancer," attended Hammer's inaugural panel meeting on October 27, 1981 and handed him a letter requesting his resignation on grounds including an "insurmountable conflict of interest" between the short term financial interests of his company and his Federal responsibilities for cancer prevention. The letter was subsequently circulated as a petition to scientific, labor, religious and public interest communities.

CHAPTER 6

Dumping Waste Oil

O il is the universal lubricant for our mechanized modern society—billions of gallons are used each year. Crankcase oils, brake fluid, transmission fluid, antifreeze, industrial oils, and transformer oils are not generally consumed or destroyed during use and, as a result, must be disposed of afterwards. In 1979 alone, some 1.4 billion gallons of waste oil were generated in this country. Each year this figure increases.[1]

Waste oils pose a significant threat to health and the environment. Unused motor oil, for example, contains high concentrations of lubricant additives, such as detergents and heavy metals—lead, zinc, phosphorus, barium, and vanadium—and trace pollutants from the machinery itself (see Table 6-1). Motor oil also contains significant concentrations of carcinogenic polycyclic aromatic hydrocarbons (PAH).

Oil's spongelike quality—its ability to soak up large quantities of ultrahazardous materials, such as polychlorinated biphenyls (PCBs), concentrated pesticide wastes, and heavy metals during use—also contributes to its potential toxicity. Moreover, after oil is used, it accumulates additional toxic contaminants.

A favored method for disposing of waste oil is using it as a dust suppressant. There are well over one hundred thousand miles of dirt roads throughout rural America. During dry months, the surface dust on these roads creates a major nuisance for people living near and traveling on them. One report estimates that some 120 million gallons of waste oil are dumped on rural dirt roads to reduce dust each year.[2] The oil does not remain immobile, and about 70 percent is eventually washed away by rain or blown off the roads with the surface dust. Soil from oiled roads retains high levels of lead, originating from the tetraethyl lead in gasoline, with an average of 209 milligrams per kilogram (mg/kg), versus an average of only 39 mg/kg in soil from unoiled roads.[3] The laxity of past controls over the dumping of used oils on dirt roads, probably the cheapest way of disposing of these oils, has led to some serious problems.

Table 6-1. Typical Waste Automotive Oil Composition

Variable	Value
Gravity, °API	24.6
Viscosity @ 100 °F	53.3 Centistokes
Viscosity @ 210 °F	9.18 Centistokes
Flash Point	215 °F (C.O.C. Flash)
Water (By Distillation)	4.4 Volume %
Sulfur	0.34 Weight %
Ash, Sulfated	1.81 Weight %
Lead	1.11 Weight %
Calcium	0.17 Weight %
Zinc	0.08 Weight %
Phosphorus	0.09 Weight %
Barium	568 ppm*
Iron	356 ppm*
Vanadium	5 ppm*

Source: Report on Waste Oil to the U.S. Congress, Environmental Protection Agency, 1974.

*ppm = parts per million.

Road Oil in Shenandoah Stables, Missouri

Shenandoah Stables, owned by Frank Hempel and Judy Piatt, was a large and successful quarter-horse breeding ranch and show arena in Moscow Hills, Missouri. Horse enthusiasts came from miles around to bid on the stables' strong stock or just to watch the more than one hundred horses canter around the arena.

Early each morning, Judy would go to the barn to feed and water the horses. During the last week in May, 1971, the usual barn smells were masked by strong chemical odors from the newly sprayed road oil in the arena. Almost 10 years later, Judy still remembers the smell, "like carbon tetrachloride, real musty, tangy, and heavy." A visitor to the stables recalled that the smell made the end of his nose tingle "as if someone was sticking pins into it." However, Judy was not concerned. She had had the arena oiled many times before. "I didn't think anything about it," she said.

The morning after she first noticed the smell, Judy found dozens of dead sparrows littering the barn's earthen floor. Within a few days, sparrows nesting in the rafters were dying by the hundreds. "It got so bad we started taking them out by the shovelful and burying them in the cornfield," she said. By mid-June, Shenandoah had lost eleven cats and five dogs.

All the animals died with the same symptoms. For no apparent reason, they started losing hair, became dehydrated and emaciated, their mouths turned white, their tongues and eyes reddened, and they howled constantly. Judy came to believe that the cats died from the same disease that had killed the sparrows. "I thought the cats got it from eating the dead birds." But when the dogs started dying too, Judy became alarmed. She knew the dogs hadn't been eating the birds. She was afraid that whatever had killed the birds, cats, and dogs was going to continue killing. And she was right.

Of the eighty-five horses being exercised in the arena, fifty-eight became ill and forty-three died within a year. Of forty-one breedings in 1971, only one foal survived. There were twenty-six spontaneous abortions, six foals died at birth, and fifteen died within four months of birth.[4]

When the problems first began, Judy's regular veterinarian, Doc Evans, was out of town. A substitute, asked to the stables when the horses began to get sick, told Judy not to be concerned, but when Evans finally returned, "he took a walk down the aisle and then walked over to my office and said, 'Oh, my God, there's something terrible wrong.'" From June to August, Evans and state vet Patrick Phillips tried in vain to diagnose and save the animals. "It was scary," Phillips said later. "Nothing that we did or tried to do worked. They just kept losing weight and dying." The deaths were unpleasant, Phillips added. "It was very painful for the horses." Like the cats and dogs, without warning, a horse would become dehydrated, lose weight rapidly, develop huge sores all over, and die within days.

Judy remembers one incident with painful clarity. Her prize junior stallion had collapsed in the pasture about one hundred yards from the house. Judy and her two young daughters, Andrea, six, and Lori, ten, spent days carrying cool water out to where the stallion lay and pouring it over him to keep from roasting in the hundred-degree heat. They smeared ointment on the horse's quarter-size sores and tried to comfort him as best they could. A few days later, the horse suddenly rose to his feet and "leapt as high as eight feet into the air. Something awful frightened him," said Judy. After a last lunge, the stallion died.

That evening, Judy took the animal to the University of Missouri veterinary school for an autopsy. Judy described how the liver, kidney, stomach, and other organs were massively swollen and hemorrhagic. The vets told Judy that they had never seen anything like it before. Later, autopsies on the other horses revealed a characteristic picture of skin lesions, severe weight loss, and liver necrosis.

Whatever was killing her animals was now beginning to affect Judy's children as well. Andrea and Lori both complained of bad headaches, and Lori developed blisters and sores on her hands. When Judy arrived home from the stallion's autopsy, she found Andrea seriously ill and with bloody urine. "Andrea was hemorrhaging," Judy said. "The blood was everywhere."

On August 23, several days after Andrea was admitted to St. Louis Children's Hospital, Judy was asked to meet with a group of doctors, including doctors from the Federal Center for

Disease Control in Atlanta. "I entered this conference room," Judy said. "It had a long table in the middle, and there were doctors on both sides. They asked me to go over everything. They asked me if Andrea had access to poisons. I said, 'of course', but told them she wasn't the kind that would take any." The doctors described Andrea's condition, and, said Judy, "something kind of rang a bell. I pulled the autopsy report on the stallion out of my purse and handed it to them." Judy then told the doctors about the mysterious deaths at her stables. The doctors finally concluded that there was some connection between the animal deaths and Andrea's near-fatal condition and that some powerful toxic chemical in the road oil must be responsible.

THE CONTAMINATION OF THE ROAD OIL

Bliss Oil and Salvage Company, a St. Louis-based waste oil and resale firm, had been mixing road oil and spreading it on dirt roads and in horse arenas in Missouri for many years. Between February and October, 1971, under contract to Independent Petrochemical Company in Verona, Texas, Bliss had hauled some 16,000 gallons of trichlorophenol (TCP) waste residues to its St. Louis facility, where they were dumped into tanks containing waste auto oil. Bliss sold the TCP-contaminated waste oil to M. T. Richards Company in Crossfield, Illinois for "re-refining." Instead, Richards spread the contaminated waste oils on rural Crossfield roads. The TCP-sludge wastes were mixed by Bliss with more waste oil and other liquid wastes for use as road oil. On May 25, 1971, Bliss sprayed some two thousand gallons of this road oil in Shenandoah Stables at a cost of $150.

Later investigations revealed that at least three other areas in rural Missouri had been sprayed. All reported widespread animal deaths. Six horses died at Bubbling Springs Ranch in Fenton. Timber Line Stables in New Bloomfield lost twelve horses, a cat, and a dog. Even Bliss was affected. One of his drivers, in an effort to lighten his load, had dumped waste from the Independent plant on a road at Bliss's farm in St. James. Within two weeks, Bliss lost all seventy of his chickens. Dozens of wild birds and other local animals were also found dead. At least ten persons reported illnesses that they believed resulted from exposure to the contaminated soil.

Independent Petrochemical Company had become involved in the TCP problem in a roundabout way. The story goes back to the Vietnam War days, when the Verona, Missouri plant of Syntex Agribusiness, Inc. was manufacturing 2,4,5-T, a powerful herbicide used by the military as a defoliant.* When the military contracts for the herbicide were not renewed, Syntex rented its facility to Northeastern Pharmaceutical and Chemical Company (NEPACCO), a small New England–based pharmaceutical supply operation, for the manufacture of hexachlorophene (HCP), a disinfectant. During the manufacturing process, about fifty gallons a day of highly concentrated still-residue (residue left after distillation) TCP wastes were pumped from the reaction vessel to storage tanks. At first, NEPACCO contracted with one of the top waste disposal firms, Rollins Environmental Services, Inc., to remove the TCP wastes. The subsequent collapse of the market, when it was discovered that HCP itself produced unexpected toxicity, forced NEPACCO to switch to a less expensive disposal firm, Independent Petrochemical Company, which, in turn, subcontracted to Bliss.

In August, 1971, samples of oil-soaked soil from the horse arena were sent for analysis to the Federal Center for Disease Control. The responsible contaminant was not identified until three years later, when it was shown to be TCDD, one of the most toxic and carcinogenic chemicals known. Samples from Shenandoah Stables, other arenas, and the Bliss farm contained TCDD levels up to about 33 ppm. Subsequent tests revealed the presence of other highly toxic contaminants, including PCBs, which were found in Shenandoah soil samples up to levels of about 1600 ppm. Exactly how the TCDD-laden TCP and the PCBs ended up in the road oil is still uncertain. As is common practice among waste-oil haulers, Bliss simply dumped a variety of liquid

---

*Use of the herbicide for domestic and most agricultural purposes was suspended in the United States in 1979, largely because of the highly toxic, carcinogenic, and teratogenic effects of its contaminant, TCDD.

wastes into the same storage tank containing the dirty crankcase oil collected from numerous service stations all over Missouri. Bliss maintains that he never knew that the wastes he had picked up from NEPACCO in Verona were so dangerous. However, according to Judy Piatt, a NEPACCO employee warned Bliss that the wastes were deadly and insisted that Bliss wear protective clothing, gloves, and an air mask when he connected a pipe from the TCP still-residue storage tank to his truck.

RESTITUTION

Judy Piatt eventually forced Bliss and NEPACCO to remove the contaminated soil from her arena. The thousands of pounds of contaminated dirt were then used as roadbed material. Contaminated soil from other affected areas was dumped into a municipal landfill and used to fill holes at developments elsewhere in Missouri. NEPACCO, however, did not recompense the numerous victims of the road oiling for livestock losses and property damage, as it went bankrupt.

Syntex, the plant owner, inherited a tank filled with an estimated 4,600 gallons of TCP still residues. Tests in late 1974 showed that the liquid contained TCDD concentrations of about 350 ppm. Syntex, while disclaiming responsibility for the tank's contents, has cooperated with the state of Missouri and the EPA in the development of a safe method of destroying the waste.

A search for the thousands of gallons of missing wastes, estimated to contain about 40 pounds of TCDD, revealed a statewide contamination problem. Almost 150 drums of waste were found at "Denny's Farm."[5] Syntex agreed to clean up those wastes.[6] That was, however, just the tip of the iceberg. In the summer of 1982, EPA experts uncovered TCDD levels in the town of Times Beach, Missouri, which were over 100 times the emergency level of 1 ppb suggested by the Centers for Disease Control, and over 10,000 times the detectable level of 10 parts per trillion. Additional tests, and the spread of the contamination by winter storms, finally forced the EPA to order an emergency evacuation of the town's 2,400 residents. On February 22, 1983, after it was determined that there was no possible way of decontaminating the town, EPA announced that the Superfund would pay an estimated $33 million to buy out the town. While it is not known just how many other Times Beaches there are, by the spring of 1983 over thirty seriously contaminated TCDD sites had been located in the state of Missouri, many with TCDD levels several times higher than those in Times Beach. At one of these sites, Imperial, intensive health screening by the Centers for Disease Control revealed, according to April 1983 press reports, abnormalities in liver function and other tests in 112 out of 130 residents.

Judy Piatt insists that there is no way her family can be adequately compensated. While her daughter Andrea has apparently recovered from the poisoning that nearly killed her in 1971, her other daughter Lori developed chronic problems, such as constant fatigue, nose bleeds, hair loss, gray color, and numbness in her hands. However, Judy's main concern, based on the very potent carcinogenicity of TCDD, is that her daughters will eventually develop cancer.

Since the incident, Judy has developed frequent angina and has had two heart attacks. She believes her condition was probably caused by exposure to the TCDD. Judy is no longer bitter. She just wants to be left alone. "You know," she said, "for over a year I refused to admit that something toxic in the oil was to blame. I didn't think that could happen in this country. I just kept saying, 'You can't go around spraying deadly chemicals on people's property, where they keep animals and kids.' I thought if you could go to the moon you ought to be able to control something like that."

Road Oil in Corrigan, Texas

On October 20, 1978, Ken Robinson, manager of Reily's Village, a small community in Corrigan, Texas, a hundred miles northwest of Nederland, awaited the arrival of road oil from Browning-Ferris Chemical Services Industries, Inc. (a BFI subsidiary).*

---

*BFI, a Houston-based corporation with assets of $415 million, is one of the state's largest haulers of waste oil and liquid and solid industrial wastes and describes itself as "the largest publicly-held company engaged primarily in the collection, process-

Robinson, a private contractor who had been dealing with BFI since 1975, managed the spreading of road oil not only at Reily's Village, but also at Barlow Lake Estates and Town Bluff, two other southeastern Texas developments. Robinson used to keep in contact with BFI through Gene Davis, the operations manager of the company's transfer station at Neederland. Davis would let Robinson know when road oil was available. The road oil cost Robinson nothing. BFI not only gave it away, but also shipped it free of charge in its own tanker trucks.

When the truckloads of BFI road oil arrived at Reily's Village, Robinson cut a trench down the middle of each strip of dirt road and supervised the pouring of oil into the trench. He then mixed the dirt dug from the middle of the road back into the trench, "let it set," and then spread it evenly over the road. When the oiling was complete, Robinson signed a special Texas Department of Water Resources shipping manifest (trip) ticket, and the empty truck returned to Nederland.* Between October 20 and November 13, 1978, approximately eighty thousand gallons of road oil were disposed of in this fashion.[8]

As soon as the road oil was laid, the air filled with unpleasant fumes smelling like shoe polish. Ricky Goodson, whose home is within a hundred feet of one of the oiled roads, said the smell burned his nose and made his family sick. Eugene Fox, another area resident, said that the smell was so bad "you could hardly stand to be around it." Dozens of other residents in the Village and in nearby Town Bluff Estates were sickened by the oil. "I've never had a headache in my life until six months ago. I would wake up in the mornings with a headache. Just terrible. Nauseous. Sick to my stomach," said George Barber.

ing, recovery, and disposal of solid and liquid wastes" in the nation. BFI has facilities in 135 towns in thirty-six states, employs some 8,000 people, and owns 3,200 "specially equipped collection trucks." In 1979, the company operated sixty-five solid-waste disposal landfill sites and disposed of liquid, chemical, and hazardous wastes at seventeen facilities, including six deep-injection wells, three "secure" hazardous waste sites, and four sanitary landfills. Although reputed by industry analysts to be most reliable, BFI has not been free of environmental problems, quite apart from road oil. In 1979 alone, BFI was a defendant in thirty-three proceedings for alleged violations of water, air, and land protection laws.[7]

*Each load of hazardous waste transported in Texas must be recorded on such a manifest.

Animals in the area were affected too. Robert Duff reported that he had lost several dogs since the oiling. He complained that "patches of hair" had come off one of his dogs which had to be destroyed. Douglas Wilder had worse luck. Soon after the road outside his farm was oiled, six calves and three cows in nearby pastures died from "apparent poisoning."

DISCOVERY OF THE CONTAMINATION

In spite of these problems, nobody complained to the local authorities. The offensive smell was just accepted as an unpleasant fact of life. Then, on April 26, 1979, Jim Carlton of the local *Port Arthur News* reported that the road oil used in Corrigan was contaminated with heavy concentrations of nitrobenzene and trace amounts of cyanide.

While reviewing the BFI file in the Orange office of the Texas Department of Water Resources, the state agency in charge of waste disposal, Carlton came across a complaint from Melvin Grizzard, previous manager and chemist in charge of the storage tanks at BFI's Nederland plant. On November 2, 1978, Grizzard had informed the Jefferson County pollution control agent, Victor Bateman, that the road oil shipped to Corrigan was probably contaminated with cyanide.[9] Grizzard said that he had been ordered by the plant operations manager, Gene Davis, to prepare a batch of road oil by mixing waste oil with cyanide-containing wastes obtained from the giant DuPont chemical complex in Orange.* Grizzard insists that when he objected, Davis told him, "Don't worry about it, Mel. We've been doing it for years." Grizzard was so upset that he called Nederland's manager, Steven Custer, at home around 2:30 A.M. that night. Custer told Grizzard to meet him at the office the next morning. When Grizzard arrived, he was told he had been fired.

Bateman immediately referred Grizzard's complaint to the Texas Department of Water Resources, which sent an inspector, Melvin Swoboda, to examine BFI's records.[10] Swoboda found trip tickets showing that the cyanide wastes from DuPont had

---

*DuPont appears to have assumed implicitly that its waste would be properly disposed of by BFI and its subcontractors.

been shipped by BFI to Sonics, Inc., a deep-well injection operation in Ranger, Texas.* The incoming and outgoing trip tickets for the cyanide wastes hauled by BFI balanced perfectly. Swoboda also checked Grizzard's unofficial records on tank contents and volumes and found that they also balanced with the trip-ticket information. As far as Swoboda could tell, all the cyanide waste seemed accounted for, so none could have been used in the road oil. However, his investigation covered only trip tickets for cyanide shipments over the preceding two months. Swoboda failed to check whether the cyanide had been received by Conservation Services and Sonics, to test the road oil being shipped to Corrigan to see if it was contaminated, and to test the oiled road surface. Furthermore, Swoboda restricted his inquiry to the possibility of cyanide contamination and did not investigate the possibility of contamination of the road oil with any other toxic waste.

Carlton was not impressed by Swoboda's perfunctory investigation of the complaint and decided to take matters further. He and other newspapermen and government officials visiting Reily's Village some five months after the roads had been oiled found that the fumes made them sick and nauseated, even though the shoe-polish-like odor had by then largely dissipated. Inquiries at BFI made it clear that no adequate records were kept on the quantities and types of wastes being received, stored, and shipped, where they were shipped, or their ultimate disposal site.

Analysis by the state of Texas of samples from the surfaces of various dirt roads in Corrigan revealed low levels of cyanide, but very high concentrations of nitrobenzene, another toxic waste stored at the Nederland BFI facility.† The state confirmed these results in eight separate areas of eastern Texas, where

---

*In deep-well injection, liquid wastes are pumped hundreds of feet under the ground, below known water tables (see Chapter 12).

†An estimated 400 million pounds of nitrobenzene are manufactured each year for use in soap, perfume, cleaners for wool, wood flooring and paneling, and as an ingredient in metal and shoe polishes. Nitrobenzene is relatively persistent and its liquid and vapor penetrates the skin rapidly. Vapor absorption by inhalation is high. Nitrobenzene is moderately toxic, and induces hemolytic anemia, hepatitis and jaundice, central nervous system damage, and skin disorders.

about nine hundred thousand gallons of BFI road oil had been spread between 1976 and 1979.[11] Nitrobenzene concentrations in dirt on these roads ran as high as 21,000 ppm, with the highest levels in Reily's Village.[12]

THE CONGRESSIONAL INVESTIGATION

In May, 1979, in preparation for hearings on hazardous wastes, Congressman Bob Eckhardt, then chairman of the House Commerce Subcommittee on Oversight and Investigations, sent a small team of investigators to examine the operations and records of the BFI Nederland facility. The investigators concluded that BFI had been "grossly negligent" in its handling of hazardous wastes.

While not charging BFI with deliberate intent to "dump" hazardous wastes on east Texas roads, Eckhardt released a staff study that showed that getting rid of nitrobenzene in road oil was far more profitable than proper disposal of the hazardous waste. Shipping the nitrobenzene waste to Conservation Services' landfill would cost BFI $526 per load. If the waste were shipped to Sonics, a deep-well injection operation, BFI would realize a profit of $291 per load. On the other hand, if BFI simply dumped the nitrobenzene waste on Corrigan roads, it could realize a profit of $1,087 per load.[13] BFI objected to this analysis at the hearings, but never subsequently provided contrary documentation.

BFI accepted full responsibility for "the serious, unfortunate incident whereby the processing of certain nitrobenzene waste streams at the company's Nederland, Texas facility resulted in contamination of waste oil . . ."[14] and agreed to undertake the large-scale removal of contaminated soil from the miles of oiled roads at a cost of about $3.3 million. However, BFI claimed that the contamination had been due to an unfortunate accident:

> The company's investigation has not uncovered any credible information that would lead to the conclusion that nitrobenzene or other hazardous substances were intentionally mixed with waste oil in order to dispose of such hazardous substances as road oil. However, improper and careless practices by company personnel in their handling of these materials unintentionally brought about this regrettable occurrence.[15]

The Corrigan roads "accident" was not unique in BFI's operations. For instance, while BFI claimed to have shipped six truckloads of cyanide wastes to Sonics and had billed DuPont for six, only four had, in fact, been received by Sonics. BFI also claimed to have shipped about 218,000 gallons of nitrobenzene to Sonics, but, when questioned, BFI retracted its statement, saying that the shipment in question had been another industrial waste. Attempts to balance the incoming and outgoing cyanide-waste ledgers resulted in a shortfall of 75,000 gallons. BFI claimed that the "missing" cyanide was in storage, to be later shipped for disposal to an unspecified site, but produced no supporting documentation.[16]

In further explaining the disposal of its waste oils and hazardous wastes, such as cyanide, nitrobenzene, and benzene, BFI noted that, during 1977 and 1978, it shipped a total of some 400,000 gallons of wastes to the L.A.&D. Company of Louisiana.* Included were 196,000 gallons of "waste oil," 36,500 gallons of "commingled waste," 28,000 gallons of benzene waste, and 6,300 gallons of "benzene asphalt" waste.[17] The Texas Department of Water Resources trip-ticket records indicated only that L.A.&D. had hauled these wastes away from BFI, but gave no information on what happened to them.

Subcommittee chairman Bob Eckhardt questioned BFI management about its relationship with L.A.&D.

> MR. ECKHARDT: Are you aware that the corporation [L.A.&D.] is not registered to do business in the state of Louisiana?
> MR. PAUL ZIMMERMAN [Regional Liquid Waste Director, BFI]: No, I am not.
> MR. ECKHARDT: You don't know that it is so registered, do you?
> MR. ZIMMERMAN: No, I don't.
> MR. ECKHARDT: Are you aware that there isn't any post-office box listing for this company?
> MR. ZIMMERMAN: No, I don't.
> MR. ECKHARDT: The two post-office box listings that they gave this committee—that they reported to the state of Tex-

---

*The only information BFI seemed to have on this contractor was that L.A.&.D. are the initials of three daughters of its owner, Frank Meyers, who lives somewhere in Louisiana.

as—were incorrect, as I understand it. Do you know what the company is and where it is located?

MR. ZIMMERMAN: No sir, I don't. I am very faintly familiar with it. Only by name.

MR. ECKHARDT: Mr. McAlpin, do you know?

MR. MARK MC ALPIN [Regional Advertising and Public Relations Director, BFI]: No, sir.

MR. ECKHARDT: Do you know that a considerable amount of wastes have been disposed of by BFI to this company?

MR. MC ALPIN: Yes, sir. I am aware that they went to the L.A.&D. Company.

MR. ECKHARDT: But you don't know where it is or what it is or how responsible it is, or have you never checked these questions?

MR. MC ALPIN: The location of the plant, as I recall, was put on the Texas Water Quality Board shipping manifest ticket. . . .

MR. ECKHARDT: Do you know what they do with these materials that you dispose of through them?

MR. MC ALPIN: We were told they went back in the fuel market.

MR. ECKHARDT: Into the fuel market. Nitrobenzene into the fuel market? Nitrobenzene with oil sold for No. 6 fuel oil?

MR. MC ALPIN: I have no idea how they treated the materials that they received over there or what their process was, Mr. Chairman. . . .

MR. ECKHARDT: When you make a contract with DuPont to get rid of something like nitrobenzene, does that contract include your commitment to dispose of it in a way which is safe to the public, or does it not include such a commitment?

MR. MC ALPIN: Mr. Chairman, I couldn't answer that. I would have to look at the contract to say just exactly what it says.[18]

When contacted by Congressional staff, the state of Louisiana had little further information to add on L.A.&D.

TEXAS STATE LAW

More hazardous waste is produced in Texas than any other state. Over 1,300 industrial facilities generate an estimated 15.2 million tons of hazardous waste each year. A congressional survey of America's top fifty-three chemical producers indicated that 159 of their 1,600 facilities were located in Texas.[19] Texas also has the nation's largest concentration of petrochemical industries, which generally account for the most highly toxic wastes.

Unlike many other states, Texas has aggressively attacked the growing hazardous waste problem. It enacted one of the first comprehensive industrial solid-waste laws in 1969. Seven years later, following California's lead, Texas established a shipping control, or manifest, system to track the generation, transportation, and disposal of industrial wastes, with which all generators of hazardous wastes (called Class I) are required to comply. The system is administered by the Texas Department of Water Resources.

> The waste generator is responsible for originating an industrial waste shipping control ticket describing the waste material and designating the authorized receiver. After signing the ticket and obtaining the signature of the carrier, the generator detaches a copy of his records.
>
> The carrier is responsible for conveying the waste materials to the designated receiver where, upon receipt, the receiver must also sign the ticket. After the receiver detaches his copy, the carrier returns a copy signed by the receiver to the waste generator, thus enabling the generator to verify that his waste was in fact received. Waste generators and authorized receivers file reports with the department on a monthly basis. These reports itemize the shipment and receipt of Class I industrial wastes, thus enabling the department to monitor these activities for compliance with the rules.[20]

Good as this manifest system seemed, it was full of potential loopholes. First, it ignored on-site disposal by the generator, which accounts for about 80 percent of all hazardous waste disposal in Texas and elsewhere. Second, generators could escape state jurisdiction and surveillance by designating out-of-state receivers. Third, waste generators could list fictitious destinations and receivers. Fourth, the manifest system failed to recognize the possibility of commingling hazardous and nonhazardous wastes by allowing the same disposal facility with the same trucks to handle both.* Finally, the original trip ticket gave no indication as to the ultimate fate of wastes passing through storage or transfer facilities, such as BFI, Neederland.

The state compounded these regulatory problems by granting BFI special treatment in view of its national prestige as a leading waste disposal company and the huge volume of wastes it handled. BFI was allowed a special category, "commingled wastes," for some liquid wastes of the same general classification. The company was thereby permitted to mix, dispose, and transport various wastes together without their individual identification and labeling.

Overview

At the present time, tracing the disposal of waste oil is an almost impossible task. A recent congressional survey of the nation's fifty-three largest chemical manufacturers showed that even the biggest industries know very little about the fate of the waste oil and sludge they generate. About 40 percent of the 1,600 facilities surveyed reported that they had no idea where their wastes ended up. The situation with small generators is even more chaotic. For decades, the vast majority of waste oil disposers, haulers, and traders have collected small amounts of oil from numerous service stations and other small customers and commingled them in the same tank. The mixture is then sold for fuel oil, for re-refining, recycling, and reprocessing, and for use as road oil.

The potential hazards posed by waste oils stem largely from the ease with which they can be accidentally or deliberately contaminated. Drawn usually from the bottoms of tanks holding various waste oils, road oil is often contaminated with heavy metals and other hazardous wastes. Sprayed untreated on roads or arenas, these toxic wastes can be carried on dust and inhaled, eaten by domestic animals or cattle, or leached into local water supplies.

---

*For instance, Texas officials calculated that failure to clean a residual 5 gallons of nitrobenzene waste from a 4,200-gallon truck subsequently used for road oil would result in contamination levels in excess of 1,500 ppm.

As early as 1972, Congress expressed concern over the disposal of waste oils. In 1974, the EPA produced the first comprehensive report on waste oil, estimating that over 28 million barrels of waste oil were generated nationwide yearly, with the energy potential to heat and cool some 675,000 homes or operate over 1.3 million cars for a year.[21] The EPA found that 43 percent of this oil was burned without regard to problems of air pollution, 18 percent was used on roads, 8 percent was re-refined, and the fate of the remaining 31 percent was entirely unknown.[22]

The careless manner in which waste oils are currently handled, even by large and apparently reliable disposers, such as BFI, in a state with tight regulations, such as Texas, raises serious questions about the adequacy of waste-oil disposal by less sophisticated haulers, such as Bliss, and in states with far less regulation, such as Missouri.

The EPA determined that there were between one thousand and two thousand waste-oil collectors in the country, "most of whom are poorly equipped and operate in urban areas only." In rural areas, "the small quantities of waste oil generated per square mile cannot economically support waste-oil collection systems."[23]

The waste-oil industry remains almost untouched by government regulation. Nor are there current plans to remedy this situation. Local service stations, which yield the largest volume of waste oil, are not required to account for its disposal. The EPA, finding that "the collection of waste oil from industrial operations and automotive service facilities is the weakest link in the overall waste oil recycling disposal scheme,"[24] and believing that attempts to enforce controls against station owners would be ineffective, shifted the burden of reporting to the waste-oil haulers involved. Under the EPA's new regulations, only small businesses and industries generating over 100 kilograms (200 pounds) of waste oil per year will have to comply with hazardous-waste regulations.

All these problems would be less acute if there were a viable used-oil recycling industry in the United States. A combination of factors has, however, led to a decline in the volume of waste oil re-refined. In 1960, for example, over 300 million gallons a year of waste oil were re-refined. By 1975, the yearly figure had dropped to 50 million gallons.[25] Some critics have blamed at least part of the decline in re-refining on "misguided" government action. A Federal Trade Commission ruling requires that all recycled waste oil carry the label "Made From Previously Used Oil."[26] The House of Representatives declared in 1980 that the "discriminatory labeling requirements issued by the Federal Trade Commission have had an adverse impact on consumer acceptance of re-refined oil."[27]

Although Congress had directed the Department of Commerce as early as 1976 to establish federal procurement guidelines for waste oil "to ensure that the government will be a market for this oil," by the end of 1980, no such guidelines had been issued.[28] And, although disposal of waste oils was to be controlled under the Resource Conservation and Recovery Act (RCRA), the EPA decided not to classify waste petroleum oil as a hazardous waste.

Frustrated with the Department of Commerce's failure to stimulate re-refining and the EPA's failure to take appropriate steps to stop unsafe waste-oil disposal, in the fall of 1980, Congress enacted the Used Oil Recycling Act. This modest piece of legislation provides the states with $5 million for 1982 and another $5 million for 1983 for the development of waste-oil recycling operations. It also specifically directs the EPA and the Department of Commerce to take aggressive action to stop the waste of used oil.

According to one recent report, such statewide re-refining operations could be carried out at minimal cost. Maryland found, for instance, that a sufficient statewide collection and storage system could be established and maintained for less than three cents a gallon. Compared to the millions of dollars of damage unsafe disposal of waste oils has already inflicted on society, this amount seems a small price to pay.

Increased re-refining is a key to reducing the indiscriminant dumping of waste oil. Re-refining is not, however, a panacea. One widely used process actually produces toxic residues that are more hazardous than the waste oil itself.[29] New and safer technologies are, however, now available, and their use should be encouraged.

Even more important is the need for comprehensive state-wide collection systems, coupled with strong enforcement against unsafe dumping. Waste oil and hazardous wastes should be rigorously segregated. They should be disposed of and handled by entirely separate haulers and facilities. As for hazardous wastes, careful tracking is needed for waste oil from individual generators, through transfer and transshipment facilities, to ultimate disposal sites. Waste oils should not be dumped, but rather should be cleansed of unwanted contaminants and re-refined. Huge quantities of waste oil could be recycled in this manner on a regional basis, especially if economic incentives could be developed.

It is difficult to envisage adequate systems for hazardous-waste disposal that do not concurrently deal effectively with disposal of waste oil. It is clear that little progress will be made until the lack of federal and state regulation of waste oil disposal, coupled with the lack of economic incentives for recycling, is remedied.

It's simply a wide open situation,
like the Wild West in the 1870s.

JAMES MOORMAN
Assistant U.S. Attorney General for
Land and Natural Resources,
May 16, 1979

CHAPTER 7

Midnight Dumping

Midnight dumping, an unsafe and unlawful method of hazardous waste disposal, has become an increasingly significant problem. Unscrupulous haulers, lured by the promise of quick profits, are continuing to dump millions of gallons of wastes each year all over the country. The destruction they have wrought has already cost the public millions of dollars. As investigations into dozens of phony operations and midnight dumps continue, many communities are finding that their land and waters have been spoiled and their health threatened.

According to Edwin Stier, New Jersey's assistant attorney general for organized crime, most illegal dumping is being carried out by "a relatively small number of people who have a certain amount of technical knowledge in the toxic waste disposal area [and who] have become very sophisticated in setting up businesses which satisfy, at least superficially, licensing requirements." Often, companies "with good reputations . . . turn out to be the most frequent offenders." The owners of these seemingly aboveboard companies, mostly operating under the guise of legitimate licensed waste recyclers or haulers, "have created a whole series of insulators between themselves and these illegal operations."[1]

New Jersey: The First Signs

In the spring of 1977, Stier, who had spent nine years investigating organized-crime activities in New Jersey, received a curious phone call from a public utilities commissioner. The commissioner requested police protection for his inspectors, who were planning to search a private landfill operation in northern New Jersey. Although Stier knew that organized crime was deeply entrenched in the state's garbage-hauling business, the commissioner told him that the inspectors were not interested in garbage, but in the dumping of hazardous wastes. The commissioner also told him that inspectors previously visiting the site had been confronted by hostile workers, who forced them off the premises. As these inspectors were leaving through the garbage dump, they spied the site owner working the grounds on a bulldozer. However, any hope of questioning him vanished as a helicopter swooped down on a heap of garbage and whisked him away.

This bizarre tale sparked Stier's interest. "At that time," he reflected, "I hadn't the foggiest idea what illegal hazardous waste disposal was." But Stier was soon to learn. He arranged for state investigators to monitor the movement of waste-carrying trucks in and out of the landfill and also throughout northern New Jersey. What they discovered sent him scrambling to the state attorney general to ask for additional staff and resources.

The investigators found haulers running rampant, dumping drums of toxic chemicals under the Pulaski skyway, in uncultivated fields, and in vacant urban lots; throwing drums off the back of moving trucks onto the shoulders of main thoroughfares; digging up streets in residential neighborhoods and filling the holes with drums; stacking countless drums in abandoned waterfront piers; abandoning stolen trucks filled with waste-

containing drums in the middle of city streets; pumping tanker
trucks full of chemical wastes into residential streets, creeks,
municipal sewers, old water wells, Newark Bay, and the Arthur
Kill, a narrow body of water between Elizabeth, New Jersey and
Staten Island, New York; mixing toxic flammable and corrosive
wastes with garbage and hauling the wastes off to municipal
landfills; filling the basements of abandoned inner-city tene-
ments with hazardous wastes, then demolishing the structures;
and creating large artificial lakes of toxic wastes in the Pine
Barrens, the site of New Jersey's future drinking water supply.

Chemical Control, Inc., Elizabeth, New Jersey

State inspection of the 3.4-acre Chemical Control facility in
Elizabeth, New Jersey in the winter of 1979 revealed approximately forty thousand rusted and leaking fifty-five-gallon drums
of highly toxic, corrosive, and flammable industrial wastes. In
some places, the drums were piled five high and packed cheek-
to-jowl, presenting "a supermarket of acrid and sickly sweet
chemical odors, the ground spotted with shiny pools of various
shades and sheens."[2]
    In a loft in the incinerator building on the site, investigators
discovered about a hundred pounds of explosive dried picric
acid; several pounds of radioactive material; several large bottles
of a liquid labeled "Nitro"; over twelve hundred "lab pacs,"
packages of material wastes from research laboratories containing toxic agents; dozens of containers of explosive compressed
gases; "leaking containers of chromic acid, isopropanol, mineral
spirits and petrochem naphtha, all designated hazardous substances"; and cylinders of mustard gas, "a highly toxic nerve
gas." Also found inside the building were two other storage
areas, labeled by the state as the "pesticide room" and the "boiler
room," each crammed with rusted and leaking drums.[3]
    The chemical wastes in the Chemical Control facility were
clearly highly hazardous and contained agents known to induce
a wide range of acute and chronic toxic effects, including
"mucous membrane and respiratory tract irritation; cardiovascular, hepatotoxic, and neurotoxic effects; blood disorders;

allergies; skin disorders; carcinogenicity; mutagenicity; terato-genicity; and embryofetal toxicity."[4]

State experts determined that there was an imminent risk of fire and explosion at the site. Located only six hundred feet away was a sixteen-foot high-pressure gas line. Less than two thousand feet from the site was a large liquid natural-gas tank with a capacity equivalent to 150 million cubic feet, several bulk gasoline storage tanks with 100,000-gallon-plus capacity, and ten 60,000-gallon propane gas tanks. If an explosion at the Chemical Control site set off any of these other highly flammable materials, tens of thousands of people could be killed within minutes. The experts also predicted that a major fire at the site would probably blanket Elizabeth with thick clouds of highly toxic smoke. A school and large residential area were located within one thousand feet of the site. In addition, these clouds could drift to Staten Island and even Manhattan, injuring or perhaps even killing thousands of people. Faced with these risks, and after several unsuccessful attempts to force the company to reduce the inventory and clean up the operation, the state finally took control of the site.

Just before 11 P.M. on Monday, April 21, 1980, Chemical Control erupted into flames. Flames jumped two hundred to three hundred feet into the air, and huge clouds of toxic smoke rolled over fifteen miles out to sea. Schools were closed, and residents were told to stay inside with their windows closed. Hundreds of firemen battled the blaze for ten hours before it was brought under control. Luckily, the wind was blowing away from the most heavily populated areas, and before the explosion took place, about ten thousand barrels of the most dangerous material had been removed from the site as a result of a year-long state cleanup.

"It went boom, boom, boom, boom," Marion McDaniel, one of the owners of Big John's Tavern, located a block from the site, told a reporter. "I thought it was thunder. It looked like an atomic blast."

Roxie West, who lived just across a parking lot from the site, said, "I heard the noise, and it just scared me to death. I looked out and saw these big barrels flying in the air like they were soda cans."

Reacting to the events, Elizabeth health director John N. Surmay remarked, "We were within a hair's breadth of disaster." Although a major public disaster was avoided, the explosion did take a toll. Some thirty firemen were injured in the blaze, and an estimated seventy residents sought medical attention at local hospitals for nausea, and throat, eye, and lung irritation.

Even before the explosion, those involved in cleanup operations had been injured by Chemical Control's toxic wastes. A few weeks after the cleanup began, several trucks loaded with chemical-waste drums belonging to the company were found in nearby warehouses and brought back to the site. Fumes from leaking drums on one truck sent two policemen to the hospital; one sustained permanent eye damage.

Following a second fire on June 4, fourteen truckloads of diluted chemical wastes and crushed fifty-five-gallon drums were shipped from the Chemical Control site to a landfill in Niagara Falls operated by Cecos International. One of the trucks was prevented from continuing to Niagara Falls after a conservation officer noticed chemicals dripping from its tailgate.

BACKGROUND AND OPERATIONS OF CHEMICAL CONTROL, INC.

William Carracino, the owner of Chemical Control, Inc., was no stranger to the chemical-waste disposal and recycling business. He learned his trade at the Kin-Buc solid-waste disposal facility in Edison, New Jersey, the only authorized dump in the state, hauling plastic and chemical wastes for large manufacturers. Kin-Buc was New Jersey's largest waste disposal site. It was forced to close in the mid-seventies when it was found that the massive volumes of chemical liquid wastes dumped there posed a serious threat to public health. According to Carracino, he quit Kin-Buc in 1968 because management pressured him "to do something I considered illegal—to add to the bills and give them kickbacks." [5] Together with a group of friends and relatives, he bought an old barrel factory on the waterfront in Elizabeth and started his own company, Chemical Waste Disposal, Inc., renamed Chemical Control, Inc. two years later.

Apparently, all went well until 1970, when Carracino decided to expand and to install an incinerator. He "walked Wall

Street" for months to raise a million-dollar loan for this purpose, but met with no success. Finally, he was put in contact with Michael Collington, president of Northeast Pollution Control, a small manufacturing concern that built and installed scrubbers in New York City housing projects, schools, and public buildings. Collington advanced the money. By the winter of 1971, Northeast Pollution owned 81 percent of Chemical Control's stock, with Carracino, his friends, and relatives now minority shareholders. Continued financial difficulties, which Carracino insists had nothing to do with the operation, forced Chemical Control into bankruptcy in the summer of 1972, when it was taken over completely by Northeast Pollution Control.

Under new ownership, Chemical Control continued to operate with Carracino as plant manager. The incinerator, installed and approved for operation in 1971, stimulated an upswing in business. Chemical Control became one of the largest waste-disposal facilities in the state. The company incinerated and processed large volumes of flammable and hazardous chemical and pharmaceutical wastes for industry and also for the federal government. Wastes that could not be burned were treated, resold, or shipped to landfills in Rhode Island. Carracino insists that he ran a clean operation. There appears to be some basis for this claim, since the Food and Drug Administration contracted with Chemical Control in 1976 to dispose of 500,000 cans of bacterially contaminated Bon Vivant vichyssoise, an operation described as "a model of recycling waste disposal."[6]

How, then, did Chemical Control become such a scandalous mess? Carracino blames Northeast Pollution Control, the major shareholder whom, he insists, forced him out of his business, bilked Chemical Control of its profits, and pressured him to stockpile more inventory than he could possibly process. Carracino insists that his dream of turning Chemical Control into a model recycling operation was not shared by its parent company, Northeast Pollution. As an example, Carracino explained how, after he successfully battled an accidental fire at the site, Collington fumed, "You should have let it burn; we have got the half a million dollars [in insurance] and we would have been out of all our troubles."[7]

According to Carracino, Northeast Pollution Control gradually tightened its grip on Chemical Control. On September 9, 1977, according to Carracino, Collington informed him at gunpoint that Northeast Pollution Control was going to take over management. Carracino objected. "I told him I didn't work for anybody. I refused to work with that. I knew what they were going to do. I took whatever papers I could and left."[8]

Two weeks later, Carracino was indicted for illegal dumping of hazardous wastes throughout northern New Jersey. He was convicted in 1978 on three counts of illegal dumping and was sentenced to a two-year prison term. Chemical Control was fined $75,000. Carracino stresses his innocence of all charges and blames the problem on the state's continued failure to provide approved hazardous waste disposal facilities anywhere in New Jersey. "Honest" recyclers have no place to dispose of their toxic wastes, complains Carracino.

Carracino says that when he left Chemical Control, there were twenty thousand barrels of waste on-site, the incinerator was in operating condition, no waste was stored in the incinerator building, nor were any radioactive or explosive materials stored.

Other Illegal Operations in New Jersey

Illegal dumping and recycling operations were being discovered almost daily in New Jersey. Further investigation of Northeast Pollution Control showed that it owned another illegal operation, the A to Z Chemical Company in New Brunswick, New Jersey. According to Glenn Paulson, then assistant state commissioner for science and research, A to Z "is really cut from the same cloth" as Chemical Control.

The state also learned that Chemical Control had "stored" some six thousand drums at Duane Marine Salvage Corporation, another company under investigation for suspected environmental violations. On September 25, 1980, the owners of Duane Marine were indicted by the state of New Jersey for illegally dumping over five hundred thousand gallons of industrial waste into a sewer in Perth Amboy. They were also indicted for allegedly dumping eighty thousand gallons of hazardous wastes into the Edgeborough landfill, which was not authorized to accept hazardous wastes.

Within a few blocks of Chemical Control, yet another illegal operation was found at Iron Oxide, a company manufacturing filtration devices for industrial air-conditioning systems. Suspicion focused on Iron Oxide after state enforcement personnel learned that an acid-waste treatment facility had supposedly been set up there, although no stockpiling of wastes could be observed on-site. In a dramatic raid, the doors of the facility were broken down, and a four-inch drainage pipe, with an external hookup for tanker trailers, was discovered. The Army Corps of Engineers traced the pipe as it snaked under the building and emptied directly into the Arthur Kill. Iron Oxide is reported to have disposed of more than sixty thousand gallons of toxic acidic chemical wastes in this way.

On February 13, 1979, the state of New Jersey indicted managers of Scientific Chemical Processing, Inc., a licensed recycling operation in Newark, New Jersey. Scientific Chemical processed approximately four million gallons of industrial wastes per year. Its license allowed it to handle explosives, acids, cyanide, alkalis, solvents, oils, paints, emulsions, and flammable liquids and solids. The state has accused the company of dumping tanker trucks of waste into an open pit connected directly to the city sewer system. Investigators raiding this facility found a five thousand gallon tanker truck backed up to a pipe discharging directly into the sewer system. The state estimates that well over one hundred thousand gallons of liquid wastes, including benzene, other suspected carcinogens and untreated highly toxic and flammable materials, were disposed of here.[9] Company management face a total penalty of eighty-five years in prison and about $800,000 in fines.

Yet another investigation uncovered an even larger illegal dumping operation. In Old Bridge, New Jersey, investigators found that Madison Industries, Inc. had been illegally dumping industrial wastes into the Old Bridge sewer system, thereby jeopardizing the health and safety of those living along the sewer route and workers at the city sewage treatment plant. Instead of properly disposing of the materials, the state charged, Madison dumped, for free, over 3.2 million gallons of dangerous liquid wastes into the sewer.

The Highway Auto Service Company, Pittston, Pennsylvania

On July 31, 1979, the EPA regional headquarters received a call from the state of Pennsylvania, alerting the agency to an oil spill in the Susquehanna River near the town of Pittston, Pennsylvania. Tom Massey, a veteran of the EPA's oil-spill program, was immediately dispatched to the scene. Massey was escorted to the river, where oil was cascading from the mouth of a mine-drainage tunnel at a rate of one thousand gallons a day, making this a major spill. Massey had originally anticipated a routine oil-spill operation, but the "odd smell, foul smell, chemical smell," said Massey, made it clear that he was dealing with a chemical-waste problem. "One sniff of it and I wasn't going to go near it again. I'd be upwind of it at all times."

Massey's workers began to lay out booms to capture the oily wastes and pump them out of the river. To keep from being overcome by fumes, workers wore gas masks and protective clothing and worked in fifteen-minute shifts. All river traffic was kept away, and state police blocked all roads leading to the spill site.

Analysis of the waste liquids revealed a complex mixture of high concentrations of dichlorobenzene, toluene, xylene, benzene, and other hydrocarbons, as well as cyanides. Of major concern was the potentially disastrous impact of the spill on the drinking water of the city of Danville, whose population of fifty thousand obtains its drinking water from the Susquehanna sixty miles below the spill site. Within a few days, trace amounts of the contaminants began to appear in Danville's tap water. Continued discharge, it was feared, could markedly raise the level of these chemicals. "No one can tell me at this minute," Massey said some six months after the spill, "that there will not be a threat at any given time."

Although the spill slowed to only a trickle by mid-August, Massey and state experts estimated there may be between three hundred thousand and five hundred thousand gallons of chemical wastes trapped somewhere in the mine shafts leading to the drainage tunnel. With each rainfall, more wastes could be flushed from the shafts into the river.

Perhaps even more serious than the drinking water problem were the possible effects of cyanide gas on local residents. "I can substantiate a high potential for a high release [of gas] causing high public health problems. . . . The doses which could come out of that mountain through natural and manmade bore holes could be substantial," Massey said.

Some fifty thousand people live on top of the hundreds of miles of abandoned mine shafts in this depressed mid-state area. Besides the vents remaining from old mine workings, thousands of residents have bored holes up to sixty feet deep into old mine tunnels for sewage-disposal purposes. Although illegal, this practice has allowed homeowners and others to avoid the expenditure of thousands of dollars on septic tanks. Everybody has a bore hole, said Massey. "The mayor has a bore hole, the police chief has a bore hole, state people who work there have a bore hole."

Preliminary EPA tests have confirmed these fears. "The cyanide was venting out and into the homes," Massey said, although only in small quantities. No one has died yet from cyanide gas, but the potential remains for massive poisoning of local residents.

During investigations into the spill, the Pennsylvania Department of Environmental Resources staked out a local truck stop, the Highway Auto Service Company, located about twenty feet off the DuPont exit of Interstate 81, as a possible illegal dump site. Dozens of out-of-state tanker trucks had been observed at the truck stop over the preceding few months. On examination of the facility, state investigators discovered a bore hole filled with liquid closely resembling the Susquehanna oil spill. When dye was dropped into the hole, it emerged sixteen hours later from the mouth of the drainage tunnel.

A year after the problem was discovered, Terry Scatena, owner of the truck stop, and his two sons were indicted and convicted on illegal dumping charges. The alleged source of most of the wastes dumped is Hudson Oil Company of New Jersey. Legal action against Hudson Oil is now pending.

ABM Disposal Company, Philadelphia, Pennsylvania

Some of the worst problems in Pennsylvania, as in New Jersey, have centered on seemingly legitimate waste disposal operations. Prominent among these is ABM Disposal, a Philadelphia-based hauling and recycling corporation and a licensed waste facility, which began operations in the early 1970s. The corporation, formed by a local garbage hauler, was sold in 1975 to its present owner, Franklyn Tyson, the company's general manager.

Like Chemical Control, ABM was not a fly-by-night operation, but a bona-fide small business that enjoyed the support of local banks and the business community. Among its customers were some of America's largest and most prestigious companies, such as Texaco, DuPont, Smith, Kline & French, Scott Paper, General Electric, Boeing-Vertol, Owens-Illinois, and Sun Oil, which contracted with ABM to dispose of their wastes.

The difficulty with the ABM operation, says Keith Welks, attorney for Pennsylvania's Department of Environmental Resources, was simple. Once ABM picked up the hazardous waste, "it didn't know what to do with it." As early as 1977, ABM haulers were convicted for three separate illegal dumping incidents. In March, 1977, ABM personnel were convicted for illegally dumping dangerous pharmaceutical wastes into a groundwater well located in a garage in Montgomery County.[10]

Another illegal ABM dumping operation was discovered by a Chester-area resident who, in the early morning hours, saw a huge quantity of red liquid pouring from the back of a tank truck into the street and draining into Ridly Creek, a favorite swimming spot for local youngsters. Police arrested the truck driver a few blocks away. "If anyone had been swimming at the time," Welks said, "it could have killed them." Tests on the spilled liquid indicated that it contained "many, many times the lethal dose" of cyanide. ABM pleaded guilty to this charge and was fined $5,000, and the truck driver was given four years probation.[11]

What ABM could not easily dump was disposed of in other ways. State inspectors found over a dozen deteriorating ABM tanker trucks filled with hazardous wastes left abandoned at an

ABM transfer station in Eddy Stone, Pennsylvania. The most favored disposal method, however, was to pass on the wastes to another disposal operation, with no questions asked. In 1974, ABM entered into a contractual agreement with Melvin Wade, the president of Eastern Rubber Reclaiming, Inc., to deposit drums loaded with wastes on Wade's property in a densely populated section of downtown Chester, almost directly under the entrance ramp to the Commodore Barry Bridge on the north side of the Delaware River. The agreement provided for approximately three hundred drums of waste per week at a cost of $1.50 each. The EPA estimates that Wade accepted as many as fifty thousand drums of waste from ABM before his operation was closed.

The huge shipments of drums were stacked in several locations on Wade's property. Wade made more money on the drums, "whenever he needed it," by opening them and pouring the contents onto the ground or into lagoons on his property and selling the empty drums at $6.00 each to a local recycler. Tanker trucks filled with hazardous wastes were also allowed to discharge their contents on the grounds of Eastern Rubber Reclaiming. Following surveillance of the open operation of Eastern Rubber Reclaiming, from the vantage point of the Commodore Barry Bridge, the facility was raided in the fall of 1977.

Wade, a well-known local entrepreneur, apparently could not understand what the fuss was all about. He had been openly carrying on this practice for years and didn't seem concerned when told the drums' contents were highly dangerous. The thousands of leaking drums found stacked at the Wade site posed a major fire and explosion hazard. State environmental officials were also concerned about toxic fumes drifting from the site into the surrounding residential area, and about the leaching and surface drainage of thousands of gallons of toxic material into the river.

On February 2, 1978, before a proper inventory and cleanup could be carried out, the site exploded into flames. It was a spectacular fire. Dozens of drums of toxic waste were hurled hundreds of feet into the air. Huge clouds of toxic smoke blanketed the area, hospitalizing some forty-two firemen sent to put out the blaze. A Philadelphia paper described the fire as "sending roaring balls of flame high into the air," closing the Commodore Barry Bridge for several hours. Most of the drums on-site were destroyed by the fire, and only about forty-five hundred remained intact. When the smoke cleared, inspectors also found several tanker trucks filled with waste abandoned at the site.

The site, in 1981, threatened the surrounding community. The ground remained saturated with high concentrations of highly toxic chemicals, including methacrylic acid, xylene, isopropyl benzene, various other synthetic organic chemicals, and oils. The EPA has estimated that it will cost taxpayers over $1.5 million to clean up the Wade site. Although court action against Wade and ABM is pending, it is unlikely that any cleanup funds will be collected, since both companies are now bankrupt.

The ease with which ABM and Eastern Rubber Reclaiming were allowed to openly operate an illegal dumping operation sparked an investigation into city inspection of the site. Two city inspectors were indicted for taking bribes to ignore the illegal Chester operations. One of the inspectors pleaded guilty to accepting $21,000; the other inspector and ABM's Tyson are awaiting trial.

Other Illegal Waste Operations in Pennsylvania

The ABM operation is just the tip of the iceberg in Pennsylvania. In Philadelphia alone, during the last three months of 1979, the state arrested two employees of other industrial-waste facilities for illegal dumping. Gray Brothers, a local trucking firm, was charged with obtaining hazardous wastes, including large quantities of trichloroethylene, from a local manufacturer and dumping them in an open field. Another company, Natural Liquid Waste Co., which hauled approximately fifteen thousand gallons of liquid industrial wastes per day from a manufacturing plant, has been accused of dumping them into a working rock quarry. State officials fear that the wastes have already contaminated local groundwater supplies.

The huge concentrations of industry, miles of open space, and lax enforcement have made Pennsylvania the new waste capital of the East. In recent years, illegal dumping of toxic wastes has taken a dramatic upturn in the state. Donald A. Lazarchik, director of Pennsylvania's Bureau of Land Protection, says, "The midnight dumper is one of our most serious problems." Keith Welks says Lazarchik's remarks are an understatement.

Who Is Responsible for Illegal Dumping?

Just who bears the major responsibility for illegal dumping is difficult to define. While there is considerable interest in the preeminent roles of high profits and crime, these factors may well be secondary to the lack of available legitimate hazardous waste disposal facilities. This deficiency is made more critical by the extreme inadequacy of regulatory resources at the state level, jurisdictional problems between states, and the failure of the federal government to implement its legislative mandate for hazardous waste disposal.

HIGH PROFITS

One lure of illegal dumping is simply high profit. Carracino, the convicted manager of Chemical Control, Inc., explains: "Wherever there's a fast buck, people are going to get involved. . . . Why treat wastes when you can get $50, $100, $200, and put it in the ground for nothing?"[12]

ORGANIZED CRIME

Is organized crime behind the illegal dumping industry? No one knows for sure. Organized crime has been closely tied to the garbage-hauling industry, especially in the Northeast. It has been further suggested that some hazardous waste operations are syndicate fronts.

Was organized crime involved in the Chemical Control operation? "I only know that I don't belong to a group. I never did and I never will," says Carracino. But when asked about his partners, Carracino says he's not sure. Some New Jersey officials believe Carracino isn't telling the whole story. They suggest that he has been told to keep quiet and that he has been warned by the "mob" that his life and his family are in danger if he says anything. They point to an incident in which they suggest "muscle" was used to let Carracino know what the score is.

On the day Carracino was scheduled to testify before a state grand jury investigating illegal dumping operations in northern New Jersey, both his legs were "accidentally" crushed. Ronald Buchanan, chief of the state Bureau of Hazardous Wastes, told a House subcommittee, "Feedback from the street was that someone drove over his legs."[13] Carracino disputes this allegation and insists that his injury was an "accident." In an attempt to help someone right a wrecked tractor trailer, says Carracino, "I slipped and the trailer turned over on top of me."[14] Accident or no accident, Carracino suddenly became "less than forthcoming in his testimony before the grand jury."*

Whether or not organized crime is a major factor in the hazardous waste disposal industry, illegal dumpers are sometimes known to use Mafia-like tactics. Peter Iacavazzi, president of the now defunct Lackawanna Refuse Removal, Inc. in Old Forge, Scranton, Pennsylvania, was indicted and convicted on several counts of operating an illegal dump. Over one hundred thousand drums filled with industrial wastes were found in an abandoned strip mine that Iacavazzi used as a dump between September, 1978 and March, 1979. The houses of two witnesses who testified against Iacavazzi were subsequently fire-bombed.

"It would be easy to say this is organized crime," said New Jersey's assistant attorney general Stier in a January, 1980 interview, but he found it hard to believe. While admitting organized-crime figures were "peripherally involved" in the mushrooming of illegal dumping operations, he maintained that the major criminal element, although sophisticated and well-financed, was not organized. However, by the fall of 1980, Stier admitted that he had miscalculated the extent to which organized crime was involved in illegal disposal.[15]

Attorney John Fine, an organized-crime investigator who conducted a year-and-a-half-long investigation into illegal haz-

---

*Carracino, who is appealing a two-year sentence for illegal waste dumping, has been a key informant to the New York State Crime Committee and the House Energy and Commerce Subcommittee on Oversight and Investigation, and appeared before a New Jersey Grand Jury several times in January, 1981. Carracino has subsequently claimed immunity as a congressional and state "legislative aide," seeking protection from New Jersey officials who he claims are trying to "suppress his revelations of corruption."

ardous waste disposal in the New York City metropolitan area under the authority of the New York State Attorney General's Office, insists that "racketeering elements dominate" the industry.[16] Fine, a biologist and former assistant to New York's Frank Hogan, a well-known crimebuster, notes that several years ago organized-crime elements firmly entrenched in the garbage-carting industry moved into hazardous waste dumping because it was so lucrative.

When Fine first began his investigation into illegal dumping, he asked New York state law enforcement officials to check the identities of the owners of some sixty New York metropolitan hauling companies. The check revealed that fifty-three of the companies were "associated" with organized crime.

In testimony before the New York State Standing Committees on Environmental Conservation and Health in March, 1980, Fine even tied "some of the same people involved in the Abscam probe" into the illegal transport, storage, and disposal of hazardous wastes. Fine testified:

> George Katz, an associate of Senator Harrison Williams and Mayor Kenneth Givons, is a partner and business colleague of certain persons associated with organized crime. In these business dealings, George Katz is a man who became involved in the waste-disposal business through John Seratelli. Seratelli was a strong-arm hoodlum before his disappearance and onetime bodyguard of underworld czar Waxy Gordon. He is associated with John Albert, Patsy Stamato, and Frank Stamato through the following companies: J&B Disposal Company of New Brunswick, Jersey Sanitation, Edgeborough Landfill, Hudson Jersey Sanitation, and American Collectors.[17]

Fine says that underworld figures have gained control over substantial parts of the hazardous waste disposal industry through the establishment of "front" organizations and the almost instantaneous replacement of companies caught illegally dumping with other phony operations. As an example of the quick-switch, Fine points to Positive Chemical Company, which was found illegally dumping in the Staten Island, New York area in December, 1978. Immediately thereafter, "the company changed its name to Chelsea Terminal, Inc. and continued to receive millions of gallons of toxic waste," Fine asserts. "John Albert, John Lynch, and others were behind the Staten Island operation."[18]

Albert is also allegedly involved in Sampson Tank Cleaning, J&B Disposal, A to Z Chemical Company, Northeast Pollution Control, and Chemical Control, serving on the executive boards of each of these allegedly violative hazardous waste disposal companies. Albert, according to Fine, "has a history of arrests for organized-crime related activities." He was indicted in Massachusetts for chemical dumping activities. And, in the fall of 1980, he was indicted for illegal activities involving the operations of Chemical Control.

New Jersey crime investigators also linked Albert, whom they identified as a "soldier for the Frank Trevi (formerly Genovese) family," with a New York Fulton Fish Market operation. According to a November, 1979 memorandum, fish dealer Joseph Lapi, reputedly another crime figure, was often seen at Chemical Control, talking to Albert.

Lapi allegedly lent money to Albert for the Chemical Control operation and "made frequent trips to the site to pick up money for organized crime."[19]

The web of illegitimate, "mob"-controlled businesses expands even further, Fine asserts, once one begins to look at the business arrangements of each of these suspect companies. Fine's investigation showed that industrial wastes were shipped by Sampson Tank Cleaning and dumped in "roll-off units, garbage bins," owned by Jersey Sanitation, Inc. of East Brunswick, New Jersey. Jersey Sanitation is owned by "George Katz and his family, Patsy Stamato, Frank Stamato, Sr., and others," Fine observes. The Stamatos, George Katz, John Albert, and Eugene Conlon all sit on the board or are officers of J&B Disposal.[20] In 1974, when a reporter attempted to obtain information from J&B Disposal and Jersey Sanitation, he was referred to Conlon and Albert by one of Stamato's accountants. One newspaper account noted: "Stamato's Bergen County operation is involved with Catena, widely regarded in law-enforcement agencies as the successor to Vito Genovese, in the Cosa Nostra, 'boss of bosses.'"[21]

According to Fine, when Chemical Control was searched, an agreement between Carracino and Anthony Rizzo of A. Rizzo Carting was discovered. Rizzo was supposed to act as a "dealer" for Chemical Control and also hauled waste to Chelsea. Rizzo was indicted by Fine's task force for landfill takeovers and illegal dumping in Rockland County, New York. Fine believes that organized-crime control of hazardous waste dumping stretches well beyond New Jersey. An investigation he began in 1977 concerning a landfill operation in Ramapo, New York convinced him that organized crime was illegally dumping toxic chemicals in several areas of New York and had tried, in some cases successfully, to take over several landfills to further its control over dumping. In July, 1980, Fine described how those associated with organized crime had used violence to take over the operation of a dump near the New York/New Jersey border:

> One of the unsuccessful bids was apparently a disguised bid for Carmine and Salvatore Franco. The surprised low bidder, however, took the contract.
>
> Carmine and Salvatore Franco, with the intervention of one George Berkowitz, a Rockland office building cleaning contractor, and the employer and close associate of Ramapo's Solid Waste Director in charge of supervising the landfill for the Town, wanted to dump New Jersey garbage in the landfill, which was a clear violation since the dump was subsidized by the Town and was only for Ramapo Town garbage.
>
> Subsequently, the Francos wanted to buy out the contractor's operation.
>
> Shortly thereafter, the original landfill operator's house was set on fire while his two little daughters were inside.
>
> After the arson, the operator sold out to Carmine and Salvatore Franco.[22]

Investigators probing the operations of the dump after the takeover occurred were also threatened. "A sheriff's car was cut off the road. A police officer was surrounded in New Jersey and he was menaced with a shotgun. A town environmental employee was threatened [and] his family was threatened," said Fine.[23]

Fine also found evidence of organized-crime involvement in the dumping of toxic wastes in Orange County, New York. In a taped interview between a supervisor of the Service Corporation of America (SCA) of Boston and a waste hauler, the hauler described the dumping of toxic wastes, including corrosives and dyes, into a pit near a hospital in Harriman, New York.* Directly across from the hospital is a municipal water well.[24]

In the interview, the hauler also described how Jeffrey Gaess, who Fine described as "proprietor of one of the toxic waste companies," C&D Disposal Service, a subsidiary of SCA, had "paid off" a local official to keep his mouth shut about the illegal dumping operation. Anthony Gaess is a defendant in the New Jersey Kin-Buc toxic waste landfill case.

Fine's investigation has disclosed other "mob figures." Matthew ("Matty the Horse") Ianello, Joseph Fiorillo (known to investigators as "Joe Garbage"), and Michael and Vincent Fiorillo (owners of Duchess Sanitation) are also involved in illegal dumping operations, says Fine. A notebook found in a New Jersey raid provided a link between Fiorillo and yet another "gangster," Charles Mucillo. The notebook allegedly contained the entry "Fiorillo friend Charles Mucillo." Mucillo's nineteen-year-old son, according to Fine, ran an illegal toxic waste dumping operation that was put out of business when his company was caught illegally dumping toxic wastes into a Connecticut gravel pit owned by C. Stanton Gallop.

Duchess Sanitation's routes were taken over by DV Waste Control, which allegedly dumped toxic wastes mixed with sewage sludge at Merion Blue Grass Sod Farm in Wawayanda, New York. DV is run by Vincent DeVito, who, according to

---

*SCA, which grossed $270 million in 1980 and is listed on the New York Stock Exchange, has been the subject of repeated federal and state investigations since its rapid growth in the 1970s. It now operates disposal facilities in thirty-two states and owns the largest waste-treatment plant in Model City, New York, near Niagara Falls. In May, 1980, SCA Services of Georgia (a subsidiary of SCA Services, Inc. of Boston) and three other waste disposal companies—Browning Ferris Industries (BFI) of Georgia, Inc., of Atlanta, Georgia; Waste Systems, Inc., of Lake City, Galveston, a subsidiary of Waste Management, Inc., of Oak Brook, Illinois; and Complete Refuse Removal, Inc., of Smyrna, Galveston—were indicted for a price-fixing conspiracy. According to testimony on May 27, 1981, by the FBI and the New Jersey State Police before the House Energy and Commerce Subcommittee on Oversight and Investigation, SCA had participated in an illegal system of territorial allocation of customers mediated by organized crime in New Jersey. More recently, Central Intelligence Agency Director William Casey's role as lawyer for SCA has been the subject of an investigation by the House Intelligence Committee.

Fine, is not only Tommy Milo's partner in the Al Turi landfill, but a "loan shark." DV was later purchased by C&D. All County Environmental, another carting company, was also found dumping alleged toxic wastes at the sod farm.

Fine asserts that his attempts to rout out the organized-crime figures involved in illegal dumping were frustrated by the political connections between alleged crime figures and powerful politicians in New York. Authority for Fine's investigation was terminated in the spring of 1980. A number of federal and state crime-investigation organizations are now looking into Fine's charges. In late 1980, a number of the individuals accused by Fine were indicted for illegal dumping and hauling as well as conspiracy.

On October 17, 1980, a New Jersey grand jury indicted two carting-company trade associations, twenty-four corporations, and twenty-eight individuals for allegedly participating in a conspiracy to control the garbage-collection industry in nine northern New Jersey counties. Duane Marine Salvage Corporation of Middlesex, New Jersey and A. Rizzo Carting of Wayne, New Jersey were among the companies indicted. According to the indictment, representatives of the companies involved in the alleged conspiracy used to meet each week either in the Crow's Nest Restaurant in South Hackensack, New Jersey or at Snuffy's II Restaurant in Somerville, New Jersey to discuss business. The indictment further alleges that a Browning-Ferris Industries (BFI) vice-president was also involved in the conspiracy.* Did this conspiracy also involve the illegal dumping of hazardous wastes? Why did it take the state of New Jersey so long to move on these companies? These questions remain unanswered.

LACK OF ADEQUATE DISPOSAL FACILITIES

At the heart of the hazardous waste disposal problem is the extreme scarcity of licensed and legitimate operations. In New Jersey, for instance, in July, 1976, the state closed Kin-Buc, the only remaining licensed hazardous waste dump. Approved as a solid-waste disposal facility in 1970, Kin-Buc is a forty-acre

---

*BFI has been cited several times for water, air, and waste-disposal violations (see Chapter 6).

landfill site in Edison Township. Through the continued dumping of solid waste, it reached a height of eighty-five feet above ground level. By 1976, the facility was accepting approximately 60 million gallons of liquid chemical waste and 110 million pounds of solid waste per year. After the site was closed, there just wasn't any other place to dump these wastes. Not surprisingly, hazardous waste generators gladly paid whoever appeared at the factory gates to haul away their ever increasing stockpiles. No questions were asked.

By 1977, state environmental officials identified the closing of Kin-Buc as the root of their illegal dumping problem. However, they insisted that illegal dumping was only a "temporary phenomenon."

The state of Pennsylvania is the nation's third-largest producer of industrial wastes. A state study estimates that Pennsylvania's seventeen thousand manufacturing plants produce as much as 3.5 million tons of waste each year, a figure expected to grow to 4.5 million by 1983. However, there are no approved hazardous-waste landfill operations in the entire state, although there are seventy-five private industrial and thirty municipal landfills that have been previously approved for solid and industrial wastes. The amount of hazardous waste accepted by these licensed landfill operations is unknown.

LACK OF ADEQUATE STATE REGULATION

The lack of adequate disposal facilities for hazardous wastes is only paralleled by the lack of regulatory mechanisms at the state level. Pennsylvania was one of the first states to crack down on unsafe dumping of garbage and other solid wastes, yet, in 1969, when Pennsylvania's waste law was passed, the problem was exclusively defined in terms of garbage and trash. The issue of hazardous industrial wastes was simply not contemplated. Aggressive enforcement of the law in the early 1970s resulted in the closure of most of the state's landfills. "Unfortunately," says Keith Welks, "there was a much greater lag in perceiving the problem of hazardous waste disposal."

Hazardous waste regulation in Pennsylvania during the 1970s was almost nonexistent. Until the fall of 1979, the agency in charge of regulating solid waste, which is also responsible for hazardous waste, had a field staff of only twenty for the entire state. In 1979, only one person handled waste disposal full time for the Philadelphia area. The state had no hazardous waste disposal law until 1980. When confronted with a list of 163 hazardous waste disposal sites, developed through a survey conducted by the House Oversight and Investigations Subcommittee, state officials admitted that they were aware of only about 20 percent of these sites. They further admitted that there are as many as one-hundred-ten thousand unapproved industrial solid-waste disposal facilities in the state and that as much as 80 percent of all industrial waste produced in the state is inadequately disposed of and inadequately regulated.

Many of the state's current problems have been blamed on Governor Thornburgh's administration's failure to provide adequate staff and resources. Less than 2 percent of Pennsylvania's environmental budget went toward waste regulation in 1978 and 1979. Although the Thornburgh administration has declared hazardous waste regulation its number-one environmental priority, a 1980 report charged that "the Secretary of the Department of Environmental Resources (DER) has also directed the DER to approve more landfill permits more quickly" in a possible effort to "beat" the issuance of federal hazardous waste disposal regulations.[25]

JURISDICTIONAL PROBLEMS BETWEEN STATES

Some states have been quick to attempt to solve their hazardous waste problems by exporting them across state lines. The crackdown on illegal dumping in New Jersey, for example, the nation's second largest generator of industrial waste, together with the continued absence of any approved hazardous waste disposal facilities in the state, has resulted in the illegal dumping in Pennsylvania of wastes that were previously illegally dumped in New Jersey.

Data from the New Jersey manifest system in 1979 indicates that 70 percent of its hazardous wastes are being shipped to dump sites in Pennsylvania. But environmental officials in Pennsylvania are skeptical:

[The manifest data provided by New Jersey] many times contain a substantial number of entries of places we've [state of Pennsylvania regulators] never heard of and cannot locate or identify and which we believe do not exist. . . . I think that New Jersey's conclusion is that the waste went to Pennsylvania. I don't know that that's true.[26]

The results of an independent investigation by the *Philadelphia Inquirer* appear to support these suspicions.

According to the New Jersey manifest system, in a brief period in 1978, 128,000 pounds of hazardous wastes were shipped from New Jersey to Reclamation Resources, Inc., in Lansdale, Pennsylvania. When asked about the 8,910 pounds of cyanide residues the manifest showed were delivered to his facility, Leroy Beaver, operator of the landfill, said, "I wouldn't touch it." With regard to the over 2,200 pounds of asbestos allegedly shipped to the site, Beaver answered, "I take none of that whatsoever. I wouldn't have any place to put it." And concerning the over 2,200 pounds of the 2,4,5-T herbicide wastes, Beaver explained, "I don't even accept that."[27] Pennsylvania environmental officials are convinced that Beaver is telling the truth.

Where did all these toxic wastes go? Keith Welks believes they never left New Jersey:

If I were a waste hauler picking something up in south Jersey and I was going to dump it illegally, I wouldn't pick a place far away outside the state. . . . We have found that waste haulers do not drive ten miles to dump illegally when they can drive five miles.[28]

The New Jersey manifest system, which tracks the movement of hazardous wastes within the state from point of generation through transportation, storage, and final recycling or disposal, is a key element in the state's hazardous waste regulatory system. It is also a key element in the federal system of hazardous waste regulations. The manifest system is not an enforcement tool and is only as good as the information plugged into it. It takes enormous staff resources and constant surveillance to ensure that the manifest entries are correct.

At the present time the manifest system is of no value [admits Assistant Attorney General Stier]. The information in the system must be constantly cross-referenced so that information that flows out of it will trigger some response. . . . The manifest system relies on the good faith of people. And if you are a recycler and you say it's been incinerated, but it's been dumped in the sewer, how do you know?[29]

The New Jersey manifest system is designed to stop at the state border. This proviso seriously impairs the effectiveness of the system. A hauler may simply indicate that he takes the wastes to a site outside the state unknown to state regulators, when in reality he's dumping them along the road. A special regional system of manifests will be needed to combat this problem.

Perhaps an even more critical element in the growing cold war between New Jersey and Pennsylvania is a law prohibiting the movement of garbage and hazardous wastes into New Jersey. The constitutionality of the law was challenged by the city of Philadelphia, which, because of this law, faced a critical solid-waste disposal problem. The matter was finally decided by the United States Supreme Court in June, 1978. The Court held that the New Jersey law was parochial, in violation of the commerce clause of the U.S. Constitution, and "protectionist." In delivering the opinion, Supreme Court Justice Potter Stewart wrote, "What is crucial is the attempt by one state to isolate itself from a problem common to many by erecting a barrier against the movement of interstate trade."[30] In its concluding paragraph, the Court foreshadowed the present flip-flop in Pennsylvania/New Jersey waste relations. "Tomorrow, cities in New Jersey may find it expedient or necessary to send their waste into Pennsylvania."[31]

Another major jurisdictional problem behind the continuing illegal dumping problem is fragmentation of waste disposal regulatory responsibilities among several agencies within each state and between state and federal agencies. There is, in many cases, an almost total lack of cross-communication between these groups. In New Jersey, for example, Stier found that he was working at cross purposes with the state Department of Environmental Protection. "We would be investigating a recycling operation while they would be licensing it," he said.

Overview

Illegal dumping is not simply a problem for New Jersey, Pennsylvania, or even the Northeast. It has become a national problem of rapidly increasing dimensions. Illegal dumping operations have been identified in Kentucky, Texas, Ohio, Michigan, California, North Carolina, and many other states. Largely as a result of recent crackdowns in New Jersey and Pennsylvania, illegal dumping operations are also becoming more sophisticated. We are now seeing a trend away from midnight dumping of drums off the backs of trucks toward more complex sewering operations, in which it is extremely difficult to locate the underground disposal line carrying the waste away from the disposal site.

To date, neither state nor federal governments have been able to make any appreciable impact on the problem. As the crackdown begins in one state, illegal operations simply move elsewhere or become more sophisticated. The lure of the fast and big buck, the lack of adequate disposal facilities, the ease with which illegal operations have secured the unofficial sanction of state regulatory agencies, the almost total lack of reliable intelligence on where and how what waste is going and when, and the paucity of enforcement action have all created a climate in which illegal disposal has been able to flourish.

Chances are that the situation will further deteriorate over the next five years as the chemical industry attempts to dispose of not only the wastes they now generate, but also the millions of tons being stored pending the development of new disposal facilities. It seems certain that more companies will try to dump their wastes wherever possible to avoid having them on hand when the new regulations become effective. It also seems certain that if the new regulations cost too much, that is, if companies wishing to dispose of their wastes legally are forced to pay what they consider prohibitively high prices, more will choose to "go outside the system" to illegal dumpers with their hazardous wastes.

In 1980 the U.S. Department of Justice began taking this matter seriously. The Land and Natural Resources Division of the department beefed up its staff from less than five to over fifteen attorneys to handle civil suits against illegal dumpers. District attorneys and Federal Bureau of Investigation staffs throughout the country were geared up to begin an all-out assault on this new form of white-collar crime. A national hazardous waste task force was created, combining the staffs of the EPA and the

Department of Justice, which works with regions and states to prepare investigations and court actions against illegal dumpers. Bills passed by Congress in late 1980 call for massive increases in investigative staffs, legal powers, and criminal penalties for illegal dumpers. These new efforts to attack the problem of illegal dumping should pay off, but it would be folly to expect any significant improvement in the near future.* There clearly are limitations to exclusively penal approaches. While the civil and criminal penalties for illegal disposal must be high enough to discourage wrongdoers, if they are too high, ultimate recovery becomes impossible.

Most analyses indicate that the major causes of illegal dumping are industry irresponsibility or ignorance, combined with government laxity. Illegal dumpers, says Stier, "have depended on government's inefficiency, inadequate resources, and unwillingness to peel away the layers of insulation" around dummy operations that protect illegal dumpers from indictment and prosecution.

Vigorous enforcement action will be an important key to reducing illegal dumping. Manifests must be cross-referenced and checked. The cop on the beat must be alert to the signs of illegal dumping. Citizens must scrutinize the movement of tanker trucks and trucks carrying drummed industrial wastes. And illegal dumpers must be stopped from obtaining loads from generators. One way of encouraging generators to be careful is for states to write laws making the generators responsible for the cleanup of any wastes that they allowed such questionable haulers to take away.

The near-future prospects for stopping the midnight dumpers are not good. The problem is urgent.

---

*While the Department of Justice in the Carter Administration brought over 60 actions against illegal dumpers between 1979 and late 1980, the Reagan Administration had brought only a single case by November, 1981.

PART III

The Law

I've probably killed more people by passing
the Resources Conservation and Recovery Act.
I worked very hard for it. As a result,
they're breeding and dumping waste as fast as
they can before it takes effect.

WILLIAM SANJOUR
former chief, Hazardous Waste Assessment Branch,
Environmental Protection Agency, October 8, 1979

CHAPTER 8

Legislation of Hazardous Wastes

Although the problem of hazardous waste disposal has been building up for over a century, government action to regulate toxic wastes from mining, agriculture, and industry has been delayed and sporadic in comparison with government action on other public health concerns. Indeed, only when the disaster at Love Canal captured the imagination of the news media and invaded the nightmares of the public did the problem attract serious attention.

Legislation before Love Canal

Before Love Canal, government had viewed toxic waste materials as an insignificant after-effect of industrial production. Officials working on the problem of toxic wastes struggled unnoticed and often alone. State policies reflected the random competence and interest of individual politicians and bureaucrats. Something industry wanted to throw away, it seemed, was unworthy of serious attention.

Love Canal changed all that, perhaps forever. Now, each new regulation, every proposed dump or incinerator, carries with it the potential of conflict and confrontation. Television crews watch orphan storage sites for signs of a spectacular fire or other disaster. Arid Federal Register notices receive front-page headlines and are immediately scrutinized by battalions of corporate lawyers. America has yet to decide what it will do with the millions of tons of poisons that no one wants. But since Love Canal, it is clear that future decisions in this area will be made after extensive, public, and noisy debate.

EVOLUTION OF PUBLIC HEALTH LEGISLATION

In 1798, Congress authorized the government to establish hospitals for American seamen, a program that eventually evolved into the present Public Health Service. More than a century later, another federal agency in this field came into being, the Food and Drug Administration, charged with preventing the adulteration of food and the sale of ineffective or dangerous medicines. A few decades passed. Public health remained largely a state and local concern, but Congress tentatively began to focus on new kinds of health problems, those associated with pollution and the environment. Air and water pollution came to congressional attention in the late 1960s. Congress became aware that, in many cases, pollutants generated by cities or industrial plants in one state were being carried by winds or currents into another. Instances occurred in which virtually all of the pollution put out by one state drifted into another, yet the state on the receiving end had no legal recourse to force a cleanup.

In 1964, Congress passed the first law aimed at interstate air-pollution problems. In 1968, the federal government assumed a role in water-pollution regulation. Public concern about environmental issues increased throughout the 1960s, peaking in 1970 with the first Earth Day.

Congress responded to this new public interest by strengthening laws that had already been passed to deal with air and water pollution. The center of most of this activity was the Senate Subcommittee on Air and Water Pollution, chaired by Senator Edmund Muskie, a Democrat from Maine. Muskie and his Republican counterpart, John Sherman Cooper of Kentucky, assembled around them a talented staff of lawyers, led by Muskie's key aide, Leon Billings, and by Tom Jorling,* who worked for Cooper, and later for Cooper's successor on the subcommittee, Republican Caleb Boggs of Delaware.

By the time the first Earth Day celebration occurred, Muskie had earned a reputation as "Mr. Clean" and was considering running for president. But Muskie's record on pollution control came under attack in the spring of 1970. A team of researchers organized by Ralph Nader published a book, *The Vanishing Air,* blasting Muskie for writing laws that were too weak and not enforceable and for paying too much attention to the views of the chairman of the Public Works Committee, West Virginia Democrat Jennings Randolph, whom the Nader researchers claimed did not want to crack down on corporate polluters.

PUBLIC HEALTH AND ENVIRONMENTAL LEGISLATION AFTER EARTH DAY

Encouraged by the new public interest displayed on Earth Day, and stung by the Nader criticism, the Subcommittee on Air and Water Pollution under Muskie and Cooper began to write a new generation of pollution-control laws, far tougher than their predecessors. Instead of focusing on the interstate features of pollution, the new environmental laws of the 1970s relied upon the general power of the federal government to regulate businesses engaged in interstate commerce. In this way, all the pollution put out by industry could be reduced, whether or not it could be shown to drift across state boundaries or to enter interstate rivers.

While the new laws used the very broad congressional power to regulate business, they initially focused on the classical interstate forms of pollution, air and water. In 1970, Congress adopted a Clean Air Act drawn up by Muskie's subcommittee and their counterparts on the Health Subcommittee of the House Commerce Committee, led by Florida Democrat Paul Rogers. The new air act promised Americans that by 1975 the air everywhere would be safe and healthy.

---

*Later assistant administrator for water and waste-management programs of the EPA.

In 1972, Muskie was able to win from a reluctant House Public Works Committee agreement on a water-pollution bill promising Americans that their waterways would be "swimmable and fishable" by 1983.* In 1973, Rogers took the initiative in obtaining passage of legislation mandating that the Environmental Protection Agency (EPA) ensure the quality of the nation's drinking water supplies, surface and subterranean.†

Thus, by 1973, Congress had enacted laws that appeared to require the rapid elimination of air- and water-pollution problems from the American scene. But while the new legislation sounded tough, those close to the problem knew that it was full of loopholes.

The air and water laws focused on cleaning up the "four pipes"—factory smokestacks, automobile tailpipes, city sewers, and factory sewers—known as "point sources." The laws required those responsible for pollution from such point sources to obtain state or federal permits limiting the allowable amount of pollution from each such source. The limits for each smokestack or drainage pipe were set pollutant by pollutant—so much carbon monoxide and sulfur oxides into the air per hour, or so many pounds of suspended solids per day into the river. By continually reducing the level of pollution permitted from each pipe, the total level of pollution discharged into the environment would also be reduced.

Unfortunately, less easily regulated "non-point" sources also play an important role in pollution. "Non-point" sources include oil wastes; asbestos from brake linings; worn tire fragments that wash off city streets into rivers or blow into the air; pesticides and fertilizers that drain off farmlands into streams or vaporize into the atmosphere; and toxic wastes stored in settling ponds or lagoons or dumped in landfills, which are carried away by the winds or rain into air and water.

Worse, while the relatively few pollutants regulated by these laws account for most of the tonnage of air and water pollution, thousands of other agents in industrial use have the

---

*The Clean Water Act of 1972.

†The Safe Drinking Water Act of 1973.

potential to contaminate the environment. And, of these agents, many are so toxic that even trace quantities are very dangerous.*

The air and water laws required the EPA to strictly limit the emissions of such toxic pollutants, but gave the agency no guidance as to what, if anything, was supposed to happen to toxic agents once industry was prevented from disposing of them into the air or the waters. Industry was required to capture toxic agents before they escaped from a smokestack or outfall. These captured agents were then designated as wastes, but there were no federal guidelines about what to do with them. Thus, the disposal of waste materials, even very toxic ones, remained to be solved well after extensive government action had been taken to regulate the same materials as air or water pollutants.

By the mid-1970s, for example, in no state was it legal to use dangerous pesticides except under restricted conditions. Yet, in thirty-one states, unused pesticide wastes or pesticide containers could legally be disposed of in any way that suited the whim of the user. And, since 1958, it has been illegal for any substance that has been found to cause cancer to be deliberately added to food. Yet forty-five states still allowed the release of such carcinogenic materials into the environment as waste, even when this meant the accidental contamination of food supplies by these wastes entering soils, air, or water.

Since 1972, the federal government has required every industry or municipality discharging toxic chemicals from a sewage pipe or outfall to have a permit specifying the nature and amounts of chemicals discharged. Yet, in the mid-1970s, less than one quarter of the states had similar discharge limits on the same toxic chemicals seeping from a dump site into the same river. The EPA had established limits on the concentration of lead particulates that may be emitted into the air from lead industries such as smelters. Yet, the state of California discovered that one

---

*For example, the Clean Air Act regulates the various chemicals formed in the air from automotive emissions of hydrocarbons and nitrogen oxides as if they were one compound—photochemical oxidants. The EPA measures the level of oxidants—the common Los Angeles smog—by measuring one of the most common compounds formed—ozone. However, the smog mixture contains other oxidants—such as peroxyacetylnitrate (PAN)—some more dangerous than ozone. And these are not effectively measured or regulated at all.

hazardous waste disposal site was emitting an atmospheric concentration of lead one hundred times as high as that allowed around a smelter. Such hazardous waste disposal sites were not required to obtain permits from the EPA.[1]

ATTEMPTED HAZARDOUS WASTE LEGISLATION IN 1974

Since the early 1970s, Senator Randolph had been calling for congressional legislation to fill the gap left by the failure to regulate dangerous materials disposed of as wastes. In 1970, Congress passed a new Solid Waste Act, a compromise that did not resolve the issue of how big the federal role in solid-waste disposal would be, but which did call for a study of hazardous waste practices in the United States, with the results to be submitted to Congress.

But hostility was building between the Nixon administration and environmentalists. The administration had created the EPA, to which authority over solid waste, as well as air and water pollution, was transferred. The EPA was not sure it really cared about its solid-waste responsibilities, including the responsibility for hazardous waste. "This program was subjected to benign as well as malignant neglect. . . . The host agency gave the Solid Waste Management Program all the tender loving care of an unwanted orphan in an institution which at that time seemed to regard only air and water pollution as legitimate offspring."[2]

As a result, the comprehensive report called for by the Solid Waste Act of 1970 was not issued until 1974, and little public attention was given to the problem. Thus, Randolph's proposal for a hazardous waste bill never developed much momentum, even though he was in a powerful position as the chairman of the Senate Public Works Committee, to which Muskie's Environmental Pollution Subcommittee* reported.

But by 1974, Congress was ready to focus on the general problem of solid-waste disposal, of which hazardous waste problems were a part. Hearings were held in both the House and Senate on proposed legislation. Paul Rogers, chairman of the Health Subcommittee of the House Commerce Committee, opened the House hearings on March 27, 1974. Rogers was

---

*Formerly the Subcommittee on Air and Water Pollution.

angry because the Nixon administration was refusing to carry out programs enacted by previous Congresses to help municipalities deal with the problem of disposing of their accumulation of garbage and other solid wastes. Rogers was also angry because the federal budget for solid-waste programs was being cut by 82 percent; because the EPA was supporting an extension of New York's and New Jersey's permits to dispose of their garbage by dumping it off the coast, even though this dumping had created "a dead sea"; because, "although EPA undertook a program to reduce the number of open dumps . . . three years ago, we now have more open dumps than we had when the program began"; and because the annual report of the president's environmental advisors, the Council on Environmental Quality (CEQ), had spent only 11 pages on solid waste, out of a total of 1,200 pages. Rogers commented that "the Environmental Protection Agency, perhaps because of the action of the Office of Management and Budget, seems to be expending more effort in dismantling this program than in administering it."[3] And, indeed, the administration was quite forthrightly trying to keep the problem of disposing of municipal trash and garbage a state and local responsibility. Nixon did not want to create a major federal role in solid-waste disposal, as Congress had already done in air and water pollution.

Instead, the administration proposed that the federal role in the solid-waste area be limited to dealing with disposal of toxic wastes. The administration submitted a law regulating hazardous waste management and suggested that this law be the substitute for a federal program in the general area of solid wastes.*

Rogers did not agree with the administration's position. He favored a comprehensive solid-waste bill, one that would require the states to develop overall plans for the safe disposal of

---

*Tom Williams, an EPA official who was close to the internal discussions of these bills, believes that many of those who supported action on hazardous waste within the Nixon administration sought to prevent the EPA from pursuing its interest in efforts to reduce the volume of solid waste generated. "Without doubt, the need for legislation to regulate hazardous waste received support from those who dislike EPA's emphasis on source reduction. They favored legislation whose commitment to resource conservation would be more titular than substantial, and probably surmised that implementing a hazardous waste regulatory program could keep all the program's employees fully occupied and then some."[4]

all their solid wastes. He wanted a strong federal role in reviewing and approving these plans and extensive federal financial assistance to carry them out.

Rogers did, however, want the federal government to ensure that hazardous wastes got special treatment. Indeed, Rogers took a much more encompassing view of what constituted "hazardous wastes" than did the Nixon administration witnesses who appeared before the Health Subcommittee. The administration took the position that only a few, exceptionally hazardous types of materials generated by selected industries needed federal attention as "hazardous."

Rogers continually pressed administration officials to justify this narrow focus. Wasn't it hazardous, he asked, when ordinary garbage caused half the fires in New York City? Didn't the EPA think it was hazardous when fires from open dumps in New Jersey sent smoke swirling over the New Jersey Turnpike and caused accidents? Wasn't it hazardous when open dumps killed children playing on them or contaminated wells? In short, as Rogers put it, "I think we have reached the point where 'hazardous' does not have much meaning when you talk about solid waste." In his view, the entire range of solid-waste problems posed hazards and required federal action.[5]

EPA witnesses responded feebly. It was common knowledge that EPA administrator Russell Train and most of his staff had not favored the Nixon-imposed cutbacks in solid-waste problems. When Train and other officials appeared, Rogers went to great lengths to show that he knew that the EPA and its experts did not agree with the position they were seeming to support, but were simply following White House orders.

The effect of the White House stance, however, was to make hazardous waste regulation seem noncontroversial. Since both congressional environmentalists like Rogers and their foes in the administration agreed that there should be a federal role in regulating hazardous waste, no one paid much attention to exactly how this should be done.

Of all the other witnesses Rogers called, only two even mentioned the hazardous waste section of the bill, and the committee failed to follow up with questions to even these two witnesses. The bulk of the hearings were spent on things that, in Washington in 1974, were seen as the real guts of the solid-waste problem—bans on throwaway bottles, the problem of finding municipal dump sites, the burning of garbage to generate electricity, the problem of how to get rid of junked automobiles, and the impact of federal tax policies on recycling.

Similar hearings were held on the Senate side in 1974 by Democratic Senator Gary Hart of Colorado. But these hearings, like those held by Rogers, were more expressive of the ongoing struggle between congressional leaders and the administration over proposed cutbacks in federal environmental programs than they were of a commitment to pass a bill. Because the administration and Congress could not agree what to do about nonhazardous solid waste, or indeed if such a thing existed, no action was actually taken on regulating hazardous waste, the one subject on which there appeared to be general agreement. Congress recessed in 1975 without passing any solid-waste legislation.

The Resource Conservation and Recovery Act of 1976 (RCRA)

HISTORY

The Congress that convened in January, 1975 faced a very different situation. Richard Nixon was no longer president. His pardon by President Ford had triggered a Democratic landslide that left lopsided Democratic margins in both houses of Congress. Prominent Democratic leaders boasted of a "vetoproof Congress." Initially it appeared that the congressional advocates of a major federal role in solid-waste management could realize their dream. Senator Randolph reintroduced his comprehensive solid-waste bill, as did Rogers and Pennsylvania Democratic Congressman Fred Rooney.

The new congressional interest in solid-waste legislation, however, was eclipsed by other pending bills. The Democratic landslide offered environmentalists the hope that Congress would finally pass controversial legislation to regulate overall toxic-substance problems. Previous proposals to pass a Toxic

Substances Control Act (TSCA) had foundered under heavy counterpressure from industry, particularly the chemical industry, led by the Chemical Manufacturing Association (CMA).* Dow Chemical continued to fight against any form of a toxic-substances law. But the remainder of the chemical industry decided that Congress would inevitably pass some law, and they combined forces to try to shape TSCA in a direction that would interfere with their practices and profits as little as possible. By contrast, the industry decided that the proposed hazardous waste sections of the solid-waste law were relatively unimportant. Only the actual haulers of hazardous waste, a small and not very influential industry, saw RCRA as a major threat.

Environmental groups also put most of their effort into the development of TSCA. Linda Billings, the Sierra Club's chief lobbyist on toxics problems, spent almost all of her time on TSCA. Environmental Action's lobbyist, Blake Early, worked closely with the Senate Public Works and House Commerce committees to write the hazardous waste sections of the solid-waste law that became RCRA. But Early made a conscious decision not to try to generate much public attention to RCRA. He feared that too much publicity would simply attract attention from industry, which otherwise might remain preoccupied with TSCA.[6]

Even the Ford administration took itself out of the action. Citing the president's opposition to any new federal programs, the new administration refused to resubmit the hazardous waste legislation proposed by its predecessor. By taking a position of simple opposition, the administration lost much of the leverage it might otherwise have had over the early drafting of RCRA.

Thus, the congressional committees in charge of solid waste were under almost no outside pressure, one way or another, in dealing with toxic wastes. Nevertheless, many of the congressional experts on solid waste were deeply concerned about the hazardous waste problem. They saw solid waste as the

---

*Originally the Manufacturing Chemists' Association (MCA), this trade association changed its title in 1979, but is consistently referred to as the Chemical Manufacturing Association (CMA) in this text.

unfinished piece of the job of environmental cleanup. They also felt that much of the hazardous waste problem was the responsibility of Congress, as wastes that previously would have been burnt or dumped into rivers were now being stored on land in response to the earlier congressional air- and water-pollution laws.*

But the leaders of the congressional committees that dealt with the environment were determined that hazardous waste problems would be only one of the subjects covered in the new solid-waste bill. Both Rogers and Randolph suggested that the new legislation should carry a provision requiring each state to develop an overall solid-waste management plan. Rogers even thought that, if a state refused, the administrator of the EPA should draft a plan for the state, just as the air act had provided.

However, in both Houses, strong voices were raised against such a federal intrusion into the management of municipal wastes, and the final bill left such matters with state and local governments, subject only to a requirement that open dumps be phased out.

Oregon Republican Senator Mark Hatfield tried to write into RCRA a ban on throwaway beverage containers, such as the states of Oregon and Vermont had already adopted. Hatfield failed to get such a ban included by the Public Works Committee. He then took his fight to the full Senate, and debate on his proposal occupied over half of the Senate's time.†

Congress also devoted its energy to debating the proper role of the federal government in encouraging or financing so-called "resource recovery" facilities, installations designed to take municipal waste and sort it into such components as glass, ferrous metals, aluminum, plastic, and paper, which could be recy-

---

*The EPA estimated that about two-thirds of the increase in industrial waste generation resulted directly from air and water pollution control regulations, and this figure was frequently cited in the congressional deliberations.[7]

†Of twenty-six pages in the *Congressional Record* devoted to the actual debate on RCRA and amendments to it, approximately fifteen are devoted to debate on the Hatfield amendment and related bottle-bill issues. The environmental movement probably worked ten times as hard on this issue as it did on the hazardous waste sections, and media coverage was at least ten times as great.[8]

cled, reused, or burned to generate electricity. Many hours were spent in committee debating the appropriate federal role in gearing municipalities up for this new wonder.*

In the end, advocates of a major federal role in solid-waste disposal lost virtually every battle in the shaping of RCRA. It was simply no longer true that Democrats in Congress would eagerly vote for any major new federal environmental programs proposed by Muskie and Rogers. But Muskie and Rogers were able to get pretty much what they wanted in the hazardous waste areas. Thus, the hazardous waste sections of RCRA are by far its most powerful and important. Strangely, these sections generated virtually no debate.

For one thing, no one took literally the opposition of the Ford administration to federal regulation of toxic wastes. The EPA still thought that toxics were the most important part of the solid-waste problem. Muskie and Rogers knew this. The declared Ford policy of "no new programs, even for hazardous wastes" flew in the face of congressional reality and the overwhelming Democratic majority.

For another, the industries that ultimately generated toxic wastes—chemicals, petroleum, and mining—were too busy fighting TSCA. They ignored RCRA. Indeed, the CMA welcomed the inclusion of hazardous wastes under RCRA. It gave the industry another reason for arguing against the inclusion of waste hazards in TSCA, which was expected to be a much tougher statute.

Efforts by the waste disposal firms and haulers to influence House and Senate deliberations on toxic wastes were ineffective. Committee staff had prepared a list of fifty-nine incidents in twenty-two states, in which the current practices of the waste disposal industry had endangered the public or the environment. Such evidence neutralized the lobbying of the waste disposal industry, lacking as they were the backing of the far more powerful waste-generating firms.

An additional factor muting controversy over the toxic-waste sections of RCRA was that industry found it almost impos-

---

*Ironically, resource-recovery facilities have proved one of the major technological busts of the 1970s. Few have been built. Fewer still have worked.

sible to argue against safe disposal of toxic waste. They had similarly failed in debates on both the Clean Air and Clean Water Acts to find a basis for arguing against controls on toxic pollutants. Muskie and Rogers knew from this experience that even the most stringently drafted language prohibiting release of toxic materials drew almost no fire from industry. And so it proved with RCRA.

Indeed, the hazardous waste section was strengthened in two important ways. Congressman Rooney wrote into the bill a specific requirement that the EPA establish a "cradle-to-grave" manifest system to keep track of hazardous wastes from the point of generation to final disposal, and the EPA succeeded in convincing the committee to include a wider range of substances in its definition of "hazardous wastes."

Only one major concession had to be made. Budget cutters in the Ford administration's Office of Management and Budget insisted on a procedure permitting hazardous waste disposal facilities to receive "interim permission" to dispose of wastes while the EPA developed regulations under the law. The administration had no intention of giving the EPA enough money and personnel to issue permits promptly to all disposal facilities. It was equally unwilling to shut the industry down for the time required to issue all the permits.

When the House and Senate debated RCRA, the hazardous waste sections were praised in passing. While Senator Randolph declared that the bill "will give the federal government strong, progressive programs in all environmental areas,"[9] virtually no one, either in Congress or among the public, had any notion of what would be required to carry out the mandate of safe disposal of hazardous wastes. Indeed, Congress viewed the problem as a petty oversight resulting from earlier pollution laws, and RCRA as a rather modest mopping-up operation in the triumphant war against pollution.*

---

*For example, the House Commerce Committee reported to other House members that "the Committee believes that the approach taken by this legislation eliminates the last remaining loophole in environmental law, that of unregulated land disposal of discarded materials and hazardous wastes. Further, the Committee believes that this legislation is necessary if other environmental laws are to be both cost and environmentally effective. At present, the federal government is spending billions of

On October 22, 1976, President Ford signed RCRA. It was not all that far from the proposals originally put forth by his Republican predecessor, and while the bill technically violated his administration's stance against "new" programs, it was seen as a small, and in budgetary terms insignificant, violation.*

If Congress had understood the costs, it might have legislated less generously. When it passed the Safe Drinking Water Act, Congress took great care to protect the oil and gas industry from the impact of regulation of deep wells. But Congress enacted RCRA in seeming obliviousness of the possibility that the oil and gas industry relied upon tons and tons of potentially hazardous chemicals, including hydrofluoric and nitric acids, to drill those wells, and that these materials (drilling muds) required disposal—somewhere.

Instead, the tone of the floor debate on RCRA suggests that the hazardous waste problem is one of carelessness, of fly-by-night operators, and poor housekeeping by industry. As we have seen, it is truly the burdensome, complex persona of modern industrialism. What goes up must come down. Congress showed almost no comprehension that, for the industrial machine, what goes in must come out.

HAZARDOUS WASTE PROVISIONS

RCRA contains eight separate titles dealing with a variety of separate issues. Title III is the major hazardous waste section, al-

---

dollars to remove pollutants from the air and water, only to dispose of them on the land in an environmentally unsound manner. The existing methods of land disposal often result in air pollution, subsurface leachates, and surface run-off, which affect air and water quality. This legislation will eliminate the problem and permit the environmental laws to function in a coordinated and effective way."[10] Thus might an engineer of an early steam locomotive have described the act of sitting on the safety valve as an abatement of noise pollution. Without public debate, without controversy, without the formation of a strongly committed and informed public constituency, Congress was shutting down the safety valve—land disposal—left by the earlier air and water laws for disposing of industry's unwanted poisons.

*This was due in large part to the lack of congressional comprehension of the dimensions of the problem. Congress passed the hazardous waste sections of RCRA almost absentmindedly. Except for the key staff and some of the more interested members like Muskie, Randolph, Rooney, and Rogers, almost no one in Congress understood just how widespread were waste disposal practices posing major threats. Congress had no collective notion, it seems, that it would cost billions of dollars to dispose safely of common industrial by-products.

though pieces of other titles also bear on hazardous waste regulation. There are eight major sections to Title III.

Section 3001 requires the administrator of the EPA to publish criteria for identification of hazardous waste materials. At the same time the administrator is required to publish a list of particular substances that fit these criteria and that are to be designated as hazardous wastes. Congress gave the EPA eighteen months to accomplish these tasks, ending in March, 1978.

On the same timetable, Section 3002 provides for the administrator to establish requirements for record keeping, labeling, packing, and transporting of hazardous wastes by the firms that generate such materials. These requirements are to provide for the use of a manifest system "to assure that all hazardous waste generated is designated for treatment, storage, or disposal in treatment, storage, or disposal facilities" for which the EPA has issued a permit. Within the same eighteen months, the EPA was to publish standards under Section 3003 to ensure that transporters of hazardous waste do not endanger "human health or the environment." Hauling firms were also to make use of the manifest system. The EPA's regulations for transporters under Section 3003 were to be consistent with those developed by the Department of Transportation under the Hazardous Materials Transportation Act.

Section 3004 requires the EPA to establish standards for hazardous waste disposal facilities, principally to ensure that all such facilities provide for "treatment, storage or disposal of all such waste received by the facility pursuant to such operating methods, techniques and practices as may be satisfactory to the Administrator."

Section 3005 requires all operators of hazardous waste disposal facilities to receive a permit from the EPA. A permit will establish what quantities of what sorts of wastes the facility is entitled to receive and dispose of, and the site and methods to be used in such disposal. However, as demanded by the Office of Management and Budget, 3005(d) states that any operator who has applied for a permit under the section shall, for the interim while the EPA processes this application, be considered to have complied with the requirements of the act and shall be authorized to receive and dispose of hazardous wastes.

Section 3006 provides for the EPA to delegate authority over hazardous waste management to states that establish programs that are at least as stringent as the EPA program.

Section 3007 requires that inspectors have access to inspect and monitor sites and that such facilities must maintain public records.

Section 3008 provides for both civil and criminal penalties for violators of the hazardous waste sections of RCRA.

Congress also gave the EPA a broader general mandate in Section 7003 of the bill, entitled "Imminent Hazard," stating:

> Notwithstanding any other provision of this Act, upon receipt of evidence that the handling, storage, treatment, transportation or disposal of any solid waste or hazardous waste is presenting an imminent and substantial endangerment to health or the environment, the Administrator may bring suit on behalf of the United States in any appropriate district court to immediately restrain any person for contributing to the alleged disposal to stop such handling, storage, treatment, transportation or disposal or to take other such action as may be necessary.

While Section 7003 broadens the EPA's general authority under Title III, other sections of the law in Title I narrow it. Thus, the definitions section of the law spells out that solid and hazardous waste provisions of RCRA do not extend to radioactive waste as regulated by the Atomic Energy Act, nor to water pollutants regulated by the Clean Water Act. Section 1006 further spells out these exemptions, and also orders the EPA not to use RCRA to regulate wastes subject to control by the Safe Drinking Water Act and the Marine Protection, Research and Sanctuaries Act of 1972 (the latter related to ocean dumping).* Since these other statutes in many cases contain far narrower

---

*Additional exemptions include small businesses generating 220 pounds of waste monthly, changed in the final regulations to 2,200 pounds, and boiler fuel incineration. The latter allows hazardous wastes to be burned in industrial or commercial boilers to recover usable energy with virtually no restrictions. This is all the more serious in view of recent EPA estimates that up to 50 percent of all hazardous wastes are disposed of in industrial or commercial boilers (Fred C. Hart, Associates. *Impact of Burning Hazardous Waste in Boilers.* Report to SCA Chemical Services, Boston, Mass., August, 1982).

regulatory authority than RCRA, the effect of this requirement is a very real limitation on the EPA's authority.

Legislative Response to Love Canal and Evolution of the Superfund

By January, 1979, enough horror stories had emerged about hazardous wastes to compel a new phase of government activism. Unlike the first government efforts to regulate toxic wastes, which had proceeded from rather abstract concerns about possible future problems, the post–Love Canal response was a concrete effort to deal with immediate, critical needs.

CONGRESS REAUTHORIZES RCRA

Congress had originally scheduled RCRA for review in 1979, intending to examine how the law was working in practice. But by 1979, the EPA had yet to issue regulations to carry out RCRA, so that Congress had no experience to evaluate. Legally, however, reauthorization was necessary; without it, RCRA would have expired. Logically, such a reauthorization might have been the place to debate the issues raised by the need to clean up Love Canal and similar abandoned dumps. But neither the House nor the Senate wished to tie up RCRA, the preventive law, in the predictably nasty debate over who was to pay for past mistakes.

Initially, the House and Senate planned a simple extension of the law without any significant changes. However, industry had other ideas. Alerted by the December, 1978 RCRA regulations proposed by the EPA, the oil and gas industry in early 1979 began a major lobbying effort to get Congress to remove from the EPA the authority to regulate hazardous wastes produced by oil and gas drilling. Environmentally sympathetic members of Congress opposed this effort, but by the end of May, 1980, both the House Commerce and Senate Public Works committees had approved such a weakening of RCRA.

Pulp and paper companies also sought relief from RCRA. They feared that unlined disposal ponds that held waste water from paper mills before treatment in sewage facilities would be subject to strict RCRA rules. Congressman Al Swift, a Democrat from the timber state of Washington, who was generally sympathetic to environmental concerns, persuaded the House Commerce Committee to pass an amendment to exempt these ponds. Whatever Swift's intent, and he appears to have been concerned only about pulp-mill ponds, he quickly found unexpected allies in such corporate interests as Union Carbide and General Motors, which scurried to Capitol Hill to lobby for his amendment. After the committee approved it, it became clear that it covered a much broader class of facilities than the lagoons of northwestern paper mills alone. The EPA warned Congress, "It means the industry is unregulated for pits, ponds and lagoons that ultimately feed waste water into on-site treatment plants, even if it takes 100 years before they are ready to treat it. That hazardous material can run off the surface, or leach out, and EPA cannot even take 'imminent hazard' action against it." George Hanks, the lobbyist for Union Carbide, supported the amendment, stating, "We have never really conceived that RCRA applied to water."[11]

Swift, however, had not intended to allow industry to transform the solid-waste problem into a liquid-waste problem by simply dumping wastes into unlined ponds to soak into groundwater. When RCRA came up on the House floor on February 20, 1980, Swift offered a new, much more limited version of his amendment.

Other industries were also getting into line for exemptions. Electrical power companies did not want the slag and ash from coal-fired power plants subject to RCRA. Cement companies sought exemptions for their kiln dust. Uranium-ore wastes were proposed for exemptions, as were phosphate rock tailings.

On February 20, the House approved the RCRA reauthorization, complete with the various exemptions. And there the reauthorization sat. Although staff conferred, Senate and House members did not get together to try to work out the differences between the bills until the fall of 1980.

Finally, in early October, 1980, the Senate and House conferees reached agreement. The long public controversy about hazardous waste problems had changed the tone of the debate. While the revised version of the bill as proposed by the conferees did remove from the EPA's regulation a number of major waste streams—including coal mine wastes and drilling-rig muds—utility wastes, cement wastes, and ore-mining wastes were left in the act, pending an EPA study. These exemptions were significantly more limited than those the Congress had appeared to favor earlier. More important, the conferees strengthened RCRA in important ways.

The Imminent Hazard section was significantly beefed up by changing the phrase "is presenting an imminent and substantial endangerment" to "may present," thus permitting the EPA and the Department of Justice to act before the hazard actually occurred.

Penalties in Section 3008 were significantly increased. A new section providing for serious penalties in cases in which individuals recklessly and knowingly endangered the public health was included, even in instances in which no damage actually resulted. This section, while somewhat limited, gave the EPA and the Department of Justice a critical new tool against illegal dumpers. Other enforcement portions of the section were also strengthened—violation of permits, for example, became a felony.

On October 10, 1980, the president signed into law this modified reauthorization of RCRA.

THE CLEANUP PROBLEM

In the wake of Love Canal, members of both the House and Senate introduced in late 1978 and early 1979 a variety of proposals for new legislation. The Carter administration threw new resources into its hazardous waste activities, and the Justice Department launched a major new effort to deal with illegal hazardous waste activities. But in spite of all this activity, government performance after Love Canal raises serious doubts about its competence to resolve this problem with conventional regulatory approaches. Indeed, there is reason to wonder if government can even successfully regulate the more egregious abuses found in the disposal of toxic materials.

With the publicity surrounding Love Canal and similar incidents, state and federal agencies began to examine the problems of cleaning up such sites. The enormous costs quickly emerged as the biggest obstacle to even minimal cleanup. Government agencies involved simply did not have the funds. In some cases, no private party could be found to bear the costs, so that there was no one to sue to recover damages. Either the responsible party was a company that had gone out of existence or, as in the case of illegal dumping, the responsible parties could not even be identified. In cases like Love Canal, dumpers had apparently successfully passed their legal liability on to someone else. In yet other cases, the company that had dumped, although still in existence, legally liable, and identifiable, did not itself possess the resources to fund a cleanup. Some technique for financing hazardous waste cleanup efforts, especially of abandoned sites, thus became a major goal of responsible federal agencies and the Carter administration.

THE OIL-SPILL CLEANUP FUND

Congress had been wrestling with a similar problem for several years. Since the Santa Barbara oil spill of 1969, the costs associated with cleaning up spilled oil had been a major concern of coastal governments. In some cases, spills washed up on beaches, and there was no evidence as to which tanker was responsible. In other cases, it was clear which tanker had spilled the oil, but there was no way to recover costs from the owner because of the complexities of maritime law. In the cases of horrendous spills, like that of the *Amoco Cadiz* off France in 1974, the costs of the cleanup were simply too large for the owner of the tanker to pay. Similar problems turned up in rivers and harbors, where the material spilled was often not oil, but some other toxic chemical.

In response to the problem of spilled oil or other hazardous material, Congress in 1977 had considered legislation to establish an industry-wide fee system. Deposited in an insurance fund, these fees would pay the unrecoverable portion of the costs of oil or hazardous materials spilled into marine or fresh waterways. The Senate Environmental Pollution Subcommittee, led by Senator Muskie, had worked to combine this concept with a cleanup fund for hazardous materials in general, including those disposed of on land as well as in the water.

Muskie's combined bill passed the Senate, but the House Committee with jurisdiction, the Merchant Marine and Fisheries Committee, did not wish to combine the oil-spill fund with other hazardous waste problems. Congress was unable to reach agreement on a final piece of legislation.

THE NEW CONGRESS

In January, 1979, a new Congress convened. Comprehensive cleanup legislation was on the agenda of a number of committees. However, by now the focus of public concern was on the hazardous waste problem. The momentum behind the oil-spill issue appeared to have diminished.

Muskie's subcommittee took the lead on the Senate side. In the House, the most intense activity was in the Commerce Committee. The new chairman of the Transportation and Commerce Subcommittee, with the authority to actually write such legislation, was James Florio, a Democrat from New Jersey, a state with one of the worst toxic waste problems in the country. And the powerful Oversight and Investigations Subcommittee was spurred by Tennessee Democratic Congressman Albert Gore, Jr., who had already held hearings in 1978 on the Hardeman dump in Toone, Tennessee (see Chapter 3). The subcommittee was chaired by Texas Democratic Congressman Bob Eckhardt, who took a strong interest in the hazardous waste problem.

WHO SHOULD PAY

The initial basis of the cleanup fund was the idea of government-required insurance. A standard fee would be levied on the industry responsible for the hazard, geared to the quantity of oil (or hazardous waste) generated by each firm. The proceeds from the fee would go into a fund. The fund would compensate government or other parties suffering damages from an oil spill or an abandoned toxic-waste dump if damages could not be recovered from the firm actually responsible. Such an insurance mechanism would effectively hold industry as a whole responsible for the risks created by any firm in the industry if collection from the firm itself was impossible.

A formula was needed for charging premiums for payment into the fund. The original oil-spill bill had levied a fixed charge per barrel of petroleum product shipped. Hazardous wastes, however, were generated by a diversity of industries. Some were more toxic than others. There were great differences in how difficult it was to clean up various wastes and various sites. No one really knew what these costs would be. No one really knew how many old sites there were to be cleaned up or how much it would cost to clean them up. A private insurance company would have had great difficulty designing a premium schedule that would accurately reflect the risk incurred by each type of waste generator.

The representative from the Niagara Falls area, Democratic Congressman John LaFalce, had introduced a bill that focused on the operators of hazardous waste treatment, storage, and disposal facilities, levying the premium on waste materials as they were disposed of, rather than as they were generated. LaFalce also suggested that industry should not bear the entire burden. His bill included contributions from both federal and state governments. However, since LaFalce did not serve on the committees with jurisdiction over hazardous wastes, his bill was never given serious consideration.

WHO SHOULD COLLECT

A second design problem was the relationship between the insurance program and the normal liability of industry for damages. Was the fund to become the primary source for cleaning up old dumps? Was it to be used only when no responsible party could be found and sued? What about industry dump sites that had complied with state laws at the time they were operated—would these be cleaned up with money from the fund? Would there be limits on the amount paid out to clean up any one site, as had been proposed earlier for the oil-spill fund?

What kind of expenses would be reimbursed from the fund? Everyone agreed that the actual costs of safely closing old, abandoned dumps and containing their contents should be covered. What about property damages suffered by homeowners in the vicinity of such dumps? Would the fund pay for the condemned houses near Love Canal? Would it pay for a new drinking water system for Toone, Tennessee? Would it compensate fishermen and others for economic losses due to contamination of fields, streams, or other economic resources? Would there be payouts to the fishermen on the Hudson cut off from their livelihood by General Electric's polychlorinated biphenyl (PCB) spills? What about medical expenses incurred by those poisoned by a dump site before it was cleaned up?

Was the fund, in short, designed to transfer to industry the costs of cleaning up, costs that would otherwise have been borne by government, or did it have a broader purpose—to ensure that all the victims of improper hazardous waste disposal, private as well as public, were properly compensated?

THE FINANCIAL STAKES

The urgency behind proposed legislation to levy cleanup fees derived from the government's fears that, without it, the bill for cleanup would become a major drain on the public purse.

These anxieties were transformed into a strong concern in February, 1979, when the consulting firm of Fred C. Hart Associates submitted its first estimate to the EPA on the nation-wide costs of cleaning up old hazardous waste sites. The firm estimated that there were roughly from thirty-two thousand to fifty-one thousand potentially dangerous sites around the country, of which from twelve hundred to thirty-four thousand might pose a major threat. Temporary cleanup at such a major-threat site was calculated at $43.6 million per site, and final disposal at an average of $25.9 million per site.[12]

Multiplying these average cleanup costs by the number of sites estimated, the firm told the EPA that it might cost as much as $44.2 billion to clean up all such sites. And it warned the agency that probably only half of this cost could be recovered from the operators of such facilities, leaving the government with a potential bill of $22 billion.

Senator Everett Dirksen once commented, "A billion here and a billion there and pretty soon you're talking about real money." Hart's figures were admittedly tenuous, the figures and estimates "soft," but if they were anywhere near the mark, hazardous waste problems were "real money," even in Washington terms. The disposal fund was promptly christened "the super-fund" because it would cover both oil spills and dump sites and because it initially appeared that an almost irresistible force would carry it through to enactment—the alternative of sticking the taxpayers with the bill. But, eager as many in Washington were to pass a superfund bill, the House, Senate, and administration had to agree to pass the same bill, and major differences remained.

The battle commenced in earnest in March, 1979. Congressional subcommittees opened their hearings on the subject, and ABC Television highlighted the issue with a documentary entitled "The Killing Ground." Muskie and the Senate Environment Committee* declared their intention to seek enactment of a hazardous-waste-only superfund financed exclusively by charges on industry.†

Gore suggested that it might be necessary to separate the oil-spill and toxic-waste funds. He feared that the influence of "those who safeguard the oil industry" might again kill a combined fund in Congress, which might fear "that the tax on the oil companies quickly would be exhausted by the massive cleanup costs of these abandoned sites."[13] But Gore did not think that industry ought to foot the entire bill. Florio was inclined to agree with the previous Senate approach of combining the oil-spill and hazardous waste funds.

THE CARTER ADMINISTRATION BILL

The Carter administration was internally divided. The EPA wanted a unified superfund; the Department of Transportation wanted to separate the two concepts in order to increase the chances of enactment of an oil-spill bill. The administration promised to announce its position in May.

Initially, the EPA floated within the administration a proposal involving annual levies of $600 million on generators of hazardous waste feedstocks. These fees would have continued until a total of $6 billion had been collected. The EPA also suggested that most of the burden for cleaning up old sites should fall on these industry fees.

Other parts of the administration disagreed with this approach. In particular, other agencies argued for a smaller fund, a

---

*Formerly the Senate Public Works Committee.

†Muskie's bill, jointly sponsored by Iowa Democratic Senator John Culver, also focused heavily on increasing the liability of anyone releasing hazardous material into the environment.

lower set of fees, and government financing of the cleanup of inactive dump sites. At the last minute, administration testimony scheduled to be sent to Congress was postponed.

The May deadline came and went while this internal struggle went on. On June 5, 1979, the *Los Angeles Times* reported that the president's advisors had given him a final proposal that was cut back to $300 million a year, allowed to accumulate only to $1.6 billion, and which placed the burden for cleaning up inactive dump sites on the taxpayers.

Carter personally stalled the proposal, asking his aides to look again at the question of industrial liability for old sites. On June 10, the EPA's proposal was reported again to be pending in the Office of Management and Budget.

On June 14, the administration announced its proposal. Domestic advisor Stuart Eisenstadt called it "the most important new environmental proposal of this administration this year." The proposal, while somewhat scaled down from the original EPA concept, still bore evidence that the President had in important ways sided with EPA administrator Douglas Costle against those in the administration who wanted the taxpayer to bear more of the burden.

The administration proposed a $1.6 billion bill, with 80 percent of the funding to come from generators of hazardous waste. The premium was set at $0.03 per barrel of oil or other raw materials used to make petrochemicals, $0.05 per pound of petrochemicals, and $2 per ton of heavy metals and inorganic chemicals. (This was about half the level originally suggested by the EPA.)

The $1.6 billion figure also represented a shortening of the authorization period; the EPA had suggested allowing the fund to accumulate to $6 billion. The practical effect of this change was small; once communities became accustomed to using the fund to pay for cleanups, Congress would be likely to extend the superfund if it should run out of money, the administration reasoned.

However, the administration stuck to its original position that the fund should be used for cleanup only. Except for fishermen, those who suffered economic or medical damages from unsafe disposal sites would be forced to try to recover their losses by suing the responsible private parties, not the fund. According to the administration's own figures, this meant that in half the cases those suffering damages would find no one from whom to collect.

Industry promptly attacked the administration's proposal. Robert A. Roland, president of the CMA, made it clear that he was not going to let environmentalists and their friends in Congress and the administration write legislation imposing heavy burdens on the chemical industry without a major battle. Roland put forth a simple industry viewpoint—the public benefits from chemicals; the public should pay to clean up chemical wastes.

> The solid waste disposal problem, including toxic or hazardous wastes, is not just the problem of the chemical industry. It is a result of society's advanced technology and pursuit of an increasingly complex lifestyle. Man has always been a messy animal. . . . Certain amounts of waste are inevitable. . . . Everyone should realize that the blame does not belong to a single company, or a single industry, but to all of us as individuals and as an advanced society. Rather than looking for scapegoats, we should recognize the dilemma and consider new ways to encourage the disclosure of dump site information and ways to limit the crushing liabilities that could result.[14]

Industry also argued that there was no crisis. Roland said, "We are not dealing with a rash, an epidemic of Love Canals. There is no need to rush to the legislature. And we are not dealing with an irresponsible industry." The National Chamber of Commerce joined the industry attack, pleading with Congress not to combine an oil-spill cleanup bill with the hazardous waste problem.

Environmental groups were more enthusiastic. They called the administration bill a good start, but urged payments from the fund to many more victims of hazardous waste, a stricter definition of industry liability, and heavier reliance on industry as opposed to government funding.

THE MUSKIE-CULVER BILL

On July 12, Muskie and Iowa Democratic Senator John Culver introduced their superfund bill (S 1480), which met many of the objectives of the environmentalists.

It contains a broader definition of hazardous substances; it contains funds for coverage of third party losses; it sets no dollar limits on emergency assistance; it provides for federal borrowing authority to start up the fund and maintain cash flow as needed; it provides for a floating fee arrangement sufficient to keep the fund solvent; it provides a stronger definition of strict liability; the operator of a facility must be financially responsible for liabilities, by insurance or bonding; and the fund must be reauthorized by Congress after seven years (instead of four).[15]

On July 19 and 20, 1979, the Senate Environment Subcommittee on Resource Protection held hearings on both the administration and the Muskie-Culver proposals. They were followed on July 31 by hearings in the House Merchant Marine and Fisheries Committee. Both House and Senate members were disappointed in the administration proposal. Especially disturbing was the fact that the administration bill only covered "emergency" action and allowed funds to be expended only to protect the public from the immediate danger posed by abandoned waste sites and spills. Also of great concern was the provision in the administration bill that limited relief to $300,000 per site or spill. Further, if the site was a municipal dump, 50 percent of the costs would have to be met by the state. If such state funds were not provided, no matching federal money would be available.

When they examined the administration proposal, members of the House Commerce Oversight and Investigations Subcommittee, which had already held twelve days of hearings on the problem, were aghast to learn that they could not legally act on the bill. The administration had written its bill as an amendment to the Clean Water Act (CWA), which governed pollution in surface waters. Under the rules of the House of Representatives, bills relating to the CWA could only be considered in the House Public Works Committee. Oil-spill legislation passed through yet another committee, Merchant Marine and Fisheries. In other words, the committee that had invested so much time investigating the issue was left out of the picture, and one that had never held a single day of hearings was handed the bill.

Irate members of the House, chief among them Bob Eckhardt, who chaired the Oversight and Investigations Subcommittee, pressed the administration for an explanation. Red-faced officials admitted that they didn't realize what they had done. As a legal vehicle, the administration bill was quickly dropped from serious consideration, and Florio wrote an abandoned-site bill of his own.

These hearings marked the end of serious congressional interest in the superfund during 1979. As swiftly as it had built up, the momentum vanished. On July 15, the president announced a major new package of energy initiatives to deal with the oil-imports problem. The president's proposed Energy Mobilization Board (EMB) could have exempted energy facilities from all or part of RCRA, and this new battle drew attention away from the superfund. The proposals threw the environmental movement and its congressional allies on the defensive. In the fall, efforts by the Senate Environment Committee staff to hold committee meetings to discuss the proposed legislation attracted only a few members, too few for further progress.

In addition to industry resistance, other serious obstacles stood in the way of the superfund. On the House side, Florio was working toward a bill very similar to that supported by the administration. But Florio had trouble getting votes in his subcommittee, which had heavy representation from congressmen supportive of the industries that generated the waste and that would have to pay the fees—particularly the oil, gas, and coal industries.

Muskie and Culver faced a different problem. Their bill attempted to deal with overall problems of liability and compensation for the victims of toxic chemicals. One observer called it "more of a toxic torts bill than a hazardous dumping proposal."[16] The issue of liability was legislatively much more complex than a simple insurance fund. The original fund concept required that Congress set a fee schedule, list the types of damages eligible for payment, and then instruct the EPA to go out and solve the technical problems of cleaning up each site. But in trying to rewrite the rules for compensating victims, Muskie and Culver were forced to solve the complicated issues directly, not by delegating them to the EPA.

The law, as they found it, provided close to perfect protection for companies that recklessly used toxic substances. Victims had first to establish that an illness or other damage resulted directly from exposure to a certain toxic chemical and not from any fault or lifestyle defect.* They also had to prove to the court which firm or company had released the chemical into the environment. Muskie and Culver argued that, under such laws, which had evolved in medieval England long before the Industrial Revolution, proof of damages and liability was almost impossible.

The legal obstacles had grown up over centuries as protection for individuals (see Chapter 10). In the nineteenth century, they were applied by the courts to huge corporations as a means of protecting them from legal liability for the consequences of their actions. However, there are exceptions to these doctrines that limit liability. Alternate legal concepts were devised by the courts over the years for situations in which it was desired to hold individuals and firms *responsible* for the outcomes of their actions, rather than to shield them from such responsibility.

Muskie and Culver set out to apply these more demanding legal concepts of responsibility to those who use toxic materials. First, S 1480 extends liability and compensation provisions to effects of all hazardous materials on health and the environment. Environmentalists supported this broadening.

It is clear that the deficiencies in existing federal and state compensation and liability laws apply to all forms of hazardous substance injury. A hazardous substance can exert its poisonous properties whether the route of entry into the body or the environment is through the air, land, or water, whether as a result of a spill, an explosion, or pesticide spraying.[18]

Second, the bill extends the legal concept of "strict liability" to toxic-substance damage cases. If toxic materials are released with resultant damage, the doctrine of strict liability says that those who released them must pay the costs, even if they did not behave negligently. This doctrine has long been applied to cer-

---

*As an extension of "blame-the-victim" strategies, industry traditionally blames personal lifestyle factors, such as smoking, alcohol, and fatty diet, as being largely responsible for most disease and cancer. Other elements in these strategies include denial or denigration of the role of occupational and environmental exposures to carcinogens; denial of evidence for increasing cancer rates; insisting that if there has been an increase in cancer rates, it is exclusively due to smoking; and denial of needs for further regulations to limit or prevent exposure to carcinogens. (For a detailed critique of the lifestyle theories, see Epstein and Swartz, 1981.[17])

tain activities, like the use of firearms, which the law judged to be "intrinsically hazardous." S 1480 puts into law the by-now evident fact that handling toxic substances is also intrinsically dangerous.

Third, the bill extends to toxic materials the idea of "joint and several responsibility." One polluter dumping benzene in a dump cannot escape being sued for resulting leukemias merely because other polluters also dumped the same chemical. Further, the bill denies to the original generator of the wastes the defense of having handed them over to someone else for disposal; the generator remains responsible.

S 1480 also makes it somewhat easier for the victim of hazardous materials to establish that his illness was caused by the substance. The bill still requires the victim to prove that the illness or other damage actually resulted from exposure to the toxic material, but the victim is required only to show a *reasonable relationship* between the damage and the exposure. This requirement encourages courts to use statistical correlations showing that the chances of contracting a particular disease are increased by a certain toxic chemical, even if some cases of the disease would occur in the absence of such exposure.

The Muskie-Culver bill also extends to the victims of toxic-substance exposure the right to collect these damages from the superfund. Victims can collect both medical costs and economic losses from the fund, which, in turn, will bring lawsuits against the parties actually responsible for releasing the materials.

The fine print of many court decisions involving toxic substances in recent years argued eloquently for just these reforms. But that eloquence did not persuade everyone of the need for such a massive shift in the handling of liability for damages due to toxic materials. The CMA made the weakening of these sections its major legislative goal, anticipating that the costs involved in such lawsuits might be far larger to industry than those of a simple superfund.*

---

*Indeed, the superfund battle came to resemble some of the early struggles over workmen's compensation programs. An insurance fund is originally proposed to provide protection for occupational victims of industrialization. Eventually, this fund is transformed into protection for industry from the increasingly broad

THE DEPARTURE OF MUSKIE

On April 14, 1980, President Carter announced that he had appointed Senator Muskie to be the new secretary of state. Muskie's departure removed from the congressional scene one of the strongest advocates of a major reform of toxic-liability laws within the superfund legislation. Initially, progress on the legislation slowed down. There was uncertainty as to how the new situation would develop. A mechanism to reconcile the different versions of the bill was needed, but could not be found.

Environmentalists attempted to provide the stimulus by organizing a "Hunt the Dump" campaign. The Sierra Club and Environmental Action prepared a four-page brochure and questionnaire designed to help citizen groups query local industries about the siting and location of their dump sites, along with a list of criteria for identifying which of these sites were likely to pose hazards (see Appendix V).

Industry, presented with the questionnaires, had a dilemma. If it filled them out, it would inevitably identify for the public many hazardous sites that had previously gone unnoticed. If it refused to fill them out, it would generate the suspicion that it was trying to conceal evidence of hazardous sites.

Industry chose concealment as the lesser of the two risks. Although thousands of kits were distributed and a great many presented to local firms, virtually none were filled out by the firms and returned to Washington. The hoped-for political result—a substantial increase in the number of localities where dangerous sites had been identified—thus never came to pass.

THE HOUSE ACTS

On April 22, 1980, the Chemical Control warehouse in Elizabeth, New Jersey blew up in a spectacular confirmation of everything that superfund advocates had said of the dangers of abandoned dump sites. One week later, the Transportation Subcommittee of the House Commerce Committee approved an abandoned-waste-site cleanup bill, limited to $600 million, of

concepts of liability that might otherwise have developed and which, in fact, have dominated the evolution of liability law in other areas, such as medical malpractice. A progressive reform is thus reversed into a conservative counterattack.

which only 50 percent was funded by industry, but containing strict standards of liability for those responsible for dump sites. Two weeks later, the House Commerce Committee approved the legislation in this form, along with pledges by environmentalists and congressmen to try to strengthen the bill on the House floor, and by the chemical industry to continue to oppose it.

Before the bill reached the House floor, however, it faced a new hurdle—the House Ways and Means Committee, which controlled tax legislation, had been given a chance to review and amend the bill.

Environmentalists initially saw this as one more possible barrier to enactment of a good measure. In a stunning rebuff to the chemical industry, however, the revenue-minded committee, led by a young Democratic congressman from Long Island, Thomas Downey, restored the superfund along the original lines abandoned by the Commerce Committee. The set of fees in the committee bill, which would only have been levied against industry if Congress appropriated the federal 50 percent, were rewritten as taxes without further congressional appropriation. The industry share was increased to 75 percent, and the amount in the fund was raised to $1.2 billion.

The Ways and Means Committee action was, in large part, an effort to protect the Treasury Department and ensure that industry would carry an adequate share of the burden to spare government the costs of cleanup. Industry, by trying to shift the burden too heavily to the taxpayer, ended up losing most of what it had gained in the Commerce Committee. Now industry anticipated that an even stronger bill might emerge from the Senate, one that would cost them even more.

On September 27, the House further surprised opponents of the superfund. HR 7020, the Commerce/Ways and Means bill, swept over opposition by a vote of 351 to 23. Eight days earlier, on September 19, the House had also passed HR 85, a separate bill dealing with a superfund for oil and chemical spills.

An important factor in the overwhelming House vote was a sudden tactical shift by the chemical industry. On September 11, Robert Roland of the CMA had announced his industry's support of the Commerce/Ways and Means draft.* This shift, combined with heavy mail from concerned citizens urging Congress to act, put strong pressure on House members.

As Connecticut Democratic Congressman Toby Moffett warned on the House floor, "We're all getting this kind of mail. For heaven's sake, don't weaken this bill. The people are willing to pay more, judging from these letters, to see that we don't destroy the planet."[19]

But as so often, the House vote had an element of charade in it. Roland of the CMA had concluded that HR 7020 was going to pass. Further, he evidently judged that Senate action on the much stronger Muskie-Culver bill was unlikely, and that if it did occur, the Senate and the House would never agree on a joint bill. Thus, CMA's grudging support for HR 7020 would have no impact on the result in the House, but might strengthen the chances of a deadlock with the Senate.

However, the results of the battles over amending the bill indicate that Roland's shift was less significant than it appeared, and that public sentiment was indeed bringing heavy pressure on Congress. Efforts to weaken the bill were persistently beaten back by large margins in voice votes, while two efforts by Gore to strengthen the liability provisions easily succeeded. One of the main efforts was led by Michigan Republican Congressman David Stockman, now head of the Office of Management and Budget (OMB), who condemned the bill as a terribly overwritten extension of federal authority. Stockman complained that the bill gave the EPA open-ended power to clean up whatever and whenever it wanted, so that members of Congress might "receive a letter from a company in their district that has just received a $5 million or $10 million liability suit that was triggered by nothing more than a decision of a GS-14 that some landfill, some disposal site, somewhere, needed to be cleaned up, and, as a result of an investigation his office did, he found out that

---

*Roland later denied support for the Ways and Means bill and stated that CMA's support only went to the bill as first passed by the House Commerce Committee.

company contributed a few hundred pounds of waste to that site thirty years ago."[20]

In the wake of the House votes, the Carter administration declared its pleasure, saying that it had gotten 85 percent of what it had originally sought. Environmental groups and consumer organizations called the House bill far too weak, and called on the Senate to insist on its stronger version. But privately, they were quite surprised and pleased at how strong the House bill was and, like Roland, thought that the real issue was whether there was enough time for the Senate to muster enough support to pass a bill and reach a final compromise with the House.

SENATE ACTION

Immediately in the wake of Muskie's departure to the Department of State, the Senate Environment Committee finally began to move on the superfund. On April 16, 1980, at the urging of Vermont Republican Senator Robert Stafford, the committee agreed to consider taking up the legislation in full committee, thus eliminating the scheduling problems and bottlenecks that had held the issue up in subcommittee.

Senator Culver declined to accept this maneuver. But Muskie's heir on his subcommittee, Alaska's Democratic Senator Mike Gravel, was absent from Washington, campaigning. Culver took advantage of Gravel's absence to get agreement from the two subcommittees involved on a scaling-back of S 1480, which still left it much stronger than any House bill or the administration proposal. Exempted from the new version were such nonhazardous waste toxic-liability issues as routine pesticide applications and discharges for which the EPA had issued permits under the Clean Water Act. The size of the fund was also halved, and the bill reported on May 22 to the full committee. Remaining issues, as Stafford had urged, were to be resolved there.

On June 26, the Environment Committee approved S 1480 on a vote of 10 to 1, with the only objection coming from Wyoming's Republican Senator Alan Simpson, who said, "It preempts state common law. It gives me the creeps." The full committee made further limitations on the broad sweep of Muskie's original concept of S 1480. In response to an amendment by New Mexico's Republican Senator Pete Domenici, payments from the fund for damage to natural resources and property before enactment of the law were eliminated, as were medical expenses of which the claimant had knowledge before Jan. 1, 1977. The burden of proof for medical causation was shifted more heavily to the victim. But what remained was still very tough. Environmental groups hailed it, with environmentalist Blake Early calling it "effective and reasonable" and the EPA's Costle saying he was "delighted."

But industry's reaction was a snarl. Roland called the bill "impractical, unnecessarily broad and punitive." He warned that "we haven't stopped a goddamn thing in that committee, but we have indications that a lot of people will support us on the floor."[21]

Supporters of the fund, however, were much more concerned about a different obstacle. Just as, on the House side, the Ways and Means Committee had claimed jurisdiction, on the Senate side, the Senate Finance Committee had claimed a right to look at the bill for sixty days.

Supporters of the fund had two concerns. The Finance Committee's powerful chairman, Louisiana Democratic Senator Russell Long, was very close to the oil industry and ran the committee with a strong hand. Long appeared to be in a position to substantially modify S 1480 as the price for letting the Senate vote on it—and such modifications could force environmentalists and Culver into a series of difficult efforts on the Senate floor to restore crucial language deleted in the Finance Committee. The Finance Committee might also be able to claim the right to seats on the conference that would resolve the disputes between the House and Senate, thus making it far harder to obtain good language on the crucial liability provisions on which the two bills differed so dramatically.

The second concern was time. Even if Long could not weaken the bill fatally in his committee, he could hold it. With

Congress aiming for a final adjournment early in October, the sixty days of review could easily make it impossible for a final bill to emerge.

The clock began to run. Supporters of S 1480 originally had hoped to get the bill to Long with an agreement that he would report the bill by mid-August, giving four weeks for a Senate-House conference. But the summer dragged on with no agreement from Long.

By the week of September 23, the bill had yet to be formally referred to the Finance Committee, and the Senate Majority Leader, West Virginia Democrat Robert Byrd, had indicated that he would not schedule the bill for action on the Senate floor at all unless a compromise was reached that guaranteed there would be no long wrangle on the floor. No such agreement was in sight, even though both the oil-spill and abandoned dump-site cleanup bills had passed the House.

The last hope for superfund supporters lay in the fact that other vital congressional business had also dragged and that Congress had decided to return for a brief "lame-duck" session after the November election.

THE LAME-DUCK SESSION

Things looked very black for superfund supporters when the lame-duck session convened in November, 1980. The Carter administration, which strongly supported the superfund, had been rejected at the polls, and replaced by a new president, viewed as uninterested in environmental protection and very responsive to industry views. John Culver, the chief Senate sponsor, had been defeated in his bid for re-election. Republicans had captured the Senate for the first time in years and had made clear their intention to prevent the Democrats from trying to rush through vital legislation in the closing days of their undisputed control. And Russell Long was still sitting on the bill.

The CMA saw this as good news. To ensure against further action, Roland withdrew the manufacturers' tepid support for the House-passed HR 7020, saying that he had only supported the original Commerce Committee version.

Culver was away for much of the session, and his power and interest had waned with defeat. Vermont Republican Senator Robert Stafford filled the void, assuming in advance the effective leadership role on environmental issues that he would formally assume in the new Congress as chairman of the Senate Environment Committee. But while Stafford tried to work out a compromise bill that the House could accept and that would not produce a filibuster by conservative Republicans, such as North Carolina Senator Jessie Helms, he still could not move such a compromise to the Senate floor without Russell Long's cooperation.

Long finally scheduled Finance Committee meetings on the superfund for November 18–20. Final action appeared very unlikely. In addition to Long's own personal history of sympathy for the oil industry, the chemical companies had made a very major investment in campaign contributions to members of the committee—over $300,000 had been given before the November elections, and it was expected that final reports on campaign contributions might show an industry investment of half a million dollars or more.

On November 14, William Stover, CMA vice-president for governmental relations, confidently said, "I feel sure that the new power figures in Washington are not going to permit the Congress to move ahead with major precedent-setting legislation. Our support or lack of support at this time is really beside the point."[22]

On November 18, Roland repeated the message to the National Press Club, urging the new Congress to avoid critical issues like the superfund. But as Roland spoke, environmental demonstrators outside the club chanted, "Hey, hey, CMA, How many drums did you dump today."

On November 18, after a few hours of rambling debate, Russell Long lifted his eyes from the draft before him and commented, "If we're going to have a bill, it's going to be ironed out in the majority leader's office—with the minority leader there. So let's get it to the floor and get into huddles, because some kind of compromise must be worked out."[23] Then, by a unanimous vote, the committee voted the bill out without recommendation, clearing the way for a final round of negotiations and a vote on the Senate floor.

Superfund supporters, earlier surprised by their success in the House Ways and Means Committee, were flabbergasted by Long's action. Neither then nor later did they express confidence that they knew what Long was up to. One theory ran that far from being grateful for the $300,000 in campaign contributions showered on his panel by the chemical industry, Long was irked at the hundreds of thousands more that had proved so critical in turning control of the Senate over to the Republicans and denying him his chairmanship. Republican Senator Charles Grassley, who had unseated Culver, for example, got more chemical money than any other candidate—$73,000—$20,000 more than Long himself had received.

While superfund supporters had not expected Long's action, they had prepared for it. On November 17, Stafford had introduced a compromise proposal. This bill cut the size of the fund to $2.7 billion, eliminated the victim compensation provisions, and deleted most of the reforms of the law of liability as it related to toxic materials. Stafford's bill, for the most part, closely resembled the House-passed bill and had been designed to be acceptable to the House without a conference and to Republican senators like Helms.

Stafford had gone through a difficult period deciding whether to compromise so far. Initially after the election, his strategy had been to let the superfund die in the lame-duck session and then, in the next Congress, to try to write a strong bill resembling the Environment-Committee-passed S 1480. Many environmentalists and House members, however, pressured Stafford into compromising further. They doubted his view that, as chairman, he could pass a strong bill in the next Senate, even with its Republican, conservative majority. And they looked at the further weakening of the environmental forces in the House as evidence that it would be even harder to move a good bill there. Further, the pressure for money for cleanup was so great that many felt some bill was needed immediately.

The victim-compensation and liability provisions, while an anathema to the chemical industry, seemed much closer to the rhetoric of the new Republican majority in the Senate—the effect of most of them would be to enable individuals to pursue relief from toxic materials without relying on government regulations—something the Republicans had nominally favored for years.

Finally, Stafford decided to take what he could get in the lame-duck session and to let an effort be made in the next Congress to enact a separate bill dealing with the deferred liability and victim-compensation issues.

Now that Long had ceased holding the bill up, Stafford had his chance. The *Wall Street Journal* fulminated on behalf of the chemical industry. The day after Long reported the bill out of the Finance Committee, the *Journal* ran an editorial called "Superfund Superrush," surely one of the most remarkable documents to emerge from the entire debate on hazardous waste materials.

No one paid much attention back in September when Congressman Dave Stockman brought up some trenchant criticisms of a $1.2 billion superfund bill for cleaning up abandoned chemical waste dumps. The bill passed the House by a whopping 351–23, many of the Congressmen no doubt taking comfort from the widespread assumption that no bill would ultimately pass because the Senate was considering a far more sweeping and expensive bill and no agreement was likely.

In the wake of a resounding national mandate against intrusive government, though, the outgoing Congress has decided to have a few for the road. After patching up similar differences to gulp down an Alaska lands bill, it is getting ready to swill the superfund. On Monday, Senators Randolph and Stafford introduced a scaled down Senate bill. . . . On Tuesday . . . the Finance Committee voted unanimously to report the original bill to the floor, indicating an urgency to pass something.

So it's worth taking a look or two at the merits of the bill. . . . To start with, dumps do not migrate. Both the public health hazards associated with chemical wastes and the environmental tradeoffs are mostly local. State and municipal governments are in the best position to determine, say, whether it's worth sprucing up an eyesore, even if that means raising production costs for local industries. . . .[24]

"Sprucing up an eyesore. . . ?" Lest anyone in Congress fail to understand that the *Journal*'s real objection was to cleaning up dumps at all, it went on to say that at Love Canal, "so far there is no hard evidence of health damage from the wastes."

But while the *Journal* appeared willing to go to the barricades to kill the compromise bill, the chemical industry was far from unanimous on this point. On November 20, Irving S. Shapiro, chairman of E.I. du Pont de Nemours, urged that Congress get on with passage of the bill. "I want legislation in this session, rational legislation dictated by the facts." He expressed his opposition to the Randolph-Stafford compromise bill, but said he could accept the House-passed bill.[25]

Pressure continued to build. Finally, Senator Helms agreed that if Stafford and Randolph would reduce the size of their bill from $2.7 billion to $1.6 billion, he would permit the Senate to vote without a filibuster. On November 24, the Senate moved to the legislation. A preliminary roll call on some technical amendments passed by a vote of 78 to 9. The Senate then by a voice vote passed the compromise legislation, with 85 percent industry funding, $1.6 billion in the fund, liability for dumpers, and no coverage of oil spills.

Maine Democratic Senator George Mitchell, Muskie's successor, regretted the fact that the changes in liability law had been withdrawn from the bill, and that victims could not recover their damages in most circumstances. Mitchell promised a new fight in the new Congress over those issues, as did conservationists, with the Sierra Club's Blake Early calling the legislation "a cleanup bill."

Anxiety then built up over whether there would be last-minute maneuvers in the House to kill the Senate compromise. But on December 3, 1980, by a vote of 274 to 94, in a spirit of desperation, the House killed both its oil-spill and abandoned-dump bills and sent the Senate version to the President. One of Jimmy Carter's last acts as President was to sign PL96-510, the superfund legislation.

The industry, acting through the CMA, never gave in. After the House vote, Roland said, "We continue to be disturbed that it established an unfortunate precedent . . . and an unnecessary new federal bureaucracy."[26] The *Washington Post* deplored the loss of the victim recovery and liability reform provision.

A superfund that fulfilled the bill's original purpose would have been just the kind of regulatory reform that many of the Senate's new leaders have been calling for: regulations based on the workings of the competitive marketplace, free of fine-print rules in the *Federal Register,* and premised on the fiscally sensible notion that a penny's worth of prevention is worth a dollar spent on cure.[27]

The Reagan Administration

Shortly after the Reagan Administration came into office in January, 1981, hopes that the new Congress would complete the reform of society's handling of toxic wastes began to fade. As the Administration launched a broadside attack on environmental laws and regulations, those in the Congress concerned with protecting the public health were thrown back on the defensive.

In 1982, however, as public outrage over the cutbacks in environmental enforcement escalated, Congress moved to undo many regulatory relaxations of the Reagan-Gorsuch team. A bill reauthorizing and amending RCRA was designed to cut back upon the small generator exemption, to prohibit the disposal of liquid wastes in landfills, phase out deep well injection of wastes into groundwater, and regulate the low temperature incineration of heating oil blended with toxic wastes. The House passed a new and stronger version of the RCRA reauthorization, 317–32.

Efforts to get a similar toughening of RCRA through the Senate failed. But the 1982 mid-term elections added substantially to environmental ranks in the Congress. Environmentalists picked up 2–3 votes in the Senate and 25–30 in the House. Those results, and the subsequent series of scandals that led to the resignation of Anne Gorsuch created enormous political pressures on Congress to take strong environmental stands.

Environmentalists took the offensive. RCRA was set to be strengthened. Senator Stafford moved aggressively with the victim-compensation provisions struck from the first Superfund legislation. Observers expected an extension of the Superfund beyond its expiration date of 1985, and the allocation of far more than the original $1.6 billion. The oil industry openly talked of shifting the basis for Superfund to a tax on wastes generated, rather than one on crude feedstocks.

Conclusions

Congress prepared in 1983 to tighten down the legislative requirements for hazardous waste disposal. But a central dilemma remains. Given the enormous volumes of hazardous waste and the rate at which its volume increases; given the extreme resistance to degradation and toxicity of much waste; and given the resistance of business to assuming costs that yield no short-term economic benefit, how realistic is it to expect EPA to compel thousands of firms to identify and use safer disposal methods? What is the incentive for firms to cooperate when they bear the costs and are protected from liability by the archaic laws limiting the rights of victims of hazardous waste to recover damages? In short, how compatible with the public health and the environment is the generation of toxic wastes in the first place?

One of the most acute frustrations I have come
to experience is the immense difficulty
associated with taking statutory mandates into
implementation. Complexity, procedures,
and shortages of resources all contribute; but
there are also larger, more pervasive
reasons related to institutional fears of changing
or altering the system.

THOMAS JORLING
EPA Assistant Administrator for Water and
Hazardous Substances, December, 1978

CHAPTER 9

Regulation of Hazardous Wastes

Congressional action is only the first stage in the regulatory process. Once a general statute is written, the agency charged with carrying it out must develop (promulgate) regulations and then enforce (implement) them. In many cases, the language of the law is deliberately broad, as Congress lacks the technical expertise to draw up the detailed specifications of exactly how to put regulations into effect. In other cases, Congress deliberately leaves language unclear or even evasive. Major disputes over exactly how to implement a program are not resolved in the political arena by elected legislators, but are passed on to be resolved by regulatory agencies or even the courts at a later date.

The Implementation of Legislation

Regulatory agencies are often unwilling to assume the burden of implementation. They are subject to heavy pressures from regulated industries not to impose some of the regulations authorized by Congress or to impose them in an attenuated form. Regulatory agencies often have as much difficulty as Congress in resolving disputes. Deadlines are hard to meet, lawyers worry about the possibility of lawsuits, and the regulatory process in reality is far less precise and exact than is suggested by the language of the law.

These problems have had an important and limiting effect on the EPA's implementation of all its toxic-pollution laws, including RCRA.

EPA'S DILATORY IMPLEMENTATION OF TOXIC-POLLUTION LAWS

The problem of obtaining prompt, effective enforcement of laws dealing with toxics had already surfaced with enactment of pollution statutes that preceded RCRA and dealt with air and water pollution, pesticides, and drinking water. As long ago as 1970, the Clean Air Act had required the EPA to publish a list of air pollutants that were particularly hazardous and to limit or eliminate their emission. While public health experts have identified dozens of such hazardous pollutants, by 1976, the EPA had listed only five—asbestos, mercury, beryllium, vinyl chloride, and benzene. Congress was so concerned by this dilatory performance that, in 1977, it specifically instructed the EPA to regulate an additional group of hazardous air pollutants: radioactive materials, cadmium, arsenic, and polycyclic aromatic hydrocarbons (PAH). These pollutants were to be regulated in accordance with a set timetable.*

In 1972, Congress revised water-pollution laws and enacted the Clean Water Act. Again, it required the EPA to set strict emission limits on discharges of toxic pollutants into the nation's waterways. And this requirement, too, sat unenforced on the shelf until a public interest group, the Natural Resources Defense Council (NRDC), successfully sued the EPA in court. This suit was finally resolved by a "consent decree" between the NRDC and the

---

*Even such a specific mandate, however, often means little. Five years later, the EPA still has not finished regulating the toxic pollutants Congress listed for it in 1977.

EPA, which established a new set of deadlines. The EPA then promptly proceeded to miss these new deadlines.[1]

In 1974, the Safe Drinking Water Act instructed the EPA to regulate deep-injection wells where necessary to protect drinking water or potential drinking water supplies. The EPA finally did propose some regulations three years later. But the government economists charged with fighting inflation, the Council on Wage and Price Stability, (COWPS), protested the costs of these regulations so forcefully that industry didn't have to enter the fray itself. The EPA backed off, started from scratch, and did not finally adopt its regulations until mid-1980.

Under the Federal Insecticide, Fungicide, and Rodenticide Act, the EPA's program to regulate hazardous pesticides has been manacled by internal resistance, lack of funding, pressure from agricultural interests in Congress, and lack of committed, trained staff. As a result, it has dealt with less than 1 percent of the five hundred pesticide ingredients that the EPA suspects may cause cancer.

Even when the EPA has authority to act under several laws, it frequently does nothing. For instance, the EPA admits that cadmium, which is becoming widely and increasingly disseminated in the environment, is linked to birth defects, cancer, and liver and kidney damage. The EPA has authority under at least three statutes to act to reduce human exposure to cadmium, yet still it finds reasons to delay. Deputy Assistant Administrator for Waste Treatment Swep Davis says that cadmium is just too tough for the agency. "I wouldn't underestimate the cadmium problem, but it is simplistic to think it can be solved easily. Because of the complexity of this, there are legitimate reasons for not moving more quickly."[2]

Sometimes Congress has been so concerned about a problem that it has literally told the EPA exactly what to do. The Toxic Substances Control Act orders the EPA to ban polychlorinated biphenyls (PCBs) and recall those in use. PCBs are thus the only chemical banned by an explicit act of Congress. Yet when the EPA issued its PCB regulations, attempting to minimize opposition to its regulations, it exempted from the requirement most of those in use—by some estimates, 85 percent of the PCBs in use currently could continue to be used.

THE EPA'S DILATORY IMPLEMENTATION OF RCRA

Congress gave the EPA eighteen months to develop and implement RCRA regulations from December, 1976. This deadline came and went in the spring of 1978. But, during these eighteen months, the agency failed to develop and publish the required regulations. (Table 9-1 shows the dates regulations were due and how long the EPA actually took to develop them.)

William Sanjour, an EPA official charged with developing the regulations, faced considerable uncertainty within the agency as to what shape RCRA regulations could take. Title III says simply that the regulations shall "minimize the risk to public health and the environment." Sanjour and his staff had almost no guidance from Congress as to how they should resolve the complex technical and economic issues they faced.

Sanjour could plausibly have presented his superiors with regulations that fell almost anywhere on the spectrum from the cosmetic to the highly rigorous. He tried to prepare a tough, comprehensive set of regulations. But his proposals were expensive—much more expensive than Congress was expecting and much more expensive than the EPA administrators were prepared to defend. Beyond that, the regulations posed complex technical issues for which the agency had no good solution. So the EPA dithered, delaying even preliminary publication of Sanjour's regulations for two years.

Meanwhile, hazardous waste problems kept coming to the attention of EPA officials in the field. On May 4, 1978, the Hazardous Waste Division sent to EPA's Chicago office an alert about a dangerous situation in Ohio. Hugh Kauffman, the official who wrote the memo, told Chicago that a hundred thousand barrels of waste were being held for incineration at the Akron, Ohio facility of the Summit National Services Corporation. However, Summit's incinerator

> can handle a maximum of 500 gallons of burnable waste per hour. Preliminary calculations indicate that it would take about two years for this incinerator to burn the wastes that are presently on the site if no further wastes are brought in. Because we feel that

Table 9-1. Timetable on EPA Regulations to Implement RCRA

Section	Description	Statutory Deadline for Promulgation	Date First Proposal	Date Final Promulgation
3001(a) and 3001(b) 42 USC §6921(a) and §6921(b)	Regulations establishing criteria for identifying characteristics of hazardous wastes, and for listing hazardous waste	4/78	12/78	5/80
3002 42 USC §6922	Regulations establishing standards applicable to generators of hazardous waste	4/78	12/78	2/80
3003(a) 42 USC §6923(a)	Regulations establishing standards applicable to transporters of hazardous waste	4/78	12/78	2/80
3004 42 USC §6924	Regulations establishing performance standards applicable to owners and operators of facilities for the treatment, storage, or disposal of hazardous waste	4/78	12/78	5/80 (interim only) 1/81 (financial requirements only)
3005(a) 42 USC §6925(a)	Regulations requiring each person owning or operating a facility for the treatment, storage, or disposal of hazardous waste to have permit issued pursuant to RCRA	4/78	2/79	5/80

Source: *Environmental Defense Fund and Environmental Action v. Steffan Plehn* (O.D.C. consent order, Sept. 13, 1978).

there may not be the financial resources available to this company to properly destroy these wastes, this facility may pose a potential imminent hazard. We request that Region V (Chicago) conduct a site investigation.[3]

Region V administrator Robert Dupree sent a note back to Kauffman chastising his Hazardous Waste Division for overreacting to the Summit situation and indicating his intent to leave the situation to the state of Ohio.

> My greatest concern is the manner in which the term "Imminent hazard" appears to have become used by headquarters staff. As we are all aware, hazardous waste management facilities are inherently hazardous. Determination of imminent hazard is, in part, a legal matter, and must in my view involve a risk of significant magnitude to warrant federal intrusion into an area that has historically been handled by the state and local sector. . . .[4]

By June, 1978, the EPA's top brass had two problems on their hands. First, Sanjour was pushing for a broad-scale, stringent set of regulations under RCRA, regulations that were likely to add substantially to the cost of disposing of waste. Second, Kauffman, who had earlier forced Dupree to press the state of Indiana to take action against a facility in Seymour, Indiana, was pushing for an aggressive use of the agency's powers under the imminent hazard section of RCRA, to take action against facilities even before the regulations had been written.

On June 15, 1978, the agency resolved its first problem. John Lehman, head of the Hazardous Waste Division, was instructed by his superiors to cut back on the scope of Sanjour's proposed RCRA regulations. Lehman ascribed the decision to the President's desire to fight inflation—the same argument that back in 1976 had been used by the EPA's John Quarles as the reason for President Ford's opposition to RCRA. Lehman said, "Based on the President's cutting back on the budget to fight inflation, you know, these sorts of societal pressures are beyond our control. I guess the bottom line is that we would probably end up doing a smaller program than the one we had been working towards."[5]

The memo that Lehman transmitted instructed Sanjour to make the regulations easier on industry and bore the signature of the EPA's assistant administrator for wastes—Tom Jorling. In previous years, Jorling had worked, as a staff member of the Senate Air and Water Pollution Subcommittee, for the enactment of solid-waste legislation far tougher than RCRA. The next day, June 16, 1978, Steffan Plehn, Kauffman's boss, sent him a memo telling him to "put a hold on all imminent hazard efforts"—in other words, to stop looking for dangerous sites among the thousands of dumps already in use. When news of the Plehn "stop looking" memo reached reporters, pressures began to build on the EPA to explain. Plehn assured the press that the problem was merely bureaucratic. The EPA was moving its resources around to improve the overall program, specifically by concentrating on the RCRA regulations as part of a "deliberate programmatic choice." Assessment of risky sites under the imminent-hazard section was being transferred to the agency's Enforcement Division.[6]

Nor did the transfer of the imminent-hazard authority to the Enforcement Division under Marvin Durning solve many problems. Durning lacked both investigators and funds to enforce the section. His 1978 budget for enforcement of the imminent-hazard section was only $100,000. Only five staff people were assigned.[*]

With these resources, Durning was responsible for locating, analyzing, and prosecuting those responsible for literally thousands of dangerous waste disposal sites all around the nation. Once Durning and his staff prepared these prosecutions, they sent them to the Land and Natural Resources Division of the Department of Justice. By November, 1978, six months after the assessment of risks under the imminent-hazards section had been transferred from Kauffman to Durning, only a few cases had been sent by the EPA to the Justice Department. The Justice

---

[*]Nor did the EPA follow up the transfer of imminent-hazards enforcement to Durning with adequate personnel or money. The 1979 budget request asked for only $1 million and a staff of twenty-three.

Department had assigned only one attorney to work on the problem and had yet to file its first legal action under RCRA.

James Moorman, former director of the Sierra Club Legal Defense Fund, an environmental law firm affiliated with the Sierra Club, was then the assistant attorney general in charge of the Land and Natural Resources Division. Moorman felt that Durning badly needed to beef up his staff to deal with hazardous dumps and that Durning needed a different kind of staff from the usual EPA lawyers and technical experts. Durning needed what Moorman called gumshoes, cops, hard-nosed investigators who knew about crime, rather than scientists who knew about poisons.*

THE ENVIRONMENTAL DEFENSE FUND AND ILLINOIS SUE THE EPA

The EPA initially rejected Moorman's suggestions and did little more with its imminent-hazards authority than to put out press releases about problems that were already public knowledge. By late 1978, the EPA still had failed to issue regulations to carry out RCRA. Since no action was evident on either regulations or hazardous-waste enforcement, the Environmental Defense Fund (EDF), which was tracking RCRA implementation more closely than any other environmental organization, brought suit in the U.S. District Court for the District of Columbia to compel the EPA to issue the regulations required by RCRA.[8]

Another lawsuit was brought against the EPA at the same time by the state of Illinois. Both environmentalists and Illinois Attorney General William J. Scott clearly felt that if RCRA was not to be treated in the same fashion as the EPA's previous mandates to clean up toxic pollutants, a federal court order instructing EPA administrator Douglas Costle to issue his RCRA regulations was going to be necessary.

---

*As Moorman later told Congress, "The EPA is in serious need of tough law enforcement investigators, investigators with training comparable to the IRS, the Customs Agents, and the FBI. While a high degree of specialized technical knowledge is also necessary for these investigations, I believe that fundamental investigative techniques and good investigative instincts are equally or more important. These investigators are needed not only to identify sites and their contents and owners, and operators, and former owners and operators, they are also needed to ferret out the elements of organized crime that are alleged to be involved in hazardous waste pollution."[7]

Post–Love Canal Implementation of RCRA

Love Canal suddenly thrust public concern over hazardous waste into sharp relief. Suddenly what was or was not being done about the problem became news—and therefore important to politicians and policy makers.

THE EPA'S PROPOSED REGULATIONS

In response to the 1978 lawsuit brought by the EDF and the state of Illinois, the U.S. District Court for the District of Columbia ordered the EPA to publish its final rules to implement RCRA by December 31, 1979. On December 14, 1978, the EPA took the first public step in meeting this order by publishing proposed regulations in the *Federal Register.*[9] In his press release, EPA administrator Costle promised that the proposed system would "ensure that more than 85 million tons of hazardous waste produced in the U.S. each year, including most chemical wastes, are disposed of safely." The regulations included a list of 158 specific wastes that EPA considered hazardous. The agency said it would also regulate wastes that were acutely toxic, chemically reactive, ignitable, or corrosive. Producers of over 250 pounds per month of such waste would be required to report on all of their waste and to use the "cradle-to-grave" manifest system pioneered in California and Texas. Standards for hazardous waste landfills were also proposed. As required by law, the EPA announced that public hearings would be held, and comments were solicited from concerned citizens and groups prior to publishing the regulations in final form and making them effective.

ENVIRONMENTALISTS' REACTION

As environmental groups read the fine print of the draft rules, they concluded that Costle's promise that wastes would be disposed of safely constituted imaginative public relations at best. Indeed, the EDF warned that the EPA's approach "makes a mockery out of Congress' intentions and the public's need for protection."[10]

Instead of listing all the chemicals that it knew to be hazardous, the EPA had simply thrown together a list of 158 chemicals already regulated under other laws, or for which it already had extensive studies. Among the chemicals not listed, or incompletely covered, were: the known "human carcinogens" benzene, benzidene, beryllium, and asbestos; the "suspect carcinogens" captan, ethylene dichloride, dibromochloropropane, and tris (2,3-dibromopropyl) phosphate; and dozens of other chemicals that the agency admitted to be dangerous.

In its comments, the EDF urged the EPA to substitute for this incomplete laundry list a systematic table of pollutants or substances already regulated, listed for regulation, or identified in the scientific literature as causing cancer, birth defects, mutations, neurological defects, or other chronic diseases.[11] The EDF pointed out that where the EPA listed only 158 chemicals, the California state regulatory program had identified over 800. Additionally, the EPA had failed to cover numerous industrial processes that California had identified as generating hazardous wastes. Examples cited were pesticides from fumigation of bakery products, xylene from the formulation of soap, heavy metals from production of plastic films, heavy metals from cleaning petroleum tanks, beryllium from metal plating of aircraft parts, even DDT left over from production for export. The EDF also pointed out that the EPA Office of Toxic Substances had issued a list of industrial processes producing toxic wastes, which EPA had omitted from the RCRA regulations. Somewhat acidly, the environmental group declined to provide the EPA with a complete list, "because this information is available to EPA."[12] But the EDF did provide "some examples, all of them known carcinogens."

The EDF also pointed out that the EPA itself admitted that it was failing to regulate many hazardous materials. The EPA's chosen definition for "toxicity," the group asserted, "exempts 65 percent of the potentially hazardous waste generated by the chemical and allied product industry. Disturbingly, even some of the chemicals which forced the evacuation at Love Canal will not be completely regulated under EPA's proposal."[13]

The environmental group also attacked the EPA for exempting generators of less than 250 pounds a month of hazardous waste, an objection later supported even by the normally anti-regulation economists in the Carter administration's regulatory review group. As the EDF pointed out, this exemption would permit firms producing "small" quantities of the most highly toxic waste to do virtually anything with them. They could throw them in an ordinary municipal dump, or leave them by the side of the road. The materials would not be covered by a manifest, with the following results:

> Without a manifest, the transporter and municipal fill operator do not know what wastes they are handling. They do not know what precautions to take in handling the wastes. Without knowing what is in the fill, the operator cannot design monitoring equipment to give accurate indication of groundwater contamination. If water supplies in the region are contaminated, the contamination cannot be traced to the landfill, because the landfill is full of unknown chemicals. . . .[14]

The EDF also ripped into Costle's proposal that industries that might be heavily impacted by the regulations could be exempted, including copper and lead smelters, electroplaters, and fabric dyers, pointing out that "a waste is no less hazardous just because it is generated by a highly impacted industry." The EDF also pointed out that the states with good programs, like Texas and California, had not provided such exemptions for small generators or heavily impacted industries. Finally, the EDF attacked the draft regulations: for failing to protect aquifers from contamination; for limiting the monitoring of sites to only twenty years after they were closed down; for exempting inactive landfills from the regulations; for inadequate monitoring; and for making it too easy for facilities to receive waivers from already inadequate standards.

A Chicago-based environmental organization, Citizens for a Better Environment (CBE), focused on a specific aspect of the EPA's overall approach to toxic wastes as expressed in the draft RCRA regulations—CBE attacked the agency's handling of the cadmium problem.

Cadmium, a carcinogenic heavy metal also associated with cardiovascular disease, enters municipal sewage sludge in particularly heavy concentrations in cities where the electroplating industry dumps contaminated wastes into public sewers. Cadmium is also left on streets as auto tires wear out, so sewers that process street runoff are also likely to produce sewage sludge with high cadmium levels.

Much of this sewage sludge has already been disposed of as fertilizer. Indeed, cities like Chicago and Washington, D.C. have processed their sludge into home garden-soil conditioners. Cadmium, deposited in the soil by such conditioners, may be present in the root zone of the plants. It is taken up by the roots and concentrated in the tissues of the plant. Some crops, particularly tobacco, leafy vegetables, and root crops, have a strong potential for concentrating cadmium.

The EPA proposed to regulate this hazard by setting limits on how much cadmium-contaminated sludge can be applied to soils used to grow such crops. Application would be permitted on soils used to grow animal feed. The EPA argued that most of the cadmium will be excreted by the animals and not remain in their meat or eggs. The EPA does require the owner of the land to show how these animal feeds will be distributed to ensure that corn, for example, is fed to pigs, and not turned into cornmeal for human consumption.

It is dubious that the EPA has, or ever will have, the resources to enforce this complicated scheme. If all of the sewage treatment plants producing cadmium-contaminated sludge, however, conscientiously, competently, and consistently followed the rules, the cadmium would not enter the food chain—for a while. But the cadmium remains hazardous for centuries—until it is leached out by rainfall or taken up by animals and then excreted. If leached by rainfall, it may migrate downward to contaminate an aquifer, some nearby wells, or a river or lake used as a water supply. If the EPA and future generations are lucky, it will be carried off and diluted into the ocean. If the cadmium is taken up by sorghum or some other fodder crop, the EPA assures us that the cows or pigs fed on it will excrete most of it—and the excreted manure in many cases will be used to fertilize land on which human food crops are grown.

INDUSTRY REACTION

As environmentalists called for the EPA to strengthen its regulations, industry unleashed a far greater assault designed to weaken them. A flood of comments was submitted to the EPA, challenging the regulations at each and every point—1,200 sets of individual industry comments.

The *Wall Street Journal* chose as its favorite target the EPA's modest efforts to ensure some control over the chemicals used by the oil and gas industry to lubricate the huge bits that cut through rock in drilling for oil and gas. The EPA had not listed such drilling "muds" as hazardous wastes per se, but did require those who used them to make their own determinations as to whether they met the EPA's hazardous criteria. Even then, *hazardous* oil and gas drilling muds were relieved of many of the requirements attached to other hazardous wastes—including the twenty-year period of financial responsibility.

But those concessions, like most of EPA's efforts to silence its industry critics, failed to appease the *Journal.* In a lead editorial entitled "EPA Runs Amuck," the paper asserted that the EPA's regulation of drilling muds, brine left over from wells, and crude-oil residues, "would soak up the profits of the entire industry and then some." The *Journal's* price tag was impressive—$45 billion.[15]

The source of this awesome sum was the oil industry itself. But while the *Journal* reprinted as gospel this figure from the American Petroleum Institute (API), it omitted to mention an extensive EPA response explaining the errors in this calculation and the generous exemptions already provided.*

The *Journal* and the API reserved their greatest scorn for the EPA's proposal to limit drilling operations on seismically active areas and flood plains. "Apparently the authors of the guidelines were not aware that it is necessary to locate oil and gas wells on the geological merit of the hydrocarbon accumulation," commented the Rocky Mountain Oil and Gas Association, "not on whether the wells would be in fault zones, regulatory floodways, 500-year floodplains, wetlands, critical habitat areas, etc."[16]

Other oil industry comments blasted the EPA for requiring industry to assure the safety of wastes for twenty years after a facility shut down, judged "impossible" for oil and gas operations in which the oil company did not own the surface rights. Independent petroleum operators complained of the proposed penalties for violation of the regulation. Finally, the *Journal* dis-

---

*The EPA's response had appeared in the same oil-industry publication, *Oil Daily,* that carried the original API figure.

missed the whole effort as "an expensive frivolity. The plain fact that we have lived with these wastes for years, is apparently irrelevant."[17]

The oil industry was not alone. Paint manufacturers lamented the inclusion in the "hazardous waste" category of sludges left over from paint manufacture. These sludges contain 39 out of 129 substances that the EPA has designated as toxic water pollutants—including chromium, copper, lead, mercury, zinc, ethylbenzene, methyl chloride, and toluene.*

The paint industry says that to dispose of their sludges as hazardous wastes would cost anywhere from $12.43 to $128 a ton. To avoid this expense, the industry asked the EPA not to list the sludges as hazardous. It asserted that "the weight" of the data does not support the EPA's judgment that the wastes produced in this process are "toxic or corrosive."[18]

It appears that under the flawed approach taken by the EPA in its draft RCRA regulations, the paint companies may well be right. The EPA chose to regulate most wastes on the basis of whether their toxic components dissolved in water at greater than a specified rate. It appears, at least from industry data, that paint sludges, chock full as they are of heavy metals, halogenated hydrocarbons, and even cyanide, do not dissolve in water fast enough to meet the EPA's standard for "toxic." The EPA had assumed that materials that are relatively insoluble could be safely disposed of in an ordinary municipal landfill or dump. Their toxic contents would be gradually leached out by rains, but so slowly, according to the EPA, that no real hazards would result.

Justice Department Enforcement of the Imminent-Hazard Section

Section 7003 of RCRA provided that even before regulations had been promulgated, the government could take action to clean up hazardous waste situations posing an "imminent haz-

---

*Concentrations of each of these chemicals in paint sludges average more than 7 ppm. These wastes are produced at 1,374 sites where paint is manufactured, and about eight hundred thousand gallons a day of waste water pour from these facilities, yielding about one hundred and twenty thousand gallons of sludge a day.

ard" to public health or the environment. As we have seen, early efforts by some EPA officials to use this power were resisted by others in the agency, and, in June of 1978, the EPA had made a basic policy choice to deemphasize the search for dangerous dump sites. Instead, the agency decided to concentrate its efforts on dealing with regulations to carry out the hazardous waste sections of Title III of RCRA. But the transfer of the authority over section 7003 to the enforcement branch brought the Justice Department into the process of carrying out the law.

James Moorman of the Justice Department wanted the EPA to hire a larger number of straight investigators. He also wanted to increase the capability of the Land and Natural Resources Division to pursue illegal and hazardous dumping cases. When Love Canal began to make national headlines in August of 1978, Moorman saw a good chance to obtain the additional staff he needed to aggressively pursue hazardous waste cases. Working with environmental organizations, he began to make the case for an expanded staff in his division.

In February, 1979, the Justice Department brought the first hazardous waste enforcement action since the passage of RCRA—against Kin-Buc, for its Raritan River landfill in Scotch Plains, New Jersey. Two months later a second suit was brought in Pennsylvania against the ABM Disposal Company for dumping wastes along the Delaware River (see Chapter 7).

In the spring, Moorman testified on Capitol Hill. His testimony before congressional committees, charging that the hazardous-waste situation was like "the Wild West," impressed Congress with the need for more lawyers and investigators. By October, 1979, Moorman was working with the EPA to bring a half-dozen additional suits. In recognition of this need, Attorney General Benjamin Civiletti created a new section within the division to deal with toxic and hazardous wastes. On December 20, the Justice Department brought four separate legal actions against Hooker Chemical for its activities at Love Canal and other Niagara sites.

By November, 1980, the new Justice Department section had a docket of thirty-one cases, eight of which had been carried through successfully. (See Appendix VI.) In addition to using his authority under Section 7003 of RCRA, Moorman's attorneys also found legal authority to clean up hazardous wastes under a variety of other statutes: the Clean Water Act,* the old Rivers and Harbors Act of 1899, the Toxic Substances Control Act, and even the common-law doctrine of nuisance (see Chapter 10). The speed with which the Justice Department was able to bring actions against many of these violators, in the light of the total lack of action in previous years, indicates the importance of leading policy makers taking a strong personal interest. True, the Justice Department needed additional attorneys and funds; but the entire budget of the Land and Natural Resources Division was very small—only $15 million. Only a small part of this needed to be spent on hazardous waste. The crucial difference that produced results was that the assistant attorney general, backed by the attorney general and others in the administration, had decided to make toxic cleanup a high priority.

The crucial element that Moorman needed from the outside, however, was identification of cases that needed to be brought. That remained the EPA's job. And throughout 1978, evidence persisted that the EPA had only sporadically or lethargically tried to identify potentially dangerous waste sites. For example, as early as January, 1979, a Rockland County, New York grand jury had assessed the adequacy of the EPA's efforts to identify hazardous waste dump sites. The grand jury report concluded that the "EPA's assessment programs are worse now than before the Resource Conservation and Recovery Act was passed."[20] One witness described the situation to the grand jury:

> We have found . . . in many instances when we discover a site where people are being poisoned, that information and decisions involved with that poisoning are on file or have been made by

---

*In July, 1980, the Justice Department sued ten chemical companies, including Dow Chemical, Allied Chemical, Shell Chemical, and Ethyl Corporation, that "knew or should have known" that their toxic wastes were being stored unsafely at two sites near Baton Rouge operated by Petro Processors of Louisiana, Inc., who were named as codefendants. According to an EPA official, the Petro Processors case was chosen as a precedential test case because of "a set of facts that clearly established a chain" between the chemical companies and the dump site and because a private suit filed in 1969 should have made the companies fully aware of the problem. The suit charged violations of the Clean Water Act and asked for a $10,000 civil fine against each defendant and for an order to halt the dumping and to clean up the sites.[19]

Environmental Protection Agency regional offices and state and local officials; and that the people have not been told by any of these officials that they are being poisoned. In some cases, those officials have been involved in decisions that allowed for them to be poisoned.[21]

The grand jury itself concluded that "employees assigned to the Hazardous Waste Damage Assessment Program were instructed not to examine regional EPA files to determine if they contained complaints of poisoning or documented accounts of disasters as a result of improper disposition of chemicals."[22] The Grand Jury dismissed the EPA's supposed survey of such sites, quoting a witness that the only information included in the survey was "information in the file that the public was aware of. For example, if there was information in the file that people were being poisoned and the public didn't know it, they were not required to give—and were dissuaded from giving—the information to the Environmental Protection Agency headquarters in Washington."[23]

By the spring of 1979, however, the agency had changed its approach. Strongly driven by a desire to encourage the enactment of the superfund, EPA officials were making a serious effort to identify and bring to the public's attention hazardous waste sites posing serious threats to health. Indeed, the EPA in some cases may have paid more attention to certain sites than the evidence later indicated was warranted. For example, the Valley of the Drums, a site in Kentucky involving the dumping of large numbers of drums on the surface, got special attention, in part because the site was out in the open, visible, and hence attractive to reporters and cameramen (see Chapter 3).

The EPA's Final RCRA Regulations

The EPA had been ordered by a federal court to publish its final RCRA regulations by December, 1979. But the storm of protest from industry that swept over the EPA after its initial, December, 1978 proposals terrified the agency out of that timetable. It appears that the fear of federal court orders weighed less heavily on Costle and the administration than the fear of industry and congressional reaction. Instead, the EPA scheduled its

regulations for spring, 1980, by which time the agency expected
that Congress would have finished reauthorizing RCRA and
would have moved on to a heavy season of election-year campaigning. However, RCRA was not, in fact, reauthorized by this
date.

Publicly, Costle defended the EPA's tardiness. He told the
court that only the pressure of 1,200 sets of industry comments
had prevented the EPA from issuing final regulations.* Indeed,
Costle complained to the court that industry was laying a "minefield" of comments. But earlier, in March, 1979, he had indicated strong sympathy for the industry position that the RCRA
regulations were too expensive. Industry argues, Costle had
said, "that the cost is too high, that we must make sure that every
existing or proposed regulation either pays its own way or addresses a critical health problem that must be met regardless of
the cost. This is a thoroughly justifiable point of view†."[24]

Costle's comments focused consistently on the need for
regulations to be cost-effective—obtaining environmental protection at minimum expense. But the EPA's actual response to its

---

*By law, a federal agency must respond in its final rulemaking to each issue raised
during the comment period. But it is not necessary that an agency respond to each
individual comment, and most of the industry comments on RCRA dealt with a relatively small number of issues, issues that the EPA had already pondered for several
years.

†What lessons might industry draw from the EPA's performance in carrying out
RCRA? If we believe Costle's claims that it was the 1,200 industry comments that
delayed the regulations from December, 1979 until May, 1980, about 150 days,
then it appears that industry can achieve one day of delay after statutory deadlines
for every eight comments it files. If we take Costle's estimate that the proposed
RCRA regulations would cost industry $750 million a year, then each day of
compliance costs about $2 million. These costs are saved even if the EPA, the courts,
and Congress totally ignore all the comments and publish final rules exactly as
tough as the initial ones. Industry saves this money by not complying during the
delay. Once the basic research has been done on a regulation, it is hard to imagine
that clever lawyers could not write a set of new comments for each of hundreds of
firms in five or ten hours per firm. Even if these lawyers are paid $200 an hour,
industry is saving more than $1,000 in compliance costs for every $1 in lawyers'
fees. This is a far higher rate of return than industry can get from investing on new
production facilities. It appears that delaying regulations by laying Costle's
"minefield" is the best investment available to American industry today and that
sabotaging the regulatory process is far more lucrative than investing in new plants
or machinery. Of course, this calculus of obstruction depends upon the response of
the agency—if it refuses to collaborate with industry's paper blizzard, issues
regulations on time, and penalizes industry for obstructionistic tacts, using "recapture" techniques, the incentive to such delays would vanish.[25]

RCRA mandate not only delayed implementation long past the legal deadlines, but also made substantial concessions to industry and other segments of the Carter administration. The result of these concessions was a set of final RCRA regulations that left intact a number of loopholes and weaknesses identified by the EDF and other environmental groups.

STRUCTURE

The EPA's final regulations are divided into six major parts. Under the authority of RCRA alone, the EPA promulgated five different regulations, covering all of the areas governed by RCRA, except the final set of standards that would have to be met by landfills to qualify as permanent disposal sites. These regulations had still not been issued as of November, 1981.

Part 260 of the regulations contains the definitions and general administrative authority of the EPA under RCRA.

Part 261, the most controversial, discusses which materials are to be treated as hazardous wastes and how these determinations are to be made.

Part 262 specifies the regulations that govern generators of hazardous wastes, as defined in part 261, and that they must keep records and prepare manifests to show that all of the material they generate has been properly disposed of in a proper site.

Part 263 governs transporters of hazardous wastes, and specifies the standards they must meet and their role in keeping the manifests that track waste "from cradle to grave."

Part 264 contains standards that apply to operators of facilities for the disposal of hazardous wastes. This part was still incomplete; by November, 1981, only certain requirements, principally recordkeeping and financial in nature, had been established for permanent disposal sites. The actual physical standards to be met had not yet been decided.

Part 265 specifies the standards to be met by interim disposal facilities during the time that elapses before they receive, or are denied, their certification as permanent disposal sites.

Then, in a separate section, the EPA "consolidates" its authority under RCRA with that under several other statutes, principally the Clean Water Act, to set up a unified program for delegating permitting authority under these statutes to the various states.

The EPA issued these final regulations in two stages. In February, 1980, regulations governing the manifest system were issued; in May, 1980, the bulk of the remaining regulations were put into place. Costle described the manifest regulations by saying that they would provide the agency with a "road map" of the nation's toxic-waste problem, by requiring firms that produced waste to obtain a signed manifest from haulers or disposal firms. If a manifest showing the disposal of the material in a safe, legally permitted disposal facility was not returned to the manufacturer within forty-five days, the manufacturer would have the obligation to inform the EPA, which could then commence action against the hauler or disposal firm. Costle said that he had assigned two hundred EPA staff members to monitor the rules and was requesting others.

REACTIONS

The manifest requirements were the least controversial section of the regulations, and the chemical industry indicated that it had no major objections to what Costle was announcing. The real battle—over which wastes would be covered, which generators must report, and how waste must be handled—remained for the other sections of the regulations.

On May 6, Eckhardt Beck, EPA administrator for water and waste management, announced the second package of regulations. These regulations laid out what substances would be considered hazardous wastes, what industries would be covered, and what monitoring would have to be done.

The rules represented significant changes from the original list promulgated in October, 1978. Most important, the definition of "minor" waste generators who would not have to comply with RCRA was changed from 220 to 2,200 pounds a month. This substantial relaxation was coupled with a new, tougher definition for producers of 118 of the most dangerous substances. These firms would have to comply with RCRA if they produced as little as 22 pounds of any of these substances.

The EPA also promulgated only part of its list of substances to be regulated, but took the same basic approach as it had in its original proposed regulation. Again, it listed only 158 chemicals, whereas California was already regulating over 800 chemicals, and only some chemical processes generating wastes were listed. The EDF summed up its view of the final regulations: "It took three and a half years for the EPA to develop these regulations. I can't say it has been worth the wait."[26] Hugh Kauffman had a similar complaint. "We could have promulgated California's regulations and saved a lot of paper," he told reporters.[27] However, in response to protests, such as those of CBE, the EPA decided in the final regulations not to exempt sewage sludges. The EPA admitted that its authority over such sludges came under several statutes—under RCRA as a hazardous waste, under the Clean Water Act, and under the Ocean Dumping Act. But the Agency decided that rather than exempting such sludges from RCRA because of the jurisdictional overlap, it would promulgate a new set of regulations under all the statutes to address the problem comprehensively. However, the EPA declined to list such sludges explicitly as hazardous wastes, and, in its comments on the issue, appeared committed to its original notion of managing cadmium-contaminated sludges by placing various legal restrictions on the use of ground fertilized with them for growing human food crops. The EPA also, in its language relating to closing of hazardous-waste facilities, lengthened the time during which groundwater must be monitored for contamination from twenty to thirty years. It argued that, since it had reduced the requirements for direct monitoring of water leaching off most dump sites, the increased monitoring time did not increase the overall burden on operators of dumps.

The EPA admitted that this thirty-year period was inadequate for dealing with heavy metals and certain organic wastes. "However, the Agency has found that it would be nearly impossible for small single facilities to finance such activities in perpetuity. . . Thus, some form of national insurance is necessary to ensure perpetual monitoring. . . ."[28] These comments are revealing, for they unveil a generally concealed awareness that, in trying to regulate hazardous waste disposal, the EPA was confronting near perpetual risks and trying to regulate them using very short-term regulatory solutions.

The EPA did weaken the original regulations in several other important respects. Controls on chemical evaporation from surface storage tanks were dropped, because, according to Steffan

Plehn, "We just don't have the technical capability to monitor and control [them]."[29] Requirements for monitoring of leachate from waste disposal sites were also weakened. All in all, advocates of strong controls felt that significant portions of the problem remained unregulated by the EPA.

Industry responded mildly, by now more concerned about the potential costs of the superfund legislation than by RCRA costs, and mollified by congressional deletion of such big-volume wastes as oil and gas drilling muds. The Chemical Manufacturer's Association's (CMA) Robert Roland, while criticizing the tone of EPA announcements on the problem, was far less hostile than he had been when the regulations were first proposed in 1978. The CMA still objected to the EPA's decision to regulate all hazardous wastes in essentially the same way. It warned that this decision meant that the volume of regulated waste would be so large that soon "you'll be out of dump sites."[30]

The Aftermath of EPA's Regulations

The promulgation of the final regulations brought bubbling to the surface the unresolved underlying issues of hazardous waste regulation. Basically, RCRA, as conceived and implemented, is an attempt to force thousands of individuals, firms, states, and communities to undertake actions that are not commercially profitable or advantageous. Firms are to register as producers of hazardous waste, when the impact of such registration is to dramatically increase their own waste disposal costs. They are to file manifest forms to track their wastes, thus exposing themselves to possible liability suits. Waste firms are to dramatically increase the level of safety and monitoring they provide on their sites. Communities, if this system is to work, must be willing to permit new waste disposal sites to be located, even though such sites are known to be hazardous and may expose local officials to both political and legal liability.* States are to dramatically

---

*These comments, and most of those which follow in the next section, treat the hazardous waste disposal problem simplistically, in terms of finding dump sites. Since waste is being generated *now*, and industry intends to dispose of most of it, at least for the immediate future, in landfills, the short-term public-policy debate is dominated by this viewpoint.

increase their funding of hazardous waste enforcement work so that they can assume from the EPA the burden of compelling through regulation and enforcement this huge array of unattractive choices for private firms and localities. At the top sits the EPA, instructed to locate those who refuse to mend their ways and bring legal action against them.

Can all of this really work? The first answers began to trickle in immediately after the EPA announced its regulations. The Associated Press reported on August 4, 1980 that the first impact of the EPA's announcement of the RCRA regulations was a scramble to get rid of as much waste as possible before the regulations took effect in November, 1980.

Illegal haulers of toxic waste are using novel methods to dump as much of their chemical contraband as possible in the next 90 days. . . . In addition to their usual midnight drops in New England, they are using other ways . . . including boxcar shipments to points around the country and abandoning trailers loaded with toxic wastes in shopping center lots or along roads. . . . A waste dealer from Jersey City told the Associated Press that some waste producers are in panic. "They're looking at thousands of drums they've been collecting for years. They're scared to death that if they don't dump them before November, they'll go broke paying to dispose of them the EPA way. It's wonderful for my business."

"Guys who refused to talk to me three months ago are now pleading with me to get rid of their drums," said a trucker from Bayonne, NJ. "Purchasing agents now call me 'mister' instead of 'hey, you.'" They said the unexpected surge in shipments has forced them and others in their unsanctioned society to "throw caution to the wind."

"We've got so many loads backed up that I'm running out of safe places to dump," says another dealer, who works out of Stamford, Connecticut. "The garages and warehouses we normally use are full, the cheap landfills have tripled their prices, and my guys are dumping anyplace they can find an empty field without too many police cars sitting in it."

One operation that allegedly runs out of Hartford, Connecticut only works in foul weather. A driver watches the forecast for rain or snow, then picks up a tanker load of chemicals. With the discharge valve open he drives on an interstate until 6,800 gallons of hot cargo have dribbled out. "About sixty miles is all it takes to get rid of a load," boasted the driver, "and the only way I can get caught is if the windshield wipers or the tires of the car behind me start melting."[31]

The EPA and state officials admitted that they were powerless to stop or even apprehend the illegal dumpers. The first effect of trying to carry out RCRA proved to be the widespread increase in the worst of the illegal waste disposal practices. The second effect of RCRA was also evident even before the rules went into effect. In April, 1980, EPA officials began saying publicly that, when the rules took effect in November, 1980, society was going to have to face the fact that it did not have nearly enough legal dump sites in place, and that community opposition was making it virtually impossible to open new ones. Eckhardt Beck estimated that there were 120 dump sites in place that could meet the requirements of the law, but that 100 new sites would be needed immediately to handle the 57 million tons of waste that the EPA estimated the RCRA regulations would cover.

Worse, many of the existing 120 sites were under heavy local and community pressure to shut down, either in the courts or before local and state government. The EPA's hazardous waste enforcement director, Doug MacMillan, admitted that actions taken against unsafe sites made the job of locating new facilities harder. "Every time we nail somebody for running a bad site, we create a public perception that none of these sites can be safe. It's a dilemma. We have to get the worst sites out of operation, but we seem to be creating a blind resistance even to well-designed sites."[32] He cited as an example a 1977 incident in which residents of Wilsonville, Illinois threatened to blow up a landfill to prevent PCB disposal, even though the EPA claimed the site to be a good one.* Minnesota received $3.7 million from the EPA to set up a model waste disposal site. Forty-four sites were initially surveyed, sixteen of them picked as the best, but all were eventually rejected by local communities, and the EPA got its money back.

In addition to citizen resistance, legal liability created an incentive for localities to reject new sites and close old ones. "A city or county that did everything known or thought to be safe at the time can end up being liable later," a representative of the Na-

---

*Evidence showed, however, that this site, located in downtown Wilsonville, was highly unsuitable.[33]

tional Association of Regional Councils commented. "Why should a place spend millions for the machinery now for the privilege of running that risk?"[34]

One possibility would have been for the federal government to assume the role of siting facilities and overriding local opposition. The EPA, understandably, declined that task. It indicated that states would have to assume the task of siting such facilities. Plehn argued that, by doing so, states could secure for themselves future economic growth, which might otherwise be stunted by a lack of waste disposal facilities. But how strongly this argument would convince states was unclear, since the courts had held in the City of Philadelphia v. New Jersey that, once a disposal site was opened, a state could not prevent wastes from other sites from being shipped to it for disposal.

The EPA also announced in April, 1980 that it would examine the possibility of financial incentives to states to encourage location of waste facilities, an idea supported by Environmental Action and other environmental groups. The agency said that direct and indirect payments were under consideration. Funds could originate with government or with the developer of the facility and could be made to compensate for lost property values, to increase local tax revenues, or as one-time payments to local residents.

But while the problem was being laid out, there was little evidence that states were rushing ahead to develop means of solving it. Everyone publicly acknowledged that new sites were needed, and everyone privately waited for someone else to site them. If enough sites were not available by October 1, 1980, the burden would then fall on the EPA and the states, where they had assumed charge of the RCRA program, to prosecute generators of hazardous wastes who did not or could not find a legal way to dispose of their materials.

It was dubious that anyone had the capability to deliver on this enforcement threat. An April, 1980 report prepared for the EPA indicated that the agency had identified nine states in which the implementation of RCRA would have to remain an exclusively federal task, because the states did not have the necessary legal authority to carry out the law: Alaska, Colorado, Hawaii, Idaho, Nevada, New Mexico, North Dakota, West Virginia, and

Wyoming. An additional seven states were borderline in terms of assuming RCRA responsibility: Arizona, Delaware, Florida, Kansas, Missouri, Nebraska, and New Jersey.[35] Whether the EPA possessed the necessary resources to carry out direct enforcement of RCRA in these sixteen states was doubtful. Worse, the remaining thirty-four states to which the EPA proposed to delegate authority had the legislative authority, but lacked regulations to carry out the legislation. Even more questionable was whether the states with the necessary legislative authority would be able to develop the necessary administrative structure, financial capability, and staffing levels to carry out the program.

Staffing levels were likely to be extraordinarily high. The Office of Management and Budget estimated the RCRA would require 5.2 million hours of labor per year from industry simply to fill out the necessary reports and manifests. At a minimum, an effective enforcement structure would require random audits of these materials by state regulatory agencies. If we assume that an adequate level of enforcement would be produced by auditing 10 percent of the reports, and that an audit requires from four to five times as many hours of work as filling out the original form, then the state burden just to audit the manifests would run on the order of 2.5 million hours of work annually.

If the average employee engaged in such auditing worked fifty weeks a year for forty hours a week, then 1,250 staff members would be required simply to audit the manifests. Additional thousands of staff would be required for dealing with on-site inspections of sites and generators, examining the condition of equipment used in shipment and disposal, handling the difficult political and scientific problems of siting waste-disposal sites, preparing evidence for prosecutions, bringing lawsuits, and administering the monitoring programs required.

Reagan and Regulation of Hazardous Wastes

I would like to suggest to the Members of this House that some day down the road about a year from now they are going to receive a letter from a company in their district that has just received a $5 or $10 million liability suit from EPA that was triggered by nothing more than a decision of a GS-14 that some landfill, some disposal site somewhere, needed to be cleaned up and, as a result of an investigation that his office did, he found out that that company in your district contributed a few hundred pounds of waste to that site 30 years ago. . . . I do not know how much damage, I do not know how much harassment we want to do to the industrial economy in this country that is literally faltering from under our feet, that is in recession, that has 8 million people unemployed. . . . We discuss and deal with these problems and we are unleashing here an enormous club. [Michigan Congressman David Stockman's comments before the House on September 23, 1980, in opposition to passage of HR 7020, the Superfund][36]

Contradictions exist concerning the amount of flexibility Colorado would be allowed in designing its own [hazardous waste] program. Several unresolved issues concerning the state's prerogatives include . . . the state's authority to issue permits; the state's latitude, if any, in determining best engineering judgment criteria; the state's ability to limit citizen suits. . . . It is not possible now to determine the cost of a state administered program in Colorado. . . . [We recommend] that Colorado not establish a program to administer RCRA at this time. . . . Board of County commissioners should be given siting authority for hazardous waste disposal sites. . . . Disposal of one's own waste on one's own property should, as the current law states, not be subject to state or local regulation . . . as long as it does not constitute a public nuisance . . . and as long as such dumping is in accord with the rules and regulations of the department. Implicit in this recommendation is that the department be given no regulatory authority which supersedes or duplicates the federal program administered by EPA. [December 1980 report of a Colorado legislative committee, authored in large part by its chairwoman, Anne McGill Gorsuch, a member of the Colorado legislature from 1976–1980][37]

The election of Ronald Reagan signalled the most ferocious political conflicts yet over the issue of hazardous wastes, as well as environmental and occupational health concerns in general. Between the Presidential inauguration of January 6, 1981, and the resignation of EPA Administrator Anne Gorsuch (Burford), the Reagan Administration went through three distinct approaches to hazardous waste regulation.

PHASE I: INTO REVERSE

In the first phase, running from January 1981 until March 1982, the Administration took its mandate from a report by the right-wing Heritage Foundation which called for the "suspension of a myriad of toxic and solid waste rules" on the grounds that the premise that "industrial chemicals pose a substantial threat to humans and the environment . . . has not been substantiated."[38]

The first budget proposals cut RCRA by 23 percent.[39] EPA proposed to delete 100 of the 550 substances regulated under the Superfund bill and raised the minimum size of toxic spills to be reported from 1 pound to 100 pounds for 80 of the 131 supertoxic substances listed under RCRA. The Agency dropped its goal of requiring that landfill operators demonstrate that their facilities would not degrade the environment in response to pressure from ARCO and other industrial giants.[40] EPA now said that "landfill may be the most acceptable management option and that 'environmentally acceptable releases' would be allowed."[41,43]

EPA regional offices were told to cease initiating hazardous waste cleanup operations; the rate of action against sites declined from 26 per month to only 7.[42] After secret meetings in which Justice Department Attorneys handling RCRA cases were excluded, EPA agreed to rewrite the RCRA regulations at industries' request, allowing, for example, 50 percent expansion at existing hazardous waste operations without agency approval.

Phase I culminated in early 1982. The Agency announced intent to weaken the Safe Drinking Water Act, and in a major shift, clearly reflecting politics and not science, EPA's John Todhunter declared that he would list chemicals for priority action under the Toxic Substances Control Act only if there was strong evidence of human health effects, not just in animal experiments. In contempt for the public policy which it inherited, EPA announced its intent to permit the resumption of the dumping in landfills of barrels filled with liquid hazardous waste—the very practice that had led to Love Canal and many such crises of the past. Under this proposal, up to 25 percent of the content of landfills could be liquids.

PHASE II: THE LOW PROFILE

But this massive counter-revolution was not going well politically. Congress had rejected the White House budget cuts and leading industrial spokesmen were beginning to fear that things had gone too far. When Lou Harris Associates released a poll showing that environmental issues could swing the 1982 elections to the Democrats, EPA began to bend. Under intense political pressures the ban on liquids in landfills was reinstated. Gorsuch abandoned earlier efforts to weaken Agency regulations on lead in gasoline. Liability insurance requirements for landfills were reinstated. The previous proposal to allow 50 percent expansions of existing dumpsites was cut back to 10 percent.

But at the same time that visible, controversial initiatives were abandoned, the basic direction did not change. OMB took issue with EPA efforts to strengthen regulation of landfills; the Agency moved to relax standards governing non-mutagenic or "epigenetic" carcinogens; the Agency again proposed to allow expansions at existing disposal sites of greater than 10 percent; emissions limits on hazardous waste incinerators were to be weakened. The general perception among those watching the Agency was that the low profile would last only through the election, when the Gorsuch team would resume the dismantling of the regulatory structure governing toxic wastes quite apart from the Agency as a whole.

PHASE III: SEWERGATE

But a new set of issues was slowly building. In the summer of 1982, Congressional committees seeking to block EPA's counter-revolution had begun probing the "whos and hows" of Agency policy making. Congressional investigators looked closely into the role played by James Sanderson. Sanderson had been nominated for the chief policy slot at the Agency, and while serving as a consultant was charged with extensive conflicts of interest with his private clients. While EPA's Investigator General cleared Sanderson, five Democratic Congressmen in June called for a Justice Department investigation.

Immediately following the November election, Representative Elliot Levitas' Investigation and Oversight Subcommittee issued the crucial subpoena for some 700,000 EPA documents relating to Superfund enforcement and cleanup. Levitas and other Congressional investigators made it clear that they suspected political meddling in the lawsuits against waste dumping and were looking for "sweetheart deals" in which industry was excused from further liability in exchange for cosmetic cleanup.

On December 2, on the advice of the Justice Department, Gorsuch refused to hand over "enforcement sensitive" documents included in the subpoena. She claimed "Executive Privilege," the same doctrine that Richard Nixon had invoked to try to protect crucial Watergate documents. By claiming Executive Privilege and denying the subpoena, the Administration blundered fatally. Congressional investigators now could charge "coverup;" a policy dispute, albeit a major one, had become a scandal. On December 16, Gorsuch was overwhelmingly cited on the House floor for contempt of Congress. Her fate, and that of her team, was sealed. On the same day, Superfund Chief Rita Lavelle denied under oath that she had ordered an investigation of EPA hazardous waste official and gadfly, Hugh Kauffman. Congress suspected perjury. By now, six committees were investigating EPA and the Superfund program. On January 4, 1983, EPA brought papershredders in to destroy "excess copies" of the subpoenaed documents. By February 2, Gorsuch asked the Justice Department to investigate Lavelle's allegedly improper business contacts. Two days later she asked for Lavelle's resignation. Lavelle refused to resign; the President fired her. She responded that she was being made a scapegoat, and began denouncing Gorsuch.

As the investigation continued it appeared that EPA officials had delayed the release of cleanup funds for Stringfellow Quarry in order to hurt Jerry Brown's Senate campaign. Lavelle continued to defy subpoenas. The Justice Department refused to carry out the contempt citation against Gorsuch. The President waffled back and forth about whether he would release the documents demanded by Dingell and other investigators.

On February 18, 1983, Representative Mike Synar (D-Oklahoma) released an audit of the Superfund Program performed by the EPA's Office of the Inspector General which found that $53 million of the $180 million obligated could not be accounted for properly. The audit provided clear and convincing evidence for major mismanagement, if not worse. The White House reaction was curious. Instead of vowing to correct the problem, it fired the Inspector General.

EPA tried to recover its credibility. On February 22, 1983, the Agency announced that it would spend $33 million to buy out the entire community of Times Beach, which had been contaminated by dioxin (see page 139). Immediately thereafter, while Gorsuch (now Anne Burford) was touring the country defending her record, the White House dismissed two of her top aides. Reporters, pressing Presidential councilor Ed Meese at a San Francisco banquet as to whether Gorsuch-Burford would leave the Agency, were told, "Not before the salad course." The President continued to defend his Administrator, but Republicans in and out of his Administration demanded her resignation. On March 6, under intense pressure, and having lost even the support of Interior Secretary James Watt, Burford resigned. The President lashed out at a press conference, saying she should leave "with her head held high," and that his environmental opponents would not rest until "they've turned the White House into a bird's nest."

But then came word that Burford's replacement would be former EPA Administrator William Ruckelshaus, a man originally squarely in the mainstream of the Agency's history, one of those that candidate Reagan clearly meant in October, 1981 when he told Steubenville, Ohio steelworkers that for ten years the nation had been in the hands of "environmental extremists." And by the first of April, the rest of the top EPA team that had dealt with toxics and hazardous waste was gone.

Ruckelshaus entered with the promise that he would have a free hand, but with few specifics on what he would do with it. Morale at the agency began to improve, but action to deal with toxic wastes was still stalled.

Despite the Administration's efforts to distance itself from the EPA scandals, the Congress and public had become convinced that they grew out of basic administration policies, rather than merely management or personnel failings. Rather than waiting for Congress to approve legislatively Reagan's promised relaxation of public health regulations, the Administration had tried surreptitiously and lawlessly to block their implementation at the agency level through budget and personnel cuts and the appointment of officials hostile to their regulatory mission. Whether Ruckelshaus can reverse such fundamental policies and acts of lawlessness is one question, given his positions and policies while serving with Weyerhauser (including potential conflicts of interest); whether he wishes to is another.

Conclusions

Four years after the passage of RCRA, the EPA finally put in place a regulatory structure to carry that law into effect. The Carter administration, the most committed environmental presidency in modern American history, found the task of writing these regulations almost beyond its administrative and political capacity. From the viewpoint of environmental organizations, the final regulations fail to control adequately many of the hazards of waste disposal. From the viewpoint of industry, the regulations present the spectacle of massive paperwork, greatly increased disposal costs, and the threat that adequate disposal facilities simply may not yet be available.

These regulations, now written, must be implemented, and, indeed, important sections of the regulations themselves are still not in final form. The new Reagan administration came into office facing this as one of its most serious environmental challenges. Outgoing EPA officials in private conversations expressed deep and profound misgivings about the danger that the regulations, mishandled, could virtually destroy the federal capability to effectively regulate hazardous waste. Now these fears have come to pass.

These delays and failures are not surprising. Nor, although

there is certainly room to criticize the roles played by the EPA, industry, public-interest groups, and other participants, is it fair to assert that the problem is exclusively any one party's fault. Proper disposal of hazardous wastes is a huge enterprise. Proper, effective administration of a statute like RCRA would have major labor requirements. Indeed, to monitor all the producers of hazardous waste materials closely enough to ensure that they complied with these regulations might, in some cases, take as much labor as is required to produce the materials in the first place. Thus, the real costs of producing such goods, and safely disposing of them, may be significantly higher than the traditional market costs, which have ignored problems of disposal.

Nevertheless, there is no question that regulation is cost effective. High as the immediate costs of regulation are, Love Canal and a growing number of other examples demonstrate that the future costs of failure to regulate now are many orders of magnitude higher and grossly inflationary. But the attempt to solve the problem of hazardous waste disposal *by regulation alone* is doomed to failure. The dike that regulation erects against the flood of toxic agents simply is not strong enough to do the job alone. If the problem is that *production* of many toxic materials is not cost effective, then this problem must be tackled directly. The failure to directly discourage the production of toxic wastes makes it difficult for regulators to subsequently tackle those tasks for which regulation is appropriate. As regulation is used on a larger and larger scale to solve more and more difficult problems, and as a substitute for more direct solutions, the apparent costs of regulation mount, as more and more costs of production are shifted to after-the-fact regulatory amelioration. The costs then appear to be regulatory, and the resistance of those who bear the costs becomes improperly focused on regulation. Regulators are denied resources and power needed to do their job, and the whole system begins to break down.

Oddly enough, this point has been made vividly by David Stockman, in opposition to the Superfund. Stockman argued that the Superfund could give EPA broad authority to clean up virtually any dump in the country:

... Let us look at some of the other hazardous materials on the
RCRA list: creosote. Creosote is part of every railroad tie, every
telephone pole in the country, and there are hundreds of thousands of them discarded every year. Most of them are thrown in
rubbish piles and junkyards that, under the definition of this act,
are hazardous material. . . . Then we have naphthalene. That is
another chemical name, and what is it? It is mothballs. Every
family throws that away every day, and it is found in every
municipal dump in the country. . . . formaldehyde. That is used in
every laboratory in the country, and it is in every high school
biology lab. It gets thrown away, and that brings the site under the
scope of the bill before us. . . .[44]

But in his lengthy floor remarks, while Stockman demonstrated clearly that materials listed as hazardous were to be
found almost everywhere, he did not attempt to deny (or perhaps did not know) that, in fact, rat poison, creosote, naphthalene, and formaldehyde are all highly toxic.

So it appears that the regulatory burden involved is far
greater than was anticipated by the concerned members of
Congress who first began to develop the ideas that led to RCRA.
The public owes them a great debt for having been willing to
proceed with the passage of RCRA because it was needed, and
vitally needed, even though they could not at the time foresee all
the consequences. But the history of the regulation of hazardous
waste disposal indicates that the problem was not the simple,
"Let's finish off what we began with the Clean Air and Clean
Water Acts" task that was referred to in the floor debates on
RCRA. Solving the problem of hazardous waste disposal will involve a far broader call on all elements of society. The problem is
not amenable to a purely regulatory solution, and it goes to the
heart of our future economy. To be effective, regulatory solutions must be complemented by a wide range of additional approaches including common-law litigation, compensatory remedies, economic incentives and disincentives, and other forms of
government influence.[45]

Salus populi suprema lex.
The people's safety is the highest law.

ANCIENT ROMAN LEGAL MAXIM

C H A P T E R   10

The Citizen's Legal Guide to Hazardous Wastes

No one really knows the overall scope of the hazardous waste problem.* The unresolved questions are both technical and practical. We do not know what wastes are being released into the environment; how and where they are being released; what their ultimate fate will be in the environment; or what their health and environmental effects are. And without answers to these questions, scientists, legislators, environmental agencies, and the public cannot agree on appropriate solutions.

This chapter was conceived and developed by Durwood Zaelke with Jeffrey Trauberman, the principal author. Barbara Shaw also collaborated with Messrs. Trauberman and Zaelke in writing the chapter.

*The term *hazardous* (or *toxic*) *wastes* generally refers to discarded materials considered to have little or no economic value; they do, however, often have substantive value for recycling and reuse. In contrast, hazardous *substances* or chemicals may have obvious economic value and can include products, as well as discarded materials. Although this chapter uses the term *hazardous wastes,* the principles discussed here generally apply to hazardous substances as well.[1]

An informed public has an important role to play in answering these questions. Although federal, state, and local governments are becoming increasingly concerned about controlling hazardous wastes, the active involvement of private citizens is critical to the discovery of specific problems and to effective solutions, including vigorous law enforcement—as can be seen in the case histories presented earlier in this book.

This chapter discusses the investigative methods and forums citizens can use to solve and prevent hazardous waste problems. While the legal process is emphasized, since it is often the most effective way of solving specific hazardous waste problems, no attempt is made to address all legal issues that can arise or to substitute for the assistance of qualified legal counsel.

General Legal Theory

The legal system regulates many formal relationships within society, including the relationships between the public and those who handle, transport, treat, store, and dispose of hazardous wastes. One of the most important concepts governing these relationships is "reasonableness."

REASONABLENESS

Where there is an "unreasonable" threat of injury, the law generally will provide a "right of action" to remedy the threat. Similarly, where injury has occurred because "reasonable" precautions were not taken, the law generally will provide a "right of action" for compensation.

In determining what is reasonable, the legal system attempts to balance the competing interests of everyone involved, in light of all the surrounding circumstances. The standards used by courts and legislatures during this balancing process make up the substantive law, as opposed to procedural law.* Substantive

---

*Procedural law generally describes the processes, forms, forums, and conventions used within the legal system. Procedural issues are often important, and may even determine the outcome of a legal dispute. Examples of procedural issues include: the proper court or courts in which to sue, the administrative process for issuing rules, and the forms to file when litigating. Because procedural requirements are so diverse and complex, this chapter does not attempt to address them in detail.

law is an amalgam of rules, requirements, and principles that come from four primary sources: the common law, which is decided by judges; statutes, which are enacted by legislative bodies; regulations, which set the specific rules and standards that carry out the statutes;* and federal and state constitutions. Of these, the first three sources are most relevant to environmental law, although constitutional questions are occasionally involved.

BASIS OF LIABILITY

A basis of liability defines when someone will be held legally responsible for actual or threatened harm. After liability against a defendant is established, the plaintiff has a right to obtain relief (a remedy) from the defendant. The substantive law—that is, the common law, statutes, regulations, and constitutions—provide the primary bases of liability in American law.

COMMON LAW

The common law is made up of rules and principles originally derived from ancient usage. Because historically the common law has been interpreted and applied by the courts, it is also known as judge-made law. An example is common law nuisance, which is the unreasonable interference with a public or private interest, such as health or property.

The hallmark of much common law is the explicit balancing of competing societal interests.[2] For example, in a nuisance action brought against a hazardous waste disposal company by its neighbors, the judge must balance various factors. On the one hand, the company has a legitimate interest in a waste disposal business, and society, represented by the government, has an interest in having workers employed and in having the company pay taxes. On the other hand, the neighbors have a legitimate interest in protecting their health and well-being and in preserving the value of their property.

Generally, the balance will be struck in favor of the neighbors if the risk from the hazardous waste site is greater than the

---

*Regulations are not actually an independent source of substantive law; in reality, regulatory authority is derived from statutory authority.

social cost of preventing that risk. Although this is a difficult balance to strike, important factors include the extent of actual or threatened harm and the expense of controlling it. Human health is often an overriding issue in this balancing process.[3]

STATUTES

Laws enacted by legislative bodies are familiar to most people. Examples include the Clean Water Act, the Clean Air Act, the Resource Conservation and Recovery Act (RCRA), state sales tax laws, and even local zoning ordinances.

The explicit balancing in most cases involving statutory law is originally done by the legislature in creating the statute, rather than by the courts, as in common law litigation. In a given hazardous waste case, the statute thus already will have established that a particular type of threat to a particular class of people, such as neighbors around a hazardous waste disposal plant, *always* outweighs the social utility of the plant. If the problem before the court is the type contemplated in the statute, the judge will not be required to do any explicit balancing.

Judges, however, are trained to balance, and many will do their own balancing implicitly. In a close case, if the judge's opinion of the proper balance conflicts with the letter of the law, he may be tempted to find that the statute does not apply to the case at hand. In other cases, the statute may not clearly specify how to weigh risks.[4,5] For this reason, it may be necessary to show, even in cases based on statutes, that the overall balance is against the defendant.

REGULATIONS

Regulations are issued by government agencies, such as the Environmental Protection Agency (EPA) to help interpret and carry out statutes. Regulations and the agencies that administer them are necessary because it is usually impossible for legislative bodies to decide each of the many specific, practical issues that can arise under a statute.

Agencies often explicitly strike the balance between conflicting societal interests when issuing regulations. For example, under a statute, the EPA may issue regulations stating that any waste containing more than "x" amount of various hazardous chemicals shall not be discharged into any body of water. In this case, the EPA will have explicitly struck the balance between the harm these chemicals would cause if dumped in the water and the additional cost of using a safer disposal technique.

Regulations are usually very specific, and a judge has even less discretion in determining the balance than when applying a statute or the common law. For example, the common law generally requires warnings of unreasonable risk, while a statute additionally might require that there always be a written warning. Regulations under the statute may further specify that the written warning must be a particular size and color and that it must be displayed in a certain location.

Proving a violation of regulations is easiest because they are the most specific of all substantive laws. Without having to consider whether the statutory requirement for the warning is reasonable in light of all the circumstances, a judge need only know that a company was responsible for the designated hazardous wastes and did not display the appropriate warning.

However, even in lawsuits where compliance with regulations is in question, judges may do their own balancing. A judge may find that, despite the fact that the regulations have been met, the company's conduct was unreasonable. On the other hand, a judge may refuse to apply regulations for various reasons. A judge may find that the regulations are not an accurate interpretation of the statute, that they go beyond the scope of the statute intended by the legislature, or that they violate a constitutional principle, such as the requirement to treat all members of a given class of people equally.

ENFORCEMENT RESPONSIBILITY

The legal system for hazardous wastes addresses the prevention and cleanup of waste problems and the compensation of injuries already inflicted. Some laws and legal theories are available only to the government, while others may be available to the public. In cases involving statutory relief, the legislature sometimes will clearly specify who can obtain relief under the statute. For example, the law may contain a specific provision authorizing citizen suits in addition to governmental actions. In such situations, it is easy to determine who has enforcement responsibility. At other times, however, it may be less obvious.

If a statute is unclear as to whether citizens can exercise enforcement responsibility, examining its legislative history can be helpful. It may be that the legislative drafter implicitly intended private citizens to be able to take advantage of the law. However, to determine who can obtain relief if the suit itself does not involve a statute (such as a common law nuisance suit), it is necessary to identify the type of injury and whether private or public interests have been harmed.

Where harm results only to the health or property of a small number of individuals, the injury is typically considered to be private, and the government is not necessarily responsible for enforcement. For example, if injury occurs only to the crops of a small number of farmers as a result of pollution, the injury is generally felt to be a private one, and the farmers would be required to pursue their own legal remedies.

In contrast, where there is an actual or threatened injury to an interest common to the general public—for example, public health or resources—enforcement responsibility traditionally has been assigned to the government, with its general duty to protect the health, welfare, and resources of its people.[6] This general rule has been established in order to avoid or limit the spate of litigation that might otherwise occur if everyone who was injured initiated a lawsuit.[7]

For example, suppose a hazardous waste disposal company is not storing its waste in a manner specified under state waste management laws and is polluting a river that is used as a local drinking water supply. In this case, the state government whose regulations were violated would be a principal plaintiff in a lawsuit against the company.*

In such a suit, the government may ask the court to issue an injunction ordering the company to cease operations until the site is cleaned up and the disposal facility meets the specified re-

---

*If federal law also were violated, then the federal government, through the EPA and the Department of Justice, could also be involved in bringing the lawsuit.

quirements. The government also may ask the court to require the company to hook up the local residents' homes to an uncontaminated water system. Furthermore, if public resources actually have been damaged, the government may seek compensation for this harm. Thus, if fish and wildlife have been contaminated or poisoned by the hazardous waste discharge, the government would be allowed to sue for damages.*

Unfortunately, however, the distinction between an incident causing private harm and one causing public harm is not always easy to make. Many environmental problems injure both public and private interests, and enforcement responsibility in such incidents may be unclear. In the above example, the pollution of the river also may have decreased the property values along the river, prevented recreational use of the water, and reduced local revenues from tourism. Injury to the river and the related fish and wildlife constitutes harm to a public resource. Contamination of drinking water may be a threat to public health. Depreciated property values, reduced recreational opportunities, and decreased tourism, however, constitute a private harm.

Historically, in such situations, private citizens were not allowed to sue when public injuries occurred unless they suffered some special injury that was "different in kind" from that incurred by the rest of the public.[9,10] In the river pollution example, some courts would not consider the property owners along the river to have suffered a different kind of harm than that suffered by the public. Such courts would deny the property owners a right to sue based on the reduced value of their land. Even fewer jurisdictions would allow them to sue because of lost recreational opportunities or decreased tourism. Fortunately, however, this situation is beginning to change, and the legal distinction between an exclusively public wrong and a privately enforceable wrong gradually is disappearing. Thus, fewer private citizens now are being denied a legal remedy just because they suffered an injury like everyone else.

---

*One problem faced in such suits is the valuation of damaged resources. Courts (and economists) still struggle with determining the value of fish, wildlife, and other nonmarket public resources, such as air and water.[8]

REMEDIES

The concept of balancing must also be used in the selection of an appropriate remedy. Generally, two types of remedies are available in an environmental lawsuit: compensation—money for harm already suffered—and preventive relief—an injunction instructing the defendant to do something to prevent further harm.

Whether an injunction to prevent further harm is appropriate typically depends upon where the balance is struck between the various costs and benefits to the plaintiff, the defendant, and society. If the threatened harm to the plaintiff far outweighs the cost of the remedy to the defendant, as may be the case with serious health threats, then the plaintiff will be entitled to the relief necessary to remove the threat.

Where the balance is close, the plaintiff often can tip the scale in his favor by asking for a reasonable remedy. For example, instead of asking for a costly remedy, such as shutting down a plant or removing all the wastes, the plaintiff may ask for a less costly remedy, such as a fence and a guard, or a court-approved plan for better management of the plant. Similarly, instead of asking for the costly remedy of purifying a contaminated aquifer, the plaintiff may ask for a less costly remedy, such as having the defendant pay for connecting his home to the municipal water system. By selecting a reasonable remedy, the plaintiff may be able to show the judge that, in contrast, the company's conduct is unreasonable.

In evaluating the merits of a lawsuit, the common law concept of balancing is often a good rule of thumb, whether the case is based on common law, statutory law, or regulations. That is, if the threatened harm is greater than the cost the defendant company would have to pay to correct the harm, and if the cost will not bankrupt the company, there is a good chance of winning. Finally, while a violation of regulations and statutes may be easier to prove, common law principles, such as nuisance and negligence, give the judge the most freedom to balance and often allow for the broadest and most creative remedies.

Common Law Liability and Hazardous Wastes

In a variety of situations, the common law can be an important tool for remedying hazardous waste problems. The most useful common law doctrines in a hazardous waste suit include nuisance, negligence, and strict liability for abnormally dangerous activities.

LIABILITY FOR NUISANCE

The common law doctrine of nuisance is probably the broadest basis of liability in environmental litigation, and has been applied to a wide variety of harmful or offensive hazardous waste activities. Nuisances are sometimes characterized as "private" or "public"; however, historically, the two were quite distinct concepts.

A public nuisance traditionally was a crime, and included activities felt to cause an unreasonable interference with a right common to the general public—such as disturbing the peace. Typically, public nuisances were enforced exclusively by the government, except when someone suffered a special injury "different in kind" from that suffered by others.

Today, however, while some laws still term certain conduct a public nuisance, the practical distinction between a public nuisance and a private nuisance is gradually disappearing. Injured private citizens generally can sue for improper disposal of hazardous wastes, despite the fact that such activities also may constitute a "public" harm.*

In a modern common law nuisance suit, citizens typically must show that they have suffered a substantial and unreasonable interference with their use and enjoyment of property. Substantial interference means that the injury cannot be trivial or idiosyncratic. It can include injury to health, or damage to property itself. Unreasonable harm is determined by balancing the interests of the plaintiff, the defendant, and society. Factors

---

*See earlier discussion of enforcement responsibility.

considered by the courts in assessing whether an injury is unreasonable include: the extent and duration of the injury; the character of the harm; the social utility of the defendant's conduct; the feasibility of preventing the injury; and the nature of the locality.* [11]

Liability for a nuisance may be based on conduct that is intentional, negligent, reckless, or abnormally dangerous. These bases of liability for nuisance can be used to prevent threatened injury or to compensate for harm already suffered; they also may be invoked independently of nuisance, although usually only to compensate for past harm.

Intentional actions are the most straightforward basis of liability for nuisance. However, the "intent" may not necessarily be to cause harm. The courts will assume intent if a *reasonable* person would believe that a particular result was substantially certain to follow from a particular act. If the operator of a hazardous waste site knows that toxic contaminants are escaping into a drinking water supply, the contamination of the water supply is considered intentional even if the operator did not mean to injure anyone. Nevertheless, to be sure of intent, it may be important to notify the operator that the escape of toxic contaminants is causing or threatening to cause harm. The operator's continuing to allow the contamination after the notice almost certainly would be considered intentional.

LIABILITY FOR NEGLIGENCE

Negligence is a broad basis of liability, but is often the most difficult to prove. A defendant who fails to act in a reasonable manner is negligent. Negligence is also described as the failure to exercise "due care." [12, 13]

The practical application of this duty to act reasonably depends on the circumstances of the case. What is reasonable in one instance may not be in another. Because this issue is ultimately a question of social policy, the courts will often look to

---

*These factors are primarily important in cases involving injunctive relief. In cases where an injured plaintiff seeks compensation, many courts do not attach overriding significance to considerations such as the social utility and the location of the defendant's conduct.

policymaking bodies for guidance. Legislative and administrative requirements regulating the defendant's activities may indicate the particular standard of care to be followed. For example, if a hazardous waste disposal firm fails to obey a statutory requirement to dispose of hazardous wastes in clay-lined vaults, this fact may be evidence of negligence or, in certain jurisdictions, may be conclusive proof of negligence. Thus, it is important in a negligence action to see whether a particular company has complied with all applicable hazardous waste laws and regulations.

In other cases, common industry practices may determine whether conduct is reasonable. For example, it may not be negligent to transport wastes in unlined fifty-five gallon cardboard containers if that is standard practice. However, a court may decide that neither the standard industry practice nor compliance with regulations is good enough and that reinforced metal drums should have been used.

If there is something that a *reasonable* person would or would not have done, and if the defendant did not do it, the defendant may be negligent. For example, a defendant may be negligent for not testing the waste to determine whether it was harmful, not monitoring a site to determine whether the waste was escaping, or not warning those exposed. Obviously, the more harmful a particular waste is, the more a reasonable person would do to protect others. Similarly, the less it costs to protect others, the more likely it is that a reasonable person would take protective measures, and the more likely it is that a defendant will be found negligent for not spending money on the protective measures.

Another factor in proving negligence is determining what a defendant knew or should have known about the risk from the hazardous waste. Again, the standard is what a reasonable person under similar circumstances should have known. Consider, for example, whether it would have been unreasonable for a real estate agent not to tell a buyer about a nearby hazardous waste disposal company. If the agent knew about the company and that its wastes were hazardous, it may be considered unreasonable that the agent failed to inform the buyer. If the agent did not know the disposal company existed or that it accepted hazardous wastes, the next question is whether the agent should have known about the disposal company and the hazardous wastes. It probably would be considered reasonable for a real estate agent not to investigate the surrounding area beyond the usual proximity of schools and parks.

On the other hand, those employed in the hazardous waste business generally are expected to know more than a real estate agent. It would be expected that reasonable hazardous waste generators should be aware that some independent transport companies do not deliver the wastes where they are supposed to; that some treatment companies do not neutralize the wastes sufficiently; and that some disposal companies do not safely dispose of their wastes. Since generators should be aware of these facts, reason would dictate that they investigate the companies they hire, and it is probably unreasonable for them not to make sure that the wastes are properly transported, stored, and disposed of.

In a negligence suit, the standard of reasonableness must be based on current information and technology. Even though a reasonable waste disposal operator may not have known of a particular risk twenty years ago, he may be negligent for not protecting against the risk once he learns of it or once he should have learned of it. Similarly, while it might be reasonable to reject a particular technology to reduce risk when it costs $1 million, it may not be reasonable several years later when the technology becomes available for only $100,000.

Proving a negligence case requires the plaintiff to persuade the court that the defendant's conduct did not conform to a standard that is socially desirable, as embodied in the concept of "reasonableness." An important issue is whether a reasonable person would have tested for risk or would have warned of risk.[14]

STRICT LIABILITY FOR ABNORMALLY DANGEROUS ACTIVITIES

Courts use the theory of strict liability when the risk involved is particularly great or when the activity causing the risk is "abnormal." In this sense, abnormal generally refers to the location and nature of the activity. For example, while blasting with dynamite might be normal practice in remote mining operations, it is abnormal in an urban setting.

When strict liability applies, a defendant will be liable regardless of whether it would have been reasonable to eliminate the risk. With strict liability, the standard of care is set so high that the defendant's actions are determined to be unreasonable if any harm occurs.[15]

In practical terms, strict liability means that a plaintiff must show only that the defendant caused his injuries, without proving that the defendant was negligent or unreasonable. Because of the unusual nature of the activity or its location, no balancing is required. The courts often justify strict liability against particular defendants by noting that the defendants may be seeking a profit from their activities; that the defendants are in a better position to control the risks than the victim; or that liability for an essentially unavoidable injury should be placed on the party who can bear it best.

OTHER COMMON LAW BASES OF LIABILITY

Besides nuisance, negligence, and abnormally dangerous activities, other bases of liability and legal strategies in common law are available in hazardous waste litigation. One of these involves liability for harmful "products."

PRODUCTS LIABILITY. Several legal avenues can be used by plaintiffs in "products liability" suits. These include negligence; breach of warranty, which involves the failure of a product to live up to an express or implied claim concerning its quality or properties; and strict liability for products.

Under the theory of strict liability for products, the seller of a product can be held liable for injuries suffered by the user or consumer if that product is "defective" and "unreasonably dangerous." One of the factors a court may consider in deciding whether a product is unreasonably dangerous is whether it bears an adequate warning label. A product generally will be considered defective if it is not as safe as an ordinary, reasonable consumer would expect.

Although strict liability has been used by consumers injured by hazardous products, such as drugs, cosmetics, asbestos insulation, and insecticides,[16] its specific application in the hazardous waste area has been limited.*

PUBLIC TRUST DOCTRINE. The public trust doctrine essentially holds that the natural resources of the country are held "in trust" for the benefit of the people. Therefore, any injury to such resources by any party may be actionable in court. This theory has been used as the basis to obtain injunctive relief and damages in a wide range of environmental lawsuits.[17]

Statutory Liability and Hazardous Wastes

It is generally possible to divide statutes imposing liability for hazardous wastes into those available only to the government and those available to the public either through a "citizen suit" provision or by the creation of a right in limited groups of private citizens, such as workers' compensation laws.

GOVERNMENT ENFORCEMENT

Many statutes regulating hazardous wastes are enforced primarily or, in some cases, exclusively by the government. Even when citizens cannot directly enforce these statutes, they can encourage the government to use its vast statutory power to solve a particular hazardous waste problem.

RESOURCE CONSERVATION AND RECOVERY ACT (RCRA). One of the most important of these statutes is RCRA. RCRA imposes an elaborate system of regulations for controlling the handling, transportation, storage, and disposal of hazardous wastes from "cradle to grave."† A principal feature is the requirement for a written "manifest" to keep track of all wastes. However, the RCRA regulatory program is still far from complete, and many regulations remain to be issued.[18]

---

*One of the reasons for the limited use of strict products liability in the hazardous waste area is that some courts allow only "users" or "consumers" of products to sue under this theory. Bystanders, who would be the most likely victims of hazardous waste exposure, may be forced to rely on other legal avenues.

†See also the discussion of RCRA in Chapters 8 and 9.

In addition to authorizing detailed regulations, RCRA contains a provision very similar to common law nuisance. Section 7003 provides that where there is evidence that the "handling, storage, treatment, transportation or disposal of any . . . hazardous waste may present an imminent and substantial endangerment to health or the environment," the courts, at the EPA's request, may take whatever actions are necessary immediately to halt the alleged cause of endangerment.

Because the RCRA regulatory program is still incomplete the government has relied heavily on this provision for enforcement. As of November, 1981, the EPA and the U.S. Department of Justice had brought sixty enforcement actions under Section 7003 or related "imminent hazard" provisions, many of which have been successful (see Appendix VI). The relief granted includes many millions of dollars for cleaning up dangerous sites, as well as orders for companies to conduct monitoring and testing at waste sites, to replant vegetation near the sites, and to develop plans for preventing future waste discharges. [19,20,21]

In addition to RCRA, over twenty federal statutes may be applicable to toxic substances or hazardous waste control. The major statutes, many of which contain "imminent hazard" provisions (see Appendices VII and VIII) similar to section 7003 of RCRA, include:

THE TOXIC SUBSTANCES CONTROL ACT. This act allows the EPA to obtain information on new and existing chemicals and mixtures and to control the manufacture, distribution, and use of such substances. A specific provision governing polychlorinated biphenyls (PCBs) is included.

THE CLEAN WATER ACT. This statute controls the quality of the nation's navigable waters. Especially relevant are Section 402, governing permits for the discharge of substances into the navigable waters of the United States, and Section 311, prohibiting the discharge of oil and about three hundred designated hazardous substances "in such quantities as may be harmful."

THE FEDERAL INSECTICIDE, FUNGICIDE AND RODENTICIDE ACT. This statute governs the manufacture, distribution, and use of pesticides. Pesticides must be registered with the EPA before distribution and ultimately must be labeled and used in an approved manner.

THE SAFE DRINKING WATER ACT. This act is administered by the EPA and is intended to control the levels of contaminants and chemicals in public water systems and underground drinking water supplies.

THE CONSUMER PRODUCT SAFETY ACT. Administered by the Consumer Product Safety Commission, this act allows the commission to set safety standards for consumer products. If standards adequate to protect the public cannot be devised, the commission may ban a product.

THE OCCUPATIONAL SAFETY AND HEALTH ACT. This statute is concerned with safety in the workplace. It authorizes the Occupational Safety and Health Administration to set standards for occupational hazards, including toxic chemicals.[22,23]

THE CLEAN AIR ACT. This act governs air quality in the United States. It authorizes the EPA to set standards for air quality and to regulate the emission of air pollutants. Section 112 of the act specifically concerns "hazardous" air pollutants.

THE SUPERFUND. The latest statute in the federal government's arsenal is the superfund legislation. Formally called the Comprehensive Environmental Response, Compensation and Liability Act, the Superfund creates a $1.6 billion fund to finance governmental responses to actual and threatened releases of "hazardous substances" and dangerous "pollutants or contaminants." The federal government is required to develop a national contingency plan, detailing specifically how it will respond to such environmental incidents. Parties causing an actual or potential release are strictly liable for specified damages, which primarily include the costs incurred by the government in pollution cleanup, removal, and natural resource restoration. Compensation to private citizens for personal injuries is not provided; however, some authority exists in the law to redress medical and other expenditures incurred by private citizens under the national contingency plan. Except in certain emergencies or where a state has agreed to cooperate in pollution cleanup, the federal government's response under the Superfund is generally limited to $1 million or to a six-month period, whichever occurs first.

Similarly, the liability of those causing the "release" is limited by the Superfund, except where the polluter fails to cooperate, where known violations of safety or other regulations are the primary cause of injury; or where the pollution results from willful negligence or misconduct. Under these circumstances, unlimited liability may be imposed. Furthermore, triple damages are available if a party fails to obey a government cleanup order.

Where those causing the release are not known or are unable or unwilling to pay, the relevant party, usually the federal or state government, may file a claim against the fund for damages. Once the fund pays such a claim, it has the right to sue the responsible private party to get the money back.[24]

CITIZEN ENFORCEMENT

Citizen enforcement of hazardous waste legislation is possible in a number of different contexts. Under some statutes, citizen suits may be used to enforce the law against the government and polluters. Other statutes, such as workers' compensation laws, specifically authorize relief to private individuals and groups.

CITIZEN SUIT PROVISIONS. All the above statutes can be enforced by citizens under "citizen suit" provisions, with the exception of the Superfund and the Occupational Safety and Health Act, which contain no such authority. Citizen suit provisions generally allow citizens to sue parties violating the statute or to sue the government when it fails to fulfill a clear statutory requirement.

For example, when the federal government failed to meet its statutory deadline to issue hazardous waste regulations under RCRA, it was sued under the citizen suit provision of that law. The result was that the courts established a schedule for issuing the regulations.[25] Other citizen suits have been brought under the Clean Water Act to prevent the discharge of radioactive wastes from Three Mile Island and under the Toxic Substances Control Act to force the government to issue rules requiring chemicals to be tested.[26]

Citizen suit provisions are not limited to federal statutes. A number of state hazardous waste and toxic substances laws also contain citizen suit provisions, which vary from state to state.[27]

RULEMAKING PETITIONS. In addition to citizen suits, some federal environmental laws, such as the Toxic Substances Control Act and the Resource Conservation and Recovery Act, authorize rulemaking petitions. Provisions in these laws allow private citizens formally to request an agency to issue, revoke, or amend a rule on a particular subject. After receiving such a petition, the agency either must initiate the requested action, or else publicly explain its failure to do so. Sometimes an agency is allowed to set aside funds specifically for citizens to sue to prove their case, and to encourage public participation in other agency decisions.

FINANCIAL DECISION MAKING. One way that some citizens have used to register their concern for environmental health and safety is by making environmentally sensitive investment and financial decisions. Such citizens have refused to invest in ventures that may damage natural resources or public health.

Furthermore, regardless of one's environmental concerns, citizens may indirectly enforce environmental laws simply by recognizing that pollution in today's legal system can be quite costly. The U.S. Securities and Exchange Commission (SEC) requires most corporations to disclose, in annual reports and other public documents, the potential for certain financial effects related to compliance with environmental laws and legal proceedings. These disclosures allow investors to make more intelligent investment decisions,[28] because a company faced with a potentially large environmental lawsuit may not be a wise investment. Investors who study and rely on the information disclosed under these rules ultimately may deter business practices that damage the environment.

OTHER STATUTES AUTHORIZING PRIVATE RELIEF. In addition to laws authorizing citizen suits, rulemaking petitions, and environmental disclosures, some laws directly allow private citizens to take legal action against polluters for damages or other forms of private relief. Most of these laws exist at the state level.[29] For example, New Jersey and Florida specifically allow citizens to recover for damages caused by hazardous substances and create industry-financed funds to ensure payment.

A more novel legal strategy that can be used by private citizens involves shareholders' rights and actions under securities laws. Rules issued by the SEC make it relatively easy for shareholders, including minority shareholders, to force a stockholders' vote on corporate practices that adversely affect the environment. While substantive actions by corporate management may not necessarily be altered by minority shareholders who pursue this route, it can provide an expanded forum for criticizing business practices as they relate to the environment and other areas of social concern.* 30

Finally, all fifty states have workers' compensation laws, which may provide a limited remedy for occupational diseases and injuries in which a particular employment can be proven responsible for the damage.† 31

Problems in Hazardous Waste Litigation

CAUSATION AND BURDEN OF PROOF

Most of the bases of liability can be used to prevent threatened harm or to compensate for harm already suffered. Regardless of their use, however, every plaintiff must also deal with the burden of proving causation.

In a civil (noncriminal) hazardous waste lawsuit, the plaintiff must prove his case by a preponderance of legally acceptable evidence. While each fact need not be established with 100 percent certainty, the plaintiff must show that, more likely than not, he is entitled to relief. In order to meet this burden of proof, both a certain type and quantum of evidence must be introduced.

Establishing causation can be described as a three-part process. First, it is necessary to identify the particular hazardous waste that caused or threatened to cause the injury. Second, the responsible party, or defendant, whose actions are an actual cause of the exposure to the harmful waste, must be identified. Third, the defendant's actions must be sufficiently connected with the injuries, so that the courts, as a policy matter, will hold the defendant liable.

Identifying the hazardous substances that caused a particular injury usually requires expert witnesses and detailed technical information. This evidence is not always obtained easily or

---

*A New York–based, church-affiliated group called the Interfaith Center on Corporate Responsibility (ICCR) has been particularly active in this regard. It has presented proposals for consideration and action at stockholders' meetings of various companies offending the ICCR's social criteria for investment, including several chemical companies.

†Although these laws vary from state to state, it is generally agreed by labor that they are grossly inadequate in addressing diseases caused by hazardous substances. 32, 33

cheaply. The number of trained toxicologists, epidemiologists, and pathologists who are competent to provide evidence in a toxic-substances case is limited. What the law typically requires is therefore an extremely scarce resource.[34] As a result, suits involving hazardous wastes and other toxic substances can be expensive and time-consuming.[35]

In addition, the courts are not always willing to accept certain data as evidence of a particular fact, because scientists simply cannot supply the kind of definitive conclusions that the law seeks. For example, although animal tests are almost invariably used by scientists to predict the toxic effects of chemicals in humans, some courts may still be unwilling to recognize animal tests as conclusive evidence of the harmful properties of these chemicals.

The legal dilemma surrounding these scientific uncertainties assumes added importance when attempting to enjoin a potentially dangerous activity that has not yet caused harm. In addition to proving that money damages will not provide an adequate remedy should harm occur, the plaintiff must show that he is subjected to a particular risk of injury. That is, to obtain an injunction against such activity, the plaintiff must show harm of sufficient likelihood and severity.

With limited scientific information, showing that a specific type of harm is likely can be difficult. The hazardous effects of certain toxic chemicals may not be known, or the toxic chemicals contained in some wastes may be difficult to identify. An example is the Shenandoah Stables case in Moscow Mills, Missouri (see Chapter 6). While it was clear that some contaminant in the waste oil sprayed on the dirt arena at the stable was highly toxic, it was not until three years after soil samples were taken that the toxic agent TCDD, responsible for the injuries, was identified.

Health injuries may involve one or a few people, such as the owners of Shenandoah Stables, or a larger segment of the public, such as the many families living around Love Canal (see Chapter 5). Symptoms may show up immediately, such as the acute nephritis suffered by Andrea Piatt at Shenandoah Stables, or they may be delayed, such as cancer. Where acute injuries are involved, it is generally easier to identify the specific toxic waste and to locate the responsible party; it is also generally easier to prove causation.

Cases involving chronic health injuries may be legally more complex. Chronic injuries can occur when someone is exposed to low levels of toxic chemicals over a longer exposure period, as in the case of asbestos workers or coal miners. The relatively low level of exposure to toxic chemicals and the long exposure make it more difficult to identify any effects; some chronic diseases, such as cancer, have latency periods that prevent them from manifesting up to forty years after exposure. Furthermore, it may be difficult to identify the effects of exposure to a chemical agent when other possible causes of injury, such as smoking, are introduced.[36,37]*

In addition to the scientific problems presented in establishing the particular toxic chemical or chemicals responsible for an injury, it is often impossible to identify the responsible party, particularly in highly industrialized states, where there are many possible sources of hazardous waste contamination. Even when this is not the case, it is often difficult to identify the offender. According to Edwin Stier, an assistant attorney general for the state of New Jersey in 1977, finding the offenders in illegal dumping cases is difficult because they frequently operate behind a reputable business, such as a recycling company, which has fulfilled all licensing requirements.

Even when a responsible party potentially can be identified, to hold a defendant liable under any legal theory, a plaintiff must show that the defendant's actions or omissions were the cause of the actual or threatened injury. A defendant generally will be found to cause an injury when the injury would not have occurred without the defendant's acts or omissions and when the defendant's acts or omissions are a substantial factor in bringing about the injury. For example, under the first part of this two-prong test, a waste-disposal operator would not be liable for failing to put up a fence, when the person complaining of injury is someone who is allowed to bring the waste into the disposal

*For a scientific discussion on problems of dual causation and on the role of lifestyle factors, such as smoking, in toxic torts, see S.S. Epstein and J. Swartz "Fallacies of Lifestyle Cancer Theories," *Nature,* 289: 127–130, 1981.

facility; the existence of a fence would not have prevented the exposure in such a case.

Under the second part of this test, although a plaintiff may be able to prove that a specific chemical and person were the *actual* cause of injury, the law further limits causation for reasons of policy. If a defendant's activities are simply too remotely connected with the plaintiff's injuries (that is, not a "substantial factor" in causing the injuries), the defendant will not be liable, because the defendant's actions are not considered the "proximate" or legal cause of harm to the plaintiff.[38]

Therefore, in all cases, a range of possible defendants may be liable as the proximate cause of harm. For instance, if a person buys property and it turns out to have contaminated well water, a number of potentially liable defendants may suggest themselves. Some states require that wells be tested by public health departments before a property sale can be completed. Failure to do this properly may implicate public health officials as liable parties.

Other possible defendants in such a case include the companies that generated, handled, treated, transported, stored, or disposed of the hazardous wastes causing the suspected contamination. In addition, the former owner of the property (or perhaps even the real estate agent) may be liable for failing to tell the buyer that there was a hazardous waste disposal company in the area sharing the same aquifer.

Of course, while the acts or omissions of one or more of these parties may be deemed the proximate cause of the problem, it is not clear who, if anyone, would be liable in the above well-pollution example. Again, the fact that various governmental and private parties have had *some* role in causing a hazardous waste problem does not mean that any one of them necessarily can be held liable.

Similarly, if a person suffers injury, the defendant will not generally be held liable if the defendant did not (1) act intentionally, (2) act negligently, (3) engage in an abnormally dangerous activity, or (4) violate a statutory, regulatory, or constitutional provision. Therefore, certain defendants are not legally responsible for injuries that, in fact, they may have caused, because the law, as a policy matter, does not consider it appropriate to hold such defendants liable for harm.

One final, practical matter should be noted regarding causality and identifying a defendant. Sometimes a company that plays a part in improperly disposing of hazardous wastes may simply declare bankruptcy to avoid liability for pollution. Thus, one thing to consider in identifying defendants is whether they are financially able to compensate for damages. Even when there may be several possible defendants whose unreasonable acts or omissions can be causally connected to the injury or the threat of injury to health or the environment, it may not be realistic to sue all of them for damages. For example, if one of the possible defendants is a transport company that is a one-person operation close to bankruptcy, it would be hardly worthwhile to attempt to obtain compensation from it. In such cases, you should again consider whether other private or governmental parties can be held legally responsible under any of the bases of liability discussed earlier.

LATENT INJURIES AND STATUTES OF LIMITATIONS

In addition to the problems of causation and burden of proof, special problems of timeliness may be encountered by victims of hazardous waste pollution in states with restrictive statutes of limitations. A statute of limitations is a law that sets the length of time after an event has occurred in which a person is allowed to sue. These time limits are established to avoid "stale" lawsuits, in which evidence is unavailable and the memories of witnesses have faded.

Because many diseases caused by toxic substances are characterized by lengthy latency periods in which the victim is unaware of any injury, those at risk from hazardous chemicals may not seek timely legal redress. Some states will start the judicial clock running only after the victim has discovered or reasonably should have discovered his injury. Other state courts, however, insist that the statute should begin running at the time of the original exposure to the chemical, thus making it extremely difficult for those victims whose injuries take years to be discovered.[39]

The statute of limitations may also be a problem in cases of groundwater contamination, in which a long period of time often elapses between the introduction of hazardous wastes into groundwater and their detection. It may take years before the groundwater contamination becomes noticeable—sometimes by a chemical taste or odor in the drinking water—and even longer before any health effects are apparent.

PREMATURE OR INADEQUATE SETTLEMENTS

The severe technical, legal, and economic disadvantages of plaintiffs in hazardous waste cases may be a deterrent to initiating valid lawsuits or an incentive to accept premature or inadequate settlements. Some victims of the well-water contamination in Toone, Tennessee, for example, signed releases in their damage suit against Velsicol Chemical Corporation once the company began taking action to "make amends" (see Chapter 3). One family, the Sterlings, accepted $1500 to "sign off healthwise" because "there were no doctors who would say anything anyway." About a year later, however, a medical study concluded that these people were at high risk from long-term health effects, "particularly cancer," because of their "prolonged ingestion of high concentrations of carcinogens."

Aside from the possibility of obtaining inadequate relief, as in the case of the Sterlings, where long-term injuries might be much more serious than anticipated, out-of-court settlements might delay enforcement of hazardous waste laws. The resulting scarcity of reported precedents could discourage other citizens and attorneys from vigorously pursuing legal remedies, since they may not believe that they can win such cases. As more and more cases are resolved in the courts, the legal responsibility of those involved with hazardous wastes will become more explicitly defined and the nation will be better able to ensure the proper handling and disposal of hazardous wastes for the protection of public health and the environment.

What the Citizen Can Do

HOW TO INVESTIGATE THE FACTS

The first thing a good lawyer will tell any client is to "get the facts straight." While the factual circumstances can be complex, without reliable information that can be used as evidence or that will lead to such evidence, it doesn't matter how much law you know. You'll probably lose your case.

Ideally, hazardous waste cases that affect the public should be investigated by government enforcement agencies. However, with the exception of emergency situations, such as oil spills and explosions or fires at hazardous waste dumps, the hazardous waste staffs of government agencies are too limited to investigate even major reported problems and it is often necessary for citizens to conduct their own initial investigations before they can get government action. Initial investigation can be done by an individual or, perhaps more effectively, by an organized group.

Once the initial investigation is complete, a concise report of the facts should be submitted to the appropriate government agency. Not only will such a report give the agency the facts it needs to begin its own investigation, it will also show the agency staff that the people involved are serious enough about the problem to contribute to its solution.

Even in a private hazardous waste case, it may be beneficial to conduct a preliminary investigation of the facts before hiring an attorney. Completing the groundwork for a case will save the cost of having an attorney do it.

In either a public or a private case, the expertise of epidemiologists, toxicologists, engineers, hydrologists, or biologists eventually will be required. Such experts will, undoubtedly, also participate in any government investigation. It may be necessary, however, to get the opinion of experts on some of the more complex scientific issues to convince the government that an investigation is warranted.

Before beginning an investigation, it is necessary to know what facts to look for and how to find them. The types of facts necessary for proving a hazardous waste case will vary, depending on whether the basis of liability is common law nuisance or negligence, a statute, or regulations. There are, however, three basic facts that are essential in any hazardous waste case, regardless of the basis of liability or the defendant. These are (1) the people or environments threatened with exposure or actually injured, (2) the hazardous wastes involved, and (3) the routes of exposure.

Most investigations of hazardous waste problems are precipitated by events that create suspicion of harm to people or the environment. These events may include unexplained health problems: unusually frequent headaches, nausea, rashes, pul-

monary and kidney diseases, birth defects, and illness or death
of animals; an unidentifiable, offensive odor, taste, or color in
drinking water; an unidentifiable odor in the air; or the death or
disappearance of marine life in nearby rivers, lakes, or other
bodies of water.

IDENTIFYING PEOPLE OR ENVIRONMENTS EXPOSED. To identify who or what environment will be exposed or has already
been exposed and possibly injured requires a detailed description of the human population and the environment surrounding
the area in question. This information should be supported by
official records, such as the most recent census figures to verify
the population of the area or school enrollment records to verify
the number of children in the local grammar school. An official
subdivision map may show the exact location of schools and
residential dwellings in relation to the company site.

The investigation should focus on the populations and
environments that are most sensitive to the wastes and most in
danger of exposure. For example, a playground or school near
an unfenced waste site should be noted. Some exposed areas
may even be located directly on top of a waste site, as was Love
Canal's Ninety-Ninth Street School (see Chapter 5).

When the group of people potentially exposed to the hazardous wastes is especially susceptible—such as pregnant
women and young children—or when the type of environment
potentially exposed is very sensitive—such as a rich wetland or a
salmon-spawning stream—even a low probability of harmful
wastes escaping may be sufficient to obtain a preventive remedy
in a nuisance action. Similarly, in the case of extremely dangerous hazardous wastes, such as TCDD, a low probability of contamination even in a less sensitive population or environment
may be sufficient to get preventive relief.

Where injury may have already occurred, medical records
of the exposed population should be examined thoroughly. If the
case involves a specific plant, such as a hazardous waste disposal
company, the medical records of those working at or near the site
and those living near the site should be examined. Medical and
insurance records from the company can be especially useful,
since a history of undisclosed worker illnesses may exist. Finally,
union health records, if applicable, and health records from
nearby schools should not be overlooked.

Since most health records are personal and not readily available, some creative investigating may be necessary, including talking to former plant workers, who may sign medical release forms necessary to gain access to health records, or who may permit an interview with their doctor. Sometimes abstracts of the data will be available, such as a list of all children at the nearby school with certain types of skin rashes.

Records from veterinarians are also useful, as well as records from the local humane society and other government agencies dealing with animals. In many cases, signs of poisoning from hazardous wastes show up first in pets and barnyard animals (see Chapters 5 and 6).

IDENTIFYING HAZARDOUS WASTES. Identifying which hazardous wastes are being released or threaten to be released into the environment will require access to technical data. When a specific company is involved, necessary records would include (1) records of the suspect company and any other businesses associated with the company, (2) government records of permits granted or refused, and (3) environmental agency enforcement files. (For preliminary EPA lists of potential hazardous waste sites, see Appendices IX and X.)

Companies that handle hazardous wastes are required under RCRA to keep records of these wastes from their generation to their final disposal. But because the requirements of RCRA are so recent, they may not be helpful in most current hazardous wastes cases. Nevertheless, if the suspect company is in the disposal business, for example, there may be invoices, manifests, or other records describing what wastes have been accepted over the past years. Where these records are not available, it may be possible to get the names of previous employees who may remember some of the hazardous contents of other companies whose wastes were accepted.

The companies that generated the wastes should know what was in them or, at a minimum, what general types of wastes the company produced during its normal manufacturing process. These chemicals can be identified by chemical analysis, by a material-balance study, or an input-output analysis: if a, b, and c chemicals go into a specific production process, then, a, b, an c chemicals, plus their by-products, will come out after the various chemical reactions.

In addition to company records, local, state, and federal governments have records of permits issued for discharging any wastes into the air or water. These would include, for example, National Pollution Discharge Elimination System (NPDES) permits issued under the Clean Water Act. These permits list the types of wastes and the quantity that can be discharged. Local, state, and federal environmental agencies also maintain enforcement files, which should not be overlooked. It is possible that the suspect company has had earlier hazardous waste problems. Furthermore, the government (EPA) has extensive files because of a number of federal laws, including RCRA, Superfund, and the Clean Water Act. These statutes require various persons who deal with hazardous substances, or who spill hazardous substances, to inform the government of this fact.

Whenever there is a suspicion of hazardous waste contamination, local public health authorities should be contacted immediately and tests conducted to determine whether any toxic chemicals are present, and in what concentrations. If the preliminary tests are negative, further testing should be requested; it is possible that something was overlooked. For example, some preliminary test results of the drinking water in Toone, Tennessee, were negative. Subsequent tests, however, revealed excessively high levels of carcinogenic chemicals (see Chapter 3).

When the case involves chronic health injuries, identifying the specific hazardous waste may require a detailed history of the plaintiff's occupational and medical history. As discussed before, the low level and long exposure generally associated with chronic injuries make it more difficult to identify the hazardous waste and the cause of exposure.

Rarely, a particular type of cancer is strongly associated with a particular hazardous waste, e.g., mesothelioma and asbestos. When this is not the case, the search for the hazardous waste and the cause of exposure can be difficult. In cases of low-level, chronic exposures, it is essential to compile a detailed chronology for the victim, listing all potential exposures—in the workplace, home, surrounding neighborhoods, and vacations—and all observable health effects. Such a chronology will help answer the questions of which hazardous wastes or chemical "agents" caused the health injury and when and where the exposure occurred.

After identifying the wastes involved and their quantities, a profile of each should be prepared, including a description of how hazardous each waste is in various quantities and its specific effects—both acute and chronic—on people, animals, plants, and the surrounding environment.

A good source of information for preparing waste and chemical profiles is the MEDLARS computer service of the National Library of Medicine in Bethesda, Maryland. For a modest fee ($4 to $10 per computer search), the library will provide a comprehensive and current review of scientific literature on a given hazardous chemical.*

LOCATING THE ROUTES OF EXPOSURE. Uncovering the routes of exposure requires a detailed knowledge of the surrounding environment, including (1) the type of soil, (2) the location of any nearby groundwater or other water, its direction and rate of flow, and its present and planned uses, and (3) the weather, including the amount of precipitation and the force and direction of the winds. If the case involves a specific company, a detailed analysis of the plant site will also be necessary, including the type of disposal processes and the type of pit linings.

In the case of a contaminated drinking water well, several possible routes of exposure might be considered. The contaminant might have entered the well water through the well itself—for example, a termite service may have spilled insecticide into the well. The contaminant may have entered through the aquifer that feeds the well. The aquifer may have been contaminated through pollution of surface water feeding into the aquifer or through leaching of pollution down through the soil into the aquifer. Leaching could have occurred when rain, melting snow, or flooding waters passed through wastes, or when a waste treatment lagoon may not have been sufficiently lined, allowing the wastes to escape into the ground.

The investigation of exposure routes should note the rate at which the wastes are migrating through the particular route and

---

*MEDLARS search request forms are available from local medical school and hospital libraries, regional MEDLARS centers, and the National Library of Medicine, Literature Search Program, 8600 Rockville Pike, Bethesda, Md. 20014. A listing of regional MEDLARS centers may be obtained from the Office of Public Information, National Library of Medicine.

when the wastes will reach the exposed population or environment. Keep in mind, however, that both the direction and the rate of groundwater movement may change, depending on the type of soil and the type of wastes leaching through the soil.

The investigation of exposure routes also should consider how the various paths can possibly be closed to prevent the wastes from migrating. Any precautions the company has taken to prevent the waste from escaping should be noted—for example, fences, settling ponds, treatment ponds, warning signs, and monitoring of nearby air and water. The company may use this as their defense, and it will be necessary to rebut it by explaining why it has not worked.

Once the initial investigative report is finished, an appeal to the suspect company should be considered. Recent government enforcement programs against hazardous waste violations have made companies, particularly those that are large and well established, aware of the need to work with local communities before recourse to litigation. Before discussing the problem with the company, however, as much information as possible should be compiled to ensure that relevant questions are asked and that any evasive responses from the company can be challenged.

While investigating these basic facts, one should keep in mind the potential or threatened harm. Although actual harm is required to obtain compensation, proof of threatened harm is sufficient for preventive relief. Finally, keep in mind that not all information is reliable enough to be used as evidence in court. To prove the facts, official records or other reliable data need to be obtained.

In addition to the specific sources suggested, several organizations may be able to provide valuable information. These organizations include national environmental organizations, industry trade groups, labor unions, the EPA, and state environmental organizations (see Appendix XI).

Many national environmental organizations are active in the hazardous waste area and regularly work with citizen groups, and most will provide general information and publications on request. Their time and other resources, however, are limited, and they often cannot provide step-by-step advice.

While industry trade groups exist to promote the interests of their companies, sometimes useful information may be found in their public disclosures. Labor unions may also be helpful in the investigation, particularly if occupational exposures to chemicals are involved or if workplace exposure to a suspect chemical has ever resulted in a labor-management dispute. In the latter case, a union already may have collected health and safety data on the chemical.

The EPA and state environmental agencies are often the best source of information because of their direct contact with hazardous waste companies through regulation. In fact, they may have already investigated the site in question and may have a file of valuable evidence. Sometimes these agencies will provide data from only a telephone request. It is generally preferable, however, to make a formal request for the information under the federal Freedom of Information Act (FOIA).[40, 41]

Under the FOIA, federal agencies must disclose all information "reasonably describe[d]" in a written request, unless the information is protected by certain narrow exemptions, such as national security files, intra-agency memoranda, investigatory files, and trade secrets. Information requested under the FOIA generally must be provided within ten business days. Agencies may charge "reasonable" fees for search and duplication costs, but fees may be waived or reduced if the information is being furnished "in the public interest." Agencies also must note the reasons for refusing to disclose any data, explain appeal rights, and provide information on fees.*

Many states have statutes similar to the federal FOIA that govern public disclosure of state information. The homeowners of Love Canal, for example, could have used a state equivalent of the FOIA to obtain data from the state health department study —data they were refused (see Chapter 5).

The Federal Advisory Committee Act[42] and the Government in the Sunshine Act[43] both require certain policy-making meetings to be announced in advance and open to the public. Meeting transcripts, minutes, and other such records are also available. Often government decisions are made with the

---

*On October 15, 1981, the Reagan Administration submitted to Congress a proposal that would drastically restrict the obligation of federal agencies to provide information on their internal operations, investigations and other activities previously subject to FOIA.

knowledge that few people are aware of what goes on behind large, institutional facades. Using these statutes, private citizens can obtain better insights on the information available to the government and the real reasons underlying government actions.

Once litigation is filed, the usual "discovery" procedures are available for gathering evidence, including written interrogatories, requests for admission, *subpoenas duces tecum* for records and other written materials, and depositions. Using these discovery procedures, the attorney can obtain evidence, such as insurance claims involving hazardous waste injuries, medical records of workers, reports of hazardous waste spills, and consultants' reports.

In addition, if the suspect company is large, general hazardous waste data may have been gathered by the company's own environmental compliance officer. In many cases, the internal report from the environmental compliance officer will set out the company's hazardous waste problems and how they can be corrected. Some hazardous waste investigations have not only discovered that such information existed, but also that it had been ignored. For example, internal memoranda at Occidental Chemical Company's Lathrop, California, plant indicated that personnel were aware of the company's waste disposal violations and their resulting harm at least two years before any action was taken to stop it (see Chapter 4).

GETTING OTHERS INVOLVED IN THE CASE

As soon as the preliminary investigation is completed, the appropriate government agencies, legislatures, the press, and other citizens should be contacted, even when private negotiations with a suspect company are making headway.* Since bureaucracies are often understaffed, they may not take immediate action, so perseverance is essential. Understaffing of the EPA's hazardous waste program contributed significantly to the

---

*In addition to the EPA, other federal agencies with a major role in controlling hazardous wastes include the Department of Justice (litigation), the Council on Environmental Quality (coordination of government environmental activities and environmental impact statements), and the Department of Transportation (transport of hazardous materials and Coast Guard spill response).

delayed action against Velsicol Chemical Corporation in Tennessee (see Chapter 3). The state of Pennsylvania also attributes much of its current hazardous waste regulation problem to inadequate staff and resources (see Chapter 7).

GOVERNMENT AGENCIES. If the initial report does not get the government enforcement agency to start its own investigation, the next step is to present the facts to the local city council, the state legislature, the U.S. Congress, and the press. Even if the agency does begin an investigation, involving legislative bodies and the press will ensure that the investigation is thorough and that any appropriate enforcement actions are promptly brought. Environmental agencies, legislative bodies, and the press have an important, interdependent role in the investigation of hazardous waste cases.

LEGISLATURES. Legislatures play an important part in the enforcement of hazardous waste laws. First, they create the laws and the agencies that enforce them. Second, they control the budgets of the agencies, and they have oversight responsibility over them. Finally, they have the power to create new statutes for solving hazardous waste problems (see Appendix XII).

Since the legislature controls an environmental agency's budget, it also controls the number of people available to investigate hazardous waste problems. In addition, the budget determines what tests and studies can be done by the agency, as these frequently require outside consultants and almost always are expensive. The budget may even determine whether the agency staff can afford to travel to the site to make a firsthand inspection. Assuming that the agency staff would investigate the site if there were sufficient funds, convincing the legislature of the urgency of a specific hazardous waste problem may result in an increase in funds to provide for the investigation.

The oversight role of the legislature ensures that the agencies are properly implementing and enforcing the statutes under their jurisdiction. Oversight hearings played an important role in getting the EPA to implement and enforce RCRA. When the EPA missed by many months the statutory deadline for issuing regulations under RCRA, the congressional committee with oversight responsibility wanted to know why. The EPA was subsequently sued by a public interest group for its delay.

The oversight committee in this case was Congressman Bob Eckhardt's Subcommittee on Oversight and Investigations. The effectiveness of the committee is demonstrated in the case studies on Love Canal, BFI waste oil in Texas, and Toone, Tennessee. The oversight hearings also helped get a significant increase in the EPA's hazardous waste budget, as well as a significant increase in the hazardous waste enforcement budget of the U.S. Department of Justice.

The final role of the legislature is its ability to enact new statutes for agencies to use in solving hazardous waste problems. For example, the overwhelming hazardous waste problems brought to light by various congressional committees, by the enforcement efforts of the EPA and the U.S. Department of Justice, and by the work of private citizens helped get the Superfund statute enacted in December, 1980.

THE PRESS. Congress and the press go hand in hand, and working with both often can increase the effectiveness of an investigation. The effectiveness of working with Congress and the press together is demonstrated by the BFI road oil incident in Texas. As a result of the combined work of Jim Carlton, a reporter for the *Port Arthur News* who inadvertently discovered evidence of contaminated road oil in Corrigan, Texas, and the subsequent investigations of Congressman Eckhardt's Subcommittee on Oversight and Investigations, BFI was forced to remove the contaminated road oil, which had been spread on hundreds of miles of roads throughout eastern Texas (see Chapter 6).

Similarly, through the persistence of local citizens and the media in Toone, Tennessee, Congress investigated the nearby Velsicol dump, which was suspected of contaminating local drinking water wells. The overwhelming evidence ultimately forced Velsicol to reverse its denial of responsibility and to "make amends" for damages (see Chapter 3).

CITIZEN ORGANIZATIONS. While one individual can investigate a hazardous waste problem, it is usually more effective to organize the people who are concerned about a particular site, as the homeowners of Love Canal did. A group has several advantages over an individual. First, it has a greater potential for raising money; the citizens of Toone, Tennessee, for example, held a dance to raise funds to pay for legal advice. Second, some members of the group may have valuable expertise; one may be a lawyer, another a scientist or writer. Third, a group simply can do more work. Finally, an organized group usually has a greater political voice than its individual members.[44]

THE COURTS. If it has been difficult or impossible to get others, including the government and the press, to focus on your hazardous waste problem, finally it may be necessary to resort to the courts. Once you have decided to take direct legal action, however, you must consider hiring an attorney. Although an attorney is not essential for citizens to bring a lawsuit, it is invariably advisable to have one. Historically, unrepresented citizens have rarely been successful in litigation. Lawsuits, especially environmental lawsuits, are complex. Even an experienced attorney frequently resorts to legal references for substantive, procedural, and strategic advice.

There are a number of ways to locate an attorney. Attorneys are now permitted to advertise, and you may be able to find one through the yellow pages of the phone book or a newspaper. Your local bar association and public interest and citizen groups may also provide referrals.

Try to locate an attorney with experience in environmental law. You should be aware, however, that the number of attorneys with such expertise is limited. To locate an attorney with environmental experience, you may wish to contact an environmental organization or ask someone with general legal experience to refer you to someone with more specialized training.

Paying for a lawyer is another important factor to be considered before initiating a lawsuit. In personal injury cases, many attorneys work for a contingent fee. In such instances, if you win or settle your suit, you pay the attorney a percentage, often one-third, of your recovery. If you lose, you generally pay nothing. If the case involves injunctive relief or only a small amount of money, or has little likelihood of success, a lawyer may not take the case on a contingent fee basis. Although a few attorneys dedicated to environmental protection may take your case for free *(pro bono)* or at reduced rates, most lawyers work at an hourly rate or for a fixed fee. In all cases the fee arrangements should be spelled out in writing before litigation commences.

To help finance such a lawsuit, you may be able to find an environmental or other organization willing to join in and assist you. Alternatively, you may be able to obtain support from others in similar situations by organizing a class action suit. The costs of such litigation can be spread among many individuals, or the potential recovery for a large number of claims may be sufficient to induce an attorney to handle the case on a contingent fee basis.[45]

Conclusions

Although plaintiffs involved in hazardous waste litigation face significant obstacles, the situation is not hopeless. Slowly, citizens and their attorneys are learning how to conduct effective hazardous waste lawsuits. Federal, state, and local governments are becoming more and more active in the hazardous waste area.* And the courts have recently shown an increased awareness of the risks posed by toxic substances in the environment and the problems faced by litigants.

The courts have been using a number of different and innovative theories to deal with the problems victims have in proving who and what caused their injuries. Identifying the source of injury is especially difficult in cases involving multiple, independent sources of toxic substances, as may occur in highly industrialized states. Some courts in such situations will impose "joint and several" liability on contributing polluters.[47,48,49] Essentially, this means that the plaintiff can sue any of the defendants for the entire amount of his damages. The particular defendant who ends up paying may sometimes proceed against other parties, using a "right of contribution" to attempt to recover a proportionate share of the payment.

---

*As of November, 1981, forty-nine states had legislation controlling some aspect of hazardous waste management and pollution.[46] Idaho is apparently the only state without such programs.

Other courts, in cases involving multiple polluters, may simply shift the "burden of proof" to the defendants. In this way, a defendant must "rebut" the presumption that he should be liable for the full amount of the plaintiff's damages, thus encouraging defendants to apportion liability among themselves.[50]

Still other courts have been willing to distribute liability among large segments of industry when it is unclear who is responsible for damage. One example of this distribution of liability is a theory called "market share" liability. This theory was used in a recent California case involving injuries caused by the drug diethylstilbestrol (DES). DES was implicated as the cause of vaginal cancer in daughters of mothers given the drug in the unfounded belief that it might prevent complications of late pregnancy. Because it was difficult or impossible to establish which drug company made the DES that caused each particular victim's injury, the California court allowed liability to be imposed on the major DES manufacturers according to their share of the market.[51,52]

Thus, the courts are beginning to show greater sensitivity to the relatively unique concerns of citizens involved in toxic substances and hazardous waste litigation. Although progress is slow, recent trends in environmental law may augur well for people who decide to take direct legal action.

Citizens have a wide range of options in addressing hazardous waste problems at the national, state, and local levels. Negotiation with industry, political advocacy, and media involvement all may prove fruitful in controlling hazardous wastes. At some point, however, it may be necessary for citizens to pursue legal avenues in order to get results. This avenue is especially significant in light of recent radical cutbacks in federal environmental enforcement activities. Private citizens can attempt to compensate for these cutbacks by assuming greater responsibility in protecting public health and the environment.

Citizens need *not* incur unreasonable risks from hazardous chemicals. The legal system is imperfect, but if one is armed with the facts, the law can be a valuable ally in securing a safe and healthful environment for current and future generations.

PART IV

Problems and Technologies

I come before you today with the distressing
news that one of this Nation's most vast
and vital resources is in serious jeopardy. Our
ground waters, long considered virtually
pollution-free, are threatened by ruinous
contamination. The problem is national, for
potential sources and routes of contamination
may be found wherever people live and work.

ECKHARDT C. BECK
Former Assistant Administrator for Water and Waste
Management, U.S. Environmental Protection
Agency. Before the Subcommittee on Environment,
Energy, and Natural Resources, July 25, 1980

CHAPTER 11

Groundwater Contamination

America is a vast reservoir of fresh water. The Great Lakes alone brim with nearly 9 quadrillion gallons, representing some 20 percent of the world's total supply of fresh surface waters.* In addition, an even greater abundance of fresh water is buried in geological formations known as aquifers, generally located within a half mile of the ground's surface.

Groundwater, water found beneath the surface of the earth, is a most precious natural resource. Over 100 million Americans depend on it for drinking, bathing, cooking, and other domestic uses. American agriculture is also highly dependent on groundwater, which accounts for nearly 41 percent of all water used in irrigation. And this dependence is growing.

As vital as groundwater is to America, it has as yet received little federal attention. For years, the United States Geological Survey (USGS) was the only federal organization that had any

*However, fresh water only constitutes about 3 percent of the world's total water supplies, 97 percent of which are salt oceans. Furthermore, 75 percent of all fresh waters are locked in glacial ice.

significant interest in groundwater. USGS's role, however, was merely to conduct research into underground waters. It had no mandate to regulate their uses.

In 1972, Congress took the first step toward recognizing the importance of groundwater by passing the Federal Water Pollution Control Act. This act explicitly recognizes a federal interest in the proper management of both surface waters and groundwaters, stating that "the objective of this Act is to restore and maintain the chemical, physical, and biological integrity of the Nation's water."

But ten years after the passage of the Federal Water Pollution Control Act, the federal agency given responsibility for protecting the nation's waters, the Environmental Protection Agency (EPA), still has no policy for protecting the nation's vital groundwater resources. Indeed, the nature of the federal role in regard to the regulation of groundwater remains a hotly debated question, and growing evidence of the dangers of groundwater contamination has added to the controversy.

Incidents of groundwater contamination are being discovered with increasing frequency. First, new technologies allow groundwater to be analyzed for chemicals with greater accuracy and at far lower chemical concentrations than technologies of only a few years ago. Second, the EPA, states, and municipalities have begun to test water supplies on a more frequent basis. Third, increasing urbanization in old industrial areas has placed drinking water wells closer and closer to sources of contamination. Industrial zones, once isolated, are commonly converted into partially or totally residential neighborhoods. Finally, increasing public awareness of the potential problems posed by hazardous wastes has stimulated many towns and private citizens to test groundwaters near old landfills and hazardous waste dump sites.

A report by the House Government Operations Committee, issued in September, 1980, noted that groundwater contamination is affecting citizens all over the country. The report states:

> In 25 states, many private and public water supply wells have been capped as a result of contamination. Last year alone, more than 300 contamination incidents were reported. This situation

has become critical in several states, most notably those where industrialization has been the heaviest.

Toxic chemical contamination of groundwater supplies in several areas of the country has reached alarming proportions. Over 200 wells in California have been contaminated by toxic wastes. In Jackson Township, N.J., 100 drinking water wells have been closed as a result of contamination from a local landfill. On Long Island, N.Y., where 100 percent of the population is dependent on ground water, 36 public water supplies and dozens of private wells have been closed because of synthetic organic chemical contamination. The water supplies for nearly 2 million Long Island residents have been affected. In the State of Massachusetts "at least one-third of the Commonwealth's communities have been affected to some degree by chemical contamination." More than 16 municipal wells have been closed in the past few years as a result. In Michigan, officials have been faced with a "virtual explosion" in the discovery of ground water contamination problems; in 1979, 278 sites were identified as being already contaminated, and 381 additional sites were classified as "suspect" contamination areas.[1]

A December, 1980 report by the Council on Environmental Quality (CEQ) has further systematized and extended these concerns. The report clearly documents "the emergence of a new threat to our ground water resources . . . widespread contamination by toxic organic chemicals. . . . Ground water contamination by synthetic organic chemicals is particularly disturbing because concentrations of the toxic contaminants are often orders of magnitude higher than those found in raw or treated drinking water drawn from the most contaminated surface supplies. . . ."[2]

The Nature of Groundwater

Groundwater is formed when precipitation in the form of rain or snow-melt infiltrates the ground under the influence of gravity. The water moves through the soil until it reaches a zone of rock strata, where it fills all the interstices in the rock formation. This water-bearing stratum of permeable soil and rock is called a saturated zone. If the saturated zone is large enough to yield significant quantities of water when pumped, it is classified as an aquifer.

Aquifers come in all shapes and sizes. They may be located from a few to several thousand feet below the earth's surface. Often an area that contains one aquifer contains others at various levels. The ability of an aquifer to store water, and thereby yield significant quantities of groundwater when pumped, is highly dependent on the porosity and permeability of the soils that compose it. The composition of soils and of aquifers varies greatly.

Aquifers also allow groundwater to be "transmitted"—to flow through soil strata—and underground flows do not respect state lines. The pooling and movement of underground waters depend on geological basins, not jurisdictional districts. Groundwater moves very slowly, in most cases, only a few feet a month. Gravity, well pumping, fissures or cracks in rock strata, and even well shafts influence this movement.

Surface and groundwaters form an integrated hydrologic system. In river valleys, for example, groundwaters tend to flow toward rivers and often "recharge" those bodies of water by seeping into them through underground springs. Rivers, on the other hand, will recharge groundwaters through seepage into aquifers from river bottoms. Marshes and wetlands are essential recharge areas for groundwater supplies. Contamination of surface waters, therefore, will in many cases directly affect local groundwater quality. At the same time, contamination of an aquifer may affect the quality of surface water recharged by that aquifer.

Dependence on Groundwater

Groundwater accounts for almost 50 percent of the nation's public water supplies. Several major cities, such as Memphis and Miami, are entirely dependent on groundwater, and the USGS estimates that 95 percent of all rural Americans obtain their drinking water from wells.[3] In over thirty states, more than a third of the population consuming public water supplies uses groundwater exclusively.[4] In total, Americans annually withdraw approximately 30 trillion gallons of water from the ground. The EPA estimates that total groundwater withdrawals for all uses are increasing at a rate of 25 percent per decade.

Groundwater is essential to American agriculture. Between 1950 and 1975, use of groundwater for irrigation increased 170 percent. In the major grain-producing states of Nebraska, South Dakota, and Iowa, over 80 percent of the population depends on groundwater.

Contamination

Although only one percent of America's 35 quadrillion gallons of economically producible groundwater is now known to be polluted, man's multifarious activities are threatening vital groundwater supplies in many regions of the country. Synthetic organic chemicals pose a special threat. Many of these are toxic chemicals that cannot be broken down by subsurface microorganisms or filtered out by soils before they reach groundwater supplies. Especially troublesome are chlorinated hydrocarbons, classes of highly resistant, nonbiodegradable, or poorly degradable compounds. Included in this class are the pesticides aldrin/dieldrin, chlordane/heptachlor, kepone, and mirex. Other dangerous chlorinated hydrocarbons are the organic solvents, such as trichloroethylene (TCE), tetrachloroethylene (PCE)—also known as perchloroethylene, and carbon tetrachloride. These solvents are used in hundreds of thousands of businesses to clean or degrease metal parts. Huge volumes of these chemicals are produced, used, and disposed of each year. Not surprisingly, samples of well water from all over the country show solvents have extensively contaminated groundwater supplies.

Many organic chemicals pose both acute and chronic risks to human health. Carbon tetrachloride, TCE, and PCE have been shown to induce cancers in experimental animals, and thus pose risks of cancer to humans. It is, however, difficult to estimate quantitatively the degree of excess cancer risk from prolonged ingestion of any one of these solvents, let alone a combination of them, at the levels at which they are now commonly found in drinking water supplies.

The cool, dark, abiotic nature of aquifers allows contaminants to be stored virtually undisturbed for "hundreds of thousands of years, if not for geologic time."[5] Two examples demonstrate the persistence of groundwater contamination. In Norwich, England, groundwater contaminated with whale oil in 1815 still contained residual poisons when wells were drilled there in 1950—135 years later. In Bellevue, Ohio, where public and private wastes of all forms were dumped in sinkholes and wells beginning in 1872, wastes have contaminated a seventy-five-square-mile area. In the early 1960s, nearly a hundred years later, some area wells gushed "raw sewage, including toilet tissue and a variety of unmentionables" when pumped.[6]

The degree of threat waste disposal and treatment sites pose to groundwater depends on the toxicity and volume of the contaminants, the characteristics of the material underlying the site, and the particular geological and hydrological conditions of the area. For instance, a waste-filled unlined lagoon underlain by two hundred feet of impermeable clay devoid of fissures or cracks could pose relatively little threat to an aquifer beneath the clay, but a landfill located on permeable soils with a shallow depth to underlying water could be a serious problem indeed.

Major aquifers have taken thousands of years to form, and, because water underground does not flow swiftly, these aquifers are vulnerable to permanent contamination. Discovery of contamination may not take place until decades after it began, and the slow movement of water often makes locating the source of contamination extremely difficult, if not impossible. Contamination may, for example, have been caused by industrial dumping decades earlier and miles away. By the time the contamination is discovered, the offending source may have disappeared, and the geology or hydrologic patterns in the immediate area may have changed. Extensive and costly geologic and hydrologic studies must be conducted; establishing proximate cause is often inordinately difficult.

The major sources of groundwater contamination include landfills, surface impoundments, mining activities, oil and gas exploration, waste-injection wells, pesticide and fertilizer use, underground storage tanks, and septic tanks. Additional secondary sources of groundwater contamination include agricultural feed lots, road de-icing salts, leaky sewers, spills, landspreading of wastes, and saltwater encroachment.[7]

LANDFILLS

Landfills* present one of the greatest threats to ground-water. The EPA estimates that there may be as many as seventy-five thousand industrial landfills and fifteen thousand municipal landfills. Many, perhaps thirty thousand of these sites, are abandoned or inactive. Especially troubling is the fact that a large percentage of the 77,000,000 pounds of hazardous wastes generated each year are dumped in landfills. Only 10 percent of these wastes have been dumped in what has been considered an environmentally sound manner. The EPA estimated in early 1980 that fourteen thousand to ninety thousand land-disposal sites were contaminating surface waters and groundwaters.[8]

A 1979 study conducted by the Oversight and Investigations Subcommittee of the House Committee on Interstate and Foreign Commerce found that the top fifty-three chemical companies, owning or operating 1,600 facilities, dumped industrial wastes in over thirty-six hundred sites. Those companies, representing only about 14 percent of the nation's chemical plants, generated 132 billion pounds of industrial wastes in 1978. The study also showed that, between 1950 and 1979, some 1.5 trillion pounds of industrial wastes were sent to over thirty-three hundred sites, 94 percent of which were owned or operated by the companies generating the wastes. Of the sites included in the survey, 32 percent were inactive at the time the survey forms were completed. Over 200 billion pounds of industrial wastes had been dumped at those closed sites.[9]

A 1977 study of landfills demonstrated that, of the fifty sites investigated, organic-chemical contamination was discovered in the groundwater at forty, and migration of at least one hazardous chemical from the site was detected at forty-three. Inorganic chemical contamination of groundwater at twenty-six of the sites exceeded EPA safety levels for heavy metals in drinking water.[10]

Improper hazardous waste disposal is not the only threat posed by landfills. Rain or snow falling on landfills can filter

---

*The term *landfill,* as used in this chapter, includes sanitary and secure landfills and open dumps.

through their contents and percolate into the ground below. As this water soaks through, it often leaches out the heavy metals, organic chemicals, and other potentially dangerous compounds contained in the variety of products dumped at the site. This leachate may find its way to groundwater below. Even after dumping at a landfill has ended, the leaching action continues. Unless measures are taken to either stop the formation of leachate or drain it away safely, inactive landfills will continue to threaten groundwater.

SURFACE IMPOUNDMENTS

Surface impoundments—natural topographic depressions, artificial excavations, or dike arrangements—can pose major threats to groundwater. Commonly referred to as pits, ponds, and lagoons, they are extensively employed for storage, treatment, and disposal of industrial, municipal, agricultural, mining, and oil- and gas-brine liquid wastes.

In 1978, the EPA began a national survey of impoundments. By August, 1980, the study had identified the existence of over 170,000 impoundments throughout the country. As part of the survey, each state assessed the information available on its own impoundments.

The September, 1980 House Government Operations Committee report on groundwater focused on the EPA data available on the 8,163 industrial sites (25,749 impoundments) assessed. That report indicated that an estimated 50 billion gallons of liquid waste per year are placed in those impoundments. According to the EPA, 90 percent of those impoundments are "virtually unmonitored," indicating that no monitoring wells have been established to assess the effects the liquids in the impoundments are having on local groundwater quality.[11] The committee noted that:

> 70 percent, or about 18,200 [impoundments] are unlined, potentially allowing contaminants to infiltrate unimpeded into the subsurface; 35 percent, or about 9,100 [impoundments], may contain potentially hazardous constituents; 30 percent, or 7,800 [impoundments], are unlined and sitting directly on top of ground water sources with no barrier reported between the wastes and

the ground water; 10 percent, or about 2,600 of the total impoundments, are unlined, sitting directly on top of ground water and are within one mile of a potential water supply well.[12]

There is every likelihood that the materials placed in those impoundments will eventually leach downward into the earth.

Although the EPA impoundment study was only a first-round approximation and not intended to produce reliable data on the threat to groundwater posed by each facility assessed, a further refinement of the data disclosed some 2,100 sites containing at least one unlined impoundment and located above a usable groundwater source, with no barrier reported between the wastes and the groundwater. Of this group, 750 contained potentially hazardous constituents," and 750 were located within a mile of a "potential water supply well."

Data not released by the committee included the portion of the survey that required state assessors to rate the groundwater contamination potential of each site on a scale from one to twenty-nine, the latter number representing the greatest contamination potential. In most reports reviewed, the highest contamination ratings were generally given to industrial impoundments. Many states explained that these high ratings were given not only because of the potentially dangerous nature of industrial wastes, but also because these impoundments tended to be located in the most populated areas. The state of Ohio, for example, found the average rating of its industrial impoundments to be twenty-one, higher than the average for any other single group. Mining, petroleum, and gas-exploration impoundments also had higher average numbers. Further evaluations by the state led to the conclusion that there was indeed a close correlation between the known instances of groundwater contamination and the high ratings. Based on this more in-depth evaluation, the Ohio EPA concluded that this correlation "indicates the rating system provides an accurate appraisal of the potential degree of contamination."[13]

It should be noted that the EPA survey was not designed to uncover the most "dangerous" sites. Only when substantial information was available were sites included. In most cases, this criterion resulted in state-permitted sites being included, while nonpermitted sites were left out. The status of the latter is, of course, unknown.

By law, EPA was required to publish findings and conclusions based upon the surface impoundment assessment data reviewed in 1980 by the House Government Operations Committee. Over a 2-year period three separate drafts of this report were prepared, but EPA was unwilling to publish a final version. In December of 1982, Congressman Moffett released a copy of the latest draft. The report painted a chilling picture. EPA found that 98 percent of the sites located were within a mile of drinking water supplies and 93 percent of sites posed a threat to underlying groundwater supplies. The authors concluded that "In general, impoundments have historically been sited and constructed without apparent regard for the protection of groundwater;" that "the practice has been virtually unregulated by the Federal Government;" and, that "many states' reports characterized their programs as having fragmented jurisdiction, inadequate funding and staffing, and a historical focus primarily toward surface water concerns."

The seriousness of those conclusions was underscored by the results of earlier EPA studies which in June, 1978 concluded that "despite the potential for attenuation of contamination in some soils, a significant volume of inorganic and organic contaminants has seeped into groundwater, as indicated by records of selected case histories of contamination from industrial impoundments in twenty-nine states."[14,15,16]

MINING

Mining presents a major threat to groundwater. The potential sources of contamination include surface and underground mining activities, refuse piles, and slurry lagoons. According to a 1980 EPA study, between 1930 and 1971 almost 200,000 acres of land were used for the disposal of coal-mining wastes alone.[17]

The EPA estimates that there are more than 170,000 active coal, metal, and nonmetal mines in the United States. A 1980 report on the potential environmental impacts of mining wastes found that 2.3 billion tons of solid and liquid wastes are produced annually by the mining industry and that some 30 billion tons have accumulated throughout the country. About one-third of the tailings from lead and zinc mines were found to contain higher levels of pollution than allowed under the newly promulgated RCRA regulations. One-third of all copper-industry "leaching liquors" were also found to exceed regulatory standards, and gold- and silver-mine wastes showed excessively high levels of cyanide.[18]

Mining may destroy underlying aquifers, change local flow patterns, and affect the quality of groundwater as highly mineralized fluids, originating in spoil materials, infiltrate the aquifers. Underground fires in mines or waste dumps produce hot, highly mineralized waters that may also leach into underlying aquifers. Intra-aquifer leakage may also take place, allowing a contaminated aquifer to bleed into a clean one.

Acid drainage, produced mostly by underground coal mines, is a major source of groundwater and surface-water contamination in the coal-mining areas of Pennsylvania and West Virginia.[19] Acid drainage occurs in both surface and underground mines when strata contain a high percentage of iron sulfides. Minerals in the soil break down into water-soluble products and are forced to the surface, forming acidic solutions that can then reenter the groundwater through recharge zones. Waste-water discharge from coal mines in five states alone was estimated to be 5 billion gallons in 1972, and the increase in the demand for coal has recently expanded those discharges.

PETROLEUM AND GAS EXPLORATION

The use of brine pits, now banned in most states, to dispose of saline by-products of drilling is a major contributor to groundwater contamination. Texas has reported over twenty-three thousand cases of groundwater and surface-water contamination linked to petroleum exploration. Secondary recovery methods for gas require the pumping of steam and other agents into wells, thereby creating a substantial threat to area groundwater. Most of the damage to groundwater caused by these operations has already taken place. Since the activities generally occur in sparsely populated areas or where groundwater is not used for human consumption, the impact, though potentially large, has not yet received much public attention.

INJECTION WELLS

An injection well is any vertical shaft used to force liquids deep into the ground. These wells allow materials to be injected directly into groundwater or some other geological strata below the surface. During the injection process, materials may leak out of the wells through the well shaft, and, once at the bottom of the well, contaminants may find their way into groundwater. Only relatively few wells inject highly toxic materials deep into the earth. Most injection wells are used for the disposal of industrial and municipal wastes that generally contain high volumes of liquid of low toxicity. A great number of injection wells are used by the petroleum industry for brine disposal, and a large volume of liquid radioactive wastes is also injected into the ground through wells.

The EPA estimates that there are four hundred thousand municipal, industrial, commercial, agricultural, and domestic wells currently injecting fluids below the surface. Five thousand new wells are built each year. Well-injection of liquid wastes poses especially high risks in unlined well casings, since cracks and fissures in the strata where wastes are disposed of may allow seepage into potential drinking water sources.

DOMESTIC SEPTIC TANKS AND CESSPOOLS

Areas with large numbers of septic tanks and cesspool disposal systems may suffer significant groundwater contamination problems. These systems pump excessive concentrations of nitrates, viruses, and microorganisms from natural wastes into the ground. Phosphates and other potentially dangerous chemicals used in the home are also pumped into the ground when they are used in the wash or dumped down the drain. High concentrations of heavy metals leached out of domestic piping have also been found in groundwater contaminated by septic tanks and cesspool wastes.

In its report to Congress on waste-disposal effects on groundwater, the EPA estimated that 29 percent of the American public utilize this form of sewage disposal. This figure includes an estimated 19.5 million single-family housing units. In New England alone, an estimated 400 million gallons of domestic sewage are pumped into the ground each year.[20]

UNDERGROUND GASOLINE STORAGE TANKS

The American Petroleum Institute (API) estimates that there are hundreds of thousands of underground gasoline storage tanks throughout the nation. Most were installed in the 1950s and 1960s, a time when the retail gasoline industry was expanding rapidly. The great majority of storage tanks were constructed of steel. These tanks and their pipe connections, designed to last, at most, twenty years, are subject to corrosion, and hundreds of leaks have been reported recently.

Between 1977 and 1979, the API canvassed service stations that had reported gasoline leaks. Over 470 leaks were assessed, 304 of which originated in steel tanks; steel piping accounted for an additional 146 leaks. The API determined that corrosion was the cause of over 80 percent of the leaks. About 50 percent of the tanks or pipes found discharging gasoline underground were located in sandy soil.

Once gasoline has leached into groundwater, it is extremely difficult, if not impossible, to completely remove. Gasoline contamination of an aquifer may render it unusable for decades.

FERTILIZER AND PESTICIDE RUNOFF

Agricultural chemicals can pose a major threat to groundwater. Use of fertilizers to improve crop yields often results in the discharge of excessive levels of nitrogen into the ground. Several studies have shown that, although plants store large amounts of nutrients during the growing season, they release excessive amounts to the soil during the nongrowing season. "During the nongrowing period," a report on groundwater pollution problems in the southeastern United States notes, "excess nitrate, associated with recharge from precipitation, is leached from soil into the groundwater at high concentrations."[21]

Expanded uses of pesticides and herbicides also subject groundwater to increased contamination risk. These products are sprayed on crops, applied directly, or buried in the earth. Depending on soil conditions, pesticide and herbicide residues may leach into the earth and into groundwater supplies. Both farm and home use of these products present a growing risk to underlying groundwater.

The Federal Government

Congress has made clear the federal interest in protection of groundwater and has granted the EPA vast monitoring, regulatory, and enforcement powers. The EPA has the authority to regulate point-source contamination from surface-water discharges, solid waste landfills, hazardous waste landfills, surface impoundments, injection wells, septic systems, surface- and deep-mining operations, oil- and gas-drilling rigs, pesticide use and disposal, and underground storage tanks, where those sources contaminate public water supplies. The EPA has also been given the authority to develop comprehensive plans for groundwater regulation and to set standards for permit programs that control the discharges of active landfills, surface impoundments, and disposal wells. It also has power to set water-quality standards for public drinking water supplies.*

The Surface Mining Control and Reclamation Act grants the Secretary of the Interior the power to stop mining and reclamation activities that contaminate groundwater and the power to require that plans to restore or protect groundwater quality be submitted before such operations are begun.[28]

Unfortunately, Congress has given the EPA no guidelines for weighing the various demands of each mandated program. Although the EPA has substantial powers under existing acts, it has restricted its groundwater protection activities to enforcement actions against polluters and the issuance of regulations under RCRA and the Clean Water Act.

Ironically, some federal environmental cleanup programs have actually increased the groundwater problem. The chief culprit is the National Pollution Discharge Effluent System (NPDES), mandated by the Clean Water Act as amended in 1972. Under the NPDES system, each liquid-waste producer discharging wastes into navigable rivers and streams must apply to

---

*Several federal statutes contain directives to federal agencies to protect groundwater resources. These statutes include: the Safe Drinking Water Act (1974);[22] the Clean Water Act as Amended (1972);[23] the Resource Conservation and Recovery Act (RCRA) (1976);[24] the Toxic Substances Control Act (1976);[25] the Surface Mining Control and Reclamation Act (1979);[26] and the Federal Insecticide, Fungicide and Rodenticide Act (1971).[27]

a state agency or EPA for a pollution-discharge permit. The permit restricts that company's waste discharges to a certain level per year, depending upon the waste burden being carried by the stream or river in question and the surface-quality improvement goals established for that body of water. If a company had been dumping one hundred pounds of carbon tetrachloride a day into a river before the program was made effective and its NPDES permit allowed a discharge of only ten pounds a day, something had to be done with the other ninety pounds of waste. Many companies, facing the problem of storing or treating surplus wastes, constructed additional storage ponds and treatment lagoons. These ponds and lagoons allowed a company to moderate its discharges, alter the chemistry of the wastes, or simply allow the wastes to evaporate or be absorbed into the ground. Unfortunately, through inadequate design or faulty construction, most of the ponds and lagoons allowed large quantities of liquid waste to soak into the earth.

Why wasn't this problem foreseen? Where did the legislators who designed the Clean Water Act think the wastes were going to go?

Lyle Silka, a former EPA geologist who was directed by the EPA to make some sense of the confusion, thinks that Congress has been "myopic." "One of the biggest problems we have is Congress writing laws which call for implementation deadlines for when regulations are to be implemented; but no one allows time either before the law is written or before the regulations have to be promulgated to study the problem and get the basic knowledge base established. . . . In an effort to get the programs on the road, Congress shot itself in the foot."[29]

Hazardous waste disposal regulation is inextricably linked to the protection of both groundwater and surface-water quality. Contaminated groundwater often repollutes the very streams and rivers the Clean Water Act was designed to clean up.

Lyle Silka points out that, typically, after laws have been passed, new problems develop. He says, "There's a lack of communication; there is a gap between the people who are responsible for instituting, implementing, and creating the regulations and the people who have the experience, knowledge, and technical background" to understand the problem. This gap, says

Silka, often leads to inadequate regulatory proposals and incorrect guidelines.[30]

While the federal government has demonstrated that it knows little about what actually is taking place underground throughout the nation, a survey by James W. Dawson finds that the states are also in the dark. Dawson's survey of all fifty state water-regulatory agencies concludes:

> A large number of states are unable to develop a sufficient data base and the data that is collected is typically spotty, inaccurate or incomplete, with collection based primarily on voluntary cooperation.[31]

Dawson found that the effort to force water users to report to state governments is minimal because the states have no laws requiring reporting. "As a result, many states do not have a realistic determination of what it is they are supposed to protect."[32]

The bottom line on hazardous waste contamination of groundwater is that most experts just do not know what is going on, although they fear the worst. Some believe that within the next decade we will begin to see a series of catastrophes. Groundwaters in the industrialized areas of the Gulf states, Northeast, and Great Lakes are now showing signs of contamination. Hundreds of wells have already been closed. Solvent wastes have begun to destroy water supplies. And solvent wastes are only the beginning—the more mobile front line of pollution. Directly behind them may come pesticide wastes and other toxic industrial wastes dumped onto or into the ground decades ago.

Currently the regulatory scheme under RCRA requires waste disposers to construct environmentally safe waste disposal landfills and lagoons. The regulations establishing design criteria go some way toward reducing—or possibly just postponing—new problems. Unfortunately, these regulations can do nothing about the damage already done. The government's only recourse in regard to past disposal practices that have resulted in groundwater destruction is to take court action or to use superfund monies (see Chapter 8).

Suing companies today for polluting aquifers through faulty waste disposal or storage practices that took place twenty years ago is similar to suing to recover cleanup costs for abandoned sites. The cost of proving that x corporation caused y pollution could easily run into hundreds of thousands of dollars. If the alleged polluter can be found and has not gone out of business in the intervening years, he may raise as a defense the fact that what he did was legal at the time or that government regulations forced him to dispose of or store his wastes in leaky pits, ponds, or lagoons. Assuming that the government suit is successful, recovery of high-enough damages to clean up the problem is unlikely. In most cases, the cost of cleaning up an aquifer, a process that might take decades, is prohibitive. The entire superfund could quicky be depleted.

The groundwater contamination problem is not, however, necessarily unsolvable. Treatment technology now exists that will at least allow water at the municipal or tap level to be partially cleansed of some contaminants. Granulated activated-carbon filters are seen as one of the more effective of these technologies. Such cleanup technologies are, however, very expensive and require continual maintenance.

A number of difficult choices now have to be made, choices requiring a vast improvement in our understanding of the nature of groundwater contamination. Although that understanding must be based on improved science, the ultimate decisions are political.

In the fall of 1979, Douglas Costle, administrator of the EPA, took a personal interest in the groundwater problem and kicked the agency into gear. In June, 1980, the EPA took the first steps toward addressing these political questions on the federal level. Congress also took new interest in groundwater protection. Congressman Toby Moffett, chairman of the Environment, Energy, and Natural Resources Subcommittee of the House Committee on Government Operations, held several days of hearings on groundwater contamination in the summer and fall of 1980. Moffett's subcommittee prepared a report in September of 1980, which concluded:

> (1) This nation is highly dependent on ground water.
> (2) Ground water destruction will be one of the most serious environmental problems of the 1980s.

(3) The health of millions of Americans is threatened by government and industry's past failure to properly protect our ground water.

(4) The destruction of our nation's ground water will continue unless we move immediately to locate all potential sources of ground water contamination and take action to block the further flow of toxic substances into the ground.

(5) We can expect hundreds of more cases of ground water contamination to be discovered as a result of our past failure to protect our ground water. Some cases will have been caused by disposal of toxic substances that took place decades ago.

(6) In many areas, cases of contamination may have resulted in irreversible damage to ground water resources or rendered them unusable for decades or perhaps even for geological time.

Failure to anticipate the potentially devastating effects disposal practices may have on ground water has been shared by government and industry. As a consequence, both the public and private sectors of our nation must work together to rectify this situation, in an atmosphere of cooperation and not one of confrontation. As our national response to these facts develops, we must remember one fundamental fact: any threat to the nation's ground water is ultimately a threat to our citizens' health and livelihoods. [33]

The report also urged the EPA to "enunciate as swiftly as possible a definitive national groundwater policy."[34] A subsequent report by the CEQ, fully supporting the findings of the Moffett subcommittee, concluded that, although a variety of toxic organic chemicals had been found in well water throughout the country, little research had been conducted to determine what impact these contaminants are likely to have on human health.[35]

Recognizing the need for a national groundwater policy and relying on its already-existing powers to regulate, the EPA published a draft groundwater policy in November, 1980. In January, 1981, six days of hearings were held and over 400 comments received.

The new Administration, while professing great interest in groundwater protection, failed to move ahead with the development of a plan until its inaction was exposed in a hearing by the Moffett subcommittee in November, 1981. John Hernandez, then Deputy Administrator of EPA, promised the subcommittee that a groundwater policy would be completed in the spring of 1982. In fact, some progress was being made toward the promulgation of a national groundwater protection policy until late October of 1982, when then Assistant Administrator for Solid Waste and Emergency Response, Rita Lavelle, waged a campaign to kill the policy. When Lavelle failed to halt action on it entirely, then EPA Administrator Anne Gorsuch took the unusual step of submitting the "controversial" policy to the President's Cabinet Council on Natural Resources for approval before proposing it for public comment.

The policy sent over to the Cabinet Council was toothless. It lacked any statutory authority; it did not provide additional resources for either state or Federal groundwater protection programs; and it contained no new controls on polluters. Nevertheless, the concept alone was enough to raise the ire of the Council's Chairman, Interior Secretary James Watt. Watt shelved the plan, and in late February, 1983 began a successful crusade to ensure that it would never again resurface. As of June 1, 1983, no action had been taken to adopt even a weak policy.

Conclusions

The big questions remain unanswered. Do we try to clean up contaminated aquifers or do we let them die? Should we place standards on them as drinking water sources, or irrigation sources, or mining water sources? Who should have the final say: federal, state, or local government?

The ideal method for controlling hazardous waste contamination of groundwater is to end the production of hazardous wastes. The next-best method is to reduce the volume of hazardous wastes and to change our concept of land-use planning. It's time to stop siting landfills and lagoons in areas where vulnerable groundwater aquifers are located. Land disposal of hazardous wastes should be restricted rigidly or banned.

Regulation of groundwater resources has traditionally been the responsibility of state governments. Yet few have utilized their police powers to do more than restrict, in some small way, the quantity of water withdrawn from aquifers. Tensions between western states, more concerned about quantity of water, and eastern states, more concerned about its quality, make a uniform national system of regulation almost impossible.

Moreover, each aquifer requires different treatment. One may carry high levels of natural radiation, another high levels of sodium. For contamination-control programs to be successful, all aquifers must be mapped and analyzed; all sources of contamination must be located; all recharge areas must be found; and groundwater supplies must be monitored on a periodic basis. A federal-state partnership is essential to the success of a contamination-control program.

Ultimately, state legislatures will be left to decide the fate of our nation's groundwaters. Nevertheless, the federal government must take the lead by establishing minimal standards and by establishing and implementing a strong national groundwater protection policy embodying the "nondegradation standard"[36] expressed in the Clean Water, Safe Drinking Water, Surface Mining Control and Reclamation, and Resource Conservation and Recovery Acts. Congress must examine and correct its environmental laws to assure that they encourage, rather than discourage, proper disposal and storage practices. Although the EPA under the Carter administration showed great enthusiasm for the development of a national groundwater protection program, the Reagan administration's budget cuts and regulations freeze have all but eliminated this effort.

> The use of waste management
> technologies to recycle, treat, and destroy
> highly toxic hazardous wastes is feasible,
> affordable, and safe.

CALIFORNIA OFFICE OF APPROPRIATE TECHNOLOGY
Sacramento, California, 1981

CHAPTER 12

The Technology of Disposal

The disposal of hazardous wastes has generally been regarded by industry as an unwelcome nuisance to be resolved as cheaply and conveniently as possible. As a result, disposal technology is poorly developed and incapable of responding to the burgeoning national concerns over the hazards of improper disposal.[1,2,3] Requirements for the proper management of hazardous wastes will have substantial future impact on industry as a whole and on the chemical industry in particular.

Problems of hazardous waste disposal will eventually require industry to search for nonhazardous or less hazardous alternatives to toxic chemicals in current use. Additionally, cradle-to-grave technologies will have to be designed into processes using toxic chemicals as raw or intermediate materials, and into processes generating toxic chemicals as accidental by-products in the course of manufacture. Another important impact will be on the hazardous waste disposal industry, which is already emerging as a major growth market.

While the majority of hazardous wastes are currently disposed of in unsecured landfills, a wide range of extensive and complex safer technologies is available in a rapidly evolving market, and even more are available at the prototype stage.[4-12] However, there is no universal disposal technology that is ideal for all categories of hazardous wastes. Rather, the appropriate technologies are, in general, specific to particular types of waste streams—although some may be effective for a wide variety of wastes.

Hazardous waste disposal technology falls logically into five major but overlapping categories: resource recovery, pretreatment, deep-well injection, incineration, and landfill or burial.

Resource Recovery

The recovery and reuse of commercially valuable materials from hazardous industrial-waste streams is the most ideal disposal method, from the criteria of safety and conservation of nonrenewable resources and energy.[13] However, for most industries, the economics of recovery have until recently been unfavorable because of lower costs of raw, compared with recycled, materials and because of continuing ease and cheapness of conventional land disposal. Other disincentives to resource recovery are depletion allowances and capital gains treatment—which place a premium on the use of raw, rather than recycled, materials—and trade secrecy, which appears to inhibit American industry from making information available to others on potentially useful waste resources. These trends are likely to be reversed by the increasing costs of energy and raw materials, particularly petrochemicals, and by pressures to reduce the volume of hazardous waste streams because of RCRA regulations.

Toxic-waste streams should be regarded as valuable crude resources, to be mined, processed, refined, and recovered. Recovery is maximized by recapture at "end of pipe"—at the earliest possible stage of producer generation, at which wastes are still relatively isolated and concentrated. Commingling of waste streams is probably the greatest single barrier to economic recycling. Recapture after wastes have been disseminated and diluted in the consumer product chain is less economic although, in some instances, it can be encouraged by a system of refundable deposits, as in the case of cadmium- or lead-containing batteries and used motor oil.

Resource-recovery technology, while usually process- and product-specific, is applicable to a wide range of industries. For instance, perchloroethylene and trichloroethylene solvents, which are extensively used in various industries for metal degreasing and textile cleaning, can be recovered from gaseous- and liquid-waste streams. Most processes involve filtration through activated charcoal, followed by solvent desorption by a flushing stream. Trichloroethylene can also be recovered from sludge-oil wastes in degreasing processes by an evaporation, two-stage stripping procedure. Solvent-waste streams from semiconductor and other specialized electronic industries are often purer than the technical grades used by most other industries and are thus clearly a useful resource.

The automobile industry generates considerable amounts of scrap car-seat fabric, containing textiles bonded to polyvinyl chloride (PVC). Incinerating the scrap releases entrapped vinyl chloride (VC), hydrochloric acid, and other pollutants in flue gases. Instead, the PVC resin can be extracted from the scrap by washing with solvent, from which clean PVC can then be recovered.

Polyvinyl alcohol is an expensive, nonbiodegradable polymer, widely used in the textile industry for sizing yarns before weaving. The free alcohol is scoured from the textile prior to dyeing and is then lost in waste streams. Recently, several companies, including Union Carbide and J.P. Stevens, have developed a hyperfiltration process for recovery and recycling of over 90 percent of polyvinyl-alcohol wastes.

Sulfur dioxide from a wide range of sources, such as utility plants and smelters, can be recovered from waste streams in several ways. For example, the gases can be scrubbed with calcium hydroxide, with the formation of calcium sulfides or sulfate. These salts can then be used for the manufacture of hydrogen sulfide or sulfuric acid.

The recent emergence of some twenty regional waste-exchange clearinghouses does not seem to have generated much industrial interest, even though confidentiality is assured. These clearinghouses are operated by trade associations, chambers of commerce, private industries, local universities, and state and local governments, and they provide their clients with updated inventories of wastes, classified by broad chemical class, without identification as to their origin from any particular company. Orders and inquiries are forwarded to the owner of the wastes, who handles subsequent negotiations directly. However, in contrast with European and Japanese practice, these waste exchanges operate minimally and passively, rather than aggressively seeking out waste generators and potential reusers, who could be linked to common advantage (see Appendix XIV).

As with other forms of disposal preferable to "secure" landfills, the future of recycling depends on the implementation of both economic and regulatory pressures. Such pressures include taxation of disposal in "secure" landfills; taxation of other disposal methods when recycling is feasible; a shift in research subsidies from disposal to recovery technologies; encouragement of active waste-exchange clearinghouses; taxation of the manufacture of toxics from virgin raw materials to reflect the full cost of their disposal, especially when these toxics could be recovered from hazardous wastes; and rigorous restriction of disposal in "secure" landfills.

Pretreatment

Hazardous wastes can be pretreated or detoxified to improve the efficiency, economics, and safety of subsequent disposal. In some pretreatments, the wastes are so completely detoxified that they may not need further treatment or monitoring. Pretreatment methods are generally process- and product-specific and are still only used for relatively few types of waste streams. However, there is now growing recognition of the critical need for research into the role of pretreatment in the overall management of hazardous wastes. Large-scale substitution of pretreatment for land disposal would achieve a wide range of benefits, including saving land space, decreasing groundwater contamination at disposal sites, and increasing possibilities for resource recovery.

Advances in pretreatment technology, which is still poorly developed, and encouragement of its increased future application are critically contingent on direct incentives, such as research subsidies, and indirect incentives, such as taxation of disposal in "secure" landfills. A wide range of biological, chemical, and physical methods is potentially available for the pretreatment of most hazardous wastes, with the exception of heavy metals and radioactive materials.

BIOLOGICAL

Biological pretreatment, or biodegradation, is applicable to only narrow ranges of waste composition. Most of these methods are restricted to dilute liquid streams of nonchlorinated organics of fairly uniform and constant composition, and which contain under 5 percent salts and low concentrations of heavy metals. Additionally, large land areas are necessary for most such forms of disposal.

In the activation process, refinery, petroleum or other organic wastes are digested aerobically by microorganisms. Incoming wastes are aerated and mixed in holding tanks with activated sludge. Undigested residues and sludge are then settled or flocculated and recycled. More effective aeration is achieved in the trickling-filter process by running wastes over beds of rocks, during which biodegradation is accompanied by filtration and adsorption on bacterial and algal surfaces. Organic wastes can also be oxidatively biodegraded by bacteria and reduced by photosynthetic algae in large, shallow stabilization basins, in smaller lagoons, or in evaporative pits, which may be aerated mechanically or by diffusion. While large volumes of materials can be handled in this way, the quality of effluent is usually lower than in activated-sludge processes.

First developed by the petrochemical industry, landfarming is another form of aerobic biodegradation that is now the most extensively used biological pretreatment method, particularly for refinery sludges. The method has also been widely applied to nonpersistent organic-chemical and pharmaceutical wastes. Thin layers of sludge are spread over large areas of land, allowed to dry for a few days, and then disked into the soil together with necessary nutrients. Depending on the rate of degradation of any particcular sludge, the process can be repeated every few months. Landfarming is typically practiced in semiarid areas of the Midwest on land of poor agricultural quality. As required by recent EPA regulations, the soil must not be used for food crops and must be carefully and regularly monitored for downward migration of nondegraded wastes and heavy metals. Of particular concern are zinc and cadmium, whose concentrations vary greatly with different types of industrial wastes and sewage sludges, and which may be toxic to plants, to animals eating the plants, and to people eating the plants or animals. Landfarming has also provided a wide range of nuisance problems, particularly malodors. It has been estimated that about 3 percent of all hazardous wastes could be landfarmed at costs, transportation aside, in the range of from $5 to $22 per cubic meter. [14,15,16]

Aerobic composting is cheaper, more versatile, and more widely applicable all over the United States than is landfarming. Composting depends on the use of elevated temperatures to increase biodegradation rates by mesophilic and thermophilic bacteria. Wastes are mixed with bulking agents, such as shredded garbage, straw, or waste paper, to maintain aerobic conditions and then composted in modified conventional pits, open tanks, or rotating drums. A wide range of degradable chemical wastes, including chlorinated-hydrocarbon and organophosphate pesticides and pharmaceuticals, has been successfully degraded by composting processes, some of which are currently under active development.

CHEMICAL

There are several forms of chemical pretreatment, designed to detoxify a wide range of hazardous waste streams or to reduce their bulk. Such pretreatment can, in some instances, be followed by recovery and recycling processes.

Waste streams can be oxidized by chlorine (chlorinolysis), hypochlorites, ozone, peroxides, or electrolysis, or they can be reduced by sulfur dioxide, ferrous sulfate, or sulfite. In wet-air oxidation, liquid waste streams are oxidized by air under pressure at temperatures from 170 °C to 340 °C. The process can be made more efficient by heat exchange of wastes with effluent streams. Wet-air oxidation has been used for a variety of hazardous wastes, including acrylonitrile.

Acid- and base-waste streams can be mixed to neutralize each other. Acid-waste streams can be neutralized by being passed through limestone beds or by being mixed with lime slurries or such concentrated alkaline solutions as caustic soda. Alkaline waste streams can be neutralized with compressed carbon dioxide or concentrated sulfuric acid. Heavy metals are precipitated by hydroxides in several of these neutralization processes. Other forms of chemical pretreatment include solvent extraction, for removal of water and oils from sludges containing organics and inorganics; ion exchange, for wastes such as cyanides and heavy metals; and precipitation, for heavy metals.

PHYSICAL

There is a wide range of physical pretreatment methods of waste streams, which are primarily designed to isolate or concentrate particular constituents for subsequent recycling or disposal, to reduce their volume, to solidify or detoxify them, or to achieve any combination of these objectives.

Volume reduction of hazardous liquid and solid wastes can achieve substantial economies in subsequent transportation, storage, and disposal costs. Slurries or solutions with high concentrations of solids can be reduced in volume by evaporation, particularly at high temperatures. Waste streams can be dewatered by combining evaporation and filtration on sludge-drying beds of gravel or stone overlaid with sand. Volatile components, such as ammonia, can be removed from aqueous liquid streams by steam stripping. Mechanical compaction is suitable for certain types of solid waste, provided none of their chemical constituents are pressure sensitive.

Only a limited number of concentration technologies have been so far applied to the treatment of hazardous liquid wastes. Dissolved organics or other constituents can be removed from liquid waste streams by carbon or resin sorption. Solid constituents of liquid wastes or sludges can also be segregated by sedimentation, centrifugation, filtration, or magnetic separation for ferromagnetic or paramagnetic particulates. In its simplest form, sedimentation involves settling of heavy solids from suspensions in tanks. The process can be improved, especially for fine particulates, by addition of flocculating agents. A more efficient method for recovery of solids is centrifugation, with techniques that can be varied to accommodate different types of sludge. While filtration techniques are used more restrictedly because of relatively high costs, they can be combined with volume reduction, as in vacuum filtration processes. Modified forms of filtration include filtration/adsorption, reverse osmosis, dialysis through semipermeable membranes, and electrodialysis.

Solidification is the process originally designed for low-level radioactive wastes, by which liquids or slurries are converted, with the addition of stabilizing or binding agents, into solid masses suitable for burial in "secure" landfills, with much reduced chances of leaching.* Solidification may be suitable for highly toxic organic-waste streams or slurries that cannot be economically incinerated or that are unsuitable for incineration because of high concentrations of heavy metals, for inorganic-waste sludges containing high concentrations of heavy metals, and for liquid streams or sludges contaminated with low-level radioactivity. Solidification is being increasingly used for hazardous chemical wastes, over forty different companies are reported to have developed different proprietary processes, largely tailored for particular types of wastes. The major outstanding questions that still have to be resolved by prolonged field tests are how long the solidified wastes will remain intact and stable and whether solidification merely postpones an inevitable toxic-leachate problem, possibly until after the thirty-year period for which EPA regulations require "secure" landfills to be monitored.

Cementation is the cheapest and most common form of solidification and appears particularly useful for wastes with high concentrations of inorganics and heavy metals and low concentrations of organics. Cement-based techniques are primarily designed for wet sludges generated by the precipitation of heavy metals. These sludges are added to cement, which binds the

---

*As all solidification processes involve addition of chemical stabilizing agents, they may be alternatively classified as physicochemical pretreatments.

metals as insoluble hydroxides or carbonates. Proprietary additives are added to bind the metals further and to strengthen the cement matrix, which can be further strengthened by certain other sludge constituents, such as asbestos, metal filings, and latex. Lime-based cementation techniques are primarily designed for wet-flue gas sludges produced by the scrubbing of sulfur oxides from effluents of coal-gas-fired plants. These sludges are mixed with lime, proprietary additives, and cement-kiln dust or fly ash from electric power plants as a source of siliceous materials that react with metals, producing insoluble metal silicates, to form pozzolanic* concrete. Both cement- and lime-based processes produce bulky and heavy solid wastes that are weakened by certain organics and that are particularly susceptible to acidic degradation.

Thermoplastic processes involve the incorporation of dried sludge wastes at elevated temperatures with setting agents, such as paraffin, bitumen, polyethylene, or asphalt, which solidify on cooling and bind the wastes tightly. The solid wastes are then transported in rigid containers for burial in "secure" landfills. Thermoplastic solidification is expensive and involves skilled labor. Its greatest potential use is to minimize or delay possibilities of leaching from very concentrated and highly hazardous buried chemical wastes. This technique is unsuitable for wastes that are volatile at setting temperatures or that contain organic solvents or other materials that can attack the setting agent.

In polymerization processes, small amounts of a monomer, such as urea formaldehyde, and a catalyst are mixed thoroughly with wet or dry sludges. As the polymer hardens, it traps solid wastes in a spongelike resin, from which most water is extruded. Since many organic polymers are biodegradable, and also for structural reasons, the resin is transported in rigid containers for burial in a secure landfill.

Encapsulation is an advanced form of solidification, done preparatory to land disposal. Wastes are bound with an atmospheric-temperature-curing or thermosetting polymeric binder,

---

*This term is derived from Pozzuoli, a city near Naples where volcanic silico-aluminate calcium ash, which has been mined for centuries, is mixed with lime and water to form a very dense concrete.

such as polybutadiene or polyolefins, followed by their cocooning in a fused, seamless polyethylene or fiberglass jacket of high compressive strength. These techniques are expensive, involve sophisticated technology, and are largely applicable to highly toxic wastes, from which any chances of leaching must be prevented or at least delayed; they also appear to be applicable to liquid wastes in corroding fifty-five-gallon steel drums. A simpler and cheaper method of encapsulation in cement is also being investigated, particularly for the disposal of small containers.

Deep-Well Injection

Deep-well injection involves pumping or draining liquid wastes through injection tubes into highly porous rock formations, at depths ranging from a few hundred to over ten thousand feet, where it is claimed that they are permanently stored. These formations have the ability to retain within their structure massive quantities of liquids or gases, petroleum, natural gas, brine, or fresh water. This method was originally developed over fifty years ago by the oil- and gas-producing industries for the disposal of brines pumped up from oil-field drilling operations that penetrated brine aquifers while seeking oil; there are now about seventy thousand such deep wells in use, mainly located in major oil-producing states. Other industries—such as the pharmaceutical, chemical, refinery, and steel industries—have over the past thirty years drilled a total of about three hundred deep wells for on-site disposal of their hazardous wastes. Additionally, a relatively small number of wells are owned and operated by major commercial waste-disposing companies.

The economics of deep-well injection seem particularly attractive. Capital and transportation costs aside, the overall costs of disposal are very cheap, in the region of about ten cents per gallon. It is estimated that about 5 percent of all hazardous wastes are currently disposed of in this manner, and the number of new wells is increasing by about 20 percent a year.[17,18,19]

Injection sites are selected for their location between impervious strata of rock in porous, brine-containing sandstone or limestone beds. These sites are claimed by the oil and gas industries to be isolated from adjacent deep aquifers of fresh groundwater by impervious formations of compressed fine-clay shale particulates known as aquacludes. It is further claimed that such suitable sites are available in as much as one quarter of the land mass of the United States. In addition to such hydrogeologic considerations, all preexisting drinking water wells in or near the sites must be located and plugged. Wastes are pretreated by a wide range of physical and chemical methods to prevent plugging or corrosion of injection tubes, plugging of injection sites, and incompatibility with water or brine in the site.*

The understandable enthusiasm of industry for deep-well disposal of hazardous wastes is not shared by environmentalists, who regard this as an indefensible short-term solution with potentially serious and irreversible consequences. Potential problems largely relate to the possibility of contamination of fresh drinking water, particularly in deep aquifers above or below injection sites. The full range of hazards includes leakage due to fractures in well casings and injection tubes; infiltration of groundwater from unplugged local wells; migration or leakage of wastes from the injection site, possibly through cracks or fissures and bore holes in aquacludes; eruption of overpressurized sites, as happened in Erie, Pennsylvania, in 1968; and earthquakes, such as those in Denver, apparently due to waste disposal in Rocky Mountain Arsenal wells.[20,21,22] Finally, the reliability of geological predictions as to whether a given injection site is sealed exclusively with shale, and thus relatively safe, or only partially sealed with water barriers, thus allowing escape of toxic wastes, is less well developed than the industry claims.

THE WYOMING EXPERIENCE

In practice, the security of deep-well disposal has proven illusory. In Wyoming, the uses of injection wells in a uranium mine, as a means of removing uranium ore out of sandstone, resulted in significant contamination of rock layers above those which were supposed to be affected.[23] A spokesman for the mine

---

*These methods include settling, centrifugation, or filtration for suspended solids; coagulation and precipitation followed by removal of suspended solids for colloidal matter; pH adjustment followed by removal of colloidal matter and suspended solids; skimming devices and oil separators for oils and oily polymers; neutralization for corrosives; and chlorination or filtration for algae and bacteria.

could offer no explanation for the contamination of the upper layers, but said that perhaps the geology of the area was different from that predicted by their experts. Wyoming Department of Environmental Quality geologists suggested that there might be seasonal fluctuations resulting in the contamination. Other state experts admitted that the process was poorly understood. Yet this project was undertaken under intense scrutiny in 1978–79.

While it was an ore-removal project, not a waste disposal one, the technical problems are identical—and it is evident that not enough is yet known to predict how such rock strata will actually behave.*

UNDERGROUND INJECTION CONTROL

Subtitle C of the Safe Drinking Water Act requires the administrator of the EPA to establish standards to protect underground drinking water sources from "endangerment by the subsurface emplacement of fluids through well injection."[25] In regulations promulgated in June, 1980, the EPA defined underground sources of drinking water to include "aquifers or their portions which currently provide water for human consumption or which are capable of yielding water containing fewer than 10,000 mg/l of total dissolved solids (TDS)."

The regulations require the director of each state program to "identify those aquifers or aquifer portions" that will be con-

---

*Another western example of the hazards of relying upon present geological knowledge, and of the extreme vigilance needed to ensure that deep-well disposal is done safely, also comes from the uranium industry. Water officials of both the state of Wyoming and the federal government reported that "uranium exploration holes may be draining underground water formations in Wyoming, turning the aquifers into colanders."[24] Uranium miners were drilling holes down through irrigation aquifers, which were then draining out the holes into formations below. State law in Wyoming requires uranium prospectors to plug their holes, but James Marie of the U.S. Geological Survey admitted that "the state doesn't have the manpower or money to enforce those regulations." Walter Ackerman of the State Department of Environmental Quality said that 20 billion feet of hole would be drilled in Wyoming in one year. "That's a lot of hole. You would have to have twenty people to monitor just that program." Even then, he admitted it would be difficult to see if holes were leaking hundreds of feet underground. "About all you can do is check one or two and hopefully the rest would see that you mean business and comply." The aquifers being affected are actually in use by Wyoming ranchers and are critical to the state's current economy. Water levels in some wells have dropped twenty or thirty feet. Men have been killed in Wyoming over less.

sidered as underground sources of drinking water. The regulations also establish five classes of disposal wells, which must each comply with different requirements. Furthermore, the regulations provide that an aquifer can be designated an underground drinking water source, "even if not affirmatively identified by the Director." The state is also allowed to exempt an aquifer from regulation under certain conditions.

The EPA has encountered great political and technical difficulties in attempts to issue regulations under this part of the act. For example, the first regulations were proposed in August, 1976, but final regulations were not issued until late 1980, and the EPA has since been forced to back off from the full thrust of its original proposed regulations.*

A major issue raised in the challenge to the proposed regulations concerned the EPA's authority to control injections into natural-gas wells and oil-production wells. In the most recent set of proposed regulations, which establish criteria for the approval of state Underground Injection Control (UIC) programs, the EPA asserts that it has such authority, but limits its coverage. The EPA has determined that most of these wells are not likely to contaminate drinking water supplies and that the owners, because of the value of the product involved, have great incentives to ensure against the leaking of these wells into underground waters. The EPA may be prevented from claiming broader authority with regard to regulation of oil and gas wells as a result of Congress' pronouncement that protective action should not "interfere with or impede oil and gas production."[26]

Imposition of these regulations will increase costs for states and industries. The EPA estimates that the regulations will result in incremental costs of approximately $775 million (in 1977 dollars) in the first five years of operation. Industry is expected to shoulder $744 million of that increased cost. Booz, Allen, and

---

*Two major omissions from these regulations are worth noting. First, under the broad definition of an injection well, the EPA could have regulated shallow-well and single-family sewage-disposal systems. It chose not to do this, but it did include industrial sewage disposal and multifamily disposal systems. Second, the EPA has declared that the mandate of the Safe Drinking Water Act is preventative control. It therefore rejected suggestions that the regulations require restoration of degraded underground drinking water aquifers.

Hamilton, a major industrial consulting firm, claims that these regulations will cause a reduction in the production of oil of twenty-nine thousand barrels per day and result in a loss of approximately six hundred jobs in this one industry.[27]

Challenges to the EPA's proposed regulations forced the agency to avoid a formal definition of "endangerment." Instead of defining "endangerment" as such, the EPA has established a "nonmigration" standard. No injection operation will be permitted if it will result in the "migration of injected or formation fluids into an underground source of drinking water."

FUTURE PROSPECTS

Disposal of hazardous wastes by deep-well injection poses insurmountable regulatory problems. While an isolated, untapped brine aquifer three thousand feet deep may be effectively sealed off for millions of years, such a formation is a very much less-reliable repository for nondegradable or poorly degradable wastes, such as heavy metals or chlorinated hydrocarbon pesticides.

Nor would the real costs be as insignificant as the industry claims. The EPA, even for its modest regulatory program, estimates that the annual monitoring costs for hazardous waste disposal in deep wells will be nearly $1 million a year. If this practice increases at its present 20 percent rate for twenty years, the annual bill in the year 2000 would be about $370 million in 1977 dollars. Even if the volume of hazardous waste does not increase over its present level, and the proportion disposed of in deep wells increases from 3 percent to 60 percent, then an annual bill of at least $20 million would be involved just for monitoring. Underground disposal seems cheap now—but it commits society to a continuing, indefinite burden of policing the vast areas that may overlie a given disposal aquifer, to ensure that its integrity is not destroyed by a wide range of variables, including the degeneration of well seals and plugs and new well drilling.

Deep-well injection is now permitted in only about twenty states, mostly those with previous experience in regulation of oil wells. However, many other states are now under considerable local pressure to permit this form of disposal. Proposed EPA regulations, while calling for more precautions, particularly monitoring for leakage, are unlikely to reverse this trend in the absence of aroused, informed public concern. The prospects of the states or the federal government monitoring drilling activities in the vicinity of waste disposal wells for centuries to come are unrealistic.

Incineration

Incineration is potentially the safest and most effective method of disposal of most types of hazardous wastes, except those with high concentrations of noncombustibles and heavy metals. However, complete incineration involves complex and sophisticated technology and expensive antipollution devices. Nevertheless, it is probable that the increasing regulatory and legal problems and costs of other disposal methods will create strong economic incentives for the large-scale use of conventional incineration techniques, and for the development of promising new techniques still at the prototype stage.

A wide range of hazardous wastes—such as organic solvents, PCB's, other chlorinated hydrocarbons, distillation residues, and oily wastes—can be incinerated. The particular process used depends on whether the wastes are gases, liquids, or solids, and on other factors, including uniformity of composition, corrosiveness, viscosity, and combustibility.

CONVENTIONAL HIGH-TEMPERATURE INCINERATION

There are currently only about fifteen controlled high-temperature incinerators suitable for disposal of hazardous wastes in the United States.[28,29,30] Most are small units, costing in the $.5–$1 million range, owned and operated by major waste-generating chemical industries—the remainder being large commercial facilities costing up to $30 million.* Because of the relatively high costs of incineration, these facilities now handle only small amounts of hazardous wastes, probably under 3 percent of all hazardous wastes. The average operating expenses of these fa-

---

*Three of these are owned and operated by Rollins Environmental Services, Wilmington, Delaware.

cilities are estimated to be about $100 per ton, with severalfold higher costs for wastes with corrosive effluents, such as highly chlorinated hydrocarbons, which need expensive abatement technology. Some reduction in operating costs can, however, be anticipated through increasing energy efficiency, particularly using effluent to heat other process streams.

The incineration process necessarily involves several sequential stages. First, the waste stream is preheated by burners or exchange with hot effluent. The stream is then fed into the primary combustion chamber, where the bulk of the incineration takes place; auxiliary fuel is added to maintain combustion if the liquid wastes are only partially combustible. The flue gas is passed through a secondary combustion chamber and then discharged through a stack, where it is cleaned up by electrostatic precipitators or other devices to trap particulates and by scrubbers to remove trace metals and acidic pollutants, such as chlorides and sulfur or nitrogen oxides.

Currently available incinerator technology is ripe for massive expansion, both on-site for large sources of producer wastes and off-site for smaller waste generators and consumer wastes. Economies of scale can be achieved through the establishment of regional units, operated either commercially or by federal or local governments, ideally located in nonpopulated or sparsely populated regions. The acceptability of such centralized units will demand strong support from the EPA. Local communities will have to be assured of rigorous control of transportation of the hazardous wastes, their storage prior to incineration, and the monitoring of stack effluents by continuous, sensitive monitoring systems, with immediate accessible readout and automated shutdown. In the near future, it is unlikely that there will be any expansion in the use of incinerators—quite apart from the development of prototype technology—in the absence of economic incentives to such technology and disincentives to cheap disposal in "secure" landfills.

MARINE INCINERATORS

There are now three functioning incinerator ships, including the *Vulcanus* and the *Matthias II*, which handle about thirty-five hundred and eleven hundred cubic meters of liquid wastes, respectively, at a cost of under one hundred dollars per ton.* These relatively low costs are achieved by relying on atmospheric dilution to deal with trace metals and acidic gases in unscrubbed stack effluents. The efficiency of combustion has been shown to be very high in both ships.

In 1977, under contract to the United States Air Force and operating under the stringent criteria of EPA ocean-dumping permits, the *Vulcanus* incinerated about ten thousand tons (2.2 million gallons) of surplus Agent Orange, a mixture of the herbicides 2,4-D and 2,4,5-T, in the mid-Pacific, about 120 miles south of the Johnston Atoll (Project Pacer HO). The Agent Orange was heavily contaminated with about forty-four pounds of tetrachlorodibenzo-para-dioxin (TCDD), with a mean concentration of about 2 ppm, which is heat-stable up to about 800°C. No TCDD was detected in the incinerator effluent.

The *Vulcanus* now has more business than it can handle, and her owners are planning to build a new incinerator ship for the North American market.† Marine incineration is a superficially attractive option for the disposal of hazardous wastes, particularly those generated in the vicinity of small seaports suitable for the construction of large storage facilities. Apart from possible problems with United States marine law (the Marine Protection, Research, and Sanctuaries Act of 1972) and international maritime law, the large-scale expansion of this form of disposal calls for critical analysis of the assumption that pollution of the marine environment with unscrubbed stack effluents containing pollutants such as halogenated hydrocarbons is insignificant and that risks of accidents from pilot error, wind, fog, reefs, and engine failure can be discounted.‡ Apart from problems of storage at seaports, marine incineration poses grave potential occupational hazards.

---

*The *Vulcanus* is owned by Chemical Waste Management, Inc., a subsidiary of Waste Management, Inc., of Oak Brook, Illinois. *Matthias II* is owned by Industrie Anlage of West Berlin.

†Additionally, Global Marine Development, Inc., Newport Beach, California is planning the refitting of surplus tankers as incinerator ships.

‡There are virtually no restrictions on incineration outside the 200-mile limit.

PROTOTYPE INCINERATORS

A wide range of prototype incinerators has been designed in efforts to reduce the relatively high costs of conventional high-temperature incinerators imposed by needs for antipollution devices. With assurances of a market and other possible economic incentives, many such prototypes could readily be developed for large-scale commercial application.

Prototype incinerators fall into two broad classes—those achieving high efficiency of combustion at reduced temperatures and those converting products of combustion from corrosive pollutants to utilizable resources. Illustrative of the former are small microwave furnaces, in which solid, liquid, or gaseous waste streams mixed with oxygen are fed into a quartz-tube reactor activated by a microwave power source, where they are ionized into a plasma at a temperature of only about 500 °C; the reaction is conducted under reduced pressure to minimize chances of leakage. At this temperature, the free plasma electrons produce a destructive energy equivalent to about 16,000 °C, which results in complete combustion without the formation of highly corrosive gases that would otherwise attack the containment vessel. This process also eliminates the need for scrubbers to neutralize these gases.* Automated monitoring systems with automatic shutdown are used to detect microwave leakage and to identify and measure reaction products. Illustrative of the latter is the use in cement manufacture of chlorinated hydrocarbon wastes at levels up to 20 percent in the boiler fuel. Apart from the energy savings, the halogens liberated during combustion become incorporated in the cement matrix and reduce the alkalinity of the cement clinker, thus obviating the need for the standard use of chloride-salt additives during the manufacture process. Combustion conditions in cement kilns are generally more rigorous than those in incinerators designed solely for hazardous waste disposal and are more than adequate for the

---

*One such microwave unit, a 15,000-watt furnace capable of incinerating seven kilograms of waste per hour, has been developed by Lockheed Research Center, Palo Alto, California. Various compounds, including kepone, PCBS, DDT, and malathion, have been successfully destroyed by such techniques.

destruction of halogenated and nonhalogenated hydrocarbons, including polychlorinated biphenyls (PCBs). However, attempts to introduce this technology in the United States have so far been defeated by the opposition of local communities.[*][31,32,33]

A more recent development is the fluidized alkaline-bed incinerator. Wastes are continuously introduced under aerated beds of molten sodium salts at temperatures of 800–1,000°C. Complete combustion is accompanied by the sorption and neutralization of acidic pollutants, such as halides and nitrogen and sulfur oxides. While highly efficient, particularly for the disposal of stable, highly chlorinated aromatic compounds, such as PCBs, this process is still comparatively expensive.

Burial or Landfills

CONVENTIONAL SANITARY LANDFILLS

Burial in landfills has been and still is the standard method for disposal of hazardous wastes. The cheapest and most dangerous form of burial is the conventional sanitary landfill, in which minimal, if any, precautions are usually taken against environmental contamination.[†] Unsecured chemical landfills are generally shallow trenches or pits dug in soils of varying porosity, into which raw wastes or cartons and drums of wastes are dumped. The wastes may then be covered with soil or clay in attempts to contain liquids and to exclude rain and surface waters, which can dissolve out soluble constituents, which together with liquid wastes produce a grossly polluted leachate. When saturated, a disposal site produces an amount of leachate equal to the amount of water entering it. The potential for leachate is thus greatest in humid areas where rainfall exceeds evaporation losses. These typically are areas of maximum population density and industrialization, such as the northeastern megalopolis.

---

[*]A cement kiln in Puerto Rico is the focus of a current $500,000 study, in which about one hundred sixty thousand gallons of medium to low toxicity hazardous wastes are being burned to determine the kiln's utility for hazardous waste destruction.

[†]Of about twenty thousand municipal-waste land-disposal sites, some six thousand are sanitary landfills, usually operated under state permits.

"SECURE" LANDFILLS

It is questionable whether any landfill, however ideally constructed and monitored, can ever be truly "secure," except on a short-term basis.[34,35] Sooner or later, toxic leachate will escape and contaminate subsurface soils. However, while landfills continue to be used, they can be made less insecure or more secure. Landfills are claimed to be "secure" when designed to prevent contamination of surface- and groundwaters and constructed to be impervious to external sources of water and to prevent accidental leakage of toxic leachate.

"Secure" landfills should be located in sites easily accessible to transportation, in areas of low population density and low alternative land value. In order to prevent leachate or runoff from accidental spills, the sites should be in poorly permeable, high-clay soils and in flat terrain and never over fractured bedrock. The sites should also be located well above the high-water table, away from drinking-water wells and floodplains, and in areas of low rainfall and high evaporation. The landfill pit should be excavated in clay, the subgrade compacted, smoothed, and fitted with an impermeable, inert liner of such materials as asphalt, concrete, rubber, or plastic, reinforced by overlaying with compacted clay soils. A system of leachate drains should be constructed adjacent to the liners at the perimeter of the landfill base to collect and treat any water leaking into the pit. In order to segregate chemically incompatible materials—such as acid- and cyanide-containing wastes, which when mixed form highly toxic hydrogen cyanide—and to facilitate possible future recovery of any particular waste, the landfill should be divided by clay dikes into a series of separate compartments, each designated for specific waste streams. When ready for closure, the landfill should be capped with a liner and layer of clay, and a fresh pit should be opened adjacently on the site. Each landfill on a secured site should be regularly monitored by a surrounding network of wells, and water from each should be regularly analyzed to check for leaching.

Under the provisions of RCRA, the EPA has proposed tough new regulations primarily designed to maximize containment.[36] These regulations include setting construction specifications;

setting operating standards—including restrictions on disposal
of liquid wastes and bans on the disposal of flammable and
highly toxic volatile materials; setting standards for closure and
sealing; setting schedules and standards for monitoring sites for
leakage up to thirty years after closure; and promulgating standards for strict financial liability of the owner and/or operator
of the site, requiring posting of a substantial bond and comprehensive insurance coverage.*[37,38,39,40] There is little question that
such regulations, if effectively implemented, would create com-
plementary powerful economic disincentives to continued on-
site disposal of hazardous wastes and incentives to the few major
commercial disposal firms capable of operating large centralized
or regional "secure" landfills.

The relatively high expense of construction and operation
of "secure" landfills has created strong interest in a wide range of
pretreatment methods, particularly those designed to achieve
volume reduction and solidification of hazardous liquid wastes.
Even with regulatory pressures and economics favorable to the
further practical development of other forms of safer disposal, it
is likely that burial in large, regional, "secure" landfills will continue in the near future to be the commonest method for disposal
of hazardous wastes. While there are no hard figures on the
number of currently operating commercial "secure" chemical
landfills, they probably number as few as twenty to forty and
handle only a small fraction of the nation's wastes.

INTERIM STORAGE SITES

For highly toxic, poorly degradable and nonreusable
wastes, for which no other practical disposal or detoxification
technologies are yet available, interim storage as opposed to
secure landfill is clearly the method of choice. Interim storage
sites ideally should be above ground level and designed for ease
of inspection, monitoring, isolation from surface waters and

---

*For each site, regulations require coverage of $2.5 million for "sudden and
accidental occurrences" and $2.5 million for "nonsudden and nonaccidental
occurrences."

groundwaters, and future waste retrieval. It is essential to avoid commingling of different waste streams, which should be stored in separate, labeled compartments. Interim storage units, preferably as above-ground, concrete mausolea, should be located on-site for large industry- or producer-generated waste streams, where they should be maintained and monitored at company cost. For consumer waste streams, which are widely disseminated and more dilute than producer streams, interim storage units should be located on a regional basis at sites that combine remoteness from population centers with accessibility to transport. Apart from the critical need for massive research efforts in waste reuse and recycling, probably the greatest immediate national priority is the shifting of emphasis from secure landfills, particularly for poorly degradable wastes, to a national network of interim storage facilities.*

DEEP BURIAL

Abandoned giant underground missile silos have recently found a use in the deep burial of toxic wastes. In 1973, Wes-Con, a hazardous waste disposal firm in Grandview, Iowa, bought an eighty-acre missile facility in the southern Idaho desert from the USAF. The facility—consisting of three silos, each 160 feet deep, 40 feet in diameter, and with a capacity of 1.5 million cubic feet—offers the extreme in safe disposal, "encapsulation" in vessels designed to withstand earthquakes and bombing attacks.[41] The facility, which is over three thousand feet above the water table, from which it is separated by impermeable clay, meets all state standards and has found eager clients among major chemical industries all over the United States. Wes-Con's 1980 base rate for disposal of hazardous wastes was six cents a pound. According to its managing partner, business is booming: "I don't need a sales staff. Every time another Love Canal is discovered, our business gets a real boost." The silo is now almost full, and Wes-Con is preparing to use a recently acquired, identical site some thirty miles away.

---

*In July, 1980, the Senate passed a bill emphasizing short-term, off-site procedures for storing radioactive waste from nuclear plants in surface or near-surface storage sites, where wastes could be constantly monitored pending future retrieval.

Conclusions

The greatest disincentive to the improvement of currently available disposal techniques, and to the development and application of resource recovery and a wide range of prototype technologies, is the ease and economy of disposal of hazardous wastes in "secure" landfills. The creation of economic disincentives to "secure" landfill disposal—to reflect the full range of their currently externalized and delayed societal costs—and the creation of economic incentives—including research subsidies—to safer forms of disposal and resource recovery are critically needed to reverse this situation (see Appendix XIII). Implementation of such economic pressures will be facilitated by the recognition that, in general, landfill is the most hazardous and least reliable method of disposal and one that inappropriately shifts the burden to future generations, even if there is uniform and complete compliance with current regulations for siting, impermeability, and isolation from groundwater and air.[42] It is even questionable whether solidification and encapsulation techniques represent any improvement, especially for poorly degradable wastes. The role of secure landfills should be restricted to fixed metals and to non-reusable wastes, which can undergo complete or near complete degradation under the conditions of burial within a maximal time frame of one or two decades, during which the site and adjacent surface and groundwaters must be rigorously monitored.

Finally, the persisting preoccupation of hazardous waste generators with disposal per se has limited recognition of the critical dual importance of resource recovery and recycling—with attendant energy conservation—and of a wide range of pretreatment methods, which can markedly improve the efficiency and safety of ultimate disposal. Reversal of these trends requires legislative and regulatory approaches that reflect the delayed and high externalized costs to health and the environment of failure to regulate, combined with direct economic-incentive programs.

PART V

The Future

It must also be said that industry has shown laxity, not infrequently to the point of criminal negligence, in soiling the land and adulterating the waters with its toxins. And it cannot be denied that Congress has shown lethargy in legislating controls and appropriating funds for their enforcement. As a result, even an extraordinary effort, commenced immediately, cannot achieve protection for the American public for years to come.

REPORT OF THE SUBCOMMITTEE ON
OVERSIGHT AND INVESTIGATIONS
U.S. House of Representatives, September, 1979

CHAPTER 13

Where Do We Go From Here?

Improper disposal of hazardous wastes is now America's number-one environmental problem. Although this problem only recently captured public attention, it has resulted from decades of negligence and lack of foresight. Clearly, it would be inaccurate, simplistic, and even unfair to burden industry with the entire blame. American society as a whole shares some responsibility. After all, the driving force behind the very existence of the hazardous waste problem is modern society's thirst for consumer products and its eagerness to purchase them at the lowest short-term market cost, even if this means generating massive quantities of dangerous by-products. We have become a society highly dependent upon toxic chemicals. We cannot, in the short run, power automobiles, paint houses, grow food, make and dye clothes, or print books without generating substantial amounts of toxic wastes.

Our technology has run away from us. It has developed far faster than our understanding of it, and far faster than our social control mechanisms, permitting society to become far more dependent upon toxic chemicals than most of us have realized. These chemicals have become deeply embedded in the very infrastructure of our economy.

Modern technology has run away because we permitted it to. Widespread public lack of interest about the underlying nature of the technical changes and a tendency to worship new materials and products uncritically have combined to ensure that anything that was technically possible would be tried.

Operational power over the pace and nature of the introduction of new chemicals and new chemical uses has been vested in a small but powerful segment of society, a network of industrial corporations, characterized by extremely short time-horizons and a very limited ethos of responsibility—one in which virtually all consequences are measured by the immediate impact on shareholder profits. A less safe guardian for Pandora's box cannot possibly be imagined. As a result of this short time-horizon and narrow sense of responsibility, industrial behavior has been generally characterized by inefficiency, malfeasance, and recklessness.

Meanwhile, even those social institutions characterized by a broader and more encompassing sense of responsibility have been neglectful, corrupt, or inefficient. Government, in particular, has acted only when literally compelled by public outrage, and has acted even then with more sloth than vigor. Even the guardians of the broadest concept of the public interest and the greatest concern for the future, the citizen health and environmental organizations, have come only belatedly to the recognition that toxic wastes are a major part of the industrial process, and one that no one was paying heed to.

Solutions to the problem are possible. The mistakes of the past must be rectified by cleaning up the residual wastes. Cleanup will be expensive, but it is, in essence, a technical and financial problem, one to be solved by engineers, chemists, and economists.

So long as we continue to produce toxic wastes, we must vigorously insist that today's problems be handled properly and that we do not repeat the mistakes of the past. Safe disposal of today's toxic wastes will also require engineering and chemical ingenuity, persistence, and caution. Technology must be set to guard technology.

But, while we must use our technology to protect ourselves and improve our capacity to do so, the temptation to define and solve these problems in purely technological terms is simplistic. Their solution will depend in the long run on a variety of technical and nontechnical fixes and, even more importantly, on changing attitudes toward our relation to the world around us.

The Political Realities

It is clear that the present political climate seriously threatens the implementation of either short or long-term solutions to problems of hazardous wastes. The Reagan administration is embarked upon the destruction of the inadequate structure erected by its predecessors under RCRA and other statutes. Indeed, it appears that the administration has launched an assault upon the entire infrastructure upon which society must rely to control toxic materials, including wastes.

Almost as soon as the administration was installed, it froze a wide range of pending federal regulations, particularly those relating to public health and environmental concerns, including several important hazardous waste regulations. The Office of Management and Budget (OMB) was assigned to review all such regulations before they could be implemented.

OMB rapidly announced that it would pursue a program of deferring industry compliance dates under RCRA, delaying the effect of the regulations until Congress could rewrite the basic statute in 1983.

This delay—and possible elimination—of aggressive regulation over hazardous wastes was not unexpected, particularly in view of the past track record of OMB Director David Stockman (see Chapter 9). But even opponents of the administration's environmental stance were stunned by the ferocity of what followed. The second target of the new administration was EPA itself. Cuts were to be expected, given that overall the administration was committed to major reductions in non-defense federal expenditures. Initial proposals were severe. The 1982 operating budget for Superfund was slashed from $250 million to $200 million.

These reduced funds were matched with significant staff cuts. Even where money had been appropriated for special new hiring under Superfund, overall EPA hiring freezes made it impossible for the agency to hire the right new staff for the job. Overall, EPA, amounting to ½ of 1 percent of the total federal budget, was slated for 12 percent of the budget cuts in round one, from $1.3 billion in fiscal 1981 to $1.19 billion in fiscal 1982. These cuts came at a time when the agency's workload was generally estimated to be doubling, as it assumed new responsibilities under RCRA, TSCA, and Superfund to deal with the chemical revolution, on top of its existing air and water pollution mission.

Then, in the wake of the summer passage of the president's proposed tax cuts, EPA observers reluctantly reached the conclusion that the administration intended not only a cut-back in the effectiveness of the agency, but also, with the active support of Gorsuch and Stockman, to destroy the agency itself.

Leaked drafts of Gorsuch's proposed 1983 budget revealed that even before OMB made its round of reductions, she was proposing to reduce EPA's 1983 spending power by 60 percent, including a reduction in the hazardous waste area from the 1981 level of $154.7 million to $108.4 million, a reduction of 50 percent after accounting for inflation.[1] In November, 1981, Stockman informed Mrs. Gorsuch that her cuts were not deep enough. He proposed that funding for the hazardous waste regulatory program be reduced by 65 percent. Stockman also suggested that the toxic substances control program be reduced by 44 percent.

The late summer and autumn of 1981 also saw repeated reports of poor morale at the agency, of unprecedented levels of turnover, of crippling declines in the agency's ability to recruit able people. Three congressional committees were so concerned about the situation that they held special oversight hearings into Gorsuch's impact on the agency, with the Republican Chairman of the Environment Committee, Robert Stafford, commenting, "I personally do not believe that the Environmental Protection Agency can continue to function if its staff and budget are cut so drastically. Decreases of such magnitude could amount to de facto repeal of some environmental laws." The third phase of the Reagan/Stockman/Gorsuch assault was on science. The heaviest burden of the early budget cuts fell on research functions, particularly those designed to measure the impact of toxic materials. The initial 1982 budget request from the administration called for a reduction in EPA's funding of scientific research by more than one-third. The draft 1983 budget leaked from the agency in October represented a 75 percent cut in EPA's support of outside research in real dollars. According to former EPA assistant administrator and chief budget officer William Drayton, "most of this country's environmental scientists, working in research institutions and universities such as Duke, the Universities of Washington and Nebraska, Harvard, etc., will discover over the coming year that they have been let go. The environmental effort will be crippled through at least the end of this decade once this scientific community, which has defined the problems and many of the solutions, has been disbanded."[2]

Gorsuch also took steps to cripple the effectiveness of the scientific research still going on. EPA's research director, Andrew Jovanovich, in the fall of 1981 circulated an agency plan to effectively muzzle EPA's scientists from informing the public of their results if top agency administrators disliked their implications. Under the plan, "every oral presentation by an EPA scientist, scientific consultant, or research contractor must be reviewed at four levels of the EPA bureaucracy. . . Scientific manuals and reports would have to follow a circuitous path through the agency involving as many as 30 steps before their conclusions became known to the general public."[3] The agency justified the plan as necessary to improve the quality of agency research, but the agency's scientists privately called it a disaster, one saying, "No published data—no new or revised pollution risks assessments—no standards which can, therefore, be defended—voila, you have instant regulatory reform."[4]

These cutbacks in funding for research, and in the ability of agency scientists and contractors to make their findings public once the research was done, seemed particularly hypocritical given the administration's repeated calls that before regulating, better scientific data and more of it be required.

These appeals culminated in the fall in a critical agency decision by Assistant Administrator for Toxic Substances, John Todhunter, not to regulate formaldehyde in spite of extensive scientific evidence that it was carcinogenic and that human exposures were widespread and heavy. Todhunter, in deciding not to regulate formaldehyde, declared that he would not regulate the substance in the absence of actual human health effects data. In response to the formaldehyde decision, Arthur Upton, former head of the National Cancer Institute, commented, "If the carcinogenicity of formaldehyde is ignored, it would mean that no agent could be regarded as carcinogenic in the absence of positive evidence in humans."[5]

Added together, the Reagan assault during the first nine months of his presidency constituted a fundamental threat to society's efforts to protect itself from hazardous waste. But by the summer of 1982, investigators were probing deeper and deeper into the Agency. They found what public health officials and environmentalists had warned for two years—that effective progress in cleaning up toxic wastes had been sacrificed to a set of incestuous relationships with former and present industry officials and waste disposal firms. Superfund chief Rita Lavelle had regularly been wined and dined by those she was charged with pursuing. Consultants still employed with private firms being investigated had helped direct EPA investigations. A report written on dioxin contamination by EPA's regional office in Chicago had been sanitized at the behest of Dow Chemical officials. A memo written by key Lavelle aides suggested that enforcement, weak as it was, was alienating the Administration's "principal constituency, business."

As the scandal, dubbed "sewergate," escalated, some in Congress moved beyond personnel issues to the heart of the matter. In October, 1982 a Sierra Club Natural Heritage Report revealed that EPA was spending Superfund money at less than half the minimum rate needed. Congressional willingness to see EPA's budget cut still further was at an end, and the Budget Committee made large increases in OMB's proposals. Finally, in March, 1983 Anne Gorsuch (now Burford) resigned. By April 1, all of the top architects of EPA toxics policy, including Assistant Administrator Todhunter, were gone from the Agency. The President, stung, attacked "environmental extremists," but his political advisors and aides maneuvered him into appointing former Administrator William Ruckelshaus to replace Burford. Even the Heritage Foundation, the ever-politically expedient right-wing think-tank that had drafted the strategic plan for weakening EPA that Burford and her aides carried out, announced that the Administration needed a new, aggressive environmental program focussed on effective enforcement.

The California Plan

Valuable time had been lost. Fortunately, outside Washington, the outlines of new strategies for dealing with the toxic waste problem had been emerging. In the early 1970s, California led the nation with the regulation of land disposal facilities for hazardous wastes and with the first cradle-to-grave hazardous waste tracking system, upon which current federal legislation (RCRA) was based. The abundance of available land, the state's favorable climate, and encouragement from state agencies resulted in the licensing of ten landfill facilities throughout the state for the disposal of all types of non-nuclear hazardous wastes, including wastes containing highly toxic and persistent chemicals. However, incidents of environmental contamination from land disposal sites in California led state officials to question the wisdom of continuing the use of "secure" landfills.

HIGH PRIORITY WASTES

In a report, *Alternatives to the Land Disposal of Hazardous Wastes: An Assessment for California,*[6] the Office of Appropriate Technology (OAT) identified six generic classes of hazardous wastes that are inappropriate for land disposal. These were designated "high-priority wastes," because they are highly toxic, persistent in the environment, bioaccumulative, and mobile in a landfill environment, such as those which contain pesticides, toxic metals, PCBs, halogenated organics, cyanides, or non-halogenated volatile organics. These wastes comprise about 40 percent of the hazardous wastes currently being disposed of in off-site land disposal facilities in California.

The OAT study demonstrated that alternatives to direct land disposal of all the state's high-priority wastes are technically feasible, commercially available, and not unreasonably costly compared to rising landfill costs and massive potential cleanup costs.

In addition, the study identified and recommended the use of alternative technologies for another 37 percent of California's off-site hazardous waste stream. In response to the OAT report, Brown, in October, 1981, issued an Executive Order phasing out the concept of land disposal facilities as repositories for any and all types of hazardous waste; the six generic categories of high priority wastes were banned from land disposal on a phased timetable. A higher fee was levied on the land disposal of these wastes in the interim to encourage construction of treatment facilities. The legislature passed a bill to create an array of financial incentives, including low interest loans, tax-exempt bond financing, and rapid amortization for alternatives to land disposal.

While Brown was establishing an intellectual framework for bold new assaults on the problem, however, administrative execution of the program lagged. A critical report by the staff Auditor General revealed that the State Health Department, charged with carrying out California's hazardous waste program during the first seven years of Brown's term, had largely failed to regulate disposal effectively.[7] The incoming Administration of Governor Deukmejian also appeared less committed to the new approaches, and thorny institutional obstacles hampered the implementation of the technically feasible approaches outlined in the OAT report.

The Danish Model

Solutions to these institutional problems have been developed in Europe, first in Denmark, and later in the West German states of Hesse and Bavaria.[8] While the Danish model emerges from a drastically different political culture, its effectiveness is so much greater than any program currently existing in the United States that it seems crucial that an effort be made to translate the model to American circumstances.

The Danish model involves the creation, in a given area, of a government or joint government-industry non-profit corporation with a monopoly over disposal and off-site treatment of hazardous waste in that area. The corporation operates a centralized treatment facility, consisting of a high-temperature controlled incinerator for organic wastes and a variety of physical and chemical treatment processes for inorganic wastes. Recycling facilities are also operated by the corporation. A network of regional collection points equipped to dewater and pre-treat wastes receives material from generators, using a manifest system similar to that required by RCRA. The corporation also operates a special fleet of railway tank cars to transport wastes from the regional collection points to the centralized treatment facility. A small landfill is also operated, but it receives only boiler slag from the incinerators and detoxified chemical residues from the inorganic waste treatment facilities.

Because these corporations have a monopoly they can charge fees adequate to cover the costs of properly incinerating, recycling, or detoxifying each waste stream. In exchange, industry receives the assurance that the corporation will treat all non-radioactive waste. Because the fees are high enough to cover the costs of detoxifying wastes, industry has a strong incentive to reduce waste generation. In Hesse, levels of waste generation have been reduced by more than one-third in five years. Liability for the waste passes to the waste disposal corporation, relieving generators of a major concern.

In Denmark local government has control of the corporation; in Hesse and Bavaria, approximately one-third of the seats on the Board of Directors are in the hands of local government. This provides the citizens of the communities where the waste disposal facilities are located with influence over operating procedures and environmental standards.

The waste disposal corporations are subject to Danish and German environmental laws governing air and water pollution; they have emission standards set by the national governments and their emissions are carefully monitored. However, the hazardous waste regulations themselves are far simpler than in the United States. This is possible because decisions about each waste stream, indeed about each shipment of waste, are made by the waste disposal firms, not the generators. These firms have no financial incentive to undertreat, and are imbued with the same broad concern for the public interest that in the U.S. is or should be reposed in regulatory agencies. But the firms are much closer to the disposal process, and can more easily make efficient, routine adjustments in procedures, prices and methods.

In Denmark, firms that misrepresent the composition of a waste shipment are informed, immediately, that their fees have increased by 30 percent. Since the Danish corporation, Kommunikem, has a monopoly, firms must pay this increased fee. Second offenses trigger a 60 percent fee increase. Danish officials report that they have never faced a second offense.

The Danish/West German model is not perfect. Newer types of waste disposal technology, like plasma gas treatment of PCBs, have not yet been installed. Heavy metal treatment is not yet satisfactory—heavy metal hydroxides, which are the precipitate from the treatment plants, are still potentially dangerous. And Danish and German officials admit that 15–25 percent of the total waste generated is still disposed of illicitly.

The Danes have established a consulting firm to spread this approach to other countries, and work is proceeding in Sweden. The model is there, working, for the United States to emulate—even though it runs into the conventional American reluctance to trust government with operating powers in the industrial sphere. (It should be noted that Bavaria, the first German state to adopt this plan, is the most conservative state in West Germany.) The head of the Danish Chamber of Commerce believes that the system is one of the best things ever to happen to Danish industry.

How to Deal with Toxic Wastes of the Past

The EPA and various states have listed and are currently investigating over eight thousand sites where hazardous wastes have been or could have been improperly dumped in past decades (see Appendices X and XIV). During early 1981, $13 million of government cleanup funds were being spent on thirty-four sites to prevent the escape of their toxic leachates into the environment. Some twenty-five additional sites were found to be

in need of emergency action and were awarded $17 million for
design and engineering studies. A total of 114 sites were on the
EPA's priority cleanup list as of August, 1981.[9] (See Appendix IX.)
National cleanup costs are estimated to range from $3.6 to
$25.5 million per site, with total national bills as high as $40 billion. Cleanup costs are $20 million for the Montague, Michigan
site alone.[10] These estimates are very crude, hardly better than
guesses. But better data are already coming in from some states.
New Jersey and New York estimate that they have some 230 and
157 sites, respectively, in need of remedial action. Michigan estimates it will require as much as $70 million just to determine the
extent of groundwater contamination at 640 of its sites.[11]

The superfund legislation authorizes funding of $1.6 billion
over three years for cleanup purposes. While this amount is
clearly inadequate to cover the multibillion-dollar estimates, it is
intended only as a supplement for those instances in which responsible parties cannot be identified and held liable. Assuming
that private parties could be held liable for half the total bill, in
the next three years, up to $3.2 billion could become available,
enough to clean up 170 of the sites.[12]

Private liability, of course, requires enforcement. The Justice Department under the Carter administration developed a
strong capability to enforce laws against those responsible for
past dumping practices and to collect damages. Some states,
particularly California and New Jersey, have been developing
their own enforcement capability. But many others still have almost no staff training and are not equipped to pursue hazardous
waste violations.

Knowledge of how best to spend these funds to achieve effective cleanup is scanty and poorly developed. Few companies
are presently equipped to carry out such projects. Recent events
further suggest that some companies that have created hazardous waste problems or that are currently involved in the operation of problem sites, are the same ones obtaining cleanup contracts. Obvious conflicts of interest are thus posed. A company
is unlikely, in cleaning up an abandoned site, to admit that hazards are posed by construction standards or work practices that
its own, currently licensed facility employs. Similarly, a firm en-

gaged in cleaning up one site may be reluctant to admit that a particular situation is hazardous if the firm is also potentially liable for another site where a similar situation may exist.

Cleaning up hazardous waste sites, even if possible, does not solve all the problems created by past practices. Many people may already have been exposed to dangerous materials dumped in the past, or may be exposed in the future before cleanup operations can be carried out. Surface and underground waters may have been contaminated, fisheries and wildlife poisoned, and land rendered unfit for agricultural purposes. Many such damages are possibly irreparable and permanent.

The superfund law of liability remains very weak in regard to the chances of financial recovery for those suffering these damages. The final legislation, unlike the original Muskie-Culver proposal (see Chapter 8), failed to make the necessary changes in the law of liability to enable victims to recover under the superfund. Furthermore, in those cases in which no private party can be found to bear the liability, the final version of the superfund prohibits most victims of toxic waste from recovering damages from the fund, except for the costs of relocation and water-supply replacement.

As a result, out-of-pocket medical expenses, lost wages due to related illnesses, reduced property values, and pain and suffering can only be redressed by private litigation. Such prosecution, even against a defendant who could be found and held legally liable, is usually unrealistic. Successful prosecution requires expensive attorneys and experts, compilation of tomes of scientific information, and protracted and burdensome litigation. As the CEQ points out, "The costs of scientific studies needed to prove a case may well be beyond the value of the case and will therefore add to the pressure on injured parties to settle."[13] Most often, the injured settle at a rate of compensation far below their legitimate entitlements and needs. Justice is only for the few who can bear the high costs of pursuing a case to fruition, or at least of presenting a credible threat of so doing.

In summary, present policies for dealing with the past heritage of abandoned hazardous wastes are grossly inadequate for a wide range of reasons. Information about the location and hazard posed by abandoned waste sites is fragmentary at best.

Only a small fraction of the federal funds likely to be needed to clean up those dump sites for which damages cannot be collected from the responsible companies has been appropriated. Most states do not have a sufficient commitment to ensure that responsible private parties who can be found and held liable are vigorously prosecuted and forced to pay for cleanup costs. Very little is still known about the best way to clean up many of these sites, and there are very few companies equipped to carry out cleanup operations. Many companies that attempt such cleanup have conflicts of interest, as they are heavily involved in past or present dumping practices that are suspect. For many kinds of medical and economic damage, current legal doctrines make it virtually impossible for many of those injured by hazardous wastes to collect for their damages. Even when private lawsuits could legally be brought by those who have suffered damages, in many cases, the delays and costs of such litigation are prohibitive and ensure that many who suffer will never be compensated.

RECOMMENDED SOLUTIONS

In the immediate future, more funds must be expended to inventory all inactive or abandoned sites and to assess the potential threats they pose. The sooner the dangers are identified, the sooner can action be taken to restrict their impacts. Nevertheless, the fiscal year 1982 Reagan budget will reduce by 600 the number of inspections carried out by the EPA. Much more severe cuts have been suggested for fiscal year 1983. Adequate funding at the state and federal levels is essential if the inventory is to be completed.

Additional funding for the superfund is essential. There is no reasonable prospect that $1.6 billion will take care of the problem. One alternative is to extend the fee system and the superfund itself after its current expiration date of 1985. Another option, under consideration in California, is for the state to levy a system of fees on waste generators to create its own "mini-superfund."[14] However, legal challenges to a New Jersey statute of this type are pending. Chemical companies claim the federal superfund precludes state action.

These public funds must be protected and reserved for only those cases in which no financially competent and liable private party can be found. Prosecution of former dumpers for damages on and off their sites must be carried out vigorously. The Reagan administration will be under heavy pressure from industry lobbies to reduce the commitment to enforcement of these laws initiated by the Justice Department under President Carter. Already there have been indications that such prosecutions will be discouraged, if not curbed. Cutbacks would be disastrous. The EPA and the Department of Justice must have the necessary funds, investigators, scientists, and lawyers to pursue toxic dumping cases. While no company wants to be sued, the realities of business will dictate cooperation with government demands for restitution only when such demands are clearly stated and backed by a strong and credible threat of prosecution. Moreover, companies that act quickly to clean up their problems benefit in terms of reduced potential for future liability. Strong prosecution of corporate malfeasance will thus not only correct such malfeasance, it will also encourage corporate good citizenship.

Research on more efficient cleanup technology designed to decontaminate or neutralize polluted groundwater is in its infancy and must be urgently increased. In addition to the recognized effectiveness of granular activated carbon filtration beds, prototype studies have demonstrated the utility of synthetic polymeric resin adsorbents and diffused countercurrent aeration. However, cleanup costs are likely to be very high. No technology is currently available for decontaminating polluted soil. The only remaining option is to physically remove it elsewhere to a "secure" landfill selected to minimize possibilities of local environmental pollution.

A radical change is needed in the institutional approach to implementing such cleanup technologies for old dump sites. Congress should create a "superfund corps," which would be in control of cleanup operations. States that already have effective and publicly accountable operations could well continue them under federal sponsorship.

The superfund corps should include engineering experts, hydrologists, engineers, chemists, and toxicologists. Service in the corps should be made into a highly sought-after career for the best qualified professionals in these fields. Technical challenge and appropriate salaries, combined with the social value of the work, could make the corps a highly professional and rewarding elite group, with much of the same *esprit de corps* that characterized the Public Health Service in the days when it fought malaria and yellow fever in Cuba and Panama under George Geothals in the early 1900s.

The corps would be responsible for implementing the highest degree of protection available in the most cost-efficient fashion. Such a corps would not be concerned about its own profits, nor about any possible consequences on its other hazardous waste operations. It could be protected from infiltration by criminal elements that are apparently a problem in at least part of the hazardous waste industry.

While this solution appears to run against the current Washington mania for exclusively private-enterprise solutions, it should be noted that the present problem has been created by private enterprise. It was corporate managers, in companies large and small, strong and weak, that chose to abandon wastes all over the countryside. When they have been apprehended, their defense has been that, however bad their practices were, they were established and standard at the time. What is now needed is a public mechanism to implement the best possible solutions, to strive continuously to improve those solutions, and to reject discredited industry practices. Private contractors tied in to the industries that generate and treat wastes cannot be expected to provide this type of leadership. Technically, cleaning up abandoned dump sites is as difficult a problem as any facing this nation and one that offers no prospect of profits to those who do the job better.

Another major unfinished task is the rewriting of the law of liability in regard to toxic wastes. The toxic torts features of the Muskie/Culver version of the superfund, for strict, several, and joint liability, should be enacted into law by Congress. If the new administration is serious about its commitment to individual initiative, the least it can do is to make it possible for individuals damaged by hazardous materials to take action to protect themselves in court.

However, in many cases, extensive court proceedings may not be the best way to pursue such problems of compensation. Even when a legal right to recovery has been established, courtrooms are often too expensive. Several other industrialized societies have created alternatives to litigation in such cases. The Japanese, for example, have a health-damage compensation law that provides individuals living in designated polluted areas with special relief when state medical examiners find that their ailments may be pollution-related.[15] Revenues for this compensation system are raised through taxes on pollution sources. If the state determines that the injury has been caused by the activities of a specific company, the company must pay the compensation costs calculated by the state.

America can surely afford and should strive for a more equitable, less burdensome, and more humane mechanism for dealing with victims of environmental pollution than is currently available or planned. Congress should reconsider proposals like the Toxic Substances Pollution Victim Compensation Act of 1977[16] as a basis for such a program. This proposed legislation was never reported out of subcommittee and was introduced too late for serious consideration in the 95th Congress. Nevertheless, the need for such a program increases daily.

How to Deal with Today's Toxic Wastes

Under the authority of RCRA, the EPA is now attempting to implement a complex system for regulating the generation, transportation, storage, and disposal of hazardous wastes. This new program will join the Clean Air, Clean Water, Safe Drinking Water, and Toxic Substances Control Acts and other related pollution control programs now mandated by federal law.

Implementing the RCRA program will not come cheaply. The EPA estimates that the first phase of the new regulations will cost some twenty-nine thousand hazardous waste generators a total of about $510 million; more than twice this number of generators are also expected to be substantially affected by the RCRA regulations. The EPA estimates that about half of this sum will be expended to upgrade the thousands of surface impoundments scattered all over the country.

Most companies affected by the new regulations, however, will be able to pass on their higher costs to consumers in the form of higher prices. It is doubtful that profit margins will be significantly reduced. While some argue that environmental regulations require the investment of inordinate amounts of scarce capital resources in nonproductive items, the EPA estimates that it will cost only $80 to dispose of a ton of materials under the new regulations, while cleanup of improperly dumped wastes costs up to $1800 a ton. Moreover, new technologies for recycling, pretreating, and incinerating wastes hold out the promise of actually increasing efficiency and productivity by cutting down on industry operating costs, generating energy, and reducing raw-material demand (see Appendix XIV).

Additional costs have been placed on industry by the Superfund. Some 87 percent of the $1.6 billion to be collected will come from industry and will also result in price increases that consumers will bear. The remaining federal share will be financed from taxes. Other direct costs will result from efforts to ensure the proper disposal of hazardous wastes. Additional investigators will be needed to police the RCRA program. More engineers and scientists will be needed to evaluate the adequacy of sites, monitor their impact on the environment, and explore preferable alternatives to land disposal. More laboratories will be required to test the soil, air, and water around dump sites. Health experts and toxicologists must be employed to determine the effect exposures to these wastes could have on human health. More attorneys will be needed to pursue enforcement action against lawbreakers. Both federal and state governments, and ultimately the public, will be forced to bear these costs.

Against these costs must be set benefits—vastly greater benefits. The easiest set of benefits to calculate is to compare the cost of proper disposal initially with the costs of cleanup later. Ton for ton, the costs society will incur under RCRA for proper disposal of hazardous waste are but a tiny fraction of those associated with attempting to clean up the problems created by improper disposal in the past. It is estimated that proper disposal of the chemicals dumped in the Love Canal decades ago would have cost less than $2 million in 1979 dollars. In contrast, the bill for Love Canal containment, relocation, and health and environmental impact studies alone topped $36 million by the end of 1980. Ultimate costs will be much higher, probably over $100 million.

The greatest benefit of proper disposal is the avoidance of future adverse effects on human health and the environment. For a whole host of reasons, both conceptual and methodological, no satisfactory system has yet been devised for calculating the benefits of regulatory programs designed to prevent future damage to people's health.[17] One figure, however, may shed some light on the probable dimensions of the savings. Thus far, those who have suffered medical and other damages from Love Canal have filed actions for $2 billion in damages. No doubt some of these claims will prove exaggerated, and others will be dramatically reduced by the courts, fairly or unfairly. But even if a small fraction of these costs are eventually judged by the courts to be accurate, the total health costs will be at least a factor of magnitude greater than the cleanup costs, which in turn are more than a factor of magnitude greater than the costs of initial, proper disposal.

RCRA, then, even in its present form, appears to be a great bargain. At $510 million a year it can prevent the persistence of past disposal practices, practices that, as we have seen, may cost $40 billion to correct. Considering the dramatic increase in the volume of hazardous waste production, it is clear that improper disposal could mean tens of billions of dollars of losses each year in the future, *just for after-the-fact cleanup,* even before the vastly larger costs of human suffering, death, and environmental destruction are taken into account.

Unfortunately, while RCRA is a bargain, it is far from an adequate preventative against future Love Canals. The program as the Carter administration left it is seriously deficient as a means of handling today's hazardous waste streams. Essentially, the problem with RCRA is that it encourages the maximum use of "secure" landfills, the least desirable of all available disposal technologies, and one that shifts the burden of proper disposal to future generations (see Chapter 12).

RECOMMENDED SOLUTIONS

James A. Rogers, Associate General Counsel of the EPA's Water and Solid Waste Division, warned in November, 1980:

Many of the thousands of synthetic organic chemicals that this country has been manufacturing in increasing amounts since

World War II last for decades. Human institutions and conventional engineering are not well suited to guard for decades against environmental dangers from these chemicals. Corporations dissolve, and key officers change positions. And steel tanks and clay landfills can start leaking before chemicals lose their toxicity.[18]

Nevertheless, RCRA encourages "secure" landfills as the disposal technology of choice. California, for example, with one of the most comprehensive programs of this type in the nation and indeed the program on which RCRA was modeled, shows how severe this bias is. Of its 5 million tons of hazardous waste generated annually, almost all are disposed of in landfills, 20 percent in licensed, "secure" facilities and 80 percent on-site. In order to break this dependence, California is trying to adopt an entirely different approach, outlined earlier in this chapter.

One of the few companies trying to develop approaches for recycling hazardous wastes into new uses has commented:

> Landfills should pay for their own demise through a system of fees intended not to subsidize resource destruction but resource recovery. This has never been done. . . . The money pouring into the landfills is going for lobbying and research into ever more fantastical ways to throw away wastes without taking responsibility for their fate. Against this kind of competition, resources recovery [programs] may be swamped. No state or federal agency has ever allocated one single dime to any research in the area of resource recovery of chemical wastes.[19]

An immediate priority should be the shift of research subsidies from landfill disposal into finding economically attractive ways of reusing producer waste streams.* This recycling is essential to make it possible for "wastes" to become "raw materials." Raw materials, expecially valuable raw materials, are far less likely to be dumped into the environment than wastes, regardless of how stringent the waste disposal regulations may be. It is always far safer to rely upon a company's safeguarding a material that has an economic value than to assume it will guard something it regards as useless. The creation of economic disincentives to "secure" landfill disposal, to reflect the full range of its

---

*Important options can also be developed for recycling of toxic chemicals in consumer waste streams, such as mercury in batteries.[20]

currently externalized costs, and of economic incentives, including research subsidies, to other forms of disposal is critically needed to reverse this situation.

The inadequacy of "secure" landfills also raises serious questions about the wisdom of legislation, such as that proposed by the Chemical Manufacturers' Association to preempt at the state or federal level the siting control over such sites.[21] Such legislation, it is argued, is needed to ensure that sites can be found, permitted, and operated in the volume needed. But the definition of volume need invariably assumes a continuation of landfilling as the disposal technology of choice, not of last resort. Such legislation thus runs the risk of institutionalizing our dependence upon landfill.

It is, however, likely that intense community resistance to the location of new "secure" landfills will provide the greatest immediate incentive to the development of better alternatives. To rebut the argument that if landfills are not licensed, generators will simply hand their toxic wastes over to midnight haulers, the immediate creation of a network of interim storage sites should be of high priority. These sites will ensure that, as technology improves, waste materials can be retrieved and recycled, reused, or detoxified. In light of recent advances—for example, in the chemical breakdown of PCBs announced by Goodyear and by SunOhio* and proposed new methods for degrading all halogenated hydrocarbons[22]—it appears fortunate indeed that, instead of licensing an "adequate" number of disposal landfills, the EPA has permitted the storage of wastes like DDT and PCBs in temporary facilities, from which they can now be removed and safely degraded.

Irrespective of the techniques used for hazardous waste disposal, pretreatment or initial detoxification can improve the efficiency, safety, and economics of subsequent disposal. Advances in pretreatment technology, which is still poorly developed, and encouragement of its increased future applications are critically

---

*SunOhio is a small operation based in Canton, Ohio. Dechlorination by the SunOhio PCBX process is highly efficient, and over five hundred gallons of contaminated oil can be handled by a portable prototype at a cost of only $3 a gallon.

contingent on direct incentives and research subsidies, and on indirect incentives, by taxation of disposal in "secure landfills." Biological, chemical, and physical methods already exist to treat virtually all hazardous wastes, with the exception of heavy metals and radioactives. Illustratively, acid and base waste streams can be easily neutralized; some organics can be rapidly degraded by composting on land farms or in concrete lined pits; PCBs can be dechlorinated, even in dilute waste streams, by reactive sodium salts; and, more simply, most liquid wastes can be dewatered to achieve substantial volume reductions.

Incineration is potentially one of the safest and most efficient disposal methods for most types of hazardous wastes, except those containing noncombustibles or heavy metals. Because of relatively high costs, there are only some fifteen high-temperature controlled incinerators available, which handle under 5 percent of the nation's hazardous wastes. New types of incinerators under development will permit efficient destruction at low temperatures in microwave plasma furnaces and the like. Other new approaches are likely to produce usable resources from the combustion products of wastes.

A massive expansion of our capacity to destroy hazardous waste in both conventional and innovative incinerators is urgently needed. This expansion can be combined with the needed network of interim storage facilities, detoxification centers, and other alternatives to "secure" landfilling, through a two-tiered network system of hazardous waste processing facilities—on-site disposal and regional centers.

The first tier would be located on the plant sites of major hazardous waste generators. The less the hazardous waste has to be moved and the fewer hands it has to pass through, the more likely it is that it will be properly handled. The major generators of hazardous waste are, for the most part, large and technologically sophisticated firms, far less likely to go out of business than specialized hazardous waste operators, with greater incentives and chances to innovate if they continue to have responsibility for their own waste. In addition, their processes are generally so stable that the relative composition of their waste streams shifts only slowly. Thus, such firms can reasonably design a combination of chemical neutralization, incineration, composting, and interim storage facilities to meet the particular requirements of their own waste streams.

The major objection to this first-tier system would be against requiring waste facilities to be located on-site in waste generators located in "high-hazard" or densely populated areas. It is highly questionable whether major generators of hazardous waste should be located in such high-hazard areas as flood-plains, downtown urban areas, and high fire- or earthquake-hazard zones in any case. Exposures from process materials in the event of a disaster are likely to be as much or more of a threat than waste exposures. But where such facilities have been improperly sited already, it is probably rash to locate their waste storage on-site. Such companies should probably locate waste storage facilities on separate sites in safer areas, still under their own ownership, responsibility, and jurisdiction. Eventually, the hazardous phases of the production process itself should be shifted to these new sites.

The second tier would be a regional network of high technology facilities, run by state governments or consortia of state and local governments, and staffed by an organization akin to the superfund corps proposed for dealing with abandoned sites, or perhaps by the corps itself. These facilities would be designed for the handling of hazardous wastes generated by smaller firms unequipped with their own processing centers, and for the collection and detoxification of consumer waste streams. Such regional centers should also serve as a focus for resource-recovery and waste-exchange operations.

These regional centers should be designed to handle a variety of hazardous wastes, using the best available technology. After preliminary sorting, hazardous wastes could be subject to the most environmentally safe and cost-effective methods of extraction, treatment, recycling, or incineration. The facilities should be funded by industry clients, based on volumes of waste initially generated and possibly also on their purity and composition. Credits could be granted to those firms demonstrating that they were safely recycling or detoxifying wastes in some manner other than in the regional center. Thus, there would be no financial disincentive to the actual use of the regional centers. The costs of collecting and processing consumer waste streams, again, should be borne by the manufacturers who initially placed the toxic material into the hands of consumers. These costs will then be passed on to the consumers, who will thus pay for the costs of reclaiming the materials at the end of the consumption cycle.

One solution to the disposal of hazardous wastes—to be avoided at all costs—is their export. With increasing restrictions on hazardous waste disposal, American corporations are increasingly looking overseas for cheap dumping sites. While it is impossible to document how much waste is now being exported, according to Richard Golob of World Information Systems Research, Cambridge, Mass., "We're seeing increasing evidence of a flow of waste from here into developing countries which usually don't have the facilities to safely handle it."*[23]

Exporting hazardous wastes is currently both legal and easy. Under regulations promulgated in November, 1980, a company merely gives four weeks' notice to the federal government, which in turn notifies the foreign country. By July, 1981, approximately thirty such notices had been filed. EPA approval is required only for export of wastes containing PCBs and dioxin.

Reflecting the concerns over the increasing export of hazardous wastes, Senator Daniel K. Inouye (Democrat-Hawaii) recently introduced legislation to amend the Export Administration Act of 1979 to include export limits on all wastes listed as hazardous by the EPA. An exporter would have to obtain a license from the secretary of commerce, who would issue it only with consent of the government of the importing country. Such legislation is clearly critical and overdue.

How to Deal with Toxic Wastes in the Future

There is a wide range of available technological options, some still at the prototype stage, for dealing with the disposal of hazardous wastes in the future. But options based on such

---

*In March, 1981, Mexican authorities jailed an American expatriate, Clarence Nugent, for illegally importing hazardous wastes, including forty-two drums of PCBs and forty drums of mercury cinders, from companies in the United States, including Diamond Shamrock and B.F. Goodrich. In another case, Nedlog Technological Services of Arvada, Colorado, which recycles wastes from mines, has confirmed that Sierra Leone rejected its $25 million offer to receive the firm's hazardous wastes.

narrowly-based technological fixes are, at best, makeshift, as they fail to confront the fundamental problem. Given the limitations of knowledge, the imperfection of institutions, the runaway nature of modern chemical technology, and the "unforgiving" nature of hazardous substances, capable of inflicting great damage at even trace levels many years after they were originally manufactured and disposed of, only one strategy can ensure the long-range protection of man and the environment from hazardous wastes. And that is not to generate them—a goal that can only be achieved by eliminating or reducing the production and use of those hazardous substances that generate toxic wastes.

At the present time, however, there are very few societal incentives to encourage such use reduction. An industry intending to manufacture a new chemical must, it is true, comply with the provisions of the 1976 Toxic Substances Control Act (TSCA). However, while TSCA nominally gives the EPA authority to regulate, and even prevent, the manufacture of new highly toxic chemicals, it explicitly excludes consideration of the dangers posed by wastes generated from them, and in fact, has proven so cumbersome and weak that it is of questionable value. It is estimated that the chemical industry releases into commerce some seven hundred new chemicals each year.[24] Since the passage of TSCA five years ago, the EPA has exempted from full testing thirty of these new chemicals and has rejected pending testing the production of only six.[25,26] An additional problem with TSCA is that it is dualistic; substances are either simply too dangerous to produce at all, in which case they can possibly be banned, or they are given the green light for unlimited production, advertising, and marketing.

THE RIGHT TO KNOW

Once industry has received authorization to manufacture a new product, it is under virtually no formal constraints on the marketing, uses, and final disposal of the product. If the product generates hazardous wastes, as defined in RCRA regulations, and in quantities the EPA regards as significant, the industry must take responsibility for disposing of the wastes left at its plant. But the basic question of whether the wastes can be safely disposed of on-site or in a "secure" landfill is not addressed before permission to manufacture is granted, nor is the company held formally responsible for the ultimate disposal of the product it sells. To compound the problem further, the company is free to slap a nondescriptive trade name on its product, thus concealing its actual chemical composition from the worker who manufactures it and the public who uses it.* Nor is the company required to disclose the specific nature of the hazards associated with a trade-name product. The chemical industry, in fact, has fought consistently and successfully against requirements for such disclosure. In this, they have been backed by the Reagan administration, which in response to intensive lobbying by the Chemical Manufacturers' Association, ordered OSHA to withdraw a January 16, 1981 proposal requesting public comments on a proposed regulation requiring the labeling of hazardous chemicals, on the grounds that it was unduly burdensome and expensive to industry. The withdrawal of this proposal has eliminated the possibility of even considering such regulations, let alone implementing them.

Mandatory requirements for explicit and noneuphemistic labeling and disclosure of ingredient identities and hazards of toxic materials in consumer products† and in the workplace are critically needed. Such labeling and disclosure would immediately create potent disincentives to the continued use of toxics and incentives for their displacement by equally or similarly efficacious, but less hazardous alternatives. The "right to know" has been generally challenged by industry, but would appear to be an inalienable and basic democratic principle, a fact recognized by the city of Philadelphia in 1980, when it became the first jurisdiction in the nation to pass a "right to know statute."[27]

USE REDUCTION

The principle of nonuse or use reduction of toxic substances has profound societal implications. Its implementation will depend on a mix of legislation, regulation, and marketplace

---

*Estimates by the National Institute of Occupational Safety and Health indicate that over 70 percent of the chemicals in trade-name products to which workers are exposed are not identified by the industries concerned.

†Illustratively, these requirements should extend to accidental food contaminants, such as pesticide residues, as well as to food additives.

pressures. The latter include economic incentives to the development and use of nonhazardous or less hazardous alternatives to toxic materials, disincentives to the use of toxic materials in the form of a user and disposal tax, roughly equivalent to a superfund, and disincentives based on legal liability. Key elements in overall use reduction are requirements for a complex of strategies, including labeling, incentives for product and process substitution, and redesign of industrial technology to encourage conservation and reuse. Application of these strategies to any particular product or process based on toxic chemicals must be individualized to reflect a wide range of factors, including toxicity, degradability, intended uses, and efficacy.

The regulatory authority for use reduction, in its broadest sense, is contained in the provisions of TSCA and RCRA. It is, however, unlikely that banning of specific toxic chemicals or products will feature prominently in the overall development of future strategies. Certain highly toxic and carcinogenic chemicals should be completely banned, especially if they are highly persistent, and especially if used for purposes for which similarly efficacious substitutes are available. The EPA's current authority under TSCA, if permitted to function by the Reagan administration or some successor, will probably identify more such products in the future. Products of this type already in commerce will not, however, be reviewed by the EPA for years under its present funding and personnel levels. And, given the Reagan administration demand for body counts before regulating formaldehyde, little is likely to happen before 1985. But, at least, the mechanism is in place.

Process- and product-substitution technologies, while still in their infancy, are of major potential importance to the future reduction of hazardous wastes. Examples include the use of man-made mineral fibers (MMF) and sintered iron for asbestos in insulation and automobile brake linings, respectively; toluene for benzene as a solvent; soap-based detergents for alkyl halide solvents and degreasing agents; chlorinated paraffins for the more expensive PCB paint additives; and mineral oil for PCBs used as heat transfer and hydraulic fluids. Careful preliminary research is, of course, essential to minimize the possibility that the substituting technology does not pose unrecognized hazards, such as the occasional problem of flammability at high temperatures of mineral oil used as a PCB replacement or, less comprehensibly, recognized hazards, such as those attendant on the replacement of the soil fumigant dibromochloroprane (DBCP) by the more carcinogenic and potent alkylating agent ethylenedibromide (EDB).

An even greater role for process and product substitution is reversal of the technological displacement of products based on natural organic materials by synthetic products—such as the replacement of paper and wood by plastics, cotton textiles by synthetics, and soap-based detergents by nitrilotriacetic acid (NTA) and optical brighteners. Questions of quality of life apart, the technological displacement of natural by synthetic products, with the advent of the petrochemical era some four decades ago, has probably been the most important example of sudden, and massive, distortions of the marketplace in the entire history of human commerce.

Substantial use reduction of toxics can also be achieved by recovery and recycling in current industrial plants, although the success of retrofit or "end-of-the-pipe" treatment is greater in newer, rather than older, plants. Material balance studies—in which raw materials and energy used are inventoried against products, by-products, and liquid and gaseous effluents and wastes—are increasingly demonstrating the inefficiency of many industrial processes due to unrecognized losses of raw material and resources. Such studies, which should be made mandatory for all industries using or manufacturing toxic chemicals, are likely to provide an important stimulus to use reduction, reuse, recycling, and reduction of accidental or unrecognized effluents. An equally important stimulus would be the introduction of a system of user fees for hazardous substances.

It is however much easier to reoptimize production processes, achieve use reduction, increase reuse, and reduce generation of hazardous wastes when these considerations are engineered into new plant design, rather than retrofitted into old plants designed in the absence of such considerations. Both regulatory and economic pressures could be potent stimuli to the routine use of closed-loop technologies in all industries using toxic materials and generating hazardous wastes.

BIOMASS TECHNOLOGY

The production of chemicals, and energy, from biomass represents an important, if not revolutionary, possibility for the replacement of petroleum feedstocks by nonfood plants and trees.[28] Vast sources of glucose are potentially available in the lignocellulose complex of biomass and, given favorable economics, could be used for a wide range of fermentation processes yielding ethyl alcohol, besides a wide range of other products in the two-to-four carbon range, such as acetic acid, acetone, butanediol, and butanol. The dehydration of fermentation alcohols could yield various short-chain olefins, which are now exclusively petroleum-derived. Butadiene obtained by industrial dehydration of butanediol could be used to manufacture styrene, which is normally derived from benzene, a highly toxic and carcinogenic petroleum hydrocarbon.

Biomass technology for large-scale chemical production, while still in its infancy, could represent a major opportunity for use reduction in toxic chemicals and intermediates and for replacement of petrochemical technology by a technology based on natural organic materials. By-products of biomass technology could be returned to ecosystems as fertilizers, in contrast to by-products of synthetic fuels and petrochemical processes, which are major sources of hazardous wastes. This is by no means pie-in-the-sky philosophy, particularly as the infrastructure of a large-scale fermentation industry is available in laboratories of pharmaceutical and major oil industries, and universities. The only major requirement is an economic incentive for a profitable biomass-derived product market, coupled with disincentives to the currently cheaper petrochemical technology.

ECONOMIC INCENTIVES AND DISINCENTIVES

Critical to these various strategies is the development of economic disincentives to the use and manufacture of toxic substances and incentives to their conservation, recycling, and reuse. These economic measures should be designed to ensure that the costs of producing or using a material reflect fully all the externalized costs, including those resulting from disposal or from risk of accident. Given a choice between a more expensive product, whose cost is increased because of the hazardous wastes generated by its manufacture, and an item that costs less because it does not entail the generation of such wastes, industry and consumers alike will choose the less expensive product. Such economic incentives and disincentives must be carefully designed to reflect the nature of the toxic materials, including specifics of their toxicity and degradation, and the nature of their intended uses, market penetration patterns, and final dissemination.

To reduce the use of toxic products, a tax or fee should be levied on those who initially produce them, as early in the manufacturing process as it is possible to identify the specific nature of the hazard posed. The superfund is a very crude variant on the idea, but it levies charges only on gross feedstocks. It provides no incentives to those using petrochemicals to produce relatively less-toxic plastics, for example, because no fee is levied at the stage of formulation of the polymer, only on the feedstock. Thus, as materials make their way through the production and formulation process, a fee would be levied at each stage at which the toxicity of a given material was increased by the manufacturer.

The system of economic incentives and disincentives would have to be carefully geared towards particular toxic chemicals and to their particular intended uses. As an example, fees could be levied on cadmium production. If these fees were high enough to fully reflect the possible costs to society of disseminating all of the cadmium or mercury into food chains, the costs of batteries containing cadmium would increase dramatically. However, since the batteries could be easily reclaimed from consumers through the payment of a fee for the return of each worn-out battery, their costs might increase only slightly, since most of the cadmium involved would be repeatedly recycled. In contrast, the use of cadmium in automobile tires would become very expensive, because most of the metal cannot be reclaimed. Other materials would over time take the place of cadmium in tire formulation, and markets might also emerge for the reclamation of cadmium from used tires (but not cadmium released into air and road dust from normal tire wear, for which collection would be virtually impossible).

It is clear that use-reduction strategies, whether by banning or by user and disposal taxes, must be individualized to reflect a wide range of considerations. The formulation of such individual strategies must dually reflect the nature of the toxic material, including its toxicity and degradability, and the specific nature of its intended use. Use reduction or nonuse is particularly critical for highly toxic and carcinogenic materials, especially when they are poorly degradable or immortal; when they are used by small, rather than large, businesses; when their use becomes progressively diluted and widespread in the consumer chain; when they cannot practically be recaptured and recycled; and when less-hazardous alternatives are available.

Questions of inherent toxicity and intended use apart, there are even more fundamental considerations relating to societal efficacy and utility. With the exception of the 1962 Kefauver-Harris amendment to the Federal Food, Drug and Cosmetic Act, which imposes the requirement that drugs must be effective, there is no requirement for efficacy of other consumer products (except Federal Trade Commission [FTC] laws that these products mush achieve their stated objective) or for efficacy of industrial chemicals. The narrow FTC requirement that products must achieve their stated objective is in no way responsive to the broader question as to whether such stated objectives have any societal efficacy or utility. The imposition of the requirement that defined categories of toxic chemicals in defined-use categories must achieve broad societal efficacy, and one that cannot be substituted by less-toxic alternatives, would be a major advance in the development of use-reduction strategies. Illustrative has been the extensive use of the chlorinated hydrocarbon pesticides, aldrin and dieldrin, which are highly carcinogenic, persistent, and poorly degradable, have bioaccumulated in the food chain, have become widespread pollutants of air, water, and food, and have produced major economic losses due to fish and poultry kills. Yet their manufacturer, Shell Chemical, was unable to produce evidence of their efficacy in 1973/74 EPA cancellation/suspension hearings. The major target insect populations, corn rootworms and wire worms, were in fact largely resistant to these pesticides.

Similar questions of lack of broad societal efficacy can be addressed to a very wide range of toxic products, such as the use of coal-tar dyes in cosmetic food additives; the use of acrylonitrile plastics instead of glass beverage containers (with the resulting leaching of the highly carcinogenic acrylonitrile into soft drinks, largely drunk by young children or teenagers); and the use of aminostilbene optical brighteners in detergents to produce the optical illusion of whiteness in clothes.

How We Should Shape the Future

It is relatively easy to conceptualize the overall societal changes that are vitally needed to reduce future threats from hazardous wastes. It is, however, less easy to set into motion the broad-ranging initiatives needed to implement such changes. The changes required to deal with past, present, and future problems of hazardous wastes will demand not only a high degree of technological innovation and political sophistication, but more importantly they will also call for some fundamental shifts in ways of thinking about the world and ourselves.

Perhaps less important than the solutions chosen to resolve problems of hazardous wastes are the ways in which such problems themselves are defined. We are all a vital and dynamic part of the world. The molecules in our bodies are not isolated entities, but engaged at every moment in complex interchanges with the external environment. With every breath we exchange oxygen with the air. With every drink of water, we incorporate part of streams and aquifers into our bodies. With every mouthful of food, we complete pathways that run from our bones, liver, and brains to rainwater and microorganisms in the soil that nurtured the crops upon which we depend. "No man is an Island, entire of it self" was for John Donne a religious principle. For us, it must become the basis for our daily lives, for it is an unrelenting and unforgiving reality.

The ecological notion that living organisms are mutually connected and interdependent is by now a commonplace. But interconnectedness in this sense goes beyond ecological interdependence to the idea that the very identity of organisms is a function only of a given moment. An organism may perceive that there is an "inside" and an "outside," but the material that is inside at one moment may be outside at the next—indeed, almost certainly will be at some future moment. Equally, things that are thrown away "outside" the boundaries of the body today will, or statistically may, turn up inside it next year.

Yet, our senses, culture, history, and Judaeo-Christian ethos encourage us to see ourselves as set apart from the rest of the world we inhabit. They foster the false sense of an "inside" and an "outside," leading to the belief that we can dominate and subjugate that which is "outside," altering and changing it to meet our needs.

No doubt this habit of thinking is of great and essential value to our survival. At any given moment, we are quite right to nurture and protect our own bodies at the expense of, say, our clothing, even though, in a few months, dust from the cloth may enter and remain in our lungs. But while the false consciousness that we are separate may be essential, it is also dangerous. It leads us to actions that are not prudent, that do not make sense, but that merely indulge transitory desires or whims.

It is in the nature of materials based upon cellulose to rot— they are made of carbon, which is food, for us, and for the myriads of smaller species that preceded us. But it is inconvenient to have fence posts eaten by termites, so we developed chlordane, a pesticide that operates by interfering in the metabolic processes of termites, metabolic processes similar to our own. And thus it develops that chlordane is a carcinogen—it triggers within us irreversible molecular changes that our bodies cannot control, just as the termites cannot, in a much briefer time, cope with what chlordane does to them. And, since we wish for our houses and fences to be protected for years, if not decades, we have devised in chlordane a persistent chemical, one that other microorganisms will not rapidly break down into simple carbon dioxide and water. But once we release such persistent chemicals into the biosphere, we are, in effect, unleashing them into our own bodies, which connect through a tangled web with the substance of the biosphere.

Social practices and regulatory mechanisms must begin to recognize and reflect that we are an integral element of the environment. Current ways of handling pesticides are spectacular examples of flaunting this reality. The EPA's pesticide regulations and the practices of farmers somehow assume that complex, persistent organic molecules can be carefully deposited on one part of a farmer's acreage at a particular point in a growing cycle and yet not become incorporated in human food chains. This attitude overlooks a wide range of phenomena, such as wind-induced drift, soil residues, runoff into streams, mistimed applications, deliberate violations of regulations, and mislabeling errors. All of these ensure that a significant fraction of the total volume of pesticides applied in this country ends up being ingested by human beings.

Another principle that future approaches to toxic wastes must incorporate is admission of ignorance. We do not even begin to have the scientific knowledge to justify the assumption that so long as we dilute our wastes below a certain threshold, they are safe. The EPA has implicitly adopted this principle of safety-by-dilution in its RCRA regulations and philosophy. Yet we know little even of the effect of loading marginally larger quantities of such nontoxic nutrients as nitrogen into the air and water. How much less well equipped are we to understand the consequences of dramatically increasing by factors of magnitude the concentrations of highly toxic chemicals in the environment. We have increased worldwide levels of lead in the biosphere, not by 10 or 20 percent, but ten- or twenty-fold; such substances as DDT and PCBs are now disseminated throughout the biosphere, which has no evolved mechanism for detoxifying them.

The idea that trace concentrations of toxic chemicals can have dangerous effects may seem farfetched—what, after all, is the real scale of such concentrations compared with the vastness of the atmosphere and ocean? But already, only forty years into the petrochemical age, the warning signs are everywhere. The relationship between exposure to a wide range of petrochemical carcinogens and an extensive array of occupational cancers are now well documented, and such studies are still in their infancy. Recent reports suggest that the concentrations of dibenzofurans, a breakdown product of PCBs, have had a significant effect in reducing the fertility of American males.[29] Other studies indicate that the average urban child carries much higher levels of body lead than previously thought and that the characteristic levels today are associated with measurable declines in IQ and other intelligence measures.[30]

Many of the chemicals released into the environment by modern technology possess the property of concentrating in body tissues, of bioaccumulating, so that predators higher up the food chain, including humans, may end up with millions of times as much of a given halogenated hydrocarbon as the environment at large. What is much less well known are the ways in which these different pollutants interact within the body and the external environment and what new and untested breakdown products they may generate.

Our own biologically determined urge to survive, the instinct that led us forth as a predator in ages gone by and that drove us to go very far down the road to the destruction of other living beings that share this planet with us, is the same force that, wisely harnessed, may turn us from destroyer to savior. And here, in the long run, is the saving grace of our interconnectedness with life—because, just as we cannot endanger life without endangering ourselves, so we cannot save ourselves without preserving the entire biosphere.

That is the challenge of our times. It is a challenge with many facets. Toxic wastes are only one. But we will not solve the problem of hazardous waste dumps and Love Canals until we recognize that we are a part of life and that we cannot destroy it for our immediate convenience and comfort without ultimately destroying ourselves.

References

Chapter 1

1. *Federal Register* 46 (Feb. 26, 1980):33119.
2. *Federal Register* 43 (Dec. 18, 1978):58947.
3. U.S. Environmental Protection Agency, Office of Water Quality Management, *Groundwater Protection.* Document No. WH-554 (Washington, D.C., 1980), p. 4.
4. Idem., Office of Public Affairs, "Waste Alert," EPA *Journal* 5:12, 1979.
5. Idem., Office of the Administrator, *Report to Congress on Disposal of Hazardous Waste,* June 23, 1973 (Washington, D.C., 1973), p. 4.
6. R. D. Lipschutz, *Radioactive Waste: Politics, Technology, and Risk: A Report of the Union of Concerned Scientists* (Cambridge, Mass.: Ballinger, 1980). See also F. C. Shapiro, *Radwaste: A Reporter's Investigation of a Growing Nuclear Menace* (New York: Random House, 1981).
7. Samuel S. Epstein, *The Politics of Cancer* (New York: Anchor/Doubleday, 1979), p. 28.
8. EPA, *Report to Congress,* p. 4.
9. U.S. Environmental Protection Agency, Oil and Special Materials Control Division, *Damages and Threats Caused by Hazardous Material Sites* (Washington, D.C., 1980), p. xiv.
10. The literature on public health effects of hazardous waste dumps is scanty and general. See, for example, the following selected references: Segal *et al.,* "The Toxic Substance Dilemma," National Wildlife Federation, Washington, D.C., 1980 (a good elementary discussion); Report of the Subcommittee on the "Potential Health Effects of Toxic Chemical Dumps" of the DHEW Committee to Coordinate Environmental and Related Problems in *Health Effects of Toxic Pollution,* Report from the Surgeon General to the U.S. Senate Committee on Environment and Public Works (Ser. No. 96-15), Washington, D.C., August 7, 1980; W. W. Lowrence, ed., "Assessment of Health Effects at Chemical Disposal Sites," Rockefeller University, New

York, 1981; National Institute of Environmental Health Sciences, "Research Needs for Evaluation of Health Effects of Toxic Chemical Waste Dumps," Symposium at Research Triangle Park, October 27–28, 1981; T.H. Maugh, "Just How Hazardous Are Dumps," *Science* 215:490–493, 1982.

11. For early warning indicators of chronic toxic effects, especially cancer, reproductive, and genetic hazards, see A.D. Bloom, ed., "Guidelines for Studies of Human Populations Exposed to Mutagenic and Reproductive Hazards," March of Dimes Birth Defects Foundation, White Plains, New York, 1981; T.H. Maugh, "Biological Markers for Chemical Exposure," *Science* 215:643–647, 1982.

12. J. Melius and W. Halperin (NIOSH), "Medical Screening of Workers at Hazardous Waste Sites," Society for Occupational and Environmental Health Conference, Washington, D.C., Dec. 9, 1980; P. Landrigan, "Chemical Wastes: Illegal Hazards and Legal Remedies," *Am. J. Pub. Health,* 71:985–987, 1981; R.J. Costello and M.V. King, "Protecting Workers Who Clean Up Hazardous Waste Sites," *American Industr. Hygiene Association Journal,* 43:12–17, 1982.

13. EPA, *Report to Congress,* p. 4.

14. Congressional Reference Service, *Resource Issues from Surface, Groundwater and Atmospheric Contamination* (Washington, D.C.: U.S. Government Printing Office, 1980), p. 75.

15. Ibid., p. 76.

Chapter 2

1. M. Brown, *Laying Waste: The Poisoning of America by Toxic Chemicals* (New York: Pantheon), 1980.

2. Congressional Research Service, the Library of Congress, *Six Case Studies of Compensation for Toxic Substances Pollution: Alabama, California, Michigan, Missouri, New Jersey and Texas.* Report to the Committee on Environment and Public Works, U.S. Senate. Ser. No. 96-13 (Washington, D.C., U.S. Government Printing Office, 1980).

3. R. Nader, R. Brownstein, and J. Richards, *Who's Poisoning America: Corporate Polluters and Their Victims in the Chemical Age* (San Francisco: Sierra Club Books), 1981.

Chapter 3

1. *Oversight: Resource Conservation and Recovery Act.* Hearings before the Subcommittee on Oversight and Investigations of the House Committee on Interstate and Foreign Commerce, 95th Cong., 2d Sess., Ser. No. 95-183, Oct. 30, 1978, p. 214.

2. For more information on this incident, see *Adverse Effects of Polybrominated Biphenyls (PBBs).* Hearings before the Subcommittee on Oversight and Investigations of the House Committee on Interstate and Foreign Commerce, 95th Cong., 1st Sess., Ser. No. 95-65, Aug. 2–3, 1977.

3. Statement of Robert Harris and Robert J. Rauch, Environmental

Defense Fund, in *Regulation of Cancer Causing Flame Retardant Chemicals: TRIS*. Hearings before the Subcommittee on Oversight and Investigations of the House Committee on Interstate and Foreign Commerce, 95th Cong., 1st Sess., Ser. No. 95-33, May 11, 1977.

4. *Resource Conservation and Recovery Act* Hearings, p. 213, 1978.

5. W. C. Galegar, Deputy Regional Program Director, Water Supply and Pollution Control, Department of Health, Education and Welfare, Dallas, Texas to L. S. Jones, Executive Secretary, Tennessee Stream Pollution Control Board, Nashville, Tennessee, July 27, 1965.

6. D. R. Rima et al., *Potential Contamination of the Hydraulic Environment from Pesticide Waste Dump in Hardeman County, Tennessee* (U.S. Geological Survey, Water Resources Division, Aug. 1967), p. 2.

7. Complaint by the Public Health Department of the state of Tennessee in the matter of Velsicol Chemical Corporation, Memphis, Shelby County, Tennessee, Division of Water Quality Control, Davidson County, Feb. 21, 1972.

8. *Resource Conservation and Recovery Act* Hearings, Oct. 30, 1978, p. 110.

9. Ibid., p. 232.

10. Ibid., p. 215.

11. Ibid., p. 427.

12. National Academy of Sciences, National Research Council, *Chloroform, Carbon Tetrachloride and Other Halomethanes: An Environmental Assessment* (Washington, D.C., 1978).

13. *Resource Conservation and Recovery Act* Hearings, Oct. 30, 1978, pp. 109–13.

14. Ibid., p. 309.

15. Christine Sterling to Lester O. Brown, Sept. 1979 (personal communication).

16. Conestoga-Rovers & Associates (Waterloo & Mincardine, Ontario, Canada), "Site Investigation and Monitoring Programs." Contract Report to Velsicol Chemical Corporation, Feb. 1979, pp. 1–20.

17. U.S. Environmental Protection Agency, Athens, Georgia, *Final Report: Hazardous Waste Site Investigation, Hardeman County, Tennessee,* Oct. 4, 1979.

18. Conestoga-Rovers & Associates (Waterloo & Mincardine, Ontario, Canada), "Hardeman County Landfill Site: Closure Plan, Concept." Contract Report to Velsicol Chemical Corporation, Oct. 1979, pp. 1–26.

19. Press release, University of Cincinnati Medical Center, Institute of Environmental Health, Kettering Laboratory, June 21, 1979.

20. C. S. Clark et al., "An Environmental Health Survey of Drinking Water Contamination by Leachate from a Pesticide Waste Dump, Hardeman County, Tennessee." *Archives of Environmental Health* 37:9–18, 1982. (These investigators were concurrently examining exposure of Memphis waste water treatment plant workers to similar Velsicol waste being then discharged into the Memphis sewage system.)

21. C. S. Clark et al., "Evaluation of the Health Risks Associated with the Treatment and Disposal of Municipal Wastewaters and Sludge." Grant

Report No. R-805445 to the Health Effects Research Laboratory, Environmental Protection Agency (Cincinnati, Ohio, 1981).

22. Press release, University of Cincinnati Medical Center, June 21, 1979.

Chapter 4

1. Memorandum prepared by J. Fred McCarthy, McCarthy Well Company, entitled "Repair Job 1933," Dec. 14, 1934, p. 1, records of the Minnesota State Department of Health.

2. Memorandum prepared by F. J. Mootz for H. L. Holstrom, entitled "Storage 3 Emulsion, Reilly Tar and Chemical Corp.," May 8, 1956, records of the Minnesota State Department of Health.

3. Eugene A. Hickok and Associates, *Ground-water Investigation at St. Louis Park, Minn.* Report to the city of St. Louis Park, Sept. 1969, p. 17.

4. G. R. Koonce and Edward A. Pryzina, *Report on Waste Disposal at Republic Creosote Co. and Reilly Tar and Chemical Corp., St. Louis Park.* Report to the city of St. Louis Park, Apr. 1970, pp. 1, 4.

5. Wayne Popham to Lester O. Brown, June 1980 (personal communication).

6. Minnesota State Department of Health, *Report on Investigation of Phenol Problem in Private and Municipal Wells in St. Louis Park, Minnesota Hennepin County,* Sept. 1974, p. 5.

7. Barr Engineering Co., *Soil and Ground Water Investigation: Coal Tar Distillation and Wood Preserving Site, St. Louis Park, Minn.* Report to Minnesota Pollution Control Agency, June 1977.

8. *State of Minnesota v. Reilly Tar and Chemical Corporation,* No. 670767 (D. Minn., filed Sept. 4, 1980).

9. *United States v. Reilly Tar and Chemical Corporation, et al.,* No. 4-80-CV-469 (D. Minn., filed Sept. 4, 1980).

10. Ibid.

11. R. T. Torkelson et al., "Toxicologic Investigation of 1,2-Dibromo-3-Chloropropane," *Toxicology Applied Pharmacology* 3:545–59, 1961.

12. N. N. Rakhmatullaev, "Hygienic Characteristics of the Nematocide Nemagon in Reaction to Water Pollution Control," *Hygiene Sanitation* 36:344–48, 1971.

13. M. B. Powers et al., "Carcinogenicity of Ethylene Dibromide and 1,2-Dibromo-3-Chloropropane after Oral Administration in Rats/Mice," *Toxicology Applied Pharmacology* 33:171–72, 1975.

14. A. Blum and B. Ames, "Flame Retardant Additives as Possible Cancer Hazards," *Science* 195:17–23, 1977.

15. M. Legator, "Chronology of Studies Regarding Toxicity of 1-2-Dibromo-3-Chloropropane," *Annals New York Academy of Sciences* 329:331–38, 1979.

16. *Hazardous Waste Disposal.* Hearings before the Subcommittee on Oversight and Investigations of the House Committee on Interstate and Foreign Commerce, 96th Cong., 1st Sess., Ser. No. 96-49, June 18, 1979, p. 1594.

17. Ibid.

18. California Regional Water Quality Control Board Resolution 69-19, Aug. 16, 1968.

19. *Hazardous Waste Disposal* Hearings, p. 1594.

20. Ibid., p. 1597.

21. Ibid., p. 1590.

22. Ibid., p. 1587.

23. Ibid., p. 1571.

24. *United States et al.* v. *Occidental Chemical Corporation,* No. 79-989-MLS (D.E. Cal., filed Dec. 18, 1979).

25. Ibid.

26. *Federal Register* 46 (Feb. 26, 1981):14229.

27. Francine Rudolph, U.S. Department of Justice to Lester O. Brown, Aug. 21, 1981 (personal communication).

28. U.S. House of Representatives, Committee on Government Operations, *Interim Report on Ground Water Contamination: Environmental Protection Agency Oversight.* House Report No. 96-1440, 96th Cong., 2d. Sess., Sept. 30, 1980, p. 3.

29. Testimony of Robert Harris for the Council on Environmental Quality, in *Toxic Chemical Contamination of Ground Water.* EPA Oversight Hearings of the Subcommittee on Environment, Energy and Natural Resources of the House Committee on Government Operations, 96th Cong., 2d. Sess., July 24, 1980, p. 13.

30. State of Connecticut, Department of Environmental Protection, "Hazardous Waste Disposal Site Inventory," Jan. 1981.

31. Ibid.

32. Thomas A. Burke and Robert K. Tucker, *A Preliminary Report on the Findings of the State Groundwater Monitoring Project* (State of New Jersey, Department of Environmental Protection, Mar. 1978).

Chapter 5

1. New York State Department of Health, *Love Canal: Public Health Time Bomb.* Special Report to the Governor and Legislature, Sept. 1978, p. 2.

2. R. Blumenthal, *New York Times,* Feb. 1, 1981.

3. *Hazardous Waste Disposal.* Hearings before the Subcommittee on Oversight and Investigations of the House Committee on Interstate and Foreign Commerce, 96th Cong., 1st Sess., Ser. No. 96-48, Apr. 10, 1979, p. 489.

4. Memorandum by Charles Thiele, school board architect, reprinted in "1954 Alarm Ignored on Canal Site," *Buffalo Evening News,* Aug. 27, 1978.

5. Ibid.

6. Memorandum from Jerome Wilkenfeld to R. F. Schultz, "Exposed Residue at the Love Canal," June 18, 1958, reprinted in *Hazardous Waste Disposal* Hearings, p. 651.

7. Ibid., p. 665.

8. Ibid., p. 666.

9. R. P. Leonard, P. H. Wertham, and R. C. Ziegler, *Characterization and Abatement of Groundwater Pollution from Love Canal Chemical Landfill, Niagara Falls, N.Y.* (Buffalo, N.Y.: CALSPAN Corporation, Aug. 1977).

10. Ibid.

11. Harvey Albond to Lester O. Brown, Oct. 14, 1979 (personal communication).

12. *Hazardous Waste Disposal* Hearings, Mar. 21, 1979, p. 60.

13. U.S. House of Representatives, Committee on Interstate and Foreign Commerce, Subcommittee on Oversight and Investigations, *Report on Hazardous Waste Disposal.* Committee Print 96-IFC-31, 96th Cong., 1st Sess., Sept. 1979, p. 21.

14. David Rall to Lester O. Brown, Oct. 19, 1979.

15. Harvey Albond to Lester O. Brown, Oct. 14, 1979.

16. Ibid.

17. Ibid.

18. *United States* v. *Hooker Chemical and Plastics Corporation,* No. 79-990 (D.W. New York, filed Dec. 20, 1979).

19. Dante Picciano, "Pilot Cytogenetic Study of Love Canal, New York." Prepared by the Biogenics Corporation for the EPA, May 14, 1980.

20. Ibid.

21. Ibid.

22. Report of the Health and Human Services Review Panel on Chromosome Aberration Study to the Environmental Protection Agency, May 21, 1980.

23. Dante Picciano, "Love Canal Chromosome Study," *Science* 209:754–56, 1980. See also Margery Shaw letter, *Science* 209:751–52, 1980.

24. Ibid.

25. *Love Canal: Health Studies and Relocation.* Joint Hearings before the Subcommittee on Oversight and Investigations and the Subcommittee on Environment, Energy, and Natural Resources of the House Committee on Interstate and Foreign Commerce, 96th Cong., 2d. Sess., Ser. No. 96-191, May 22, 1980, p. 31.

26. *Congressional Record* 126:H9468, 1980.

27. Lewis Thomas et al., "Report of the Governor's Panel to Review Scientific Studies and the Development of Public Policy on Problems Resulting from Hazardous Wastes," Oct. 8, 1980, State of New York, Office of the Governor.

28. Ibid., p. 22.

29. Ibid., p. 9.

30. Ibid., p. 20.

31. Ibid., p. 16.

32. Ibid., cover letter to Governor Hugh L. Carey, Oct. 8, 1980, p. 1.

33. Irwin Bross, "Muddying the Water at Niagara," *New Scientist,* p. /28, Dec. 11, 1980.

34. D. T. Janerich et al., "Cancer Incidence in the Love Canal Area," *Science* 212:1404–7, June 19, 1981.

35. U.S. Environmental Protection Agency, *Carcinogen Assessment Group's Cancer Risks Estimation Procedure for Selected Carcinogens in Love Canal Area Housing,* Nov. 14, 1979.

36. *Hazardous Waste Disposal* Hearings, Apr. 10, 1979, p. 489.

37. Letter to Steve King, New York State Department of Health, from Cornell University Remote Sensing Program in *Hazardous Waste Disposal* Hearings, Mar. 21, 1979, pp. 113–15.

38. *Hazardous Waste Disposal* Hearings, Apr. 10, 1979, p. 656.

39. Donald L. Baeder, President, Hooker Chemical and Plastics Corporation, to Members of Congress, Aug. 14, 1980.

40. *Chemical Waste: Fact Versus Perception: Remarks by Donald L. Baeder, President, Hooker Chemical and Plastics Corporation, before the Commonwealth Club of California, Apr. 11, 1980* (Niagara Falls: Hooker Chemical and Plastics Corp., 1980).

41. Ibid.

42. *Love Canal: The Facts (1892–1980),* Hooker Fact Line, June, 1980 (Niagara Falls: Hooker Chemical and Plastics Corp., 1980).

43. Baeder to Member of Congress, Aug. 14, 1980.

44. Ansley Wilcox II, Vice President and General Counsel of Hooker Chemical and Plastics Corporation, to the Niagara Falls Board of Education, Nov. 21, 1957.

45. *United States* v. *Hooker Chemical and Plastics Corporation* (102d St. Landfill), No. 79-987; Ibid. ("S" Area Landfill), No. 79-988; Ibid. (Hyde Park Landfill), No. 79-989 (D.W. New York, filed Dec. 20, 1979).

46. Testimony of Elliot J. Lynch in *Hazardous Waste Disposal* Hearings, Mar. 22, 1979, p. 200.

47. *United States* v. *Hooker Chemical.*

48. Testimony of Howard K. Allen in *Hazardous Waste Disposal* Hearings, Mar. 22, 1979, p. 210.

49. *United States* v. *Hooker Chemical,* No. 79-988.

50. *Hazardous Waste Disposal* Hearings, Mar. 22, 1979, p. 277.

51. Ibid., p. 280.

52. *United States* v. *Hooker Chemical,* No. 79-988.

53. Letter reprinted in *Hazardous Waste Disposal* Hearings, Apr. 10, 1979, p. 634.

54. M. Singal *et al.,* NIOSH Health Hazard Evaluation, "Composite Report on Hyde Park Landfill," National Institute for Occupational Safety and Health, Cincinnatti, Ohio, Dec. 1980.

55. *Hazardous Waste Disposal* Hearings, Apr. 10, 1979, p. 640.

56. Ernest R. Gedeon, Acting Assistant Commissioner for Environmental Health, Niagara County, N.Y., Department of Health, to John Judy, Works Manager, Hooker Chemical and Plastics Corporation, in *Hazardous Waste Disposal* Hearings, Apr. 10, 1979, pp. 636–37.

57. Ibid.

Chapter 6

1. U.S. Environmental Protection Agency, *Report on Waste Oil to the U.S. Congress* (Washington, D.C., 1974).

2. Mark S. Rudolph, "Road Oiling: An Example of Environmental Mismanagement," *Alternatives*, vol. 9(Spring), 1980.

3. U.S. Environmental Protection Agency, *Runoff from Rural Roads Treated to Suppress Dust* (Washington, D.C., 1972), p. 4.

4. Renate D. Kimbrough et al., "Epidemiology and Pathology of a Tetrachlorodibenzodioxin Poisoning Episode," *Archives of Environmental Health*, 28:77-85, 1977.

5. *United States v. North Eastern Pharmaceutical and Chemical Co., Inc., Syntex Agribusiness Inc., et al.,* Aurora, Missouri, No. 80-5066-CV-SW (D. filed Aug. 1, 1980). EPA Hazardous Waste Enforcement Task Force Case Summary, Sept. 18, 1980.

6. Ibid.

7. Browning-Ferris Industries, Inc., *1980 Annual Report* (Houston, Texas, 1980).

8. *Hazardous Waste Disposal.* Hearings before the Subcommittee on Oversight and Investigations of the House Committee on Interstate and Foreign Commerce, 96th Cong., 1st Sess., Ser. No. 96-49, May 30, 1979, p. 912.

9. Ibid., p. 1012.

10. Ibid.

11. *Hazardous Waste Disposal* Hearings, June 18, 1979, p. 1459.

12. Ibid., p. 906.

13. Ibid., p. 1537.

14. Statement of Browning-Ferris Industries, Inc., Ibid., p. 1429.

15. Ibid., p. 1445.

16. Ibid., p. 1526.

17. Ibid., p. 1489.

18. Ibid., pp. 1490–91.

19. U.S. House of Representatives, Committee on Interstate and Foreign Commerce, Subcommittee on Oversight and Investigations, *Waste Disposal Site Survey.* Committee Print 96-IFC-33, 96th Cong., 1st Sess., Oct. 1979, p. xv.

20. *Hazardous Waste Disposal* Hearings, June 5, 1979, p. 1351.

21. Hearings before the Subcommittee on Advanced Energy Technologies and Energy Conservation Research, Development and Demonstration of the House Committee on Science and Technology, 95th Cong., 1st Sess., Dec. 12, 1977, p. 77.

22. Ibid., p. 203.

23. EPA, *Report on Waste Oil.*

24. Ibid.

25. *Waste Oil* Hearings, p. 271.

26. U.S. House of Representatives, Committee on Interstate and Foreign Commerce, *Report on the Used Oil Recycling Act of 1980* [S.2412]. House Report No. 96-1415, 96th Cong., 2d. Sess., Sept. 12, 1980.

27. Ibid.

28. Ibid.

29. *Waste Oil* Hearings, Dec. 12, 1977.

Chapter 7

1. Edwin Stier to Lester O. Brown, Jan. 1980 (personal communication).

2. Status Report to Robert Hunt by Glenn Paulson, Assistant Commissioner of Environmental Protection, State of New Jersey, May 31, 1979, New Jersey Department of Environmental Protection.

3. Ibid.

4. Reporter's Transcript of the Hearings on Chemical Control Corp., Feb. 8, 1979, p. 40, in *State of New Jersey Department of Environmental Protection* v. *Chemical Control Corp.; Northeast Pollution Control; Michael Colleton; Eugene Conlon; John Albert; Robert J. Day; and Charles Day* (Superior Court of New Jersey, Chancery Division, Union County, filed Jan. 19, 1979).

5. William Carracino to Lester O. Brown, Sept. 1979 (personal communication).

6. *New York Times,* May 29, 1975.

7. William Carracino to Lester O. Brown, Sept. 1979 (personal communication).

8. Ibid.

9. *State of New Jersey* v. *Scientific Chemical Processing, Inc., et al.,* complaint, New Jersey Superior Court, Nov. 1978, S.G.J. 51-78-2, Feb. 8, 1979.

10. Keith Welks to Lester O. Brown (personal communication).

11. Ibid.

12. William Carracino to Lester O. Brown, Sept. 1979.

13. *Hazardous Waste Disposal.* Hearings before the Subcommittee on Oversight and Investigations of the House Committee on Interstate and Foreign Commerce, Apr. 5, 1979, p. 430.

14. William Carracino to Lester O. Brown.

15. Public Hearings on Organized Crime and Toxic Wastes, New York State Senate Select Committee on Crime, Its Causes, Control and Effect on Society, July 8, 1980.

16. Testimony of John Fine before the New York State Standing Committees on Environmental Conservation and Health, March 14, 1980, p. 1.

17. Ibid.

18. Public Hearings on Organized Crime and Toxic Wastes.

19. *Hazardous Waste Disposal* Hearings, Dec. 1980.

20. Public Hearings on Organized Crime and Toxic Wastes.

21. Toxic Waste Hearings before the New York State Standing Committees on Conservation and Health, Mar. 14, 1980.

22. Ibid.

23. Ibid.

24. Ibid.

25. "As New Jersey Gets Tough, Waste Slips Across River," *Philadelphia Inquirer,* Sept. 27, 1979.

26. Keith Welks to Lester O. Brown.

27. *Philadelphia Inquirer.*
28. Keith Welks to Lester O. Brown.
29. Edwin Stier to Lester O. Brown.
30. *Philadelphia* v. *New Jersey,* 430 U.S. 141, 97 S. Ct., 987, 1977.
31. Ibid.

Chapter 8

1. Testimony of Alvin Gordon in Hearings on S.1480 before the Subcommittee on Environmental Pollution of the Senate Environment and Public Works Committee, 96th Cong., 1st Sess., San Francisco, June 29, 1979.
2. Tom Williams, *Hazardous Waste, 15 Years and Still Counting.* U.S. Environmental Protection Agency, Office of Public Affairs, Document No. 98/10 (Washington, D.C., 1980).
3. *Amendments to the Solid Waste Disposal Act.* Hearings before the Subcommittee on Public Health and Environment of the House Committee on Interstate and Foreign Commerce, 93rd Cong., 2d. Sess., Ser. No. 93-78, Mar. 27, 1974, p. 1.
4. Williams, *Hazardous Waste,* p. 2.
5. *Solid Waste* Hearings, p. 5.
6. Blake Early interview, Oct. 10, 1979.
7. Committee on Interstate and Foreign Commerce, *Report on H.R.14496.* House Report No. 76-7260, 94th Cong., 2d. Sess., Sept. 9, 1976, p. 52.
8. *Congressional Record* 122:S11061–11105, June 30, 1976.
9. Ibid. 121:S3850, July 21, 1975.
10. *Report on H.R.14496,* p. 4.
11. Ward Sinclair, "Industry Lobby Loosens Waste Controls," *Washington Post,* May 20, 1979.
12. Fred C. Hart Associates, *Preliminary Assessment of Cleanup Costs for National Hazardous Waste Problems* (U.S. Environmental Protection Agency, Feb. 23, 1979).
13. Dick Kirschten, "The New War on Pollution is Over the Land," *National Journal,* Apr. 4, 1979, p. 605.
14. Robert A. Roland, "Toxic Scapegoats," *Washington Post,* Apr. 21, 1979.
15. Cliff Curtis, Memo to Environmental Groups (Washington, D.C.: Center for Law and Social Policy, July 12, 1979).
16. Lester O. Brown, staff member House Commerce Committee Subcommittee on Investigations, May 6, 1980.
17. Samuel S. Epstein and J. B. Swartz, "Fallacies of Lifestyle Cancer Theories," *Nature* 289:127–30, 1981.
18. Testimony of James Barnes before the Subcommittees on Resource Protection and Environmental Pollution of the Senate Public Works Committee, 96th Cong., 1st Sess., July 19, 1979, p. 7.
19. *Congressional Quarterly,* Sept. 27, 1980, p. 2819.
20. "Superfund, SuperRush," *Wall Street Journal,* Nov. 20, 1981.

21. Joanne Omang, "Senate Unit Wants Industry to Pay," *Washington Post,* June 28, 1980.

22. Edward Roeder, "Chemical Industry Money Compounds Cleanup Issue," *Sacramento Bee,* Nov. 17, 1980.

23. "Bill for Cleanup of Dump Sites Cleared," *Wall Street Journal,* Nov. 19, 1980, p. 14.

24. "Superfund, SuperRush."

25. Phillip Shabecoff, "Dupont Head Backs a Cleanup Fund," *New York Times,* Nov. 20, 1980.

26. Idem., "Fund of 1.6 Billion for Waste Cleanup Accepted by House," *New York Times,* Dec. 4, 1980.

27. "Semi Mini Superfund," editorial, *Washington Post,* Nov. 26, 1980.

Chapter 9

1. *National Resources Defense Council et al.* v. *Train,* 8 E.R.C. 2120 (D.D.C., 1976).

2. "Toxic Substances: EPA and OSHA Are Reluctant Regulators," *Science* 203:28, 1979.

3. Michael Brown, *Laying Waste* (New York: Pantheon, 1980) p. 306.

4. Ibid., p. 307.

5. Rod Nordland and Josh Friedman, "Fearing Inflation, Government Has Braked Cleanup Effort," *San Francisco Examiner,* Oct. 14, 1979.

6. Ibid., p. 16.

7. Testimony of James Moorman before the Senate Judiciary Committee, 96th Cong., 1st Sess., Apr. 11, 1979.

8. *Environmental Defense Fund and Environmental Action* v. *Steffen Plehn* (D.D.C. consent order, Sept. 13, 1978).

9. *Federal Register,* Dec. 14, 1978.

10. "Comments on EPA's Draft RCRA Regulations," (Washington, D.C.: Environmental Defense Fund, undated), p. 5.

11. Ibid., p. 8.

12. Ibid., p. 19.

13. Ibid., p. 4.

14. Ibid., p. 27.

15. "EPA Runs Amuck," *Wall Street Journal,* May 9, 1979.

16. Ibid.

17. Ibid.

18. Russell Dawson, "Sludge Management in the Paint and Coating Industry," *Sludge* (Sept.–Oct., 1979), p. 37.

19. *Wall Street Journal,* July 16, 1980.

20. Rockland County, N.Y., Grand Jury, "In the Matter of the Special Grand Jury for Investigation into Organized Criminal Activity of the County of Rockland," Aug. 7, 1979, p. 41.

21. Ibid., p. 42.

22. Ibid., p. 44.

23. Ibid., p. 43.

24. Nordland and Friedman, "Fearing Inflation."

25. William Drayton, "Economic Law Enforcement," *Harvard Law Review,* vol. 4, no. 1, 1980.

26. Joanne Omang, "Rules to Control Hazardous Waste Unveiled by EPA," *Washington Post,* May 6, 1980.

27. Ibid.

28. *Federal Register,* Dec. 14, 1978, p. 33197.

29. Jeffrey Smith, "EPA Announces Toxic Waste Controls," *Science,* vol. 208, May 9, 1980.

30. Joanne Omang, "Rules to Control Hazardous Waste."

31. Andrew Schneider, Associated Press wirestory, Aug. 4, 1980. See also Michael Knight, "Toxic Waste Hurriedly Dumped," *New York Times,* Nov. 16, 1980.

32. Joanne Omang, "U.S. Faces Toxic Waste Disposal Crisis," *Washington Post,* May 21, 1980.

33. "Wilsonville Battles a Landfill," *Illinois Issues,* Aug. 1977, pp. 4–6.

34. Omang, "Toxic Waste Crisis."

35. General Accounting Office, *Hazardous Waste Management Programs Will Not Be Effective; Greater Efforts Are Needed* (Washington, D.C., Jan. 23, 1979).

36. *Congressional Record,* V126,#148, P H 9466, Sep 23, 1980.

37. *Inside EPA,* Mar 20, 1981, SV 2 #12, P. 8.

38. *Inside EPA,* Nov 21, 1980, "Reagan's Starting Point," P. 5.

39. *Inside EPA,* Apr 10, 1981, V 2, #15, "OMB Heading for Major RCRA Overhaul," P. 1.

40. *Inside EPA,* May 1, 1981, V 2, #18, "Industry Blasts Landfill Rules," P. 6.

41. *Inside EPA,* May 29, "EPA Reopens RCRA Land Disposal Rules," V 2, #22, P. 1–2.

42. Ralph Blumenthal, "EPA Restricts Regional Orders on Toxic Wastes," *New York Times,* June 21, 1981.

43. *Inside EPA,* Aug 14, "CMA, API Blast Disposal Rules," P. 9.

44. Stockman, David, *Congressional Record,* V 126, #148, P H 9439, Sep 23, 1980.

45. Michael S. Baram, *Alternatives to Regulation: Managing Rights to Health, Safety, and the Environment* (Lexington: Lexington Books, 1981).

Chapter 10

1. V. Yannacone, Jr., B. Cohen, and S. Davidson, *Environmental Rights and Remedies,* (Rochester, New York: Lawyers Cooperative Pub. Co. and Bancroft Whitney Co., 1972), 1973–81 cumulative supplement, pp. 666–719. This reference contains a useful bibliography on toxic substances and hazardous wastes.

2. W. Prosser, *Law of Torts* (St. Paul, Minn: West, 1971), pp. 6–7.

3. *Village of Wilsonville v. SCA Services, Inc.,* 426 N.E. 2d 824 (Ill. Sup. Ct., May 22, 1981) (enjoining operation of waste disposal site). *Environmental Law Reporter* 11:20698, 1981.

4. *United States* v. *Reserve Mining Co.*, 543 F. 2d. 1210 (8th Cir., 1976). *Environmental Law Reporter* 7:20051.

5. *Ethyl Corp.* v. EPA, 541 F. 2d. 1 (D.C. Cir., 1976).

6. J. Bryson and A. Macbeth, "Public Nuisance, the Restatement (Second) of Torts, and Environmental Law," *Ecology Law Quarterly* 2:241, 1972.

7. W. Prosser, *Law of Torts* (St. Paul, Minn.: West, 1971), p. 587.

8. *Commonwealth of Puerto Rico* v. *S. S. Zoe Colocotroni*, 628 F. 2d 652 (1st Cir., 1980). *Environmental Law Reporter* 10:20882, 1980.

9. W. Prosser, "Private Action for Public Nuisance," *Virginia Law Review* 52:997, 1966.

10. *Union Oil* v. *Oppen*, 501 F. 2d. 558 (9th Cir., 1974) (allowing fishermen to recover for water resources damaged by oil spill). *Environmental Law Reporter* 4:20618, 1974.

11. "Private Nuisance Law: Protection of the Individual's Environmental Rights," *Suffolk University Law Review* 8:1162, 1974.

12. Prosser, *Law of Torts*, pp. 139–204.

13. "The Viability of Common Law Actions for Pollution Caused Injuries and Proof of Facts," *New York Law Forum* 18:946–48, 1973.

14. *Borel* v. *Fibreboard Products Corp.*, 493 F. 2d. 1076 (5th Cir., 1973) cert. denied 419 U.S. 869 (1974) (liability involving failure to warn of hazards from asbestos insulation). *Environmental Law Reporter*, 4:20133, 1974.

15. "Strict Liability for Generators, Transporters, and Disposers of Hazardous Wastes," *Minn. Law Review* 64:949, 1980.

16. "Compensating Victims of Occupational Disease," *Harvard Law Review* 93:926–28, 1980.

17. W. Rodgers, *Environmental Law* (St. Paul, Minn.: West, 1977), p. 173.

18. J. Rogers, "Hazardous Waste Regs Increase in Complexity," *Legal Times*, Feb. 9, 1981, p. 17.

19. *United States* v. *Solvents Recovery Service of New England;* 496 F. Supp. 1127 (D. Conn., 1980) *Environmental Law Reporter* 10:20796, 1980.

20. *United States* v. *Vertac Chemical Corporation;* 489 F. Supp. 870 (E.D. Ark., 1980) *Environmental Law Reporter* 10:20709, 1980.

21. *United States* v. *Midwest Solvent Recovery, Inc;* 484 F. Supp. 138 (N.D. Ind., 1980) *Environmental Law Reporter* 10:20316, 1980.

22. *American Textile Manufacturers Institute* v. *Donovan,*—U.S.— 69L. Ed 2nd 185 (1981) (cotton dust standard).

23. *Industrial Union Dept.*, AFL-CIO v. *American Petroleum Institute,* 448 U.S. 607 (1980) (benzene standard).

24. J. Trauberman, "Superfund: A Legal Update," *Environment* 23:25–29,1981.

25. *Illinois* v. *Castle, Environmental Law Reporter* 9:20243 (D.D.C. Jan. 3, 1979). See also *Illinois* v. *Gorsuch* (D.D.C. Dec. 7, 1981), denying federal governments motion to reconsider deadlines for regulations on hazardous waste land disposal facilities. *Environmental Law Reporter*, 12:20101, 1980.

26. R. Sandler, "Citizen Suit Litigation," *Environment* 23:38–39, 1981.

27. K. Kamlet, *Toxic Substances Programs in U.S. States and Territories: How Well Do They Work?* (Washington, D.C.: National Wildlife Federation, 1980), p. 8.

28. "Environmental Disclosure Rules: Despite Court Win, SEC Adopts Broad New Standard for Corporations," *Environmental Law Reporter* 9:10222, 1979. See also "SEC Proposes Cutting Environmental Reporting Rules," *National Law Journal* 3:4, (June 8, 1981), p. 4.

29. *Hazardous Waste Management: A Survey of State Laws 1976–1980* (Washington, D.C.: National Conference of State Legislatures, 1980).

30. J. Esposito, "Air and Water Pollution: What to Do While Waiting for Washington," *Harvard Civil Rights–Civil Liberties Law Review* 5:40, 1970.

31. "Compensating Victims of Occupational Disease," *Harvard Law Review* 93:916, 1980.

32. Samuel S. Epstein, *The Politics of Cancer* (New York: Anchor / Doubleday, 1979), p. 504.

33. "Compensating Victims of Occupational Disease," p. 916.

34. Samuel S. Epstein, "The Role of the Scientist in Toxic Tort Case Preparation," *Trial* 17:38–53, 1981.

35. Congressional Research Service, the Library of Congress, *Six Case Studies of Compensation for Toxic Substances Pollution: Alabama, California, Michigan, Missouri, New Jersey and Texas.* Report for the Committee on Environment and Public Works, U.S. Senate. Ser. No. 96-13 (Washington, D.C.: U.S. Government Printing Office, 1980).

36. League of Women Voters, *A Toxics Primer* (Washington, D.C., 1980).

37. "Judicial Attitudes Toward Legal And Scientific Proof of Cancer Causation," *Columbia Journal of Environmental Law* 3:344, 1977.

38. Prosser, *Law of Torts,* pp. 244–70.

39. S. Birnbaum, "Statutes of Limitations Problems in Environmental Tort Suits," in *Toxic Torts,* ed. P. Rheingold, N. Landau, and M. Canavan (Washington, D.C.: Association of Trial Lawyers of America, 1977), p. 412.

40. 5 *U.S.C.* §552.

41. A sample FOIA request appears in *The Toxic Substances Dilemma* (Washington, D.C.: National Wildlife Federation, 1980), p. 52.

42. 5 *U.S.C.* Appendix I, §1 et seq. (1976).

43. 5 *U.S.C.* §552b.

44. For a good guide to citizen group action see *The Toxic Substances Dilemma.*

45. For a good discussion of the ways in which an environmental attorney can be hired, see P. Rheingold and N. Landau, *The Environmental Law Handbook* (New York: Friends of the Earth / Ballantine Books, 1971), pp. 16–19.

46. *Hazardous Waste Management: A Survey of State Laws, 1976–1980* (Washington, D.C.: National Conference of State Legislatures, 1980), p. I-32.

47. *Landers* v. *East Texas Salt Water Disposal Co.,* 151 Tex. 251, 284 S.W. 2d. 731 (1952).

48. *Phillips Petroleum Company* v. *Hardee,* 189 F. 2d. 205 (5th Cir., 1951).

49. "Allocating the Costs of Hazardous Waste Disposal," *Harvard Law Review* 94:588–90, 1981.

50. *Michie* v. *Great Lakes Steel,* 495 F. 2d. 213 (6th Cir., 1974), cert. denied, 419 U.S. 997 (1974).

51. *Sindell* v. *Abbott Laboratories,* 26 Cal. 3d. 588, 607 P 2d. 924, 163 Cal. Rep. 132, cert. denied. 449 U.S. 912 (1980).

52. "Market Share Liability: An Answer to the DES Causation Problem," *Harvard Law Review* 94:668, 1981.

Chapter 11

1. House Committee on Government Operations, *Interim Report on Ground Water Contamination: Environmental Protection Agency Oversight.* House Report No. 96-1440, 96th Cong., 2d. Sess., Sept. 30, 1980, p. 3.

2. Council on Environmental Quality, *Contamination of Ground Water by Toxic Organic Chemicals* (Washington, D.C., 1981).

3. U.S. Geological Survey, *Water Used for Public Supplies by States: Estimated Use in U.S. in 1975.* USGS Circular No. 765, 1977, pp. 20–21.

4. Ibid.

5. *Interim Report on Ground Water Contamination,* p. 4.

6. Wayne A. Pettyjohn, "Ground-Water Pollution: An Imminent Disaster," in *Proceedings of the Fourth National Ground Water Quality Symposium.* Document No. 600/9-79-029 (Washington, D.C.: U.S. Environmental Protection Agency, 1979).

7. U.S. Environmental Protection Agency, Office of Drinking Water, *Planning Workshops to Develop Recommendations for a Ground Water Protection Strategy* (Washington, D.C., 1980), p. III-13.

8. Ibid.

9. House Committee on Interstate and Foreign Commerce, Subcommittee on Oversight and Investigations, *Waste Disposal Site Survey.* Committee Print 96-IFC33, 96th Cong., 1st Sess., Oct. 1979.

10. U.S. Environmental Protection Agency, Office of Solid Waste, *The Prevalence of Subsurface Migration of Hazardous Chemical Substances at Selected Industrial Waste Land Disposal Sites* (Washington, D.C., 1977).

11. *Interim Report on Ground Water Contamination,* p. 6.

12. Ibid.

13. Ohio Environmental Protection Agency, Division of Ground Water, *Surface Impoundment Assessment for the State of Ohio,* Feb. 1980, p. 18.

14. U.S. Environmental Protection Agency, Office of Drinking Water, *Surface Impoundments and Their Effects on Ground-Water Quality in the United States: A Preliminary Survey.* Document No. 570/9-78-004 (Washington, D.C., 1978), p. 2.

15. Ibid.

16. U.S. Environmental Protection Agency, Office of Solid Waste, *Report to the Congress on Waste Disposal Practices and Their Effects on*

Ground Water. Document No. WH 554 (Washington, D.C., 1977), p. 322.

17. Bureau of National Affairs, *Environment Report* (Current Developments) 2:928, 1980.

18. Ibid.

19. National Academy of Sciences, National Research Council, *Draft Report of the Committee on Ground-Water Resources in Relation to Coal Mining* (Washington, D.C.: National Academy of Sciences, 1980).

20. EPA *Report to Congress on Waste Disposal Practices,* p. 196.

21. John C. Miller et al., *Groundwater Pollution Problems in the Southeastern United States.* Document No. 600/3-77-012 (Washington, D.C.: U.S. Environmental Protection Agency, 1977), p. 201.

22. Safe Drinking Water Act, 42 U.S.C. §300f et seq. (1976).

23. Clean Water Act, 33 U.S.C. §§1251 et seq. (1978).

24. Resource Conservation and Recovery Act, 42 U.S.C. §§6901–6987 (1976).

25. Toxic Substances Control Act, 15 U.S.C. §§2601–2619 (1976).

26. Surface Mining Control and Reclamation Act, 30 U.S.C. §§1201 et seq. (1979).

27. Federal Insecticide, Fungicide and Rodenticide Act, 7 U.S.C. §§136 et seq. (1971).

28. Surface Mining Control and Reclamation Act, 30 U.S.C. §§1201–1328 (1978).

29. Lyle Silka to Lester O. Brown, Feb. 1980 (personal communication).

30. Ibid.

31. James W. Dawson, "State Ground Water Protection Programs—Inadequate," in *Proceedings of the Fourth National Ground Water Quality Symposium,* p. 104.

32. Ibid.

33. *Interim Report on Ground Water Contamination,* pp. 10–11.

34. Ibid.

35. Council on Environmental Quality, *Contamination of Ground Water by Toxic Organic Chemicals.*

36. For an excellent discussion of the nondegradation concept and its essential role in protecting groundwater supplies, see James T. B. Tripp and Adam B. Jaffee, "Preventing Groundwater Pollution: Towards a Coordinated Strategy to Protect Critical Recharge Zones," *Harvard Environmental Law Review,* vol 3, no. 1, 1979.

Chapter 12

1. General Accounting Office (GAO), *Report to the Congress of the United States: Waste Disposal Practices—A Threat to Health and the Nation's Water Supply.* CED-78-120, June 16, 1978.

2. Ibid., *How to Dispose of Hazardous Waste—A Serious Question That Needs to be Resolved.* CED-79-13, Dec. 19, 1978.

3. Ibid., *Hazardous Waste Management Programs Will Not Be Effective: Greater Efforts Are Needed.* CED-79-14, Jan. 23, 1979.

4. T. H. Maugh II, "Toxic Waste Disposal: A Growing Problem," *Science* 204:819–23, 1979.

5. Idem., "Hazardous Wastes Technology Is Available," *Science* 204: 930–33, 1979.

6. Idem., "Incineration, Deep Wells Gain New Importance," *Science* 204:1188–90, 1979.

7. Idem., "Burial Is Last Resort for Hazardous Wastes," *Science* 204: 1295–98, 1979. Provides an excellent summary review.

8. R. B. Pojasek, ed., *Processes and Stabilization/Solidification,* Toxic and Hazardous Waste Disposal, vol. 1 (Ann Arbor, Mich.: Ann Arbor Science, Inc., 1979). A good ongoing series that is detailed and highly technical.

9. Idem., *Options for Stabilization/Solidification,* Toxic and Hazardous Waste Disposal, vol. 2, 1979.

10. Idem., *Legislation,* Toxic and Hazardous Waste Disposal, vol. 3, 1980.

11. U.S. Environmental Protection Agency, "Treatment of Hazardous Waste," in *Proceedings of the Sixth Annual Research Symposium, Chicago, Ill., Mar. 1980.* Document No. 600/9-80-011 (Cincinnati, Ohio: Environmental Protection Agency, 1980).

12. "Disposal of Hazardous Waste," in *Proceedings of the Sixth Annual Research Symposium.* Document No. 600/9-80-010.

13. M. G. Royston, "Making Pollution Prevention Pay," *Harvard Business Review,* Nov.-Dec. 1980, pp. 6–22.

14. GAO Report, *Waste Disposal Practices.*

15. Idem., *How to Dispose of Hazardous Waste.*

16. Idem., *Hazardous Waste Management Programs.*

17. Idem., *Waste Disposal Practices.*

18. Idem., *How to Dispose of Hazardous Waste.*

19. Idem., *Hazardous Waste Management Programs.*

20. Idem., *Waste Disposal Practices.*

21. Idem., *How to Dispose of Hazardous Waste.*

22. Idem., *Hazardous Waste Management Programs.*

23. W. Wilson, "In Situ Mine Contamination Worse Than Expected, DEQ," *Caspar* [Wyoming] *State Tribune,* May 15, 1979.

24. "Uranium Holes May Be Draining Water," *Gillette* [Wyoming] *News Record,* Apr. 24, 1979.

25. U.S. Environmental Protection Agency, "Water Programs; Consolidated Permit Regulations and Technical Criteria and Standards; State Underground Injection Control Programs," *Federal Register* 45 (Part II): 42472–512, June 24, 1980.

26. *Safe Drinking Water Act.* House Report No. 93-1185, 93rd Cong., 2d. Sess., 1974, p. 31.

27. *Federal Register,* pp. 42493–98.

28. GAO Report, *Waste Disposal Practices.*

29. Idem., *How to Dispose of Hazardous Waste.*
30. Idem., *Hazardous Waste Management Programs.*
31. Idem., *Waste Disposal Practices.*
32. Idem., *How to Dispose of Hazardous Waste.*
33. Idem., *Hazardous Waste Management Programs.*
34. Toxic Waste Assessment Group, Governor's Office of Appropriate Technology, *Alternatives to the Land Disposal of Hazardous Wastes: An Assessment for California* (Sacramento, 1981).
35. P. Montague, "Do Any Secure Landfills Exist?" *New Jersey Hazardous Waste Review* 1:July, 1980.
36. U.S. Environmental Protection Agency, "Hazardous Waste: Proposed Guidelines and Regulations and Proposal on Identification and Listing," *Federal Register* 43(Part IV):58946–59028, Dec. 18, 1978.
37. Idem., "Hazardous Waste and Consolidated Permit Regulation," *Federal Register* 45(Part II):33066–84, May 19, 1980.
38. Idem., "Hazardous Waste Management System," *Federal Register* 45(Part VII):33154–259, May 19, 1980.
39. Idem., "Standards and Interim Status Standard for Owners and Operators of Hazardous Waste Treatment Storage and Disposal Facilities," *Federal Register* 45(Part VIII):33260–79, May 19, 1980.
40. Idem., "Proposal to Modify 40 C.F.R. Part 265, Subpart II, Financial Requirements," *Federal Register* 45(Part VIII):33260–78, May 19, 1980.
41. "Burying Waste in Titan Silos," *New York Times,* July 10, 1980.
42. Office of Technology Assessment (OTA), *Technologies and Management Strategies for Hazardous Waste Control*, Congress of the United States, 1983; National Materials Advisory Board, *Management of Hazardous Industrial Wastes: Research and Development Needs*, National Academy Press, Washington, D.C., 1983.

Chapter 13

1. *Inside* EPA 2:1, 1981.
2. William Drayton, Memorandum to the Environmental Community, Sept. 30, 1981.
3. Jeffrey Smith, "Tight Screening Plan for EPA Data," *Science* 213: 1345–46, 1981.
4. Ibid., p. 1345.
5. Joanne Omang, "EPA Staff Finds Formaldehyde No Great Cancer Risk," *Washington Post,* Sept. 19, 1981.
6. Toxic Waste Assessment Group (see above).
7. Auditor General of California, Report to the Joint Legislative Audit Committee. "California's Hazardous Waste Management Program Does Not Fully Protect the Public from the Harmful Effects of Hazardous Wastes," Sacramento, California, 1981.
8. Discussion of Danish/German models is based on visits to Europe in the spring of 1983 by Carl Pope.
9. *New York Times,* Oct. 24, 1981. "114 Toxic Waste Dumps Listed as the Nation's Worst."

10. *Toxic Chemical Contamination of Ground Water.* Hearings before the Subcommittee on Environment, Energy and Natural Resources of the House Committee on Government Operations, 96th Cong., 2d. Sess., July 25, 1980, p. 201.

11. Ibid., p. 204.

12. *Inside* EPA, July 31, 1981, p. 11; v. 2, No. 31.

13. Council on Environmental Quality, *Environmental Quality 1980; The Eleventh Annual Report of the Council on Environmental Quality,* Dec. 1980, p. 228.

14. California *Assembly Bill AB 69,* 1981–1982 Sess.

15. *Environmental Quality 1980,* p. 229.

16. U.S. House of Representatives, "Toxic Substances Pollution Victim Compensation Act of 1977." H.R.9616, 95th Cong., 1st Sess. Hearings were held on the bill, but no legislation ever emerged from the House Commerce Subcommittee on Consumer Protection.

17. Carl Pope, "Risk Benefit Analysis; Locke, Bentham and Hobbes." Paper delivered to the Technical Information Project Conference on Toxic Substances: Decisions and Values, Washington, D.C., Feb. 1, 1979.

18. Letter to the editor, *New York Times,* Nov. 28, 1980.

19. Paul Palmer to the Sierra Club, Aug. 20, 1980 (personal communication), p. 2.

20. John Abbots, *Disposable Consumer Items: The Overlooked Mercury Pollution Problem* (Washington, D.C.: Center for Responsive Law, Apr. 1981).

21. Chemical Manufacturers Association, "A Statute for Siting, Construction and Financing of Hazardous Waste Treatment, Disposal and Storage Facilities," monograph (Washington, D.C., undated).

22. Peter Behr, "Goodyear Claims Breakthrough," *Washington Post,* Aug. 22, 1980.

23. *New York Times,* June 18, 1981, p. 15.

24. Samuel S. Epstein, *Politics of Cancer* (New York: Anchor/Doubleday, 1979), p. 69.

25. Richard Severo, "EPA Slow to Act on 3-Year-Old Law," *New York Times,* May 6, 1980.

26. Morton Mintz, "EPA Blocks Production of 6 Chemicals," *Washington Post,* Apr. 29, 1980.

27. "Law Regulation Chemicals Wins in Philadelphia," *New York Times,* Jan. 23, 1981.

28. B. O. Pallson et al., "Biomass as a Source of Chemical Feedstocks: An Environmental Evaluation," *Science* 213:513–17, 1981.

29. Bill Richards, "Drop in Sperm Count is Attributed to Toxic Environment," *Washington Post,* Sept. 12, 1979.

30. Herbert Needleman, *New England Journal of Medicine,* Mar. 29, 1979.

APPENDIX I

Sources and Composition of Nonradioactive Hazardous Wastes

Waste stream title	Standard industrial code	Percentage by geographic area*									Volume (lb/yr)	Remarks
		NE	MA	ENC	WNC	SA	ESC	WSC	M	W		
Aqueous inorganic												
Chromate wastes from textile dyeing	22	0.101	0.178	0.034	0.005	0.563	0.034	0.014	0.006	0.060	2×10^7	maximum
Chlorine production brine sludges	2812	.02	.11	.10	—	.19	.22	.24	—	.12	1×10^8	
Potassium chromate production wastes	2819	.19	.06	.015	.005	.60	.10	.01	.01	.01	1×10^8	
Cellulose ester production wastes	2821	.10	.21	.21	.16	.14	.07	.10	—	.02	5×10^7	
Intermediate agricultural product wastes (nitric acid)	287	.005	.075	.145	.074	.299	.207	.090	.047	.058	2×10^5	
Production works from ammonium sulfate	2873	—	—	.040	—	—	—	—	.96	—	1×10^3	
Copper- and lead-bearing petroleum refinery wastes	291	.001	.102	.175	.056	.019	.031	.417	.039	.160	8×10^8	
Chrome tanning liquor	31	.22	.29	.29	.03	.086	.05	.004	—	.03	2×10^7	
Mirror production wastes	3231	.09	.25	.23	.01	.28	.10	.04	—	—	9×10^8	
Cold finishing wastes	331	.03	.34	.43	.01	.07	.02	.05	.04	.01	5×10^9	

*NE = New England: Connecticut, Maine, Massachusetts, New Hampshire, Rhode Island, and Vermont; MA = Mid Atlantic: New Jersey, New York, and Pennsylvania; ENC = East North Central: Illinois, Indiana, Michigan, Ohio, and Wisconsin; WNC = West North Central: Iowa, Kansas, Minnesota, Missouri, Nebraska, North Dakota, and South Dakota; SA = South Atlantic: Delaware, District of Columbia, Florida, Georgia, Maryland, North Carolina, South Carolina, Virginia, and West Virginia; ESC = East South Central: Alabama, Kentucky, Mississippi, and Tennessee; WSC = West South Central: Arkansas, Louisiana, Oklahoma, and Texas; M = Mountain: Arizona, Colorado, Idaho, Montana, Nevada, New Mexico, Utah, and Wyoming; W = West (Pacific): Alaska, California, Hawaii, Oregon, and Washington.

Waste stream title	Standard industrial code	Percentage by geographic area									Volume (lb/yr)	Remarks
		NE	MA	ENC	WNC	SA	ESC	WSC	M	W		
Consolidated steel plant wastes	331	.02	.33	.42	.02	.09	.02	.03	.05	.02	5×10^8	
Stainless steel pickling liquor	3312	.050	.259	.404	.026	.068	.055	.044	.028	.067	5×10^7	
Brass mill wastes	333	.04	.29	.01	.25	.01	.04	.04	.13	.19	5×10^7	
Metal finishing wastes:	33	.115	.179	.379	.046	.050	.015	.036	.011	.169	4×10^7	Cyanide solution
Aluminum anodizing bath with drag out		.115	.179	.379	.046	.050	.015	.036	.011	.169	8×10^6	Metal sludges
Brass plating wastes		.115	.179	.379	.046	.050	.015	.036	.011	.169	Not available	
Cadmium plating wastes		.131	.285	.321	.045	.049	.023	.036	.007	.103	1×10^6	
Chrome plating wastes		.115	.179	.379	.046	.050	.015	.036	.011	.169	Not available	
Cyanide copper plating wastes		.115	.179	.379	.046	.050	.015	.036	.011	.169	2×10^6	
Finishing effluents		.115	.179	.379	.046	.050	.015	.036	.011	.169	Not available	
Metal cleaning wastes		.115	.179	.379	.046	.050	.015	.036	.011	.169	Not available	
Plating preparation wastes		.115	.179	.379	.046	.050	.015	.036	.011	.169	Not available	
Silver plating wastes		.115	.179	.379	.046	.050	.015	.036	.011	.169	Not available	
Zinc plating wastes		.115	.179	.379	.046	.050	.015	.036	.011	.169	Not available	
Metal finishing chromic acid	34	.244	.198	.149	.095	.081	.032	.031	.041	.031	4.4×10^7	
Graphic arts and photography wastes	3555	.06	.19	.20	.08	.15	.06	.09	.13	.04	4×10^3	
Electronic circuitry manufacturing wastes	36	.143	.342	.170	.037	.053	.019	.032	.039	.165	5×10^5	
Aircraft plating wastes	372	.123	.158	.117	.093	.057	.013	.095	.019	.325	4×10^7	
Cooling tower blowdown	—	.005	.150	.170	.060	—	.58	—	.035	—	2×10^7	As chromate
SUBTOTAL											7×10^9	

Organic

Cosynthesis methanol production wastes	2818	—	.05	—	.05	—	.90	—	—	1×10^6	Sludge
Formaldehyde production wastes	2818	—	.02	—	.05	—	.93	—	—	8×10^5	Sludge
n-Butane dehydrogenation butadiene production wastes	2818	—	.03	—	.11	—	.02	—	.05	3×10^5	Sludge
Rubber manufacturing wastes	2822	.07	.14	—	.11	.11	.50	—	.07	1×10^6	
Benzoic herbicide wastes (DOD)†	2879	.168	.130	.009	.447	—	—	—	.246	3×10^3	
Chlorinated aliphatic herbicide wastes (DOD)	2879	.196	.062	.027	.649	.010	.057	—	—	5×10^3	
Phenyl urea herbicide wastes (DOD)	2879	.539	.059	—	.343	.059	—	—	—	2×10^3	
Halogenated aliphatic hydrocarbon fumigant wastes (DOD)	2879	1.0	—	—	—	—	—	—	—	2×10^2	
Organophosphate pesticide wastes (DOD)	2879	.0007	.014	.010	.033	—	—	.014	.929	1×10^6	
Phenoxy herbicide wastes	2879	.0002	.0001	.0007	.0008	.849	.149	.0002	.0004	8×10^6	
Carbonate pesticide manufacturing (DOD)	2879	—	—	.006	.848	—	—	—	.145	3×10^2	
Polychlorinated hydrocarbon pesticide wastes (DOD)	2879	.097	.142	.003	.096	.004	.033	.017	.591	1×10^5	
Miscellaneous organic pesticide manufacturing waste (DOD)	2879	.026	.012	.002	.257	—	—	—	.702	3×10^4	

†Department of Defense

Waste stream title	Standard industrial code	Percentage by geographic area									Volume (lb/yr)	Remarks
		NE	MA	ENC	WNC	SA	ESC	WSC	M	W		
Contaminated and waste industrial propellants and explosives	2892	—	—	—	—	—	—	—	.344	.655	3×10^5	
Contaminants and waste from primary explosives production	2892	—	.096	.001	.898	—	.001	—	.003	.001	4×10^6	
Nitrocellulose base propellant contaminated waste	2892	—	.041	—	.457	.492	—	—	.009	—	9×10^6	
High explosive contaminated wastes	2892	—	.005	.094	.394	.397	.027	.004	.023	.012	1×10^7	
Incendiary contaminated wastes	2892	—	—	—	—	—	—	1.0	—	—	6×10^5	
Production of nitroglycerin	2892	—	—	—	—	.42	.19	—	—	.39	7×10^5	
Solid waste from old primers and detonators	2892	—	.005	.430	.454	.001	.006	—	.084	.014	3×10^5	
Wastes from production of nitrocellulose propellants and smokeless powder	2892	—	.060	.046	.387	.477	—	.006	.025	—	6×10^6	
Waste high explosives	2892	.002	.006	.346	.174	.218	.104	.127	.010	.001	1×10^7	
Waste incendiaries	2892	—	.014	.002	.002	—	—	.718	.009	.255	8×10^5	
Waste nitrocellulose and smokeless powder	2892	—	—	—	—	—	—	—	.406	.594	2×10^6	
Waste nitroglycerin	2892	—	—	.01	—	.50	.22	—	.004	.266	5×10^5	
Nonutility polychlorinated biphenyl wastes	2899	.037	.221	.372	.153	.040	.041	.057	.009	.072	8×10^6	
Gasoline blending wastes	2911	.006	.086	.159	.055	.025	.025	.477	.033	.134	4×10^8	
Reclaimers residues	2992	.040	.120	.205	.081	.135	.082	.139	.044	.155	3×10^8	

Coke plant raw waste	3312	.02	.33	.41	.01	.07	.02	.06	.06	.02	8 × 10⁷	
Military arsenical wastes	9711	—	.002	.001	—	.015	.031	.001	.024	.926	3 × 10⁶	
Outdated or contaminated tear gas	9711	—	.138	.189	—	.022	.044	.252	.144	.209	3 × 10⁸	
SUBTOTAL											1 × 10⁹	
Aqueous organic												
Dimethyl sulfate production wastes	2611	—	‡	—	—	‡	—	—	—	—	2 × 10⁵	Still bottoms
Acetaldehyde via ethylene oxidation	281	.015	.170	.156	.047	.156	.111	.265	.020	.060	8 × 10⁷	
Residue from manufacture of ethylene dichloride/vinyl chloride	2821	—	.021	.015	—	.163	.171	.533	—	.097	2 × 10⁷	
Nitrobenzene from rubber industry wastes	2822	—	.07	.14	—	.11	.11	.50	—	.07	5 × 10⁹	Probably too dilute to be of concern
Drug manufacturing wastes	283	.056	.348	.183	.089	.100	.033	.060	.011	.115	5 × 10⁹	Probably too dilute to be of concern
Chlorinated hydrocarbon pesticide production wastes	2879	.115	.148	.136	.073	.141	.057	.093	.054	.183	2 × 10⁸	
Miscellaneous organic herbicide production wastes	2879	.076	.135	.124	.080	.156	.062	.108	.059	.200	4 × 10⁸	
Organophosphate pesticide production wastes	2879	.115	.148	.136	.073	.141	.057	.093	.054	.183	6 × 10⁷	

‡Exists but quantity is unknown.

Waste stream title	Standard industrial code	Percentage by geographic area									Volume (lb/yr)	Remarks
		NE	MA	ENC	WNC	SA	ESC	WSC	M	W		
Organic pesticide production wastes	2879	.115	.148	.136	.073	.141	.057	.093	.054	.183	3×10^8	
Phenoxy herbicide production wastes	2879	.076	.135	.124	.080	.156	.062	.108	.059	.200	4×10^7	
SUBTOTAL											1×10^{10}	
Solid, slurry, or sludge												
Recovered arsenic from refinery flues (stored)	1021	—	—	—	—	—	—	—	—	1.00	4×10^7	Tacoma, Wash.
Sodium dichromate production wastes	2819	—	.150	.243	—	.437	—	.170	—	—	3×10^8	
Solvent-based paint sludge	285	.044	.243	.269	.072	.103	.041	.069	.012	.147	4×10^7	
Water-based paint sludge	285	.044	.243	.269	.072	.103	.041	.069	.012	.147	3×10^7	
Tetraethyl and tetramethyl lead production wastes	2869	—	—	—	—	—	—	.63	—	.37	3×10^5	Dry basis
Urea production wastes	2873	—	.05	.09	.18	.09	.15	.29	—	.14	2×10^5	
Benzoic herbicide contaminated containers	2879	—	—	.655	.154	.006	.017	—	.009	.160	2×10^4	
Calcium arsenate contaminated containers	2879	.03	.02	.08	.07	.16	.16	.35	.09	.03	6×10^3	
Carbonate pesticide contaminated containers	2879	.0008	.016	.382	.070	.022	.108	.321	.020	.060	5×10^4	
Chlorinated aliphatic pesticide contaminated containers	2879	.381	—	.076	.418	—	.105	.010	—	.010	1×10^4	
Dinitro pesticide contaminated containers	2879	.496	.168	.023	.017	.228	—	.003	.006	.165	2×10^4	

Lead arsenate contaminated containers	2879	.03	.02	.08	.07	.17	.17	.35	.03	.08	1×10^4
Mercury fungicide contaminated containers	2879	.02	.03	.04	.03	.28	.32	.05	.01	.22	5×10^2
Miscellaneous organic insecticide contaminated containers	2879	.148	.084	.054	.039	.197	.143	.148	.017	.170	4×10^4
Organic arsenic contaminated containers	2879	—	.007	—	—	.011	.764	.218	—	—	5×10^3
Organic fungicide contaminated containers	2879	.048	.125	.047	.028	.441	.001	.036	.007	.266	8×10^4
Organophosphorus contaminated containers	2879	.043	.050	.018	.125	.139	.192	.175	.049	.208	1×10^5
Phenoxy contaminated containers	2879	.035	.033	.196	.321	.031	.030	.067	.141	.146	2×10^5
Phenyl urea contaminated containers	2879	.106	.085	.106	.033	.106	.424	.042	.003	.095	9×10^3
Polychlorinated hydrocarbon contaminated containers	2879	.017	.107	.019	.138	.306	.211	.133	.024	.044	2×10^5
Triazine contaminated containers	2879	.147	.121	.320	.372	.013	.003	.011	.002	.011	6×10^4
Miscellaneous organic pesticide contaminated containers	2879	.014	.162	.385	.068	.162	.123	.041	.014	.034	1×10^4
Petroleum refining still bottoms	2911	.006	.086	.159	.055	.025	.025	.477	.033	.134	2×10^4
Petroleum waste brine sludges	2911	.002	.06	.09	.011	.12	.10	.55	.022	.045	4×10^6
Iron manufacturing waste sludge	331	.05	.05	.56	.02	.12	.03	.09	.05	.03	6×10^6
Arsenic trioxide from smelting industry	333	—	.03	.015	.07	.005	.01	.10	.70	.07	2×10^7

Waste stream title	Standard industrial code	Percentage by geographic area									Volume (lb/yr)	Remarks
		NE	MA	ENC	WNC	SA	ESC	WSC	M	W		
Selenium production wastes	3339	—	.75	—	—	—	—	—	.25	—	2×10^4	
Duplicating equipment manufacturing wastes	3555	—	1.00	—	—	—	—	—	—	—	7×10^5	Upstate New York
Refrigeration equipment manufacturing wastes	3585	.013	.232	.408	.096	.040	.069	.086	.011	.045	2×10^8	
Battery manufacturing waste sludge	3691	.117	.043	—	.118	.117	—	—	.118	—	5×10^7	
Arsenic trichloride recovered from coal	49	.05	.23	.07	.05	.33	.25	—	.07	—	6×10^6	
Military paris green (stored)	9711	—	—	1.00	—	—	—	—	—	—	3×10^4	
Stored military mercury compounds	9711	.47	—	—	.51	—	—	—	—	.02	2×10^2	
SUBTOTAL											7×10^8	
Aqueous inorganic (insufficient quantity or distribution data)												
Zinc ore roasting acid wash	1031				Not available						Not available	
Mercury ore extraction wastes	1092	—	—	—	—	—	—	—	.28	.72	Not available	
Cadmium ore extraction wastes	1099				Not available						2×10^8	
Mercury bearing textile wastes	22				Not available						Not available	
Wastes from pulp and paper industry	26	.11	.11	.19	.04	.23	.08	.10	.03	.11	Negligible	

	SIC										Not available
Cadmium selenium pigment wastes	28	Not available									Not available
Waste or contaminated perchloric acid	28	Not available									Negligible
Arsine production wastes	2813	‡	—	‡	—	‡	‡	—	‡	‡	1 × 10⁴
Borane production wastes	2813	1.0	—	—	—	—	—	—	—	—	Negligible
Nickel carbonyl production wastes	2813										Negligible
Waste bromine pentafluoride	2813	1.0	—	—	—	—	1.0	—	—	—	Negligible
Waste chlorine pentafluoride	2813	—	—	‡	—	—	‡	—	—	—	Negligible
Waste chlorine trifluoride	2813	—	—	‡	—	—	‡	—	—	—	Negligible
Chromate wastes from pigments and dyes	2816	.015	.170	.156	.047	.156	.111	.265	.020	.060	1 × 10¹¹§
Arsenic wastes from purification of phosphoric acid	2819	.015	.170	.156	.047	.156	.111	.265	.020	.060	Negligible
Contaminated fluorine	2819	.007	.101	.166	.075	.147	.207	.147	.054	.096	Negligible
Cyanide production wastes	2819	.007	.101	.166	.075	.147	.207	.147	.054	.096	2 × 10¹¹§
Waste from manufacture of mercuric cyanide	2819	—	1.0	—	—	—	—	—	—	—	Negligible
Waste from production of barium salts	2819	.007	.101	.166	.075	.147	.207	.147	.054	.096	Negligible
Urethane manufacturing wastes	2821	.046	.121	.101	.018	.404	.182	.101	—	.027	2 × 10¹²§
Wastes from polycarbonate polymer production	2821	.046	.121	.101	.018	.404	.182	.101	—	.027	2 × 10¹²§
Pharmaceutical arsenic wastes	283	.056	.348	.183	.089	.100	.033	.060	.011	.115	Negligible

§Total liquid discharge for the larger 3-digit standard industrial code category (SIC).

Waste stream title	Standard industrial code	Percentage by geographic area									Volume (lb/yr)	Remarks
		NE	MA	ENC	WNC	SA	ESC	WSC	M	W		
Pharmaceutical mercurial wastes	283	.056	.348	.183	.089	.100	.033	.060	.011	.115	Negligible	
Wood preservative wastes	2865	.007	.029	.117	.060	.267	.141	.174	.042	.162	2×10^{11} §	
Contaminated antimony pentafluoride	2869	—	‡	‡	—	—	—	‡	—	—	Negligible	
Contaminated antimony trifluoride	2869	—	‡	‡	—	—	—	‡	—	—	Negligible	
Hydrazine production wastes	2869	‡	‡	—	—	‡	—	‡	—	—	Not available	
Agricultural chemical production wastes	287	.005	.075	.145	.074	.299	.207	.090	.046	.058	2×10^{12} §	
Agricultural pesticide arsenic wastes	2879	.005	.075	.145	.074	.299	.207	.090	.046	.058	2×10^{12} §	
Mercuric fungicide production wastes	2879	.005	.075	.145	.074	.299	.207	.090	.046	.058	2×10^{12} §	
Pesticide arsenate wastes	2879	.005	.075	.145	.074	.299	.207	.090	.046	.058	2×10^{12} §	
1080 production wastes and contaminated lots	2879	—	‡	—	—	‡	1.0	—	—	—	Negligible	Production of sodium fluoracetate
Wastes from pesticide-herbicide manufacture (arsenites)	2879	.005	.075	.145	.074	.299	.207	.090	.046	.058	2×10^{12} §	
Electrical fuse manufacturing wastes	2899	.037	.221	.372	.153	.039	.040	.057	.009	.072	2×10^{12} §	
Beryllium salt production wastes	3339	—	1.0	—	—	—	—	—	—	—	Negligible	

Waste type	Code	—	—	—	—	—	1.0	‡	—	Negligible	Small amount in Colorado
Thallium production wastes	3339	—									Small amount in Colorado
Rotogravure printing plate wastes	3555	.105	.446	.320	.051	.019	.028	—	.031	1×10^{12}§	
Computer manufacturing wastes	3573	.143	.342	.170	.037	.053	.032	.039	.165	1×10^{12}§	
Electronic tube production wastes	367	.143	.342	.170	.037	.053	.032	.039	.165	Not available	
Magnetic tape production wastes	3679	.171	.336	.165	.120	.077	.060	—	.060	Not available	
Battery manufacturing wastes	3691	.030	.236	.289	.111	.103	.056	.012	.134	1.1×10^{12}	
Mercury cell battery wastes	3692	.060	.138	.556	.049	.074	.017			1.1×10^{12}§	
Railroad engine cleaning	40				Not available					Not available	
Arsenic wastes from transportation industry	40				Not available					Not available	
Military cadmium wastes from plating	9711				Not available					Not available	
Military sodium chromate	9711				Not available					Not available	
SUBTOTAL										2×10^{8}	
Organic (insufficient quantity or distribution data)											
Spent wood preserving liquors	2491	.007	.029	.117	.060	.267	.174	.042	.162	2×10^{12}§	
Off-specification "agent orange" defoliant	9711				Not available		1.0			Not available	
Paint stripping wastes, Vance Air Force Base, Oklahoma	9711									Not available	
SUBTOTAL											

Waste stream title	Standard industrial code	Percentage by geographic area									Volume (lb/yr)	Remarks
		NE	MA	ENC	WNC	SA	ESC	WSC	M	W		
Aqueous organic (insufficient quantity or distribution data)												
Synthetic fiber production wastes	2824	.046	.121	.101	.018	.404	.182	.101	—	.027	2×10^{12} §	
Dye manufacturing wastes	2865	.015	.170	.156	.047	.156	.111	.265	.020	.060	1×10^{11} §	
Nitrile pesticide wastes	2879	.005	.075	.145	.074	.299	.207	.090	.046	.058	2×10^{12} §	
Organic arsenicals from production of cacodylates	2879	—	.200	.800	—	—	—	—	—	—	Not available	
Torpedo process wastes	2879	—	—	—	—	—	1.0	—	—	—	Negligible	
Utilities and electrical station waste	49	Not available									3×10^{7}	
Wastes from production of chloropicrin	9711	—	‡	—	—	—	—	‡	—	‡	Negligible	
SUBTOTAL											3×10^{7}	
Solid, slurry, or sludge (insufficient quantity or distribution data)												
Wastes from seed industry	011	.017	.088	.371	.213	.053	.060	.081	.023	.094	Not available	
Contaminated orchard soil	0175	.05	—	.15	—	.33	—	.35	.03	.09	Unknown	
Old or contaminated thallium and thallium sulfate rodenticide	2879	.005	.075	.145	.074	.299	.207	.090	.046	.058	Not available	
Highly contaminated soil	9711	—	—	—	—	—	—	—	1.00	—	3×10^{9} (not included in total)	Stored at Rocky Mountain Arsenal

Spent filter media from military operations	9711	Not available	Not available
Waste chemicals from military	9711	Not available	3×10^5
Explosives from military ordnance	9711	Not available	4×10^8
Drugs and contraband seized by customs	—	Not available	Not available
Etiological materials from commercial production	—	Not available	3×10
SUBTOTAL			4×10^8
TOTAL			2×10^{10}

Source: EPA report to Congress on the disposal of hazardous wastes, Washington, D.C., June 20, 1973. Pp. 50–53.

APPENDIX II

Estimated Industrial Hazardous Waste Generation

	Quantity (tonnes)			Universe
State[1,2]	EPA estimate	State estimate	Same as EPA	State additions[3]
Alabama[2]	730,000	265,680		PCBS.
Alaska[2]	130,000	360		PCBS.
Arizona[2]	160,000	4,280,000		PCBS, waste oil.
Arkansas	370,000	No data[4]		PCBS, waste oil.
California[5]	2,630,000	15,000,000		Approximately 4 mmt is oilfield waste; also includes mining waste, small generators, PCBS.
Colorado[2]	180,000	775,490		PCBS.
Connecticut[2]	610,000	102,000	●	Extrapolated from 3 months manifest data.
Delaware[1]	300,000	272,000	●	—
Florida	960,000	No data	●	—
Georgia[2]	700,000	38,500,800		Some delisted waste; 99.7% is high volume, aqueous solutions, neutralized on site and discharged to sewers and receiving waters.
Hawaii	30,000	No response		—
Illinois[1]	2,530,000	1,810,000		Manifest data only.
Indiana	1,280,000	94,900,000		Includes 92.3 mmt of steel industry wastes, pending delisting and currently regulated under NPDES permit.
Idaho	80,000	No response		—
Iowa	300,000	No response		—
Kansas[1]	350,000	45,300		Refinery waste, small volume generators.
Kentucky[1]	700,000	415,000	●	
Louisiana[1]	1,250,000	38,800,000		Fly and bottom ash, small volume generators, substances with LD_{50}.
Maine[2]	130,000	5,290		Mineral spirits, tanning industry waste, small volume generators, infectious waste.
Maryland[1]	590,000	272,100		Waste oil, PCBS, fly ash, and other unspecified waste.
Massachusetts[2]	820,000	172,000		Waste oil.
Michigan[2]	1,990,000	408,000		Extrapolated from manifest data; 280 compounds (including waste oil) not on EPA list.
Minnesota[2]	360,000	181,000		PCBS, crank case oil.
Mississippi[1]	340,000	1,810,000	●	—
Missouri[1]	910,000	658,930		Waste oil.
Montana[1]	50,000	91,200	●	
Nebraska[2]	120,000	0.5% of national total		Special waste including infectious waste.
Nevada	50,000	No response		—

State[1,2]	Quantity (tonnes)		Universe	
	EPA estimate	State estimate	Same as EPA	State additions[3]
New Hampshire[1]	100,000	9,980		Imported PCBs, waste oil.
New Jersey[1]	3,120,000	855,000		Manifest data only; waste oil, PCBs, some delisted waste, and other unspecified compounds.
New Mexico	60,000	No data		Small volume generators, PCBs, waste oil.
New York[2]	2,320,000	1,270,000		PCBs.
North Carolina	1,330,000	No response		—
North Dakota[1]	30,000	125,000	•	—
Ohio[1]	2,570,000	3,260,000		Solid waste on a case-by-case basis.
Oklahoma[2]	230,000	3,570,000		PCBs.
Oregon[2]	200,000	19,100		PCBs and other unspecified compounds.
Pennsylvania[2]	2,550,000	3,628,000		Other unspecified compounds.
Rhode Island[1]	190,000	1,600		A generally broader definition which includes waste oil, low-level radioactive.
South Carolina[2]	1,140,000	1,587,000		Waste oil, paint waste, unstabilized sewerage sludge.
South Dakota[2]	10,000	1,590		Waste oil.
Tennessee[1]	1,820,000	4,300,000	•	—
Texas[1]	3,010,000	29,146,960		Generally different definition which includes sludge, fly and bottom ash, water soluble oils, boiler sludges, PCBs, and other solid waste.
Utah[1]	110,000	558,000	•	—
Vermont[2]	30,000	9,070		Waste oils, infectious waste, PCBs, industrial laundries, some waste delisted by EPA, and other unspecified compounds.
Virginia[2]	1,220,000	181,000		PCBs.
Washington[2]	380,000	616,000		Additional unspecified waste.
West Virginia	790,000	No response		—
Wisconsin[1]	630,000	81,600		—
Wyoming	40,000	No response		—
Guam[2]	n/a	1,450	•	—
Puerto Rico[2]	560,000	417,000	•	—
North Mariana Is.	n/a	No response		—
American Samoa	n/a	0	•	—
Dist. of Columbia	140,000	No data	•	—
Virgin Islands	n/a	No response		—
TOTAL	41,200,000 (excl. 2 territories)	250,000,000 (excl. 10 states, 3 territories)		

1. State data based on inventory. 2. State data based on consultant and/or State agency estimates. 3. PCBs are currently regulated under TSCA. EPA is considering transferring regulation of this substance to RCRA jurisdiction. 4. A few States did not supply information to this survey. 5. The State figure of 15 million tonnes is from the testimony of S. Kent Stoddard, California Office of Appropriate Technology, House Subcommittee on Natural Resources, Agriculture Research and the Environment, Dec. 8, 1982; it is based on a recent State study. Conversions: gallons × 0.00378 = metric tons; tons × 0.907 = metric tons; cubic feet × 0.02828 = metric tons; cubic yards × 0.76441 = metric tons.

Source: State estimates and associated information by ASTSWMO unless noted otherwise; EPA estimates by Office of Solid Waste for 1980. From *Technology and Management Strategies for Hazardous Wastes*, Office of Technology Assessment, Congress of the United States, 1983, pp. 121–122.

APPENDIX III

Comparability of State Hazardous Waste Programs to the Federal RCRA Program

State	Universe of waste	Generators	Transporters	Facilities
AL	RCRA	RCRA	Permit required	RCRA
AK	.... COOPERATIVE ARRANGEMENT			
AZ	Equivalent, plus expanded reactivity criteria	Annual reports Manifest copies to State	RCRA	Proof of financial responsibility; quarterly report
AR	RCRA plus PCBs	RCRA by regulation	Permit and State manifest	RCRA
CA	RCRA plus PCBs, metals, waste oil, mining waste, some recycled wastes, and more stringent toxicity criteria	Monthly reports for storage of less than 60 days	Registration, insurance inspection	No exemptions in general. Special permits for disposal of certain high-hazard waste
CO	Some recycled/reused materials covered by RCRA excluded under State law	RCRA by statute	RCRA by statute	Disposal sites revert to State ownership at closure
CT	RCRA by statute	N.E. manifest	License, insurance, bonding for hauler storage	Licenses; special requirements for dewatered sludges
DE	RCRA	Annual report, copy of manifest to State	License	Special groundwater monitoring requirements
FL	RCRA by reference	RCRA by reference; generator inspections	RCRA; inspections	RCRA by reference; liability insurance required
GA	RCRA by reference	RCRA by reference	RCRA by reference; permit required	RCRA by reference
HI	.... COOPERATIVE ARRANGEMENT			
ID	.... COOPERATIVE ARRANGEMENT			
IL	RCRA plus special wastes, infectious hospital wastes	State manifest tracking system	Permit required; all shipments must be manifested	Prohibits landfilling unless facility has appropriate permit for each waste stream received
IN	RCRA	More stringent recycling requirements	Liquid industrial waste haulers must have a permit	RCRA
IA	RCRA by reference	RCRA by reference	RCRA by reference	Facility must establish financial responsibility consistent with risk
KS	RCRA	Must obtain disposal authorization from State before waste shipment	Registration, insurance; State approval of disposal requests before transport	Waste disposal must be authorized
KY	RCRA by reference	Equivalent	Equivalent	RCRA by reference
LA	RCRA plus State waste list; more stringent toxicity test	State manifest system	Permit required	Each TSDF unit permitted separately; liability insurance required; quarterly reports for onsite disposal
ME	RCRA	N.E. manifest	License, insurance	Licenses
MD	RCRA plus PCBs	RCRA	License	State permit
MA	RCRA plus waste oil, PCBs and radioactive waste	N.E. manifest	License, bond	License; liability insurance
MI	RCRA plus waste oil, additional toxic wastes, recycled wastes must be sold for gain	State manifest system	License	License; certificates of waste disposal, more frequent inspections

State	Universe of waste	Generators	Transporters	Facilities
MN	RCRA plus waste oil, recycled wastes, additional waste characteristics	Manifest returned to State; generator waste disclosure and management plan	RCRA	Monthly reports for offsite TSDFS
MS	Equivalent	Equivalent	Equivalent	Equivalent
MO	Waste oil, State-listed wastes	Manifest returned to State; generator registration	License, insurance	Similar to RCRA, monthly reports, certification of recyclers
MT	RCRA	RCRA	RCRA	RCRA
NE	RCRA by reference	RCRA by references	RCRA by reference	Equivalent
NV	. . . . COOPERATIVE ARRANGEMENT			
NH	RCRA	N.E. manifest	License and insurance	Permit by rule
NJ	RCRA plus waste oil, PCBs, recycled wastes	State manifest; manifest copies to State	License, operating requirements	Monthly groundwater monitoring reports
NM	. . . . COOPERATIVE ARRANGEMENT			
NY	RCRA by statute	—	License	RCRA
NC	RCRA	RCRA by reference	RCRA by reference	RCRA
ND	RCRA	RCRA	RCRA	RCRA
OH	RCRA	RCRA	Transporter registration	RCRA
OK	RCRA plus PCBs, no exemption for recycled wastes	RCRA	Registration, manifest for recycled wastes	RCRA; storage requirements for recyclers
OR	No waste listing, regulate by waste characteristics	Manifest exemption for generators shipping less than 2,000 lb/load	RCRA	Substantially equivalent
PA	Primary neutralization units	Quarterly reports; manifest to State; must get authorization from TSDF before waste shipment	License	Facility must authorize that it is capable of handling wastes before shipment
RI	9 waste characteristics	N.E. manifest	License; liability insurance	
SC	No exemption for recycled waste; additional listed wastes; more stringent corrosivity test	Manifest copies to States; must obtain authorization from TSDF before waste shipment	Permit	Licenses; recycling regulated; quarterly reports for onsite TSDFS
SD	. . . . NO PROGRAM			
TN	Equivalent	Equivalent	Equivalent	Groundwater monitoring wells approved by State geologist
TX	RCRA plus halogenated hydrocarbons	RCRA	RCRA, hauler storage is regulated	RCRA, liability endorsement
UT	RCRA, waiver for some recycled wastes	RCRA	RCRA	RCRA
VT	19 classes of hazardous wastes, additional wastes regulated	N.E. manifest	License	Permit by rule, recovery operations regulated
VA	RCRA	RCRA	Permit	RCRA
WA	Larger universe of waste, mining wastes, and degree of hazard system for extremely hazardous wastes	RCRA	RCRA	Insurance; location restrictions for extremely hazardous waste facilities; buffer zones
WV	. . . . COOPERATIVE ARRANGEMENT			
WI	RCRA, more stringent recycling provisions	Manifest to State, annual report	License	License, quarterly report, treatment at wastewater treatment facilities must be permitted
WY	. . . . NO PROGRAM (EPA PROGRAM OPERATING IN STATE)			

Notes: RCRA = State program is nearly identical to Federal regulations. Equivalent = State program is equivalent, but not identical to Federal regulations. RCRA by reference = State program adopted Federal regulations by reference. — = not classified.

Sources: Robert A. Finlayson, "Should State Rules Be Tougher Than EPA's?" Solid Waste Management, vol, 25, pp. 78, 80–82, May 1982; Hazardous Waste Regulatory Guide: State Waste Management Programs (Neenah, Wis.: J. J. Keller & Associates, Inc., 1982); and Citizens for a Better Environment, Approaches to Hazardous Waste Management in Selected States, OTA Working Paper, December 1982. From Technologies and Management Strategies for Hazardous Waste, Office of Technology Assessment, Congress of the United States, 1983, pp. 349–350.

Toxicological Effects of Hazardous Chemicals Found at the Love Canal

Chemical	Toxicological Effects*							
	Mutagenicity	Carcinogenicity	Teratogenicity	Fetotoxicity and/or Embryotoxicity	Neurotoxicity	Hepatotoxicity	Renal Toxicity	Pulmonary Toxicity
Acenaphthene								
Acetaldehyde	+	−	+	+				
Acetic acid	−	−						
Acetone	−	−						
Acetylchloride		−						
Alkyl butyrate								
Aluminum chloride	+							
Aniline	−	+					+	
Anthracene	−	−						
Antimony trichloride								
Arsenic trichloride								+
Benzaldehyde	−							
2-Chlorobenzaldehyde								
4-Chlorobenzaldehyde								
2,4-Dichlorobenzaldehyde								
2,6-Dichlorobenzaldehyde								
3,4-Dichlorobenzaldehyde								
Benzene	+	+	+	+				
1,2-Benzene dicaboxylic acid, dibutylester	−	−	−	+				

* + = at least one report of positive listed effect; − = only negative data; absence of sign = no data in the literature.

Chemical	Toxicological Effects							
	Mutagenicity	Carcinogenicity	Teratogenicity	Fetotoxicity and/or Embryotoxicity	Neurotoxicity	Hepatotoxicity	Renal Toxicity	Pulmonary Toxicity
1,2-Benzene dicarboxylic acid, diethylester	−		−	+				
1,2-Benzene dicarboxylic acid, di-l-octylester	−		−	+				
Benzene hexachloride. *See* Hexachloro-cyclohexane	−		+					
Benzo-a-anthracene	+	+						
Benzo-a-pyrene	+	+						
Benzodisulfide								
Benzo-8-fluoranthene	−	+						
Benzo-K-fluoranthene		−						
Benzo-E-phenanthrene	−	−						
Benzopolysulfide								
1,2,3,-Benzothiazole								
Benzotrichloride. *See* α,α,α-trichloro-toluene		+						
Benzotrifluoride								
Benzyl acetate								
Benzoyl chloride	+							

Toxicological Effects

Chemical	Mutagenicity	Carcinogenicity	Teratogenicity	Fetotoxicity and/or Embryotoxicity	Neurotoxicity	Hepatotoxicity	Renal Toxicity	Pulmonary Toxicity
Chlorobenzofluorene								
Chlorobenzoic acid								
α-Chlorobenzotri-fluoride								
o-Chlorobenzotri-fluoride								
p-Chlorobenzotri-fluoride								
Chlorodibromo-methane	+							
Chlorocresols					+			
Chloroethylene (vinyl chloride)	+	+	+	+	+	+		+
Chloroform	–	+		+		+		
1-Chloronaphthalene								
2-Chloronaphthalene								
α-Chlorotoluene	+	+						
p-Chlorotoluene	–							
Cyclohexanol								
Cyclohexenol								
Cyclopentaphenan-threne		+						
DOM Residues. See Diaminodiphenyl-methane								

Compound							
Decane						−	−
Dechlorane				+	+	+	
2,4'-Diaminodiphenyl-methane							
4,4'-Diaminodiphenyl-methane		+			−	+	+
1,2-Dibromoethane		+	+				+
1,2-Dibromomethane			+		−	+	+
Dibutyl oxide. See di-n-butyl ether							
Di-n-butyl phthalate							−
Dichloroaniline				+	−	−	−
Dichlorobenzaldehyde See Benzaldehyde							
1,2-Dichlorobenzene							+
1,4-Dichlorobenzene	+	+	+				+
1,3-Dichlorobenzene							+
Dichlorobenzoic acid							
Dichlorobiphenyl							
Dichlorobromometh-ane. See Bromodi-chloromethane.							
Dichlorocyclohexane							
2,7-Dichlorodibenzo-p-dioxin				−	−		
Dichloroethane			+		−		−
1,1-Dichloroethane			+	+		+	+
1,2-Dichloroethane			+	+		+	+
Dichloroethylcyclo-propyl pentane							
1,1-Dichloreothylene	+	+	+	+		+	+

Toxicological Effects

Chemical	Mutagenicity	Carcinogenicity	Teratogenicity	Fetotoxicity and/or Embryotoxicity	Neurotoxicity	Hepatotoxicity	Renal Toxicity	Pulmonary Toxicity
1,2-Dichloroethylene (cis isomer)	+				+			
1,2-Dichloroethylene (trans isomer)	−							
Dichloromethane	+	−	−		+			
Dichloronaphthalene(s)				−	+			
2,4-Dichlorophenol	−	+						
2,6-Dichlorophenol		+						
1,2-Dichloropropane	+							
α,α-Dichlorotoluene				+				
Diisobutylphthalate	−	−	+					
Dimethyl benzene. *See* xylene								
2,2-Dimethylbutane								
2,3-Dimethylbutane								
2,5-Dimethyl Furan								
2,3-Dimethylhexane								
2,4-Dimethylhexane								
1,6-Dimethyl-naphthalene		−						
1,3-Dimethyl-naphthalene		−						
2,6-Dimethyl-naphthalene		−						

2,3-Dimethyl-l-pentanol						−	−
Dimethyl Phenol	+			+	+		
Di-n-octyl phthalate	+						−
Diphenyl ether		+					
Dodecyl Mercaptans							
Eicosane							
Ethyl Alcohol			+	+	+	−	
Ethyl Acetate							
Ethyl Benzene						−	
Ethyl Phenol			+	+	+		
bis (2-Ethylhexyl)-phthalate							+
Fluorene						−	+
Fluoranthene						−	
Furan							
Furfural			+	+		−	+
Heptachlor			+			+	+
Heptachlorotoluene							
n-Heptanal							
Heptanoic acid						−	
Het Acid (Chlorendic acid)		+					
Hexachloroanthracene							
Hexachlorobenzene			+	+	+	+	+
Hexachlorobicyclo-heptadiene							
Hexachloro-1,3-Butadiene	+			+	−	+	+
1,2,3,4,5,6-Hexachlorocyclohexane						−	

	Toxicological Effects							
Chemical	Mutagenicity	Carcinogenicity	Teratogenicity	Fetotoxicity and/or Embryotoxicity	Neurotoxicity	Hepatotoxicity	Renal Toxicity	Pulmonary Toxicity
1,2,3,4,5,6-Hexachlorocyclohexane (mixed isomers)		+						
α-1,2,3,4,5,6-Hexachlorocyclohexane		+						
β-1,2,3,4,5,6-Hexachlorocyclohexane		+						
δ-1,2,3,4,5,6-Hexachlorocyclohexane		−						
γ-1,2,3,4,5,6-Hexachlorocyclohexane	−	+						
1,2,3,4,5,6-Hexachlorocyclopentadiene	−	−			+			
Hexachlorodibenzo-p-dioxin				+				
Hexachlorotoluene			+			+		
Hexachlorophenanthrene								
Hexamethylcyclotetrasiloxane			−		+			
Hexane	−	−						
Hexylbenzoate								
Isobutyraldehyde	+							
Isophorone							+	

Isopropanol

Isopropyl Acetate

Lauryl Chloride

L.D.S. Liquid disulfide

Lindane. *See* γ-Hexa-
chlorocyclohexane

meta Nitrobenzoic acid.
See m-Nitrobenzoic
acid

MNBC. *See*
m-Nitro-
benzoyl chloride

Methanol

Methylbenzene. *See*
Toluene

Methylbenzoate

5-Methyl Benzacridine

Methyl Biphenyl

4-Methyl-2,6-di-tert-
butylphenol

Methylcyclopentane

Methyl Dichloro
Stearate

2,2¹-Methylene-
bis (4-chlorophenol)

Methylene chloride. *See*
Dichloromethane

2-Methyl-2-Ethoxy
propane

Methyl Ethyl Ketone

Methyl Fluorene

| Chemical | Toxicological Effects | | | | | | | |
	Mutagenicity	Carcinogenicity	Teratogenicity	Fetotoxicity and/or Embryotoxicity	Neurotoxicity	Hepatotoxicity	Renal Toxicity	Pulmonary Toxicity
Methyl Formate								
Methyl Furan						+	+	
Methyl Isopropyl Ketone								
Methyl Naphthalene	−							
Methyl Pentachloro-Stearate								
4-Methyl-2-Pentanone (Methyl isobutyl ketone)								
Methyl Phenanthrene	+							
m-Methyl Phenol								
o-Methyl Phenol								
p-Methyl Phenol								
Methoxy-di-tert-Butylphenol								
Methyl Phthalate				+				
Methyl Pyrene								
Methyl Salicylate			+				+	
Methylvinyl Ketone								
Naphthalene	−					+		
m-Nitro benzoic acid		−						
m-Nitrobenzoyl chloride	−							
m-Nitrophenol								

o-Nitrophenol

p-Nitrophenol

Nonane

Octachlorocyclopentane

1,1-Oxybis Methylene, bis benzene

Polychlorinated Biphenyls

Pentachloroanthracene

Pentachlorobenzene

Pentachlorobiphenyl

Pentachlorobutadiene

Pentachloroethane

Pentachlorophenan-threne

Pentachlorophenol

Pentachloropropane

Pentachlorotoluene

Pentanal

2-Pentanone

Phenol

(PNBC) Paranitroben-zoylchloride

Sodium Hypophosphite

Sodium Sulfide

Sodium Tetrasulfide

Sulfene

Sulfur Dichloride

Sulfur Chloride

Tetrachloroanthracene

| | Toxicological Effects | | | | | | | |
Chemical	Mutagenicity	Carcinogenicity	Teratogenicity	Fetotoxicity and/or Embryotoxicity	Neurotoxicity	Hepatotoxicity	Renal Toxicity	Pulmonary Toxicity
2,3,7,8-Tetrachlorodibenzo-p-dioxin	+	+	+	+	+	+		
1,2,3,4-TCDD				−				
1,2,4,5-Tetrachlorobenzene	+							
1,2,3,4-Tetrachlorobenzene								
1,2,3,5-Tetrachlorobenzene								
Tetrachlorobutadiene						+		
Tetrachloroethane					+			
1,1,1,2-Tetrachloroethane	−							
1,1,2,2-Tetrachloroethane		+			+			
Tetrachloroethene. See Tetrachloroethylene								
Tetrachloroethylene	−	+	−	−	+	+	+	
Tetrachloromethane. See Carbon Tetrachloride								
Tetrachlorophenanthrene								
Tetrachlorotoluene								
Tetrahydropyridine								

Tetramethyl Hexadiene							
Tetraphenyl tin							
1,1-Thiobis methylene, bis benzene			+				
Thionyl Chloride							
2,4,6-Tetrachloroaniline	−						
1,2,4-Trichlorobenzene	−	−					
1,2,3-Trichlorobenzene	−						
1,3,5-Trichlorobenzene	−			+			
1,1,1-Trichloroethane	+	+		+			
Trichloroethylene	+	+		+			
Trichloromethane. *See* Chloroform							
2,3,6-Trichlorophenol	+	+		+			
2,4,5-Trichlorophenol	−	−		+			
2,4,6-Trichlorophenol	+	+		+			
3,4,5-Trichlorophenol	+			+			
α,α,α-Trichlorotoluene	−				+		
Toluene	+	+		+	+	+	+	+
Vinyl Acetate	+						
Xylene (mixed)	−	+		−	+		
Xylene					+		
m-Xylene					+		
o-Xylene					+		
p-Xylene					+		

Source: Report of the Subcommittee on the "Potential Health Effects of Toxic Chemical Dumps" of the DHEW Committee to Coordinate Environmental and Related Problems, in *Health Effects of Toxic Pollution*, Report to the U.S. Senate Committee on Environmental and Public Works (Ser. 96–15). August, 1980, Washington, D.C.

APPENDIX V

Hunt the Dump: An Environmental Action, Inc., and Sierra Club Campaign to Locate and Expose the Nation's Unsafe Hazardous Waste Sites

In July, 1979, the Massachusetts Department of Environmental Quality Engineering ordered the W. R. Grace Chemical Company to eliminate the dumping of hazardous wastes at its plastic plant in Acton, Massachusetts. The order was the culmination of excellent "sleuthing" and citizen activism led by a core group of Sierra Club members. The order was the first that the state had issued to control hazardous waste disposed at the plant site.

It all started when Sierra Club members, investigating the source of odors that had long bothered local residents, hiked along a railroad spur and photographed colorful open lagoons into which odorous chemicals from the plant were being discharged. These photos were shown to the public, press, and town officials, raising public awareness of the possible dangers of an operation that had previously been unknown to most residents.

And they didn't stop there. When samples of water from a well that supplied the town's drinking water revealed the presence of vinyl chloride, a virulent cancer-causing agent, W. R. Grace claimed it was no longer using the chemical. Citizens hiked back to the site with a reporter and photographed tank cars stencilled with the words *vinyl chloride* on the side.

This is just one of many stories that illustrate what citizens can do to shock public officials and the public at large into addressing the serious threats posed by the improper disposal of hazardous chemical wastes. Citizens must organize and force government and industry to act to protect our public health and environment. To help enable citizens to do just that, the Sierra Club and Environmental Action have launched a national Hunt the Dump campaign. Designed to give citizens the tools to track down these chemical nightmares, the campaign will focus national attention on the real culprits—the polluters themselves. But before we look at the campaign, let's first take a look at the problem.

Ton upon Toxic Ton

How big a problem is hazardous industrial waste? The U.S. Environmental Protection Agency (EPA) estimates that approximately 77 billion pounds of hazardous waste are generated annually. While the EPA has the authority to regulate future hazardous waste disposal, the disasters at Love Canal, Valley of the Drums, and elsewhere raise major concern about the threats from the billions of pounds of hazardous wastes disposed in the past. The EPA estimates that there are roughly 32,000 abandoned or closed (inactive) dumpsites. However, since over 90 percent of all hazardous industrial waste disposal occurs at the site of generation, no one knows how many closed sites exist or how many threaten health or the environment.

The House Commerce Committee's Subcommittee on Oversight and Investigation was so concerned with the lack of information that it conducted its own survey of 1,605 facilities owned by the 53 largest chemical companies. The survey revealed that 762 million tons of chemical process waste, not all of it hazardous, have been disposed at 3,308 facilities since 1950. Thirty-two percent of these facilities are closed and are not being monitored for possible health and environmental hazards.

The survey did *not* reveal how safe any of the sites are, particularly the closed sites where encroachment by residences and human activity is more likely.

Citizen inquiry about the sites used by hazardous waste generating companies in their communities will help ensure that these companies shoulder their responsibility to safeguard disposal facilities. Citizens can focus public attention on potential problems and encourage remedial action before additional Love Canals, on a more modest scale, can occur. We urge you to use the Hunt the Dump campaign to target the hazardous waste generators in your community that may be improperly disposing of their wastes.

Goals of the Hunt

The Hunt the Dump Campaign involves four parts:

1. Targeting manufacturing companies for the survey
2. Submitting a questionnaire to each company
3. Evaluating each company's disposal sites
4. Creating public and governmental awareness of potentially hazardous disposal sites.

The basic objective of Hunt the Dump is to determine where past and present hazardous waste sites are and whether the sites are likely to leak dangerous chemicals that could cause health or environmental problems.

Government officials are moving very slowly to address the hazardous waste problem, partly because they fear the problem is too big to handle with existing resources. By using the enclosed questionnaire to ask local hazardous waste generators about their disposal practices, citizens can protect themselves by identifying actual and potential hazardous disposal sites long before the government will. In addition, by sending the questionnaire to us, you can assist in defining the seriousness of the hazardous waste problem nationwide.

Step 1: Targeting Manufacturing Companies

The House of Representatives' survey provides the best starting point for your hunt; however, surveys of facilities not listed are of greater value. (For copies of the House lists, write to Blake Early, Sierra Club, 330 Pennsylvania Ave., S.E., Washington, D.C. 20003.)

Most chemical waste disposal occurs at the site of generation. Therefore, those enterprises that are located near routes of human exposure pose the gravest threat. Table IV-1 lists the categories and the standard industrial code numbers of those industries that the EPA has found to generate the most hazardous waste. Using various sources (Thomas Register of American Manufacturers, Dalton's Directory, local Chamber of Commerce publications, publications of state and local government economic agencies, etc.), you should be able to find out if any of these industries operates in your locale. With the aid of a zip-coded street map, you can then pinpoint the enterprises and determine just where you might find a hazardous dump.

After this list of targets is identified, water supplies and community activity centers require special detective work.

SURFACE WATER

First check where your source of public water supply is located. If it is a river, concentrate on those enterprises located upriver from the drinking

Table IV-1

Category	Standard Industrial Code No.
Organic chemicals manufacture	2861
Pesticides manufacture	2865–2869
Explosives manufacture	2892
Ferrous metals	3312, 3313, 3399
Electroplating	3471
Inorganic chemicals manufacture	2812–2819
Nonferrous metals	3331–3341
Textile mill products	2201–2295
Petroleum refining	2911
Plastics & synthetics manufacture	2820–2829
Special machinery	3550, 3570
Leather tanning	3111
Paint & allied products	2851
Pharmaceutical manufacture	2831–2834
Petroleum refining	2992
Rubber goods	3011, 3021, 3031, 3041, 3069
Electronic components	3670
Battery manufacture	3691, 3692

water intake. Also target facilities located on the banks of major tributaries. If your municipality uses a reservoir for drinking water, the job is more complicated, for you will need to target facilities located in the reservoir's "watershed," or water collection basin. Local drinking supply officials should be able to help you identify all major sources of water supply. Also ask these officials for information regarding what contaminants have been identified in your drinking water.

GROUNDWATER

Your drinking water may come from wells drilled into underlying groundwaters. Find out where these wells are located. Identify target companies that are "upgradient" (the equivalent of upstream) from these wells. Also learn how deep this groundwater is and where the "recharge" zones are located. Recharge zones are the areas that allow surface water to enter the groundwater. Learn where nearby private wells are located. Ask local drinking supply and public health officials if owners of these private wells have complained of contamination. Questions that local drinking water officials either will not or cannot answer should be directed to state water survey or geological survey organizations. Also check with the U.S. Geological Survey and state universities—some of these officials may be able to identify target companies for you. Ask state water pollution control agencies and the regional U.S. EPA for the location of target companies that have waste water discharge permits. Often these companies are dumping on the land the hazardous wastes that these agencies have prohibited from being discharged directly to the water.

COMMUNITY ACTIVITIES

You will also need to determine areas of your community where residential or recreational facilities are in close proximity to industrial companies. These areas are where direct human contact with hazardous waste is most likely.

Step 2: Submitting the Questionnaire

The next step involves presenting the questionnaire to the target companies. While this can obviously be done by mail, we suggest that an interview be arranged with the plant manager or other appropriate official to review the concerns you and other representatives from the community may have. Gather as many prominent citizens as you can interest. The nature of the response is dependent upon a number of factors. The company wants to maintain a favorable public image. On the other hand, it does not want to reveal information that will be of use to competitors or subject it to civil action from governmental authorities. The more information you have gathered about the target company, the less likely it is that you will be persuaded to accept phony information. During the interview, let the official know that:

1. There is a real need to ascertain the size and scope of the hazardous waste problem to avoid over and under reacting;

2. There is a need to reduce public paranoia regarding hazardous waste disposal by forthrightly investigating and addressing the problems. This will help reduce public resistance to the siting of new disposal facilities;

3. You have information about the enterprise and you are aware that more can be researched;

4. Enterprises that are viewed as uncooperative will be subject to greater scrutiny.

The questionnaire at the end of this appendix focuses on toxic wastes that are regarded as among the most dangerous in terms of human toxicity. Included are chemical categories that appear on numerous governmental "most dangerous" lists. You may wish to broaden the list to include substances of particular concern to you or your community. If you wish to add to the questionnaire, please do so at the end. (Please do not reorder the substances currently on the list, or we will have difficulty merging the information on your questionnaire with others). The glossary of terms included here briefly describes many of the priority substances appearing on the questionnaire.

A Toxics Lexicon

Amides, amines, and imides are basic chemical building blocks in chemical and plastics production. Various members of this class of chemicals cause cancer, birth defects, and genetic damage in test animals or test organisms. Many are toxic to aquatic life at low concentrations.

Arsenic is used in the production of boric acid and pharmaceuticals. Arsenic can cause brain damage, nervous system damage, gastrointestinal damage, and skin lesions. There is epidemiological evidence of carcinogenic action of arsenic in skin and lung of humans. Arsenic causes birth defects and genetic damage in test animals.

Benzene is used widely as a solvent in chemical processes. Benzene exposure to humans in the workplace is known to cause leukemia.

Cadmium is used in industry, principally in electroplating, cadmium–silver oxide battery production, in pigment manufacture, and as a plasticizer, chiefly in polyvinyl chloride. Low-level intake of cadmium over a long period of time is known to cause damage to kidney function. Cadmium has also been associated with hypertension. It has caused tumors in rats and is also known to be teratogenic (cause birth defects) in rats.

Carbon tetrachloride is used in numerous chemical processes, dry cleaning, and degreasing operations. Carbon tetrachloride has caused acute poisoning through liver and kidney damage. It is a carcinogen in laboratory animals and a suspected human carcinogen.

Chromium is principally used in electroplating processes and paint pigments. Hexavalent chromium has long been recognized as a toxic substance. It produces hemorrhages of the gastrointestinal tract after ingestion. Airborne chromium has caused cancer of the respiratory tract in occupationally exposed humans.

Copper is a gastrointestinal tract irritant and can be highly toxic. Acute episodes have been reported from ingestion of carbonated beverages that were in contact with copper vessels.

Esters and ethers are a family of hydrocarbons, most commonly used in pesticides and herbicides, and generated during petroleum refining. Some have caused cancer in test animals and are highly toxic to mammals.

Land farming is the application of wastes onto land or incorporation into the surface soil, including the use of waste as a fertilizer or soil conditioner.

Landfill is a land area that may or may not be excavated, where solid, semisolid, or liquid wastes are emplaced for permanent deposition. Such wastes may or may not be compacted or segregated by soil barriers.

Leachate is the liquid that has percolated through or drained from hazardous waste and contains components removed from the waste.

Lead is used in the manufacture of pigments and lead acid batteries and is found as a by-product in metal smelting. While acute lead poisoning is extremely rare, exposure to low levels of lead over long periods of time can cause brain and bone damage. Lead has caused malignant tumors in test animals.

Manganese is found in metallurgical processes, including steel making, aluminum manufacture, and also in electroplating. Chronic exposure may result in permanent crippling. Symptoms include sleepiness, leg cramps, increased tendon reflexes, emotional disturbances, and spastic reflexes. Chronic manganese poisoning results in progressive deterioration of the central nervous system.

Mercury is used in the production of chlorine, caustic soda, electrical apparatus, as a plasticizer, in metallurgical processes, and in chemical production. Hexavalent mercury is known to cause brain damage and damage to the central nervous system. It is also teratogenic and can cause genetic damage in humans.

Pits, ponds, and lagoons are a natural topographic depression, artificial excavation, or dike arrangement above, below, or partially in the ground for holding, treating, or storing waste.

Selenium is used in manufacture of electronics equipment, steel, pigments, glass, and ceramics. Acute exposure to selenium can cause eye, lung, and heart damage.

Trichloroethylene (TCE) is used as a solvent. TCE is toxic to both aquatic organisms and humans. It has been shown to be an effective carcinogen in test animals.

Step 3: Evaluating a Company's Disposal Site

The Toxics Lexicon also briefly describes the type of disposal facilities that are in the questionnaire. Obviously, you cannot make an expert assessment of the adequacy of an enterprise's disposal practices unless you have professionals advising you. (We recommend a search for volunteer experts at local universities and among community organizations). You should be

able to raise some hard questions and prod governmental officials into ensuring that adequate answers are obtained.

Hazardous waste generators can minimize the amount of waste created
initially through changes in production processes and waste recycling. The
amount of waste destined for land disposal can be further minimized by
offering wastes for recycling by other enterprises and by incineration. Where
feasible, hazardous wastes should be neutralized. The irreducible amount of
hazardous waste remaining must be encapsulated so it will not threaten
human health or the environment. The following describes the safety needs
for those types of land disposal.

LANDFILL

Water is the biggest enemy in ensuring that land emplacement of hazardous waste will remain safe. The most important characteristics of any
site are those that prevent water from penetrating the site, coming into
contact with hazardous waste, and then escaping the site. The principles
here should be incorporated in any land disposal site.

1. The bottom of the site should be a minimum of five feet above the
underground water table. If the site is located in sandy type soils, it should be
at least ten feet above groundwater, especially if the groundwater is a source
of drinking water. Active sites over aquifers that provide the sole source of
public drinking water should be eliminated.

2. No site should be in contact with any surface waters, including seasonal streams and springs. Sites located on a flood plain represent an obvious hazard.

3. No site should fail to have an impermeable "cover" made of eighteen
inches of clay soil or some plastic or other man-made material. In addition,
the surface of the site should be graded to drain rain water away from the
site. Ponding on the surface of the site is a sure sign of trouble.

4. Sites without a cover or located in sandy soil should have a leachate
collection and treatment system. Such a system catches contaminated water,
or "leachate," as it penetrates the bottom of the site and pumps it to the surface for neutralization before it is discharged.

5. Sites located in sandy soil without a leachate collection system
should have a groundwater monitoring system. Such a system consists of
wells surrounding the site, from which groundwater samples are periodically taken and tested for organic and inorganic chemical contamination.

Other signs of more gross contamination can be found in the form of
oily or discolored surface waters, withered vegetation, and yellow streaks in
foliage (a sign of cadmium and zinc toxicity) nearby the site.

Other factors that should cause concern are

1. The proximity of a disposal site to residential areas where lateral
movement of escaping waters either above or below ground result in direct
human contact.

2. The absence of any financially viable owner of a site who can be
pressed to prevent or abate hazardous waste releases.

3. If the disposal site accepted a variety of wastes without testing them for reactivity and segregrating incompatible wastes, concern should be raised concerning possible adverse chemical reactions if wastes escape and mix.

PITS, PONDS, AND LAGOONS

Because of the high water content of these wastes at their inception, pits, ponds, and lagoons pose an inherently greater threat of escape. Many of these sites have been created to comply with water pollution control requirements. The ponds allow some pollutants to settle out and others to oxidize during long-term exposure to the air. Few of these sites were built with impermeable bottoms or sides because the underlying soil acts as a sponge, absorbing pollutants as the waste passes through. Unfortunately, just as a sponge stops absorbing when it is full of water, the soil stops absorbing pollutants.

Groundwater monitoring around these facilities should be established to measure the movement of pollutants out of the ponds.

A special case is that of carcinogens, which are a threat to humans even when diluted; pit and pond owners should be encouraged to empty those sites containing carcinogens.

LAND FARMING

The principle in land farming is similar to pits, ponds, and lagoons in that the wastes mix with soil and degrade naturally. In land farming the microbial action in the soil enhances the degradation process. Again, however, the disposal technique is used with highly liquid wastes that can run off or percolate to underlying groundwater. In either case, barriers are desirable. Where barriers do not exist, groundwater monitoring is advisable.

STORAGE

Land emplacement is overwhelmingly the most common type of disposal used. Hazardous waste storage must meet fundamentally the same requirements.

Surface runoff tends to be the greatest problem of concern. Waste is not in place long enough to penetrate groundwaters; however, continuous changeover may mean there is equal danger.

Storage of quantities of waste greater than the treatment or disposal capacity of a facility is a sure alarm signal. It may indicate that the site owner is intentionally, or because of insolvency, abandoning responsibility for the site soon.

Step 4: Raising Public Awareness

Once "problem" hazardous waste sites are identified, citizens' options vary greatly.

In the ideal situation, the site owner will cooperate in investigating the potential threats. While the potential for liability for a toxic waste release does exist, unfortunately it is not great. Even assuming the site owner is held strictly liable, or liable regardless of fault, plaintiffs have difficulty proving that the release was the cause of their injury. The most effective tools to encourage cooperation from the site owner are adverse publicity, public pressure, and rigorous state or local enforcement of pollution control laws.

If you have questions about the safety of a site, you must raise them with other citizens, local officials, and local media. Start with citizens' groups. Where a nucleus of groups assisted in the initial survey, work with them to expand your network. Familiarizing the media with potential problems before a network of community groups has been established can help in the creation of the network. Sometimes, however, it is not until community interest has been demonstrated that media interest can be raised.

The rest of the process is simply dependent upon the persistence and ingenuity of the individuals and organizations involved. You can make a difference in the safeguarding of hazardous waste disposal sites in your community and nationwide. Please don't forget to send copies of responses to the questionnaire to either of the following:

A. Blakeman Early   Marchant Wentworth
Sierra Club   Environmental Action
330 Pennsylvania Ave., S.E.   1346 Connecticut Ave., N.W.
Washington, D.C. 20003   Washington, D.C. 20036
(202) 547-1141   (202) 833-1845

Finally, be sure and involve congressmen and senators from your state. They can assist in obtaining action at all levels of government, but acquainting them with problems of hazardous waste in their own communities will improve the chances of obtaining their support for comprehensive national legislation.

Stopping Future Hazards

The "technical" response needed to safeguard an actual or potentially threatening hazardous waste site is highly dependent upon the individual circumstances. Most remedies are not remedies at all, but minimize damage. The ultimate solution to a problem site is the removal of the waste for neutralization, destruction or encapsulation in a safer site. However, often this option will be too costly. The alternative is a combination of actions to contain further waste escapes and monitor for leaking wastes to warn those who may come into contact with them. Containment usually involves digging around and under the site and emplacing leachate collection and pumping devices. All too often, containment involves little more than placing an impermeable "cap" on the site to prevent further infiltration of surface water. The latter effort in most cases is unacceptable because usually large volumes of liquids are already within the site and will escape. The major strategy should be to press for the most effective containment and monitoring system feasible. The monitoring system is key because it can warn of escapes that have already occurred as well as future escapes that indicate a failure of the containment structure.

Once groundwater has been contaminated, remedies are limited. Under some conditions, it is possible to "counter pump" the contaminated water from the aquifer, assuming the underlying structure has not allowed widespread contamination of the "plume." Pumping out the water may be used to either slow the movement of the contaminated plume toward downgradient drinking water wells, or to remove the major part of the contaminants. This option is most viable in circumstances where alternatives to the threatened wells are difficult and costly to acquire. In all cases, the "writing-off" of an aquifer should be resisted. Every effort should be made to maintain the highest quality feasible of underground supplies, for they remain our only hedge against future shortages.

For More Information

National Cancer Institute
9000 Rockville Pike
Bethesda, Md. 20014
(301) 496-5615
Conducts cancer research.

National Institute of Environmental
Health Sciences
P.O. Box 12233
Research Triangle Park, N.C. 27709
(919) 541-3345
Conducts research on environmental hazards.

National Institute for Occupational
Safety and Health
Parklawn Bldg.
5600 Fishers Lane
Rockville, Md. 20857
(301) 443-2140

National Solid Waste Management
Association
1120 Connecticut Ave., N.W.
Washington, D.C. 20036
(202) 659-4613
Represents the major commercial hazardous waste disposal firms—good source on disposal technology.

Occupational Safety and Health
Administration
3rd St. and Constitution Ave., N.W.
Washington, D.C. 20210
(202) 523-9362
Deals with workplace standards to control toxics.

U.S. Environmental Protection Agency
401 M. St., S.W.
Washington, D.C. 20460
Environmental regulations development and enforcement—most regulatory efforts are directed by regional administrators in the ten federal regions headquartered in Boston, New York City, Philadelphia, Atlanta, Kansas City, Dallas, Chicago, Denver, San Francisco, and Seattle.

U.S. Geological Survey
Water Resources Division
National Water Data Exchange
Reston, Va. 22092
860-7444 or 860-6031
Knowledgeable on geology and groundwater nationwide.

Questionnaire

Complete this form for every site (including the location of this facility as one site) used for the disposal of process wastes generated by this facility since 1950.

Company Name
_____

Division/Subsidiary
_____

Facility Name
_____

Name of Site
_____

Address of Site
_____

Name of Owner (while used by facility)
_____

Address
_____

Current Owner (if different from above)
_____

Address
_____

1. Location (1 = the property on which facility is located; 2 = off-site) ..... _____

2. Ownership at time of use (1 = company ownership; 2 = private but
   not company ownership; 3 = public ownership; 9 = don't know) .... _____

3. Company status (1 = closed; 2 = still in use; 9 = don't know) .... _____

   IF CLOSED, specify year closed .... 19_____

4. Year first used for process waste from this facility .... 19_____

5. Year last used for process waste from this facility .... 19_____

6. Total amount of process waste from this facility disposed at site
   IF POSSIBLE, USE TONS

   thousand gallons .... _____

   hundred tons .... _____

   thousand cubic yards.................................... _____

7. Specify type(s) of disposal method(s) used at site and whether method
   is still in use (1 = currently in use; 2 = no longer in use; 3 = never
   used; 9 = don't know)

   landfill, mono industrial waste........................... _____

   landfill, mixed industrial waste .... _____

   landfill, drummed waste .... _____

   landfill, municipal refuse co-disposed.................... _____

   pits/ponds/lagoons .... _____

   deep well injection .... _____

   land farming .... _____

incineration . . . . _____

treatment (e.g. neutralizing) . . . . _____

reprocessing/recycling . . . . _____

other (specify)_____ . . . . _____

8. Users of this site (1 = this facility; 2 = this facility and other company facilities only; 3 = this company and others; 9 = don't know) . . . . _____

LIST NAMES AND ADDRESSES OF OTHER KNOWN USERS BELOW

Company Name _____

Division/Subsidiary _____

Facility _____

Site Name _____

9. Components (or characteristics) of process waste from this facility disposed at site (1 = present in waste; 2 = not present in waste; 9 = don't know) FILL IN EVERY SPACE

Acid solutions, with pH <3 . . . . _____

Base solutions, with pH >12 . . . . _____

Heavy metals & trace metals (bonded organically & inorganically) . . . . . _____

    arsenic, selenium, antimony . . . . _____

    mercury . . . . _____

    iron, manganese, magnesium . . . . _____

    zinc, cadmium, copper, chromium (trivalent) . . . . _____

    chromium (hexavalent) . . . . _____

    lead . . . . _____

Organics . . . . _____

    insecticides & intermediates . . . . _____

    herbicides & intermediates . . . . _____

    fungicides & intermediates . . . . _____

    rodenticides & intermediates . . . . _____

    chlorinated hydrocarbons . . . . _____

    PCBS/PBBS . . . . _____

    amides, amines, imides . . . . _____

    plasticizers . . . . _____

    resins . . . . _____

    solvents polar (except water) and nonpolar . . . . _____

    oils and oil sludges . . . . _____

    esters and ethers . . . . _____

    alcohols . . . . _____

    ketones & aldehydes . . . . _____

dioxins . . . . ____

Inorganics . . . . ____

   salts . . . . ____

   mercaptan . . . . ____

Misc . . . . ____

   pharmaceutical wastes . . . . ____

   paints & pigments . . . . ____

   catalysts (e.g., vanadium, platinum, palladium) . . . . ____

   asbestos . . . . ____

   shock sensitive wastes (e.g., nitrated toluenes) . . . . ____

   air water reactive wastes (e.g., P_6 aluminum chloride) . . . . ____

   wastes with flash point below 100 °F . . . . ____

Source: "Hunt the Dump," by the Sierra Club and Environmental Action, 1980.

Location of Sites Subject to Legal Action by the Hazardous Waste Enforcement Effort of the U.S. Environmental Protection Agency

Acton, Mass.
W. R. Grace & Co. (filed 4/17/80)
Waste migration and seepage from lagoons and a landfill on site have resulted in contamination of soil and a major aquifer supplying 40 percent of the town's drinking water.

Atlantic City, N.J.
Charles Price *et al.* (Price's Landfill) (filed 12/22/80)
Hazardous wastes from the landfill have contaminated soil and numerous private drinking water wells and threaten contamination of the city's public water supply.

Aurora, Mo.
North Eastern Pharmaceutical and Chemical Co., Inc., Syntex Agribusiness, Inc. *et al.* (filed 8/1/80)
Dioxin, 2,4,5-trichlorophenol, and 1,2,4,5-tetrachlorobenzene wastes from a hexachlorophene manufacturing operation threaten contamination of soil, groundwater, and surface water. Defendants have entered into a consent decree with the United States to abate the hazard.

Bristol, Tenn.
Automated Industrial Disposal and Salvage Co., Inc., Tipton Investment Service Co. (filed 8/1/80)
On-site storage and salvage of industrial hazardous wastes have contaminated a nearby creek, soil, and possibly local groundwater. Defendants have entered into a consent decree with the United States to abate the hazard.

Bucks County, Pa.
Fischer and Porter Company, Inc. (filed 10/8/80)
Manufacturing operations utilizing trichloroethylene and perchloroethylene as solvents and degreasers have contaminated groundwater, public and private drinking water wells, and the public sewer system.

Calumet Park, Ill.
Ciszar *et al.* (filed 6/30/80)
Storage of some nine hundred drums containing mostly paints and paint sludges poses a threat of fire and explosion and has contaminated the underlying soil.

Chester, Pa.
Wade Landfill (filed 4/20/79)
Is a hazardous waste storage and disposal facility with deteriorating and mislabeled hazardous waste and a history of fire. There is a continuing fire hazard and threatened contamination to groundwater and surface water.

Chicago, Ill.
Acme Refining Company *et al.* (filed
6/20/80)
  Wastes leaking from barrels stored
on site have contaminated soil and
entered the sanitary sewer system. The
site poses a threat of fire resulting from
proximity to a liquid-oxygen storage
tank.

Cleveland, Ohio
Chemicals and Minerals Reclamation,
Inc. (filed 7/10/79)
  Improper storage of approximately
six thousand 55-gallon drums containing hazardous waste crowded into an
abandoned warehouse poses an imminent threat of fire and explosion.

Columbia, S.C.
South Carolina Recycling and Disposal, Inc. *et al.* (filed 7/7/80)
  Storage, treatment, transport, and
disposal of solid and hazardous wastes
have contaminated soil, caused fires
and explosions, and pose threats of
additional fires, explosions, and
groundwater contamination.

East Baton Rouge, La.
Petro Processors of Louisiana, Inc. *et al.*
(filed 7/15/80)
  Improper storage and disposal of
wastes by owner/operator and eleven
named generators have resulted in surface water and soil contamination and
threaten contamination of drinking
water and the food chain.

East Chicago, Ind.
Lloyd L. Hodges *et al.* (filed 8/25/80)
  Improper storage of asbestos from
the dismantling of an oil refinery poses a
threat to the project workers and to the
neighboring community.

Elyria, Ohio
Chemical Recovery Systems, Inc. (filed
10/7/80)
  Wastes from a chemical processing
and disposal operation have polluted
soil, a nearby river, and threaten to
contaminate groundwater.

Flemington, N.C.
Waste Industries, Inc. (filed 1/11/80)
  Improper disposal of liquid and solid
hazardous waste into a landfill has resulted in toxic chemicals leaching into
nearby private residential wells.

Gary, Ind.
KOR Corporation and David Suhm
(filed 9/12/80)
  Chemical wastes from production of
industrial cleaners and rust removers
have created a health and fire hazard to
nearby residents.

Gary, Ind.
Midwest Solvent Recovery, Inc. (Mid
Co.) (filed 11/16/79)
  Approximately fourteen thousand de-
teriorating 55-gallon drums are stored
on site, which has had at least one fire.
There is imminent threat of further fire
and/or explosion.

Gary, Ind.
Steve Martell, Irvin Clark, *et al.* (9th
Avenue Site) (filed 8/26/80)
  Waste disposal operations at this
twenty-acre site have created a fire
hazard and present an imminent and
substantial hazard to health and the
environment.

Hamilton, Ohio
Chem-Dyne Corporation (filed
12/19/79)
  Improper storage and disposal of hazardous waste in drums and tanks have
resulted in past fires and continued
threat of explosion and fire, as well as
contamination of groundwater and surface water.

Hammond, Ind.
Ken Industries, Inc. *et al.* (filed 8/1/80)
  Operations at a scrap metal facility
have caused one major fire, threaten
future fires, and continue to release
toxic chemicals into the environment.

Jacksonville, Ark.
Vertac Chemical Corporation and
Hercules, Inc. (filed 3/4/80)
  Improper disposal of hazardous
wastes at various locations on site has

resulted in contamination of surface waters, surrounding soil, and municipal sewage system with various hazardous chemicals, including dioxin.

Jefferson, Ohio*
Laskin Greenhouse and Waste Oil Co. (filed 4/24/79)

Owner/operator has spread oil contaminated with PCBs onto county roads (Ashtabula County); burned similar oil in his boiler, thereby contaminating the air; and allowed PCB-contaminated water to enter a nearby creek.

Jefferson County, Colo.
American Ecological Recycle Research Corporation, Donald K. Gums (filed 6/24/80)

Reclamation and storage of waste solvents and oil have resulted in one fire and threaten future fires, explosions, and emissions of toxic fumes.

Kansas City, Mo.
Conservation Chemical Company et al. (filed 9/29/80)

Wastes from a hazardous waste storage, treatment, and disposal facility have contaminated groundwater, adjoining agricultural land, and threaten contamination of the Missouri and Blue rivers.

King of Prussia, Pa.
Stanley Kessler Company, Inc. et al. (filed 9/2/80)

Organic solvents used in the production of welding rod wire have contaminated an aquifer and threaten a reservoir that supplies drinking water for approximately eight hundred thousand people.

Kingston, N.H.*
Ottati and Goss, Inc. et al. (filed 5/15/80)

Activities at a waste storage and disposal site and a drum reconditioning facility have created a fire hazard and have contaminated soil, surface water, and groundwater.

LaPorte County, Ind.
Fisher-Calo Chemicals and Solvents Corporation et al. (filed 7/3/80)

Wastes from a storage, disposal, and reclamation facility disposed in unlined lagoons, drum burial sites, and aboveground areas have resulted in groundwater and soil contamination.

Lathrop, Calif.
Hooker (filed 12/18/79)

On-site disposal of wastes from production of agricultural products and pesticides has resulted in contamination of groundwater used as a public drinking water source.

Logan Township, N.J.
Bridgeport Rental and Oil Services, Inc. et al. (filed 10/2/80)

Wastes from an eleven-acre waste-oil storage lagoon and a fifty-eight tank storage area have contaminated soil, groundwater, and a tributary of the Delaware River.

McClain County, Ok.
Royal N. Hardage (filed 9/8/80)

Waste-disposal operations at this sixty-acre facility threaten continued release of dioxin, asbestos, cyanides, and other toxic chemicals into the air, soil, groundwater, and a nearby creek.

---

*"Uncontrolled sites" subject to ongoing emergency response action by the EPA (see Appendix IX). Other uncontrolled sites not yet subject to legal action by the EPA include: Chemical Control Co., Elizabeth, N.J.; Cordova Chemical, North Muskegon, Mich.; French Ltd., Barrett, Tex.; Gilson Road (Sylvester) Site, Nashua, N.H.; Goose Farm, Plumstead, N.J.; Gurley Refinery, West Memphis, Ark.; Holden Municipal Landfill, Holden, Mass.; Mottollo Site, Raymond, N.H.; National Wood Preservers, Haverford, Pa.; Ohio Steel Drum, Cleveland, Ohio; Old Mill Site, Rock Creek, Ohio; Old York Oil Co., Moira, N.Y.; Outboard Marine Co., Waukegan, Ill.; Picillo Site, Coventry, R.I.; Pollution Abatement Services, Oswego, N.Y.; and Summit National Liquid Services, Deerfield, Ohio.

Malvern, Iowa
Robert Richter (filed 3/21/80)
Storage of drums of solid and hazardous chemical wastes in an old warehouse presents an imminent and substantial endangerment of fire, explosion, and generation of toxic gases.

Mantua and Harrison Townships, N.J.*
Li Pari Landfill (filed 3/21/80)
The owner/operator of the landfill accepted hazardous chemical wastes, which have contaminated adjoining streams, a nearby lake, and soil and which have emitted noxious odors that have affected the health of area residents.

Mission, Tex.
Franklin J. Dusek, Helena Chemical Co., Tex-Ag., Inc. (filed 5/5/80)
Pesticides and related chemicals from an inactive pesticide production facility have contaminated soil and are being transported by the wind into the surrounding residential neighborhood, threatening the health of area residents.

New Castle County, Del.
New Castle County, William C. Ward, *et al.* (Tybouts Landfill) (filed 10/8/80)
Wastes migrating from an inactive fifty-acre municipal sanitary landfill have contaminated portions of the Columbia and Potomac aquifers and at least one private drinking water well.

Niagara Falls, N.Y.*
Hooker Love Canal (filed 12/20/79)
Hooker 102nd Street (filed 12/20/79)
Hooker "S" Area (filed 12/20/79)
Hooker Hyde Park (filed 12/20/79)

Nitro, W. Va.
Fike Chemicals, Inc., C.S.T., Inc., and Coastal Tank Liners, Inc. (filed 12/5/80)
Chemicals manufacturing, transport, and treatment by three associated defendants have contaminated soil, surface water, and groundwater.

Painesville, Ohio
Diamond Shamrock Corporation (filed 10/7/80)

Operations at an inactive facility that processed chemicals containing chromium have contaminated groundwater, surface water, and soil.

Philadelphia, Pa.
Union Corporation, Metal Bank of America (filed 4/23/80)
PCB-contaminated oil has leached from an underground storage tank, contaminating soil, underlying groundwater, and the Delaware River, threatening the water supply of Philadelphia's Torresdale Drinking Water Plant.

Providence, Md.
Spectron, Inc., Paul J. Mraz (filed 6/17/80)
Operations at an industrial-solvent recycling facility engaged in storing and processing spent organic solvents for reuse by industry have resulted in contamination of soil, surface water, and groundwater.

Reserve, La.
2001 Inc., Southeastern Chemical Company, Inc., and two individuals (filed 3/5/80)
Storage of incompatible and hazardous substances in leaking or deteriorating containers is threatening the release of poisonous gases, explosion, fire, and air, water, and soil contamination.

Richland and Cumberland Counties, Ill.
A & F Materials Company, Inc. *et al.* (filed 9/3/80)
Discharges of oil and other pollutants at two waste-disposal sites owned by A & F Materials Company, Inc. have contaminated soil and surface waters and possibly groundwater.

Riverview, Mich.
BASF Wyandotte Corporation and Federal Marine Terminals, Inc. (filed 9/30/80)
Wastes dumped at this thirty-acre site near the Detroit River have contaminated soil, surface water, and groundwater.

Romulus, Mich.
Chemcentral-Detroit Corporation (filed 10/3/80)

Operations at this chemical distribution facility have led to contamination of the soil, surface water, and groundwater.

St. Louis Park, Minn.
Reilly Tar and Chemical Corporation *et al.* (filed 9/4/80)
Operations at a coal-tar refining facility have contaminated soil and groundwater, polluting an aquifer system that supplies drinking water to the Minneapolis–St. Paul metropolitan area.

Scotch Plains, N.J.*
Kin-Buc Landfill (filed 2/7/79)
Hazardous waste landfill. Improper disposal of liquid and solid hazardous waste over nearly a decade has contaminated groundwater and surface water.

Seattle, Wash.
US *vs.* Ronald S. West *et al.* (Chemical Processors, Inc.) (filed 12/31/80)

Seffner, Fla.
County of Hillsborough (Taylor Road Landfill) (filed 10/9/80)
Landfill operations in a forty-two-acre section of a two-hundred-and-seventy-two-acre site have contaminated soil, groundwater, and private drinking water wells and threaten contamination of a public water system.

Seymour, Ind.*
Seymour Recycling Corporation *et al.* (filed 5/9/80)
Leachate from forty thousand to sixty thousand barrels of solid and hazardous wastes has contaminated a navigable waterway of the United States and polluted soil and shallow groundwater.

Southington, Conn.
Solvents Recovery, Inc., Lori Engineering (filed 12/17/79)
Improper disposal of industrial solvents and waste chemicals on the ground and in lagoons has resulted in contamination of groundwater used as a public drinking water source.

Tampa, Fla.
Gulf Coast Lead Company (filed 10/9/80)
Wastes from a secondary lead smelting and reclaiming facility have contaminated soil and shallow groundwater and threaten the Floridian aquifer, the principal drinking water source of the city of Tampa.

Waynesboro, Tenn.
Waynesboro *et al.* (filed 5/30/80)
Disposal of wastes containing PCBs and trichloroethylene at an old dump has resulted in contamination of a United States waterway and threatens contamination of groundwater.

Youngsville, Pa.*
Robert J. Burns, Daniel Dracup, Robert E. Ward, Jr., *et al.* (filed 10/3/80)
Storage and disposal of PCB-contaminated fluids at a warehouse in Youngsville have contaminated soil, surface water, groundwater, and potential drinking water.

Federal Statutes Governing Toxic Wastes and Substances

Statute	U.S. Code
Comprehensive Environmental Response, Compensation, and Liability Act	42 U.S.C. §9601
Resource Conservation and Recovery Act	42 U.S.C. §6901
Toxic Substances Control Act	15 U.S.C. §2601
Clean Water Act	33 U.S.C. §1251
Clean Air Act	42 U.S.C. §7401
Safe Drinking Water Act	42 U.S.C. §300(f)
Federal Insecticide, Fungicide, and Rodenticide Act	7 U.S.C. §136
Consumer Product Safety Act	15 U.S.C. §2051
Occupational Safety and Health Act	29 U.S.C. §651
Hazardous Materials Transportation Act	49 U.S.C. §1801
Federal Hazardous Substances Act	15 U.S.C. §1261
Uranium Mill Tailings Radiation Control Act	42 U.S.C. §7901
Federal Food, Drug, and Cosmetic Act	21 U.S.C. §301
Poison Prevention Packaging Act	15 U.S.C. §1471
Lead-Based Paint Poisoning Prevention Act	42 U.S.C. §4801
Federal Disaster Relief Act	42 U.S.C. §5121
Marine Protection, Research, and Sanctuaries Act*	33 U.S.C. §1401
Deepwater Ports Act*	33 U.S.C. §1501
Outer Continental Shelf Lands Act*	43 U.S.C. §1801
Intervention on the High Seas Act*	33 U.S.C. §1471
Trans-Alaska Pipeline Act*	43 U.S.C. §1651
Ports and Waterways Safety Act*	33 U.S.C. §1221

*These statutes relate primarily to oil as a hazardous substance.

Source: U.S. Code.

APPENDIX VIII

Imminent-Hazard Provisions of Federal Statutes

Statute	U.S. Code
Comprehensive Environmental Response, Compensation, and Liability Act	§§9604, 9606
Resource Conservation and Recovery Act	§6973
Toxic Substances Control Act	§2606
Clean Water Act	§1321(e)
Clean Air Act	§7603(a)
Safe Drinking Water Act	§300(i)
Federal Insecticide, Fungicide, and Rodenticide Act	§136(e)
Consumer Product Safety Act	§2061
Occupational Safety and Health Act	§662(a)
Hazardous Materials Transportation Act	§1810(b)
Federal Hazardous Substances Act	
Uranium Mill Tailings Radiation Control Act	
Federal Food, Drug, and Cosmetic Act	
Poison Prevention Packaging Act	
Lead-Based Paint Poisoning Prevention Act	
Federal Disaster Relief Act	
Marine Protection, Research, and Sanctuaries Act*	§1415(d)
Deepwater Ports Act*	§1511(b)

*These statutes relate primarily to oil as a hazardous substance.

Source: U.S. Code.

APPENDIX IX

Proposed Superfund Priorities List, December 1982

Alabama: Mowbray Engineering, Greenville; Perdido Groundwater Contamination, Perdido; Triana-Tennessee River, Limestone and Morgan Counties. **Arkansas:** Cecil Lindsey, Newport; Crittenden Co. Landfill, Marion; Fritt Industries, Walnut Ridge; Gurley Pit, Edmondson; Industrial Waste Control, Ft. Smith; Mid-South, Mena; Vertac Inc., Jacksonville. **Arizona:** Indian Bend Wash Area, Scottsdale; Kingman Airport Industrial Area, Kingman; Litchfield Airport Area, Goodyear; Mt. View Mobile Home, Globe; Tucson Int'l Airport, Tucson; 19th Ave. Landfill, Phoenix. **California:** Aerojet, Rancho Cordova; Celtor Chemical, Hoppa; Coast Wood Preserving, Ukiah; Iron Mt. Mine, Redding; Jibboom Junkyard, Sacramento; Liquid Gold, Richmond; McColl, Fullerton; MGM Brakes, Cloverdale; Purity Oil Sales Inc., Fresno; Selma Pressure Treating, Fresno; Stringfellow, Glen Avon Heights. **Colorado:** California Gulch, Leadville; Central City-Clear Creek, Idaho Springs; Denver Radium Site, Denver; Marshall Landfill, Boulder; Sand Creek, Commerce City; Woodbury Chem., Commerce City. **Connecticut:** Beacon Heights, Beacon Falls; Laurel Park Inc., Naugatuck; Solvents Recovery System Inc., Southington, Yaworski, Canterbury. **Delaware:** Army Creek, New Castle; DE City PVC Plant, Delaware City; Delaware Sand and Gravel, New Castle; Harvey Knott Drum Site, Kirkwood; New Castle Steel Site, New Castle; Tris Spill Site, New Castle; Tybouts Corner, New Castle County; Wildcat Landfill, Dover. **Florida:** Alpha Chemical, Galloway; Amer. Creosote, Pensacola; Brown Wood, Live Oak; Coleman Evans, Whitehouse; Davie Landfill, Davie; Florida Steel, Indiantown; Gold Coast Oil, Miami; Hollingsworth, Ft. Lauderdale; Kassauf-Kimerling, Tampa; Miami Drum, Miami; Munisport, North Florida; NW 58th St., Hialeah; Parramore Surplus, Mt. Pleasant; Pickettville Landfill, Jacksonville; Pioneer Sand, Warrington; Reeves SE Galvanizing, Tampa; Sapp Battery, Cottondale; Schuylkill Metals, Plant City; Sherwood Medical, Deland; Taylor Rd. Landfill, Seffner; Tower Chemical, Clermont; Varsol Spill, Miami; Whitehouse Oil Pits, Whitehouse; Zellwood; 62nd St. Dump, Tampa. **Iowa:** Aidex Corp., Council Bluffs; Dico, Des Moines; Labounty Site, Charles City. **Idaho:** Arrcom, Rathdrum; Bunker Hill, Smelterville; Flynn Lumber Co., Caldwell. **Illinois:** A&F Materials, Greenup; Acme Solvent/Morristown, Winnebago; Belvidere; Byron Salvage Yard, Ogle County; Cross Bros/Pembroke, Pembroke; Galesburg/Koopers, Galesburg; Johns-Mansville, Waukegan; Lasalle Elec. Util., La Salle; Outboard Marine Corp., Waukegan; Velsicol Ill., Marshall; Wauconda Sand and Gravel, Wauconda. **Kansas:** Arkansas City Dump, Arkansas City; Doepke Disposal, Holiday; John's Sludge Pond, Wichita; Tar Creek, Cherokee County. **Kentucky:** A.L. Taylor, Brooks;

Airco, Calvert City; B.F. Goodrich, Calvert City; Distler Brickyard, West Point; Distler Farm, Jefferson County; Lee's Lane Landfill, Louisville; Newport Dump, Newport. **Louisiana:** Bayou Bonfouca, Slidell; Bayou Sorrel; Cleve Reber, Sorento; Old Inger, Darrow. **Massachusetts:** Baird & McGuire, Holbrook; Cannon Engineering, Bridgewater; Charles-George, Tyngsboro; Groveland Wells, Groveland; Hocomoco Pond, Westborough; Industrial-Plex, Woburn; New Bedford; Nyanza Chemical, Ashland; Plymouth Harbor/Cordage, Plymouth; PSC Resources, Palmer; Re-Solve, Dartmouth; Silresim, Lowell; W. R. Grace, Acton; Wells G&H, East Woburn. **Maryland:** Limestone Rd., Cumberland; Middletown Rd. Dump, Annapolis; Sand, Gravel & Stone, Elkton. **Maine:** McKin Co., Gray; O'Connor Site, Augusta; Pinette Salvage Yard, Washburn; Saco Tanning, Saco; Winthrop Landfill, Winthrop. **Michigan:** Anderson Development, Adrian; Auto Ion, Kalamazoo; Berlin & Farro, Swartz Creek; Butterworth #2 Landfill, Grand Rapids; Cemetery Dump, Rose Township; Charlevoix Municipal Well, Charlevoix; Chem Central, Grand Rapids; Clare Water Supply, Clare; Cliff/Dow Dump, Marquette; Duell & Gardner Landfill, Muskegon; Electrovoice, Buchanan; Forest Waste Products, Otisville; G&H Landfill, Utica; Grand Traverse Overall Supply Co., Greilickville; Gratiot Co. Golf Course, St. Louis; Gratiot Co. Landfill, St. Louis; Hedblum Ind., Oscoda; Ionia City Landfill, Ionia; K&L Avenue Landfill, Kalamazoo; Kentwood Landfill, Kentwood; Liquid Disposal Inc., Utica; Littlefield Dump, Oden; Mason Co. Landfill, Ludington; McGraw Edison, Albien; Northernaire Plating, Cadillac; Novaco Ind., Temperance; Organic Chemicals, Grandville; Ossineke, South Ossineke; Ott/Story/Cordova, Muskegon; Packaging Corp. of America, Filer City; Petoskey Mun. Wells, Petoskey; Rasmussen's Dump, Brighton; Rose Township Dump, Rose Township; SCA Landfill, Muskegon; Shiawassee River, Livingston Co; SW Ottawa Landfill, Park Township; Sparta Landfill, Sparta: Spartan Chem. Co., Wyoming; Spiegelburg Landfill, Brighton; Springfield Township Dump, Davisburg; Tar Lake, Mancelona; U.S. Aviex, Niles; Velsicol Mich., St. Lewis; Verona Well Field, Pennfield Township; Wash King Laundry, Pleasant Plains TWP; Whitehall Wells, Whitehall. **Minnesota:** Burlington Northern, Brainerd/Baxter; FMC, Fridley; Kopper's Coke, St. Paul; Lehillier; National Lead Taracorp, St. Louis Park; New Brighton; Oakdale; Reilly Tar, St. Louis Park; South Andover Site, Andover; Waste Disposal Engineering, Anoka Co. **Missouri:** Arena 1, Moscow Mills; Arena 2; Fills 1&2, Imperial; Ellisville Site, Ellisville; Fulbright Landfill, Springfield; Syntex Facility, Verona; Times Beach. **Montana:** Anaconda, Anaconda; Libby Ground Water, Libby; Milltown; Silver Bow Creek, Silver

Bow/Deer Lodge. **North Carolina:** Chemtronics, Inc.,
Swannanoa; Martin Marietta, Sodyeco, Charlotte; PCB
Spills, 210 Miles of Roads. **New Hampshire:** Auburn Rd.
Landfill, Londonderry; Dover Landfill, Dover; Kes-
Epping, Epping; Ottati & Goss, Kingston; Somersworth
Landfill, Somersworth; Sylvester, Nashua, Nashua;
Tinkham Site, Londonderry. **New Jersey:** A.O. Polymer,
Sparta; American Cynamid, Bound Brook; Asbestos
Dump, Millington; Beachwood/Berkley Wells, Berkley;
Bog Creek Farm, Howell Township; Brick Township
Landfill, Brick Township; Bridgeport Rent. & Oil,
Bridgeport; Burnt Fly Bog, Marlboro Township; Caldwell
Trucking, Fairfield; Chemical Control, Elizabeth;
Chemsol, Piscataway; Combe Fill North Landfill, Mt.
Olive Township; Combe Fill South Landfill, Chester;
CPS/Madison Industries, Old Bridge Township; D'Imperio
Property, Hamilton Township; Denzer Schafer X-Ray,
Bayville; Dover Municipal Well 4, Dover; Ellis Property,
Evesham; Evor Phillips, Old Bridge; Fair Lawn Wellfield,
Fair Lawn; Friedman Property, Freehold Township; Gems
Landfill, Gloucester Township; Goose Farm, Plumstead
Township; Helen Kramer Landfill, Mantua; Hercules,
Gibbstown; Imperial Oil, Marlboro Township; Jackson
Township Landfill, Jackson Township; JIS Landfill, South
Brunswick TWP; Kin-Buc Landfill, Edison; King of
Prussia, Winslow Township; Krysowaty Farm, Hillsbo-
rough; Lang Property, Pemberton Township; Lipari Land-
fill, Pittman; Lone Pine Landfill, Freehold; M&T Delisa
Landfill, Asbury Park; Mannheim Avenue Dump, Gallo-
way Township; Maywood Chemical Sites, Maywood &
Rochelle Pk; Metaltec/Aerosystems, Franklin Township;
Monroe Township Landfill, Monroe Township; Mont-
gomery Housing Dev., Montgomery Township; Myers
Property, Franklin Township; N.L. Industries, Pedrick-
town; Pepe Field, Boonton; Pijak Farm, Plumstead; PJP
Landfill, Jersey City; Price Landfill, Pleasantville; Reich
Farms, Dover Township; Renora, Edison; Ringwood
Mines/Landfill, Ringwood; Rockaway Boro Wellfield,
Rockaway Boro; Rockaway Township Wells, Rockaway
Township; Rocky Hill Municipal Well, Rocky Hill;
Roebling Steel Co., Florence; Sayreville Landfill,
Sayreville; Scientific Chemical Processing, Carlstadt;
Shakey Landfill, Parsippany, Troy Hls; South Brunswick
Landfill, South Brunswick; Spence Farm, Plumstead;
Swope Oil and Chemical, Pennsauken; Syncon Resins,
South Kearny; Toms River Chemical, Dover Township;
Universal Oil Products, East Rutherford; US Radium,
Orange; Vineland State School, Vineland; Williams
Property, Swainton. **New Mexico:** ATSF/CLOVIS , Clovis;
Homestake, Milan; South Valley, Albuquerque; United
Nuclear Corp., Churchrock. **New York:** American
Thermostat, South Cairo; Batavia Landfill, Batavia;
Brewster Well Field, Brewster; Facet Enterprises, Elmira
Heights; Fulton Terminals, Fulton; GE Moreau Site,
South Glens Falls; Hooker-Hyde Park, Niagara Falls;
Hooker-S Area, Niagara Falls; Hooker-102nd Street,
Niagara Falls; Kentucky Ave. Wellfield, Horseheads; Love
Canal, Niagara Falls; Ludlow Sand & Gravel, Clayville;
Marathon Battery, Cold Springs; Mercury Refining,
Albany; Niagara County Refuse, Wheatfield; Old Beth-
page Landfill, Oyster Bay; Olean Wellfield, Olean;
Pollution Abatement Services, Oswego; Port Washington
Landfill, Port Washington; Ramapo Landfill, Ramapo;
Sinclair Refinery, Wellsville; Solvent Savers, Lincklaen;
Syosset Landfill, Oyster Bay; Vestal Water Supply, Vestal;

Wide Beach Development, Brant; York Oil Company,
Moira. **Ohio:** Allied Chemical, Ironton; Arcanum Iron &
Metal, Arcanum; Big D Campgrounds, Kingsville; Bowers
Landfill, Circleville; Buckeye Reclamation, St. Clairsville;
Chem Dyne, Hamilton; Coshocton City Landfill, Coshoc-
ton; E.H. Schilling Landfill, Ironton; Fields Brook,
Ashtabula; Fultz Landfill, Byesville; Nease Chemical,
Salem; New Lyme Landfill, Dodgeville; Poplar Oil, Jeffer-
son; Pristine, Reading; Rock Creek/Jack Webb, Rock
Creek; Skinner Landfill, West Chester; Summit National,
Deerfield; Van Dale Junkyard, Marietta; Zanesville Well
Field, Zanesville. **Oklahoma:** Criner/Hardage, Criner;
Tar Creek, Ottawa County. **Oregon:** Gould, Inc., Port-
land; Teledyne Wah Chang, Albany. **Pennsylvania:**
Blosenski Landfill, West Chester TWP; Brodhead Creek,
Stroudsburg; Bruin Lagoon, Bruin Boro; Centre County
Kepone, State College; Craig Farm Drum Site, Parker;
Douglasville Disposal, Douglasville; Drake Chemical Inc.,
Lock Haven; Enterprise Avenue, Philadelphia; Fischer &
Porter, Warminster; Havertown PCP Site, Haverford;
Heleva Landfill, West Ormrod; Hranica, Buffalo; Kim-
berton, Kimberton; Lackawanna Refuse, Old Forge;
Lehigh Electric, Old Forge; Lindane Dump, Harrison
Township; Lord Shope, Girard Township; Malvern TCE
Site, Malvern; MCADOO, McAdoo; Metal Banks, Philadel-
phia; Moyers Landfill, Lower Providence TWP; Old City
of York Landfill, Seven Valleys; Osborne, Grove City;
Palmerton Zinc Pile, Palmerton; Presque Isle, Erie; Resin
Disposal, Jefferson; Stanley Kessler, King of Prussia;
Voortman, Upper Saucon TWP; Wade (ABM), Chester;
Westline, Westline. **Puerto Rico:** Barceloneta Landfill,
Florida Afuera; Frontera Creek, Rio Abajo; GE Wiring
Devices, Juana Diaz; Juncos Landfill, Juncos; RCA Del
Caribe, Barceloneta. **Rhode Island:** Davis Liquid, Smith-
field; Forestdale, North Smithfield; L & RR-N Smithfield,
North Smithfield; Peterson/Puritan, Cumberland; Picillo
Coventry, Coventry; Western Sand & Gravel, Burrillville.
South Carolina: Carolawn, Inc., Fort Lawn; SCRDI Bluff
Road, Columbia; SCRDI Dixiana, Cayce. **Tennessee:**
Amnicola Dump, Chattanooga; Galloway Ponds, Gal-
loway; Lewisburg Dump, Lewisburg; Murray Ohio
Dump, Lawrenceburg; North Hollywood Dump, Mem-
phis; Velsicol Chemical Co., Toone. **Texas:** Bio-Ecology,
Grand Prairie; Crystal Chemical, Houston; French, Ltd.,
Crosby; Harris (Farley St), Houston; Highlands Acid Pit,
Highlands; MOTCO, LaMarque; Sikes Disposal Pits,
Crosby; Triangle Chemical, Orange County. **Virginia:**
Chisman, York County; Matthews, Roanoke County;
Saltville Waste Disposal, Saltville; US Titanium, Piney
River. **Vermont:** Old Springfield Landfill, Springfield;
Pine Street Canal, Burlington. **Washington:** Colbert Land-
fill, Spokane; Com. Bay, Near Shore Tide Flat, Tacoma;
Com. Bay, S. Tacoma Channel, Tacoma; FMC Yakima,
Yakima; Frontier Hard Chrome, Vancouver; Harbor
Island Lead, Seattle; Kaiser Mead, Mead; Lakewood,
Lakewood; Pesticide Pit, Yakima; Western Processing,
Kent. **West Virginia:** Fike Chemical, Nitro; Follansbee
Sludge Fill, Follansbee; Leetown Pesticide Pile, Leetown;
West VA Ordnance, Point Pleasant. **Other State Sites:**
Plastifax, Gulfport, Mississippi; Arsenic Trioxide Site,
Southeastern, North Dakota; Phillips Chemical, Beatrice,
Nebraska; Whitewood Creek, Whitewood, South Dakota;
Rose Park Sludge Pit, Salt Lake City, Utah; Baxter/Union
Pacific, Laramie, Wyoming.

Source: U.S. Environmental Protection Agency, Proposed Superfund List, December, 1982.

EPA's Listings of Potential Hazardous Waste Disposal Sites

Alabama

Bishop's Ldfl.
Rte. 7
Albertsville

Alexander Ppty.
Rte. 2
Alpine

Anniston Plant Ldfl.
Hwy. 202 W.
Anniston

Kevlar Waste Stge.
Hwy. 62
Anniston

Monsanto Waste
Anniston

Plant Ldfl.
Hwy. 202 W.
Anniston

Cuttler Hammer
Box 951
Athens

Jefferson Elect.
Athens

Petro Prod., Inc.
Hwy. 72
Athens

Brine Sludge Pond
Box 100
Axis

Mobile Plant
Box 525
Axis

Stauffer Plant Ldfl.
Box 100
Axis

Alpine Labs
Bay Minette

Baldwin Coun.
Ldfl.
Box 150
Bay Minette

Bolon Ppty.
Rabun Rd.
Bay Minette

City Dump
W. 7th St.
Bay Minette

E. R. Brantley
Newport Pkwy.
Bay Minette

Kilcrease Rd. Ldfl.
Stockton Hwy./
Kilcrease Rd.
Bay Minette

Red Hill Ldfl.
Dobson Ave.
Bay Minette

Bessemer Plant
Box 190
Bessemer

By-Product Lake
Box 752
Bessemer

Jefferson Coun.
Ldfl.
Bessemer

Koppers Co.
(plus 1 other site)
Woodward Rd.
Bessemer

Alabama Testing
Lab
Central Ave.
Birmingham

Allied Chem. Corp.
Center St.
Birmingham

Baptist Med. Ctr.
Montclair Rd.
Birmingham

Birmingham
Platting
N. 17th St.
Birmingham

Buckner Barrel
Birmingham

Dolomite
Tin Hill Rd.
Birmingham

Edgewater
Canada-Jamaica
Birmingham

McWane Cast Iron
Pipe
Vanderbilt Rd.
Birmingham

New Georgia Ldfl.
47th St.
Birmingham

Shannon Ldfl.
(plus 1 other
site)
Shannon Rd.
Birmingham

Swift Agri-Chem.
14th Ave.
Birmingham

U.S. Steel
Tin Mill
Birmingham

H&S Chem.
Blountsville

Stauffer Chem.
Corp.
Box 32
Bucks

Cherokee Ala.
Box 250
Cherokee

American
Cyanamid
Plant Rd.
Childersburg

Goins Ppty.
Hwy. 235/Forest
Hills
Childersburg

Henderson Ppty.
Birmingham Hwy.
Childersburg

Osborne Ppty.
Birmingham Hwy.
Childersburg

Randle Ppty.
Birmingham Hwy.
Childersburg

Tennis Ct. Sport
N. Sports Complex
Childersburg

Tuscaloosa Coun.
  Ldfl.
Coker

City of Decator
Old Moulton Rd.
Decator

Creosote
Tenn. R.
Decator

Decator Munic.
Hwy. 31
Decator

Decator Plant
Finley Is. Rd.
Decator

Decator Site
Decator

Goodyear Incin.
19th Ave.
Decator

Johnson Ldfl.
Decator

Monsanto Plant
Box 2204
Decator

Munic. Ldfl.
Decator

3-M Co.
Hwy. 20/State
Decator

Borden Chem Plant
Lock/Dam Rds.
Demopolis

City of Demopolis
McDowell Ferry
  Rd.
Demopolis

City Dump
  Compton
Demopolis

City Dump Lagoon
McDowell Ferry
  Rd.
Demopolis

Demopolis Plant
N. Jeff. St.
Demopolis

Carter Ppty.
Rte. 8
Dolomite

Edwards Ppty.
Dennison Ave.
Dolomite

Estech Gen. Chem.
E. Bundershaw
Dothan

County Ldfl.
Elmore Coun.

Chem. Waste
Hwy. 17
Emelle

Waste Mgt. Ala.
Hwy. 17
Emelle

Crow Ldfl.
Rte. 1
Fackler

Fairfield City Dump
Cherokee-Crest
Fairfield

Florence Ldfl.
Florence

Intl. Min. & Chem.
Commerce &
  Union
Florence

Foley Site
  (plus 1 other site)
Foley

Fovil Mfg.
S. Bay St.
Foley

Gadsden Raceway
Rabbitt Town Rd.
Gadsden

M & M Chem.
Gadsden

Spill Site
Hwy. 116

Martin Town Ldfl.
1st & Sheridan
Hollywood

AAA Septic Tank
  Serv.
Box 704
Huntsville

Redstone Arsenal
Huntsville

Technical Micronics
Wynn Dr.
Huntsville

Bucknen Barrels
Irondale

Johns Ldfl.
Jefferson Cn

Spill Site
Lawrence

Monsanto Waste
Limestone

Maringo Coun.
  Ldfl.
Linden

Livingston Site
Livingston

Crenshaw Coun.
  Ldfl.
U.S. 331
Luverne

Anhydrite Ponds
Olin Rd.
McIntosh

Ash Pond & Ldfl.
Off Hwy. 43
McIntosh

Ciba-Geigy
Hwy. 43
McIntosh

Olin Corp
McIntosh

Olin Corp. Lime
Off Hwy. 43
McIntosh

Olin Corp.
  Mercury
Off Hwy. 43
McIntosh

Olin Corp. Old
  Plant
Off Hwy. 43
McIntosh

American
  Cyanamide
Cyanamide Rd.
Mobile

Diamond Shamrock
  (plus 2 other
  sites)
Mobile

Mobile Plant
Cyanamide Rd.
Mobile

Mobile Plant
Jarvis Rd.
Mobile

Southland Pearson
Anton St.
Mobile

Thompson-
  Hayward
Mobile

Crenshaw Coun.
  Ldfl.
Montgomery

Koppers
Louisville St.
Montgomery

Montgomery City
Montgomery

N. Montgomery
  Ldfl.
Davidson St.
Montgomery

Plant Facil.
Louisville St.
Montgomery

Muscle Shoals
  Plant
Muscle Shoals

Gulf Oil Chem. Co.
Parrish

Stauffer Chem. Co.
Main St.
Pennington

Gerald Willis
  Lumb.
Rte. 3
Piedmont

Allied Chem. Corp.
Pleasant Grove

Wylam Hgts.
Pleasant/Main
Pleasant Grove

Bruman Clay Pits
Saraland

Scottboro Plant
Hwy. 79 By-Pass
Scottboro

Strip Mines
Selfville

Diamond Shamrock
  Ldfl.
Wilson Dam Rd.
Sheffield

Browning-Ferris
Ind.
Theodore

Dequssa
Box 606
Theodore

Kerr-McGee
Rangeline Rd.
Theodore

Dump Site
Trinity

Johnson Ldfl.
Johnson Rd.
Trinity

EPC
Turnerville

Reichold Chem.
Reichold Rd.
Tuscaloosa

Diamond Shamrock
Corp.
Box 454
Tuscumbia

Robin Tire
6th St.
Tuscumbia

Birmingham Works
Watson

Koppers Co.—
Coke Plant
Woodward

Alaska

Alaska Electropl.
15th Ave.
Anchorage

Alaska Husky
Battery
Mountain View
Anchorage

Alaska R.R.
1st Ave.
Anchorage

Frontier Tanning
Klatt Rd.
Anchorage

Intl. Airpt.
Anchorage

Liquid Air, Inc.
Arctic Spur Rd.
Anchorage

Merrill Fd. Sanit.
15th/Debar
Anchorage

M&M Ent.
Wyoming St.
Anchorage

Red Devil Waste
Pond
Bethel

Alaskan Battery
Ent.
Richardson Hwy.
Fairbanks

Alaska R.R.
N. Cushman St.
Fairbanks

Earth Movers of
Fairbanks
Aurora St.
Fairbanks

Fairbanks City
Dump
2nd Ave.
Fairbanks

Fairbanks Daily
News
N. Cushman St.
Fairbanks

Fairbanks N. Star
Cushman St. Ext.
Fairbanks

Fairbanks R.R.
Fairbanks

Fairbanks Sand &
Gravel
Richardson Hwy.
Fairbanks

Gerstle R. Test Site
Ft. Greely

Juneau Ldfl.
Juneau

Chevron U.S.A.,
Inc.
Kenai

Collier Carbon &
Chem.
Kenai

Kenai City Dump
Kenai

Old Kenai Dump
Kenai Spur Hwy.
Kenai

Tesco-Alaskan Petr.
N. Kenai Rd.
Kenai

Union Oil Co.
Rte. 1
Kenai

Louisiana-Pac.
Ketchikan

Energy Co.
N. Pole

N. Pole Ref.
Richardson Hwy.
N. Pole

Arco–Prudhoe Bay
Prudhoe Bay

Mukluk Dump
Prudhoe Bay

Sterling Ldfl.
Swanson R. Rd.
Sterling

Arizona

Phelps Dodge Corp.
Well Rd.
Ajo

El Paso Nat. Gas
Avra

Cypress Mine-
Smelter
Baghdad

El Paso Nat. Gas
Benson

Pima Chandler Ind.
Blackwater

Asarco, Inc.—
Sacaton
Casa Grande

Pinal Coun. Dump
S. Chu Chu Rd.
Casa Grande

Ariz. Aerochem.
E. Germann Rd.
Chandler

Midland Ross
Corp.
S. Arizona Ave.
Chandler

Rogers Corp.—
Circut
Williams F. Rd.
Chandler

Duval Corp.—Min.
Chloride

Inspiration Consol.
Christmas

Inspiration Consol.
Claypool

Congress Consol.
Congress

Diamond Drum
Stge.
Burridge St.
Coolidge

Ariz. Tanning Co.
Santan Ind. Pk.
Dock

Phelps Dodge Corp.
Don Luis

Bisbee-Douglas
Intl.
U.S. 666
Douglas

Phelps Dodge Corp.
U.S. 80/Hwy. 66
Douglas

Ponderosa Paper
Prod.
Butler Ave.
Flagstaff

Ariz. Fuels Corp.
Fredonia

Asbestos Mfg. Co.
Hwys. 70 & 77
Globe

Bluebird Mine
Globe

Jaquay's Asbestos
Co.
Box 328
Globe

Metate Asbestos
Co.
Globe

Mtn. View Est.
Rte. 77
Globe

Unidynamic
Phoenix
N. Litchfield Rd.
Goodyear

Midland Ross
Corp.
Kyrene Rd.
Guadelupe

Hella Min. Co.—
  Lake
Gu Komelik

Asarco Copper
  Smelt
Hayden

Kennecott Copper
Hayden Jct.

Cyprus Johnson
  Corp.
Johnson

Black Mesa Coal
  Mine
Kayenta

Gen. Cable Corp.
Ind. Blvd.
Kingman

Zonia Copper Mine
Star Rte.
Kirkland

Marathon Steel Co.
Kyrene Rd.
Kyrene–S. Temple

Citizens Util.
Lake Havasu City

Lake Havasu Sanit.
Lake Havasu Ave.
Lake Havasu City

El Paso Nat. Gas
Littletown

Terminal Sta.
Wilmot Rd. & I-16
Littletown

Ak Chin Ind.
Ak Chin Ind. Pk.
Maricopa Ind.

Mesa Facil.
W. Broadway
Mesa

Talley Ind.
E. McKellips Rd.
Mesa

Cities Serv. Mine
Miami

Inspiration City
Copper Mine
Miami

Nogales Ldfl.
Ariz. 93
Nogales

Ocotillo Pow. Plant
Hayden Rd.
Ocotillo

Salt R. Proj.
Hwy. 22
Page

Palo Nuclear Gen.
Palo Verde

Palo Verde Nuclear
Box 49
Palo Verde

Agua Fria Steam
  Plant
75th/Northern
Peoria

Anocad Plating Co.
W. Cypress Ave.
Phoenix

Ariz. Plating
Central Ave.
Phoenix

Ariz. Sand & Rock
E. Univ. Dr.
Phoenix

Coun. Mdws.
  Unit 9
Phoenix

Fisher Heat
  Treating
W. Mohave
Phoenix

Honeywell Info.
N. Black Cyn.
Phoenix

Kenworth Motor
  Trk.
S. 19th Ave.
Phoenix

Liquid Air, Inc.
W. McDowall Rd.
Phoenix

Lower Buckeye
Lower Buckeye
Phoenix

Nursery
Phoenix

Osborn Prod., Inc.
W. Clarendon
Phoenix

Potential Site
Phoenix

Potential Site
Lower Buckeye
Phoenix

Reynolds Metal
  Perk
Phoenix

Rinchem
15th Ave.
Phoenix

Salt R. Ldfl.
16th/19th/27th
  Aves.
Phoenix

Sperry Flight Sys.
19th Ave.
Phoenix

Union Oil Co.
S. 51st Ave.
Phoenix

Wayne Oxygen Co.
S. 40th St.
Phoenix

Phelps Dodge Corp.
Plantsite

Ariz. Portland
Rillito

Anamax Mining
  Co.—Twi
Box 127
Sahurita

Cypress Met.
Pima Mine Rd.
Sahurita

Duvall Mine—
  Smelter
Sahurita

Apache Powder Co.
Saint David

Salt R.—Coronado
Saint Johns

Tri City Ldfl.
Beeline Hwy.
**Salt River Indian
  Res.**

Magma Copper Co.
  Mine
San Manuel

Asarco, Inc.—
  Mission
San Xavier

Cypress Pima Min.
San Xavier

Motorola Govt.
E. McDowell Rd.
Scottsdale

Asarco, Inc.—
  Silver
Aura Valley Rd.
Silver Bell

Southwest For. Ind.
Snowflake

Somerton Ldfl.
16th St.
Somerton

Kennecott Copper
Sonora

El Paso Nat. Gas
Stanfield

Magma Copper Co.
Superior

Kyrene Steam Plant
Kyrene/Rural
Tempe

Salt R. Proj.
Project Dr.
Tempe

Farmers Agdustries
Tollen

Pure Gro. Co.
99th/Harrison
Tolleson

Res. Chem.
83rd Ave.
Tolleson

Tolleson Plating
W. Polk
Tolleson

Tubac Ldfl.
Frontage Rd.
Tubac

Hughes Aircraft
  Co.
Nogales Hwy.
Tucson

Pac. Fruit Express
E. Fairland Ave.
Tucson

Pioneer Paint &
  Yarn
W. Congress St.
Tucson

Univ. of Arizona
Tucson

Duval Corp.
  Sierrita
Twin Buttes

Potential Site
Wilmot Rd.
Wilmot

Yucca Power Plant
Yuma

Arkansas

Little R. Coun.
Ldfl.
Ashdown

Cent. Ark. Trash
Coll.
Box 432
Bald Knob

Ark. Eastman Co.
Box 2357
Batesville

Banquet Food
Corp.
Louis St.
Batesville

City of Batesville
N. of Hwy. 69
Batesville

Gen. Tire Dump
Box 72501
Batesville

Indedendence
Coun. Ldfl.
Batesville

White Rodgers Co.
Box 2117
Batesville

Reynolds Metals
Co.
Box 97
Bauxite

City of Beebe
Beebe

Bella Vista Sanit.
Hwy. 71
Bella Vista

Benton Salv.
Box 72
Benton

City of Benton
Ldfl.
Benton

Farrow Sanit.
Elm/S. Main
Benton

Agrico Chem. Co.
Hwy. 18 E.
Blytheville

Blytheville City
Dump
S. Ruddle Rd.
Blytheville

Blytheville Dump
Coun. Rd.
Blytheville

Goolsby Salv. Yd.
Hwy. 18 W.
Blytheville

Larimore Crop
Supp.
Henderson St.
Blytheville

Miss. Coun. Ldfl.
S. of Bly.
Blytheville

Riverside Chem.
Blytheville

Sparton Mfg. Co.
Box 657
Blytheville

S. Farmers Assoc.
N. 5th St.
Blytheville

Booneville Sanit.
Hwy. 18 W.
Booneville

Brinkley Sanit.
Ldfl.
Hwy. 49
Brinkley

Camden Sanit.
Ldfl.
Camden

Naval Ord. Plant
Off Hwy. 274
Camden

Carlisle City Dump
Carlisle

England City
Dump
City of England

Piper's Ind., Inc.
Box 111
Clarendon

Cameron Disp.
Serv.
Box 51
Clarksville

Clarksville Ldfl.
Clarksville

Clinton Cord Prod.
Clinton

Clinton Dump
Hwy. 65
Clinton

Daling Store Fix
Corning

Georgia-Pac. Corp.
Hwy. 82
Crossett

Sevier Coun.
Ldfl.
Hwy. 24 N.
De Queen

Weyerhauser Wood
Box 387
De Queen

Dewitt Ldfl.
Dewitt

Diaz Dump
Diaz

Diaz Ref. Co.
Diaz

NLR Bulky Waste
Facil.
Dulaski Coun.

Highland Disp.
Box 3017
E. Camden

Transitank Car
Corp.
E. Camden

Ark. Chem.
Hwy. 155
El Dorado

El Dorado Chem.
Ind. Rd.
El Dorado

El Dorado Ldfl.
El Dorado

Energy Sys. Co.
Am. Oil Rd.
El Dorado

Gt. Lakes Chem.
Rte. 15
El Dorado

H. Blacker Prtg.
Box 608
El Dorado

Lion Oil Co.
Lion Oil Bldg.
El Dorado

Monsanto
Hwy. 7
El Dorado

Velsicol Chem.
Rte. 2
El Dorado

Delta Specialty,
Inc.
Emmett

Recycling Ctr.
Fayetteville

Fordyce City Dump
Fordyce

Forrest City Ldfl.
Forrest City

Ft. Smith
P St.
Ft. Smith

Griffin-Srygley
Towson Ave.
Ft. Smith

Ind. Waste
Off Rte. 71
Ft. Smith

Seco
S. 6th St.
Ft. Smith

Gravette City
Dump
Hwy. 59
Gravette

Hoskin Fill
Greene Coun.

Stinger Dump
Greene Coun.

Garner Sanit.
Hwy. 63
Hardy

Heber Springs
Sanit.
S. of Hwy. 25
Heber Springs

Agric. Div.
Box 825
Helena

Helena Coun. Ldfl.
Helena

Bulk Transport,
Inc.
Hwy. 67 N.
Hope

Hempstead Coun.
Sanit.
Hope

Hope Proving Gds.
Hope

Coun. Ind. Ldfl.
Rte. 6
Hot Spr.

Old Chem. Fab.
Dump
Hwy. 70
Hot Spr.

Solid Waste Bldg.
Valley/Runyan
Hot Spr.

Union Carbide
Rte. 6
Hot Spr. Pk.

Hatcher Waste
Old Jacksonville
Hwy.
Jacksonville

Vertac Ind.
Marshall Rd.
Jacksonville

City of Sanit.
Jonesboro

E. I. Dupont
Box 2038
Jonesboro

Kerr McGee
Buchanan Rd.
Keo

Chicot Coun.
Sanit.
Hwy. 65
Lake Vill.

Leachville City
Ldfl.
Off Hwy. 77
Leachville

Tri-Star Chem.
Leachville

Ark. Disp. Co.
Scott Hamilton
Little Rock

Bierman Nine Site
Ironton Rd.
Little Rock

Ldfl. Office
Hwy. 365 S.
Little Rock

Metro Waste, Inc.
Little Rock

P. F. Harris Co.
W. 8th St.
Little Rock

Piper Ind.
Box 111
Little Rock

Recycling Ctr.
E. Capitol
Little Rock

Security Prod. Co.
Box 72203
Little Rock

Stauffer Chem.
Ironton Rd.
Little Rock

Stauffer Ind.
Arch St.
Little Rock

Teletype Corp.
I-30
Little Rock

Thompson-
Hayward
Little Rock

Lonoke Dump
Off Hwy. 70
Lonoke

Remington Arms
Co.
Remington Rd.
Lonoke

Dow Chem. Co.
Box 520
Magnolia

Ethyl Corp.
Hwy. 79
Magnolia

Magnolia City
Dump
Magnolia

Farrow Sanit.
E. Page
Malvern

NL Ind., Inc.
Box 10
Malvern

Reynolds Metals
Co.
Box 128
Malvern

Manila City Dump
Manila

Douglas &
Lomason Co.
Box 628
Marianna

Marianna Ldfl.
Marianna

Crittenden Coun.
Ldfl.
Marion

McCrory Dump
Outside McCrory
McCrory

Seco, Inc.
Hwy. 45
Midland

Monette City
Dump
Box 382
Monette

Monark Boat Co.
Patton St.
Monticello

Tri-Coun. Disp.
Hwy. 289
Morriston

Baxter Lab Div.
Hwy. 201 N.
Mn. Home

R.L.M., Inc.
S. Church St.
Mn. Home

Am. Lantern Co.
Box 280
Newport

MacMillan
Ringfree
MacMillan Rd.
Norphlet

Agri-Chem. Div.
E. 12th St.
N. Little Rock

Brushy Is. Sanit.
Rixey Rd.
N. Little Rock

Kopper Co., Inc.
Edmonds St.
N. Little Rock

N. Little Rock Acid
Plant
E. 5th St.
N. Little Rock

NLR Ash Disp.
Site
N. Little Rock

Ozark Chem. Corp.
Murphy Dr.
N. Little Rock

Union Carbide
Films
San Souci Rd.
Osceola

Darline Store Fix.
Paragould

Monroe Pit Site
Hwy. 358
Paragould

Allied Chem. Corp.
Fairfield Rd.
Pine Bluff

CP&W Printing
Catalpa St.
Pine Bluff

Pine Bluff Arsenal
Pine Bluff

Riverside Chem.
Box 8369
Pine Bluff

Randolph Coun.
Pocahontas

Waterloo Ind.
Box 486
Pocahontas

Animal Feed Lot
Waste
Pope Coun.

Duffield Bonnie
Hwy. 64
Pottsville

Benny Stovall Ldfl.
Prescott

Bentley-Miller
Dump
Pulaski Coun.

Rison/Cleveland
Dump
Rison

Old Hope Dump
E. of Hope
Rocky Mound

Fulton Sanit. Ldfl.
Box 207
Rogers

Hyrum Smith
Dump
Rte. 2
Royal

Ark. Pow. & Light
Russellville

Dow Chem. Co.
River Rd.
Russellville

Russellville City
Dump
Russellville

Searcy Ldfl.
Main St.
Searcy

Sheridan Dump
Sheridan

Cross Oil & Ref.
Box 105
Smackover

MacMillan
Ringfree
Stamps

Star City Dump
Star City

Callahan Dump
Texarkana

N. Am. Car Co.
N. Cutter/N. Oats
Texarkana

Singer Ldfl.
Trumann

Cement Asbestos
Prod.
Box 423
Van Buren

Van Buren Sanit.
Hwy. 59
Van Buren

Frit Ind., Inc.
P.O. Box 149
Walnut Ridge

Wiggins, Jimmy
Loggin
Rte. 2
Warren

Helena Chem. Co.
Hwy. 49
W. Helena

Vertac, Inc.
Box 2648
W. Helena

W. Helena Sanit.
Off Hwy. 242
W. Helena

Gurley Oil Co.
S. 8th St.
W. Memphis

Vertac, Inc.
Box 914
W. Memphis

Watts Dump
W. Memphis

W. Memphis Ldfl.
W. Memphis

W. Memphis Ldfl.
S. 8th St.
W. Memphis

California

City Bur. Elec.
Webster St.
Alameda

Cerro Metal Prod.
Alameda Coun.

Delaval Turbine
Ind.
Alameda Coun.

Albany Ldfl.
Buchanan St.
Albany

Buen Aventura
Albany

Alhambra PCB
Dump
W. Missouri
Alhambra

Don & Dick Mine
Alleghany

9 Par Dump
Los Esteros Rd.
Alviso

Amador Coun.
Amador Coun.

Natl. Distil. &
Chem.
N. Kemp St.
Anaheim

Desert Site
Andrade

Antelope Valley—
Ille
175 Sts./Y-S Aves.
Antelope Valley

Antioch Wks.
Bridgeland Rd.
Antioch

Auburn Sanit. Ldfl.
Shale Ridge Ln.
Auburn

Azusa Ice
Martinez
Azusa

Azusa Land Recl.
W. Gladstone Blvd.
Azusa

Oil & Solv. Proc.
10th St.
Azusa

Paradise Lake
N. Todd Ave.
Azusa

Arco
(plus 7 other
sites)
Box 147
Bakersfield

Arco
(plus 3 other
sites)
Box 147
Bakersfield

Bob Ferguson Ind.
Truxton Ave.
Bakersfield

Chevron U.S.A.
Inc. (plus 5 other
sites)
Box 5355
Bakersfield

Envir. Protect.
19th St.
Bakersfield

Getty Oil Co.
Rte. 1
Bakersfield

Kern Coun. Airport
Bakersfield

Kern Coun. Ref.
Bakersfield

Kern Front Oil Fd.
Bakersfield

Los Lobos Oil Fd.
Bakersfield

Magma Corp.
(plus 1 other site)
Pacheco & Gosford
Bakersfield

Marathon Oil Co.
Box 2348
Bakersfield

N. Antelope Hills
Bakersfield

PCB Dump Site
White La./
Wible Rd.
Bakersfield

Pioneer Oil Fd.
Bakersfield

Pleito Oil Fd.
Bakersfield

Round Mtn. Disp.
Round Mtn. Rd.
Bakersfield

San Emido
Bakersfield

Superior Oil Co.
Box 1031
Bakersfield

Tejon Oil Fd.
Bakersfield

Tennaco Oil Co.
Box 1996
Bakersfield

Tri State Petr.
Bakersfield

Union Oil Co.
F St.
Bakersfield

Valley Waste Disp.
Box 5368
Bakersfield

Williams Bros. Eng.
U.S. Naval Petr.
Res.
Bakersfield

Yowlumne Oil Fd.
Bakersfield

Ft. Irwin Rd. Disp.
Ft. Irwin Rd.
Barstow

Benecia Dredge
Disp.
Benecia

Benecia Munic.
Benecia

Berkeley Ldfl. Co.
Univ. Ave.
Berkeley

Pine Creek
**9 mi. N.W. of
Bishop**

Riverside Co. Dump
Lemon St.
Blythe (S.)

Brea—Olinda Cyn.
E. Cerritos
Brea

Camp Pendleton—
PCB
Ditch Drains
Camp Pendleton

Santa Susana File
Ldfl.
DeSoto Ave.
Canoga Pk.

Joe & Brown
Brown Ranch
Capitola

Beckman Instr.
Carlsbad

Alameda
S. Alameda St.
Carson

Borden Chem.
S. Wilmington
Carson

Cal. Compact
S. Main
Carson

GBF Pittsburg
Dump
Carson

Johns-Mansville
Plant
223rd St.
Carson

L.A. Coun. Intl.
Water
S. Figoura
Carson

Shell Chem. Oil Co.
Carson

Neary Cattle Ranch
Chico

Naval Weapons Ctr.
China Lake

Marsh Ck. Rd.
Box 133
Clayton

Atlas Asbestos
Corp.
Los Gatos Cyn. Rd.
Coalinga

Coalinga Asbestos
Co.
Pine Cyn.
Coalinga

Envir. Disp. Serv.
W. Elm
Coalinga

Colton Ldfl.
Colton

San Bernadino
Lacadena Ave.
Colton

U.S.S. Chem.
W. Adams St.
Colton

Randolph Ref.
Randolph St.
Commerce

MSTR Lubricants
N. Alameda
Compton

Crown Zellerbach
**Contra Costa
Coun.**

Union Oil Co.
**Contra Costa
Coun.**

Calaveras Asbestos
Copperopolis

Lakeland Aerial
Appl.
Corcoran Apt.

Am. Smelting
Crockett

Crockett-Valona
Crockett

Kern Coun. Dump
Woolomes Rd.
Delano

Del Rey Site
Am. Ave.
Del Rey

New Idria Mine
Diablo Mine

Union Carbide
Mine
Diablo Min. R.

Dinuba Munic.
Dinuba

Newby Is.
Dixon Landing

Deepwater Chem.
Dominquez

Dos Palos Airpt.
Folson/Merrill
Aves.
Dos Palos

Union Chem. Co.
I-152/33
Dos Palos

Chem-Tronics
El Cajon

FMC Res. Fm.
Mace Rd.
El Macer

Chevron Ref.
El Segundo

El Segundo Wks.
Sepulveda Blvd.
El Segundo

Dave Carlson
Eureka

James Clary
Box 1006
Eureka

Fairfield Sip
Bush Rd.
Fairfield

City of Farmsville
Farmsville

LFL Fontsite—San
Bernardino
Highland Ave.
Fontana

Chem-Serve
E. Pico
Fremont

E. Bay Disp. Co.
Durham Rd.
Fremont

FCW Beverage
Fremont

Fremont
Royce Rd.
Fremont

McMonterego-
Middle
Durham Rd.
Fremont

Carbarry Corp.
E. Clinton
Fresno

Chateau Fresno
Chateau Fresno Rd.
Fresno

FMC Corp.
Box 1669
Fresno

Lee Gibson Oil Co.
Fresno

Orange Ave. Disp.
Site
S. Orange Ave.
Fresno

City of Kerman
Sew.
Fresno Coun.

Texaco, Inc.
Fresno Coun.

Grass Valley Gp.
Bitney Spr. Rd.
Grass Valley

Mercury Mine
Tailing
Fife Creek
Guerneville

Bay Area Rapid
Trans.
Ind. Pkwy. N.
Hayward

Lumber Yd.
W. Jackson St.
Hayward

Rohm & Haas Co.
Whitesell St.
Hayward

San Fran
Hayward

Valley Nit. Prod.
Box 128
Helm

Bethlehem Steel
Corp.
Hercules/Pinole

Hercules Powder
Co.
Hercules

Pac. Ref. Co.
Box 68
Hercules

Sterpa Army Depot
Herlong

Hirshdale Dump
Hwy. 80
Hirshdale

John Smith Solid
Waste
John Smith Rd.
Hollister

Commander Oil
Co.
Hopper Cyn.

Art Henry
Humboldt Coun.

Bolsa Chica
Wetlands
Huntington Beach

Huntington Beach
Site
Bolsa Chica St.
Huntington Beach

Ignacia Substa.
Ignacio

Imperial Coun.
Dump
Worthington Rd.
Imperial

Brawley City
Imperial Coun.

Jessen & Co. Ind.
Imperial Coun.

Val Air Co., Inc.
Imperial Coun.

W. R. Grace
Centinola
Industry

Dow Chem.
Inglewood

Jack D. Mill Ref.
Iowa Mill

Coyote Cyn.
W. Centingla
Irvine

Nu-Way Ind. Ldfl.
E. Live Oak
Irwindale

Kerman City Dump
Am. Ave.
Kerman

Union Carbide
Corp.
Kern Coun.

Powers
Kettleman City

Union Carbide
King City

Air Prod. & Chem.
E. Louise Ave.
Lathrop

Occidental Chem.
Howland Rd. /
Louise Ave.
Lathrop

U.S. Naval Air Sta.
Lemore

Foothill Sanit. Ldfl.
Waverly Rd.
Linden

Live Oak
Live Oak

Loma Rica ADM
Site
Loma Rica Apt.
Loma Rica

PPG Ind.
Bartlett Plant
Lone Pine

Dominquez Plant
S. Wilmington
Long Beach

Long Beach Site
Vail Ave.
Long Beach

Monsanto
N. Paramount
Long Beach

Atlantic Richfield
Los Angeles

Capri Tank Fm.
Whittier Blvd.
Los Angeles

PCB Spill Site
N. Alameda
Los Angeles

Scholl Ldfl.
N. Figueroa
Los Angeles

Olin Corp.—Daves
Los Gatos

City of Madera
Airpt.
Madera

Madera Coun.
Dump 1
Ave. 16/Rd. 24
Madera

Madera Coun.
Dump 11
Rd. 19/Ave. 24
Madera

Mirex-Contam.
Madera Coun.
Airpt.
Madera

West Fm. Serv.,
Inc.
Madera

Wing & Curtis
Madera Coun.

Central Valley
Hide
Manford

Bendix Forest Prod.
Hwy. 49
Martell

Acme Ldfl. Corp.
Arthur Rd.
Martinez

IT Envir.-Con
Arthur Rd.
Martinez

Martinez Regen.
Sulfur
Mococo Rd.
Martinez

Menlo Pk. Disp.
Marsh Rd.
Martinez

Monsanto-Avon
3rd Ave.
Martinez

Shell Oil Co.
Box 711
Martinez

U.S. Dept. of
Energy
Menlo Pk.

Delhi Coun.
Water
Merced Coun.

Middletown Loran
Sta.
Middletown

Miller & Gibson
Ind.
Bothelo Ln.
Milpitas

Cash Ind.
Box 5505
Mission Hills

KMT Oil Co., Inc.
Anapola Ln.
Mission Viejo

FMC—Modesto
McHenry Ave.
Modesto

Modesto Sand &
Gravel
Hammet Rd.
Modesto

City Serv. on
Site Ldfl.
United St.
Mojave

Fleta
United St.
Mojave

Abandoned Oil
Well
Montebello

Operating Ind., Inc.
Portrero Gr. Rd.
Monterey Pk.

Olin Corp.
Tennant Ave.
Morgan Hill

Union Oil Co.
Mtn. Pass

Mtn. View Ldfl.
Shoreline Pk.
Mtn. View

Needles—Private
Land
Needles

Land-O-Gold, Inc.
Nevada Coun.

Columbus Coated
Fabr.
Cherry St.
Newark

FMC—Magnesia
Enterprise Dr.
Newark

FMC–Newark
Phosphate
Enterprise Dr.
Newark

Newberry Dump
Hwy. 66/Mtn.
  View
Newberry Spr.

Newberry Plant
Mtn. View/Pioneer
  Rd.
Newberry Spr.

Am. Pac. Intl.
Towsley Cyn.
Newhall

Newhall Ref. Co.
Newhall

Bendix For. Prod.
  (plus 1 other site)
Rd. 225
N. Fork

S. Pac. R.R.
Stromm
N. Hollywood

Bay City Disp.
Peralta Blvd.
Oakland

Bayside Oil Co.
Alameda Ave.
Oakland

Carter Pk.
Oakland

Gen. Elec. Fac.
Oakland

L&M Platting Co.
54th St.
Oakland

Oakland
Oakland

Ranrob
Oakland

Sunkist Growers
Sunkist St.
Ontario

Ct. Alloy
  Sprochets
Box 577
Oregon House

Borg Warner Facil.
Oxnard

Carney & Son Ldfl.
W. Fifth St.
Oxnard

Diamond Shamrock
Arcturus Ave.
Oxnard

Feather R. Plant
Baggett Manville
  Rd.
Oroville

Halico Eng. Co.
Oxnard

Oxnard City Dump
Oxnard

Oxnard Pub. Dump
Gonzales Rd.
Oxnard

Santa Clara Sanit.
  Ldfl.
N. Ventura Rd.
Oxnard

Standard Oil Co.
Browns Cyn.
Oxnard

Ventura Coun.
  Ldfl.
Gonzales Rd.
Oxnard

Contra Costa
  Coun.
Pacheco Rd.
Pacheco

Aydin
Palo Alto

Aydin Energy
Hanover St.
Palo Alto

City Dept. of Util.
E. Bayshore
Palo Alto

Ford Aerospace—
  PCB
Palo Alto

Ldfl. 2
S. Crenshaw
Palos Verdes

City Wire &
  Power Dept.
W. Mtn.
Pasadena

Glendale Pub. Serv.
Air Way
Pasadena

Penrose Pit Class
Penrose

Allied Chem.
  Corp.
Nichols Rd.
Pittsburg

Bay Point Wks.
Nichols Rd.
Pittsburg

Crown Paints Lot
  (plus 1 other site)
Front St.
Pittsburg

Dow Chem. Co.
Loverridge Rd.
Pittsburg

Stauffer Chem.
Loverridge Rd.
Pittsburg

West Chem. Co.
Nichols Rd.
Pittsburg

Mono Belting
  Corp.
Placer Coun.

Armin Mine
Plumas Coun.

Meyer's Mine
Plumas Coun.

Mono
Plumas Coun.

Robin R. Jeskey
  Mine
Plumas Coun.

Robert P. Wilson
  Mine
Plumas Coun.

J. S. Bowers Assoc.
N. Towne Ave.
Pomona

Spaora Ldfl. 2
W. Valley Blvd.
Pomona

Quincy Sanit.
  Disp.
N. Church St.
Quincy

U.S. For. Serv.
Box 1500
Quincy

Aerojet Gen. Corp.
Rancho Cordova

Billington Elec.
Folsom Blvd.
Rancho Cordova

E Prod.
Rancho Cordova

Afterthought Mine
Redding

Iron Mtn. Mines
Redding

Safety Kleen
S. I St.
Reedley

Del Norte Coun.
Klamath Rd.
Requa

Arsenic Sulfide
  Filt.
Mass Ave.
Richmond

Blair S. Pac. Ldfl.
S. 51st
Richmond

Chevron Chem.
  Co.
Hensley St.
Richmond

Chevron U.S.A.
Box 1272
Richmond

Coopers Chem. Co.
Richmond

FMC Corp.
Parr Blvd.
Richmond

Richmond Wks.
Castro St.
Richmond

Stauffer Chem.
47th St.
Richmond

W. Contra Costa
Parr Blvd.
Richmond

Highgrove Sanit.
  Ldfl.
Box 1090
Riverside

Public Util. Dept.
Lincoln
Riverside

Springfellow
Riverside Coun.

Palos Verde Ldfl. 1
Crenshaw Blvd.
Rolling Hills

Palos Verde Ldfl. 4
Hawthorne Blvd.
Rolling Hills

Roseville Car
  Repair
S. W. of Roseville

McClellan AFB
Sacramento

Sacramento Depot
Sacramento

Tenco Tractor, Inc.
Pacific Ave.
Sacramento

Dept. of Fish &
  Game
Sacramento Coun.

Crazy Horse Sanit.
  Ldfl.
Salinas

Munic. Disp. Site
Davis Rd.
Salinas

Staff Eng. Mg.
  Coun.
Box 204
Salinas

U.S. Bur. of Land
San Bernardino

Gen. Atomic Co.
John Hopkins
San Diego

Miramar N.E.
San Diego

U.S. Navy
San Diego

William C. Lettin
San Diego

R. S. Hazard Ind.
San Diego Coun.

Streuter Ind.
San Diego Coun.

Decca Xagon
Market St.
San Francisco

Emeryville Facil.
Shellhound St.
San Francisco

Mine Devel. Corp.
Union St.
San Francisco

PG&E
San Francisco

Vacant Lot
Jerrold St.
San Francisco

San Joaquin Airpt.
W. Manning
San Joaquin

Tranquility Munic.
Colorado Ave.
San Joaquin

Arcady Oil Co.
San Joaquin Coun.

Pac. Gas. Co.
San Joaquin Coun.

Raisch Quarry
S. 1st St.
San Jose

San Jose Dept. of
N. 6th St.
San Jose

San Jose State
  Univ.
San Jose

Singleton Disp.
Singleton Rd.
San Jose

Liquid Gold Oil
  Co.
Martine
San Leandro

Marina Disp. Site
Marina Blvd.
San Leandro

Solid Waste Disp.
Davis St.
San Leandro

Lou Amir
San Luis Obispo

Richmond Sanit.
  Co.
Rd. 20
San Pablo

Calif. Salv. Co.
N. Lagoon St.
San Pedro

Dew Corp.
Box 1734
San Pedro

Electro-Test, Inc.
Fostoria Way
San Ramon

U.C.S.B. Campus
Santa Barbara

City Elec. Dept.
Martin Ave.
Santa Clara

City Ldfl. Disp.
Lafayette St.
Santa Clara

James Lick
  Mansion
Montague Ext./1st
Santa Clara

Monsanto Chem.
  Co.
Lafayette St.
Santa Clara

Olin Corp.
Montague Ext.
Santa Clara

G. N. Wagner
Santa Cruz Coun.

PGP Ind., Inc.
Alondra Blvd.
Sante Fe Springs

Aminoil
Box 11279
Santa Rosa

WM House
Box 11279
Santa Rosa

Keysor Century
Springbrook Rd.
Saugus

Parker Aircraft Co.
A Sand Cyn. Rd.
Saugus

Seal Beach Plant
Pac. Coast Hwy.
Seal Beach

Am. Smelting
Selby

Walsh & O'Brian
Shasta Coun.

Washington Mine
Whiskeytown Res.
Shasta Coun.

Jack Cronhardt
Shell Rd.
Shell

Del Phete Mine
Sierra Coun.

Mannix Mines
Sierra Coun.

Michael Meister
  Mill
Sierra Coun.

Pemighem Metal
  Mine
Sierra Coun.

Plumbago Mines,
  Inc.
Sierra Coun.

Simi Valley Ldfl.
Los Angeles Ave.
Simi Valley

Christ & Kingdom
  Ch.
Siskiyou Coun.

GHI Mine
Siskiyou Coun.

Hyde Waldkirch
  Min.
Siskiyou Coun.

J. M. Kunkel Mine
Siskiyou Coun.

R. W. Parker Mine
Siskiyou Coun.

Agua Clear
Solano Coun.

City of Benecia
Solano Coun.

Aminoil U.S.A.,
  Inc.
Sonoma

Burman Oil & Gas
Box 11279
Sonoma

Louisiana Pac. Co.
Hwy. 70
Sonoma

Sullivan Filters, Inc.
Fremont Dr.
Sonoma

David K. Pitcher
Sonoma Coun.

G. T. Karnes
Sonoma Coun.

Russ Snider
Sonoma Coun.

Union Oil
Sonoma Coun.

S. San Francisco
Linden Ave.
S. San Francisco

Southgate Plant
Ardine
Southgate

Forward, Inc.
Austin Rd.
Stockton

Johns-Mansville
Plant
Sperry Rd.
Stockton

McCormick &
Baxter
Stockton

Valimet
Sperry Rd.
Stockton

Sunnyvale Ldfl.
Sunnyvale

S. Calif. Waste
Degarmo St.
Sun Valley

D. J. Pickbell
Chapin Ave.
Burlingame

Montrose Chem.
Co.
Normandie Ave.
Torrence

Shell
Torrence

Torrence City Ldfl.
Madrona/Del Amo
Blvd.
Torrence

Union Carbide
Corp.
Del Amo Blvd.
Torrence

Cody & Weber
Mine
Trinity Coun.

Hoffman Mine
Trinity Ctr.

Larry Riley
Box 22
Trinity Ctr.

MA Trinity Mine
Trinity Coun.

Mueller Mine
Trinity Coun.

Robert Nichols
Mine
Trinity Coun.

Verden Hurst
Trinity Coun.

Kerr–McGee Argus
(plus 1 other site)
Box 367
Trona

Onosi Pub. Util.
Tulare

Tulare Coun. Dump
Tulare

Tulare Munic.
Kern Ave.
Tulare

J. W. Larson
Tulare Coun.

Valley Wood Proc.
Golden State
Turlock

Orsetti Trucking
Union City Blvd.
Union City

Turk Is. Ldfl.
Union City Blvd.
Union City

Solano Co. Dump
Parker
Vacaville

Mare Is.
Vallejo

Dow Chem. Co.
43rd/Pacific
Venice

Union Oil Co.
Ventura Coun.

U.S. Nat. Gas
Corp.
Ventura Coun.

W. P. Barker
Ventura Coun.

S. Calif.
E. Vernon Ave.
Vernon

Kern Coun. #5
Wasco

Dick Baker, Plant
Mgr.
Yosemite
Waterford

R. A. Shaw Frozen
Foods
Harvest Dr.
Watsonville

Watsonville Ldfl.
San Andreas Rd.
Watsonville

Contl. Diver.
Maple Ave.
Westbury

BKK Corp.
(plus 1 other site)
Azusa Ave.
W. Covena

Mission Cyn. Ldfl.
Sepulveda Blvd.
W. Los Angeles

C&S Battery &
Lead
Riske Ln.
W. Sacramento

Puente Hills #6
S. Workman Rd.
Whittier

Ascon Ldfl.
N. Alameda St.
Wilmington

Calif. Carbon
E. Grant St.
Wilmington

Falcon Trans Sta.
E. I St.
Wilmington

IT Yard
N. Lagoon Ave.
Wilmington

Koppers Co.
Avalon Blvd.
Wilmington

Port Disposal
Wilmington

TCL
Anaheim St.
Wilmington

Terminal Hwy.
Anaheim St.
Wilmington

Colorado

Tri-Coun. Ldfl.
62nd St.
Adams Coun.

Colo. Circuits Co.
W. 56th
Arvada

Bank–Boulder
Creek
Cyn. Blvd.
Boulder

Rocky Flats Plant
Boulder

Marshall Ldfl.
S. 66th St.
Boulder Coun.

Potential site
Hwy. 85—E. Side
Brighton–Ft. Lup

Weld Coun. Ldfl.
Hwy. 85
Brighton–Ft. Lup

Pinello Ldfl.
Hwy. 94
Colorado Spr.

Colorado Methane
Delaware
Commerce City

Colorado Org.
Chem.
Dahlia
Commerce City

E. 48th/Holly
E. 48th/Holly
Commerce City

Globe Chem. Co.
Dahlia St.
Commerce City

LC Corp
Dahlia St.
Commerce City

Rocky Mtn.
Arsenal
Commerce City

Shell Chem. Co.
Rocky Mtn.
Arsenal
Commerce City

Tri-County Lfdl.
62nd St.
Commerce City

Woodbury Chem.
Jackson St.
Commerce City

Northgate Plant
Cowdrey

Aero Chem. Co.
N. Fed. Blvd.
Denver

Allied Chem.
Lincoln
Denver

Asanco
E. 51st St.
Denver

B & C Metal Prod.
12th Ave.
Denver

Brannan Sand &
  Gravel
Bryant St.
Denver

Card Co. Pitt
  Radium
W. Evans
Denver

Cedar Run Apts.
Leetsdale Dr.
Denver

Colorado Org.
  Chem.
Dahlia
Denver

Colorado South
  R.R.
W. 15th St.
Denver

Creative
  Illumination
S. Kalamath St.
Denver

Duwald Steel Corp.
Umatille St.
Denver

8th / Wolff
W. 9th / Tennyson
Denver

Exposition &
  Harrison
Colorado Blvd. /
  Cherry
Denver

Gen. Elec. Co.
Kingston St.
Denver

G&L Granite Co.
Quivas St.
Denver

Happy Church
S. Platte R. Dr.
Denver

Intl. House
E. Colfax
Denver

Mat. Handling
W. 13th Ave.
Denver

Parking Lot
Yuma Ct.
Denver

Place Jr. High
Cherry C. Dr. / 17th
Denver

Riverside Baptist
  Ch.
South Platte R. Dr.
Denver

Robinson Brick &
  Tile
S. Santa Fe
Denver

Rocky Mtn. Res.
Yuma
Denver

Ruby Hill Pk.
Jewell / S. Platte
Denver

Rudd Invest. Co.
Quivas St.
Denver

Shattuck Chem.
  Co.
S. Bannock
Denver

6th Ave.
Denver

Street-Corona / 7th
Corona / 10th / 7th
Denver

Street-11th
11th / York /
  Cheesem
Denver

Street- Lafayette /
  7th
Lafayette St.
Denver

Street-Marion / 6th
Marion / 6th / 10th
Denver

Street-9th Ave. /
  Lafay
Denver

Street-9th Ave. /
  Ogden
Denver

Street-23rd / Stout
23rd / Stout /
  Lawrence
Denver

Street-York
York / 6th / 13th
Denver

Univ. Bldg.
16th St.
Denver

Vacant Lot
Arizona / Peco
Denver

Vacant Lot
W. Louisiana St.
Denver

Vacant Lot
S. Santa Fe Dr.
Denver

W. Elec.
W. 4th St.
Denver

Wholesale Off.
  Eq.
18th St.
Denver

Durango Ldfl.
Durango

Laposta Rd. Site
Laposta Rd.
Durango

Estes Park Ldfl.
  (plus 1 other site)
Hwy. 36
Estes Pk.

Am. Eco. Recycle
Hwy. 72
Golden

Frontier For. Prod.
Hwy. 72
Golden

Western Inorg.
W. Hwy. 72
Golden

Potential Site
W. Hwy. 72
Golden

Rooney Rd. Ldfl.
Roosevelt Rd.
Golden

Thoro Prod.
Umber Ct.
Golden

J&J Enterprises
Main St.
Grand Junction

Orchard Mesa
Hwy. 50
Grand Junction

Greeley-Milliken
  Ldfl.
77th Ave.
Greeley

Weld Coun. Ldfl.
77th Ave.
Greeley

Henderson Site
124th Ave.
Henderson

Am. Eco. Recycle
Hwy. 72
Jefferson Coun.

Waste Disp.
Hwys. 72/93
Jefferson Coun.

Wayne Darling Res.
Baseline Rd.
Lafayette

Denver Fed. Cent.
Lakewood

W. 1st Ave. / Sher
Lakewood

Louviers Wks.
Louviers

Moly Corp., Inc.
Box 607
Louviers

Lowry Ldfl.
Lowry

Arapahoe Chem.
  Dump
Hwy. 66
Lyons

Highland Elec. Co.
S. Highland Ave.
Madison

Hill Petr. Bldg.
S. Grand
Montrose

R.R. Loading Dock
Silig Ave.
Montrose

Small Bldg.
W. of Montrose

Old Mine Tram
Placerville

Pueblo Army Depot
Pueblo

Anvil Pt.
Rifle

Cliffs Copper Corp.
Box 1211
Rifle

Ft. Lupton Ldfl.
Rural

Transformers
Unltd.
I-25/Rte. 6
Rural

Salida Plant
Salida

Ore Stge.
Sawpit

52nd/Harland
52nd/Harland
Sheridan

Slickrock Site
Slickrock

Uravan Uranium
(plus 1 other site)
Uravan

Vanadium Radium
Mill
Vanadium

31 Water Disp.
Coun. Fds. 18/31
Weld Coun.

Weld Coun. Disp.
Rtes. 12/35
Weld Coun.

Connecticut

Beacon Falls Oak
Beacon Falls

Beacon Hgts. Ldfl.
Beacon Falls

Reliable Ind. Waste
Disp.
Railroad Ave.
Beacon Falls

Pk. Area Lead
Styph.
Asylum St.
Bridgeport

Pk. Area Waste
Trmt.
Asylum St.
Bridgeport

Warehouse
Bridgeport

Bristol Solid Waste
Bristol

Exxon Ent.
Fed. Rd.
Brookfield

Potential Site
Rte. 7/Meadow &
Brook
Brookfield

Yaworski Waste
Ldfl.
Packer Rd.
Canterbury

J. M. Swift Ind.
Rte. 44/Colonial
Canton

Roy's Mobile Gas
Sta.
Rtes. 16/2
Colchester

Munic. Ldfl.
Danbury

Unknown—Near
Lakevie
Danbury

Deep R. Dump
Deep River

Delta Ind.
Bradley Pk. Rd.
E. Granby

Solid Waste
Trans.
E. Haddam

Kement Ldfl.
N. Rd.
E. Windsor

Town Scale Dump
One Roo Hwy.
Fairfield

Unknown
Farmington
Farmington

Munic. Ldfl.
Flanders Rd.
Groton

Pfizer, Inc.
E. Pt. Rd.
Groton

Pine Swamp
Hamden

Ledyard Ldfl.
Avery Hill Ext.
Ledyard

Upjohn Co.
N. Haven

Unknown Norwalk
Site
Norwalk

Stonington Munic.
Sanit.
Greenhaven Rd.
Pancatuck

Plainfield Site
Rte. 12/Tarbox Rd.
Plainfield

Mott
Metallurgical
Johnson Ave./Hyde
Rd.
Plainville

Unknown—
Prospect
Prospect

Town Dump
Chase Rd.
Putnam

Town Dump
Town Farm Rd.
Putnam

Rocky Hill Ldfl.
Rocky Hill

Lori Corp.
Old Turnpike Rd.
Southington

Solvents Rec. Inc.
Lazy Ln.
Southington

Southington Ldfl.
Southington

Town Dump
S. Killingly

Stamford—
Shiffan
Magee Ave.
Stamford

Ross & Roberts
W. Broad St.
Stratford

Uncertain—
Thomaston
Thomaston

Tolland Ldfl.
Old Stafford Rd.
Tolland

S. Cherry St. Site
S. Cherry St.
Wallingford

Scotch Cap Serv.
Sta.
Old Norwich Rd.
Waterford

Ldfl. (Hilton)
Mather St.
Wilton

Cedar Crest Apt.
Windham

Hamilton Std.
Windsor

Well 42
Near S. Pomperaug
Rd.
Woodbury

Delaware

Cokers Ldfl.
Rte. 92
Cheswold

Cokers Ldfl.
(plus 1 other site)
Rte. 152
Cheswold

Reichold Chem.
Rte. 133
Cheswold

Delaware Wks.
6300 Phil. Tnpk.
Claymont

Olin Corp.
P.O. Box F
Claymont

Delaware Facil.
Governor Lea Rd.
Delaware City

Potential Site
River Rd.
Delaware City

Stauffer Chem.
Box 320
Delaware City

Kent County Ldfl.
U.S. Rte. 113
Dover

Kent Coun. Ldfl.
Rte. 397
Houston

Porters Ldfl.
Houston

Sussex Coun. Ldfl.
Laurel

Barcroft Co.
Lewis

Delaware Farms,
  Inc.
Millsboro

FMC Corp.
1301 Ogletown
Newark

Chicago Bridge &
  Iron
New Castle

Delaware Sand &
  Gravel
New Castle

Denton Ldfl.
Rte. 9
New Castle

Harry Wood Ldfl.
Rte. 273, S. of
  Rte. 9
New Castle

Ind. Prod.
New Castle

Vincent
  Dellacersano
New Castle

Witco Chem.
900 Wilmington
  Rd.
New Castle

Army Ck. Ldfl.
Rtes. 13/40
New Castle Coun.

Koppers
James & Water Sts.
Newport

Seaford Plant
Seaford

Smyrna Plant
Smyrna

Capitol Rec.
Wilmington

Cherry Is. Ind.
  Ldfl.
12th St./Hay Rd.
Wilmington

Dover AFB
Wilmington

Exper. Sta.
Wilmington

Fiber Proc.
Garashies Ln.
Wilmington

Municipal Sew.
Wilmington

Pidgeon Pt. Sanit.
Wilmington

Tybouts Corner Ld.
Tybouts Corner Rd.
Wilmington

District of Columbia

James Warring &
  Sons
S. Capitol St.
**Washington,
D.C.**

Florida

Sapps Battery
Coun. Rd. C-280
Alford

Coun. Ldfl.
Anthony

S. W. Sanit. Ldfl.
Hwy. 24
Archer

Bartow Plant
Box 1480
Bartow

Bartow Plant
Box 150
Bartow

Bonnie Plant E.
  Gypsum
Bonnie Mine Rd.
Bartow

802 Scrubber Cir.
Hwy. 60
Bartow

Farmland Ind.
Box 960
Bartow

Phosphate Unit—
  Gypsum
Bartow

S. Pierce Chem.
  Wks.
Hwy. 630
Bartow

U.S.S. Agri-Chem.
Hwy. 60
Bartow

U.S.S. Agri-Chem.
Hwy. 630
Bartow

W. R. Grace & Co.
Hwy. 60
Bartow

Chem. Op.
Bradley

Sydney Mine
Dover/Turkey
Brandon

Brighton City
  Dump
Hwy. 721
Brighton

Gulf Oil Chem.
Brookville Rock
  Rd.
Brooksville

Brold & Co. Dump
N. Broward
Broward Coun.

Broward Ind.
  Platting
Broward Coun.

Cramer & Maurer
Broward Coun.

St. Regis Paper Co.
Box 87
Cantonment

Tower Chem. Co.
Montverde Rd.
Clermont

Kerr McGee Chem.
  Corp.
Main St.
Cottondale

Aluminum Smelters
Dade Coun.

Dade Coun. Pub.
  Wks.
Dade Coun.

58th St. Dump
58th St.
Dade Coun.

Broward Coun.
  Pub. Wks. Ldfl.
Dania

Fairbanks
Fairbanks

Cities Serv. Co.
Fernandina Beach

Broward Chem.
W. Prospect Rd.
Ft. Lauderdale

Univis
Ft. Lauderdale

Uniweld Prod., Inc.
Ft. Lauderdale

Alcoa
Ft. Meade

U.S.S. Agrichem.
Hwy. 630
Ft. Mead

Ohio Med. Prod.
Tice St.
Ft. Meyers

W. R. Grace
Old Dixie Hwy.
Ft. Pierce

K Mart
23rd Ave.
Gainsville

Pensular Chem. Res.
Gainsville

Gibsonton Ldfl.
Gibsonton

Fla. Solite
Box 297
Green Cove Spr.

Pembroke Pk.
  Whse.
Pembroke Rd.
Hallandale

Miami Battery &
  Elec.
River Dr.
Hedley

Pepper's Steel &
  Alloys
River Dr.
Hedley

Vinylex Corp. of
  Fla.
W. 2nd Ct.
Hialeah

N.W. Ldfl.
Hillsborough Coun.

Santa Rosa
Combust. Ldfl.
Hilton

Monico Res. Prod.
Janice Dr.
Hollister

Allied Chem. Corp.
Soutel Dr.
Jacksonville

Alton Boxboard
Box 150
Jacksonville

Clean River, Inc.
Parker St.
Jacksonville

Container Corp. of
Am.
N. 8th St.
Jacksonville

Fasco-Jacksonville
Fert.
Talleyrand
Jacksonville

FMC Jacksonville
Plant
Talleyrand Ave.
Jacksonville

Imeson Ldfl.
Gun Club Rd.
Jacksonville

Jacksonville Elec.
Hecksher Dr.
Jacksonville

Jacksonville Naval
Jacksonville

Jacksonville Plant
Talleyrand Ave.
Jacksonville

Jacksonville
Shipyd.
Jacksonville

Northside Ldfl.
Is. Dr.
Jacksonville

Owens Ave. Ldfl.
Owen Ave.
Jacksonville

Pickettville Ldfl.
Pickettville Rd.
Jacksonville

Regency Sq. Shop
Atlantic Blvd.
Jacksonville

Sandler Rd. Ldfl.
Sandler Rd.
Jacksonville

Solid Waste Res.
Sunbeam Rd.
Jacksonville

Alpha Chem. Co.
Lakeland

Az Prod. Co.
Lakeland

City of Lakeland
Dump (plus 1
other site)
Lakeland

Landia Chem. Co.
Lakeland

Cook Ind.
Lake Worth

Gen. Comp.
124th Ave.
Largo

Coun. Ldfl.
Rd. 40
Martel

Pepper's Steel &
Alloys
River Dr.
Medley

Dyna Tech.
Melbourne

Assoc. Paint &
Plastic
Miami

Ind. Vinyls
30th St.
Miami

Miami Drum Serv.
Miami

S. Steel Drums
Miami Springs

Santa Rosa
Milton

Electro Phos. Co.
Pebbledale Rd.
Mulberry

Layco Chem. Co.
Pebbledale Rd.
Mulberry

New Wales Chem.,
Inc.
Box 1035
Mulberry

Mobile Chem. Co.
Box 311
Nichols

Munisport Ldfl
N. Miami

Envian Rd. Substa.
Ocala

Coun. Ldfl.
Rd. 441
Ocala

McArthur Dairy
Okeechoree

Woodbury Chem.
Orange Coun.

Orlando Plant
Lee Rd.
Orlando

PPG Ind.
Pace

Hudson Pulp &
Paper
Box 919
Palatka

Dyer Ldfl.
Palm Beach

Lantana Ldfl.
Palm Beach

Pratt & Whitney
Box 2691
Palm Beach, W.

Piney Pt.
Phosphoric
Box 908
Palmetto

Burke Chem. Co.
Pampano Beach

Masette Tower
Sanit. Ldfl.
Panama City

S.W. For.
Panama City

Air Pro. & Chem.,
Inc.
Box 467
Pensacola

Beulah Ldfl.
U.S. 90
Pensacola

Klondike Ldfl.
Box 905
Pensacola

Monsanto
Box 12830
Pensacola

Pioneer Sand Co.
Warrington
Pensacola

Reichold Chem.
Jackson St.
Pensacola

Reichold Chem.
Pace Blvd.
Pensacola

Motorola, Inc.
Plantation

Asgrow
Plant City

Feed Phos.
Box 790
Plant City

Natl. Oil
Michigan St.
Plant City

Plant City Ldfl.
Plant City

Plant City Phos.
Plant City

Schurykill Metals
Woodrow Wilson
Plant City

Howard Vroom
Well
Polk Coun.

Polk Coun.
Polk Coun.

Allied Chem. Corp.
Hwy. 71
Port St. Joe

City of Port St. Joe
Port St. Joe

Woodbury Chem.
Co.
Princeton

Harnesco, Inc.
Riviera Beach

Waste Oil Ser.
Rudd

Olin Corp.
Hwys. 363/98
St. Marks

Chase & Co. S.
Sanford

Sarasota Coun.
  Ldfl.
Sarasota

Chloride, Inc.
50th St.
S. Tampa

Chloude Metals
50th / 35th
Tampa

City of Tampa
Cypress Ave.
Tampa

FMC Tampa P
5th St.
Tampa

Gulf Coast Lead
66th St.
Tampa

MRI Corp.
Stannom St.
Tampa

Stauffer Plant
Orient Rd.
Tampa

Southern Mill
56th
Tampa

Tampa Munich
  Incin.
34th St.
Tampa

Tampa Plant
Orient Rd.
Tampa

Taylor Rd. Ldfl.
Taylor Rd.
Tampa

Stauffer
Anclota Rd.
Tarpon Spr.

Reichold Chem.,
  Inc.
Box 83
Telogia

Vero Beach
Box 1389
Vero Beach

C. F. Ind.
Wauchula

Coleman-Evans
U.S. 90
Whitehouse

Whitehouse
Whitehouse

#1 Gypsum Stack
Box 300
White Spr.

Occidental Chem.
Box 300
White Spr.

Georgia

Cook Coun. Airpt.
Box 53
Adel

Air Prod. & Chem.
Gillionville Rd.
Albany

City of Albany Ldfl.
  (plus 1 other site)
Albany / Front St.
Albany

Co. Ppty.
Albany

Musgrove Ppty.
Albany

Scrub Waste Mold
  Pond
Old Leesburg Rd.
Albany

Swift Agrichem.
  Corp.
N. Jackson St.
Albany

U.S.S. Agri-Chem.
Old Leesburg Rd.
Albany

Vandy Musgrove
Oakridge Dr.
Albany

Intl. Min. & Chem.
Oak Ave.
Americus

Bankhead Ldfl.
Watts Rd.
Atlanta

BFI (Bankhead)
Marietta Blvd.
Atlanta

BFI Watts Rd.
Watts Rd.
Atlanta

Borden Chem.
Near Westvw. Cem.
Atlanta

Browning-Ferris
  Ind.
Atlanta

Cascade Rd. Ldfl.
Cascade Rd.
Atlanta

Dettelbach
Peachtree St.
Atlanta

Fulton Co. Merck
  Rd. Ldfl.
Merk Rd.
Atlanta

H&D Barrel / Drum
Redstone Arsenal
  Cpx.
Atlanta

Intl. Min. & Chem.
  Corp.
Oak Ave.
Atlanta

M&J Solvent (plus
  2 other sites)
Marietta St.
Atlanta

W. View Ldfl.
Atlanta

W. H. Allgoods
  Ldfl.
Cleveland Ave.
Atlanta

Acidulation Dump
Molly Pond Rd.
Augusta

Augusta Plant
  (plus 1 other site)
Marvin Griffin Rd.
Augusta

Augusta Plant Site
Columbian Nitro
  Rd.
Augusta

Coun. Ldfl.
Hwy. Loop 56
Augusta

Dump #1
Hwy. Loop 56
Augusta

Dump #2
Hwy. Loop 56
Augusta

Dump #3
Hwy. Loop 56
Augusta

Dump #4
Hwy. Loop 56
Augusta

E. I. Dupont—
  Augusta
Marvin Griffon Rd.
Augusta

Intl. Min. & Chem.
Molly Pond Rd.
Augusta

Monsanto—Atlanta
  Plant
Marvin Griffon Rd.
Augusta

Moreland
  McKesson
Augusta

Youngbloods
Chesterfield Rd.
Augusta

Austell City Dump
Bagley Ln.
Austel

Arivec Chem.
Huey Rd.
Austel

Arrivec Corp.
Austel

Polymers Div.—
  Austel
Kensington Rd.
Austel

Bainbridge Mills
U.S. 27
Bainbridge

Decatur Coun.
  Ldfl.
Spring Ck. Rd.
Bainbridge

Decatur Ind. Pk.
  Ldfl.
Hwy. 27
Bainbridge

FRP Co.
U.S. 341 E.
Baxley

Brunswick Plant Site
Cook / L St.
Brunswick

Brunswick Wks.
Ross Rd.
Brunswick

Cate Rd. Ldfl.
Cate Rd.
Brunswick

4th St. Ldfl.
4th St.
Brunswick

T St. Dump
(plus 2
other sites)
Brunswick

009 Ldfl.
Benedict Rd.
Brunswick

Bona Allen
Buford

Artizans Plant Site
River Rd.
Calhoun

Calhoun-Gordon
Co. (plus 3 other
sites)
South of Hwy. 156
Calhoun

CPC
Cartersville

Cedar Spr. Sludge
Pond
Box 156
Cedar Spr.

Gt. Southern Corp.
Box 156
Cedar Spr.

Cedartown Ldfl.
10th St.
Cedartown

Diamond Shamrock
Wissahickon Ave.
Cedartown

Pastures (various)
Cedartown

Polk Coun. Hwy.
278
Hwy. 278
Cedartown

Polk Coun. Ldfl.
Cedartown

Dekalb Co. Ldfl.
Chamblee

Murray Coun. Ldfl.
Chatsworth

Bainbr-Afton-Guil
Chenango Coun.

Tommy Duncan
Indian Ck. Dr.
Clarkston

Borden Chem.
Sullivan Rd.
Coll. Pk.

Rolling Hills &
Ldfl.
Sullivan Rd.
College Park

Browning-Ferris
Ind.
Henrico Rd.
Conley

Cottage Ln.
Cottage Ln.
Conley

Gold Kist
Cordele

Helena Chem. Co.
Adkins Comm.
Cordele

Covington Ldfl.
Covington

Newton Coun.
Ldfl. (plus 2
other sites)
Lackey Rd.
Covington

McCluskey's Farm
Luke Edwards Rd.
Dacula

Chem. Proc. Ga.
Mill
Coronet Dr.
Dalton

City of Dalton Ldfl.
Brooklyn Dr.
Dalton

Dalton
(plus 2
other sites)
Prosser Rd.
Dalton

Dow U.S.A.—
Dalton
Prosser Dr.
Dalton

Southeastern Waste
New S. Harris St.
Dalton

Stevens Ind.
Dawson

Crymes Ldfl.
Buford Hwy.
Decatur

Dekalb Coun. Ldfl.
Buford Hwy.
Decatur

Arivec Chem.
Douglasville

Allied Chem. Corp.
Central Ave.
E. Pt.

Atlanta Util. Wk.
Washington Ave.
E. Pt.

Crosby Stevens Co.
Central Ave.
E. Pt.

W. C. Meredith Co.
Lawrence St.
E. Pt.

Oconee Coun. Ldfl.
Mayme Mill Rd.
Farmington

Aries Alpha Corp.
Fispon

Bag Craft Corp.
Royal Dr.
For. Pk.

Ft. Gillem
For. Pk.

Rolling Hills Ldfl.
Sullivan Rd.
For. Pk.

S.E. Drum Co.
Ft. Oglethorpe

BFI Ldfl.
Fulton Coun.

Westview Ldfl.
Fulton Coun.

Clifton Eq. Rental
Hwy. 21
Garden City

Garden City Plant
Foundation Tract
Garden City

M.C. Anderson,
Inc.
Hwy. 21
Garden City

Romine Eq. Rental
Hwy. 21
Garden City

W. A. Porter Ppty.
Hwy. 17
Garden City

Gordon Serv. Co.
(plus 1 other site)
Box 433
Gordon

City of Griffin
Shoal Ck. Rd.
Griffin

Griffin/Spalding
Ldfl.
Griffin

Crymes Ent.
Gwinnett Coun.

Crymes Ldfl.
Gwinnett Coun.

Hazelhurst Mills
(plus 1 other site)
Hazelhurst

New City Ldfl.
Hazelhurst

New Hazelhurst
Sanit. Ldfl.
N. William St.
Hazelhurst

Old City Ldfl.
Hazelhurst

Old Hazelhurst
Solid
McEachin Rd.
Hazelhurst

Waste Latex Evap.
U.S. 23
Hazelhurst

City of Ideal
City Hall
Ideal

Shavers Farm
Shavers Farm Ppty.
Kensington

Steele Brothers
Ldfl.
Hwy. 341
Kensington

Whites Ldfl.
Cold Spr. Rd.
Kensington

Arnolds Ldfl.
Arnold Rd.
Lawrenceville

Clayton Coun.
Ldfl.
Hwy. 3
Lovejoy

Allied Chem. Corp.
Guy Paine Rd.
Macon

Allied Chem. Corp.
(plus 1 other site)
Mead Rd.
Macon

Ficklin and Walker
Macon

Macon Prestres
Mead Rd.
Macon

Triangle Chem. Co.
Macon

Cobb Coun. Baler
Bldg.
County Farm Rd.
Marietta

Cobb Coun. Ldfl.
County Fm. Rd.
Marietta

Cobb Coun. Solid
Waste
Marietta

Koppers Co., Inc.
Owenby Dr.
Marietta

Berrien Coun.
Hwy. 168
Nashville

Berrien Coun.
Sanit. Ldfl.
Hwy. 547
Nashville

City of Nashville
Tifton Rd.
Nashville

Coun. Farm
Nashville

Enigma Rd. Coun.
Ldfl.
Nashville

Homerville Hwy.
Coun. Ldfl.
Nashville

Nashville City Ldfl.
Old Valdosta Rd.
Nashville

Tifton Rd. City
Ldfl.
Nashville

John Smith Disp.
Nellister

Flantco
Peachtree City

Thompson-
Hayward
U.S. 278
Powder Spr.

Powersville Ldfl.
Powersville

Goodyear Tire &
Rubber
Goodyear St.
Rockmart

Floyd Coun. Ldfl.
Rome

Ldfl.
Chatham
Rome

On Site Ldfl.
Rome

Potts Rd.
Off Potts Rd.
Rome

Rome City Ldfl.
Rome

St. Mary's Ldfl.
Inside City Limit
Saint Marys

Allied Chem. Corp.
Brampton Rd.
Savannah

Am. Cyanamid
Deptford Tract
Savannah

Cherokee Ldfl.
Hwy. 21
Savannah

City of Savannah
Ldfl.
E. President St.
Savannah

City of Savannah
Ldfl.
Hwy. 17
Savannah

City of Savannah
Ldfl.
Stiles Ave/37th St.
Savannah

Hercules
Old Louisville Rd.
Savannah

Hercules Disp Serv.
1 Foundation Tract
Savannah

Jordan Sign Co.
President/Rudolph
Savannah

Savannah
Old Louisville Rd.
Savannah

Savannah
(plus 8 other sites)
Brampton Rd.
Savannah

Swift Agri-Chem.
Corp.
Lathrop Ave.
Savannah

New Sterling Ldfl.
Hwy. 99
Sterling

Old Sterling Ldfl.
Old Hwy. 99
Sterling

Acidulation Pond
E. 2nd St.
Tifton

Tift Coun. Ldfl.
Tifton

Ben Gober Ldfl.
Mimosa Dr.
Tucker

Crymes Ldfl.
(plus 3
other sites)
Lawrenceville
Tucker

Barker Chem. Co.
Azalea Ind. Pk.
Valdosta

Griffin Corp.
Plant 2
Valdosta

Ramsey Salv.
Rte. 2
Valdosta

White Coun.
White Coun.

Union Carbide
Harriets Bluff Rd.
Woodbine

Woodbine
Box 428
Woodbine

Guam

Diesel Pow. Plant
Dededo

Ordat Disp. Site
Guam

Dept. of Agric.
Whse.
Guam

Hawaii

Mililani Ldfl.
(plus 1 other site)
Ewa

Brewer Chem. Co.
Plant
Kaomi Loop
Ewa Beach

Energy Rec. Sys.
Kaomi Loop
Ewa Beach

Honolulu Wood
Trmt.
Ewa Beach

Kawailoa Ldfl.
Kawailoa Rd.
Haleiwa

DBCP Drums
Box 87
Haliimaile

Hana Ldfl.
Maui
Hana

Hanalei Ldfl.
Kauai Belt Rd.
Hanalei

Hilo Rubbish
Dump
Leilani St.
Hilo

ABC Disp.
Kam Hwy.
Honolulu

Atlas Elec. Co.
Halekauwila
Honolulu

Brewer Chem.
Corp.
Pacific St.
Honolulu

Del Monte
Honolulu

Dept of Trans. ·
Kakoi St.
Honolulu

Diamond Hd.
  Creator
Diamond Hd. Rd.
Honolulu

Gaspro, Inc.
Kam Hwy.
Honolulu

Hawaiian Elec.
Box 2750
Honolulu

Hawaiian Ref.
Box 29789
Honolulu

Kewalo Incin.
Ala Moana Blvd.
Honolulu

Occidental Chem.
Waiwai Loop
Honolulu

Pac. Concrete Ldfl.
Barbers Pt.
Honolulu

Shell Oil Co.
Nimitz Hwy.
Honolulu

Stan Shinkawm,
  Inc.
Kala Kava Ave.
Honolulu

Univ. of Hawaii
East-West Rd.
Honolulu

Waikapu Dump
Kahului

Kailua Ldfl.
  (plus 1 other site)
Kailua

Kalamaula Ldfl.
Molokai
Kalamaula

Kalaupapa Ldfl.
Molokai
Kalaupapa

Kaneone Marine
  Corps.
Mokapu Penin.
Kaneone

Kapaa Ldfl.
Opala Rd.
Kapaa

Brewer Chem.
  Corp.
Pumi
Kauai

Kekaha Ldfl.
Kekaha

Kokee Ldfl.
Kokee

Dole Plantation
Plantation
  Washwater
Lanai

Lanai Ldfl.
Lanai
Lanai

Halehaka Ldfl.
Halehaka Rd.
Lihue

Makani Ldfl.
Maui
Makani

Maunaloa Ldfl.
Maunaloa

Barbers Pt.
Naval Air Sta.

Olowalu Ldfl.
Olowalu
Olowalu

Pearl City Navy
Lehua Ave.
Pearl City

Pearl Harbor Naval
Pearl Harbor

U.S. Dept. of Navy
Pearl Harbor

Schofield Ldfl.
Wahiawa

Jaymer, Inc.
Hale Elua St.
Waianea

Waianae Ldfl.
Wainae Valley Rd.
Waianea

Waikoloa Ldfl.
Waikoloa

Waiohina Ldfl.
Hawaii Belt Rd.
Waiohina

ABC Chem. Corp.
Leonui St.
Waipahu

Waipahu Ash Dump
Depot Rd.
Waipahu

P&S Sanit. Haul.
Kauapuu
Watanea

Idaho

Poles, Inc.
Blanchard

Min. States Paint
  Mfg.
Box 5465
Boise

Pre-Cote Ind.
Wise Way
Boise

L. D. McFarland
Boville

Grandview/
  Bruneau Ldfl.
Bruneau Grandview

Central Cove Sanit.
Caldwell

Deming Ind.
Govt. Hwy.
Coeur D'Alene

City Abandoned
  Dump
Franklin

Franklin
  Abandoned
  Dump
Franklin

Garage Over Ldfl.
Main St.
Franklin

Ritewood
Main St.
Franklin

Abandoned Silo
  Site
Box 393
Grandview

Grangeville Sanit.
Grangeville

Timber Craft Prod.
Box 908
Hayden Lake

Garland Call Pole
  Co.
Rte. 7
Idaho Falls

Jerome Co. Weed
  Ctl.
Jerome

Kellogg Trans., Inc.
Box 70
Kingston

Lewiston Airport
Lewiston

Omark CC Ind.
20th and Snake R.
  Ave.
Lewiston

Marsing Airpt.
Marsing

Wilson Ck. Mod.
Marsing

Ada Coun.
Meridian

Latah Co. Sanit.
  Ldfl.
Troy Hwy.
Moscow

Univ. of Idaho Ldfl.
N. of Hwy. 8
Moscow

Valley Plating
Garrity Blvd.
Nampa

Am. Microsys.
Buckskin Rd.
Pocatello

Dykes Poleline
  Elec.
Poleline Rd.
Pocatello

Pocatello Sanit.
  Ldfl.
Ft. Hall Mine Rd.
Pocatello

Union Pac. R.R.
Pocatello

Paul Lower
W. Oneida Rd.
Preston

Paul Lower Salv.
Parkinson Rd.
Preston

Trend, Inc.
Pleasant Way
Roper

Paul Airport
Rupert

Butcher Wood
  Preserv.
Sandpoint

L. D. McFarland
  Co.
N. 2nd Ave.
Sandpoint

For. Prod.
Smelterville

Georgetown Cyn.
Soda Springs

Monsanto Co.
Box 816
Soda Springs

Soda Springs Kerr-
  McGee
Box 478
Soda Springs

Cinnabar Mine
Stibnite

Superior Min.
Stibnite

Yellow Pine Mine
Stibnite

Illinois

Edwards Coun.
  Ditch
Red Mill Rd.
Albion

Alton Ldfl.
N. Alby St.
Alton

Henry Coun. Ldfl.
  (plus 2 other sites)
Rte. 1
Atkinson

Hopkins
W. Arch St.
Atlanta

Grayslake
Avon

White Septic Co.
Bartlett Rd.
Bartlett

Chicago Acetylene
Bedford Pks.

Amoco Oil Co.
Belleville

Belvidere Munic.
Appleton Rd.
Belvidere

Boone Coun. Ldfl.
Belvidere

Dewane Ldfl.
Bus. 20 E.
Belvidere

Sexton Ldfl.
Central Rd.
Bensenville

Logan Stge. Sites
Rte. 1
Bethalto

Mallard Lake For.
Schick Rd.
Bloomingdale

Welco Truck Stop
Joliet Rd. & 155
Boling Brook

Brighton Ldfl.
Rte. 1
Brighton

Brighton Ldfl.
Box 401
Brighton

Byron Salv. Co.
Byron

Estech Gen. Chem.
Calumet City

Vermont
Vermont Ave.
Calumet Pk.

Plant Facil.
Box 270
Carbondale

Ordill D—Area 12
  (plus 1 other site)
Crab Orchard
Carterville

Ordill Fire Sta.
Carterville

Ordill I—Area
Carterville

Ordill—Ogden Rd.
Carterville

Ordill Water Tower
Carterville

Amoco Chem.
  Corp.
U.S. 6/I-55
Channohon TWP

A&B Cont.
42nd/Knox
Chicago

Acme Barrel Co.
13th St.
Chicago

Acme Refin.
22nd Place
Chicago

Armstrong Cont.
Kilbourn Ave.
Chicago

Barker Chem. Co.
E. 138th St.
Chicago

J-P Refuse Disp.
W. 65th St.
Chicago

Battaglia Dist.
S. Ashland
Chicago

Cal Harbor Ind.
Hoxie
Chicago

Calumet Wks.
S. Gorondolet
Chicago

Custom Org.
W. 42nd St.
Chicago

Earth II
S. Yates
Chicago

Enterprise Co.
Ashland Ave.
Chicago

Fisher-Calo Chem.
W. 41st St.
Chicago

Ft. Madden Ind.
S. New England
Chicago

Hyon Waste
S. Stonyis. St.
Chicago

MSDGC "New
  Earth"
E. Erie
Chicago

Name Unreported
Chicago

Name Unreported
138–141/Calumet
Chicago

Peterson Coal Co.
S. State St.
Chicago

Riverdale Plating
S. Halstead
Chicago

Stauffer Chem.
E. 138th St.
Chicago

U.S. Drum Disp.
S. Oglesby
Chicago

Waterway Plant
E. 138th St.
Chicago

W. Chicago–Kerr
  McGee
Ana St.
Chicago

W. Pullman Iron
120th/Peoria
Chicago

Al's Sand Pit
Rte. 30
Chicago Hgts.

Columbia Tool Steel
14th/State St.
Chicago Hgts.

Dow Ind. Serv.
Saulk Tr./Bend
Chicago Hgts.

Gaby Iron & Metal
  Co.
E. End Ave.
Chicago Hgts.

Hall Aluminum Co.
State Rd.
Chicago Hgts.

Roadway Truck
  Term.
Rte. 30/Torrence
Chicago Hgts.

Std. T. Chem.
10th/Washington
Chicago Hgts.

Stauffer Chem.
Chicago Hgts.

IMC Chem. Gp.
Crab Orch. Ref.
Potential Site
Rte. 1
Crossville

Danville City Dump
Danville

Danville H&L 1
Danville

Danville Wks.
Brewer Rd.
Danville

H&L Disp. Site 2
Murray Clarke Rd.
Danville

McKinney Ldfl.
Decatur

Macon Coun. Ldfl.
Hill Rd., Rte. 8
Decatur

Deerfield Met.
Pfingsten/LK Cook
Deerfield

A. O. Smith Co.
Rte. 23
Dekalb

Custom Can
Box 248
De Land

Sexton Ldfl.
Central Rd.
Des Plains

Land & Lakes
E. 138th St.
Dolton

Powder Op. Site
E. Alton

Olin Corp.
Patterson-Laraway
E. Alton

Zone 4 Scrap Gds.
E. Alton

Tazwell Coun. Ldfl.
Farmdale Rd.
E. Peoria

E. St. Louis Plant
Lynch Ave.
E. St. Louis

E. St. Louis Plant
N. Kings Hwy.
E. St. Louis

Shippers Carline
Trendly Ave.
E. St. Louis

ESL Waste Mgt.
Laraway Rd.
Elwood

Allied Chem.
Carondolet
Fairmont

Conrail Train Yd.
Fairmont

E. St. Louis Wks.
Fairmont Coun.

Thomas Garage
Collunsville Rd.
Fairmont Coun.

Logan Stge. Sites
Box 216
Franklin Grove

Liquid Waste, Inc.
Lucyland
Franklin Pk.

Old Knox Coun.
Henderson Rd.
Galesburg

Plant Facil. Hwy.
Hwy. 415
Galesburg

Lawrence &
Ahmans
Gallagan/Huntley
Gilberts

Litter Brick Yd.
W. Lake Ave.
Glenview

Litter Dump
Glenview

Granite City Police
E. Glenview Naval
Granite

Granite City Dump
Granite City

Milan #1
Rte. 1
Granite City

ARF Ldfl. Corp.
Rte. 83
Grayslake

A&F Mat. Co.
Hwy. 121
Greenup

Macon Coun. Ldfl.
Harristown

Henry Plant
Rte. 1
Henry

Hindsdale/Sexyon
Ldfl.
31st St.
Hindsdale

Beaver Tank &
Sludge
Lenzi
Hodgkins

Wabash Tape Corp.
E. Main St.
Huntley

Borden Chem.
Box 27
Illiopolis

Illiopolis City
Dump
Illiopolis

Amoco Chem.
Corp.
Joliet

Banner Disp. Serv.
Moen
Joliet

Bennitt's Ppty.
W. Mien Ave.
Joliet

Joliet Army Ammo
Plant (plus 1
other site)
Joliet

Joliet Illinois
McKinley Ave.
Joliet

Olin Corp.
Patterson/Laraway
Joliet

RHO Chem Co.,
Inc.
Industry Ave.
Joliet

Stauffer
Ingalls/Broadway
Joliet

Joseph Arnove
Box 305
Kankakee

Medusa Aggregates
Rte. 6
Kankakee

Lake Zurich Vill.
Lake Zurich

Bee Chem. Co.
E. 170th
Lansing

Kingery Devel.
E. Torrence
Lansing

Browning-Ferris
Main/Parker
Lemont

Hannah Intl.
Waterway
Rtes. 83 & 107
Lemont

Union Chem.
Lemont

Peterson Sand &
Gravel
Milwaukee
Libertyville

Bill's Excav.
Lockport Rd.
Lockport

Lockport
Waterwks.
State St.
Lockport

Armak, Inc.
47th St.
McCook

Kearney Co.
Joliet Rd.
McCook

Motor Oils Ref.
47th St.
McCook

Crab Orchard Natl.
Marion

Energy Burning Pad
Marion

Energy Lagoon
Marion

Incin. Co.
Marion

Dump
159th Pl.
Markham

Dump near
Marshall
Rte. 4
Marshall

Vesticol Chem.
Corp.
Box 39A
Marshall

John Sexton
Contract
Saulk Trail &
Central
Matteson

Crystal Mfg.
W. Lake St.
Melrose Pk.

Trekker Chem. Co.
Hwy. 51 S.
Mendota

Metropolis Wks.
U.S. 45
Metropolis

Morris City Dump
Morris

Plant Ppty.
Collins Rd.
Morris

Reichhold Chem.
Collins Rd.
Morris

Ldfl. Area
Morrison

Whitside Coun.
Ldfl.
Hwy. 30 E.
Morrison

Illinois
Commonwealth
N. Chicago

Lake Ldfl., Inc.
Frontage Rd.
Northfield

Sexton, John
Jorie Blvd.
Oak Brook

Orland Barrel &
Drum
Ridge Ave.
Orland Pk.

Closed Dump at
105th
Palos Hills

Peru Munic. #2
Box 299
Peru

John Sexton
Contract
Saulk Trail
Richton Pk.

Richton Pk.
Saulk Trail
Richton Pk.

Morton Chem. Co.
Barnard Mill Rd.
Ringwood

Carlstrom Ldfl.
Rock Is. Ave.
Rockdale

C&H Co.
Mobile Oil Co.
Rockdale

M&W Ldfl. Co.
Moen Rd.
Rockdale

DBA Roto-Rooter
18th Ave.
Rockford

Interstate Pollution
9th St.
Rockford

Rockford/Tipton
Rural Winnebago
City
Rockford

Andalusia/Watts
4th St.
Rock Is.

Pettifer Is.
Rock Is.

Roadway Exp. Co.
78th Ave.
Rock Is.

Watts Disp.
Rock Is.

Watts Ldfl.
4th St.
Rock Is.

Dorian Drum Co.
135th & Des Plaines
Romeoville

Rosiclare Plant
Box 57
Rosiclare

Dump
9th St.
Russell

Met. Ldfl.
St. Clare Coun.

Milam
St. Clare Coun.

Clayton Chem. Co.
Sauget

Deed Ck.
Sauget

Krummich
Sauget

Monsanto Co.
Rte. 3
Sauget

Russell Bliss Waste
Sauget

Sauget & Co. Ldfl.
Monsanto Ave.
Sauget

Sauk Vill.
Gailine
Sauk Vill.

Savanna Army
Depot
Savanna

E. I. Denemours,
Dupont
Dupont Rd.
Senaca

Hooker Chem.
W. Kilkapoo Ck.
Senaca

Seneca Wks.
Box 68
Senaca

Bend Robert Farm
Mobile Oil Corp.
Shabonna

Am. Louver Co.
Austin Ave.
Skokie

Skyline Disp.
28th/E. End
S. Chicago Hgts.

Tri-County Ldfl.
S. Elgin

Mr. Frank
W. 155th St.
S. Holland

S&L Ldfl.
Sparta

Chicago Met. Sanit.
Stickney

Koppers
S. Caramie
Stickney

Borden Chem.
Streator

Green Pond
Smith-Douglass
Streator

Gypsum Settling
Pond
Smith-Douglass
Streator

KSF Pond
Smith-Douglass
Streator

Summit/Am. Grad.
U.S. 66/Lawndale
Summit

Plow Ck. Farm
Tiskilwa

Romaine Fly Ash
Pile
Tuscola

Pool Area Fly Ash
Tuscola

Tuscola Ind.
Box 218
Tuscola

Multi-Co.
Rte. 1
Villa Grove

McHenry Sand &
Gravel
Rte. 120
Volo

Lakeland Est.
S. Lakeview
Waconda

Waconda Sand &
Gravel
Bonner/Garland
Rds.
Waconda

Chem. Waste Mgt.
138th
Waste Hgt. of Ill.

Knox Coun. Ldfl.
Wataga

Dexter Chem. Co.
Waukegan

Sexton, John
31st/Wolf
Westchester

Kerr McGee
Factory/Ann
W. Chicago

N. Shore Natl.
W. Chicago

C. L. Hale Co.
Rte. 1
Wilmington

Chemtrol Pollution
Wilsonville

Earthline Corp.
Box 38
Wilsonville

Rockford/Tipton
Rte. 2
Winnebago

Browning-Ferris
Ind.
Green Bay Rd.
Winthrop Harbor

IMC Chem. Gp.
Hwy. 3
Wolf Lake

Venus Labs
Lively Blvd.
Wooddale

Amoco Oil Co.
Box 182
Wood R.

Wood R. Ref.
Wood R.

FMC Corp.
Hwy. 17 E.
Wyoming

Indiana

Indiana
  Woodtreating
St. Roger/Clear
Bloomington

City of
  Bloomington
Bloomington

Westinghouse
Bloomington

Essex Intl.
Boonville

Enviro-Chem.
Boston

Bethlehem Steel Co.
U.S. 12/149
Burns Harbor

Privately Owned
  Farmland
Central

Ind. Army Ammun.
Charleston

Clark-Floyd
  Sanit.
Wilson Switch Rd.
Clarksville

Ind. Liquid Waste
Rte. 3
Columbus

Burning Plant
Covington

Olin Corp.
Hwy. 136
Covington

Neutralization
  Pond
Covington

Spoil Ldfl.
Covington

Wet Waste
Covington

Crane Naval
  Weapons
Crane

American Rec. Co.
Riley Rd.
E. Chicago

E. I. Dupont
Kennedy Rd.
E. Chicago

E. Chicago City
  Dump
Michigan St.
E. Chicago

E. I. Dupont
  Denemours
E. Chicago

M&T Chem., Inc.
E. 151st St.
E. Chicago

Union Carbide–
  Linoy
Kennedy Ave.
E. Chicago

Gen. Am. Trans.
Railroad Ave.
E. Chicago

Ind. Disp.
Gary Ave.
E. Chicago

Inland Steel Plant
Blast Furnace 7
E. Chicago

U.S.S. Lead Ref.
Kennedy Ave.
E. Chicago

Cities Serv. Co. 1
E. Chicago

Floyd Coun.
Edwardsville

Circle R
Circle R Ln.
Elkhart

Himco
Coun. Rd. 10
Elkhart

Martin Dunn
Grove St.
Evansville

Fortville Plant
Fortville

Transenviron.
Ft. Wayne

Tri-Tech
Commercial Rd.
Ft. Wayne

Montgomery Sanit.
Rte. 7
Frankfort

Garrett Flex Prod.
S. Cowen St.
Garrett

Gary City Ldfl.
15th/Colfax
Gary

Garyland Devel.
N. Cline
Gary

Anderson Devel.
W. 4th Ave.
Gary

Ind. Cinders
S. of Pa. Cent.
Gary

Bongi Cartage
N. Clark
Gary

Ninth St. Dump
W. 9th St.
Gary

Calumet Inds.
W. Industrial
Gary

N. Indiana
Clark St.
Gary

Kor Corp.
9th Ave.
Gary

N.W. Ind. Site
I-94/Colfax
Gary

R. J. Connor
15th Ave.
Gary

Samocki Bros.
  Trucking
Gary

Site 10
Corner Cline
Gary

Sandy Joe Lake
W. 25th Ave.
Gary

Site 18
Frontage Rd.
Gary

Site 75
Clark Ind. Hwy.
Gary

Site 9
5th/In. Toll
Gary

Site 76
Clark St.
Gary

Topo. Site 15 D
I-94/GA
Gary

Topo. Site 15
Harrison/29th/
  Grant
Gary

Vulcan Mat. Co.
N. Cline Ave.
Gary

95
N. of Gary Ave.
Gary

Aerial Photo Site 1
32nd/Chase
Gary

Aerial Photo Site 2
I-94/I-65
Gary

Conservation
  Chem. Co.
Ind. Hwy.
Gary

Lakemar
Gary

Mid-Continent
Coke Co.
N. Clark Rd.
Gary

Midco
W. 15th Ave.
Gary

Midco II
Ind. Hwy.
Gary

Midwest Ind. Waste
Ind. Hwy.
Gary

Midwest Solv.
W. 15th Ave.
Gary

Mobile Chem. Co.
Gary

Kapica Drum
Arbogast
Griffith

Griffith Ldfl.
S. Colfax
Griffith

Am. Chem. Serv.
Colfax Ave.
Griffith

Keen Cast
E. Main
Griffith

Transenviron.
Hamilton

Amoco Tank Fd.
129th/Calumet
Hammond

Ace Welding
Sheffield
Hammond

Calumet Cont.
136th/State
Hammond

Am. Maize
113th/Indian
Hammond

Chem. Haulers
Kennedy Ave.
Hammond

Ashland Chem.
167th St.
Hammond

Fed. Metals
Indianapolis
Hammond

Davies Imperial
State St.
Hammond

Flexiflo
Kennedy
Hammond

Dombrowski &
Holmes
Columbia
Hammond

Griffin Wellpoint
Co.
Calumet Ave.
Hammond

H. Bairstown
129th/Calumet
Hammond

Hammond Plant
Hammond

Illiana Trans. Corp.
Calumet Ave.
Hammond

Hammond Sew.
Trmt.
Columbia Ave.
Hammond

Post Whse. Corp.
Sheffield
Hammond

J&L
Hammond

Shell Oil
Kennedy/160th
Hammond

Ken Ind.
Sheffield
Hammond

Wolf Lake Term.
Box 565
Hammond

Ruan Trans. Co.
Kennedy
Hammond

Stauffer Chem. Co.
(plus 1 other site)
Michigan St.
Hammond

W. Shore Trkg.
Hoffman St.
Hammond

CES, Inc.
54th St.
Indianapolis

Southside Sanit.
Indianapolis

Kentucky Ave. Ldfl.
Kentucky Ave.
Indianapolis

McKinley-
Thompson Ldfl.
Harding St.
Indianapolis

Res. & Devel.
Indianapolis

96th St. Dump
96th/465
Indianapolis

Conrail Derailment
Inwood

Seymour Recycl.
Co.
Freeman
Jackson

Jeffersonville
Jefferson

Graves Rock
Quarry
Jeffersonville

Hooker Chem.
Dump
Hwy. 131
Jeffersonville

Past Part of Base
Jeffersonville

Howard Coun.
Ldfl.
Kokomo

Wildcat Ck. Fms.
Kokomo

Crossroads Truck
I-80
Lake Sta.

Fisher Calo Chem.
Box 684
La Porte

City Dump
McClung/Hwy. 39
La Porte

GTI Corp.
School/Smith St.
Leesburg

Gen. Elec.
12th St.
Linton

On-Site Deep Well
Michigan City

On-Site Lagoon/
Ldfl.
Michigan City

Waste, Inc.
U.S. 12
Michigan City

Kordell, Inc.
Clover/Jefferson
Mishawaka

Montezuma Fly
Ash Plant
Montezuma

Gen. Elec. Site
Mt. Vernon

Mt. Vernon City
Dump
Mt. Vernon

Indiana Steel &
Wire
E. Jackson
Muncie

Am. Brick
Calumet/45th
Munster

Elko
Nappanee

Kentucky Liquid
Recyl.
Willow St.
New Albany

Newport Army
Ammun.
Newport

Black Oxide Co.
Palestine Lake
Palestine

Own Coun. Ldfl.
Beverly Rd.
Patricksburg

Plant Site
Peru

Brown Trkg. Co.
U.S. 20/520
Pines

Enamel Products
U.S. 12
Portage

Wayne Wks.
Rte. 35/I-70
Richmond

Four Coun. Ldfl.
Rochester

J. L. Manley
Rosedale

Distler Fm.
Salem

By Prod. Mgt.
Jct.
Schererville

Mason Metal
Rte. 41
Schererville

Intec Ind.
Schererville

Chemdyne Corp.
Seymour

Seymour Recycl.
Freeman
Seymour

Salumet
Seymour

H&R Prod.
Ireland Rd.
S. Bend

Ldfl.—Victory Dis.
Sugar Ck.

Potential Site
Dombay
Sugar Creek

Green Coun. Ldfl.
Switz City

J. A. Sears Off.
Site
Terre Haute

Ldfl. Margaret Ave.
Terre Haute

Privately Owned
Gds.
Terre Haute

Radioactive Waste
Terre Haute

Terre Haute E.
Terre Haute

Terre Haute Nit.
Terre Haute

Terre Haute Sanit.
Terre Haute

Terre Haute Trmt.
Terre Haute

Vego Chem. Co.
Terre Haute

Victory Mine
Sanit.
Bloomington Rd.
Terre Haute

Vego Coun. Ldfl.
Terre Haute

Vego Plant Ldfl.
Terre Haute

Y—Ldfl. W.
Terre Haute

49er Sanit. Ldfl.
Valparaiso

Koppers
(plus 1 other site)
Raystone Dr.
Valparaiso

Valparaiso Plant
Valparaiso

Ldfl. Linton-Sout.
Vigo Coun.

Y—Ldfl.
W. Terre Haute

Westville Oil Div.
Westville

Amoco
Whiting

Whiting Site
Schrage Ave.
Whiting

Calumet Coll.
N. Y. Ave.
Whiting

Enviro-Chem.
Corp.
Rte. 1
Zionsville

Hazardous Waste
Hwy. 67
Zionsville

N. Side Ldfl.
Rte. 1
Zionsville

Iowa

Davenport Plant
Box 500
Buffalo

Occidental Chem.
Box 500
Buffalo

Bonewitz Chem.
Serv.
N. Roosevelt
Burlington

Burlington Basket
Bluff/Oak St.
Burlington

Determann Inds.
(plus 1 other site)
N. Washington
Blvd.
Camanche

Dupont EI
Hwy. 67
Camanche

Lawrence Todiz
Fm.
Rte. 1
Camanche

McManus Ldfl.
9th St.
Camanche

Cedar Rapids Pub.
Ldfl.
A St. S.W.
Cedar Rapids

Cedar Rapids Sanit.
Ldfl.
C St. S.W.
Cedar Rapids

Cedar Rapids Sew.
A St./Burlington
Cedar Rapids

Hennessey Bros.
Quarry
River Rd.
Cedar Rapids

Unreported
Wilson Ave.
Cedar Rapids

W. R. Grace Co.
Wilson Ave.
Cedar Rapids

C St. Ldfl.
C St.
Cedar Rapids

McManus Ldfl.
Hwy. 218
Charles City

Chemplex Co.
Box 819
Clinton

E. I. Dupont
Box 451
Clinton

Clinton Coun. Ldfl.
Elvira Rd.
Clinton

Clinton Ldfl.
Rte. 1
Clinton

Clinton Corn Proc.
Beaver Channel
Clinton

Clinton Plant
Box 451
Clinton

Collis Corp.
S. 19th St.
Clinton

Aidex Corp.
7 mi. S. of
Council Bluffs

Drumco, Inc.
(plus 1 other site)
29th Ave.
Council Bluffs

Davenport Ldfl.
Davenport

Walnut Grove Prod.
21st St.
Des Moines

Des Moines Barrel
S.E. 19th/Scott
Des Moines

Dico Co., Inc.
16th St.
Des Moines

Polaris Plating
W. Bridge St.
Elkador

Ft. Dodge Nit.
Plant 2
Hwy. 20
Ft. Dodge

Farmland Inds.
Ft. Dodge

Chevron Chem.
Co.
Box 282
Ft. Madison

Dupont Denemours
35th/Ave. H
Ft. Madison

Ft. Madison
  Munic. Ldfl
Denmark Rd.
Ft. Madison

Ft. Madison Plant
Ortho Way
Ft. Madison

Jerome Strunk
Ft. Madison

Glenwood Iowa
  Dump
N. edge of town
Glenwood

Iowa Coun. Ldfl.
Homestead

Midwest Inds.
Ohio St.
Ida Grove

Iowa City Sanit.
  Ldfl.
Rte. 1
Iowa City

Smith-Jones, Inc.
High St.
Kellogg

Midwest Carbide
  Corp.
Main St.
Keokuk

Norbert Nejdl
Linn Coun.

Malvern Drum Site
W. edge of
Malvern

Vogel Plant Waste
  Disp.
Maurice

I. A. Army
  Ammun. Plant
Rte. 1
Middleton

U.S. Nameplate
Hwy. 30 W.
Mount Vernon

Monsanto Co.
Box 473
Muscatine

Muscatine Coun.
  Sanit. Ldfl.
Hwy. 61 N.
Muscatine

Muscatine Plant
Rte. 5
Muscatine

Thermo Gas Co.
Brick Plant Rd.
Ottamwa

Iowa Ind.
Industrial Pk. Rd.
Pocahontas

Mid Am. Tanning
Box 668
Sergeant Bluff

FMC Corp.–Agric.
Port Neal Ind.
  Area
Sergeant Bluff

Arnold Jensen
RFD
Shellsburg

Sioux City Ldfl.
Sioux City

Chas. Knoch Fm.
W. Point

James Baier Fm.
W. Point

Kansas

Arkansas City
  Dump
S. of Hwy. 166
Arkansas City

Mobile Oil Corp.
Second/Oak Sts.
Augusta

Old Mobile Oil
  Ref.
N. of U.S. 54
Augusta

Deffenbaugh Ldfl.
Loring Dr.
Bonner Spr.

Old Mobile Oil
Bruno TWP

Neosho Coun. Site
  (plus 1 other site)
Chanute

Nat. Zinc Co.
Cherryvale

Abandoned Sinclair
Coffeeville

Sherwin William
  Co.
Fourth St.
Coffeeville

National Distillers
  & Chem.
Desoto

U.S. Ind. Chem.
Desoto

Sunflower Army
  Ammun. Army
Box 640
Desoto

Farmland Ind.
  Dodge
U.S. 50
Dodge City

Pester Ref. Co.
N. Topeka St.
El Dorado

Doepke Disp. Serv.
S.W. of I-635
Holiday

Joe Wendell's Fm.
6 mi. N. of
Hutchinson

Soda Ash Waste
  Disp.
Hutchinson

R&K Mfg.
Rte. 4
Hutchinson

Browning-Ferris
  Ind.
N. 7th St.
Kansas City

S&G Metals Disp.
  (plus 1 other site)
S. Bethany
Kansas City

S&G Metals Disp.
40th/Gibbs
Kansas City

S&G Metals Disp.
Ruby Dr.
Kansas City

S&G Metals Site 7
State Ave.
Kansas City

S&G Metals Disp.
Pacific Ave.
Kansas City

S&G Metals Site 1
14th/State Ave.
Kansas City

S. Bank Missouri R.
Behind Fairfax Ind.
Kansas City

Thompson-
  Hayward CHE
Speaker Rd.
Kansas City

Turkey Ck.
  Dumping
Merriam Dr.
Kansas City

PBI-Gordon, Inc.
S. 3rd St.
Kansas City

Parking lot
Fairfax Rd.
Kansas City

Kansas City Ref.
Fairfax
Kansas City

Heatwood Oil Co.
12th St./Kansas R.
Kansas City

Fairfax Ind. Area
  Dump
Fairfax Trafficway
Kansas City

Fairfax Drainage
River Levee
Kansas City

Doepke Disp. Serv.
Funston Rd.
Kansas City

Coral Ref. Corp.
Kansas City

Kingman Coun.
  Ldfl.
Kingman

Farmland Inds.
Box 308
Lawrence

FMC Corp.
9th/Maple
Lawrence

Old Callery Chem.
Lawrence

Victorian Marble
  Co.
139th/Antioch Rd.
Leawood

City of Neodesha
  Lag.
11th/Illinois
Neodesha

Chemical
Commod.
S. Blake
Olathe

N. R. Hamm—
Williamstown
S.E. Douglas
Perry

Jayhawk Plant
Box 62008
Pittsburg

Old Vickers Ref.
Potwin

Greenwood Helium
Plant
Star Rte.
Richfield

Cities Serv. Helex
U.S. 160
Satana-Rte.

Johnson Coun.
Ldfl.
53rd St.
Shawnee

Solomon Elec.
W. Main
Solomon

E. I. Dupont
Denemours
Box 481
Topeka

Goodyear Tire &
Rubber
Hwy. 24
Topeka

Cities Serv. Co.
U.S. 60
Ulysses

N. R. Hamm
Quarry
Hwy. 24
Williamston

Derby Ref. Co.
E. 21st
Witchita

Johns Sludge Pond
Hydraulic/29th
Witchita

Kansas Ind.
Environ.
N. 127th St.
Witchita

Kentucky

Armco
Russell Rd.
Ashland

Olin Chem. Corp.
(plus 9 other
sites)
Hwy. 933
Brandenburg

Unconfirmed site
Brandenburg

Air Prod. Ldfl.
Hwy. 1523
Calvert City

B. F. Goodrich
Box 527
Calvert City

Calvert various site
Calvert City

Ind. Waste Haul.
Hwy. 1523
Calvert City

Ind. Waste Disp.
Hwy. 1523
Calvert City

Liquid Waste Disp.
Hwy. 1523
Calvert City

Sanit. Ldfl.
Hwy. 1523
Calvert City

Penwalt Corp.
Hwy. 1523
Calvert City

Dow Corning
Corp.
Hwy. 42
Carrolton

Covington Ldfl.
U.S. Hwy. 42
Covington

Hardin Coun. Ldfl.
Springfield Rd.
Elizabethtown

Kentucky Ind. Serv.
Hawkins Dr.
Elizabethtown

Raymond
Carpenter Ldfl.
No. 9
Flemingsburg

Whitefeather Fm.
Hwy. 68
Gracie

Koppers, Inc.
Merriweather Rd.
Guthrie

Hancock Coun.
Dump
Hawesville

Wilson's Well
Hawesville

PB&S Chem. Co.
N. Adams
Henderson

Oil Fds.
Henderson

Maxey Flats
Radioact.
Maxley Flats Rd.
Hillsboro

Hopkinsville Ldfl.
(plus 2 other
sites)
Mt. Zoar Rd.
Hopkinsville

Phillips Petr.
Calvin Dr.
Hopkinsville

Brantley Ldfl.
Hwy. 85
Island

Reichold Chem.,
Inc.
Waterson Trail
Jeffersontown

Finley Mill Rd.
Finley Mill Rd.
Lagrange

Ind. Plating
Lexington

Old Lexington
Ldfl.
New Circle Rd.
Lexington

Greenup Ldfl.
Hwy. 42
Lloyd

B. F. Goodrich
Bells Ln.
Louisville

Borden Chem.
Campground Rd.
Louisville

Bramers
Lake Dreamland
Louisville

Campground Rd.
Grade Ln.
Louisville

Cooks Ldfl.
Ralph Ave.
Louisville

E. I. Dupont—
Louisville Wks.
Louisville

Evap. Pond
Campground Rd.
Louisville

Kentucky Petr.
Prod. Co.
Blanton Ln.
Louisville

Landfill, Inc.
Grade Ln.
Louisville

Lee's Ln. Ldfl.
Lee's Ln. at Ohio R.
Louisville

Liquid Waste Disp.
Fern Valley
Louisville

Louisville Wks.
Campground Rd.
Louisville

Mobile Waste Ctl.
Grade Ln.
Louisville

Pit—Jct. Bells
S.W. of Bells
Louisville

Pits—S.W. Jct. Bells
S. of Bell Ln.
Louisville

Rohm & Haas
(plus 5 other
sites)
Vogt Ave.
Louisville

Rohm & Haas
Campground Rd.
Louisville

Smith Fm.
Louisville

S. Mat.
Louisville

Stauffer Chem. Co.
Campground Rd.
Louisville

Triangle Ref.
Louisville

Upper Pond Ck.
Louisville

Wood & Fuel
Griffith / 3000th
Louisville

Woodland Dr. Mill
Woodland Dr.
Louisville

Green R. Disp.
Ldfl.
Kelly Cem. Rd.
Maceo

Allen Chem. Dump
Marion

Pennwalt Corp.
Rte. 10
Marion Coun.

Cooksey Bros.
Disp. Co.
Big Run Rd.
Meads

Inland Chemicorp
New Castle

Newport Dump
Newport

Owensboro City
Ldfl.
Burton Rd.
Owensboro

Owensboro Plant
Site
Rte. 1 / Hwy. 60
Owensboro

Allen Chem. Dump
Raywick

Borden Fert.
Morgantown Rd.
Russelville

Griffin Ind.
Borden Dr.
Russelville

Russelville City
Dump
Morgantown Rd.
Russelville

Russelville Sanit.
Co.
Coppertown Rd.
Russelville

Russelville Sanit.
Co.
Hopkinsville Rd.
Russelville

Sand Gap Dump
Chestnut Flat
Sand Gap

A. L. Taylor site
Hwy. 1020
Shepardsville

N/L Ind.–Didier
Taylor
S. Shore

Field off Mitchell
Tip Top

Brantley Ldfl.
Utica

Messinochlager
Dump
Utica

Bavarian Trkg. Co.
Dump Rd.
Walton

Distler Brickyd.
U.S. 31 / 60
W. Point

Distler Fm.
W. Point

Epperson Trash
Haul
Kells Rd.
Williamstown

E. I. Dupont
Harris Rd.
Wurtland

Jeff Mead's Ldfl.
Uhlen Branch Rd.
Wurtland

Louisiana

John Nunez Ppty.
Abbeville

PAB Oil & Chem
Jean Edias
Abbeville

Roy Young Yd.
Charity
Abbeville

Galveston-
Houston
Off Hwy. 335
Abbeville

Missouri-Pac.
Terminal Rd.
Alexandria

Rax Timmy Garb.
Evangeline Ln.
Alexandria

Leon Lowe & Sons
15th St.
Alton

St. Bernard
St. Claude
Arabi

B.W.S. Basile
Basile

White Ollie Harvey
Hwy. 139
Bastrop

Stauffer Chem. Co.
N. Washington
Bastrop

Allied Chem. Corp.
Scenic Hwy.
Baton Rouge

Browning-
Ferris Ind.
Seigen Ln.
Baton Rouge

Atlantic Waste
Environ.
Kincaid
Baton Rouge

B.R. Polyolefins
Box 53006
Baton Rouge

Allied Chem. Corp.
Scenic Hwy.
Baton Rouge

Catalyst Handle
Sys.
Main St.
Baton Rouge

Grant Chem.
Baton Rouge

Ethyl Corp.
Box 341
Baton Rouge

Exxon Co.
Scenic Hwy.
Baton Rouge

Lens-Wicks Co.,
Inc.
Halsey St.
Baton Rouge

Maclan Serv. Co.
Daradelle Rd.
Baton Rouge

Pearce &
Leblanc
Baton Rouge

Petro Proc.
Brooklawn Dr.
Baton Rouge

Petro Proc.
Brooklawn Dr.
Baton Rouge

Rollins Environ.
Serv.
Scenic Hwy.
Baton Rouge

Sanfil Ld. Recl.
Airline Hwy.
Baton Rouge

Schylkill Prod.
Brooklawn Dr.
Baton Rouge

S. Vac.
Jeffery Dr.
Baton Rouge

Stauffer Chem. Co.
Box 828
Baton Rouge

U.S.S. Chem. Div.
Box 73496
Baton Rouge

Glenmore Pltn.
Augusta Rd.
Bayou Goula

Rollins Environ.
Serv.
Bayou Sorrel

Environ. Pur.
Box 2868
Bayou Sorrel

Alliance Rec.
Hwy. 23
Belle Chasse

Oak Pt. Plant
Box 70
Belle Chasse

Tom Hicks Oil Fd.
Belle Chasse

Grand Bois Water
Disp.
Hwy. 24
Berwick

Potential Site
Hwy. 24
Berwick

Harold White Ldfl.
Boutte

I.T. Corp.
Burnside

Browning-Ferris
Ind.
Carlyse

Chem. Waste Mgt.
John Bramon Rd.
Carlyse

F.&L. Sanit. Co.
Pt. Noir
Church Pt.

Burnside Plant
Rte. 1
Convent

Texaco, Inc.
Box 37
Convent

Crowley City
Dump
Northern Ave.
Crowley

Frenchies Oil Co.
Hwy. 1112
Crowley

Four Way Haul.
Rte. 1
Darrow

Inger Oil Co.
Hwy. 85
Darrow

Browning-Ferris
Ind.
S.E. of Geismar
Darrow

Sun Oil Co.
Box 67
Delhi Fd.

Combustion, Inc.
Denham Spr.

Lockharts Waste
Disp.
Hwy. 16
Denham Spr.

March Chem.
Box 1197
Denham Spr.

B.W.C. Corp.
Dequincy

Harold William
Fm.
Dequincy

Boise S.
Taylor Rd.
De Ridder

Agrico Chem. Co.
Box 71
Donaldsonville

C.F. Inds., Inc.
Hwy. 18
Donaldsonville

Eola Plant 94
Gen. Deliv.
Eola

Southeast, Inc.
Hwy. 190
Erwinville

N. Bend Plant 95
N. Bend Rd.
Franklin

Nalco Chem. Co.
Garyville

Shreveport Plant
Hwy. 1
Gayles

Allied Chem. Corp.
Box 226
Geismar

Borden, Inc.
Box 427
Geismar

Inger Oil Co.
Hwy. 75
Geismar

Shell Chem. Co.
Hwy. 75
Geismar

Vulcan Mat. Co.
River Rd.
Geismar

Good Hope Ref.
Prospect Ave.
Good Hope

Kaiser Aluminum
River Rd.
Gramercy

Colonial Sugars Co.
Gramercy

Mermentau Res.
Grand Chenier

Greenwood Sanit.
Serv.
Church/Nixon St.
Greenwood

Browning-
Ferris Ind.
Hwy. 27
Hackberry

Argus Chem. Corp.
Box 310
Hahnville

Becker Inds.
Hwy. 18
Hahnville

Hooker Chem. Co.
Box 74
Hahnville

Shell Oil Co.
Hahnville

Taft Plant
Hwy. 18
Hahnville

B.&F. Rural Sanit.
Baton Rouge Hwy.
Hammond

Graphic, Inc. Corp.
River Rd.
Harahan

Hydril Co.
Destrehan Ave.
Harvey

Metroplex Ldfl.
Peters Rd.
Harvey

Natl. Environ.
Peters Rd.
Harvey

Malone Disp. Site
Hatch

Delta Iron Wks.
Ind. Blvd.
Houma

Reliable Disp. Co.,
Inc.
Iris Ave.
Jefferson

Evangeline Ref.
Jennings

Curtis Simon Pit
Hwy. 335/Parish
Kaplan

Alton Romero Site
Kaplan

Tower Pit, Inc.
Kaplan

Forked Is. Shipyd.
Hwy. 82
Kaplan

A-1 Disp.
Clay St.
Kenner

Dubois
Dawson
Kenner

W. Disp. Co.,
Inc.
Kenner Ave.
Kenner

Disp. Serv. of
Lafayette
Bertrand Dr.
Lafayette

Calcasieu—Parish
Dump
Lake Charles

Calcasieu Sanit.
Broad
Lake Charles

Cities Serv. Oil
Box 1522
Lake Charles

Hercules
Cities Serv. Hwy.
Lake Charles

Lake Charles Ldfl.
Broad St.
Lake Charles

Lake Charles Plant
(plus 1 other site)
Box 3247
Lake Charles

Nederland Facil.
Box 3044
Lake Charles

W. R. Grace & Co.
Box 3247
Lake Charles

PPG Inds.
Columbia S. Rd.
Lake Charles

Ponchartrain Wks.
Box 2000
La Place

W.J. Oils
Larose

Gulf Fab Salvors
Larose

Lelieux Disp. Co.
Hwy. 13
Lelieux

S.W. Environ. Co.
Hwy. 190 W.
Livingston

Unidentified Site
Livingston

Conserv. Sp.
Box 16
Livonia

Lockport Chem.
  Co., Inc.
Elm St.
Lockport

Fordoche Gas Plant
Lottie

Monsanto Co.
Hwy. 18
Luling

Mansura Ready
  Mix
Stess St.
Mansura

Marrero Site
Miss. R.
Marrero

New Orleans Wks.
4th St.
Marrero

Guthrie Oil
Maurice

Lee Sanit. Serv.
Ridge Lake Rd.
Metairie

M.&W. Disp.
Mistletoe St.
Metairie

Waste Sys. Div.
L.&A. Rd.
Metairie

Allied Chem. Corp.
Central Ave.
Monroe

Hearold Disp. Co.
Timberline Dr.
Monroe

Monroe Wks.
Central Ave.
Monroe

W.R. Grace Co.
Box 4751
Monroe

W.R. Grace Co.
Sterlington Rd.
Monroe

Ivanhoe Plant
Box 1328
New Iberia

Am. Cyanamid
River Rd.
New Orleans

Bionuclear, Inc.
Jefferson Hwy.
New Orleans

Waste Land, Inc.
Florida Ave.
New Orleans

Algiers Ldfl.
Woodland Hwy.
New Orleans

Conaway Truck
  Serv.
Elysian Fds.
New Orleans

Gentilly Ldfl.
Old Gentilly
New Orleans

Natl. Oil of La.
Intracoastal Dr.
New Orleans

Recovery I
Chef Menteur
New Orleans

Shell Chem. Co.
Box 10
Norco

Reichold Chem.
Box 685
Oakdale

Newport Div.
Box 685
Oakdale

Robbins Bldrs.
Oil City

Agric. Chem.
Box 588
Opelousas

St. Landry Parish
Main St.
Opelousas

Prairie Comm.
  Ldfl.
Opelousas

St. Landry Parish
Prudhomme Ln.
Opelousas

Prudhomme Ln.
Opelousas

Delaney Chem. Co.
Esler Fd. Rd.
Pineville

Louisiana Div.
Box 150
Plaquemine

Hercules, Inc.
Box 716
Plaquemine

Georgia-Pac. Corp.
Box 629
Plaquemine

McLean Trkg.
Box 149
Port Allen

Sugarland Disp.
Hwy. 90
Raceland

Jones Chem. Disp.
Reserve

S.E. Chem. Co.
Hwy. 61
Reserve

Browning-Ferris
  Ind.
Hwy. 61
St. Charles Parish

E. St. Charles Ldfl.
Hwy. 61
St. Charles Parish

Pelican State
  Environ.
Hwy. 61
St. Charles Parish

W. St. Charles Ldfl.
Hwy. 90
St. Charles Parish

Air Prod. & Chem.
Box 1
St. Gabrial

St. Gabrial Plant
  (plus 1 other site)
Hwy. 30
St. Gabrial

Ciba-Geigy Plant
Box 11
St. Gabrial

Gulf Oil Chem.
St. Gabrial

Gulf Oil Chem.
Hwy. 18
St. James

Cambre Carl Contr.
Rose St.
St. Rose

Gleason Crater Site
James Deal Ppty.
Shongaloo

Ldfl.
Bagley Rd.
Shreveport

La. Army Ammun.
Shreveport

Roadway Exp.
Shreveport

S.C.A. Serv. of La.
Tulsa
Shreveport

W. Elec.
Shreveport

Univ. Oil Prod.
Box 21566
Shreveport

Braselman Corp.
Slidell

Cleve-Reber Site
Sorrento

Arizona Chem. Co.
Minden Rd.
Springhill

Gulf Oil Chem.
Box 857
Springhill

IMC Fert. Corp.
Hwy. 2
Sterlington

Browning-Ferris
  Ind.
I-10 Serv. Rd.
Sulphur
B.W.S. Tate Cove
Tate Cove
Sheffield Petr.
Hwy. 447
Walker
Australia Pt.
W. Baton Rouge
Cont. Carbon
Westlake
Jefferson Disp.
Hwy. 90
Westwego
Campesi Fm.
Rte. 1
White Castle
Calcasieu Disp. Site
Willow Spr. Rd.
Willow Spr.
Mud Pits, Inc.
Hwy. 308

Maine

Daulphin Dump
Bath
Callahan Min.
Cape Rosier
McKin Co.
Gray
Eastern Surplus
Heddybemps
Howland—Tris
  Spill
Howland
Security Hill
Mill St.
Lewiston
Harry's Pit
Limerick
Chem-Waste, Inc.
Varney Crossing
N. Berwick
Inc. Orrington Plant
Orrington
Orrington Plant
Rte. 15
Orrington

Quarry
Old Country Rd.
Rockland
Crockett Pt.
Rockland
Ldfill
Rockport
Gravel Pit
Box 591
Sanford
New Dump Solid
  Waste
Rushton St.
Sanford
Old Dump Solid
  Waste
Rushton St.
Sanford
Rear 82
Box 591
Sanford
Sanford Munic.
  Ldfl.
Rushton St.
Sanford
Union Chem. Co.
S. Hope
S. Portland Ldfl.
Highland Ave.
S. Portland
S. Maine Fin.
Rte. 5
Waterboro
W. Lagoon
Wells
Winthrop Dump
Annabessacook
Winthrop

Maryland

Aberdeen Dump
Aberdeen Coun.
Busk Ldfl.
Abingdon Coun.
Naval Acad.
Annapolis
Naval Sta.
Annapolis
Hawkins Pt. Imd.
  Port
Ann Arundel

Johnson & Speak
Salley Rd.
Ann Arundel
Allied Chem. Agric.
Race St.
Baltimore
Am. Chem. Rec.
Birch St.
Baltimore
Baltimore Smelting
Baltimore
Baltimore Wks.
Block St.
Baltimore
BFI Norris Fm. Ldfl.
Trappe Rd.
Baltimore
BFI Ross-Tyl-Quar
Quarantine Rd.
Baltimore
Browning-Ferris
  Ind.
Trappe Rd.
Baltimore
SCM-Robb-Tyl-
  Quar Rd.
Quarantine Rd.
Baltimore
Chemetals Corp.
Baltimore
Curtis Bay Plant
Pennington Ave.
Baltimore
Dump Area
Chemical Rd.
Baltimore
Dundalk Marine
  Team
Baltimore
FMC Corp.
Patapsco Ave.
Baltimore
Hous & Auth.
Baltimore
Koppers Dump Site
Child St.
Baltimore
Md. Sludge Disp.
  Site
Baltimore
Mid-Atlantic Wood
  Pres.
Baltimore

Pemco Prod.
Baltimore
Reedbird Ldfl.
Reedbird Ave.
Baltimore
Robb-Tyler
Morris Ln.
Baltimore
Buck's Steel Drum
Baltimore Coun.
Bata Shoe Co.
Belcamp
VS Beltsville Agri
Beltsville
Anacostia R. Pk.
Bladensburg
Gen. Serv. Admin.
Bladensburg
Cambridge Site
Trenton
Cambridge
City Disp. Plant
Cambridge
Cecil Coun. Ldfl.
Cecil Coun.
Naval Res. Lab
Chesapeake
Chestertown Plant
Rte. 297
Chestertown
Munic. Dump
Chestertown
Bio-Quest
Schilling Ck.
Cockeysville
Boehm Dump
St. Stephens Ch. Rd.
Crownsville
Amoelle
Box 444
Cumberland
Edgewood Arsenal
Edgewood
Elkton Quarry
Elkton
Old Elkton Dump
Jones-Chapel Rd.
Elkton
Rte. 7 Chem. Dump
W. of Rte. 40
Elkton

Rte. 7 Chem. Dump
Elkton

Spectron, Inc.
Rte. 8
Elkton

Howard Coun.
Ldfl.
Montgomery Rd.
Ellicott City

Hoffman Ldfl.
Rte. 36/48
Frostburg

Cabin Run Rd.
Ldfl.
Cabin Run Rd.
Frostburg

Vale Summit Ldfl.
Rte. 36/38
Frostburg

Ann Arundel Co.
Ldfl.
Patapsco Ave.
Glen Burnie

BFI Solley Rd. Ldfl.
Solley Rd.
Glen Burnie

Browning-Ferris
Ind.
Solley Rd.
Glen Burnie

Joy 2 Joy/Hamlen
Arundel Corp. Rd.
Glen Burnie

Fairchild Ldfl. Disp.
Hagerstown

Koppers Co., Inc.
St. Clair St.
Hagerstown

Mack Trucks, Inc.
Hagerstown

Havre de Grace
Dump
Havre de Grace

Mullins Ldfl.
Old Post Rd.
Havre de Grace

Bladensburg Plant
52nd Ave.
Hyattsville

Naval Ord. Sta.
Indian Head

Koppers Co., Inc.
U.S.1/Contee Rd.
Laurel

Ninamar Corp.
Odenton

Odenton Plant
Telegraph Rd.
Odenton

Chevron Chem.
Telegraph Rd.
Odenton

Koppers Co., Inc.
Old Town

Naval Air Test Ctr.
Patuxent
River

Baltimore Galv.
Quad Ave.
Rosedale

Salisbury Plant
Quantico Rd.
Salisbury

Grigco Waste Oil
Co.
Sharptown

Naval Surface
Weapons
Solomons Is.

Naval Support
Facil.
Thurmont

Naval Surface
Weapons
White Oak

Woodlawn Ldfl.
(plus 1 other site)
Woodlawn

Massachusetts

W. R. Grace
Independence Rd.
Acton

Sanit. Ldfl.
East Rd.
Adams

Pfizer Co.
Columbia St.
Adams

Andover Plant
Lowell Jct. Rd.
Andover

Town Dump
Chandler Rd.
Andover

Nyanza Chem.
Corp.
Megunlco Rd.
Ashland

Attleboro Ldfl.
Peckham St.
Attleboro

Shpack Dump
Union Rd.
Attleboro

Auburn Site
Rochdale St.
Auburn

Hybrid Sys.
Bedford

BASF Ind.
Crosby Dr.
Bedford

Bedford Site
Bedford

V.A. Hosp.
Springs Rd.
Bedford

Belchertown Site
Bay Rd.
Belchertown

Benzenold Org.
Mendon St.
Bellingham

Charleston Navy
Yd.
Boston

Recycl. Ind.
Braintree

Cannon Eng.
First St.
Bridgewater

Burlington Site
Burlington

Burlington Cesspool
Muller Rd.
Burlington

Kendall Sq.
Whitemore Ave.
Cambridge

W. R. Grace Co.
Cambridge

Uncertain Site
Canton

Plymouth Rubber
Co.
Canton

Fastener Corp.
Crescent Ave.
Chelsea

Ahearn Trucking
Co.
Burnett Rd.
Chicopee

Grattan
Chicopee

M. T. Sullivan
Burnett Rd.
Chicopee

Partyka Ldfl.
Lombard Rd.
Chicopee

Creese & Cook Co.
Water St.
Danvers

Uncertain Site
Rte. 114
Danvers

H&M Drum Co.
Dartmouth

Dedham Water Co.
Dedham

Liquidator, Inc.
Dorchester

Hile Rd. Dump
Dorchester

E. Bridgewater
Bridge St.
E. Bridgewater

Monsanto Co.
Mustic Vw. Rd.
Everett

Tilliston Co.
Ferry St.
Fall River

Otis AFB
Falmouth

Lott Ppty.
Fitchburg

Freetown/H&M
Drum Co.
Rtes. 24/79
Freetown

Groveland Site
Groveland

Haverhill Ldfl.
Old Groveland Rd.
Haverhill

Vernon Plastics
  Corp.
Shelley Rd.
Haverhill

Holden Dump
River St.
Holden

Mobile Chem. Co.
Hanover St.
Holyoke

Monson Chem.
South St.
Hopkinton

Potential Site
Rte. 3
Kingston

Munic. Ldfl.
Mechanic St.
Leominster

Borden Co.
Lancaster St.
Leominster

H.S. Gravure
Willard St.
Leominster

Roche Bros. Barrell
Phoenix Ave.
Lowell

Lalla's Garage
Middlesex St.
Lowell

Silresin Chem. Co.
Tanner St.
Lowell

Hickory Hills
Lunenburg

Gen. Elec. Co.
Turbine Bldg.
Lynn

E. Smelting
Rubier St.
Lynn

Compo Ind.
Branch St.
Mansfield

Mansfield Town
  Dump
East St. / Rte. 106
Mansfield

Pleasant Trkg.
Fitchburg St.
Marlboro

Allied Chem.
Corp. Way
Medford

Methuen Dump Site
Burnham Rd.
Methuen

New Bedford Ldfl.
Shawmit Ave.
New Bedford

Camger Chem.
Main St.
Norfolk

STP (closed)
Massachusetts Ave.
N. Adams

Sanit. Ldfl.
W. Shaft Rd.
N. Adams

N. Andover
Sharpners Pond Rd.
N. Andover

Town Ldfl.
Holt Rd.
N. Andover

Unknown Site
No. 3 & 4
N. Reading

Ellis Wellfield
Norwood

Ldfl.
Oxford

L. Fine Co.
Lynnfield St.
Peabody

Eastman Geletine
  Co.
Kingston St.
Peabody

Gen. Elec.
Plastics Ave.
Pittsfield

Munic. Ldfl.
East St. / Hubbard
Pittsfield

Pittsfield Sew.
Holmes Rd.
Pittsfield

Potential Site
Plymouth

Cedarville Ldfl.
Plymouth

Components Mfg.
  Serv.
Polasset

Randolph Sanit.
Ldfl.
Johnson Dr.
Randolph

Trancoa Site
Ash St.
Reading

Rehoboth-Silva-
  Bosco
Providence St.
Rehoboth

Machine Shop
Rowley

S. Essex Sew.
Fort Ave.
Salem

Refuse Energy Sys.
Salem Tnpk.
Saugus

Southington Ldfl.
Southington

Ldfl.
Turnboll / Cottage
Springfield

Monsanto Co.
Worcester St.
Springfield

Monsanto Co.
Grochmal St.
Springfield

Taunton Ldfl.
Winthrop St.
Taunton

Templeton
Hubbartson Rd.
Templeton

Lily Chem. Co.
Athol Rd.
Templeton

Ldfl.
Tisbury

Charles George
  Ldfl.
Dunstable Rd.
Tunesboro

Thermo Electron
First Ave.
Waltham

Star Chem.
Rtes. 225 / 110
Westford

Surface Coating,
  Inc.
Eames St.
Wilmington

Olin Chem.
Eames St.
Wilmington

Ritter Trkg. Co.
Woburn St.
Wilmington

Wilmington Site
Wilmington

MDC Septage
  Receiv.
Woburn St.
Wilmington

Edward C. Whitney
Woburn St.
Wilmington

New England
  Resins
New Boston St.
Woburn

Severance Trucking
Walnut Hill Rd.
Woburn

Whitney Barrell Co.
Salem St.
Woburn

Woburn Sanit. Ldfl.
Merrimack St.
Woburn

Woburn Steel Drum
Harlow Ct.
Woburn

Ind.-Plex 128
Commerce / Atlantic
Woburn

Aberjona Auto Parts
Salem St.
Woburn

Atlantic Gelatin
Hill St.
Woburn

Ind. Tallow
Cedar St.
Woburn

Sanit. Ldfl.
Yarmouth

Michigan

Buena Vista Twp.
Sutton Rd.
Adrian

SWS Silicones
Sutton Rd.
Adrian

Lenawee Disp. Serv.
N. Ogden Hwy.
Adrian

Anderson Devel.
E. Michigan St.
Adrian

Huitt & Sons, Inc.
Rte. 2
Allegan

Alpena & Wiss
Off Rte. 32
Alpena

Edward C. Levy Co.
Ash Twp.

Arkona Rd. Ldfl.
Augusta Twp.

Christianson Dump
Hamlin Rd.
Avon

Dump C Proposed
Hamlin/Adams Rd.
Avon

M.A.L. Ent.
Hamlin Rd.
Avon

Oakland City Dump
Avon

Sandfill, Inc.
Hamlin Rd.
Avon

Sandfill Ldfl. #2
Hamlin Rd.
Avon

S.E. Oakland
Avon Twp.

Huron Coun. Solid
Waste
Bad Ax

Bimba Wash King
Baldwin

Neway Laundry
Baldwin

G&G Disp.
Bath Rd.
Bancroft

Du-Well Prod., Inc.
Cemetary Rd.
Bangor

Raymond Rd. Ldfl.
Six Mile Rd.
Battle Ck.

Thomas Solv. Co.
N. Raymond Rd.
Battle Ck.

Bay City Plant
Bay City

Lamina, Inc.,
Div. of
Fairground Rd.
Bellarie

N.E. Gravel Co.
Cannonsburg Rd.
Belmont

N.W. Berriew Co.
Benton Harbor

Eaton Coun.
Disp. 1
Windsor Hwy.
Benton Twp.

E. E. Oakland
Berkley

Wayne Disp.
Berlin Twp.

Tri-Township Ldfl.
Rte. #1
Berrien Ctr.

Clarence Brubaker
Ldfl.
Blissfield

Howes Leather Co.
W. Front St.
Boyne City

Brighton Town
Dump (plus 1
other site)
Alpine Rd.
Brighton

Bronson Resident
Well
Mill St.
Bronson

Bronson Platting
Ind. Ave.
Bronson

Heiden Fm.
Brownston

Thorton Ldfl.
Telegraph Rd.
Brownstown Twp.

Cadillac City Airpt.
Cadillac

Northerpaire
Plating
6th St.
Cadillac

K&J Ldfl.
Lilly Rd.
Canton Twp.

Crystal Ref. Co.
N. Williams
Carson City

S.W. Cass Coun.
Ldfl.
Anderson Rd.
Cass Coun.

Cedar R. Solid
Cedar R.

Charlotte Disp.
Stine Rd.
Charlotte

Clinton R. Rd. Ldfl.
Clinton R.
Clinton

Dependable Ldfl.
Palmer Rd.
Columbia Twp.

Consumers Pow.
Co.
Morrow Steam
Plant
Comstock

Drake Inds.
Water St.
Constantine

Newell Sanit. Ldfl.
28th Ave.
Covert Twp.

Cent. Rd. Dump.
Cent. Rd.
Dalton

Oakland Coun.
Ldfl.
Davis

Thermal
Conversion
Dearborn

Wayne Disp., Inc.
Kinsbury Rd.
Dearborn

Reichold Chem.
Derndale

Allied Chemicorp.
Detroit

Detroit Plant
Incline
Detroit

Holloways
Detroit

Koi Petrol Co.,
Inc.
Lycaste
Detroit

Michigan Petr.
Detroit

Nelson Chem. Co.
Detroit

Site on I-2
Detroit

Waste Acid Serv.
Detroit

Gen. Motors Corp.
Grand Blvd.
Detroit

Wayne Disp.
Detroit

Chase Mfg.
Chase Rd.
Douglas

Dowagiac Sanit.
Nebour Rd.
Dowagiac

Simons Sanit. Ldfl.
Bigelow Rd.
Dundee

E. Jordan City Ldfl.
E. Jordan

E. Rapids Ldfl.
Hogback Rd.
Eaton Rapids

Am. Cyanamid Co.
Escanaba

Am. Cyanamid 2
Escanaba

Am. Cyanamid 1
Escanaba

Consol. Metal
Halstead Rd.
Farmington Hill

Packing Corp. of
Am.
Filer City

Brey Fm.
Flatrock

G.M.C. Fisher
Body
E. Coldwater Rd.
Flint

Grand Blanc Ldfl.
Grand Blanc Rd.
Flint

For. Waste Disp.
Section 8
For. Twp.

Hoover Ball &
Bearing
Frank St.
Fowlerville

Stanley Wks.
Frank St.
Frankenmuth

San Juan Subdiv.
Fruitland

Noster Ind.
Ind. Rd.
Garden City

Champion Intl.
Corp.
Gaylord

Gladstone Ldfl.
Gladstone

George Westcoff
Site
Pine Grove
Gobles

Claud Rd. Ldfl.
Grand Blanc

Nevilles Waste
Jordan Rd.
Grand Blanc

Atco Rubber Prod.
Marion St.
Grand Haven

Butterworth Ldfl.
Grand Rapids

Fenske Ldfl.
Kenowa
Grand Rapids

Foam Tech. Insul.
Kirtland
Grand Rapids

Guard Chem. Co.
Grand Rapids

Guard Chem. Co.
Steele St.
Grand Rapids

Lack's Inds.
Gabraith Ave.
Grand Rapids

Sparta Ldfl.
Alpine Ave.
Grand Rapids

Wolverine Chem.
Grand Rapids

Lindberg Plast.
U.S. 31/Sullivan
Grand Traverse

Organic Chem.,
Inc.
Chicago Dr.
Grandville

James Spiegelburg
Spicer Rd.
Green Oaks

Ferro Tech.
Agglomer
Ind. Pk.
Grosse Ile

Am. Cyanamid Co.
Hannibal

Harbor Spring Pub.
E. Bluff St.
Harbor Beach

Pond 2 & Pond 1
Harbor Beach

Burrows Sanit.
Orland Rd.
Hartford

Du-Well Metal
Prod.
Haywood St.
Hartford

Private Fm.
Haslett

Hastings Mfg.
N. Hanover
Hastings

Hastings Sanit.
Serv.
N. Broadway
Hastings

Newton Lumber
Co.
S. Michigan Dr.
Hastings

Viking Corp.
N. Ind. Pk.
Hastings

Private Homes—
Jones
W. George
Hazel Pk.

Jones' Residence
Hazel Pk.

Hemlock City Area
Hemlock

Hemlock
Semiconductor
Hemlock

Lear-Siegler
W. Clark St.
Hendon

Henrietta Twp.
Ldfl.
Bunker Rd.
Henrietta Twp.

Hi-Mill Mfg.
Highland
Highland

Numatics, Inc.
N. Milford Rd.
Highland

RGCW Disp. Ldfl.
Teeple Lake Rd.
Highland

Williard Ldfl.
Teeple Lake Rd.
Highland

Lucas Ldfl.
Mauck Rd.
Hillsdale

Rozema Ind. Waste
Hodnanville

Facil. Ppty.
Holland

Holland Die
Casting
E. Lakewood Blvd.
Holland

Holland Twp. Ldfl.
Holland

Jacobusse Refuse
Serv.
N. 168th Ave.
Holland

Vanguard Glass
Fab.
Elm Lake
Holland

Cast Forge, Inc.
W. Highland Rd.
Howell

Howell Sanit. Co.
Howell

Intl. Paper
McPherson Pk.
Howell

Ben Powell Ldfl.
Clarkston Rd.
Independence

Reilly Tar & Chem.
S. Tibbs Ave.
Indianapolis

Am. Anodco Alum.
N. Beadslee
Ionia

Am. Anodco. Auto.
N. Beadslee
Ionia

Ishpeming
Ishpeming

Pluto Plant
Ishpeming

Libra Ind.
Jackson

Sherrod Refuse
Sheffield Rd.
Johnstown

Addison Prod. Co.
Gauge St.
Jonesville

A&B Septic Tank
Serv.
Kalamazoo

Abandoned Ldfl.
Kalamazoo

Alum. Impounds
Kalamazoo

Impounds 3 & 4
Kalamazoo

Kalamazoo Wks.
Kalamazoo

Nazareth Ldfl.
W. South St.
Kalamazoo

Roto-Finish Co.
Milham Rd.
Kalamazoo

Spoil Pile
Kalamazoo

Sulfur Plant
Kalamazoo

Viking Die Caste
Corp.
W. Michigan Ave.
Kalamazoo

W. K L Ave. Ldfl.
W. K L Ave.
Kalamazoo

1952 Site
Kalamazoo

1955 Site
Kalamazoo

1958 Site
Kalamazoo

1961 Site
Kalamazoo

1964 Site
Kalamazoo

1968 Site
Kalamazoo

1969 Site
Kalamazoo

1976–77 Site
Kalamazoo

Kalkaska Co. Rd.
Is. Lake Rd.
Kalkaska

Hartley & Hartley,
Inc.
Kawkawlin

Kentwood Ldfl.
Walma Ave.
Kent

St. Clair Coun. Rd.
Smith Ck. Rd.
Kimball

Privately Owned
Fm.
Lansing

Lansing Sanit. Ldfl.
(plus 1 other site)
Aurelius Rd.
Lansing

Lansing City Disp.
Comfort St.
Lansing

Dump Site
Hamlin / Adams
Lawrence Twp.

Leighton Twp.
Dump
130th / 140 Sts.
Leighton

Ind. Heat
Dexter-Chelsea
Lima

Rasmussens Sand
& Gravel
Spicer Rd.
Livingston

Sun-Livonia
Livonia

Attwood Corp.
Monroe St.
Lowell

C&O R.R. Yard
First St.
Ludington

Dow Chem.
S. Madison St.
Ludington

Ind. Plating
Harrison St.
Ludington

S. Mad.
Ludington

Straits Steel & Wire
N. Rowe
Ludington

Gulf & W. Stamping
Antrim Coun.
Mancelona

Manchester Dump
Schlweiss
Manchester

Sycor Corp.
Manchester

Morton Chem. Co.
6th St.
Manistee

Consumer Pow. Co.
Marion

Intl. Res. & Devel.
N. Main St.
Mattawan

Lear-Siegler
W. Clarke
Mendon

Metamora Fm.
Thornville Rd.
Metamora

Metamora Sanit.
Ldfl.
Dryden Rd.
Metamora

Getty Street Plant
Getty St.
Michigan

Midland Plant
Midland

Window Ldfl.
Midland

City of Midland
Ldfl.
Midland

Dow Corning
Midland

Milford Ldfl.
Old Plank Rd.
Milford

S.W. Ldfl.
Anderson Rd.
Milton

Colormetric
Mishawauka

Ford Motor Co.
E. Elm Ave.
Monroe

Heckett Eng. Ldfl.
E. Front St.
Monroe

Monroe City Ldfl.
Monroe

Port of Monroe
Ldfl. (plus 1
other site)
I-75 / Front St.
Monroe

E. I. Dupont
(plus 1 other site)
Old Channel Rd.
Montague

Hooker Chem. Co.
Whitebeck Rd.
Montague

Montague Wks.
Montague

Muskegon Coun.
Apple Ave.
Moorland Twp.

Morenci Town
Dump 1
W. Main St.
Morenci

Dean Bros. Co.
Clinton R.
Mt. Clemens

Quarry
Mt. Clemens

Lake States Wood
Munising

Am. Soil Spring
E. Keating Ave.
Muskegon

Bofors Lakeway
Chem. (plus 1
other site)
Evanston Ave.
Muskegon

Consumers Pow.
Co.
Muskegon

Cordova Chem. Co.
Muskegon

Duell Gardner Ldfl.
E. Bard Rd.
Muskegon

Johnson Prod. Div.
E. Keating Ave.
Muskegon

Private Well
Theresa
Muskegon

Whitehall Leather
Lake St.
Muskegon

Judson Road Yd.
Muskegon

Lorin Inds.
Muskegon

Lou Anodizers, Inc.
Robert's
Muskegon

Muskegon Pistol
Ring
6th St.
Muskegon

Private Well
Theresa
Muskegon

Storychem. Co.
Muskegon

Peck St. Ldfl.
Sanford St.
Muskegon

Story Chem.
Muskegon

Thomas Solv. Co.
Raymond Rd.
Muskegon

Systech, Inc.
Muskegon

Tech. Caste, Inc.
Whit
Muskegon

Teledyne Contl.
N. Getty St.
Muskegon

Browne-Morse Co.
E. Broadway
Muskegon Hgts.

Muskegon Hgts.
Seaway Dr.
Muskegon Hgts.

Macoms Coun.
New Haven

Acme Disp.
Reum Rd.
Niles

Aviax
Niles

S.E. Berrien Coun.
Niles

S.E. Berrien Coun.
E. Main St.
Niles

Terminal Rd. Ldfl.
Reum Rd.
Niles

Vulcan Cincinnati
Near Airpt.
Northport

Anderson Munic.
West/Mile Rd.
Novi

Cardinal Ldfl.—
Veterans
W. Hamlin Rd.
Oakland

Gerald Fons Mobile
Lapeer/Silver Bell
Oakland

S.E. Oakland Coun.
Oakland City

Richard's Refuse
W. Covert
Onondago

Garavaglia Ldfl.
Brown/Joslyn Rds.
Orion

Wurtsmith AFB
Oscoda

Wurtsmith AFB
Oscoda

Labell Oliver
Ossineko

For. Waste Disp.
Ldfl.
E. Farrand Rd.
Otisville

Menasha Corp.
N. Farmer
Otsego

Diamond Shamrock
Corp.
Painesville

Plant Dump
Parchment

Parkville Dump Site
Parkville

Plattco Ldfl.
Parkville

Lockwood Ent.
Squawfield Rd.
Pittsford

State Disp. Corp.
Ldfl.
E. Beltline Rd.
Plainfield Twp.

A-1 Disp.
Beard St.
Plainwell

Commercial
Pumping
Plainwell

Sunrise Ldfl.
(plus 1 other site)
Plainwell

Salem Ldfl.
Five Mile/Chubb
Plymouth

Ankerson Res.
Pontiac

Collier Rd. Ldfl.
Collier Rd.
Pontiac

Gt. Lakes Cont.
Collier Rd.
Pontiac

J. Fons Co., Inc.
Joslyn Rd.
Pontiac

Joslyn Rd. Ldfl.
Pontiac

Nat. Res.
Lapele/Rte. 1
Pontiac

Oakland Coun.
Ldfl.
Pontiac

Pontiac Lake Rd.
Pontiac

Oakland Coun. Rd.
Bald Mtn. Rd.
Pontiac

Sanicem
Lapeer Rd.
Pontiac

Ankerson Res.
Pontiac

Portage City Sanit.
Ldfl.
Portage

Wayne Disp. Co.
Rawsonville

Gen. Oil
Redford

Kopper's Co., Inc.
Reed City

Smith-Douglas
Riga

Detroit Wks.
R. Rouge

Zug Is.
R. Rouge

Fed. Marine
Jefferson Ave.
Riverview

Firestone Co.
Jefferson Ave.
Riverview

Firestone Site
Detroit/R. Shore
Riverview

McLouth Steel
Corp.
Jefferson Ave.
Riverview

Riverview Ldfl.
Riverview

Sibley Quarry
Riverview

Natl. Twist Drill
N. Rochester Rd.
Rochester

Six Star Ltd.
Rochester

Michigan Silica Co.
Rockwood

Western-Eaton Solv.
Huron R. Rd.
Romulus

Rose Twp. Cem.
W. of Milford Rd.
Rose

Rose Twp. Dump
Demode Rd.
Rose

Oakland Coun.
Rose Twp.

Buena Vista Twp.
Ldfl.
Hack/N. Outer Dr.
Saginaw

Agrico Chem.
Saginaw

City Disp. Coun.
Ldfl. (plus 1
other site)
Saginaw

Fm. Bur.
Saginaw

Green Pt. Ldfl.
Saginaw

Saginaw Plant
Saginaw

Mr. Fleischman
Saginaw

Saginaw Twp. Ldfl.
(plus 1 other site)
Saginaw

Taymouth Twp.
Ldfl.
Saginaw

Bourdou Tr. Co.
Saginaw

Agrico Chem. Co.
Saginaw

Sanit. Ldfl. 2
Thomas Rd.
St. Clair Coun.

S. Macomb Disp.
Pleasant St.
St. Claire Shore

Bendix Corp.
Maiden Lane
St. Joseph

Bendix Corp.
(plus 1 other site)
Red Arrow Hwy.
St. Joseph
Gratiot City Ldfl.
E. Jackson Rd.
St. Louis
Dustmasters Div.
Watson St.
St. Louis
Vesticol Chem. Co.
Bankson St.
St. Louis
Hoover Ball &
Bearing
Monroe St.
Saline
Cent. Sanit. Ldfl.
Rte. 1
Sand Lake
Lack's Inds.
Riverside Dr.
Sarenac
Saugatuck Twp.
Ldfl.
134th Ave.
Saugatuck
Hamlin Ldfl.
Hamlin Rd.
Shelby
Albion-Sheridan
Ldfl.
Div. Dr.
Sheridan Twp.
Dickerson Rd. Auto
Dickerson Rd.
Springfield
Oakland Coun.
Springfield
Springfield Twp.
Shindlee Rd.
Springfield
Grand Garb.
144th St.
Spring Lake
Star Inds., Inc.
Van Wagoner Rd.
Spring Lake
S. Macabe Coun. 6
Sect. 25
Sterling Twp.

City Sand & Ldfl.
Willow Rd.
Sumpter
Hard Fill Ldfl.
Judd Rd.
Sumpter
Sumpter Ldfl.
Elwell/Willow
Sumpter
Berlin & Farro Liq.
S. Moorish Rd.
Swartz Ck.
Edward Levy Ind.
Ldfl.
Penn. Rd.
Taylor
S.W. Berrien Ldfl.
Box 253
Three Oaks
Three Rivers
Anodizi
Rte. 2
Three Rivers
Detroit Edison Co.
Quarry Rd.
Trenton
J. R. McCalla
Trenton
Trenton Inorg. Plant
Trenton
Trenton Resins Plant
Trenton
Vulcan Mold & Iron
Fort St.
Trenton
McLouth Steel
Corp.
Sibley Ave.
Trenton
Fons Sanit. Ldfl.
Onenges Rd.
Troy
H&M Disp.—
Closed
Higgens/Walker
Tuscola Twp.
Chem. Met.
Tyler
Prod. Rec.
Arbogast Rd.
Union

Am. Legion Ppty.
Cass Ave.
Utica
Hamlin Devel. Co.
Hamlin Rd.
Utica
Liquid Disp. Co.
Hamlin Rd.
Utica
Ramona Pk. Sanit.
Ldfl.
Auburn Rd.
Utica
Stan's Trkg. Co.
Ryan Rd.
Utica
Wayne Disp. Co.
Van Buren Twp.
Vermontville Ldfl.
W. Vermontville
Hwy.
Vermontville
Macomb Coun.
Dump
Warren
Warren Mfg. Plant
Warren
Walker Ld. Recl.
Mile Rd.
Washington Twp.
Ford Motor Co.
Factory
Washtenau
Osceola Ref.
W. Branch
Old Dump
Weston
Stauffer Chem. Co.
Sand Ck. Hwy.
Weston
Waste Water Trmt.
Weston
Dupont, Whitehall
Whitehall
Muskegon Chem.
Co.
Warner St.
Whitehall
White Hall Ldfl.
Whitehall
Hoover Chem. Co.
Mile Rd.
Whitemore Lake

Suburban Sanit.
Ldfl.
24th/Garfield
Wright Twp.
BASF-Wyandotte
Corp.
Biddle Ave.
Wyandotte
Chemmet Serv., Inc.
Allen Rd.
Wyandotte
Wyandotte Plant
Biddle
Wyandotte
Rozema's Ind. Waste
Thornwood St.
Wyoming
Spartan Chem. Co.
28th St.
Wyoming
Wolverine Solv.
Stafford Ave.
Wyoming
Pighins Sand Pit
Willis/Crane
York Twp.
Norris Inds.
E. Michigan
Ypsilanti
Wayne Disp.
Ypsilanti
Wolverine
Disp.
Ypsilanti

Minnesota

Musket Ranch &
Trade
Andover
Pumpkin City
Invest.
Bunker Blvd.
Andover
Waste Disp. Eng.
Rd. 18
Andover
Anoka Elec. Co-op
N. Ferry St.
Anoka
Cedar Serv., Inc.
Bemidji

John's Manville
 Plant
Natchez

Jackson Coun.
 Ldfl.
Pascagoula

Allied Chem. Co.
Hwy. 3
Redwood

Lee Coun. Ldfl.
Skyline
Sky Line

Leland City Dump
Stoneville

Desoto Coun.
 Airpt.
Hwy. 51
Southhaven

Kopper, Inc.
Box 160
Tie Plant

Intl. Min. &
 Chem.
Pk. Ln. Rd.
Tupelo

Vertac Chem.
Box 3
Vicksburg

Halls Ferry Rd.
 Dump
Warren Coun.

Missouri

Antonia Drum
 Burial
Antonia

Abandon Ppty.
Arnold

Charles Defrenne
 Ppty.
Hollywood Beach
Arnold

Hollywood Beach
 Rd.
Hollywood Beach
 Rd.
Arnold

NL Inds.
Arnold

Swaller Rd. Dump
Near Arnold

William Hilse Ppty.
Hollywood Beach
 Rd.
Arnold

Aurora Dump Site
N. edge of Aurora
Aurora

Fm. 1
Barry Coun.

Big Three
 Enterprise
Birmingham Rd.
Birmingham

Birmingham School
Birmingham

Westlake Ldfl.
St. Charles
Bridgeton

Buckman Lab.
S.E. of St. Louis
Cadet

Carthage City
 Dump
Rte. 31
Carthage

Hercules Explos.
 Burn
Box 717
Carthage

Orange Substance
 Spi
Rural Area
Caruthersville

Ldfl.—
 Centerville
Centerville

Owens Fm.
Chilhowee

Ford Motor Co.
Hwy. 69
Claycomo

Agronomy Res.
Columbia

Chapman Salv. Yd.
Rte. 2
Cuba

Defiance Dump Site
Old Colony Rd.
Defiance

Kramer Drum
 Burial
Elvins

Movesian Site
Saline Creek
Fenton

Festus City Ldfl.
Festus Airpt.
Festus

Marnati Quarry
Parker Ave.
Frontenac

Russell Bliss
 Drain
German Blvd.
Frontenac

Oakland Cem.
W. Wall St.
Harrisonville

Latty Ave. Site
Latty Ave.
Hazelwood

St. Joe Lead Co.
Herculaneum

Moberly Sanit.
 Ldfl.
Rte. 1
Huntsville

City of Moberly
 Ldfl.
Rte. 1
Huntsville

Swaller Rd. Dump
Hwy. 21
Imperial Area

Frost Rd. Exec.
 Est.
Holland Rd. &
 Frost
Independence

Lake City Army
 Ammun.
Hwys. 7/78
Independence

Rumble Serv. Co.
S. Brookside
Independence

Red Bird Ldfl.
Jefferson City

Dittmer
Near Hwy. 30
Jefferson Coun.

Jeffco Land Recl.
Jefferson Coun.

Atlas Powd. Co.
Box 87
Joplin

Eagle-Picher Ind.
C/Porter Sts.
Joplin

Gypsum Disp. Pond
Joplin

W. R. Grace & Co.
AA Hwy.
Joplin

Browning-
 Ferris Ind.
N. 7th St.
Kansas City

Chem. Sealing
 Corp.
Banks
Kansas City

CNSRVTH
 Chem. Co.
Front St.
Kansas City

Corn Prod. Co.
Bedford Ave.
Kansas City

Koppers Co., Inc.
Stadium Dr.
Kansas City

Hamilton Haul.
Kansas City

Midnight Dumping
28th St./Mayview
Kansas City

Horse Stable
Spruce
Kansas City

Mobay Chem.
 Corp.
Hawthorne Rd.
Kansas City

Plant Facil.
Stadium Dr.
Kansas City

Landfill
Hwys. 40/170
**Kansas City/
 Independence**

Rural Drum Disp.
 Site
Kidder

Lebanon
Phosphorus
Lebanon

Woods Chapel Ldfl.
Woods Chapel Rd.
Lee's Summit

Melody Lake Site
Rte. 1
Leslie

Hercules, Inc.
Hwy. 79 S.
Louisiana

Salv. Yd.
S. 6th St.
Louisiana

Show-Me Power
Coop.
Marshfield

Chevron Chem.
Co.
Adie Rd.
Maryland Hgt.

Nit. Tetroxide
I-270/Old Dorset
Maryland Hgt.

Ldfl. 8
Missouri City

Morse Mills Drum
Site
Brinley St.
Morse Mills

Three M
Nevada

Corn Prod. Co.
N. Kansas City

Burlington N.
N. Kansas City

R&E Ldfl.
Wabash
O'Fallon

BFI Ldfl.
Coun. Rd. FF
Parkville

Dow Chem. Co.
Box 387
Pevely

Riverside Plant
Pevely

Orange Substance
N. of Hwy. 162 E.
Portageville

Junk Yard—Mr.
Grear
Randolph

Phizer Inc., Baker
Tr.
Richwoods

Phizer, Inc.—
Kingston
Richwoods

Nepacco Fm. Site
Rural Area

Van Dyke Site
N. State Fair Blvd.
Sedalia

Alcolac, Inc.
Randall Rd.
Sedalia

Esser St. Lagoon
Rte. 6
Sedalia

Sloan's Auto.
Sikeston

Cummings Diesel,
Inc.
Springfield

Litton Sys., Inc.
Kearney St.
Springfield

Syntax Holding
Pond
W. Bennett
Springfield

G. W. Fiberglass
Co.
N. Second St.
St. Charles

Raffinate Pits
St. Charles Coun.

Weldon Spr. Chem.
Plant
St. Charles Coun.

Vaughn Open
Dump
N. Outer Rd.
St. Clair

A. J. Gray
Dumpsite
St. James

Amchem. Prod.
Florence Ave.
St. Joseph

City Ldfl.
Rosecrans Fd.
St. Joseph

City Ldfl.
Water Wks. Rd.
St. Joseph

City Ldfl.
Lower Lake Rd.
St. Joseph

City Ldfl.
Pigeon Hill
St. Joseph

Farmland Inds.
4th/Seneca
St. Joseph

Genefield Rd.
Genefield Rd.
St. Joseph

Norris Disp. Site
S. Leonard Rd.
St. Joseph

Open Dump
N. of St. Joseph
St. Joseph

St. Joseph Sew.
Lower Lake Rd.
St. Joseph

Wheeling Disp.
N. of St. Joseph
St. Joseph

Carondelet Plant
Idah Ave.
St. Louis

City Ldfl.
Near Hall/
Hambolt
St. Louis

Flyer & Hampton
Ldfl.
Flyer/Hampton
Aves.
St. Louis

Gt. Lakes Cont.
Ferry St.
St. Louis

Jefferson Barracks
Grant Rd.
St. Louis

Lambert–St. Louis
Apt.
Brown Rd.
St. Louis

Mallinckrodt, Inc.
Second/
Mallinckrodt
St. Louis

Midwest Oil Ref.
Walton Rd.
St. Louis

Monsanto Co.
Idaho Ave.
St. Louis

NL Ind., NL Chem.
Div.
Manchester
St. Louis

P. O. George Paint
Co.
N. 2nd St.
St. Louis

Queeny Plant
S. Second St.
St. Louis

St. Louis Ord.
Goodfellow Blvd.
St. Louis

St. Louis School
23rd/Cones Sts.
St. Louis

U.S. Polymers
E. Primm St.
St. Louis

Maryville Coll.
St. Louis

Workhouse Quarry
Gasconade St.
St. Louis Coun.

Tyson Valley
St. Louis Coun.

Amoco Ldfm.
Sugar Ck.

Amoco Oil Co.
Kentucky Rd.
Sugar Ck.

Stanley Wks.
N. side of
Elizabeth
Sugar Creek

Sugar Creek Ref.
Kentucky Rd.
Sugar Ck.

Ramsey Corp.
Ramsey St.
Sullivan

Drum Dumping
  Area
2 mi. W. of St.
  Clair
Union

Syntex Dump
Verona

Rusha Fm. Site
Verona

Bob Rusha Fm.
Verona

Bill Ray Site
Verona

Crider Site
Rte. 1
Verona

Phoenix School
Walnut Grove

Pfizer Kingston &
  Arna
Washington Coun.

East End of 1st St.
1st St.
Webb City

G&H Ready Mix
Webb City

BMS, Inc. Haz St.
  Ldfl.
Rte. 1
Wright City

Bueneman Ldfl.
Rte. 1
Wright City

Montana

Anaconda Co.
Anaconda

Deer Lodge Coun.
Anaconda

Comet Oil Co.
N. of I-90
Billings

Exxon Old Flare
  Site
  (plus 1 other site)
Box 1163
Billings

Ref. Dumps
  (plus 1 other site)
Billings/Laurel

Asbestos Mine
  (plus 1 other site)
Karst Kamp Dist.
Bozeman

Developmental
  Techno
  (plus 1 other site)
N. Rouse
Bozeman

Stauffer Chem. Co.
Ramsay Mtn.
Butte

Silver Bow Coun.
Butte

Diamond Asphalt
  Co.
E. of Chinook

Mouat Ind.
Columbus

Cooke City Arsenic
  (plus 1 other site)
Near Soda Butte Ck.
Cooke City

Daniels Coun.
  Poisoned
Daniels Coun.

C&C Plywood Co.
  (plus 1 other site)
Sunset Dr.
Evergreen

Rocky Mtn. Phos.
  (plus 1 other site)
Garrison
Garrison

Falls Chem. Corp.
Gt. Falls

Gt. Falls City Ldfl.
25th Ave.
Gt. Falls

Morgan Chem. Co.
I-15
Gt. Falls

Western By-
  Products
I-15
Gt. Falls

Helena Ldfl.
N. of Lynndale
Helena

Jardine Arsenic
  (plus 1 other site)
Bear Creek
Jardin

Big West Oil
Hwy. 215
Kevin

Libby Pesticides
  (plus 1 other site)
Libby Townsite
Libby

Borden Chem. Co.
Missoula

Philipsburg Min.
  (plus 1 other site)
Upper Clark Fork
Philipsburg

Plant Site
Box 3146
Ramsey

Silverbow Ck.
Rocker Mtn.
Rocker

Tyson Valley
St. Louis Coun.

Paradise Tie Trmt.
  (plus 1 other site)
Thompson Falls

Nebraska

Plant Site
Rte. 2
Aurora

Beatrice Potw
Beatrice

Cominco Am.
Beatrice

Dempster Inds.
Beatrice

Kees (FD) Mfg.
Beatrice

Phillips Petr.
Box 666
Beatrice

Plant Site
Rte. 3
Beatrice

Stone Kraft Mfg.
  Co.
Beatrice

Tote Sys., Div. of
Beatrice

Bellevue Blueing &
  C
16th St.
Bellevue

Omaha Papillon Ck.
Harlan Lewis
Bellevue

Monroe Auto Eq.
Meridian St.
Cozad

CF Inds.
Box 68
Fremont

Fremont Mfg.
Fremont

A-1 Fiberglass
Hastings

AG-Tronics, Inc.
Hastings

Bruckman Rubber
  Co.
Hastings

City Ldfl.
Hastings

Dutton-Lainson
  Co.
Hastings

EBCO Inds.
Hastings

Hastings Ind.
Hastings

Hastings Nit. Plant
Box 949
Hastings

Hastings Potw
Hastings

Perfect Circle Co.
Hastings

TL-Irr. Co.
Hastings

W. Landroller
W. 2nd St.
Hastings

AG-Tronics
Kearney

Allied Chem. Corp.
Box 7354
Laplatte

Reach Elec.
Lexington

Lincoln Ldfl.
Lincoln

Elec. Hose & Ru.
McCook

Burgess Well
  Drilling
Minden

3-M Plant
Norfolk

TRW Capacitor
  Div.
Ogallala

Acetylene Plant
Grace St.
Omaha

Air Prod.
Grace St.
Omaha

Closed Plant Site
Gibson Rd.
Omaha

Control Data Corp.
Omaha

Keith Yosten
  Residence
58th St.
Omaha

Nashua Corp.
Omaha

Sarpy Coun. Ldfl.
Capehart Rd.
Omaha

Sarpy Coun. Ldfl.
Cedar Is. Rd.
Omaha

Stauffer Chem. Co.
Gibson Rd.
Omaha

370 Ldfl.
Omaha

Sarpy Coun. Ldfl.
Box 26
Papillon

Plattsmouth Ldfl.
Rte. 1
Plattsmouth

Hjerstedt Fm.
Rulo

Am. Cyanamid
Weeping Water

Nevada

Union Carbide
  Corp.
Alamo

Min. Invest.
Austin

New Pass Res.
Austin

GE Anne Foster
Baldwin Pk.

Dresser Min.
Battle Mtn.

Duvall Corp.
Battle Mtn.

IMCO Serv., Inc.
  (plus 1 other site)
Box 861
Battle Mtn.

Lyle Malone
Battle Mtn.

Milchem, Inc.
  (plus 1 other site)
Battle Mtn.

New Pass Res.
Box 69
Battle Mtn.

NL Inds.
  (plus 1 other site)
Battle Mtn.

Silver King Mines
Battle Mtn.

Tom Norris
Battle Mtn.

BKK Stge. Platform
Post Ranch
Beatty

Nuclear Eng.
  (plus 1 other site)
Box 578
Beatty

Intermtn. Explor.
Boulder City

Bar Res., Inc.
Carlin

Carlin Gold Min.
  (plus 1 other site)
Carlin

Eisenman Chem.
  Co.
Carlin

Nevada Barth
  Corp.
Carlin

Cyprus Explor.
Carson City

Houston Oil &
  Min.
Carson City

Cortez Gold Mines
Cortez

Aaron Min., Inc.
Crescent

Gold Cyn. Placers
Dayton

Douglas Coun.
  Sanit. Ldfl.
Douglas Coun.

Min. Mgt.
  (plus 1 other site)
Dyer

Stored
  Transformers
Dyer

Western Mgt.
Dyer

Chromalloy Min.
  (plus 1 other site)
Elko

Pancana Ind.
Elko

Egan Milling, Inc.
Box 415
Ely

Ely Crude Oil Co.
Ely

Mt. Hope Mine
Ely

Taylor Min., Inc.
Ely

Treasure City Mines
Ely

Idaho Min. Corp.
Eureka

Mt. Hope Mines
Eureka

Gold Ck. Corp.
Eureka

Fallon Pest
Fallon

Basic, Inc.
Box 4
Gabbs

Vita Gradde Min.
Garderville

Goldfield Ltd.
Goldfield

Kemco Buster Mine
Box 464
Goldfield

Pyramid Min. Co.
Box 52
Goldfield

Candelaria Part.
Hawthorne

Hawthorne Army
  Ammun.
Hawthorne

PM Min.
Hawthorne

Basic Mgt.
Box 2065
Henderson

Joe Min. Co.
Henderson

Kerr McGee Chem.
  Co.
Box 55
Henderson

Montrose Chem.
  Co.
Box 37
Henderson

Pepcon-Pac. Eng.
Henderson

State Inds., Inc.
Henderson

Stauffer Chem. Co.
Box 1029
Henderson

Timet
Box 2128
Henderson

Std. Gold Mine
Imlay

Tungsten Ppty.
  (plus 1 other site)
Imlay

Utah Intl.
Imlay

Antelope V. Pest
  Contr.
Lander Coun.

Gold Ck. Corp.
Las Vegas

IBEX Min. Corp.
Las Vegas

Nevada Pow. Co.
    (plus 1 other site)
Industrial Rd.
Las Vegas
Showboat Hotel
    Pest.
Las Vegas
Nevada Test Site
Las Vegas
Am. Borate Corp.
Lathrop Wells
Mohave Generating
Box 505
Laughlin
Aaron Min. Co.
Lovelock
Colorado Oil &
    Min.
Lovelock
D&Z Explor.
Lovelock
Double Eagle, Inc.
Lovelock
FM Wright Min.
    Co.
Lovelock
Lovelock Pest.
Lovelock
Eq. Specialty
Lunina
BML Min. Co.
Manhatten
McDermitt Mine
McDermitt
Kennecott Copper
    Smelter
McGill
Alan Chambers
Mina
Civic Cat Mines
Mina
Mina Milling &
    Min.
Mina
Union Carbide
Mina
Bentley Nevada
    Corp.
Box 157
Minden

Norman Ludwig
Montello
Rio Tinto Copper
    Mine
Mtn. City
Orovada Pest
    Contr.
Orovada
Bunker Hill Co.
Pioche
Std. Slag Co.
Pioche
Frank Lewis
Reno
Ladd Ent., Inc.
    (plus 1 other site)
Reno
Sand Spr. Silver
Reno
A&B Min. &
    Milling
Round Mtn.
Smokey V. Min.
Round Mtn.
Crescent Min.
    Limit
Search Light
Jesse R. Wilson
Sparks
W. Coast Oil &
    Gas
Sparks
Mineop Corp.
Tonopah
Rock Hill
    Tungsten
Tonopah
Viking
    Metallurgical
Verde
Anaconda Copper
    Co.
Weed Hgts.
Ranchers Explor.
Winnemucca
Min. Concentrate
Winnemucca
Juniper Gold Co.
Winnemucca

Milton Calder
Box 258
Yerrington
Tri-State Min.
Yerrington
Tamico, Inc. /
    Bunnslop
Box 256
Zephyr Cove

New
Hampshire

Ldfl.
Boscawen
Concord Manor
    Dump
Off Abbott Rd.
Concord
Ldfl.
Old Tnpk. Rd.
Concord
Old Suncook Rd.
    Dump
Old Dump
Concord
Transf. Serv.
Concord
Keefe Environ.
    Serv.
Rte. 101
Epping
Mdws.
Rte. 111
Hudson
Kingston Steel
    Drum
Kingston
Otatti & Goss
Rte. 125
Kingston
Senter Trans.
Rte. 125
Kingston
Londonderry Ldfl.
Old Dary Rd.
Londonderry
Ryder Concrete,
    Inc.
Milford
Grugnale Ppty.
Jennison Rd.
Milford

W. R. Grace Co.
Poisson Ave.
Nashua
Sylvester Site
Gilson Rd.
Nashua
Koppers Co., Inc.
Hills Ferry Rd.
Nashua
Peterboro Site
Peterboro
Pease AFB
Portsmouth
Pub. Serv. Co.
Seacrest Vill.
Portsmouth
Raymond Haz.
    Waste
Blueberry Hill Rd.
Raymond
Sandwich Site
Sandwich
K. J. Quinn
Folly Mill Rd.
Seabrook

New Jersey

Riegel Prod. Corp.
Frenchtown Rd.
Alexandria Twp.
M&M Mars
Box 87
Allamuchy Twp.
Jem Ldfl.
Almonesson
Alpha Quarry
Alpha
FAA NAFEC—
    Pomona
Atlantic City
Bayonne City Ldfl.
Lower Hook Rd.
Bayonne
Bayonne Inds.
Bayonne
Bayonne Munic.
    Ldfl.
22nd St.
Bayonne
Std. Tank Term.
Bayonne

Camp Kilmer
Edison

Edison Twp. Ldfl.
Meadow Rd.
Edison

GSA Raritan Depot
Edison

Stauffer Chem. Co.
Meadow Rd.
Edison

Ind. Ld. Rec.
Edge of Mill Ln.
Edison Twp.

Kin-Buc Ldfl.
Mill Rd.
Edison Twp.

Bay City of Serv.
Elizabeth

Chem. Contr.
Corp.
S. Front St.
Elizabeth

City of Elizabeth
North Ave. E.
Elizabeth

Coastal Environ.
Serv., Inc.
S. Front St.
Elizabeth

Disposal Areas,
Inc.
North Ave.
Elizabeth

Elizabeth Plant
Magnolia Ave.
Elizabeth

Elizabeth Wks.
North Ave. E.
Elizabeth

Iron Oxide Corp.
Front St.
Elizabeth

Jt. Meeting Sew.
Elizabeth

Present Port Eliz.
Elizabeth

Rollins Ent.
Elizabeth

S. Side Carting
Elizabeth

Tenneco Chem.
Elizabeth

Perk Chem. Co.,
Inc.
S. First St.
Elizabeth City

Agway Coun.
Foods
Elmer

Gloucester
Environ. Memt.
Hicktown Rd.
Erial

Borden Chem. Co.
Fairlawn

Belray Co., Inc.
Bowman Rd.
Farmingdale

Frequency Eng.
Lakewood Rd.
Farmingdale

Tenneco R. Rd.
River Rd.
Flemington

Florence Ld.
Recon.
Cedar Ln.
Florence

Ashland Chem. Co.
Meadow Rd.
Fords

Fords Plant
Meadow Rd.
Fords

Ft. Dix
Ft. Dix

USCG—Sandy
Hook
Ft. Hancock

Ft. Monmouth
Ft. Monmouth

Cellite
Franklin

Metaltec Co.
Wildcat Rd.
Franklin

N. Fines Chem.
Main St.
Franklin

Cellite
Work Hill Rd.
Franklin Bor.

Franklin Twp. Ldfl.
Pennsylvania Ave.
Franklin Twp.

Franklin Twp. Ldfl.
Marshall Mill Rd.
Franklinville

Franklin Twp. Ldfl.
Williamstown Rd.
Franklinville

Franklinville Twp.
Ldfl.
Lake Rd.
Franklinville

Lake Rd. Site
Lake Rd.
Franklinville

Marshall Mill Rd.
Marshall Mill Rd.
Franklinville

Penn. Ave. Site
Penn. Ave.
Franklinville

Williamstown Rd.
Site
Wmstown Rd./
Leonard
Franklinville

Freehold Sanit.
Ldfl.
Freehold

Lone Pine Ldfl.
Burke Rd.
Freehold

Garfield Plant
River Dr.
Garfield

Tenneco Chem.
Garfield

Buzby Sanit. Ldfl.
Marlton Rd.
Gibbsboro

Higgins Plant
N. Market St.
Gibbstown

Repaune Plant
Ldfl.
Repauno Ave.
Gibbstown

Hawshaw Chem.
Co.
Water St.
Gloucester City

Gem Lamader
Hickstown Rd.
Glouster Twp.

Southland Chem.
Gt. Meadows

Green Vill. Dist.
Co.
Green Vill.

E. I. Dupont
Denemours
Repauna Ave.
Greenwich Twp.

Eugene Pks.
S. Broad St.
Groveville

Ventron
Hackensack

Triad Plast.
Box 664
Hackensack

M&M Mar. Ind.
Sludge
High St.
Hackettstown

Somers Pt. Rd.
Somers Pt.
Hamilton Twp.

Colloid Chem.
Cedar Knolls Rd.
Hanover Twp.

Harmony Twp.
Ldfl.
River Rd.
Harmony Twp.

J. T. Baker Co.
River Rd.
Harmony Twp.

Nehanic Sta.
Hockenbury
Hillsborough

Swoco-Smith-
Wyman
Auten Rd.
Hillsborough

Contract Towing
Holmdel

Bog Creek Fm.
Lakewood-
Squankum Rd.
Howell

El Cid Contr.
Lemon Rd.
Howell Twp.

Waste Disp., Inc.
Allenwood-
Lakewood Rds.
Howell Twp.

Air Prod. &
Chem., Inc.
Oak Tree Rd.
Iselin

Waste Site
Oak Tree Rd.
Iselin

Hayden Chem.
Jackson

Powers Fm.
Jackson

Jackson Twp. Ldfl.
Lakehurst Ave.
Jackston Twp.

BASF Wyandotte
Corp.
Jamesburg

J.I.S. Ind. Serv.
Cranbury Rd.
Jamesburg

Princeton Disp.
Spotswood-Gravil
Jamesburg

Black Tom Munit.
Black Tom Rd.
Jersey City

Caven Pt. Mar.
Term.
Jersey City

Claremont Term.
Linden Ave.
Jersey City

Diamond Shamrock
Corp.
Tonnelle Ave.
Jersey City

Erie Lackawanna
R.R.
Pacific Ave.
Jersey City

Gordon Serv., Inc.
Pacific Ave.
Jersey City

Greenville Yds.
Jersey City

Ideal Cooperage
New York Ave.
Jersey City

Jersey City
12th/Monmouth
Jersey City

Liberty State Pk.
Statue of Liberty
Dr.
Jersey City

Munic. Sew. Tr.
Jersey City

PJP Corp. Ldfl.
Sip Ave.
Jersey City

Sampson Tank
Cleaning
Pacific Ave.
Jersey City

City of Kearny
Dump
Harrison Ave.
Kearny

Diamond Shamrock
Kearny

Drum Disp. Area
Belleville Tnpk.
Kearny

Edgewater Term.
Harrison Tnpk.
Kearny

Franklin Plast.
Passaic Ave.
Kearny

Harrison St. Drum
Harrison St.
Kearny

Kearny Plant
Belleville Tnpk.
Kearny

Kopper Co., Inc.
Harrison Tnpk.
Kearny

MSLA
Harrison Ave.
Kearny

St. Johnsbury Truck
St.
O'Brien/Sellers St.
Kearny

Std. Chlorine
Belleville Tnpk.
Kearny

Munic. Sanit. Ldfl.
Belleville Pike
Kearny

Elizabeth Disp. Co.
King George–
Clearvie
Keasbey

Elizabeth Waste
Disp.
Crows Mill Rd.
Keasbey

Hercules Sanit.
Ldfl.
Howard Blvd.
Kenvil

Waste Disp., Inc.
Locust St.
Keyport

NAS-Lakehurst
Lakehurst

Scott Paper Co.
Landisville

Blackwood Carbon
Fairmont Ave.
Laurel Spr.

Burlington Environ.
Mgt.
Leisuretown

Bayway Chem.
Plant
Park Ave.
Linden

Grassvelli Plant
Linden

Linden Site
S. Wood Ave.
Linden

Merch & Co.
Linden

U.S. Steel Corp.
W. Elizabeth Ave.
Linden

Warners Plant
Linden

Am. Cyanamid Co.
Wood Ave.
Linden City

Redcole Fm.
High Hill Rd.
Logan Twp.

Harbsron–Walker
Cape
Sunset Blvd.
Lower Twp.

N.W. Magnesite
Sunset Blvd.
Lower Twp.

Avon Sanit. Ldfl.
Valley Brook Ave.
Lyndhurst

V.A. Hospital
Lyons

Abex Corp.
Mahwal

Hayden Chem.
Manchester

Mannington Mills,
Inc.
Mannington Mills
Rd.
Mannington Twp.

Kramers Ldfl.
Jessup Mill Rd.
Mantua

Marvin Jonas, Inc.
Park Ridge Rd.
Mantua Twp.

Nick Li Pari
Lot 7, Block 261
Mantua Twp.

Johns Manville
Corp.
Dykes Pkwy.
Manville

Burnt Fly Bog
Tylers Ln.
Marlboro Town

Pfizer, Inc.
Maywood Ave.
Maywood

Metuchen Plant
Lake/Whitman
Metuchen

Metuchen Wks.
Prince St.
Metuchen

Borden Ppty.
Lincoln Blvd.
Middlesex

Middlesex Boro
Dump
Mountain Ave.
Middlesex

Middlesex Plant Site
Old New Market
Rd.
Middlesex

Murisol, Inc.
Factory Ln.
Middlesex

Reagent Chem.
Factory Ln.
Middlesex

SCA Chem. Waste
Serv.
Balmer Rd.
Model City

New Road Ldfl.
New Road
Monmouth Jct.

Columbia Chem.
Stouts Ln.
Monmouth Jct.

Marico Plant
Stouts Ln.
Monmouth Jct.

Landfill & Devel.
Co.
Hwy. 38
Mt. Holly

Henry Harris Ldfl.
Bridgeton Rd.
Mullica Hill

U.S. Moeral Prod.
Furnace St.
Netcong Boro

Avenue P
Newark

Brill Eq. Co.
Jabaez St.
Newark

Earthline Co.
Lister Ave.
Newark ·

Edgeboro Disp.
Doremus Ave.
Newark

Engelhard Ind., Inc.
Delancey St.
Newark

H. Gross & Co.
Doremus Ave.
Newark

Munic. Sanit. Ldfl.
Doremus Ave.
Newark

Natl. Dist. & Chem.
Doremus Ave.
Newark

Newark Plant
Lister Ave.
Newark

Newark Stamp &
Die
McCarter Hwy.
Newark

Newco Chem. Waste
Doremus Ave.
Newark

Peter Divino
Foot of Delancey St.
Newark

Sci. Chem. Proc.
Wilson Ave.
Newark

T. Fiore Demo.
Delany
Newark

Thomas H. Cook
Newark

Troy Chem. Co.
Ave. L
Newark

V. Ottilio & Sons
Blanchard
Newark

Zamilsky Scrap Co.
Fretinghysen
Newark

Celanese Chem.
Co., Inc.
Doremus Ave.
Newark

Daj, Inc.
Central Ave.
Newark

Diamond Alkali
Lister Ave.
Newark

A to Z Chem. Co.
New Brunswick

Rhone-Poulenc
New Brunswick

Borough of
Newfield
Catawba/
Weymouth
Newfield

Newfield Ldfl.
George Ln.
Newfield

Shield Alloy Corp.
N.W. Blvd.
Newfield

P&M Sanit.
Blk. 177–183
N. Arlington

N. Bergen Drum
50th St.
N. Bergen

Seaview Sq. Mall
Rtes. 66/35
Ocean Twp.

CPS Chem. Co.
Old Wtw. Rd.
Old Bridge

Global Ldfl. Rec.
Ernston St.
Old Bridge Twp.

BF Goodrich Chem.
Div.
Rte. 130/Porcupine
Rd.
Oldman Twp.

Browning-Ferris
Ind.
Porcupine Rd.
Oldman Twp.

NL Inds., Inc.
Penns Grove Rd.
Oldman Twp.

Parlin Plant
Minnisink
Parlin

Dupont Co.
Cheesequake Rd.
Parlin

Parlin F&F
Washington
Parlin

Galaxy Chem.
Cheesequake Rd.
Parlin

Parsippany
Redeposit
Off Edwards Rd.
Parsippany

Parsippany WPC
Parsippany

Parsippany-A
Jefferson Rd.
Parsippany

Gaess Environ.
River Dr.
Passaic

Essex Chem. Sanit.
Ldfl.
Thomas Ln.
Paulsboro

Paulsboro Plant
Paulsboro

Mobile Oil Ref.
Paulsboro

Plant Site
Thomas Ln.
Paulsboro

Browning-Ferris
Ind.
Pedricktown

Cesco, Inc.
Porcupine Rd.
Pedricktown

Pedricktown Plant
Rte. 130/
Porcupine
Pedricktown

Pedricktown Sup.
Fac.
Pedricktown

Pemberton Twp.
White Boys Rd.
Pemberton

Lang Chem. Dump
Off Rte. 70
Pemberton Twp.

Chevron Oil
Perth Amboy

Duane Mar. Corp.
Washinton St.
Perth Amboy

Celotex Corp.
Herbert/Market
Sts.
Perth Amboy

J. T. Baker
Red School Ln.
Phillipsburg

Sharkeys Disp.
Pine Brook

Bubenick Ppty.
St. Marks St.
Piscataway

Chemsol, Inc.
Fleming St.
Piscataway

CBS Records
Pitman

Atlantic Elec. Co.
Fire Rd.
Pleasantville

Price Chem. Dump
Mill Rd./Leeds Ave.
Pleasantville

Lenox China, Inc.
Pomona

Pompton Lakes
Wks.
Cannonball Rd.
Pompton Lakes

Port Reading
Roosevelt Ave.
Port Reading

Browning-Ferris
Ldfl.
Princeton

Ringwood Ldfl.
Cannon Mine Rd.
Ringwood

Ameliotex Co.
Crescent Ave.
Rocky Hill

Allco Environ.
Swcs.
Highland Cross
Rutherford

Altman St. Drum
Altman St.
Rutherford

Atlantic Devel.
Horseshow Rd.
Sayreville

Sayreville Munic.
Dump
Vernees Mill Rd.
Sayreville

Valumet Corp. of
N.J.
Quigley Ln.
Sayreville

Wooded Area
Sayreville

E. I. Dupont
Denemours (plus
1 other site)
Washington Rd.
Sayreville Boro

HL Inds., Inc.
Chevalier Ave.
Sayreville Boro

Pub. Serv. Elect. &
Gas
County Rd.
Secaucus

Jonas Co.
Barkridge Rd.
Sewell

Bound Book Plant
Somerset City Ldfl.
Somerville

Gov. Serv. Admin.
Stge.
Somerville

V. A. Depot
Somerville

Titanium Pigment
Plant
Box 58
S. Amboy

Big Hill Sanit.
Ldfl.
Big Hill Rd.
Southampton Twp.

IBM Corp.
S. Brunswick

J. I. S. Sanit. Ldfl.
Cranbury Rd.
S. Brunswick

Mod. Trans. Co.
Jacobs Ave.
S. Kearney

Plating Ref. Lab
S. Clinton Ave.
S. Plainfield

S. Plainfield Plant
Metuchen/
Harmich
S. Plainfield

S. Plainfield Ldfl.
Kenneth Ave.
S. Plainfield

AO Polymer
Station Rd.
Sparta

Ft. Monmouth
Tinton Falls

Toms River Chem.
Box 71
Toms River

Duck Is.
Lamberton St.
Trenton

Hmadei Ldfl.
Turmersville

Intl. Flavors & Frag.
Rose Ln.
Union Beach

Upper Penns Neck
Ldfl.
Upper Penns

Barrier Chem.
Rte. 515
Vernon

Vineland Chem.
Co.
Wheat Rd.
Vineland

Monitor Devices,
Inc.
Monmouth City
Airpt.
Wall Twp.

High Point Ldfl.
Franklin/Asbury
Rd.
Warren Coun.

Texaco Sludge Disp.
Rte. 130/295
W. Deptford

L.E. Carpenter Co.
N. Main St.
Wharton

Hoffman-Laroche
(plus 1 other site)
Lot 10, Blk. 47
White Twp.

King of Prussia
Disp.
Piney Hollow Rd.
Winslow Twp.

Winslow Township
Sanit. Ldfl.
Piney Hollow Rd.
Winslow Twp.

Atteburys Sew. Serv.
Colhune St.
Woodbine Boro

Wood Ridge
Munic. Dump
Main St., Lot 1
Woodbridge

Ventron Plant Site
Woodbridge

Woodbridge Plant
Gutters Dock Rd.
Woodbridge

New Jersey Site
S. Columbia/R.R.
Woodbury

Polyrez Co., Inc.
S. Columbia/R.R.
Woodbury

Shell Chem.
Matua Grove Rd.
Woodbury

W. Deptford Munic.
(plus 1 other site)
Woodridge Terr.
Woodbury

Woodland Twp.
Dump
Rte. 72
Woodland Twp.

Woodland Twp.
Dump
Rte. 532
Woodland Twp.

McGuire AFB
Wrightstown

Blauths Lumb. &
Bldg.
S. Broad St.
Yardville

Yardville Plant
Box 296
Yardville

New Mexico

Albuquerque Ldfl.
(plus 2 other sites)
Los Angeles Ave.
Albuquerque

Albuquerque Refuse
Pino
Albuquerque

Bernalillo Coun.
Broadway
Albuquerque

Brothers Plating
4th St.
Albuquerque

City of Albuquerque
Ldfl.
Los Angeles Ave.
Albuquerque

Gulton Inds.
Gulton Ct.
Albuquerque

Trmt. Plant 1
2nd S.W.
Albuquerque

Trmt. Plant 2
North S.W.
Albuquerque

Van Waters &
Rogers
Edmunds
Albuquerque

Wellborn Paint Mfg.
Rossmoor Rd.
Albuquerque

Kerr McGee
Ambrosia Lake

Mini Mart Gas Sta.
Angel Fire

Arch Ldfl.
2 mi. S. of Arch
Arch

Navajo Ref.
E. Main St.
Artesia

Old Artesia Ldfl.
(plus 1 other site)
Artesia

Phillips Evap.
Artesia

Aztec Ldfl.
(plus 1 other site)
Aztec

Delta & Sons Disp.
Cambridge
Belen

Atchinson, Topeka
E. of I-25
Belen

Bloomfield Ldfl.
(plus 1 other site)
Bloomfield

Harris Well
Carlsbad

N-Ren S.W.
Hobos Hwy.
Carlsbad

Amax Chem.
Hwy. 360
Carlsbad

Beker Ind. Corp.
Box 1598
Carlsbad

Duval Co.
20 mi. E. of
Carlsbad

Potash Co. of Am.
Hwy. 31
Carlsbad

Natl. Potash
Box 731
Carlsbad

S.W. Min. Corp.
E. Hwy. 380
Carrizozo

Cedar Mills Ldfl.
(plus 1 other site)
Off Hwy. 550
Cedar Hill

United Nuclear
Corp.
Church Rock

Clayton Light &
Water
One Chestnut St.
Clayton

Atchinson-Topeka
R.R.
Santa Fe Lake
Clovis

C&C Meat Prod.,
Inc.
Mitchell
Clovis

Corrales Corrals
Star Rte.
Corrales

Am. Smelting
Box 1037
Deming

Barite of Am.
Box 1602
Deming

E. Farmington Ldfl.
Farmington

Western Co. of N.
Am.
Hwy. 550
Farmington

Anaconda Co.
(plus 1 other site)
Box 638
Grants

Waste Contr. of
N.M.
Lovington Hwy.
Hobbs

Climax Chem.
Corp.
Box 1595
Hobbs

Hobbs Potash Facil.
Cobbsbad Hwy.
Hobbs

Lowell Stout
Hobbs

S. Union Truck
Hobbs

N.M. Elec. Serv.
Co.
Hobbs

Two Mile Pit
West Lea St.
Hobbs

S. Union Ref.
Hobbs

Two Mile Pit
W. Lea St.
Hobbs

White Well
Hollywood

Kennecott Copper
Hurley

Kirtland Ldfl.
(plus 1 other site)
S. of Hwy. 550
Kirtland

Las Crusas Ldfl.
Las Cruces

Morton Bros.
Rte. 1
Las Cruces

Loco Hills Ldfl.
Loco Hills

Los Alamos Sci.
Los Alamos

Malco Gas Sta.
Los Lunas

Cobb Nuclear
Milling
Magdalena

Grace Nuclear Site
Box 100
Magdalena

Hydro Nuclear
Corp. (plus 1
other site)
Cibola Natl. For.
Near Magdalena

Agric. Prod.
Mesquite

Milan Ldfl.
Milan

United Nuclear
Homes
Milan

Milan Uranium
Mill
Milan

Cities Serv. Co.
Gen. Deliv.
Milnesand

Lexco, Inc.
Moriarity

Prewitt Ref.
I-40
Prewitt

Kaiser-York Cyn.
40 mi. N. of
Raton

Raton Abandoned
Ldfl.
Raton

Molycorp., Inc.
Hwy. 30
Questa

Kennecott Copper
Santa Rita

Ariz. Pub. Serv.
Shiprock

Domestic Well
Taos

Gas Sta. Site 1
Tucumari

Gas Sta. Site 2
Tucumari

Gas Sta.
Hwys. 47/346
Turn

Phelps-Dodge Corp.
Tyrone

Pub. Serv. Co.
Waterfall

Sierra Blanc Min.
Off Hwy. 54

New York

Amax Specialty
Metal
Clarence Ctr./Hale
Akron

Houdailles Ind.
Clarence Rd.
Akron

Natl. Gypsum Co.
Alabama

Albany Sanit. Ldfl.
Rapp Rd.
Albany

N.E. Solite Corp.
Albany

Putts Fm.
W. Branch Rd.
Alleghany

Sarney Ppty. Fm.
Amenia

Town of Amenia
Amenia

Bayshore Inds.
Willow St.
Amsterdam

Modern Waste Serv.
Sand Pit Rd.
Amsterdam

Montgomery City
Ldfl.
Off Antlers Rd.
Amsterdam

Ardsley Plant
Lawrence St.
Ardsley

Nuclear Fuel Serv.
Ashford

Chem. Waste Disp.
19th Ave.
Astoria

Westinghouse Elec.
Attica

Singer Co.
Columbus St.
Auburn

Bags Ldfl.
Rte. 8
Bainbridge

Bainbridge Ldfl.
Case Rd.
Bainbridge

Bainbridge Resin
Johnson St.
Bainbridge

BMPO Ldfl.
Rte. 8
Bainbridge

Borden, Inc.
Johnson St.
Bainbridge

Jardine Bronz &
Alum.
E. Gennessee St.
Baldwinsville

Agway Store
Science St.
Ballston Spr.

Batavia Ldfl.
Galloway Rd.
Batavia

Edwin B. Stimpson
Sylvan Ave.
Bayport

City Waste Oil
Bergin

Grumman
Aerospace
Bethpage

Gordon Gardner
Ppty.
Rte. 352
Big Flats

Wolf Fm.
Halderman Hollow
Rd.
Big Flats

Bladell Site
Lake Ave.
Blasdell

Brown Dayton, Inc.
Bohemia

Dayton T. Brown,
Inc.
Church St.
Bohemia

Industrial Patterns
Bolivar

Brewster Transit
Mix
Fields Ln.
Brewster

Conrail Harlem Div.
Brewster

N.Y. State Elect.
Brewster

Casting Corp.
Dikeman St.
Brewster

Owens-Illinois
Brockport

Gen. Elec. Co.
State St.
Brockport

Pelham Bay Pk.
I-95/Pelham Pkwy.
Bronx

RCA—Rocky Pt.
Ld.
Brookhaven

Apex Thermoplast.
(plus 1 other site)
Bridge St.
Brooklyn

Borden Chem.
Nostrand Ave.
Brooklyn

City Barrel Co.
Meeker St.
Brooklyn

Fountain Ave. Ld.
Brooklyn

Jones Motor Site
Brooklyn

Lombardy St.
Ft. Newton C.
Lombardy
Brooklyn

NAS—Floyd Bennett
Flushing/
Washington
Brooklyn

N.Y. City Dump
Penna Ave.
Brooklyn

NPS Jamaica Bay
Pennsylvania Ave.
Brooklyn

N.Y.C. Dept. of
Sanit.
Fountain Ave.
Brooklyn

Allied Chem. Ind.
Lee St.
Buffalo

Allied Chem. R&D
S. Park Ave.
Buffalo

Anaconda Co.
Military Rd.
Buffalo

Buffalo Chem. Plant
Lee St.
Buffalo

Buffalo Color Corp.
S. Park Ave.
Buffalo

Buffalo Ldfl.
Hopkins St.
Buffalo

Buffalo Squaw Is.
Buffalo

Dayton Malleable,
Inc.
Tonawanda St.
Buffalo

E. I. Dupont
Buffalo Ave.
Buffalo

E. I. Dupont Co.
Sheridan Dr.
Buffalo

Empire Waste
Skillen Rd.
Buffalo

Evie Lackawanna
R.R.
Clinton St.
Buffalo

Fedders Auto.
Comp.
Tonawanda St.
Buffalo

Ford Motor Co.
Fuhrman Blvd.
Buffalo

Georgia Pac.
Buffalo

Hanna Furnace
Fuhrman Blvd.
Buffalo

Houdaille Ind.
Babcock St.
Buffalo

Houghton Pk. Ldfl.
Spann/Casmir St.
Buffalo

Lancaster Sanit.
Ldfl.
Bailey Ave.
Buffalo

Lasalle Reservoir
E. Aurora/Pk.
Ridge
Buffalo

Lehigh Valley R.R.
Tifft St.
Buffalo

Macnaughton-
Brooks
Bolton Place
Buffalo

Mobile Oil Corp.
Elk St.
Buffalo

Mollenberg-Betz
Mach.
Scott St.
Buffalo

Niagara Frontier
Fuhrman Blvd.
Buffalo

Otis Elevator Co.
Dutton/Northland
Buffalo

Pennwalt Corp.
Military Rd.
Buffalo

R. P. Adams
E. Park Dr.
Buffalo

Ramco Steel
Hopkins St.
Buffalo

Republic Steel
Marillo/Hopkins
Sts.
Buffalo

Snyder Tank Co.
Lake Shore Rd.
Buffalo

Squaw Is. Ldfl.
Squaw Is.
Buffalo

Tifft St. RDA
Tifft St.
Buffalo

TRW, Inc.
Vulcan St.
Buffalo

Yerkes
Riber Rd.
Buffalo

Nairy Chem.
Behind Bldg. 20
Burt

Tri-James
Hoag Rd.
Busti

Old Greene City
Ldfl.
E. of Ross Ruland
Cairo

Monroe-Livingston
South Rd.
Caledonia

Mumford-
Caledonia
Caledonia

Camden Wire
Masonic Ave.
Camden

Camden Wire Co.
Lovers Lane
Camden

Haz-O-Waste Corp.
Canal Rd.
Canastota

Recycling Labs, Inc.
Canal Rd.
Canastota

Lemay Optical
Corp.
Horsepound Rd.
Carmel

Old Caroga
Lane/Averson Rds.
Caroga

Vacuum Air Alloy
Rte. 317
Carroll

VA Hospital
Rte. 9D
Castle Pt.

Townley Hill Rd.
Ldfl.
Townley Hill Rd.
Catlin

Vanderhorst Co.
Cattaraugus

Morrison Brook
Dump
Rte. 30 E.
Centerville

Hubbard-Wilson
Wicks Rd.
Central Islip

Louchs Septic Site
Saratoga Coun.
Charleton

Columbia Corp.
Sanit.
Hwy. 295
Chatham

Chautauqua Ldfl.
Dinshier Rd.
Chautauqua

Aero Drive Dump
Aero Dr./Transit
Cheektowaga

Ernst Steel
Walden Ave.
Cheektowaga

Land Rellam, Inc.
Broadway/Indian
Rds.
Cheektowaga

N.Y. State Thruway
Exit Dump
Exit 52
Cheektowaga

Pfhol Bros. Ldfl.
Aero Dr.
Cheektowaga

Spencer-Kellog Res.
Genesee St.
Cheektowaga

Westinghouse Elec.
Genesee St.
Cheektowaga

Niagara Mohawk
Cherry Fm.

Gold Bond Bldg.
Prod.
Roll Rd.
Clarence Ctr.

XAR Corp.
Wood Rd.
Clifton Pk.

Now Corp.
Clinton

Atlantic Cement
Coeymans

Montagnon-Ricci
Rishkill Tnpk.
Cold Spr.

Marathon Battery
Kemble Ave.
Cold Spr.

Colonie Sanit. Ldfl.
Rte. 9/Crescent
Colonie

Intl. Paper
Off Pine St.
Corinth

Edward Allen Ldfl.
Bailey Creek Rd.
Corning

Am. Valve Mfg.
Mansion St.
Coxsackie

Crogham Town
Ldfl.
Indian R. Rd.
Crogham

Croton Ldfl.
Croton

Westchester Coun.
Croton

Croton Pt. Ldfl.
Croton Pt. Pk.
Croton on Hudson

Foster-Wheeler
Corp.
Dansville

Peter Cooper Corp.
Markham Rd.
Dayton

St. Regis Paper
Deferiet

Owens-Corning
Fiber
Rte. 32
Fuera Bush Rd.
Delmar

Land Recl.
Indian Rd.
Depew

Dresser Inds.
Main St. W. of Trnst.
Depew

Dewitt Sanit. Ldfl.
Fisher Rd.
Dewitt

Vill. of Dobbs Ferry
Hudson R.
Dobbs Ferry

Transelco, Inc.
Curry Pt. Rd.
Dresden

Dunkirk Ldfl.
S. Roberts Rd.
Dunkirk

Robin Steel
Urban/S. Roberts
Sts.
Dunkirk

Durham-Greenville
Ldfl.
Hwy. 145
Durham

Stiefel Labs
Rte. 145
Durham

Sinclair Ref.
W. of Genessee R.
N. of Jct. D

Sterling Drug 2
East Greenbush

Mitchell Manor
Merrick Ave.
E. Meadow

Deutsch Relays
Daly Rd.
E. Northport

Sigismundi
Linden Ave.
E. Rochester

St. Joe Zinc Co.
Edwards

V.A.W. of Am.
U.S. 209
Ellenville

Facet Ent.
18th/Oakland Sts.
Elmira

Kennedy Valve
E. Water St.
Elmira

IBM
North St.
Endicott

Kevtronics
North St.
Endicott

Erwin Ldfl.
Erwin

High Acres Devel.
Corp.
Budlong Rd.
Fairport

Carborundum
New York Ave.
Falconer

Fairchild Repub.
Broad Hollow Rd.
Farmingdale

Liberty Ind. Finish
Motor Ave.
Farmingdale

Texaco, Inc.
Old State Glenham
Fishkill

Keymark Corp.
Fonda

Ft. Edward Ldfl.
John St. Ext.
Ft. Edward

Ft. Miller Ldfl.
Ft. Edward

Gilbert Shortsleeves
Argyle Rd.
Ft. Edward

Old Ft. Edward
Ldfl.
McIntyre St.
Ft. Edward

Joseph Ferdula
Disp.
Frankfort

Ontario Knife
Empire St.
Franklinville

Hempstead Incin.
Freeport

Macher Inds.
Rte. 408
E. of Friend

Fulton Coun. Ldfl.
Flood Rd.
Fulton

Keck Fm. Rte. 3
Rte. 3
Fulton

Mirabito Ppty.
S. First St.
Fulton

Plant Yd.
S. First St.
Fulton

Raponi Ppty.
Maple Ave.
Fulton

Sixth Ward
S. First St.
Fulton

Taylor Ppty.
S. River Rd.
Fulton

White Mop Wringer
Co.
Fultonville

Geneseo Plant
Box 188
Geneseo

Marker 331.5
E. Lane N.Y. State
Thruway
Geneva

GFIM Ldfl.
Mortz Rd.
German Flats

Photocircuit
Sea Cliff Ave.
Glencove

Ames Chem. Wks.
Roger St.
Glen Falls

Ciba Geigy
Warren St.
Glen Falls

Hercules, Inc.
Lower Warren St.
Glen Falls

Hercules Sec. Ld.
Ridge Rd.
Glen Falls

Glenville Town Ldfl.
Barhydt Rd.
Glenville

Mattiace Chem.
Shore Rd.
Glenwood Ldg.

Harrison St. Sew.
Gloversville

Al Turi Ldfl.
Hartley Rd.
Goshen

Orange Coun.
Sanit.
S. of Rte. 17
Goshen

Moench Tanning
Co.
Palmer St.
Gowanda

Pas Clothier Site
S. Granby Rd.
Granby

Norton-Telescope
Ldfl.
Dump Rd.
Granville

Granville Ldfl.
Fox Rd.
Granville

Allied Chem. Corp.
Semet Solvoy
Tarbeds
Greddes

Ford-Green Is.
Tibbetts Ave.
Green Is.

Hazeltine Corp.
Cuba Hill Rd.
Greenland

Greenport Ldfl.
Rte. 9/Ten Brook
Rd.
Greenport

Greenwich Ldfl.
Bald Mtn. Rd.
Greenwich

SCM Corp.
Groton

Burns Ppty.
Rte. 201
Guilderland

Nepera Chem.
Hwy. 17
Harriman

Clarkstown Ldfl.
Grassy Pt. Rd.
Haverstraw

Haverstraw Ldfl.
River Rd.
Haverstraw

Mitchell Fd.
Stewart Ave.
Hemstead

Servo Corp. of Am.
New South Rd.
Hicksville

Hooker Chem. &
Plast.
New South Rd.
Hicksville

Hooker Chem. &
Plast.
New South Rd.
Hicksville

Holsville Ldfl.
Holtsville

Brake Hill
Brake Hill Rd.
Homer

Vill. Dump
(plus 1 other site)
Oshea Rd.
Homer Cortland

Hoosick Falls Ldfl.
Rte. 22
Hoosick Falls

Oak Mat. Gp.
River Rd.
Hoosick Falls

Hopewell Precision
Ryan Rd.
Hopewell Jct.

Conrail Demolition
Loder St.
Hornellsville

Treating Plant
Horseheads

Westinghouse Elec.
Westinghouse Ck.
Horseheads

Gen. Elec.
John St.
Hudson Falls

Kingsbury Ldfl.
Burgoyne Ave.
Hudson Falls

C&D Batteries
Rte. 209
Huguenot

Huntington Twp.
Deposit Rd.
Huntington

Is. Pk. Liquid
Is. Pk.

Blydenburg Rd. Ld.
Blydenburg Rd.
Islip

Islip Sanit. Ldfl.
Blydenburg Rd.
Islip

Sonia Road Ldfl.
Islip

Allied Chem.
Jamesville

Alpha Portland
Cement
Jamesville

Cyadutta Ck.
Across Old
Gloversville
Johnstown

Gloversville Ldfl.
E. Fulton Ext.
Johnstown

Johnstown Ldfl.
W. Fulton St. Ext.
Johnstown

Miller Street
Miller St.
Johnstown

Old Johnstown
Dump
Maple Ave. Exit
Johnstown

Pyramid Mall
Johnstown

Yost St.
Yost St.
Johnstown

Edon Wire Co.
Beaver St.
Jordan

AF—Plant 4
Kenmore Ave.
Kenmore

Alum. Match Plate
Military Rd.
Kenmore

Ottati & Gross
Kingston

IBM Corp.
Neighborhood Rd.
Kingston

Bethlehem Steel
Corp.
Lakeshore Rd.
Lackawanna

Ferro Corp.
Willet Rd.
Lackawanna

Knuco Home
Improve.
Transit Rd.
Lancaster

Lancaster Recl.
Pavement Rd.
Lancaster

N.Y. State Elec.
Lansing

Leicester Ldfl.
Leicester

Leroy Machine Co.
E. Main Rd.
Leroy

Lake Ontario Ord.
Wk.
Balmer Rd.
Lewiston

Lewiston Qua.
Lewiston

Mt. St. Mary's
Hosp.
Lewiston

Niagara Falls Stge.
Plecher Rd.
Lewiston

Old Stauffer Chem.
Old Lewiston Rd.
Lewiston

Pasny Site
S. of Upper Min. R.
Lewiston

State Pow. Auth.
Site
Old Lewiston Rd.
Lewiston

Upper Mtn. Rd.
Whittakes St.
Lewiston

Solv. Savers
Lincklaen

William J. Benson
Richmond Hill
Livonia

Gen. Motors Corp.
Upper Mtn. Rd.
Lockport

Guterl Steel
Ohio St.
Lockport

Harrison Radiator
Upper Mtn. Rd.
Lockport

Lockport City Ldfl.
Oakhurst St.
Lockport

Diversified Mfg.
Ohio St.
Lockport

Dussault Foundry
Corp.
Washburn St.
Lockport

Lockport Plant
Ohio St.
Lockport

Lockport RDA
Off Richfield St.
Lockport

Niagara City Dump
Richfield St.
Lockport

Norton Labs.
Mill St.
Lockport

Stauffer Chem. Co.
Upper Mtn. Road
Dump
Lockport

Van De Mark
Chem.
N. Transit Rd.
Lockport

Hudson Ref.
Boreview Ave.
Long Is.

Newton Ref.
Boreview Ave.
Long Is.

Jilson's RDA
Hwy. 17
Lowman

Lyndonville Ice &
Co.
West Ave.
Lyndonville

Novac's Fm.
McDonough

Alcoa
Massena

GMC Chevolet Div.
Massena

Reynolds Metals
Massena

Nepura Chem.
Rte. 4
Maybrook

Dyer Ldfl.
Mechanicville

Pas Holbrook Dairy,
Ontario St.
Mexico

FMC Middleport
Site (plus 1 other
site)
Niagara St.
Middletown

Middletown City
 Dump
Dolson Ave.
Middletown

J. T. Baker Co.
Milo

Fawthurp
Rtes. 43/50
Milton

Kesselring Site
 Sanit.
Milton

Columbia Mills
Off Rte. 48
Minetto

AF 68
Model City/Ridge
Model City

Millmaster Chem.
 Co.
Balmer Rd.
Model City

Modern Disp. Serv.
Model City Rd.
Model City

SCA Chem. Waste
Balmer Rd.
Model City

Moreau Ldfl.
W. of U.S. 9
Moreau

Monsanto Co.
N.E. Lolite
Mt. Marion

N.E. Solite Corp.
Box 437
Mt. Marion

Oldover Corp.
Old Kings Hwy.
Mt. Marion

Dewey-Leoffel
Mead Rd.
Nassau

Kerr McGee Chem.
Welcher Rd.
Newark

Duramate
Newburgh

Newburgh Incin.
Renwick/Front Sts.
Newburgh

Newburgh Ldfl.
Pierces Rd.
Newburgh

Newburgh Plant
 Ldfl.
Dupont Ave.
Newburgh

Stauffer Chem. Co.
Winser Rd. off Rte.
 52
Newburgh

USMA Stewart
 Annex
Rte. 17 K
Newburgh

Orange Coun.
 Sanit. Ldfl.
New Hampton

Special Metals
 Corp.
Middlesettlement
 Rd.
New Hartford

Denton Ave. Ldfl.
New Hyde Pk.

N. Hempstead
 Town
Denton Ave./
 Hillside
New Hyde Pk.

Newton Falls Paper
Newton Falls

Jones Motor Site
Lombardy St.
New York City

Kills Ldfl.
Brkfld/Arthur
New York City

Sta. Is. Ldfl
Borough of
 Richmond
New York City

Newco Waste
 System
Packard Rd./I-90
Niagara

Olin Corp.
102nd/Buffalo
Niagara

Union Carbide
Hyde Park Blvd.
Niagara

Airco Speer Intl.
 Grph.
Packard Rd.
Niagara Falls

Bell Aerospace Div.
Rte. 62
Niagara Falls

Cayuga Is.
Niagara Falls

Carborundum
S. of Blvd. 89
Niagara Falls

Carborundum
64th St.
Niagara Falls

Cayuga Is. Ld.
Niagara Falls

Chem. Waste Ld.
Niagara Falls

Chisolm Ryder Co.
College/Highland
Niagara Falls

Dibacco Site
Porter/Tuscarora
 Rds.
Niagara Falls

E. I. Dupont—
 Necco Pk.
Niagara Falls

Frontier Bronze
Packard Rd.
Niagara Falls

Frontier Chem. Co.
Royal Ave.
Niagara Falls

Great Lakes Carbon
Pine Ave.
Niagara Falls

Harshaw Chem.
 Co.
Royal Ave.
Niagara Falls

Hooker Chem.—
 Love Canal
Frontier
Niagara Falls

Hooker Chem. &
 Plast.
Hyde Park Blvd.
Niagara Falls

Hooker Chem. &
 Plast.
"S" Area
Niagara Falls

Hooker Chem.
Buffalo Ave.
Niagara Falls

Hooker Chem.—
 102nd St.
Buffalo Ave.
Niagara Falls

Ind. Welding
Packard Rd.
Niagara Falls

Land Recl.
56th/Pine Sts.
Niagara Falls

NL Inds., Inc.
Hyde Pk. Blvd.
Niagara Falls

Newco Chem.
 Waste
Royal Ave.
Niagara Falls

Niagara Falls Plant
Buffalo Ave.
Niagara Falls

Niagara Recycl.
Pine Ave./56th St.
Niagara Falls

Niagara R. Site
E. of Olin/102nd St.
Niagara Falls

Old Love Canal
97th–99th Sts.
Niagara Falls

Olin Corp.
Ind. Welding
Niagara Falls

Olin-Mathieson
 Dump
River Rd./102nd St.
Niagara Falls

Packard Rd. Site
Packard Rd.
Niagara Falls

Parking Lots
Buffalo Ave.
Niagara Falls

Plant Ppty.
Hyde Park Blvd.
Niagara Falls

Plant Site Pond
Buffalo Ave.
Niagara Falls

Reichold Chem.
Packard Rd.
Niagara Falls

Stauffer Chem. Co.
Jordan Rd.
Skanfateles
Courtland Coun.
Ldfl.
Town Line Rd.
Solon
Frazer & Jones Fov.
Milton Ave.
Solvay
Caputo Disp. Site
Ft. Edward/Wm.
S. Glen Falls
RCA Riverhead
S. Hampton
Al Hubbard Old
Brook
Spafford
Winsmith Div.
Umc. Co.
Enton St.
Springville
Claude Pulver Ldfl.
Starley
Chelsea Term.
Meredith Ave.
Staten Is.
Nassau Recycl.
Richmond Valley
Staten Is.
Torne Valley RDA
Rte. 59
Sterlington
Palmer Site
Rte. 75
Stillwater
Stillwater Dump
Site
Rte. 75
Stillwater
S. Stockton Ldfl.
Rte. 86
Stockton
K-Freeze Chem.
Stony Pt.
Syosette Ldfl.
Miller Place/
Robbins
Syosette
Lipe-Rollway Co.
Emerson Ave.
Syracuse

Oberdorfer
Foundries
Thompson Rd.
Syracuse
Prestolite Elec.
Lamson St.
Syracuse
Intl. Paper
Shore Airport Rd.
Ticonderoga
Greenwich Pulp &
Paper
Rte. 113
Thompson
Hudson Pulp &
Paper
Rte. 113
Thompson
Fed. Govt. Facil.
Three Rivers
Allied Chem. Plst.
West of River Rd.
Tonawanda
Bisonite Co., Inc.
Military Rd.
Tonawanda
Chem. Leaman
Tank
Fillmore Ave.
Tonawanda
Huntley Pow. Sta.
River Rd.
Tonawanda
INS Eq. Corp.
River Rd.
Tonawanda
Niagara Mohawk
Pow.
Huntley Pow. Sta.
Tonawanda
O-Cel-O Prod.
Sawyer Ave.
Tonawanda
Polymer Appl.
River Rd.
Tonawanda
Spaulding Fiber
Wheeler St.
Tonawanda
Ashland Petr.
River Rd.
Tonawanda

Columbus-
McKinnon
Fremont St.
Tonawanda
Dunlop Tire
Sheridon Dr.
Tonawanda
Exolon Corp.
E. Niagara
Tonawanda
FMC Corp. Ind.
Chem. Div.
Sawyer Ave.
Tonawanda
Robin Steel
River Rd.
Tonawanda
Seaway Ind. Pk.
Dev.
River Rd.
Tonawanda
Shanco Chem. &
Plast.
Wales Ave.
Tonawanda
Tonawanda Coke
(plus 1 other site)
River Rd.
Tonawanda
Town Incin.
Park Dr.
Tonawanda
Union Carbide
Lind.
E. Park Dr.
Tonawanda
St. Joe Zinc Co.
Old Beach Rd.
Towler
Portec, Inc.
Burden Ave.
Troy
Troy Munic. Incin.
Oakwood Ave.
Troy
Tully Ldfl.
Tully
Cortese Sanit. Ldfl.
Int. Wayne & Pike
Co.
Tusten

Minisink Rubber
Co.
Jersey Ave.
Unionville
Brookhaven Natl.
Wm. Floyd Pkwy.
Ext.
Upton
Chicago Pneumatic
Bleecker St.
Utica
Westinghouse Elec.
Genesee St.
Utica
Univ. Waste &
Paper
Leland/Norton
Ave.
Utica
Monarch Chem.
Co.
Prentice Rd.
Vestal
Robintech
Old Vestal Rd.
Vestal
Armstrong Cork
Co.
Off Rte. 57
Volney
Volney Ldfl.
Silk Rd.
Volney
Montgomery Ldfl.
Lake Osiris Rd.
Walden
Delaware Coun.
Ldfl.
Rte. 10
E. of Walton
Huff Bros. Refuse
Walworth
Warrensburg Board
Thurman Rd.
Warrensburg
All Coun. Serv.
Warwick
Georgia Pac. Corp.
Forester Ave.
Warwick
Waterford
Hudson R. Rd.
Waterford

Gen. Elec.
Hudson St.
Waterford

Evans Chemetics
E. Main St.
Waterloo

Black Clawson Co.
Pearl St.
Watertown

Camp Drum
Watertown

Fisher Cage Co.
Watertown

N.Y. Air Brake
Starbuck Ave.
Watertown

Adirondack Steel
Shaker Rd.
Watervliet

Al Tech Specialty
Sta.
Spring St.
Watervliet

Norton Co.
10th Ave./25th St.
Watervliet

Passano Corp.
Broadway
Watervliet

Jameco Ind.
Wayandanch Ave.
Wayandanch

Wellsville Ldfl.
Snyder Hill Rd.
Wellsville

Bainbridge Vill.
Case Rd.
W. Bainbridge

Knolls Atomic Pow.
West Milton

Oneida Coun.
Airpt.
Westmoreland

USMA—W. Point
Rte. 9 W.
W. Point

Madison Wire
Indian Church Rd.
W. Seneca

Harvey Newman
Shawnee Rd.
Wheatfield

Carborundum Co.
Walmore Rd.
Wheatfield

Lynch Pk. Ldfl.
Williams/R. Rd.
Wheatfield

Niagara Coun.
Refuse
Witmer Rd.
Wheatfield

Niagara Sanit.
Off Nash Rd.
Wheatfield

Cole-Zaiser
Little Pond Rd.
Williamstown

Wilson—Newfane
Ldfl.
Chestnut St.
Wilson

Jamelco Ind.
Wyandanch Ave.
Wyandanch

North
Carolina

N.C. Nit. Cpx.
Box 2500
Ahoskie

N.C. Nit. Cpx.
Box 2500
Ahoskie

Apex Sanit. Ldfl.
Hwy. 55
Apex

Sorrell Ldfl.
(plus 1 other site)
Hwy. 1303
Apex

Wake Coun. Ldfl.
Hwy. 1172
Apex

Potential Site
Hwy. 2035
Belmont

Jadco-Hughes
Hwy. 2035
Belmont

Brevard Plant
Buck Forest
Brevard

Camp Strauss
Bolyeston Hwy.
Brevard

Knob Ck.
Hwy. 1540
Brevard

Osheilds Fly Ash
Hwy. 1015
Brevard

Owens Ldfl.
Brevard

Bridgetown Site
Bridgetown

J. Lee Pharr Fm.
Cabarrus Coun.

New Hanover
Coun. Ldfl.
Hwy. 1534
Carolina Beach

Martin Marietta
Quarry
Hwy. 1002
Castle Wayne

Waste Lag.
Box 368
Castle Wayne

Am. Cyanamid
Wilkinson Blvd.
Charlotte

Budd Lee Paving
Holly Rd.
Charlotte

Dow Chem. Corp.
Woodlawn Green
Rd.
Charlotte

Harrisburg Pk.
Ldfl.
Petice Rd.
Charlotte

Kelly Rd.
Bailey Rd.
Charlotte

Mallard Ck. Rd.
Mallard Ck.
Charlotte

Martin-Marietta
Texland Blvd.
Charlotte

Mostellar Oil
(plus 1 other site)
N. Trylin St.
Charlotte

Academy Steel
Drum
Ridge Rd.
Charlotte

Statesville Rd. Ldfl.
Hwy. 21
Charlotte

Story Burial Areas
Orr Rd.
Charlotte

Thonit & Simmons
Co. (plus 1 other
site)
Steel Ck. Rd.
Charlotte

Winston Cont. Co.
Charlotte

Smith Pk. Colfax 3
Rte. 2
Colfax

Cabarrus Coun.
Ldfl.
Concord

Cabarrus Disp.
Co., Inc.
Box 2411
Concord

S. Latex Corp.
Buffalo Ave.
Concord

S. Latex Corp.
Central Rd.
Concord

Cumberland Coun.
Ldfl.
Cumberland Coun.

Hope Mills Ldfl.
Hwy. 1003
Cumberland

E. I. Dupont Co.
Rte. 1
Denton

Healing Spr. Plant
Denton

Amore Chem.
E. Pettigrew St.
Durham

Durham Whse.
Durham

Southchem.
E. Markham Ave.
Durham

Worth Chem. Corp.
E. Pettigrew St.
Durham

Cleveland Cont. &
Waste
Earl

Sparton Waste
Contr. (plus 2
other sites)
Earl

Elizabeth City
Elizabeth City

Herpert Cgas
Elizabeth City

Bladen Coun. Ldfl.
U.S. 7015
Elizabeth Town

Carolina Transf.
Fayetteville

Ck. Bridge
Fayetteville

Cumberland Coun.
Ldfl.
Cliffdale Rd.
Fayetteville

Fayetteville Ldfl.
(plus 1 other site)
Gray St.
Fayetteville

Fayetteville Plant
Box 2307
Fayetteville

Fayetteville Plant
Industrial Dr.
Fayetteville

Fayetteville Wks.
Fayetteville

Milan Yd. Ldfl.
Fayetteville

Rohm & Haas, Inc.
Cedar Ck. Pond
Fayetteville

New Hanover Ldfl.
Flemington

Ft. Bragg Ldfl.
Ft. Bragg

Biggerstaff Ldfl.
Hwy. 274
Gastonia

S&S Metals Recycl.
Shortcut Rd.
Gold Mill

Agrico Chem.
Corp. (plus 1
other site)
Patton Ave.
Greensboro

Greensboro City
Ldfl.
White St.
Greensboro

Greensboro Plant
S. Oxygen
Greensboro

Holding Pond
Broome Rd.
Greensboro

Holding Pond for
Waste
Hwy. 74
Greensboro

Hubert Atkins Ppty.
Rte. 9
Greensboro

N. Buffalo Pollut.
White St.
Greensboro

Pfizer, Inc.
Block High Pt.
Greensboro

City Ldfl.
Greensboro

Worth Chem. Co.
Greensboro

Carolina Tank
Hwy. 68
Greensboro

Burroughs-
Welcome
Hwy. 68
Greenville

City Ldfl.
Greenville

Coastal Chem.
(plus 1 other site)
Evans St. Ext.
Greenville

Greenville City
Ldfl.
Cemetary St.
Greenville

Halifax Coun. Ldfl.
Hwy. 1103
Halifax Coun.

Duke Ref. Co.
Jarrell St.
High Pt.

High Pt. Site
Hwy. 1145
High Pt.

City of High Pt.
Riverdale Rd.
High Pt.

Renrom
Hwys. 50/17
Holly Ridge

Jacksonville Ldfl.
Jacksonville

Seaboard Chem.
Co.
Jamestown

Carolawn Co.
W. Mtn. St.
Kernersville

Destructo
Chemway
Kernersville

Kernersville Rubble
Dump
Kernersville

Foote Min.
Kings Mtn.

Elmer Catch Pond
Bow 1577
Kingston

Kingston City Ldfl.
Davie St.
Kingston

Kingston Plant
Disp.
Box 800
Kingston

Kingston Plant
Incin.
Box 800
Kingston

Munic. Ldfl.
Kingston

City Ldfl.
Kingston

Lenor Coun. Ldfl.
Kingston

Carr-Michael Firm
Rd. 3
Laurinsburg

Plant Mgrs. &
Prod.
Rd. 3
Laurinsburg

Brunswick Coun.
Ldfl.
Hwy. 1438
Leland

W. Bank
Nauhssa Rd.
Leland

Caldwell Sys., Inc.
Mt. Hermon Rd.
Lenoir

Whittaker Chem.
Co.
Lenoir

Gulf Oil Chem.
Box 83
McLeansville

Academy Steel
Drum
Ridge Rd.
Mattews

Walden Ppty.
**Mecklenburg
Coun.**

Allied Chem. Fibers
Box 166
Moncure

Moncure Plant
(plus 1 other site)
Hwy. 1916
Moncure

Reichold Chem.,
Inc.
Hwy. 1916
Moncure

Union Coun. Ldfl.
Monroe

Koppers Co., Inc.
Hwy. 54 W.
Morrisville

Old Hwy. 27
Mt. Molly

Wilmington Branch
Wilmington Rd.
Navaasa

C. A. Hughes Co.
N. Belmont

PCB Spill
N.C. Hwy.

Koppers
Seaboard Coastline
Paw Creek

Brown 1
Hwy. 1504
Pigsah For.

Film Incin.
Vanderbilt Rd.
Pigsah For.

Is. Incin.
Vanderbilt Rd.
Pigsah For.

Is. Ldfl.
Vanderbilt Rd.
Pigsah For.

Orig. Ldfl.
Vanderbilt Rd.
Pigsah For.

Sludge Disp. Area
Hwy. 1504
Pigsah For.

S.E. Poll.
Pineville

S.E. Pl.
Box 67
Pineville

Reichold Chem.,
   Inc.
Dorman Rd.
Pineville

Chatman Co. Ldfl.
Hwy. 1513
Pittsboro

Plymouth Shopping
   Ctr.
Hwys. 32/64
Plymouth

Weyerhauser
Hwy. 1565
Plymouth

Watts Retreat
Purlear

Chloride, Inc.
Raleigh

Mallinkrodit, Inc.
Raleigh

Rowland Ldfl.
Hwy. 2013
Raleigh

Red Spr.
Red Spr.

Acme Wks.
W. of Wilmington
Reigel Wood

Fed. Paper Board
   Co.
W. of Wilmington
Reigel Wood

Rocky Fiber Dump
Atlantic Ave. Ext.
Rocky Mtn.

Rocky Mtn. Waste
   Trmt.
Box 1180
Rocky Mtn.

Reeves Bros.
Rutherfordton

Sanit. Serv. Ldfl.
St. Pauls

Benefield Site
Salisbury

Fiber Ind., Inc.
   (plus 1 other site)
Hwy. 70 W.
Salisbury

Lee Coun. Ldfl.
Hwy. 1177
Sanford

Pfizer, Inc.
Rte. 42
Sanford

Gurley Milling Co.
Selma

Fiber Ind.
Box 87
Shelby

Jones Fm.
S. Port

McCracken Fm.
S. Port

Numerous Small
   Fms.
S. Port

Pfizer, Inc.
Moore St.
S. Port

Pfizer Off-Site Fm.
S. Port

Plant Site Fm.
Moore St.
S. Port

Stevens Fm.
S. Port

Paul Love's Pit
Spencer Coun.

Private Fm.
Rte. 1
Stokesdale

Chemtronics, Inc.
Box 436
Swannanoa

Edgecombe Co.
   Ldfl.
Hwy. 1601
Tarboro

Proposed PCB
   Disp. Site
Warrenton

Schulhoffer Junkyd.
Box 314
Waynesville

Lackey Ind.
Whitesville

Amaco
River Rd.
Wilmington

Cape Fear
Box 2042
Wilmington

Hanover Plt. Waste
   (plus 2 other sites)
Hwy. 421 N.
Wilmington

Kerr McGee
Wilmington

Holding Pond for
   Waste
Hwy. 74
Wilmington

Swift Agri. Chem.
   Corp.
Azelea Sta.
Wilmington

Intl. Min.
Glenn Ave. Ext.
Winston-Salem

North Dakota

Belfield N. Ashing
**6 mi. N.W. of
   Belfield**

Belfield S. Ashing
S.E. end of Belfield

Husky Briquetting
E. of Dickinson

Sodium Chromate
Dickinson

NDSU Radioact.
   Waste
Fargo

Ldfl. Near Arsgo
N. Mill Rd.
Grand Forks

Ldfl. Near Arsgo
N. Mill Rd.
Grand Forks

Und. Radioactive
   Waste
**14 mi. W. of Grand
   Forks**

Bowman Lignit
   Ashing
7 mi. W. of Bowman
Griffin

Arsenic Disp.
Varied Locations

Ohio

Akron Chem. Plant
W. Emerling
Akron

Akron Ldfl.
Hazel St.
Akron

B. F. Goodrich
   Chem.
Moore & Walker
Akron

J. B. Lockhart
   Constr.
Waterloo Rd.
Akron

Seiberling St. Corp.
E. Market St.
Akron

Keyboard Lounge
W. Ohio Pike
Amelia

Performance
   Polymers
Bach/Buxton Rd.
Amelia

Amherst Quarry
Quarry Rd.
Amherst

Ashland Coun.
Ldfl.
Coun. Rd. 1754
Ashland

Ashtabula City
Dump
Lake Ave.
Ashtabula

Acme Scrap Metal
State Rd.
Ashtabula

Brenkus Shop
Ashtabula

Ashtabula Hide &
Leather
N. Main St.
Ashtabula

Brenkus Shop
E. 15th St.
Ashtabula

Hooker Chem.
Minnesota Ave.
Ashtabula

Detrex Chem. Ind.
State Rd.
Ashtabula

IMC Chem. Group
Ashtabula

Middle Rd. for
Brenkus
Middle Rd.
Ashtabula

Reserve Environ.
Serv.
Woodman Ave.
Ashtabula

RMI Co.
E. 21st St.
Ashtabula

Rockwell Inter.
Corp.
N. Ridge W.
Ashtabula

Semi-Wks. Plant
Ashtabula

Old Ohio Univ.
U.S. 50
Athens

Ashtabula Coun.
Waste
Rtes. 307/45
Austingburg Twp.

Chemtron Corp.
Schneider
Avon

Avon Lake Gen.
Walker Rd.
Avon Lake

B. F. Goodrich
Chem.
W. Emerling
Avon Lake

Avon Lake City
Dump
Clinton/Miller
Avon Lake

Barberton Plant
Barberton

Chemtrol Co.
Aber Rd.
Batavia

Ferro Corp.
Krick Rd.
Bedford

S. K. Wellman
Egbert Rd.
Bedford

Erieway Pollut. Co.
Industry Rd.
Bedford

Am. Steel Drum
Northfield Rd.
Bedford

Hukill Chem. Corp.
(plus 1 other site)
Krick Rd.
Bedford

Ben Venue Lab.
Northfield Rd.
Bedford

Bedford Hgts. Mat.
Perkins Rd.
Bedford Hgts.

Mayer China
Solon Rd.
Bedford Hgts.

Shell Chem. Co.
Hwy. 7
Belpre

U.S. Wrecking
Broadview Rd.
Brecksville

Modiglass Ldfl.
Oak Mill Rd.
Breman

Reichold Sanit.
Ldfl.
Cnty. Rd.
Breman

Buckeye Recl.
Rte. 1
Bridgeport

Norton Constr.
E. Royalton Rd.
Broadview Hgts.

N. Constr.
Rte. 82
Broadview Hgts.

Brook Pk.
Brookpk.

Contl. Water
Brookpk. Rd.
Brookpk.

HRM Inds., Inc.
(plus 1 other site)
Rte. 3
Bryan

Shenango Res.
Box 5
Burghill

Statewide Ldfl.
Duebar Ave.
Canton

Lake Coun. Ld.
Improve.
Brookland
Chesterland

Chillicothe Wks.
Washington Ave.
Chillicothe

City of Chillicothe
(plus 1 other site)
Renic Ave.
Chillicothe

City of Chillicothe
Narrows Rd.
Chillicothe

Canal Ridge Rd.
Dump
Canal Ridge Rd.
Cincinnati

Cincinnati MSD
Incin.
Gest St.
Cincinnati

Cincinnati Plant
Paddock Rd.
Cincinnati

City Dump
Cincinnati

City of Cincinnati
Mill Creek Rd.
Cincinnati

Crookshank Dump
Cincinnati

Clarke Incin.
E. Kemper Rd.
Cincinnati

Elda Ldfl.
Este Ave.
Cincinnati

Este Ave. Dump
Este/Township
Cincinnati

Gray Rd. Ldfl.
Cincinnati

Hughes Rd. Sanit.
Ldfl.
Hughes Rd.
Cincinnati

Keenan Reprocess.
Seymour Ave.
Cincinnati

Klor-Clean
Cincinnati

Laidlaw Ave. City
Dump
Laidlaw Ave.
Cincinnati

Metro Sew. Dist.
Gest St.
Cincinnati

MSD Hamilton Co.
Gest St.
Cincinnati

Newberry Co.
Crookshank Rd.
Cincinnati

N. Bend Dump
W.N. Bend Rd.
Cincinnati

Potential Site
Beckman/
Springrove
Cincinnati

Rumpke, Inc.
Hughes Rd.
Cincinnati

Sharonville Plant
E. Kemper
Cincinnati

West & Sons
Hazardous
Harrison Pike
Cincinnati

Pickaway Coun.
Ldfl.
Rte. 104
Circleville

Bowers Ldfl.
Is. Rd.
Circleville

Dupont
Circleville

Warehouse
Stone Levee
Cleveland

Usher Waste Oil
Serv.
W. 3rd
Cleveland

Trisket Ave. Site
Cleveland

Steel Drum
Exchange
W. 140th
Cleveland

Std. Pail & Drum
Cleveland

Warner Hill Ldfl.
Warner Rd.
Cleveland

Sohio
E. 49th
Cleveland

Sherwin Williams
Canal Rd.
Cleveland

Shell Oil Co.
W. 3rd St.
Cleveland

M. Cohen & Sons
St. Clair
Cleveland

Northway
W. 4th St.
Cleveland

Reily Tar & Chem.
Independence
Cleveland

Repub. Steel
45th St.
Cleveland

Wean Port Ltd.
Jennings Rd.
Cleveland

Mobile Tank Car
Serv.
Brookside Pk.
Cleveland

Abandoned Drums
Platt Ave.
Cleveland

Advance Barrel &
Drum
Beaver
Cleveland

Ashland Oil Ref.
Poplar Rd.
Cleveland

Air Prod. & Chem.
Quigley Rd.
Cleveland

Alchemtron
Train Ave.
Cleveland

Aronson Drum
Canal Rd.
Cleveland

Arrow Alum. Cast.
Berea Rd.
Cleveland

Beck Chem., Inc.
137th St.
Cleveland

Burdett Oxygen
Co.
Bradley Rd.
Cleveland

Cleveland Right of
Way
Broadway Ave.
Cleveland

City Barrel & Drum
E. 91st St.
Cleveland

E. 49th St.
Cleveland

Cleveland Site
Trisket Ave.
Cleveland

Erie Way Pollut.
Train Ave.
Cleveland

Cleveland-West
W. 110
Cleveland

Harry Rock
Cleveland

Dump of Trkg. Co.
Bradley & Jennings
Cleveland

Natl. Wks.
Warner Rd.
Cleveland

J. Frank Barrel
51st St.
Cleveland

Ohio Drum Recon.
Pearl Rd.
Cleveland

Jones & Laughlin
Site
Jennings Rd.
Cleveland

Ohio Drum Recon.
Cleveland

L. Gray Barrel
75th St.
Cleveland

3 C Hwy. Trans.
Cleveland

Borden, Inc.
W. Mound St.
Columbus

City Ldfl. Corp.
Alum. Ck. Dr.
Columbus

Ecol. Bedford Site 1
Claycraft Rd.
Columbus

G. Frederick Smith
McKinley Ave.
Columbus

Franklin Coun.
Ldfl.
Jackson Pike
Columbus

J. Texas Howard
Dublin Rd.
Columbus

J. Texas Howard
Jackson Pike
Columbus

MCQ Marble Cliff
Trabue Rd.
Columbus

New Columbus
Ldfl. (plus 1
other site)
Alum. Ck. Dr.
Columbus

Potential Site
Morrison Rd.
Columbus

Welch Dump
Refugee Rd.
Columbus

Potential Site
Rte. 2
Coolville

Coshocton City
Ldfl.
Hwy. 83
Coshocton

Coshocton Plant
S. Second St.
Coshocton

Otsego Ave. Dump
Hwy. 83
Coshocton

Alside, Inc.
Cuyahoga Falls

Ashland Chem. Co.
71st St.
Cuyahoga Hgts.

E. 49th St.
E. 49th St.
Cuyahoga Hgts.

Clark Oil Co., Inc.
W. End Ave.
Dayton

Dayton
Fairfield Rd.
Dayton

Summit Natl.
Alliance Rd.
Deerfield

City of Delaware
Ldfl.
Delaware

Old Delaware City
Ldfl.
Curve Rd.
Delaware

Pennwalt—Del.
Plant
London Rd.
Delaware

Fulton Coun.
Delta

Kimble Coal Co.
Rte. 1
Dover

Dover Chem. Co.
15th St.
Dover

Nela Pk. Dump
E. Cleveland

Demilta-Mahon
Ldfl.
Erie Rd.
Eastlake

Wallover Oil Co.
Virginia Ave.
E. Liverpool

Browning-Ferris
Ind.
Glenwood Ave.
E. Palastin

Ford Rd. Dump
Ford Rd.
Elyria

Garden St. Ldfl.
Middle Rd.
Elyria

Woodford Rd.
Quarry
Woodford Ave.
Elyria

Harshaw Chem.
E. 29th St.
Elyria

Elyria Fd.
W. Ridge Rd.
Elyria

Chem. Recov.
Elyria

Quarry Pit
Woodward Ave.
Elyria

Aztec Chem.
Garden St.
Elyria

Lincoln Elec.
St. Clair Ave.
Euclid

Browning-Ferris
Ind.
Bobmeyer Rd.
Fairfield

Diamond Shamrock
Co.
Second St.
Fairport

Morton Salt
Fairport Harbor

Fairport Ldfl.
East St.
Fairport Harbor

Miller Stge. Sites
Rte. 1
Felicity

W. R. Grace Co.
E. Bigelow
Findlay

Terry Little
Fostoria

Gahana Ldfl.
N. of Hampton Rd.
Gahana

Tx. & Ass. Sanit.
Gahana

Conti
Wagner Rd.
Garfield Hgts.

Allied Chem. Corp.
Warner Rd.
Garfield Hgts.

Rockside Ldfl.
Rockside Rd.
Garfield Hgts.

Dumping into Lake
Broadway/Henry
Garfield Hgts.

True Temper Corp.
Water St.
Geneva

Glenwillow Wks.
Pettibone Rd.
Glenwillow

Inland Ldfl.
Richmond Rd.
Glenwillow

Chemdyne Corp.
Grafton

Robert Ross & Sons
(plus 1 other site)
Giles Rd.
Grafton

Chem-Dyne
Ford Blvd.
Hamilton

Bond Rd. Sanit.
Ldfl.
Bond Rd.
Harrison

Browning-Ferris
Ind.
Bond Rd.
Harrison

Liberty Twp. Dump
Hartford

Haverhill Plant
Haverhill

Ashland Oil Ref.
Heath

Sys. Tech. Corp.
Edgwin
Hilliard

Sys. Tech.
Hilliard

Dupont Huron
Plant
Huron

Maint. Constr.
Rockside Rd.
Independence

E. H. Schilling Ldfl.
Patrick St.
Ironton

Gulf Chem. & Met.
S. 2nd St.
Ironton

Hanging Rock Ldfl.
N. 2nd St.
Ironton

Ironton Tar Plant
S. Third St.
Ironton

Ironton Coke Corp.
S. Third St.
Ironton

Alaskan
Greenhouse
N. Poplar St.
Jefferson

Laskin Waste Oil
N. Poplar
Jefferson

Hardin Coun. Ldfl.
Coun. Rd. 143A
Kenton

Ck. Rd. for Brenkus
Ck. Rd.
Kingsville

Whitman's Ck.
Rte. 531
Kingsville

Kingsville Twp.
Dump
Middle Rd.
Kingsville

Lake Coun.
Brooklane
Kirkland

Greenslopes Ldfl.
Rte. 3
Lancaster

Bland Trkg., Inc.
Hwy. 59
Linton

Chemline Corp.
Lisbon

Cozart Ldfl.
Applegate Rd.
Lisbon

Green Ldfl. 11
Twp. Rd. 353
Logan

U.S. Steel Plant
Lorain

City of Lorain
Dump
Root Rd.
Lorain

Ray Dingus
McKay

Abandoned Bldg.
Madison

Am. Cyanamid
Greene St.
Marietta

Gulf Oil Chem.
(plus 1 other site)
Hwy. 7
Marietta

Marietta Plant
N. Elmwood
Marietta

Marietta Sanit.
Rte. 3
Marietta

Union Carbide
Corp.
Box 176
Marietta

Donn Corp.
W. Smith Rd.
Medina

High Voltage
 Maint.
Ind. Pk. Blvd.
Mentor

Mentor Marsh
 Dump
Mentor

Mentor Headlands
Rte. 44/Headlands
Mentor

Shoreline Trkg.
Richmond Rd.
Mentor

Eastland Rd.
Eastland Rd.
Middleburg Hgts.

Lake Abrams
Eagle Rd.
Middleburg

City of Middletown
 Ldfl.
Carmody Blvd.
Middletown

Middletown Wks.
Middletown

Middletown Ohio
 Facil.
Middletown

Ohio Facil.
Yankee Rd.
Middletown

Thermo Chem.
 Corp.
Evanston Ave.
Muskegon

Newark Sew. Proj.
Newark

Closed Sanit. Ldf.
Rte. 44
Newbury

Ashtabula Coun.
 Waste
New Line

City Dump
New Philadelphia

Browning-Ferris
 Ind.
Pine St.
Niles

Hardy Rd. Ldfl.
Hardy Rd.
Northampton

James Cobbs Whse.
Rte. 76
N. Eaton

Universal Trkg.
Main St.
N. Kingsville

Spr. St. Dump
Dirt Rd.
Oberlin

Browning-Ferris
 Ind.
Rte. 10
Oberlin

Fondessy Ent.
Otter Ck. Rd.
Oregon

Orrville Plant
Box 107
Orrville

Orville Plant
Burton City Rd.
Orrville

Lake Coun. Baler
Blaze-Nemeth Rd.
Painesville

Lake Coun. Baler
Rtes. 2/20
Painesville

Ash Settling Pond
Bacon Rd.
Painesville

Ldfl.
Bacon Rd.
Painesville

Coe Mfg. Co.
Bank St.
Painesville

Painesville
Painesville

IRC Fibers, Inc.
Bacon Rd.
Painesville

Diamond Shamrock
Second St.
Painesville Twp.

Parma City Ldfl.
W. Ridgewood
Parma

Plant Site—Closed
Shepard Rd.
Penny

Plant Site—Open
Shepard Rd.
Penny

J.D. Hershberger
 Ldfl.
Crottinger Rd.
Plain City

Unico Ldfl., Inc.
Taylor Rd.
Plain City

Carbon Limestone
 Ldfl.
Poland Twp.

Name Unreported
Jct. Hwys. 36/16
Pt. Washington

Duralote
Ravinnia

Pristine, Inc.
 (plus 2 other sites)
Big Four/Smalley
Reading

Krause Disp. Site
 (plus 1 other site)
Mill Rd./Station
Rock Ck.

Mr. Webb
Mill Rd./Station
Rock Ck.

Oil Well
Hattrick Rd.
Rootstown

Cin-Made Corp.
E. Ross Ave.
St. Bernard

Buckeye Ldfl.
Rte. 214
St. Clairesville

Belmont Coun.
 Ldfl.
St. Clairesville

Ashtabula Coun.
 Waste
N. Bend Rd.
Saybrook Twp.

Zircoa
Solon
Saylo

Shelby Coun. Sanit.
 Ldfl.
Hwy. 47
Sidney

Zircoa
Solon

Anthony Min. Co.
Box 1289
Steubenville

Swanton Plant
E. Broadway
Swanton

Coulten Chem.
Sylvania Rd.
Sylvania

Benton Vill.
Wiles Rd.
Toledo

Dura Ave. Sanit.
Dura Rd.
Toledo

Tyler St. Dump
Tyler St.
Toledo

Ray Oberly Disp.
Twining St.
Toledo

Toledo Plant
Toledo

Toledo Sew. Plant
Bay View Pk.
Toledo

King Rd. Lucas
 Coun.
King Rd.
Toledo

Wis. Ave. Toledo
 Ldfl.
S. Ave./Maumee
Toledo

Toronto
Titanium Way
Toronto

Shenango Res.
Kingsman Rd.
Trumball Coun.

Liberty Solv.
Ravenna Rd.
Twinsburg

City Dump
Uhrichsville

Ind. Excess Ldfl.
Cleveland Ave.
Uniontown

Ohio Liquid Disp.
Hwy. 412
Vickery

Buckeye Trans. Sta.
Pine Rd.
Warren

Steam Discharge
Warren

Std. Transf.
Dana St.
Warren

Thomas Steel Strip
Delaware Ave.
Warren

Skinner Ldfl.
   (plus 1 other site)
Cinn-Dayton Rd.
Westchester

U.S. Steel Plant
28th St.
Westlake

Newco Chem.
   Waste
Aber Rd.
Williamsburg

Sys. Tech.
N. Valley Rd.
Xenia

Ohio-Xenia
Hawkin Rd.
Xenia

Xenia City Ldfl.
Towler Rd.
Xenia

Ohio-Xenia
N. Township Rd.
Xenia

Koppers Co., Inc.
Logan Ave.
Youngstown

Norris Ldfl.
Twp. Rd. 129
Zanesville

Oklahoma

Brockway Glass Co.
Ada

City of Altus Ldfl.
Altus

Jackson
Altus

Helena Chem. Co.
Box 814
Altus

W. Farmers Fuy.
Anadarko

Morris Post Co.
Antlers

Bacon Trans. Co.
Hwy. 142 E.
Ardmore

Old Ardmore
   Dump
Box 3246
Ardmore

Big Chief Roofing
   Co.
Box 908
Ardmore

Stromberg-Carlson
Ardmore

Vickers Petr.
142 Bypass
Ardmore

Ardmore State Pk.
S. of Ardmore

Baker Tri-City Ldfl.
S. of Ardmore

Lake Murray State
3 mi. S. of
Ardmore

Atoka 1 & 2
Atoka

Tatoms
Atoms

Petrolite Corp.
Barnsdall

Natl. Zinc. Co.
W. 11th St.
Bartlesville

Somex Ltd.
S. Virginia
Bartlesville

Ck. Coun. Haz.
   Waste
Beggs

Central Ok. Sanit.
   Ldfl.
Bethany

Acme Foundry
Blackwell

Blackwell-Tonkawa
Blackwell

Blain Coun. Solid
   Waste
Blain

Ind. Waste Disp.
Blanchard

Mackey Packing,
   Inc.
Box 101
Boise City

Strip Pits
Broken Arrow

Anderson-Dunham,
   Inc.
Broken Bow

Weyerhaeuser Co.
Broken Bow

Huffman Wood
   Preserve
Broken Bow

Thompson Lumb.
   Co.
Broken Bow

Burns Flat Dump
Burns Flat

Flat Sys., Inc.
Clinton Sherman
Burns Flat

Caddo
Caddo

Childless Chem. Co.
Cardin

Tulsa Recon. Co.
Catoosa

Tulsa Cont. Co.
Hwy. 33
Catoosa

Robert Attus Ppty.
Cedars

Chandler Ldfl.
Chandler

Seaba Mfg.
Box 211
Chandler

Maremont Corp.
Box 988
Chickasha

Carnes Disp. Site
Cleveland

Kellwood Co.
Clinton

Hub Cities Trans.
Commerce St.
Clinton

Comanche Co.
Comanche

Royal N. Hardage
Hwy. 59
Criner

Cushing Railcar Co.
Box 1354
Cushing

Hudson Ref. Co.
Box 111
Cushing

APCO Oil Corp.
S. Basket St.
Cyril

Arbuckle
E. Main St.
Davis

Sooner Rock &
   Sand
3 mi. S.W. of
Davis

Del City Dump
Del

Bond's Custom
Box 112
Delaware

Abandoned—Del
   City
Del City

M&E Oil Service
U.S. 70
Devol

A.T.&S.F.
S. of Dibble

Dover Site
Dover

Drumright Ldfl.
Drumright

Halliburton Serv.
Duncan

Sun Oil Soil Fm.
   (plus 1 other site)
S. of Duncan

Stephens Co.
Duncan

Sunray Ref. Dump
Duncan

Eaker Airpt.
Durant

S.W. Pickiling
Durant

Marathon Rankin D
Edmund

El Reno By Prod.
Box 195
El Reno

Bert Smith Diesel
Enid

Bond Baking Co.
N. Independence
Enid

Champlin Petr.
Oil Ref.
Enid

Enid Nit. Plant
S. Van Buren
Enid

Garfield 2
Enid

Raleigh Inds.
Box 3307
Enid

Old B. R. Smith
Lag.
Erick

Stapp Disp. Pit
Erin Spr.

Muskogee Environ.
Ft. Gibson

U.S. Pollut. Contr.
Grass-Mt.-W.-Fair

Dave L. Roberts
5 mi. N.E. of
Grove

Sherman Helium
Plant
Star Route
Guymon

Abandoned Strip
Mine
Haskill

Wells Coal Co.
Box 421
Haskill

Brady Welding &
Machin.
Box 788
Healdton

Healdton Dump
N. 4th St.
Healdton

Eagle Pitcher
Henrietta

Real Scrap Metal
S. Eastern
Hobart

Harmon 1 & 2
Hollis

Cent. For. Prod.
Box 392
Hugo

Hugo Waste Disp.
Hugo

Hugo Rail Car, Inc.
Rte. 1
W. of Hugo

Mixin Bros. Wood
Preserv.
Idabel

Regin Trkg. Co.
Itrorial

P.S.O. Riverside St.
Jenks

Dowell Truck
Driving
Kellyville

Black Mesa State
Pk.
Kenton

Berkenbile Unit 1
Kink Hicker

U.S. Army Fd.
Artill.
Feed Bldg.
Lawton

S.W. Disp.
Hwy. 53
Loco

McAlester Army
Ammun.
McAlester

Kay's Foundry, Inc.
Maid & Pryor

Aerial Survey Dump
(plus 3 other sites)
Maid near Pryor

Carborundum, Inc.
Maid near Pryor

Cherokee Nit.
Dump
Maid near Pryor

Kay's Foundry, Inc.
Maid near Pryor

Natl. Gypsum Co.
Maid near Pryor

Old Quarry Dump
Maid near Pryor

Oowa Steam &
Pow.
Patrol Rd.
Maid near Pryor

Oowa Waste Trmt.
Maid near Pryor

Oowa Lag.
Patrol Rd.
Maid near Pryor

Poly Guard &
Pipeline
Maid near Pryor

Pryor Automatic
Tool
Maid near Pryor

Pryor Foundry
Maid near Pryor

Red Devil, Inc.
Maid near Pryor

Underground Stge.
Maid near Pryor

B. F. Goodrich
Tire Co.
Box 31
Miami

Assoc. Milk Prod.
Midwest City

Tinker AFB
Midwest City

Pennsylvania Glass
Mills Ck.

Harmon 1 & 2
Mollis

Ok. Tank Serv.
S.W. 24th
Moore

Lone Ck. Injection
Mooreland

Consol. Cleaning
Serv.
181st St.
Mounds

Brockway Glass
Co. (plus 1 other
site)
Muskogee

Fansteel Metals
Rte. 5
Muskogee

Muskogee Env. Fly
Ash
Muskogee

Ft. Howard Paper
Co.
Muskogee

G. T. Metals
Rd. 4
Muskogee

J. W. Worley
Battery
Madison St.
Muskogee

Madewell Metals
Disp.
E. Shawnee
Muskogee

Smokey's Inds.
E. Broadway
Muskogee

Yaffee Iron &
Metal
Corner/Lexington
Muskogee

Wayman Solid
Waste Disp.
W. Edge of Nash

Acme Fence & Iron
Box 876
Norman

Nowata 2
Oak St.
Nowata

Abandoned Dump
Oklahoma City

Alliance Wall
Waste
Oklahoma City

Alpha Drum Co.
Oklahoma City

Am. Disp. Serv.
74th/Bryant
Oklahoma City

Anco Serv. Co.
30th St.
Oklahoma City

Ashland Chem.
Oklahoma City

Assoc. Milk Prod.
Oklahoma City

Bucket Shop
N.W. 5th
Oklahoma City

Browning-Ferris,
Inc.
W. I-40
Oklahoma City

Browning-Ferris,
Inc.
Exchange Ave.
Oklahoma City

Canadian Truck
Oklahoma City

Cimmaron Airpt.
Oklahoma City

Custom Eq. Co.
74th/Bryant
Oklahoma City

Double Eagle Ref.
N. Rhode Is.
Oklahoma City

Eastside Colby
Ldil.
W. Reno
Oklahoma City

Frac. Tank
Oklahoma City

Hanger 8 Wiley
Post
Oklahoma City

915 S. Fairmont
Oklahoma City

N.E. 10/Grand
Blvd.
Oklahoma City

N.E. 50/Bry
Oklahoma City

Midwest Machine
Melrose Ln.
Oklahoma City

Ok. City. Disp. Co.
15th St.
Oklahoma City

Ok. City Reagent
Plant
Sunnylane
Oklahoma City

Ok. City Disp.
36th St.
Oklahoma City

Ok. City Dump
Oklahoma City

City of Oklahoma
9th St.
Oklahoma City

Paia Electr.
W. Wilshire
Oklahoma City

Paraway Ref.
S.E. 7/Irving
Oklahoma City

Phillips 66
S. Fairmont
Oklahoma City

Potential Site
Box 14566
Oklahoma City

Prestolite Lag.
Oklahoma City

Rose Eq. Co. Ppty.
Linwood
Oklahoma City

S&W Oil Fds.
S. Eastern
Oklahoma City

S.E. 29th/Minasse
Rd.
Oklahoma City

S.E. 29th/Minasse
Rd.
Oklahoma City

S.W. Electronic
Oklahoma City

Star Mfg.
I-35
Oklahoma City

Time—DC
S.E. Skyline
Oklahoma City

Tulsa, City of
Mohawk
Oklahoma City

Unident. Dump Site
Oklahoma City

Union Carbide
S. Agnew
Oklahoma City

Unident. Site
Oklahoma City

U.S. Pollut. Cont.
Oklahoma City

Wall Colmonoy
Corp.
S.E. 59th St.
Oklahoma City

Walnut Grove Salt
Wa.
Oklahoma City

1700 S. Agnew
S. Agnew
Oklahoma City

2200 Blk. N.E.
Blk. N.E.
Oklahoma City

4 Star Sand Co.
Dump
Oklahoma City

S. Missouri
S. Missouri
Oklahoma City

Old Ok. Dump
Oklahoma City

N.E. 23rd
N.E. 23rd
Oklahoma City

Hasley Rd. Sanit.
Ldfl.
Hasley Rd.
Oklahoma City

Madewell &
Madewell
Oklahoma City

Pond
E. Reno
Oklahoma City

Kerr McGee
Kerr McGee Ctr.
Oklahoma City

Keller Furniture
Box 14504
Oklahoma City

Intl. Environ.
Oklahoma City

Hendershot Tool
Co.
S.E. 29th
Oklahoma City

East Side Colby
Ldfl.
W. Reno
Oklahoma City

Conoco Chem.
Oklahoma City

Concho Constr.
Oklahoma City

23rd/Sconer Rd.
Ldfl.
Oklahoma City

Kelco Basin
Okmulgee

Alliance Wall Co.
Hwy. 75
Okmulgee

Thompson Pump
Co.
Okmulgee

OK. City Ref. Tank
N. of Okmulgee

Cavington Aircraft
N. of Okmulgee

Pub. Serv. Co.
(plus 1 other site)
Oolagan

Irwin Sand Co.
Lag.
Perkins

Nuble
Perry

Charles Machine
Wk.
W. Fir Ave.
Perry

City Dump
Ponca City

Eastside, Colby
Ldfl.
Hwy. 60
Ponca City

Conoco, Inc.
S. Pine
Ponca City

Ponca City Sanit.
U.S. 60
Ponca City

Poolville
Poolville

U.S. Army Field
Artill.
Port Sill

Muskogee Environ.
Porum

Georgia Pac. Corp.
Pryor

Liquid Air Ind.
Pryor

Mid-Am. Ind.
Corp.
Patrol Rd.
Pryor

Kaiser Agri-Chem.
Pryor

Mid-Am. Yarn
Box 1028
Pryor

Midwest Carbide
 Corp.
Box 518
Pryor

N-Ben Corp.
Box 429
Pryor

Nipak, Inc.
 Injection
Pryor

Nipak, Inc.
 Injection
Pryor

Ord. Wks. Chem.
Pryor

Pryor Foundry
 Drum
Pryor

Pryor Foundry
 Sand
Pryor

Pryor Munic.
 Dump
S. of Pryor

Ryals Junk &
 Salvage
Hwy. 169
Pryor

Nipak, Inc.
 Injection
Pryor

Renfro Trkg.
Hwy. 20
Ralson

Ratcliffe City
Ratcliffe

Julian Wood Trtg.
Boxy 146
Rattan

Conrad Dump
S. of Reijdon

Roger Mills 3
Reydon

Roger Mills 1 & 2
Reydon

Petro Tech., Inc.
Box 38
Salina

John Scoggins
Rte. 4
Sallisaw

Big Three Inds.
S. Main St.
Sallisaw

Hissom Ldfl.
Sand Spr.

Old Sinclair Ref.
E. Morrow
Sand Spr.

Solv. Rec.
Adams Rd.
Sand Spr.

Shell Ck. Sanit.
 Ldfl.
Rte. 1
Sand Spr.

Raymond Wiley
Box 256
Sand Spr.

Fair Oil Injection
Sapulpa

Intl. Metals
Sapulpa

Dolese Co.—Sayre
 Plan
Sayre

Byron-Jackson
Seminole

Allen-Bradley
Shawne

Butler Res. Ltd.
Sheidler

U.S.P.C. 1 Ck. Co.-
 Haz.
Slick

Blain Coun. Solid
 Waste
Southard

Philips Petr. Co.
Hwy. 136
Star Rte.
Guymon

Stillwater Munic.
Stillwater

Mercury Mar.
Perkins Rd.
Stillwater

Swan Hose Ldfl.
Stillwater

Fugate Lumb. Lag.
Stringtown

Allied Mat. Corp.
Allied Rd.
Stroud

Regins Trkg. Co.
E. of Stroud

Hoot Stallings Eq.
Tishmingo

Consol. Oil Sale
Dirt Rd.
N.W. of Tulsa

Dowell Ck. Co.
 Plan
N.W. of Tulsa

Consol. Oil
N.W. of Tulsa

Acme Brick Co.
Tulsa

Am. Airlines
Tulsa

Anchor Stone Co.
Box 6130
Tulsa

Apt. Ctr. Trash
 Serv.
S. 99 Ave.
Tulsa

Ark. Wrecking Co.
49th W. Ave.
Tulsa

B.R.M. Corp.
E. 7th St.
Tulsa

Browns Trash Serv.
91st E. Ave.
Tulsa

Centr. Sanit. Ldfl.
N. Erie
Tulsa

Cities Serv. Oil
Box 300
Tulsa

Chandler Ldfl.
49th W. Ave.
Tulsa

Compass Inds.
W. 26th St.
Tulsa

Compass Inds.
W. 49th St.
Tulsa

Chromium Platting
 Co.
Box 1183
Tulsa

Cupp Clean Up
 Serv.
49th W. Ave.
Tulsa

Compass Inds.
W. 26th St.
Tulsa

Dow Chem. Corp.
Tulsa

Discount Sanit.
 Ldfl.
Tulsa

Environ.
N. Sheridan Rd.
Tulsa

George & Rudy's
 Sanit.
Tulsa

Hollis Martin
91st St.
Tulsa

Low Range
 Injection
Tulsa

Mohawk Ldfl.
E. Mohawk Blvd.
Tulsa

N. Am. Rockwell
N. Mingo Rd.
Tulsa

N. Tulsa Sanit.
 Ldfl.
56th St. N.
Tulsa

Ok. Grain Whse.
Channel Rd.
Tulsa

Ozark-Mahoning
 Co.
S. Boulder
Tulsa

PSO Tulsa Sta.
Tulsa

Rockwell Intl.
Tulsa

Spartan Refuse
 Dump
N. Vale
Tulsa

Sun Petr. Prod.
S. Union
Tulsa

Texaco, Inc.
W. 25th St.
Tulsa

Tulsa Ind. Serv.,
Inc.
S. Norwood
Tulsa

Tulsa Ldfl. 1
Tulsa

U.S. Pollut. Contr.
W. 71st St.
Tulsa

Unnamed Haz.
Waste
Tulsa

Veale Bros.
Concrete
Tulsa

Jim Carroll Site
Tulsa

Joe Brown Trkg.
Tulsa

Lamber Div.
Tulsa

United Plating
Wks.
N. Mingo Rd.
Tulsa

David L. Wallace
N. College
Tulsa

Weyerhaeser Co.
Valliant

Lake Wapanucka
Wapanucka

Imperial Coal Co.
Warner

Pub. Serv. Co.
Washita

Trojan Trans., Inc.
Watonga

Vacco Corp.
East Eads
Weatherford

Coster 1
Weatherford

Russell Ck. Coal
Box 418
Welch

Westville City
Dump
Westville

Ballard Tank
Truck Co.
Wilson

Wilson Dump
Wilson

Amoco/PPG Well 1
Woodward

Amoco/PPG Well
1D
Woodward

Amoco/PPG Well 2
Woodward

Amoco/PPG Well 3
Woodward

Amoco/PPG Well 6
Woodward

Amoco/PPG Well 7
Woodward

Jerry Pinckley
Trans.
Box 544
Woodward

Phillips Cattle
Woodward

PPG Inds., Inc.
Box 1245
Woodward

Terra Nit., Inc.
Box 1286
Woodward

Unident. Private
Con.
Woodward

Woodward City
Ldfl.
Woodward

Weyerhaeuser Co.
Box 269
Wright City

Conoco-Garbin Co.
Wynnewood

Kerr McGee
Injection
(plus 1 other site)
Box 305
Wynnewood

Oregon

Albany Ldfl.
Albany

Teledyne Wah.
Chang
Box 460
Albany

Chem-Nuclear
Star Rte.
Arlington

Reichhold Chem.,
Inc.
Box 43
Arlington

Taylor Lumb. Sales
Box 567
Beaverton

Nosler Bullets, Inc.
Parrell Rd.
Bend

Globe Union
N.W. 3rd
Canby

Bethel-Danero
5th/Beltline Hwy.
Eugene

Day Is. Ldfl.
Day Is. Rd.
Eugene

J. H. Baxter
Baxter St.
Eugene

Eugene, Oregon
Plant
Seneca Rd.
Eugene

S. Willamette St.
52nd/Willamette
Sts.
Eugene

Short Mtn.
Goshen

Oregon Tech. Prod.
Wash. Blvd.
Grants Pass

Septic Tank Serv.
Co.
Grants Pass

Umatille Depot
Hermiston

Union Pac. R.R.
Hermiston

LaGrange Plant-
Borden
Box 1028
La Grange

Alkali Lake
Lakeview

Lakeview, Oregon
Dumps
Lakeview

Uranium Mill
Tailing
Lakeview

Bloomberg Rd.
Ldfl.
Bloomberg Rd.
Lane Coun.

N.W. Printed
S.E. Pac. Hwy.
Medford

Chevron Chem.
Co.
Harvester Dr.
Milwaukie

Caron Chem.
Suver Rd.
Monmouth

Dant & Russell
Hillcrest Ave.
N. Plains

Rossman Ldfl.
17th St.
Oregon City

Ace Galvan.
14th St.
Portland

Ace Sanit.
91st St.
Portland

Alexander Paper
Prod.
N. Hunt
Portland

Allied Plating, Inc.
N.E. Union
Portland

Assoc. Chem.
Johnson Blvd.
Portland

Charles H. Lilly
Co.
Killingsworth
Portland

City Ldfl.
Columbia Blvd.
Portland

Columbia Slough
Portland Rd.
Portland

Columbia Wood
Working
Columbia Blvd.
Portland

Crosby & Overton
Swan Is.
Portland

Doane Lake Area
Portland

Drum Rec.
Holman
Portland

Electroplating
Waste
N. 46th Ave.
Portland

Hercules, Inc.
N.W. Yeon Ave.
Portland

Ind. Air Prod.
N.W. Yeon Ave.
Portland

Johnson Ck. Ldfl.
Johnson Ck. Blvd.
Portland

Koppers Co., Inc.
Helens Rd.
Portland

Krishell Lab.
S.E. Powell
Portland

Lavelle Ldfl.
King Rd.
Portland

McCormick &
Baxter
N. Edgewater
Portland

Miller Prod.
Caruthers St.
Portland

Nu Way Oil Co.
46th Ave.
Portland

Nurnberg Sci.
N. Williams
Portland

Oeco
Hawthorne Blvd.
Portland

Pac. Carbide
N. Hurst Ave.
Portland

Pope & Talbot
S.W. 4th
Portland

Rhone-Poulene
St. Helens Rd.
Portland

Spe-De-Way Prod.
14th Pl.
Portland

St. John's Ldfl.
N. Columbus Blvd.
Portland

Schultz Sanit.
Ankeny
Portland

Stauffer Chem.
Corp.
N. Suttle Rd.
Portland

Van Waters &
Rogers
N.W. Yeon
Portland

Widing Trans.
N. Portland
Portland

Wilbur-Ellis
N.W. Marshall
Portland

Zehrung Corp.
N.W. 20th
Portland

Plant Site
Box 810
St. Helens

Sanit. Serv. Co.
Salem

Salem Ldfl.
Salem

Frontier Leather
E. Pac.
Sherwood

Springfield Plant
Second St.
Springfield

Martin-Marietta
Alum.
Box 711
The Dalles

Farmcraft, Inc.
Commercial
Tigard

Koppers-For. Prod.
Greenburg Rd.
Wauan

White City Plant
Antelope Rd.
White City

Pennsylvania

Canastrales Ldfl.
Box 14
Allegheny Coun.

Seiple Plant
Allentown

Pine Ck. Prod.
Allison Pk.

Altoona Sludge
Disp.
Altoona

Amchem Prod.
Brookside Ave.
Ambler

Nicolet/Certain
Teed
Ambler

Audubon Munic.
Water
Box 151
Audubon

Enirotol, Inc.
24/31st St.
Beaver Falls

City of Bethlehem
Bethlehem

Reichard-Coulston
Bethlehem

Synthane-Taylor
Corp.
Betzwood

W. Berks Sanit.
Birdsboro

Roland Michael
Bloomsberg

Boyertown Ldfl.
Boyertown

Treating Plant
Bradford

Bridgetown Twp.
Bridgetown Twp.

Bridgeville Glass
Mayer St.
Bridgeville

Bridgeville Plant
Box 219
Bridgeville

Bristol
Bristol

Rohm & Hass
River Rd.
Bristol

Boro Water
Pond/Mulberry
Bristol

Rohm & Haas
Ldfl.
Box 219
Bristol

Sweeney Ldfl.
Brookhaven

Koppers Co., Inc.
Bruin

Bruin Lag.
Rte. 268
Bruinborough

Fairview Vill.
Bucks Coun.

Bulger Plant
Bulger

Mill Serv.
Bulger

Stravaggi Ldfl.
Rd. 1
Burgettstown

Joy Mfg. Co.
Canonsburg

Vitro Corp.
Canonsburg

BFI Imperial Site
Rte. 980/Baggs
Carnegie

Browning-Ferris
Ind.
Box 448
Carnegie

Waste Conversion
Sandstone Dr.
Hatfield

Natl. Wood Preserv.
Eagle Rd.
Haverford

Tar Pond
Hayberg

Recl. Serv.
Hazleton

Oswald's Ldfl.
Hertztown

U.S. Util.
Holsopple

Mountaintop Ldfl.
Rte. 2
Honeybrook

Plasti-Seal Corp.
Republic Rd.
Huntingdon Valley

ABM-Wade
I Flower St.
Imperial

Ind. Waste, Inc.
Imperial

EBAR Corp.
Richard Rd.
Ivyland

Alan Wood Steel
Ivy Rock

Penn. Ind. Chem.
Glen Circle Rd.
Jefferson

Castilio, Onitsa &
Unit
E. Center St.
Johnsonburg

Johnsonburg Wks.
Ridgeway Rd.
Johnsonburg

William Clark Ppty.
Ridgeway Rd.
Johnsonburg

Kennett Square
Junkyd.
Rte. 1
Kennett Sq.

Valley Forge Lab
King of Prussia

Valley Forge Water
King of Prussia

Weldwire
Queen Dr.
King of Prussia

Kimmel Iron Metal
Lancaster Pike
Lancaster

Bucks City Ldfl.
Langhorn

Leeds &
Northrop-ANA
Church Rd.
Lansdale

N. Penn. Water
Auth. (plus 1
other site)
Chestnut St.
Lansdale

Kennametal, Inc.
Latrobe

Liquid Carbonic
Corp.
Laurel Run

Bethlehem
Lebanon

ABM Disp. Serv.
N. Governor Printz
Lester

Geol. Recl.
Levittown

Levittown Dump
Rte. 13
Levittown

Evansburg
(plus 1 other site)
W. Ridge Pk.
Limerick

Oswald's Ldfl.
Rd. 1
Longswamp Town

McAdoo Assoc.
Site 929-1998
McAdoo

Hauto-
Metallurgical
I-800
McAdoo-Kline

Aloe Ldfl.
Rte. 980
McDonald

J. Phillips Ppty.
(plus 1 other site)
Rte. 51
McKees Rocks

Mazarro Ldfl.
McKees Rocks

Buck Mtn. Ldfl.
Strip Mine
Mahandy

Knickerbocker
Sanit.
Morhill Rd.
Malvern

Allied Chem.
Wilmington Tnpk.
Marcus Hook

Baker & Adamson
Wk.
Wilmington Tnpk.
Marcus Hook

Marcus Hook Ref.
Market St.
Marcus Hook

Hafco Cinder Stge.
Fairview Hgts.
Masontown

Tar Pond
Mayberg

Atlas Min.
Mertztown

Avery Intl.
Rd. 2
Mill Hall

Bald Eagle Corp.
Mill Hall

Arco Polymer
Frankford
Monaca

Beaver Valley Plant
Frankfort
Monaca

Interstate Amiesite
Monaca

Matthew
Canastrale
Monessen

Monongahela
Rte. 481
Monongahela

U.S. Util.
Monroeville

Mongomery Coun.
Ldfl.
Montgomery Coun.

Pottstown Disp.
Rte. 20
Montgomery Coun.

Grows Ldfl.
Box 180
Morrisville

Stauffer Chem.
Morrisville

Morrisville Plant
(plus 1 other site)
Penn. Ave.
Morrisville

Bradley Hershey
Rte. 1
Mount Wolf

Herbert Poe
Rte. 1
Mount Wolf

J. R. Opp Ppty.
Muncy

Log Cabin Inn
Rd. 4
Muncy

Muncy Borough
Div. St.
Muncy

21 E. Water
E. Water
Muncy

Old Ft. Nursery
Muncy

Stout-Waldron
Plant
Sherman St.
Muncy

Clyde Thompson
Rtes. 405/422
Muncy Twp.

C. E. Cast Inds.
Box 457
Muse

Ind. Tr.
Naginey

Univ. Refractory
Box 97
Nampaw

Walter Kurtz Ppty.
Rd. 1
Narvon

Herceg Ldfl.
W. Beil Ave.
Nazareth

Neville Is. Plant
Neville Is.

Ohio River Pk.
Neville Is.
Bell's Sanit. Ldfl.
(plus 1 other site)
New Albany
Newberry Twp.
Newberry Twp.
Allied Chem.
5th St.
Newell
Superior Tube Co.
Box 191
Norristown
Mays Haul.
N. Fayette
P. A. Gypsum Co.
N. Hampton Co.
Russell Std.
N. Huntingdon
N. Schykill Ldfl.
N. Schykill
Noxen Tannery
Noxen
Combustion Eq.
Oaks
Synthane-Taylor
Corp.
Oaks
Oil City Plant
Rouseville
Oil City
Heleva Ldfl.
N. Whitehall Twp.
Ormrod
New Jersey Zinc
Palmerton
Chem-Clear
Chestnut Rd.
Paoli
Conrail
Paoli
Craig Fm.
Rd. 2
Parker
Craig Lag.
Rd. 2
Parker
Wade Disp. Ldfl.
Rte. 729
Parker

Allied Steel Corp.
Rte. 724
Parkerford
Rockwell Intl.
Rte. 724
Parkerford
Grand Cent. Sanit.
Box 211
Pen Argyl
Perkins Ldfl.
Pen Argyl
Shangrila Sod Fm.
Apple Butter
Perkasie
Bush Wellman, Inc.
Perry Twp.
Craig Fm.
Perry Twp.
Jameson
Petrolia
Penna. Coal Prod.
Petrolia
Petrolia Plant
(plus 2 other sites)
Petrolia
Koppers
Petrolia
Fairview Rd. 1
Rd. 1
Petrolia
Budd Co. Dump
Sandmeyer/Red
Lion
Philadelphia
ABM 58th St.
58th St.
Philadelphia
B&P Motor Exp.
Philadelphia
Bob O'Donnell Steel
62nd/Kingessing
Philadelphia
Conrail
Philadelphia
Fort Mifflin Ldfl.
Philadelphia
Frankford Plant
Margaret/Bermuda
Philadelphia
Ind. Wiring
2nd/Tioga
Philadelphia

Manayunk Canal
Umbria/Domino
Philadelphia
Metal Bank of Am.
Cottman/State
Philadelphia
Phila. Plant
Richmond St.
Philadelphia
Phila. Redevel.
9th/Columbia
Philadelphia
Phila. S.W. Site
Enterprise Ave.
Philadelphia
Quickway Trash
Removal
Orthodox St.
Philadelphia
Schiavo Bros., Inc.
Ind. Hwy.
Philadelphia
Shiavo Ldfl.
Eastwick
Philadelphia
Marathon Serv. Co.
Spring Garden
Pittsburgh
Mill Serv.
Washington Rd.
Pittsburgh
Neville Chem. Co.
Neville Is.
Pittsburgh
Ohio R. Pk.
Neville Is.
Pittsburgh
Pittsburgh, Pa. Air
Prod.
34th/Carson
Pittsburgh
Carbon Regin—
Neville
Pittsburgh
Calgon Corp.
Rte. 60
Pittsburgh
Butler Tunnel
Susquehanna R.
Pittstown
F&R Refuse Co.
Kunz Rd.
Pleasantville

Pottstown Disp.
Rte. 20
Pottstown
Sanit. Ldfl. Co.
Tyrol Rd.
Pricedale
Tech Alloy
Rahns
Rahns-Ice
Rahns
Lackawanna Refuse
Old Forage Borough
Ransom Twp.
Pfeiffer Ldfl. Co.
Reading
Watson Johnson
Richlandtown
Clark Ldfl.
Rte. 219
Ridgeway
Frye Tract Ldfl.
Rte. 209
Riley Twp.
Mobile Chem. Co.
Cleveland St.
Rochester
Sanit. Ldfl.
Monessen Hwy.
Rostraver Twp.
Sanit. Ldfl., Inc.
Rostraver Twp.
E. Mines
St. Clair
Stackpile Carbon
Ldfl.
St. Mary's
Hranica Ldfl.
Gastown Rd. 1
Sarver
Yelenich & Smith
Scottsdale
Allen Lunkins
Simons Rd.
Sellersville
Reichold Chem.,
Inc.
Ohio R. Blvd.
Sewickley
Reichold Chem.,
Inc.
Haysville Rd.
Sewickley

Westinghouse
Sharon

River Rd. Ent.
Rte. 846
Sharpsville

Wolf Die & Beach
Shoemakersville

Leesport Ldfl.
Rd. 1
Shoemakersville

Hoffman Ind.
Sinking Spr.

Berks Ldfl.
Sinking Spr.

Gibbs Electronics
Edgewood Ave.
Somerset

Nuclear Res. Corp.
Ind. Hwy.
S. Hampton

Twp. Munic. Auth.
Cherry Ln.
S. Hampton

Novak Ldfl.
Allentown
S. Whitehall Twp.

United Piece Dye
Wor.
Spring Garden Twp.

Springdale Plant
Colfax St.
Springdale

Nease Chem.
Rtes. 26/64
State Coll.

Bell's Sanit. Ldfl.
Terry Twp.

Titusville Plant
Hydetown Pond
Titusville

Tobyhanna Army
Depot
Tobyhana

Caloric Corp.
Topton

E. I. Dupont
James St.
Towanda

GTE Sylvania
Towanda

Towanda Ldfl.
Bride St. Hill
Towanda Borough

Grows Ldfl.
Louderbach Rd.
Tullytown

Kennedy Sanit.
Ldfl.
Haupwood-
   Coalspring
Uniontown

McNeil Labs
Upper Dublin

Natl. Pk. Serv.
Upper Merion

Keystone Coke
Upper Merion

ABM-Ohara
Henderson Rd.
Upper Merion

Airco Acetylene
Upper Merion

Vortman Fm.
Haupwood-
   Coalspring
Upper Saucon

Upper
   Southampton
**Upper
   Southampton**

Univ. Refractory
Box 97
Wampum

Warminster Hgts.
Warminster

Warminster Munic.
Auth.
Warminster

Pennsbury Coatings
New Britain
   Borough
Warminster

Pennsbury Co.
Rte. 202/Sand Hill
Warminster

Hatboro Munic.
Auth.
Coun. Line/
   Jacksonville
Warminster

NADC
Jacksonville
Warminster

Warrington Twp.
Munic. Auth.
(plus 1 other site)
Box 368
Warrington

Drakenfield Colors
W. Wylie Ave.
Washington

U.S. Util.
Washington

W. Argo Chem.
Washington

Washington, Pa.
Plant
W. Wylie Ave.
Washington

William Martin
Ldfl.
N. Main St.
Washington

Accurate Brass
Corp.
Wayne Twp.

Keystone Sanit.
W. Conshohocken

Waste Tech. Corp.
River Rd.
W. Conshohocken

Turkey Run Ldfl.
Strip Mine
W. Mahonoy

Simon Wrecking
Co.
Trenton Ave.
Williamsport

Chrin, Inc.
Ind. Dr.
Williams Twp.

Eastern Mat.
Brent Wood Dr.
Willow Grove

Variety Club Camp
Potshop Rd.
Worchester

Modern Sanit. Ldfl.
York

Mundis Mills 1
N. Sherman St.
York

Mundis Mills 2
N. Sherman St.
York

Std. Concrete
N. Sherman St.
York

Union Oil Co. of
Cal.
Sherman St.
York

Transf. Serv.
Rte. 6/R.R. Ave.
Youngsville

Mill Serv., Inc.
Spring St.
Yukon

Puerto Rico

Aiborito Blvd.
Waste
Robles
Aibonito

Anasco Solid Waste
Anasco

Anasco Solid Waste
Anasco

Hernandez Site B
Areciro

Areciro Plant
Areciro

Aquada Solid Waste
Aquada

Aquas Buenas
Sumidero
Aquas Buenas

Aquadilla Solid
Waste
Caimital Base
Aqundilla

Barceloneta Ldfl.
Barrio Las Tosas
Barceloneta

Pfizer Pharm.
St. Rd. 2
Barceloneta

Barceloneta Munic.
Sanit. (plus 1
other site)
St. Rd. 665
Barceloneta

Barceloneta Solid
Waste
Horida Atuera
Barceloneta

Utuado Solid Waste
Arenas
Utuado

Vega Baja Solid
    Waste
Rio Abajo
Vega Baja

Vega Baja Solid
    Waste
Cibuco
Vega Baja

Navy Ammun.
Vie Ques

Camp Garcia
Vie Ques

Villalba Solid Waste
Hato Puerco Arriba
Villalba

Rhode Island

Bristol Ldfl.
Minturn Rd.
Bristol

Western Sand &
    Gravel
Douglas Pike
Burrillville

Pincillo Ppty.
Perry Hill Rd.
Coventry

Sanit. Ldfl.
Cranston

Cumberland Ldfl.
Mendon Rd.
Cumberland

Auralux Chem.
    Assoc.
Main St.
Hopkinton

Town of Lincoln
Lincoln

Brenton Pt. State
Newport

Ldfl. & Res. Recov.
N. Smithfield

Bosco Trkg.
Rugby/Pavillion
Providence

William Davis
    Liquid
Tarkiln Rd.
Smithfield

Photex, Inc. Ppty.
Liberty Ln.
S. Kingstown

South Carolina

Abbeville Coun.
    Ldfl.
Abbeville

Paul Graham Ldfl.
Abbeville

David Beatty Ldfl.
Rte. 3
Abbeville

Savannah R. Plant
Aiken

Aiken Coun. Ldfl.
Aiken Coun.

Anderson Plant
Pearman Diary Rd.
Anderson

Chem-Nuclear Sys.
Box 726
Barnwell

Blackfield Cherokee
I-85/Rd. 99
Beaufort

Kalama Specialty
Box 908
Beaufort

City Dump
Hwy. 5
Blacksburg

Sci. Serv.
Blackstock

May Plant
Rte. A
Camden

Charleston Ldfl.
Haygood St./
    Ashley
Charleston

Treating Plant
Charleston Hgts.
Charleston

Plant Spill Area
E. Bay St.
Charleston

Charleston Coun.
    Solid Waste
Romney St.
Charleston

Fain Septic Dump
Charleston

Std. Oil Co.
Bridge St.
Charleston

Mobile Chem. Co.
King St. Ext.
Charleston Hgts.

Ind. Chem. Co.
Chester Coun.

Allied Chem. Co.
Box 1788
Columbia

Carolina Eastman
    Co.
Box 1782
Columbia

Chem-Nuclear
    Snelling
Columbia

Richland Coun.
    Ldfl. (plus 1
    other site)
Columbia

S.C. Recycle &
    Disp.
Columbia

Darlington Coun.
    Ldfl.
Rte. 5
Darlington

Dorchester Ldfl.
Dorchester

Potential Site
W. of Hwy. 78
Dorchester

Chapel Est.
Easley

Latex Ponds
Old Pendleton Rd.
Easley

E. I. Dupont
Hwy. 301 N.
Florence

Facil. Plant
Florence

Fiber Inds., Inc.
Box 2000
Florence

Florence Coun.
    Ldfl.
N. Irby St.
Florence

Florence Plant
Florence

Koppers Co.
Box 1725
Florence

Carddawn
S. of Hwy. 9 W.
Ft. Lawn

Potential Site
S. of Hwy. 9 W.
Ft. Lawn

Charlie Bell
Rte. 3
Fountain Inn

Cherokee Coun.
    Dump
E. Jr. High Rd.
Gaffney

Cherokee Coun.
    Ldfl.
Off Hwy. 18
Gaffney

Am. Cyanamid Co.
S. Frazer St.
Georgetown

Georgetown Plant
Frazer St.
Georgetown

Georgetown Steel
Georgetown

Goose Ck. Site
Goose Ck.

Austin Browning
    Co.
Govan

Blackberry Valley
    Rd.
Greenville

Carolina Plating
White Rd.
Greenville

Greater Greenville
Blackberry Valley
    Rd.
Greenville

Greenville Plant
Box 1208
Greenville

Greenwood Nylon
    Plant
Hwy. 246
Greenwood

Gen. Battery Corp.
Old Chick Spr. Rd.
Greer

Auto Auction Lot
Greer

Chemfix Disp. Area
Hood Rd.
Greer

Former Groce Lab
Hood Rd.
Greer

Celenese Plast.
Hood Rd.
Greer

Frank Elmore
Hwy. 290
Greer

Groce Lab.
Hwy. 290
Greer

Mason & Elmore
Oil Co.
Highland St.
Greer

Plant Ldfl.
Hood Rd.
Greer

Reichold Chem.
Box 547
Hampton

Charleston Disp.
Hanahan

Intl. Min.
Society Ave.
Hartsville

United Pollut.
Contr.
Hollywood

John's Is. Site
John's Is.

Trideot Ldfl.
John's Is.

S. Agric.
Kingstree

Ladson Ldfl.
Ladson

Ladson Ldfl.
Ladson

Spring Mills
Lancaster

Lexington Coun.
Ldfl.
Hwy. 321
Lexington

Kershaw Coun.
Ldfl.
Lugoff

Palmetto Ldfl.
Rte. 2
Lyman

Amaco Chem.
Corp.
Box 987
Mt. Pleasant

Cooper R. Plant
Box 987
Mt. Pleasant

N. Charleston Ldfl.
(plus 1 other site)
N. Charleston

Seaboard R.R.
N. Charleston

Swift Agri-Chem.
Corp.
N. Charleston

Berkeley Coun.
Ldfl.
Oakley

Oconee Coun. Ldfl.
Oconee Coun.

Ethyl Corp.
Hwy. 49
Orangeburg

On-Plant Disp.
Facil.
Box 1028
Orangeburg

Greenville Coun.
Ldlf.
Pelzer

Tri-City Serv., Inc.
Box 485
Pelzer

Sangamo
Pickens

Greenville Coun.
Ldfl.
Hwy. 25
Piedmont

Piedmont Ldfl.
Piedmont

Greenville Coun.
Sanit.
Piedmont

Hexa Octa
Piedmont Area

Pinewood Site
Pinewood

SCA Chem. Serv.
Pinewood

W. R. Grace & Co.
Pinewood

C&M Oil
Rantoules

Celanese Fibers
Cherry Rd. Sta.
Rock Hill

Ferguson Ppty.
Hwy. 5
Rock Hill

Ind. Chem. Co.
Hwy. 998
Rock Hill

Quality Drum
Rock Hill

Roebuck Sys., Inc.
Roebuck

Abco & Roebuck
Box 188
Roebuck

Ruby Ldfl.
Ruby

Company Ppty.
Shilo Rd.
Seneca

Phillips Fiber Corp.
Shilo Rd.
Seneca

Surburban Sanit.
Seneca

Simpsonville Cpx.
N. Maple St.
Simpsonville

Chem-Nuclear
Serv.
Snelling

Camp Croft Ldfl.
Spartanburg

Intl. Min. & Chem.
N. St. Ext.
Spartanburg

Spartanburg Coun.
Ldfl.
Spartanburg

Spartanburg Sanit.
N. Converse
Spartanburg

Statewide Waste Oil
Spartanburg

Unisphere Chem.
Co.
Box 2871
Spartanburg

Anderson Coun.
Ldfl.
Starr

Browning-Ferris
Ind.
Summerville

Plant Site
Hwy. 78 W.
Summerville

Potential Site
Hwy. 29
Wellford

Spartanburg Coun.
Ldfl.
Wellford

York Coun. Ldfl.
Rte. 161
York

South Dakota

T&R Elec.
Colman

Edgemont
Edgemont

V.A. Ctr.
Hot Spr.

Black Hills Ord.
Igloo

Leroy Barnhardt
Ppty.
Hwy. 44 E.
Rapid City

Rapid City
Acetylene
S. Hwy. 79
Rapid City

Redfield Iron &
Met.
Redfield

Sioux Falls Ldfl.
E. Side of Fairgrd.
Sioux Falls

Watertown City
Ldfl.
Watertown

Tennessee

Aids
(plus 1 other site)
Cedar Valley Rd.
Bristol

Shelby Drive Ldfl.
Capleville

Old Bemburg
Dump
Carter Coun.

East Disp. Area
Lower R. Rd.
Charleston

Misc. Disp. Areas
Lower River Rd.
Charleston

S. Disp. Area
Lower River Rd.
Charleston

Waste Disp. Site
Lower River Rd.
Charleston

Chattanooga Plant
N. Hawthorne St.
Chattanooga

Chattanooga Plant
Box 71
Chattanooga

E. I. Dupont
Denemours
Box 71
Chattanooga

Hawthorne Ave.
Dump
Hawthorne Ave.
Chattanooga

Impound 1
Pineville Rd.
Chattanooga

Impound 2
Pineville Rd.
Chattanooga

Impound 3
Pineville Rd.
Chattanooga

Impound A
Pineville Rd.
Chattanooga

Impound B
Pineville Rd.
Chattanooga

Impound C
Pineville Rd.
Chattanooga

Impound D
Pineville Rd.
Chattanooga

Impound E
Pineville Rd.
Chattanooga

Nat. Waste Oil
Stewart St.
Chattanooga

TVA Test Well
Chattanooga

J. R. Grace Pond
N. Hawthorne St.
Chattanooga

Arnold Eng. Devel.
Coffee Coun.

Columbia Plant
(plus 2 other
sites)
Columbia

E. I. Dupont
(plus 1 other site)
Santa Fe Pike
Columbia

Hooker Chem.
Santa Fe Pike
Columbia

Kenneth Harris Oil
Carters Ck. Pike
Columbia

Maury Coun. Sanit.
Ldfl.
N. By-Pass
Columbia

Monsanto
Columbia

Copperhill Site
Copperhill

Stauffer Chem. Co.
Rte. 1
Counce

Arnold Ppty. Ldfl.
Dayton

Carter Ppty. Ldfl.
Dayton

City Brush Dump
Dayton

City Dump
Dayton

Montgomery Ppty.
Dump
Dayton

Bumpus Cove
Embreeville

Nuclear Fuel Serv.
Erwin

Rhea Coun. Sanit.
Ldfl.
Evansville

Milan Arsenal
Gibson Coun.

Hickman Ppty.
Dump
Graysville

Acidulation Dump
Greenville

Velsicol
Hardeman Coun.

C. F. Inds., Inc.
Box 87
Harrison

Chattanooga Nit.
Box 87
Harrison

Southern Ind.
Iron City

Bumpas Cove Ldfl.
Jonesboro

Washington Coun.
Ldfl.
Jonesboro

Ashworth Ldfl.
Kingsport

Holliston Mills
Kingsport

I.G.D. Kingsport
Acetyl
Industry Rd.
Kingsport

Tennessee Eastman
Co.
(plus 1 other site)
Box 511
Kingsport

Spill Site
Kingstown

Ashville Hwy.
Knoxville

Badgett Dr. Ldfl.
Knoxville

Knoxville Plant
Dale Ave.
Knoxville

Milligan St.
Knoxville

Petro Recycling
Corp.
Knoxville

Pickel Is.
Knoxville

Rose Fm.
Knoxville

Rutledge Pike
Knoxville

Walker Fm.
Knoxville

Witherspoon Ldfl.
Knoxville

R. T. Smith Ldfl.
Lagrange

James Smith Ppty.
Lagrange

Lawrence Burg
Ldfl.
Lawrenceburg

Due Waste Dump
Site
Old Due West
Madison

Hawkins Ldfl.
Near River
Madison

N. Am. Environ.
Contr.
(plus 1 other site)
Marion Coun.

Hickory Specialties
Maryland

Air Prod. & Chem.
E. Bodley
Memphis

Arlington Blending
Memphis

Bellevue Dump
(plus 2 other
sites)
N. Bellevue
Memphis

Brook Rd. Site
Memphis

Browning-Ferris
Ind.
Shelby Dr.
Memphis

Chromium Min. &
Smelt.
Fite Rd.
Memphis

E. I. Dupont
Denemours
Fite Rd.
Memphis

Environ. Sys.
Tulane
Memphis

Hollywood Dump
Memphis

Jackson Pits
Memphis

Memphis Cont. Co.
Memphis

Memphis Plant
Fite Rd.
Memphis

On Site Memphis
Plant
Old Millington
Memphis

Swift Agri-Chem.
Corp.
N. Collins Ave.
Memphis

U.S.S. Agri-Chem.
Pond
Weaver Rd.
Memphis

Watkins Ldfl.
Memphis

W. R. Grace Co.
Old Millington
Memphis

Browning-Ferris
Ind.
Sykes Rd.
Millington

Millington Ldfl.
Millington

Chickasaw Ord.
Millington

Mitchie Dump
Hwy. 22
Mitchie

Am. Recycle Co.
Arrow Mines Rd.
Mt. Pleasant

Mobile Chem.
Corp.
(plus 1 other site)
Arrow Mines Rd.
Mt. Pleasant

Stauffer Furnace
(plus 2 other
sites)
Mt. Joy Rd.
Mt. Pleasant

Stauffer Org. Plant
Mt. Joy Rd.
Mt. Pleasant

Deepwell 4
Mt. Pleasant

Stauffer Deepwell
3 & 4
Mt. Pleasant

Bordeaux Ldfl.
Old Hospital Rd.
Nashville

Buzzard Hollow
Old Hickory Blvd.
Nashville

Couchville Pike
Dump
Couchville/Daniel
Pk.
Nashville

Metro Dept. of
Water
Nashville

Metro Nashville
Dump
Nashville

Metro Sew. Trmt.
Second Ave. N.
Nashville

Metrocenter
Munic. Ldfl.
9th Ave.
Nashville

Munic. Ldfl.
(plus 3 other
sites)
Nashville

Pulley Ldfl.
Couchville Pike
Nashville

Reichold Chem.
Co.
Fiberglass Rd.
Nashville

Saad Oil Recycler
Nashville

Stauffer Chem.
Plant
Centennial Blvd.
Nashville

Sulfur Dell Dump
Site
Harrison
Nashville

E. I. Dupont
Rte. 219
New Johnsonville

Cook Coun. Sanit.
Ldfl.
Newport

Oakridge Site
Oak Ridge

Union Carbide
Corp.
Oak Ridge

E. I. Dupont Site 2
Old Hickory
Old Hickory

E. I. Dupont Site 1
Old Hickory
Old Hickory

E. I. Dupont—Golf
Club
Old Hickory
Old Hickory

Hawkins Fm.
Swinging Bridge
Old Hickory

Tenn. Oil & Ref.
Hwy. 109 S.
Portland

Saad Oil Recycler
Rutherford Coun.

Billy Ray Patterson
Saulsbury

C. C. Jones Fm.
Saulsbury

Former James
Smith Fm.
Saulsbury

James Smith Fm.
Saulsbury

John W. Parham
Saulsbury

Sykes R. Ldfl.
Shelby Coun.

3rd St./R.R. Ave.
S. Pittsburg

E. E. Culver
Tipton Coun.

Area
Tiptonville

Tiptonville Area
Site
Tiptonville

Washington Coun.
Washington Coun.

Waynesboro Coun.
Ldfl.
Waynesboro

Texas

Mat. Rec.
Abilene

Continuity Corp.
Addison

Starr Ind. Serv., Inc.
Alice

Holbert James
Commer.
Main St.
Alvarado

Amoco Chem.
Corp.
Alvin

Chocolate Bayou
Plant
Box 1488
Alvin

Customized Serv.
3rd
Amarillo

Amarillo City of
San
Amarillo

Andrews Sulfur
Plant
Andrews

Richmond Tank
Car Co.
Angleton

Force Oil &
   Vacuum
Arcola

Denton Coun.
   Sanit.
Hwy. 377
Argyle

Arkansas Pass
   Plant
Box 1300
Arkansas Pass

Arlington Disp.
Harrison
Arlington

Berryman Prod.
E. Rando
Arlington

Grano Prairie Disp.
Harrison
Arlington

Jet Res. Ctr.
S. Bowen Rd.
Arlington

Sanit. Ldfl.
Hwy. 157 N.
Arlington

Acock Labs.
E. 5th St.
Austin

Austin Comm.
   Disp.
Manor Rd.
Austin

Clevepak Corp.
E. 4th
Austin

Comm. Disp.
Manor Rd.
Austin

Constr. Chem.
Austin

Disp. Sys. Inc.
Shoal Creek
Austin

IMC Chem. Group
Hwy. 290 W.
Austin

Reichold Chem.,
   Inc.
Box 9405
Austin

S.W. Anal. Chem.
E. Woodward
Austin

Speciality Chem.
   Div.
Box 9405
Austin

St. Edwards Ldfl.
Mable Davis Pk.
Austin

Tiger Corp. DBA
Beck Circle
Austin

Whisenmunt Disp.
Dalten
Austin

Lower Colorado R.
Bastrop

Swiftex, Inc.
Hwy. 71 W.
Bastrop

Celanese Chem.
   Co.
Box 509
Bay City

Hoffman Disp. Co.
Donna Ln.
Baycliffe

Baytown Chem.
   Plant
Box 4004
Baytown

Baytown City
   Dump
Coady Rd.
Baytown

Baytown Ref.
Box 3950
Baytown

Brownwood
   Addition
Baytown

Carbon Black Div.
Box 149
Baytown

Div. Gulf Oil Corp.
I-10
Baytown

Gulf Coast Waste
   Disp.
Baytown

Ind. Chem. Div.
Box 4125
Baytown

Shield Disp.
Wade Rd.
Baytown

ABC Exterm. Co.
Prairie St.
Beaumont

Beaumont Chem.
   Plant
Box 3687
Beaumont

Beaumont Plant
Gulf States Rd.
Beaumont

City of Beaumont
Pine St.
Beaumont

Div. of Mobile Oil
   Co.
Beaumont

Doucette
Beaumont

Dupont Beaumont
   Wk.
Old Port Arthur
   Rd.
Beaumont

Elray, Inc.
E. Lucas
Beaumont

HK Chem.
   (plus 1 other site)
Lindberg Dr.
Beaumont

Intl. Galvan.
Industry Rd.
Beaumont

Kilpatrick, Inc.
Carroll
Beaumont

Mobile Chem. Co.
Box 3311
Beaumont

Neches R.
Beaumont

Olin Chem.
Box 30
Beaumont

Sanit. Chem.
Port Arthur Rd.
Beaumont

Terry Sparkmen
Box 2175
Beaumont

Velsicol Chem. Co.
Beaumont

Estech Gen. Chem.
Gulf States Rd.
Beaumont

R-Tec
Reliance Pkwy.
Bedford

Whobrey Site
Bedford Rd.
Bedford

Subsurface, Inc.
W. Loop S.
Bellair

Unident. Site
Big Spr.

Cosden Oil &
   Chem. Co.
Box 1311
Big Spr.

Sid Richardson
   Carbo.
Big Spr.

Celanese Chem.
   Co., Inc.
U.S. Hwy.
Bishop

Hale Sanit. Serv.
W. 6th
Bonham

Borger Ref. & NGL
Box 271
Borger

Camex, Inc.
Box 5067
Borger

Phillips Petr.
   (plus 1 other site)
Box 1231
Borger

Copolymer Plant
Box 1231
Borger

Philblack Plant
Box 1526
Borger

Phillips Petr.
Box 271
Borger

Plains Butadiene
   Plant
Box 357
Borger

Waste Water, Inc.
Brazoria

Ind. Waste
Box 3151
Bridge City

Triangle Chem.,
Inc.
Rte. 5
Bridge City

Brownfield
12 mi. S.E. of
Brownfield

Brownsville Plant
Brownsville

Brownwood Site
Hoover St.
Brownwood

Texas Brick Plant
(plus 1 other site)
Camp Bowie Ind.
Pk.
Brownwood

Browning-Ferris
Ind.
Bryan

Pennwalt Chem.
Co.
Box 3608
Bryan

GE Huebiner
Concrete
Bullville

Canton Site
Box 576
Canton

Cities Serv.
Canton

Deep Well
Injection
Canton

Food & Agric. Div.
Dodge St.
Canton

Jarrell Thompson
Canton

Murtle Spr. Gas
Canton

City Dump
Carrollton

Unident. Site
Carrolton

Laddie Williams
Gar.
Wood Dr.
Channelview

Mocherman
Resident
Channelview

Lyondell Plant
Sheldon Rd.
Channelview

Modern Sanit.
Serv.
N. Walnut
Clarksville

Goex, Inc.
Johnson Co. Rd.
Cleburne

Brazoria Co.
Box 788
Clute

Brazoria City Disp.
Stratton Ridge
Clute

Texas A&M Fire
College Station

Malloy Ldfl.
Commerce

Latex Glove Mfg.
Commerce

Canaan Corp.
Lyons
Commerce

Hepner Disp. Site
Commerce

City Sanit.
Mallory Rd.
Commerce

Hi Yield Chem.
Co.
Commerce

Cockfield Co.
Humble Pipeline
Conroe

Columbian Chem.
Div.
Box 1018
Conroe

Metts Rd.
Conroe

Conroe Plant
Box 219
Conroe

Clarke Bottling Co.
Conroe

Am. Chrome &
Chem.
Lawrence Dr.
Corpus Christi

Am. Disp.
Apollo
Corpus Christi

Coastal Sts. Petr.
Corpus Christi

Corpus Christi
Plant
Lawrence Dr.
Corpus Christi

Corpus Christi
Naval
Corpus Christi

Delta Sanit. Serv.
Sunrise
Corpus Christi

Intl. Pollut.
Greenwood
Corpus Christi

Nueches City
Navig.
N. Ship Channel
Corpus Christi

Crane Sulphur
Plant
Box 1087
Crane

Austin Sanit. Fill
Elroy Rd.
Creedmore

Crosby Plant
Crosby/Eastgate
Rd.
Crosby

French Ltd. Site
San Jacinto R.
Cross.
Crosby

Sikes Disp. Site
Hwy. 90
Crosby

Deloach Vacuum
Box 220
Daisetta

Boydstun Bill
Hwy. 875
Dalhart

Brookhollow Ind.
Disp.
Singleton
Dallas

BFI of Texas
Willow Brook Rd.
Dallas

City of Dallas
Linfield
Dallas

Atlas Pow. Co.
Park Cent.
Dallas

Browning-Ferris
Plantation
Dallas

City Dump—
Lenfield
E. Loop 12
Dallas

Joe Colt Trash
Removal
Bellefonte Dr.
Dallas

Dal-Worth Ind.,
Inc.
Chippewa
Dallas

Dallas Silicate
Plant
Lenway
Dallas

Dallas Steel &
Drum
Dallas

Dixie Metals Ind.
McGowan St.
Dallas

Dubois Chem.
S. Center Expwy.
Dallas

Eckhardt List
Sargent Rd.
Dallas

Evergreen Press
Dallas

Hooker Chem.
Corp.
S. Central Expwy.
Dallas

Kelly Cont. Serv.
Spring Valley
Dallas

Mollenhour Trkg.
Y Street
Dallas

Moore Ind. Disp.,
Inc.
Hawes
Dallas
Poco-Am., Inc.
Fidelity Bldg.
Dallas
Sabine R. Auth.
Dallas
J. E. Smith & Sons,
Inc.
E. 12th St.
Dallas
S.W. Nuclear Co.
LBJ Fwy.
Dallas
Storm Vulcan, Inc.
Burbank
Dallas
Texas Ind. Disp.,
Inc.
S. Lamar
Dallas
Unident. Site
Dallas
Waste Mgt., Inc.
Singleton
Dallas
Valcar Ent.
Sargent Rd.
Dallas
Yancy-Camp Whse.
Dallas
Zogcon
Dallas
Liberty Waste Disp.
Dayton
Arco Polymers, Inc.
Ellsworth
Deer Pk.
Deer Pk. Mfg. Cpx.
Hwy. 225
Deer Pk.
Deer Park Wks.
Box 500
Deer Pk.
La Porte
Battleground Ave.
Deer Pk.
Lubrizol Corp.
Tidal Rd.
Deer Pk.

Natl. Distillers
Miller Cutoff Rd.
Deer Pk.
Rohm & Haas Co.
Box 672
Deer Pk.
Rollins Environ.
Serv.
Battleground Rd.
Deer Pk.
Texas Alkyls, Inc.
Battleground Rd.
Deer Pk.
Boydstun
Hwy. 875
Delhar
Moore Serv., Inc.
Margarita
Del Rio
Johns Manville Site
Denison
Ohio Rubber Co.
Denton
Turbo
Refrigerating
Shady Oaks Dr.
Denton
Vulcan Mat. Co.
Box 1060
Denver City
Borden Chem.
W. Borden Dr.
Diboll
City Dump
Beech St.
Diboll
Goodpasture, Inc.
S. of
Dimmitt
Cactus Plant
Box 277
Dumas
Phillips Petr.
Box 277
Dumas
Dumas Helium
Plant
Box 277
Dumas
M. Store
Hwy. 80/Gross Rd.
E. Dallas

Milchem, Inc.
E. Schunier
Edinburg
Asarco, Inc.
W. Paisano
El Paso
El Paso Smelting
Wks.
W. Paisano
El Paso
Moon City Rubbish
Old Hueco Tanks
Rd.
El Paso
Moore Serv., Inc.
Montwood
El Paso
Parker Bros. Slag
El Paso
RM Trash Collect.
N. Loop
El Paso
Ras Sanit., Inc.
Gareway
El Paso
Phelps Dodge
Copper
Hawkins
El Paso
W. Disp., Inc.
Humble
El Paso
Wilcox CE Coml.
Garb.
Rosedale
El Paso
Sanit. Ldfl.
Valley View
Farmers Branch
John Stacy
Main St.
Florence
Robbins Pump Sta.
Flynn
Crow & Sons Ldfl.
Box 434
Ft. Worth
Am. Waste Disp.
Trail Lake Dr.
Ft. Worth
Estes Serv. Co.
Elliot Reeder
Ft. Worth

Capital Supply Co.
W. Hurst Blvd.
Ft. Worth
Globe Labs
Commerce
Ft. Worth
Gray's Cont. Serv.
Nichols St.
Ft. Worth
Gray's Cont. Serv.
Roberts Cut-off
Ft. Worth
N. Cent. Ldfl.
Ft. Worth
One Way Serv.
Elliot Reeder
Ft. Worth
Sangamon Grain
Co.
S. Main
Ft. Worth
S.W. Oil Serv.
Jones St.
Ft. Worth
Stauffer Chem. Co.
Deen Rd.
Ft. Worth
Thomas Steel
Drums
Ft. Worth
Fullerton Sulfur
Plant
Box 66
Franklin City
Phillips Petr.
Franklin City
Brazos R. Levee
Freeport
Bryan Mound Tar
Pits
Freeport
Dow Chem. Texas
Div.
Box 88
Freeport
Freeport Term.
Quintana Rd.
Freeport
Gulf Chem. &
Met.
Freeport
Min. Res.
Freeport.

Nalco Chem. Co.
N. Coun. Rd. 229
Freeport

Oyster Ck. Div.
Freeport

Plant B
Hwy. 288
Freeport

Smith's Welding
Wk.
South Ave.
Freeport

Specialty Chem.
Div.
E. 2nd St.
Freeport

Town Dump
Bryan
Freeport

Romer Sanit.
Mesquire
Fulton

W. Refuse Co.
Federal Rd.
Galena Pk.

Browning-Ferris
Ind.
Port Ind.
Galveston

Todd Shipyd. Plcn.
Isc.
Box 1550
Galveston

Centex
W. Walnut
Garland

Goldsmith Sulfur
Box 66
Goldsmith

Phillips Petr. Co.
Box 66
Goldsmith

Chem. Waste Mgt.
Grand Prairie

MC Bay Recl.
Grapeland

S. Sanit.
Lee
Greenville

Chemall, Inc.
Hogaboom Rd.
Groves

Riverside Chem.
Hwy. 66
Groves

Niagara Chem. Co.
North C St.
Harlingen

Farmers Supply Co.
Hwy. 87
Hartley

Sheridan Disp.
Box 42
Hempstead

Hempstead Site
Hempstead

Unknown—
Battering
Henderson Coun.

Joe C. Revelette, Jr.
Intl.
Hidalgo

Highlands Ldfl.
Thompson
Highlands

Johnson Acid Pit
Battlebell
Highlands

Liberty Waste Disp.
Ellis Sch. Rd.
Highlands

Tidwell Disp. Site
Hillsboro

Billy Tidwell Ppty.
Hwy. 22
Hillsboro

McGinnes
Hitchcock

Galveston City
Ldfl.
Hitchcock

Red R. Army Depot
Hooks

Lone Star Army
Ammun.
Hooks

Am. Gen.
W. Dallas
Houston

Ash Oil Serv.
Eagle
Houston

B&R Oil Co.
Sunnycrest
Houston

Browning-Ferris
Ind.
Holmes Rd.
Houston

Charter Intl. Oil
Manchester
Houston

Church Rd. Site
Church Rd.
Houston

Cameron Iron Wks.
Houston

A-1 Lee Oil Serv.,
Inc.
North H
Houston

Alamo Explosive
Co.
Clinton
Houston

Albert J. Jackson
Conklin
Houston

Alvin E. Folley
Richmond Ave.
Houston

Ampak, Inc.
Houston

Armco Steel Ppty.
Greens Bayou Dr.
Houston

Clear Lake Plant
Box 58009
Houston

Cloverleaf Sand Co.
Greens Bayou
Houston

Coastal Vacuum
Tank
Hansen Rd.
Houston

Coles Disp. Serv.
Rodney
Houston

Comm. Disp. Sys.
Wilcrest Dr.
Houston

Compounding Div.
Polk St.
Houston

Doty Sand Pit, Inc.
Bissonnett
Houston

Dukes Disp. Serv.
N.W. Fwy.
Houston

Houston Treating
Plant
W. Hardy St.
Houston

Hughes
(plus 1 other site)
Almeda/Genoa
Rds.
Houston

Ind. Chem. Div.
Haden
Houston

Ind. Chem. Div.
Manchester Rd.
Houston

Intl. Disp.
S. Loop W.
Houston

Jones Chem., Inc.
Haden Rd.
Houston

Kocide Corp.
Almeda Rd.
Houston

Koppers Co.
Box 9742
Houston

Koppers Co., Inc.
Industrial Rd.
Houston

Livingston Constr.
Bissonnet
Houston

Max-Bob Refuse
Co.
Brownwood
Houston

MBM Ent., Inc.
Jensen
Houston

McDonald-Traman
Trash
Belgrad
Houston

McCarty-Ward
Vacuum
Houston

McKinnon Serv.,
Inc.
St. Augustine
Houston

Meklo Proc. Co.
Dallas
Houston

Merichem. Co.
Haden Rd.
Houston

Metro Waste Mgt.,
Inc.
St. Augustine
Houston

Natl. Disp. Serv.
Holcombe Blvd.
Houston

Nuclear Sources
Etheridge
Houston

Nutro Oil Fd.
Chem.
Houston

Occidental Petr.
3 mi. N. of
Houston

Pac. Intermountain
Houston

Pollut. Packers of
E. Harwin Dr.
Houston

Prof. Solid Waste
Holmes Rd.
Houston

Res. Rec., Inc.
Lawndale
Houston

S&R Oil Co.
Minetta St.
Houston

Space City Disp.
Serv.
Old Span. Trail
Houston

Statewide Ind. Serv.
Houston

Stevens Solid Waste
Hempstead Hwy.
Houston

Tal Waste Sys., Inc.
N. Edgewood
Houston

Tex Haul, Inc.
River Falls
Houston

Texas Waste Sys.
W. 34th
Houston

Unident. Site
Arbour Dr.
Houston

Unident. Site
Near I-10 E.
Houston

Wallace Waste
Cont.
Laura Koppe
Houston

Waste Oxidation
Sys.
Bryant
Houston

G. O. Weiss, Inc.
Addicts Satsuma
Houston

Western Ld. Rec. 1
Church
Houston

Witco Chem.
Box 45296
Houston

Woodforest Sanit.
Maxey Rd.
Houston

Waste Disp. &
Regen.
Hillcroft 510
Houston

Trumball Asphalt
Div.
Clinton Dr.
Houston

Addiks Fairbk.
Addiks
Houston

BFI of Texas
Canyon
Houston

Crockett Serv.
Caplin
Houston

Crystal Chem. Co.
Blankenship
Houston

Crystal Chem. Co.
Rogersdale
Houston

Crystal Chem. Co.
N. Post Oak
Houston

Dixie Chem. Co.
N. Drennan
Houston

Eckhardt List
(plus 2 other
sites)
Tanner Rd.
Houston

Emsery, Inc.
S. West
Houston

Esco Plast. Co.
Amanda
Houston

Exxon Chem.
Stedman St.
Houston

Jr. Flix, Wh.
Theresa
Houston

Force, Inc.
Lawndale
Houston

Gen. Elec. Serv.
Wallisville Rd.
Houston

Goodyear Tire &
Rubber
Fannett Rd.
Houston

Goodyear Tire &
Rubber
Goodyear Dr.
Houston

Greens Bayou Plant
Haden Rd.
Houston

Gulf Coast Disp.
Fauna
Houston

Gulf Coast Waste
Disp.
Houston

Gulf Electro Quip.
N. Wayside
Houston

Hardin Marvin
Smith Rd.
Houston

Harrison Jet Guns
McGowan
Houston

Haul Away Trash
Serv.
Hwy. 75
Houston

Haul Away, Inc.
Holcombe
Houston

Hempstead Rd.
Plant
Hempstead Rd.
Houston

Herring Serv.
Maury
Houston

Houston Greens
Bayou
Haden Rd.
Houston

Houston Ind.
Manchester St.
Houston

Houston Plant
Haden Rd.
Houston

Houston Plant
Wallisville Rd.
Houston

Houston Reception
Old Beaumont
Hwy.
Houston

Houston Ref.
Box 2451
Houston

Triple C Sanit.
Main
Idalou

Corpus Christi
Plant
Ingleside

E. I. Dupont
Ingleside

Iowa Pk. Ldfl.
Iowa Pk.

Trinity R.
Irving

Irving Dump
S. & S.W. of
Irving

Echo Plant
Echo Comm.
Orange

JWC Site
Orange

Orange Coun.
Sanit.
Between Vidor &
Orange
Orange

Orange Coun.
Precinct
W. Bluff Rd.
Orange

Orange Plant
W. of Orange
Orange

Orange Spec.
Chem. Plant
Orange

Orange Wks.
Orange

Winters Ldfl.
Orange

Sabine R. Wks.
Orange

Cisco-Tex. Ind.
Waste
Hwy. 62
Orangefield

Hu-Mar Corp.
Palacids

Alcoa-Anderson
Palestine

Abandoned Bldg.
Palmer

Celanese Chem. Co.
Box 937
Pampa

Adams Term. Plant
Jefferson St.
Pasadena

Bayport Plant
Bay Area Blvd.
Pasadena

Celanese Chem. Co.
Bayport Blvd.
Pasadena

Ethyl Corp.
Houston
Hwy. 225
Pasadena

Fert. Co. of Tex.
Jefferson St.
Pasadena

Gulf Coast Waste
Disp.
N. Richey
Pasadena

Dixie Chem. Co.
Bay Area Blvd.
Pasadena

Lawrence Henley
Burchwood
Pasadena

Hercules, Inc.
Bay Area Blvd.
Pasadena

Pasadena Chem.
Co.
Jackson Rd./1st
Pasadena

Pasadena Plant
Davidson Rd.
Pasadena

Tenneco Chem.
Box 849
Pasadena

Culligan Water Con.
S. Hackberry
Pecos

Unident. Site
Peoria

Phillips Camp
Dump
N. of
Phillips

Phillips Onsite Ldfl.
Box 271
Phillips

Philtex Caustic
Evap.
Plemmons Rd.
Phillips

Philtex Drum Disp.
Phillips

Hooker Chem.
Dimmitt Hwy.
Plainview

Plainsman Supply
Co.
E. 5th St.
Plainview

City of Plano
Plano

AAA Wire Prod.
Hwy. 69
Point

Alum. Co. of Am.
Pt. Comfort

BP Oil Co.
Box 849
Port Arthur

Burton Shipyd.
Proctor-Main
Port Arthur

Common Ldfl.
Hoeaboom
Port Arthur

Conserv. Serv.
Hwy. 73
Port Arthur

Gulf–Port Arthur
Refin.
Box 701
Port Arthur

Gulfport Ship Bldg.
Port Arthur

Port Acres Site
Beaxart Garden Rd.
Port Arthur

Port Arthur Chem.
Plant
Box 712
Port Arthur

Port Arthur Plant
Port Arthur

Port Drum Co.
W. 9th St.
Port Arthur

Renners, Inc.
W. Port Arthur Rd.
Port Arthur

Texaco, Inc.
Box 712
Port Arthur

Seadrift Plant
Hwys. 35/185
Port Lavaca

B. F. Goodrich
Box 697
Port Neches

Common Ldfl. Site
Orchard Ave.
Port Neches

Jefferson Chem.
Box 847
Port Neches

Synpol, Inc.
Port Neches

Neches Butane
Prod.
Port Neches

Port Neches Dump
Grisby
Port Neches

C&S Market
Powderly

Unident. Site
Quinlan

Cherokee Cove
Quinlan

Sonics Intl., Inc.
Ranger

Unident. Sand Pt.
Teague Rd.
Rendon, N.E.

Texas Ecologists,
Inc.
Robstown

Howmet Alum.
Corp.
Box 96
Rockwal

Rusk Ldfl.
Rusk

Angelo Sanit. Serv.
N. Oaks
San Angelo

Garb. Serv.
N. Oakes
San Angelo

Aggie Chem. Co.
Sequin Rd.
San Antonio

A-1 Garb. Disp.
E. Houstin
San Antonio

Browning-Ferris
Warfield
San Antonio

Coastal Bend Refuse
Canterbury Hill
San Antonio

Ind. Disp.
Leal
San Antonio

Kelly AFB
Military Dr.
San Antonio

Moore Ind. Disp.,
Inc.
Luke Blvd.
San Antonio
Moore Serv., Inc.
Holbrook Rd.
San Antonio
Newman Ent.
Ima Ruth Pkwy.
San Antonio
Pearl Brewing Co.
Pearl Pkwy.
San Antonio
San Antonio City
Dump
San Antonio
Sanitas Waste Disp.
San Antonio
Timber Lake
San Antonio
Silva Disp. Serv.
Arkansas
San Antonio
Tansey Co.
Sanger
Union Y. Dignidad,
Inc.
San Juan
Gutierres Disp.
Farm Rd. 3009
Schertz
Browning-Ferris
Port Rd.
Seabrook
NASA Disp. Serv.
Meyer Rd.
Seabrook
Ozark-Mahoning
Co.
Box 1477
Seagraves
Seagrave Plant 64
Box 637
Seagraves
Seminole Plant 66
Box 547
Seagraves
Cities Serv. Mgl.
Box 306
Seminole
Unident. Site
Seminole

Saenz Sanit. Serv.
Nagel St.
Sequin
Structural Metals
Sequin
Ashland Chem. Co.
Rte. 3
Shamrock
Shamrock Plant
Hwy. 36
Shamrock
Frank Little Ppty.
Sherman
Franklin Kelly Disp.
Box 1095
Sinton
Sinton Ind. Waste
Disp.
Sinton
Hereford Bi-Prod.
Spearman
Best Garb. Serv.
I-45
Spring
Birch Site
Spring
Char Lake Site
U.S. 90A
Sugarland
Sugarland Dump
Old Fd. Rd.
Sugarland
Oil & Gas Div.
Hwy. 119
Sunray
Phillips Petr.
Box 866
Sweeny
Sweeny Ref.
Box 866
Sweeny
Temple Iron &
Metal Co.
Katy
Temple
Dump Site
Hwy. 34
Terrell
For. Prod.
Texarkana
Koppers Co.
Texarkana

Am. Oil Co.
Box 401
Texas City
Malone Serv. Co.
Texas City
Amoco Oil Co.
5th Ave. S.
Texas City
City Ldfl.
Bay St. Ext.
Texas City
GAF Corp.
Box 2141
Texas City
Gulf Chem. &
Metall.
Box 2130
Texas City
Gulf Coast Waste
Disp.
Texas City
Monsanto Co.
Bay St.
Texas City
Motco Corp.
Hwy. 3/I-45
Texas City
Swan Lake Plant
Loop 197 S.
Texas City
Texas City Plant
Fifth Ave.
Texas City
Waste Chem. Disp.
Box 210
Texas City
Anderson Clayton
Thorndale
Thom. Whitfield
Haul.
Carter Rd.
Tomball
Travis Coun. Site
Travis Coun.
Sector Ref.
Hwy. 79
Tucker
Film Prod. Div.
N. Lynon St.
Tyler
Natl. Distillers
Tyler

Pan Am. Petr. Co.
Box 660
Tyler
Tyler Sanit. Ldfl.
Kilgore Hwy.
Tyler
Vernon Ldfl.
(plus 1 other site)
Vernon
Johnson's Disp.
N. Laurent
Victoria
Victoria Plant
Box 2626
Victoria
Victoria Rendering
Houston Hwy.
Victoria
Cent. Waste Cont.
S. Valley Mills
Waco
M. Lipsitz & Co.
Elm St.
Waco
Waste-Pac Serv. Co.
Hanger Rm. 11
Waco
Sani-Serv.
Main St.
Weatherford
Redicon, Inc.
Industrial
White Oak
Unident. Cyn.
Wade Estate
Witchita Falls
Witchita Falls Ldfl.
Witchita Falls
Chem. Recycl.
Wylie
J. R. Siemoneit
Kirby St.
Wylie
Unident. Site
Zapata
U.S. 90 Site

Utah

Bauer Dump
Bauer
Blackhawk Resin
Bauer

Abandoned Ore
  Buying
Blanding

Dougway Proving
  Gd.
Dougway

Duchesne Site
  (plus 1 other site)
W. side of
Duchesne

U.S. Steel Wks.
Geneva

Kamas-Soapstone
Kamas

N. Davis Coun.
  Ldfl.
N. Layton
Layton

Bacchus Wks.
Magna

Atlas Min. Corp.
Moab

Inactive Aec. Mill
  St.
Monticello

Geneva Wks.
Box 510
Provo

Randolph Plant Site
Star Rte.
Randolph

Rawley Ldfl.
West
Rawley

Roosevelt Site
E. Side of Neola
  Hwy.
Roosevelt

Coun. Ldfl.
  (plus 1 other site)
Temple
Salt Lake City

Rose Pk. Oil Sludge
Salt Lake City

Salt Lake Plant Site
Salt Lake City

Stauffer Chem.
Salt Lake City

Trojan Div.
Box 310
Spanish Fork

All Min., Inc.
W. Murray

Bay Area Refuse
  Disp.
West
W. Bountiful

Lower 40—
  Woodcross
W. Bountiful

Virginia

Washington Coun.
  Sanit.
Abingdon

Illegal Dump
Arcadia

Baughn Fm.
Rte. 624
Augusta Coun.

T.O. Tech Fm.
Rte. 624
Augusta Coun.

Ft. Pickett
Blackstone

Chesterfield Coun.
  Ldfl.
Old Bon Air Rd.
Bon Air

Oldover Corp.
Cascade

Schneider Ldfl.
Charles City

Air Prod. Dump
Rtes. 614/5
Charles City

State Rte. 614
Charles City Co.

Chesapeake Ldfl.
Chesapeake

Chesapeake Plant
Hwys. 13/158
Chesapeake

Chesapeake Plant
Douglas Rd.
Chesapeake

City Ldfl.
Albermarie
Chesapeake

Fds. Est. Ppty.
Buell St.
Chesapeake

Browning-Ferris
  Ind.
Chester

Chesterfield Coun.
  Ldfl.
Chester

Chesterfield Coun.
  Ldfl.
Chesterfield Coun.

Chesterfield Plant
Rte. 827
Chesterfield Coun.

BFI — Sludge Disp.
Clark Coun.

Henry Coun. Ldfl.
Collinsville

W. Virg. Pulp &
  Paper
Covington

City Ldfl.
Covington

City Coun. Ldfl.
Rte. 220
Covington

Covington Plant
Edgemont Dr.
Covington

Covington Wks.
N. Magazine Ave.
Covington

Ky. Nite Min.
  Corp.
Cullen

Am. Cyanamid Co.
Shady Ave.
Damascus

Airpt. Dump
Danville

Marshall Constr.
  Dump
East St.
Danville

Wren Dr. Site
Danville

City Dump
Danville

Danville Branch
  Plant
U.S. 360
Danville

Disston Lag.
Rte. 29 W.
Danville

First Piedmont Ldfl.
Danville

Naval Weapons
  Supp. Ctr.
Delgren

City of Dublin
Near Rte. 611
Dublin

Ft. Belvoir
Dept. of Defense
Ft. Belvoir

U.S. Army Spill Site
Ft. Belvoir

Ft. Eustis
Ft. Eustis

Franklin VA
  (plus 1 other site)
Franklin

Hercules Plant
Box 656
Franklin

Front Royal Wks.
Front Royal

Goochland Coun.
Goochland Coun.

Langley AFB
Hampton

Sew. Conn. - 411
Rotary
Hampton

Williams Paving
  Co.
Armstead Ave.
Hampton

Hampton Paint
  Mfg. Co.
Hampton

End of Andrews St.
Andrews St.
Hampton

Hanover Coun.
  Incin.
Hanover Coun.

Hercules Ind.
Hiwassee

Hopewell Chem.
  Plant
Hopewell

Hopewell City Ldfl.
Hopewell

Hopewell—Alum.
  Wks.
Hopewell

Lot Adjacent to
   Rand
Hopewell

Plant Ldfl. Hercules
Hopewell

Wilson SR. Fm.
Hwy. 10
Hopewell

Norwood Wilson
   Ppty.
Hopewell

Appalachian Pow.
Independence

Naval Air Base.
Little Ck.

Va. Oak Tannery
Luray

ACDFGH & Inc.
Box 4831
Martinsville

Celco
Box 1000
Narrows

New Kent Ldfl.
New Kent

Naval Shipyd.
Norfolk

Pub. Wks. Ctr.
Norfolk

Naval Air Sta.
Oceana

Cary's Chapel
Poquoson

Off Ridge Rd.
Ridge Rd.
Poquoson

Va. Chem.
W. Norfolk Rd.
Portsmouth

Hercules
Commerce St.
Pulaski

Pulaski Ldfl.
Pulaski

Marine Corps T-D
Quatico

Radford Army
   Ammun.
Radford

James River
U.S. 15
Richmond

Liquid Waste Disp.
Richford Rd.
Richmond

On-Site Fill
Charles City Rd.
Richmond

Schneider Disp.
Charles City Rd.
Richmond

U.S. 1
U.S. 1
Richmond

E.I. Dupont
Jefferson Davis
   Hwy.
Richmond

Matthews Electro
Salem

Olin Corp.
Saltville

Saltville Town
   Dump
Saltville

Well Disp.
Saltville

Waste Disp. Pond 6
Saltville

Kim-Stan Ldfl.
Selma

S. Boston Sludge
   Disp.
S. Boston

Lee Hill Disp.
Spotsylvania

Am. Safety Razor
Box 500
Staunton

Suffolk Chem. Co.
Suffolk

Swift Agri. Chem.
   Corp.
Box 1609
Suffolk

Autex Fibers
Valley Forge

Ft. Story
Virginia Beach

Heinrich Fm.
Waynesboro

Waynesboro
   Dupont
Waynesboro

Waynesboro
   Nurseries
Box 987
Waynesboro

City Ldfl.
Waynesboro

E.I. Dupont Co.
Dupont Blvd.
Waynesboro

Armed Forces Tr.
Williamsburg

Naval Weapons Sta.
Yorktown

Yorktown Ref.
Rte. 173
Yorktown

Washington

N.W. Alloys
Addy

Texaco
Box 622
Anacortes

Anacortes Wks.
Texaco Rd.
Anacortes

Skagit Co. Dump
Old Hwy. 20
Anacortes

J.H. Baxter & Co.
Box 325
Arlington

Argent Lab.
40th/148th
Bellevue

Poles, Inc.
102 N.E.
Bellevue

Crosby & Overton,
   Inc.
Humbolt
Bellingham

Frank Brooks Mfg.
Iowa/Orleans
Bellingham

Georgia Pac.
Laurel St.
Bellingham

Haley Intl.
Bellingham

Lummi Res.
Bellingham

Oesar Cedar Co.,
   Inc.
Bellingham

Old Bellingham
   City
Bellingham

Uniflite, Inc.
9th/Harris
Bellingham

Wilder Ldfl.
Slaten Rd.
Bellingham

Black Diamond
   Disp.
Black Diamond

Palmer Coke &
   Coal
Black Diamond

Puget Sound Naval
   Yd.
Bremerton

Lewis Coun. Dump
Centralia

Am. Crossarm
Chehalis Ave.
Chehalis

Phoenix Res.
Box 93
Chewelah

Asotin Coun. Ldfl.
Clarkston

Colbert Dump
Chatteroy Rd.
Colbert

Abandoned Elec.
Concrete

Univ. of Wash.
   Dump
Eatonville

Union Oil Co.
Edmonds

Ellisford Ldfl.
Ellisford

Ballestrasse Logging
432nd St.
Enumclaw

Boeing Commer.
Prine Fd.
Everett

A. J. Zinda
Pacific Hwy.
Federal Way

Potential Site
Hwy. 18/I-5
Federal Way

Puyallup Disp.
Hwy. 18/I-5
Federal Way

Intalco Alum. Co.
Box 937
Ferndale

Mobile Oil Corp.
Unick Rd.
Ferndale

Starvation Valley
Evergreen St.
Fredericks

Martin Marietta
Rte. 677
Goldendale

Metzger Fm.
Grand Coulee

Holden Mine
    Tailing
Holden

Palmer Coking Coal
New Castle Site
Issaquah

Potential Site
N.W. 3rd
Kalama

Kalama Disp. Site
Kalama

Kelso Ldfl.
Kelso

Allied Chem. Corp.
Washington/1st
Kennewick

Allied Chem.
Medger Rd.
Kennewick

Chevron-
    Kennewick
Box 1648
Kennewick

Phillips-Petr.-
    Coulee
Kennewick

Tri-City Herald
N. Cascade
Kennewick

Borden Chem. Co.
First Ave.
Kent

Borden, Inc.
Pacific Hwy.
Kent

Central Solv.
190th St.
Kent

Borden-Kent
Military Rd.
Kent

Heath Plating
S. 200
Kent

Koppers Co.
Fifth Ave.
Kent

Liquid Waste Disp.
Kent

Union Oil Co.
196th St.
Kent

W. Proc.
196th St.
Kent

Widing Trans.
Kent

Golden Penn Oil
    Co.
Place N.E.
Kirkland

Lake Stevens Ldfl.
Lake Stevens

Greenacres Ldfl.
Spokane Coun.
Liberty Lane

Am. Cyanamid
    Coal Ck. Disp.
Longview

Am. Cyanamid
Brinton Pl.
Longview

Intl. Paper
Box 579
Longview

Reynolds Metal
Longview

Weyerhaeuser
Box 188
Longview

Spokane Coun.
    Ldfl.
Box 10
Marshall

Monsanto-Tulalip
Indian Res.
Marysville

Kaiser-Mead Wks.
Mead

Mico Ldfl.
Hwy. 27
Mica

Phillips Petr.
Kahloths Hwy.
Pasco

Res. Rec.
Hwy. 12
Pasco

Wash. State Univ.
Pullman

Hidden Valley
Meridian S.
Puyallup

Old Puyallup Ldfl.
Puyallup

Sunstrand Data
    Contr.
Redmond

J. H. Baxter & Co.
Lake Washington
Renton

J. J. Jackson Septic
Kathleen Rd.
Renton

Bur. of Recl.
Richland

Nuclear Eng.
Manford Res.
Richland

Am. Bitum
Box 125
Richmond Beach

Grant Coun. Pest.
Royal City

Royal Camp
Royal City

Univ. of Wash.
    Montlake Dump
Seattle

Ace Galvanizing
S. 96th
Seattle

Airco Welding Prod.
Marginal Way
Seattle

Am. Tar Co.
N. Lake Way
Seattle

Boeing Aerospace
E. Marginal Way
Seattle

Chem. Proc.
Airport Way
Seattle

Chempro-Waste Oil
Pier 91
Seattle

Crosby-Overton,
    Inc.
13th S.W.
Seattle

Fiberlay, Inc.
Fairview Ave.
Seattle

Gas Generator
Marginal Way
Seattle

Kenworth Trucks
E. Marginal Way
Seattle

King County Ldfl.
Seattle

Magnolia Fert.
Ballard Way
Seattle

Monsanto Co.
E. Marginal Way
Seattle

Pacific Chem. &
    Co.
4th
Seattle

Preservation Paint
Airport Way
Seattle

Puget Sound Tug &
    Barge
Seattle

Quemetco
16th St.
Seattle

Queen City Disp.
    Site
Seattle

Seattle Post
Wall St.
Seattle

Sunset Pk.
136th/15th Aves.
Seattle

Todd Shipyd. Corp.
16th S.W.
Seattle

United Serv.
16th W.
Seattle

Goose Lake
Shelton

Aluminum Recycl.
Wellesley
Spokane

BPA-Bell Substa.
Hawthorne Rd.
Spokane

Carney & Co.
Funcher
Spokane

Columbia Lighting
20 mi. N. of
Spokane

Draper Tractor Parts
Freya
Spokane

Hegler-Kronquist
Spokane

Linde Div.
N. Market
Spokane

Spokane Transf.
E. Springfield
Spokane

Linde Div.
N. Market
Spokane

Spokane Transf.
E. Springfield
Spokane

Tosco Corp.
Hillyard
Spokane

Midget Oil Co.
N. Market
Spokane

Sumner Plant
Sumner

Koppers Co.-West
Eighth Ave. E.
Sumner

Aladdin Plating Co.
Center St.
Tacoma

Alpine Plating Co.
Center
Tacoma

Asarco Tacoma
Smelt
51st N. Baltimore
Tacoma

Buffalo Don
Murphy
Waller Rd.
Tacoma

Center/Mullen
Sanit. Ldfl.
Center/Mullen Sts.
Tacoma

Chempro
Alexander
Tacoma

Coski Ind. Dump
Pendle Long Rd.
Tacoma

Draper Tractor Parts
Freya
Tacoma

Dauphin Site
Pacific Hwy.
Tacoma

Ft. Lewis, U.S.
Army
Tacoma

General Plast. Mfg.
35th St.
Tacoma

Girard Custom
Coater
Port Tacoma Rd.
Tacoma

Hooker Chem.
Alexander
Tacoma

Kaiser Tacoma Plant
Taylor Way
Tacoma

1972 Lime Ponds
Alexander
Tacoma

Lilybald Petr.
Port of Tacoma
Tacoma

Marine View Dr.
Marine View Dr.
Tacoma

N. Tacoma Ldfl.
Tacoma

Pac. Resin & Chem.
Thorne Rd.
Tacoma

Petarcik Site
Pacific Hwy. E.
Tacoma

Petr. Recl.
Taylor Way
Tacoma

Pittsburgh Coke &
Coal
Tacoma

Reichold Chem.,
Inc.
Lincoln Ave.
Tacoma

Reichold Chem.,
Inc. (plus 1
other site)
Taylor Way
Tacoma

Sound Ref.
Box 1372
Tacoma

Stauffer Chem.
(plus 2 other sites)
Lincoln
Tacoma

Tacoma Ldfl.
Center/Mullen St.
Tacoma

Tacoma Wks.
Thorne Rd.
Tacoma

Tide Flats
Lincoln Ave.
Tacoma

Trojan U.S. Powder
Box 44546
Tacoma

Water Front Bank
Alexander St.
Tacoma

1950 Lime Ponds
Alexander
Tacoma

Hillyard Proc.
Sullivan St.
Trentwood

Kaiser-Trentwood
Wks.
Trentwood

English Ldfl.
192nd Ave.
Vancouver

Vancouver Plant
Broadway
Vancouver

Vancouver Plant
Access Rd.
Vancouver

Vancouver Sanit.
Serv.
94th
Vancouver

Vancouver Wks.
26th St.
Vancouver

Borden Chem.
63rd St.
Vancouver

Alcoa-Vancouver
Box 120
Vancouver

FMC Corp.
S. Access Rd.
Vancouver

Alcoa
Box 221
Wenatchee

Wykoff
Winslow

Univ. Mfg. Corp.
190th
Woodenville

Binn & Son
Woodland

Arrcom, Inc.
Bozasth
Woodland

FMC Corp.—Agri.
Chem.
N. Washington
Yakima

Rainier Plast. Co.
Box 1743
Yakima

Yakima
W. Washington Ave.
Yakima

Terrace Hgts. Solid
   Waste
Roza Hill Dr.
Yakima

West Virginia

Manilla Ck.
Amherst
Belle 901
   McDupont
McDupont
Belle

Diamond Shamrock
W. Dupont Ave.
Belle

Dupont
Belle

Ben's Run
Ben's Run

Mercer Coun. Ldfl.
Bluefield

Harrison Coun.
   Ldfl.
Bridgeport

Chelyan Oil Co.
Box 426
Cabin Ck.

Charleston Munic.
   Ldfl.
Charleston

Don's Disp. Serv.
Box 1426
Charleston

Holmes & Madden
   Ldfl.
Wolfpen Rd.
Charleston

Institute Plant
Box 2831
Charleston

Kanawha Block Co.
Kanawha Tnpk.
Charleston

Kanawha City
   Block
Charleston

Mink Shoals Ldfl.
Mink Shoals Br.
Charleston

Koppers Disp.
Coketown

Unreported Archer
   Hgts.
Archer Hgts.
Colliers

Valero Munic. Ldfl.
Morton Ln.
Colliers

Sharon Steel
Fairmont

Koppers
Follansbee

Unreport.—
   Hooverson Hgts.
Rockdale Rd.
Follansbee

Wheeling
   Pittsburgh
Follansbee Coke
   Plant
Follansbee

Galliopolis Ferry
   Plant
Galliopolis Ferry

Kopper For.
Box 98
Green Spr.

Munic. Ldfl.
Huntington

Craddock Sanit.
Sycamore Rd.
Hurricane

Goff Mtn. Ldfl.
Institute

Ron's Dump
Jackson Coun.

Don's Disp.
Kanawha Coun.

Three B's Ldfl.
Coun. Rd. 892
Larkmead

Letart Ldfl.
Letart

3 B's Ldfl.
Lost Pavement

Dupont Potomac R.
Martinsburg

Borg-Warner
Box 816
Morgantown

Ind. Ldfl.
Box 816
Morgantown

Martin Hollow
   Ldfl.
Morgantown

Plant
Morgantown

Unreported
Box 683
Morgantown

Allied Chem.
Moundsville

Liquified Coal
Moundsville

Moundsville Plant
Rte. 2
Moundsville

New Cumberland
   Sanit.
New Cumberland

Foote Min.
New Haven

New Cumberland
   Sanit.
Gas Valley Rd.
New Manchester

Mobay
New Martinsville

Natrium Plant
Box 191
New Martinsville

PPG
New Martinsville

Aytex Fibers
Plant Rd.
Nitro

Chem. Formulators
Nitro

Fike Chem.
Nitro

FMC
Box 547
Nitro

Monsanto, Inc.
Nitro

Montgomery Ward
   Site
Rock Branch Ind.
   Pk.
Nitro

Nitro Ldfl.
   (plus 1 other site)
N. of I-64
Nitro

Nitro Plant
Viscoe Rd.
Nitro

Nitro Sanit. Sump
Main/Locks
Nitro

Nitro Wks.
Box 487
Nitro

Vimasco
Box 516
Nitro

Holders, Inc.
Howells Mill Rd.
Ona

City Ice
Jeanette St.
Parkersburg

Air Products &
   Chem.
Camden St.
Parkersburg

Marbon
Parkersburg

Parkersburg Disp.
Camden St.
Parkersburg

Sanit. Sys.
Parkersburg

Shorty Graham
   Ldfl.
Elder St.
Parkersburg

Three B's Ldfl.
Parkersburg

Lubeck Ldfl.
Hwy. 2
Parkersburg

Washington Wks.
Box 1217
Parkersburg

Goodyear
Box 9
Pt. Pleasant

Pantasote Co.
Pt. Pleasant

Ellers Ldfl.
Proctor

Kaiser Alum.
Ravenswood

Tacketts Ck.
St. Albans

Allegheny Ballistics
Short Gap

Union Carbide
Box 180
Sistersville

Barium Reduction
S. Charleston

FMC
S. Charleston

Mallory Airpt. Ldfl.
S. Charleston

Smith Ck. Dump
Rte. 12
S. Charleston

S. Charleston Plant
(plus 1 other site)
Box 8361
S. Charleston

Tech. Ctr.
Box 8361
S. Charleston

Union Carbide
S. Charleston

Upton Ck. Dump
Kanawha Tnpk.
S. Charleston

Appalachian
Timber
Old Fairgrounds
Sutton

Okey Meredith
Valley Grove

Borg-Warner
Washington

Dupont Chem.
Ldfl.
Washington

Woodmar Plant
Box 68
Washington

Colliers Ldfl.
Weirton

Nat'l Steel
Box 431
Weirton

Wheeling Site
Wheeling

Am. Cyanamid
U.S. 2
Willow Is.

Wisconsin

Nitroglycerin Waste
Baraboo

Badger Ammun.
Plant
Hwy. 12
Baraboo

Plant Waste Water
Baraboo

Site No. 3 Plant Site
Baraboo

Gridanis Ent.
Hwy. 11
Darien/Delavan

Better Bright Plating
S. 6th St.
Depere

Rock Paint &
Chem.
Box 76
Ft. Atkinson

Milwaukee Coun.
Ldfl.
Old Loomis Rd.
Franklin

Waste
Germantown

Waste Mgt., Inc.
Granville

Nardi Elec. Corp.
67th N.E.
Kenosha

Ansel Chem. Co.
Marinette

Menasha Wks.
Menasha

Waste Mgt. Lauer 1
Boundry Rd.
Menomonee Falls

Milwaukee Coun.
Ldfl.
S. 124th St.
Milwaukee

Met. Disp.
S. 124th St.
Milwaukee

Waher Ldfl., Inc.
Muskego

Bergstrom Paper
Larson Rd.
Neenah

Carl Jacobson Fm.
W. Larsen Rd.
Neenah

Weiselar Constr.
Neenah

Weiselar Constr.
Neenah

Meyer Sand &
Gravel
New Berlin

Jaeger Sand &
Gravel
W. Coffee Rd.
New Berlin

Bodus Ldfl.
New Bren

Theim Corp.
10th St.
Oak Ck.

Keno Trkg., Inc.
Paris

Poy Sippi
Poy Sippi

Caledonia Dump
Site
Racine

Oches
Racine

United Waste
S. 43rd
Racine

United Waste
Townlin
Racine

Logeman Bros.
Saukville

Freeman Chem.
Corp.
Railroad St.
Saukville

Shawana Ldfl.
Shawana

Borden Chem.
S. 24th St.
Sheboygan

Al-Chroma, Inc.
Chambers
Stevens Pt.

Rock Ref. Co.
Rte. 1
Stratford

Abandoned City
Dump
Superior

Koppers Co., Inc.
Waukesha

Theim Corp.
W. Rogers St.
W. Allis

Tork Truck &
Excav.
Engel Rd.
Wisconsin Rapid

Wyoming

Amoco Ref. Dump
W. Yellowstone
Casper

City of Casper Ldfl.
Bryan Stock Trail
Casper

El Rancho Bridge
El Rancho St.
Casper

Pacer Corp. Pine
Casper Mtn.
Casper

Old Interceptor
Pond
Green River

Plant Site—Closed
Box 513
Green River

N. Disp. Site
Green River

Horse Ck.
Horse Ck.

Split Rock Uranium
(plus 1 other site)
Jefferson City

Kemmerer Coke
Plant
Kemmerer

Lander Lag.
S. Pass
Lander

Johnnie Lee Ranch
S. of Lander Pass
Lander

UPRR Creosote
Plant
Laramie

Leefe Wyoming	Bucknum Site	Wyoming Ref.	Worland Water
Plant	Box 1960	Box 820	Supply
Star Rte.	**Mills**	**New Castle**	**Worland**
Leefe	Homa Mills	Riverton Sulfur-	
Porcupine Ck. Mine	Salt Creek Hwy.	Acid	
Porcupine Ck.	**Mills**	Hwy. 789	
Lovell		**Riverton**	

Source: Based on EPA listings of January 1, 1981, excluding sites listed "no further action"; sites with unidentified location; and locations with unnamed sites.

Note: Identification of potential site does not necessarily imply evidence of illegal activity or public health or environmental hazard. All identified sites are scheduled to be assessed under the EPA's Hazardous Waste Site Enforcement and Response System to determine if a hazardous waste problem actually exists.

With the enactment of the Superfund Legislation, Comprehensive Environmental Response, Compensation, and Liability Act, "all companies which owned or operated or who at the time of disposal owned or operated or accepted hazardous substances which are or have been stored, treated, or disposed of, unless such a facility was granted a permit to operate under Subtitle C of the Resource Conservation and Recovery Act," were required to report to the Environmental Protection Agency where that facility is located or where the wastes were transported to. After compiling those data, EPA developed a list of approximately 14,000 sites where hazardous substances had been dumped, stored, or treated. While no copies of that list had been made available for general distribution at the time of this writing, one may obtain such information from the Environmental Protection Agency in Washington. A complete listing may be obtained by asking for the ERRIS print out.

Organizations with Information on Toxic Wastes and Substances

Environmental Organizations

Association of New Jersey Environ-
mental Commissions
ANJEC Resource Center
P.O. Box 157
Mendham, N.J. 07945

The Conservation Foundation
1717 Massachusetts Ave., N.W.
Wash., D.C. 20036
(202) 797-4300

Environmental Action, Inc.
Room 731
1346 Connecticut Ave.
Wash., D.C. 20036
(202) 833-1845

Environmental Action Foundation, Inc.
724 Dupont Circle Bldg.
Wash., D.C. 20036
(202) 659-9682

Environmental Defense Fund, Inc.
475 Park Ave. South
New York, N.Y. 10016
(216) 686-4191
    Additional offices in Wash., D.C.;
Berkeley, Calif.; Denver, Colo.; and
Richmond, Va.

Environmental Law Institute
1346 Connecticut Ave., N.W.
Wash., D.C. 20036
(202) 452-9600

Izaak Walton League of America
1800 North 10th St.
Arlington, Va. 22209
(703) 528-1818

League of Women Voters
1730 M St., N.W.
Wash., D.C. 20036
(202) 296-1770

National Audubon Society
950 3rd Avenue
New York, N.Y. 10022
(212) 832-3200

National Wildlife Federation
1412 Sixteenth St., N.W.
Wash., D.C. 20036
(202) 797-6800

Natural Resources Defense Council
122 E. 42nd St.
New York, N.Y. 10168
(212) 949-0049
    Additional offices in Wash., D.C.;
Natick, Mass; and San Francisco, Calif.

Rachel Carson Council, Inc.
8940 Jones Mill Road
Wash., D.C. 20015
(301) 652-1877

Resources for the Future
1755 Massachusetts Ave., N.W.
Wash., D.C. 20036
(202) 328-5000

Sierra Club*
530 Bush St.
San Francisco, Calif. 94108
(415) 981-8634

Sierra Club Legal Defense Fund
2044 Fillmore St.
San Francisco, Calif. 94104
(415) 567-6100
    Additional offices in Denver, Colo.;
Wash., D.C.; and Juneau, Alaska

Public Interest Organizations

Citizens Clearinghouse for Hazardous
    Wastes, Inc.
P.O. Box 7097
Arlington, VA 22207
(703) 532-6816

Citizen Action
1501 Euclid Ave.
Suite 500
Cleveland, OH 44115

Inform
381 Park Avenue South
New York, NY 10016
(212) 689-4040
This public interest group is engaged in
studies on waste reduction in organic
chemical industries; publishes a
newsletter.

New Jersey Citizen's Hazardous Waste
    Directory
P.O. Box 6483
Lawrenceville, NJ 08648
Publishes a newsletter.

Labor Organizations

AFL-CIO
815 16th St., N.W.
Wash., D.C. 20005
(202) 637-5000

Workers Institute for Safety and Health
1126 16th St., N.W.
Wash., D.C. 20036
(202) 887-1983

Industrial Organizations

American Petroleum Institute
2101 L St., N.W.
Wash., D.C. 20036
(202) 457-7000

Chemical Manufacturers Assoc.
2501 M St., N.W.
Wash., D.C. 20037
(202) 887-1100

Hazardous Waste Treatment Council
P.O. Box 57212-0202
Wash., D.C. 20037
(202) 233-4155
A lobbying group for industries
advocating disposal technologies
alternative to secure landfill.

National Solid Wastes Management
    Assoc.
1120 Connecticut Ave., N.W.
Wash., D.C. 20036
(202) 659-4613

---

*Available for purchase is "Training Materials on Toxic Substances: Tools for Effective
Action," which includes information on how to organize citizens for action as well as
educational materials on many aspects of the subject.

Congressional Committees Dealing with Toxic Wastes and Toxic Substances Legislation

Senate

Committee on Agriculture, Nutrition, and Forestry
  Subcommittee on Forestry, Water Resources, and Environment

Committee on Commerce, Science, and Transportation
  Subcommittee on Consumer
  Subcommittee on Science, Technology, and Space
  Subcommittee on Surface Transportation

Committee on Environment and Public Works
  Subcommittee on Environmental Pollution
  Subcommittee on Toxic Substances and Environmental Oversight
  Subcommittee on Transportation

Committee on Finance
  Subcommittee on Health

Committee on Foreign Relations
  Subcommittee on Arms Control, Oceans and International Operations, and Environment

Committee on Government Affairs
  Permanent Subcommittee on Investigations

Committee on Labor and Human Resources

House

Committee on Energy and Commerce
  Subcommittee on Commerce, Transportation, and Tourism
  Subcommittee on Health and the Environment
  Subcommittee on Oversight and Investigations

Committee on Government Operations
  Subcommittee on Environment, Energy, and Natural Resources

Committee on Interior and Insular Affairs
  Subcommittee on Energy and the Environment

Committee on Merchant Marine and Fisheries
  Subcommittee on Fisheries
  Subcommittee on Oceanography

Committee on Science and Technology
  Subcommittee on Natural Resources, Agriculture Research, and Environment

Committee on Public Works and Transportation
  Subcommittee on Investigations and Oversight
  Subcommittee on Water Resources

Disposal
Cost Comparison

Quoted Prices for Major Hazardous Waste Firms in 1981[1]

Type of waste management	Type or form of wastes	Price 1981	$/tonne[2] 1981
Landfill	Drummed	$0.64–$0.91/gal ($35–$50/55 gal drum)	$168–$240
	Bulk	$0.19–$0.28/gal	$55–$83
	Type: Acids/alkalis		$13–$210
	Odorous waste	.	$30
	Low risk hazardous waste (e.g., oil and gas drilling muds)		$13–$29
	Hazardous		$30–$80
	Extremely hazardous		$50–$140
Land treatment	All	$0.02–$0.09/gal	$5–24
Incineration clean	Relatively clean liquids, high-Btu value	$(0.05)[3]–$0.20/gal	$(13)[3]–$53
	Liquids	$0.20–$0.90/gal	$53–$237
	Solids, highly toxic liquids	$1.50–$3.00/gal	$395–$791
Chemical treatment	Acids/alkalines	$0.08–$0.35/gal	$21–$92
	Cyanides, heavy metals, highly toxic waste	$0.25–$3.00/gal	$66–$791
Resource recovery	All	$0.25–$1.00/gal	$66–$264
Deep well injection	Oily wastewater	$0.06–$0.15/gal	$16–$40
	Toxic rinse water	$0.50–$1.00/gal	$132–$264
Transportation		$0.15/ton mile	

1. Interviews were conducted in May of 1980 and February of 1982. 2. Factors used to convert gallons and tons into tonnes are described in reference 42 (OTA), page 394. 3. Some cement kilns and light aggregate manufacturers are now paying for waste.

Source: Booz, Allen & Hamilton, Inc.

Incineration v. Treatment: Range of Estimated Post-RCRA Charges for Selected Waste Types

	Costs per tonne	
	Incineration	Treatment
Waste oils	$94	$40
Paint sludges	453	94
Nonchlorinated solvents	94	61
Chlorinated solvents	206	161
Cyanides	211	297

Note: Cost estimates are based on surveys of commercial treatment and incinerator facilities in the Great Lakes regions. Costs reported reflect the surveyed industries' estimates of their charges based on compliance with RCRA regulatory requirements for *Interim Status* facilities. No specific information provided about type of process or incinerator used, or characteristics of waste residuals.

Source: Office of Technology Assessment, from *Hazardous Waste Management in the Great Lakes Region,* Department of Commerce, September 1982.

APPENDIX XIV

Bibliography on Hazardous Waste Exchange Technology

Name	Source of Information
Acrylic resins, acid recovery by Röhm	Bundesverband der Deutschen Industrie, *Antworten auf eine Herausforderung* (Cologne: der Verband, 1977).
Adhesive pollution in the 3M Company	Ling, Joseph T., "Pollution Prevention Pays: 3M Resource Conservation Program Attacks Pollution at Its Sources," *Pollution Engineering*, September 30, 1977, p.46.
Alcohol effluent in the 3M Company	See reference for adhesive pollution.
Alcohol from industrial wastes by Georgia Pacific, Bellingham, Washington	"Money from Waste," *Development Forum*, January-February 1977, p.3.
Alumina manufacture: conversion of red mud to building materials	Gutt, W. et al., "A Survey of the Location, Disposal and Prospective Uses of the Major Industrial By-Products," in *Non-Waste Technology and Production* (Oxford: Pergamon Press, 1978).
Aluminum industry: fluoride recovery	Nestaas, I., "A Survey of Pollution Problems in the Aluminum Industry," U.N. Environment Program Aluminum Seminar, Paris, October 1975.
Aluminum industry: fluoride recycling by Vereinigte Aluminum Werke	See reference for acrylic resins.
Aluminum industry: red mud to iron and cement by the Pederson process	See reference for aluminum industry: fluoride recovery.

Name	Source of Information
Ammonia manufacture on closed cycle in the Soviet Union	See in reference for alumina "Introductory Report," by M. F. Torocheshnikov.
Antibiotic production upgrading of mycelial wastes	Private communication with Dr. R. N. Greenshields, Department of Biochemistry, University of Aston, Birmingham, England.
Automobile catalytic mufflers in Ford Motor Co.	Leung, K. C. and Klein, J., "The Environmental Control Industry," in *Annual Report of the Council of Environmental Quality* (Washington, D.C.: U.S. Government Printing Office, 1975).
Automobile industry: waste oil in Volkswagen AG	See reference for acrylic resins.
Automobile industry: plastic waste recycling by Gebr. Holzapfel KG	See reference for acrylic resins.
Bleaching (displacement) in Finland	See in reference for alumina "Displacement Bleaching," by J. Gullichser.
Bottles: plastic to replace glass	See in reference for alumina "Packaging Alternatives for Wine," by W. P. Fornerod.
Bottles: reuse	See in reference for alumina "The Recovery of Glass in Switzerland," by Y. Maystre.
Brown coal power plant by Rheinische Braunkohlwerke	See reference for acrylic resins.
Cables: recovery of copper and lead in Bex, Switzerland	Waller, J. G., "New Fluidized Bed Recycle System," *The Chemical Engineer,* October 1975, p.596.
Caprolactam black liquor to energy	"Conversion of Refuse to Energy," First International Conference, Montreux, Switzerland, November 1975.
Carbohydrate residues by Battelle, Geneva	"Considerations Concerning the Upgrading of Cellulosic Wastes and Carbohydrate Residues from Agriculture and Agro-industries." U.N. Environment Program/U.N. Food and Agricultural Organization Seminar on Utilization of Agricultural and Agroindustrial Wastes, Rome, January 1977.
Cellulosic wastes by Battelle, Geneva	See reference for carbohydrate residues.

Name	Source of Information
Cellulosic wastes to gasoline in the United States	See in reference for alumina: "Programme Considerations and Experiences in Optimizing Industrial Materials Flow and Utilization of a Non-waste Technology," by J. F. Collins.
Cement dust recovery	Coskuner, U., "Treatment of Solid Waste at Source: Industrial Wastes," U.N. Economic Commission for Europe Seminar on Solid Wastes Handling, Hamburg, 1975.
Cement dust recovery by Forschungsinstitut der Zementindustrie	See reference for acrylic resins.
Cheese whey recovery by ultrafiltration	Information available from Alfa Laval A/B, Lund, Sweden.
Cheese whey recovery by reverse osmosis	Information available from Reverse Osmosis Ltd., Whitchurch, Hampshire, England.
Cheese whey recovery by gel filtration in New Zealand	Information available from the New Zealand Dairy Research Institute, Auckland, New Zealand.
Cheese whey recovery by the Société Lacto-Centre	*Usines Propres* (Paris: Ministère de la Qualité de la Vie, 1976).
Chemical plant solvent recovery in Finland	See in reference for alumina "Methods of Conserving Raw Materials and Energy and Protecting the Environment in Chemical and Electro-plating Plants," by B. Westerholm.
Chemical wastes to fine chemicals by Westvaco	See reference for alcohol from industrial wastes.
Chemical wastes to flavors by Union Camp	See reference for alcohol from industrial wastes.
Chicken manure to pig feed by Frigoscandia	Information available from Frigoscandia A/B, Malmö, Sweden.
China clay wastes combined with waste paper	See reference for alumina.
China clay wastes to houses by English Clays	Information available from English Clays, Lovering Pochin, Ltd., St. Austell, Cornwall, England.
Chip-board effluent recycling in Finland	See reference for bleaching (displacement)

Name	Source of Information
Chlorinated plastics to carbon tetra-chloride at Hamburg University	See in reference for cement dust recovery, "On the Pyrolysis of Plastic Wastes," by H. Sinn.
Chlorinated residues to chlorine and hydrochloric acid at Solvay/Rhone Poulenc	See in reference for cement dust recovery, "Disposal of Chlorinated Organic Waste with Pure Hydrochloric Acid Recovery," by F. Prudhon.
Chlorinated solvents at Dow in Free-port, Texas	Rauch, R., "Are Environmental Regu-lations a Prime Cause of Inflation?" Environmental Defense Fund Memo-randum, mimeographed document (Washington, D.C.: Environmental Defense Fund, 1979).
Chromium "6" recovery by the 3M Company	See reference for adhesive pollution.
Citrus wastes to feed by Tate & Lyle	Imrie, F., "Single Cell Protein from Agricultural Wastes," New Scientist, vol. 66, 1975, p.458.
Coal-fired power plant: sulphur dioxide to gypsum and sulphur	See in reference for acrylic resins, "Gesamtverband der Deutschen Steinkohlenberghaus."
Coal-mine wastes plus gypsum waste to cement	See reference for alumina.
Coal-mine waste to bricks	See reference for alumina.
Coconut husk to synthetic fuel	See reference for caprolactam black liquor to energy.
Coke ovens: dry extinction	See in reference for alumina "The Iron and Steel Industry; Pollution Control and Recycling," by Y. Hellot.
Coke-oven quench heat and gas recovery	See in reference for acrylic resins "Gesamtverband der Deutschen Steinkohlenberghaus."
Containers' reduced weight	See in reference for alumina "The Heye-EPB Process: A Low Waste Technology," by V. Hallensleban.
Cooling water in the 3M Company	See reference for adhesive pollution.
Cooling water to agro-industry at Oak Ridge, Tennessee	Yee, W. C., "Estimate of Cost/Benefit for Aquacultural Operations in an Agro-Industrial Complex," occasional paper, Oak Ridge National Labora-tory, Tennessee, September 25, 1968.
Cooling water for eels at Tomatim Distilleries, Invernesshire, Scotland	"Whisky Firm to Sell Eels," Daily Tele-graph, London, April 26, 1978, p.3.

Name	Source of Information
Cooling water to fish farming at Hinckley, United Kingdom	Information from N. M. Kerr, White Fish Authority, Edinburgh, Scotland.
Cooling water to fish farming at Hunterston, United Kingdom	Kingwell, S. J., "The Use of Artificially Warmed Water for Marine Fish Cultivation." Pro Aqua–Pro Vita Conference, Basel, 1974.
Cooling water to space heating in Ageste, Sweden	Bell, S. F., "Waste Heat Uses Cut Thermal Pollution," *Mechanical Engineering,* July 1971, p.15.
Cooling water to space heating in Battersea, London	Information available from Central Electricity Generating Board, London, United Kingdom.
Copper smelting and wastes to metals by-products in Port Kembla, Australia	"Making a Residue Pay," *ECOS,* East Melbourne, February 15, 1978, p.24.
Copper smelter sulphur dioxide recovery at Outokumpu, Finland	See reference for alumina and S. Harkki, "Outokumpu Flash Smelting Method," in *Non-Waste Technology and Production* (Oxford: Pergamon Press, 1978), p.379.
Copper recovery	"Squeezing New Uses Out of Materials," *Chemical Week,* September 17, 1975, p.43.
Cow manure to cattle feed	Information available from Battelle Pacific North West Laboratories, Richland, Washington.
Cow manure to gas	See reference for carbohydrate residues and "Bio-gas (Gobar Gas) and Manure from the Wastes of Farm Animals," by H. R. Srinavasar.
Curing oven pollution at the 3M Company	See reference for adhesive pollution.
Degreaser solvent in the 3M Company	See reference for adhesive pollution.
Distillery wash to animal feed at North British Distilleries, Edinburgh, Scotland	Gray, R. M., "Cut Evaporation Costs," *Chemical Processing,* September 1974, p.76; reprint available from APV Co. Ltd., Crawley, Sussex, England.
Domestic furnace pollution avoidance	See reference for acrylic resins and "Gewerkschaft Sophia-Jacoba in Huckeloven."
Domestic waste to fish farms and vegetables	Information available from The Ark, Prince Edward Island, Canada.

Name	Source of Information
Domestic waste to water and energy in Canada	See reference for alumina and "Non-waste Technology: Comments on the Canadian Scene," by A. J. McIntyre, in *Non-Waste Technology and Production* (Oxford: Pergamon Press, 1978), p.73.
Electrostatic precipitators in Canadian pulp mills	See reference for automobile catalytic mufflers.
Electroplating waste recovery	See reference for acrylic resins and "Fa. W. Reffelmann Metallverarbeitung KG."
Electroplating works water recovery in Finland	See reference for chemical plant solvent recovery.
Etching and plating wastes: metals recovery by Westinghouse	"There's Gold in Them Thar Recycled Products," *New Scientist,* vol. 69, 1976, p.571.
Fiberboard water recycling by Isorel	See reference for cheese whey recovery.
Fiber manufacture: steam to dry distillation	See reference for cement dust recovery and "Treatment of Industrial Wastes at Source," by J. Allen, U.N. Economic Commission for Europe Seminar on Solid Wastes Handling, Hamburg, 1975.
Film material reclaim by the 3M Company	See reference for adhesive pollution.
Flue-gas pollution from incineration in the 3M Company	See reference for adhesive pollution
Fly ash to bricks	See reference for alumina.
Food industry wastes to animal feed by Findus	Jarl, K. and Tulit, M., "Symbiotic Fermentation of Food Industry Wastes," *Handinger II* (Stockholm), vol. 18, no. 2, 1963.
Food wastes to chemicals	Malcher, F., "Upgrading Food Industry Wastes," *Die Stärke* (Frankfurt), vol. 20, 1968, p.85; Surazynski, J., et al. "Recovery of Biomass from Industrial Wastes," *Przem. Ferment. Rolny* (Warsaw), vol. 14, 1970, p.21; Heisler, E. G. et al., "Fermentation of Potato Industry Wastes," *American Potato Journal,* vol. 47, 1970, p.326.

Name	Source of Information
Food wastes to feed	Information available from Dr. R. N. Greenshields, Department of Biochemistry, University of Aston, Birmingham, England.
Forest products: integrated production in Finland	Information available from Ahlstrom O/Y, Yarkaus, Finland.
Formaldehyde recovery in the United States and Australia by the 3M Company	See reference for adhesive pollution.
Freon propellant replacement by the 3M Company	See reference for adhesive pollution.
Glass recycling in Germany	See reference for acrylic resins and "Studiengruppe Altglasse."
Glass recycling in France	Information available from Chambre Syndicale des Verreries Mecaniques en France.
Glucose to chemicals by Battelle in Geneva, Switzerland	Battelle, "Non-fossil Carbon Sources," research report (Geneva: Geneva Research Centre, 1978).
Glue and gelatin water recycling	See reference for cheese whey recovery and Société des Ets. Georges Alquier.
Gravel pits to sports centers in the United Kingdom	Information available from Ready Mixed Concrete Co. and Consolidated Goldfields, United Kingdom.
Hierarchic energy use between industries in the United States	See reference for cellulosic wastes to gasoline.
Hierarchic water use between industry and community in the Soviet Union	See reference for alumina and U.N. Yevstratov and M. I. Klevsky, "Experience in Designing a Complex Scheme for Refining and Re-use of Waste Water and Creation of a Drainage Free Scheme of Water Supply and Sewerage in an Industrial Enterprise," in *Non-Waste Technology and Production* (Oxford: Pergamon Press, 1978), p.301.
Hydrocarbon recovery from mixer reflux systems, polymerized coatings, reactive coatings, and solid coatings in the 3M Company	See reference for adhesive pollution.
Industrial wastes at Hercules	See reference for chlorinated solvents.
Latex effluents at Dow	See reference for chlorinated solvents.

Name	Source of Information
Leaks to sewers at Dow Midland	See reference for chlorinated solvents.
Leaks of vapor at Union Carbide Lignin	"How Union Carbide Has Cleaned Up Its Image," *Business Week*, August 2, 1976, p.46; information also available from Battelle, Geneva Research Centre, Geneva, Switzerland.
Lignin to chemicals	See reference for glucose to chemicals.
Lubricating oil reclaim in the United Kingdom, West Germany, and the United States	Thomas, C., *Material Gains, Reclamation, Recycling and Re-use* (London: Friends of the Earth, 1974).
Manioc to petroleum in Brazil	Hawrylyshyn, G., "Brazil Spends $500 MM on Use of Alcohol for Automotive Fuel," *World Environment Report,* vol. 12, 1976, p.1.
Materials saving in the 3M Company	See reference for adhesive pollution.
Mercury from resin manufacture in the 3M Company	See reference for adhesive pollution.
Methionine recovery	See reference for cheese whey recovery and Société Alimentaire Equilibre de Commenty, *Usines Propres* (Paris: Ministère de la Qualité de la Vie, 1976).
Milling wastes to food at Rank, Hovis, MacDougal	Spicer, A., "Fungal Protein as a Source of Complete Food" (London: Food Group of the Society for Chemical Industry, 1968), unpublished paper.
Mine wastes to building materials in Poland	"Some Examples to Illustrate the Concept of Non-waste Technology," Document No. ENV/SEM6/PMR3 (Geneva: U.N. Economic Commission for Europe, 1975).
Mine wastes and furnace ashes to building materials in China	Orleans, L.A., "China's Environomics: Backing into Environmental Leadership," *Environmental Policy and Law,* vol. 2, 1976, p.28 and p.98.
Mining areas to recreational areas in the United States	Information available from AMAX Inc., Denver, Colorado.
Mining areas to recreational areas in Malaysia	Information available from Ministry of Science, Technology and Environment, Kuala Lumpar, Malaysia.
Mining areas to recreational areas in the Wigan Alps, Lancashire, England	Information available from National Coal Board, North Western Division, United Kingdom.

Name	Source of Information
Municipal wastes to chemicals	See reference for carbohydrate residues.
Oily ballast water in Ashkelon, Israel	Izraeli, O., "The Cost of Inport Disposal and Purification of Oily Ballast Water in Ashkelon Port," report (Haifa: Israel Shipping Research Institute, 1975).
Oil waste to fuel in Canada	See reference for domestic waste to water and energy.
Organic wastes to animal feed in the United Kingdom	Hughes, D., "Waste Not, Want Not," *New Scientist,* vol. 65, 1975, p. 705.
Organic wastes (low boiling point) at Chemstar Ltd., Stalybridge, Cheshire, England	"Where There's Chemical Muck," *London Sunday Times,* June 11, 1978, p. 32.
Palm oil waste to feed in Malaysia	Information available from Dunlop Bioprocesses Ltd., London, England.
Paper mill: closed white water system	Information available from Nils Jirval, Swedish Environmental Protection Board, Stockholm, Sweden.
Paper recycling in Germany	See reference for acrylic resins and "Verband Deutscher Papierfabriken."
Petrochemical residues to fuel	See reference for fiber manufacture: steam to dry distillation.
Petroleum refinery catalyst recovery	See reference for automobile catalytic mufflers.
Petroleum refinery hydrocarbon recovery at Elf Feyzin	See reference for cheese whey recovery.
Pewter furnace dust recovery	See reference for cheese whey recovery and "Société des Alliages d'Etain et Derivés."
Phosphoric acid wastes to plaster board	See reference for cheese whey recovery and "Rhone Progil."
Photographic films: silver recovery	See reference for alumina and "Non-waste Technology in Belgium," by Van Baerenbergh and A. G. Buekens, in *Non-Waste Technology and Production* (Oxford: Pergamon Press, 1978), p. 147.
Pickle liquor to pigments	Information available from Tubemakers of Australia, Sydney, Australia.

Name	Source of Information
Pig manure to fertilizer	Information available from Ministry of Agriculture and Fisheries, London, United Kingdom.
Plastic waste to energy	See reference for caprolactam black liquor.
Plastic waste incineration	See reference for acrylic resins and "Verband Kunstofferzeugende-industrie," in *Antworten auf eine Herausforderung* (Cologne: Der Bundesverband der Deutschen Industrie, 1977), p. 50.
Plastic waste reuse by foam production: pyrolysis to monomer and remolding	See reference for acrylic resins and "Verband Kunstofferzeugende-industrie" in plastic waste incineration.
Plum juice recovery	See reference for cheese whey recovery and Et. Laparre Castelnaud de Gratecombe, *Usines Propres* (Paris: Ministere de la Qualite de la Vie, 1976).
Pollution control with brown coke	See reference for acrylic resins and "Rheinische Kohlwerke."
Polymer scrap in the 3M Company	See reference for adhesive pollution.
Potato industry wastes to feed in the Netherlands	Information available from CIVO, Food Industry Research Laboratory, Zeist, Netherlands.
Poultry processing wastes at Goldkist	See reference for alcohol from industrial wastes.
Product reformulation in the 3M Company	See reference for adhesive pollution.
Pulp mill conversion in France	See reference for cheese whey recovery and "La Rochette-Cenpa."
Pulp mill: kraft closed cycle at Great Lakes Paper Company, Canada	See reference for alumina and "Nonwaste Production of Bleached Kraft Pulp," by H. Rapson and W. Reeve, in *Non-Waste Technology and Production* (Oxford: Pergamon Press, 1978), p. 379.
Pulp mill liquor to methane in the United States	See reference for cellulosic wastes to gasoline.
Pulp mill liquor to protein in United Mills, Finland	See reference for citrus wastes to feed.

Name	Source of Information
Pulp mill magnesium-based sulphite process at Hylte Bruk Mill, Sweden	Information available from Nils Jirval, Swedish Environmental Protection Board, Stockholm, Sweden.
Pulp mill recovery	See reference for glucose to chemicals.
Pulp sludge reuse and bark burning	Information available from Nils Jirval, Swedish Environmental Protection Board, Stockholm, Sweden.
Pyrolysis: Andco-Torrax, Destrugas, Garrett, Landgard, Lanz, Purox, Sodeteg, waste plastic to oil products	See reference for caprolactam black liquor to energy.
Quarry washings	See reference for cheese whey recovery and "Société d'Exploitation de l'Enterprise Mir-Saint-Lary," *Usines Propres* (Paris: Ministere de la Qualité de la Vie, 1976).
Quebacho sawdust to synthetic fuel	See reference for caprolactam black liquor to energy.
Rayon and zinc recycling in Germany	See reference for acrylic and to ENKA-Glanzstoff AG, in "Conversion of Refuse to Energy," First International Conference, Montreux, Switzerland, November 1975.
Rayon and zinc recycling in the United States by FMC Corp	"Recycling Zinc Shenandoah Style," *The Guardian,* London, July 16, 1975, p. 5.
Refuse to energy in Chicago, Hamburg, Munich, Norfolk, Paris, Switzerland, and Vienna	See reference for caprolactam black liquor to energy.
Refuse to heat and power in Italy and Switzerland	See reference to caprolactam black liquor to energy.
Refuse to methanol	See reference for caprolactam black liquor to energy.
Refuse to power and drinking water	See reference for cement-dust recovery and "Energy from Waste," by B. G. Kreiter, U.N. Economic Commission for Europe Seminar on Solid Wastes Handling, Hamburg, 1975.
Refuse segregation center in Lowell, Massachusetts	See reference for caprolactam black liquor to energy.
Refuse segregation center at La Rochelle, France	Hammond, B., "Recycling Begins at Home," *New Scientist,* vol. 67, 1975, p. 152.

Name	Source of Information
Refuse segregation centers in Sweden run by PLM	Flory, I., "Separation of Paper, Glass and Tinplate from Waste in Residential and Industrial Areas," ECMIA Conference, October 1976.
Refuse segregation centers in Switzerland and the United States	Stein, J., "Recycling Plans are Piling Up to Handle Mountainous Nationwide Problem of Bottles and Cans," *The Smithsonian*, vol. 5, 1974, p. 62.
Refuse segregation centers in the United Kingdom	"The Megabuck Revolution," *The Guardian*, London, October 13, 1977.
Refuse segregation power production and sale in Memphis, Tennessee	See reference for caprolactam black liquor to energy.
Refuse segregation, value in France to Ugine Kuhlmann	See reference for refuse segregation center at La Rochelle.
Refuse to synthetic fuel and synthetic natural gas	See reference for caprolactam black liquor to energy.
Refinery sludge to soil conditioner in Canada	"Growth from Waste," *Bulletin of the Shell Environmental Conservation Committee*, vol. 27, December 1976, p. 7.
Refinery waste heat for tomatoes with Mobil Oil and van Heyningen Bros. in the United Kingdom	"Mobil Weighs Tomato Project," *Newsweek*, June 12, 1978, p. 38.
Rice milling in Thailand by Kamchai Iamsuri	"A Farm Which Thrives on Waste Recycling," *Bangkok Post*, November 26, 1976 and Butler, V., "No Place for Unsoiled Hands," *Business Times*, June 18–24, 1978, p. 6.
Rubber tire reclamation by British Reclaim Ltd. and incineration by Avon Rubber Co.	*Environmental Pollution Management*, May–June 1974.
Scrap polymer marketing by the 3M Company	See reference for adhesive pollution.
Sewage used for fish farming in the London area	Noble, R., "Growing Fish in Sewage," *New Scientist*, vol. 67, 1975, p. 259.
Sewage used for irrigation of vegetables and for vehicle propulsion	Information available from Voirie de la Ville de Paris, France.
Sewage for steel mills in Naples, Italy	Information available from Techint, SpA, Milan, Italy.

Name	Source of Information
Sewage for steel mills in Nippon Steel Works, Kawasaki City, Japan	"Utilization of Waste Water by Japanese Steel Makers Ranks Highest in the World," *The Japan Economic Journal,* December 3, 1974, p. 20.
Silicon manufacture: chlorine and hydrogen recovery by Dow Corning, Hemlock, Michigan	See reference for alcohol from industrial wastes.
Slag to building materials in the Soviet Union	Scholes, S., "Blast Furnace Slag to Build On," *New Scientist,* vol. 59, 1973, p. 206.
Slag to construction material	See reference for alumina.
Slate waste to cement	See reference for alumina.
Slaughterhouse wastes to protein developed by ECOTECH/NZDSIR	Grant, R. A., "Protein Recovery from Meat, Poultry and Fish Processing Effluents"; reprint from *Chemistry and Industry* available from ECHO-TECH Systems, 145 Sterle Road, Poole, Dorset, United Kingdom.
Sludges to chemicals	See reference for carbohydrate residues.
Soap factory glycerine recovery	See reference for cheese whey recovery and "Savonnerie de Lutterback," in *Usines Propres* (Paris: Ministère de la Qualité de la Vie, 1976).
Solvent dyeing in France	See reference for alumina and "Dyeing in a Solvent Medium," by M. Laurent, in *Non-Waste Technology and Production* (Oxford: Pergamon Press, 1978), p. 221.
Solvent recovery in Australia and the United Kingdom by 3M companies	See reference for adhesive pollution.
Spray booth scrap in the 3M Company	See reference for adhesive pollution.
Starchy wastes to chemicals	See reference for carbohydrate residues.
Steel mills: chemical recovery and closed water system	See reference for coke ovens: dry extinction.
Steel mills: closed water system at Fos	"Solmar to Install Unique System," *Journal of Commerce (New York),* September 9, 1974, p. 14A.

Name	Source of Information
Steel mills: dust recovery in France	See reference for cheese whey recovery and "Sacilor."
Steel mills: dust recovery in Germany	See reference for coke ovens: dry extinction.
Steel mills: gas washing, sludge, and pickle-liquor recovery and rolling-mill water recycling	See reference for alumina and "Treatment and Preparation of Dusts and Sludges in the Steel Industry," by M. Haucke and W. Theobald, in *Non-Waste Technology and Production* (Oxford: Pergamon Press, 1978), p. 481.
Steel mills: solid waste recovery	See reference for alumina and "Disposal of Iron Works Waste," by R. Roth.
Steel mills: solid waste reuse and water recycling	See reference for acrylic resins and "Verein Deutscher Eisenhüttenleute," *Antworten auf eine Herausforderung* (Cologne: Der Bundesverband der Deutschen Industrie, 1978), p. 44.
Styrene from polystyrene	See reference for mine wastes to building materials.
Sugarcane to petrols in Brazil	See reference for manioc to gasoline.
Sugarcane to polyethylene in Kenya and India	See reference for glucose to chemicals.
Sugar to detergent in Austria and Germany	See reference for carbohydrate residues.
Sugar wastes to citric acid in Belgium	See reference for photographic films' silver recovery.
Sugar wastes to citric acid in Germany	See reference for acrylic resins and "Joh. A. Benickser," *Antworten auf eine Herausforderung* (Cologne: Der Bundesverband der Deutschen Industrie, 1978), p. 44.
Sugar waste recycling	See reference for acrylic resins and "Institut für Landswirtschaft Technologie und Zuckerindustrie," *Antworten auf eine Herausforderung* (Cologne: Der Bundesverband der Deutschen Industrie, 1978), p. 114.
Textile waste water to fish ponds	See reference for acrylic and "Herm Windel GmbH."

Name	Source of Information
Trees, fast-growing	Information from Governor A. Leviste, Batangas City, Philippines.
Tires, long-lived	See reference for alumina and "Non-waste Technology: The Case of Tyres in the United States," by H. C. Goddard, in *Non-Waste Technology and Production* (Oxford: Pergamon Press, 1978), p. 463.
Tires: rubber reclaim	See reference for acrylic resins and "Wirtschaftsverband der Deutschen Kautschukindustrie."
Vapor recompression by APV Co., England	Cole, J. W., "Mechanical Vapour Recompression for Evaporators," *The Chemical Engineer,* February 1975, p. 76.
Waste exchanges in Hamburg	See reference for alumina and "Waste Exchanges Improved Management for a New Type of Growth," by J. C. Deloy, in *Non-Waste Technology and Production* (Oxford: Pergamon Press, 1978), p. 247.
Wastepaper to cattle feed	See reference for cow manure to cattle feed.
Waste water in the 3M Company, United Kingdom	See reference for adhesive pollution.
Water hyacinth	Wolverton, B. and McDonald, R. C., "Don't Waste Water Weeds," *New Scientist,* vol. 71, 1976, p. 318.
Water savings with cooling towers at Dow Midland	See reference for chlorinated solvents.
Weeds to food by the U.N. Food and Agricultural Organization	Bergéret, A. and Théry, D., "Weeds into Crops," *Ceres,* vol. 9, 1976, p. 29.
White water in the 3M Company	See reference for adhesive pollution.
Wildlife cropping	Information available from Ministry of Tourism and Wild Life, Nairobi, Kenya.
Wood wastes to fuel by Moore Gasifier in Canada	See reference for domestic waste to water and energy.
Xylose to chemicals	See reference for glucose to chemicals.

Name	Source of Information
Yeast factory waste recovery	See reference for cheese whey recovery and "Société Industrielle de Levure, Fala," in *Usines Propres* (Paris: Ministère de la Qualité de la Vie, 1976).
Zinc salts and zinc oxide in the 3M Company	See reference for adhesive pollution.

Source: *Harvard Business Review,* Nov.–Dec., 1980, pp. 18–22. Copyright©1980 by the President and Fellows of Harvard College; all rights reserved. Reprinted by permission.

Note: For incomplete references in this bibliography please contact author at the Center for Education in International Management, 4, chemin des Conches, 1231 Conches-Geneva, Switzerland.

Ranking of Hazardous Waste Disposal Sites by Hazard and Risk

A. Ranking by Hazard of Toxic Chemical Constituents

I. Acute Toxicity

Score*	Oral LD$_{50}$ mg/kg	Dermal LD$_{50}$ mg/kg	Aquatic 96 hour LC$_{50}$ mg/l
7	< 5	< 5	< 1
3	5–50	5–200	1–10
2	> 50–500	> 200–500	> 10–100
1	> 500–5000	> 500–5000	> 100–1000
0	> 5000	> 5000	> 1000
•	Insufficient information		

Category†

II. Carcinogenicity

Score	Category
7	Human positive; human suspect; animal positive
3	Animal suspect
2	Carcinogenic by route other than oral or dermal; strong potential carcinogen by accepted mutagenicity screening tests or accepted cell transformation studies
1	Potential carcinogen by accepted mutagenicity screening tests or accepted cell transformation studies
0	Not carcinogenic
•	Insufficient information

III. Hereditary Mutagenicity

Score	Category
7	Confirmed
4	Suspect-multicellular organisms
2	Suspect-micro-organisms
0	Not a hereditary mutagen
•	Insufficient information

IV. Teratogenicity

Score	Category
7	Confirmed
3	Suspect
0	Not teratogenic
•	Insufficient information

V. Persistence

Score	Category
4	Very persistent
3	Persistent
2	Slowly degradable
1	Moderately degradable
0	Readily degradable
•	Insufficient information

VI. Bioaccumulation

Score	Bioaccumulation
7	>4000
3	1000–3999
2	700–999
1	300–699
0	<300
•	Insufficient information

VII. Esthetics

Score	Fish tainting/taste and odor (threshold level in water—mg/l)	Foaming, floating film, and/or major color change
3	0.0001–0.001	
2	>0.001–0.01	
1	>0.01–0.1	Yes
0	>0.1	No

VIII. Chronic Adverse Effects

Score	Category
4	Irreversible effects
2	Reversible effects
1	Adverse effects by route other than oral, dermal or aquatic
0	No detectable adverse effects
•	Insufficient information

Source: Michigan Department of Natural Resources, "Critical Materials Register," Lansing, Michigan, 1980.

*The higher the score ranking, the greater or more intense the listed effect.

†LD_{50}, a standard measure of acute toxicity, is the dose (usually expressed on a body weight basis as mg/kg) required to kill 50% of the test population of animals exposed by oral or dermal routes; LC_{50} is the equivalent value for fish expressed as the lethal concentration (in terms of mg/liter of water). The higher the LD_{50} or LC_{50} the lower is the acute toxicity, as a higher concentration is required to produce a 50% kill.

B. Ranking by Risk to Environment and Population

Rating factors	Rating scale levels			
	0	1	2	3
Population within 1,000 ft	0	1 to 25	26 to 100	Greater than 100
Distance to nearest drinking-water well	Greater than 3 miles	1 to 3 miles	3,001 ft to 1 mile	0 to 3,000 ft
Distance to nearest offsite building	Greater than 2 miles	1 to 2 miles	1,001 ft to 1 mile	0 to 1,000 ft
Land use/zoning	Completely remote (zoning not applicable)	Agricultural	Commercial or Industrial	Residential
Critical environments	not a critical environment	Pristine natural areas	Wetlands, flood-plains, and preserved areas	Major habitat of endangered or threatened species
Distance to nearest surface water	Greater than 5 miles	1 to 5 miles	1,001 ft to 1 mile	0 to 1,000 ft
Depth to ground water	Greater than 100 ft	51 to 100 ft	21 to 50 ft	0 to 20 ft
Net precipitation	Less than 10 inches	−10 to +5 inches	+5 to +10 inches	Greater than +20 inches
Soil permeability	Greater than 50 percent clay	30 to 50 percent clay	15 to 30 percent clay	0 to 15 percent clay
Bedrock permeability	Impermeable	Relatively impermeable	Relatively permeable	Very permeable
Depth to bedrock	Greater than 60 feet	31 to 60 ft	11 to 30 ft	0 to 10 ft

Source: Based on JRB Associates, "Methodology for Rating the Hazard Potential of Waste Disposal Sites." Report to EPA, 1980.

Index